A THOUSAND DAYS

JOHN F. KENNEDY IN THE WHITE HOUSE

Winner of the Pulitzer Prize

A THOUSAND DAYS

JOHN F. KENNEDY IN THE WHITE HOUSE

ILLUSTRATED AND ABRIDGED

ARTHUR M. SCHLESINGER, JR.
ABRIDGED BY DAVID SOBEL

BLACK DOG
& LEVENTHAL
PUBLISHERS
NEW YORK

PUBLISHED BY: Black Dog & Leventhal Publishers, Inc. / 151 West 19th Street / New York, NY 10011

DISTRIBUTED BY: Workman Publishing Company / 708 Broadway / New York, NY 10003

Manufactured in China
Cover and interior design by Andy Taray
Cover photographs courtesy AP / Wide World Photos
ISBN: 1-57912-449-6
h g f e d c b a

Library of Congress Cataloging-in-Publication Data available on file.

IN MEMORY OF
JOHN FITZGERALD KENNEDY

If people bring so much courage to this world the world has to kill them to break them, so of course it kills them. The world breaks every one and afterward many are strong at the broken places. But those that will not break it kills. It kills the very good and the very gentle and the very brave impartially.

–HEMINGWAY

AUTHOR'S NOTE

THIS ILLUSTRATED AND ABRIDGED EDITION is not intended as a substitute for the original text but rather as a complement to it. *A Thousand Days* was first published in 1965, which was, as I write, forty years ago. The Spanish-American War took place only nineteen years before my birth in 1917. For my generation, that war seemed ancient history. After twice nineteen years, people may well lack knowledge of events and personalities of the early 1960s. The hope is that this edition will give faces to the many figures discussed in the text and provide images that help the events come more vividly to life.

The abridged edition is faithful to the original. The central themes and basic outlines of all the events have been preserved. Missing from this edition, regrettably, are some of the details that add nuance, complexity, and shading to history. Much of the observations, reminiscence, commentary, and analysis by participants that enriched the original text is pared down. Readers are encouraged to read the original text to experience this period in all its suspense and fullness.

The nature of the abridgment process is that it often shows President Kennedy only at the end of a long road of consultation and debate. But no decision was reached, nor action taken, nor statement made that was not the result of extensive deliberation. It is in no way the intent of the author or abridger to disparage the efforts of cabinet members, legislators, foreign-service and military professionals, and others both inside and outside the administration who made contributions to the Kennedy presidency. It is because space did not allow for the inclusion of the character profiles that brought these personalities to life in the original. Again, readers should refer to the unabridged text for a deeper understanding of these figures.

After forty years, two things stand out in the thousand days. In domestic policy, the Kennedys in 1963 at last confronted the tragic racism that had shamed and disgraced American life since the birth of the nation. In foreign policy, the Cuban missile crisis provided the most dangerous moment in the Cold War. Indeed, it is not an exaggeration to say that it was the most dangerous moment in all human history. Never before had two contending powers possessed between them the technical capacity to blow up the world. The world is very lucky that the two rival states were led by two men passionately determined to avoid nuclear war, John F. Kennedy and Nikita S. Khrushchev.

I am grateful for the fine work of the abridger, David Sobel, a man of conscience and of taste, who has made possible this handsome illustrated volume by making drastic cuts while preserving the essence of a lengthy book.

ARTHUR M. SCHLESINGER, JR.
May 2005

FOREWORD TO THE 2002 EDITION

THIS BOOK WAS WRITTEN in the grim months after John F. Kennedy's assassination on November 22, 1963. *A Thousand Days* has the advantages and disadvantages of a book composed so soon after the fact. Immediacy gives it vividness. It also gives a kind of knowledge denied those who were not around when history happened. As Alexis de Tocqueville once observed, participants understand better than posterity "the movements of opinion, the popular inclinations of their times, the vibrations of which they can still sense in their minds and hearts." Posterity of course has its compensating advantages—a cooler perspective, knowledge of consequences, access to declassified documents and private papers, the diverse illuminations of hindsight. Also, as Mr. Dooley pointed out, "Ye are not subjict to interruptions be people who were there."

History is a permanent debate—"an argument without end," as Pieter Geyl, the eminent Dutch historian, put it. Historians, like everyone else, are prisoners of their own experience. Their priorities are shaped by the pressures of their time. Each new generation of historians has its distinctive preoccupations in the present, and, consequently, its distinctive demands on the past. The result is chronic fluctuation in historical verdicts. Reputations rise and fall like stocks on Wall Street, determined by the supply and demand equations of a later age. The reputation of American presidents is particularly dependent on the climate in which historians hand down their judgments.

In the conservative 1950s, I published *The Crisis of the Old Order*, the first volume of *The Age of Roosevelt*. The bitter politics of the 1930s had not yet abated, and many Americans still loathed "that man in the White House." Conscious of the continuing hatred, I noted in the foreword that this was, I supposed, "a bad time" to be writing about FDR. "The reputation of a commanding figure is often at its lowest in the period ten to twenty years after his death. We are always in a zone of imperfect visibility so far as the history just over our shoulder is concerned. It is as if we wrote in the hollow of the historical wave; not until we reach the crest of the next one can we look back and estimate properly what went on before." Today, of course, recollected in tranquility, FDR is routinely rated, by conservatives as well as by liberals, as one of the three greatest American presidents.

Some years after the publication of *A Thousand Days* in November 1965, President Kennedy was in the hollow of the historical wave. His reputation was further buffeted by external events. The Vietnam War persuaded some scholars that U.S. foreign policy was inherently imperialistic. Watergate disillusioned them about presidential power. Kennedy revisionism gathered force. Critics dismissed him as charming but superficial, a triumph of style over substance, concerned with image rather than achievement, a man who talked big but accomplished little. In the darker version, Kennedy became an incorrigible philanderer, a reckless risk taker in both private and public life, a bellicose fellow who ordered the assassination of foreign leaders, almost provoked a nuclear war with the Soviet Union, plunged the nation into the Vietnam morass and, between needless international crises, turned the White House into a virtual bordello.

When *American Heritage* magazine asked scholars in 1988 to name the single most overrated figure in American history, JFK received more votes than anyone else. One historian summed up the revisionist case: "His public relations approach to the presidency was an almost total disaster for the nation.... The revelations of his private life have added more tarnish to the once golden image."

Revisionism, it should be said, did not affect popular admiration of Kennedy. Ordinary Americans remembered a strong and stirring president who saved the peace in the most dangerous moment of the Cold War, assumed leadership in the struggle for racial justice, initiated the exploration of space, laid the foundation for federal aid to the arts and humanities, tapped the republic's latent idealism and infused a generation with a passion for public service. They cherished the idea of Camelot and its brief shining hours.

And recent years have seen a perceptible recovery of Kennedy's reputation among scholars. This is partly due to the passage of time; we are now on the crest of the next wave. And it is especially due to the documentation of Kennedy's leadership in the Cuban missile crisis in *The Kennedy Tapes* (1997), edited by Ernest May and Philip Zelikow. Their three-volume set, *The Presidential Recordings: John F. Kennedy, The Great Crises* (2001), further enhances Kennedy's standing as a calm, thoughtful, resolute and, above all, substantive president.

He glittered when he lived, and the whole world grieved when he was killed. Grief nourishes myth. The slain hero, robbed of fulfillment by tragic fate, is the stuff of legend. Myth breeds countermyth. With the perspective of forty years we can perhaps disentangle myth and reality.

Let us first dispose of Camelot. JFK had gone to Choate and Harvard with Alan Jay Lerner. He liked Lerner, and he liked the songs Lerner wrote with Frederick Loewe for the popular 1960 musical. But during his lifetime no one spoke of Kennedy's Washington as Camelot. Had anyone done so, no one would have been more derisive than JFK. Nor did those of us around him see ourselves for a moment as knights of the Round Table. You will note the absence of Arthurian allusions in the text that follows.

Camelot was Jacqueline Kennedy's grieving thought to the journalist Theodore H. White a week after her husband was killed. She thereby launched a myth that time turned into a cliché. Later she told John Kenneth Galbraith that she feared she had overdone Camelot. For that matter, King Arthur's Camelot was hardly noted for marital constancy and concluded in betrayal and death.

Then a word about the 1960 election. A recurrent myth is that the Kennedys stole the election in Illinois and that Richard Nixon's finest hour was his patriotic refusal to upset the nation by contesting the result. In fact, Illinois was not crucial to Kennedy's victory. Had he lost Illinois, Kennedy still would have won the electoral college—and the presidency—by 270 to 246. And if Mayor Richard Daley's men stole votes in Cook County, Republicans stole votes downstate. The state electoral board, 4 to 1 Republican, voted unanimously to certify the Kennedy electors.

An associated myth is that Joseph P. Kennedy made a deal in the winter of 1959–60 with a Chicago gangster named Sam Giancana to use trade unions under mob control to turn out the Chicago vote for his son. In fact, the only big union under mob influence was the Teamsters Union—and the Teamsters, led by Robert Kennedy's enemy Jimmy Hoffa, were for Nixon.

Giancana was known to the Kennedy family but hardly in a way that would have made him an ally. Robert Kennedy, as counsel to the Senate Rackets Committee in 1958, succinctly described Giancana as "chief gunman for the group that succeeded the Capone mob." Called before the Rackets Committee, Giancana declined to answer questions on the grounds that his answers might tend to incriminate him—and giggled as he declined. Robert Kennedy said bitingly, "I thought only little girls giggled, Mr. Giancana." In his book *The Enemy Within*, published in February 1960, Robert Kennedy portrayed Giancana in the most contemptuous terms. The idea is preposterous that a shrewd and experienced man like Joe Kennedy would make a deal with Sam Giancana and would regard the gangster and not Dick Daley as the key to Chicago politics.

Fifteen months after Giancana giggled before the Rackets Committee, the Central Intelligence Agency in its wisdom signed him up in a plot to murder Fidel Castro. The Mafia had flourished in Havana under the indulgent Batista dictatorship, but Castro, after he came to power in 1959, closed the casinos and whorehouses and drove the mobsters from Cuba. This gave the Mafiosi, as the CIA saw it, both the motives and the contacts to do the dirty deed without implicating the United States government.

It was the Eisenhower administration that made the decision to bring in the mob, not, as the myth goes, the Kennedy administration. In September 1960, months before Kennedy became president, the CIA recruited Giancana. In October the CIA installed him in a Miami hotel. My guess is that the CIA was doing all this on its own, confident that it knew the requirements of national security better than transient elected officials and invoking the excuse of "plausible deniability" to justify the concealment of their plans from higher authority. No one has discovered that Eisenhower—or Kennedy after him—authorized the assassination projects.

There is more to the Giancana story. In the course of the 1960 campaign, Frank Sinatra, a pal of Giancana's, introduced John Kennedy to an attractive young woman named Judith Campbell. Though her later claims were contradictory and her story escalated with every telling, it seems that their affair extended into his presidency. She also had an affair with Giancana. How much did she tell Giancana about Kennedy? Did the Mafia have blackmail power over the president?

If they did, they neglected to use it. Giancana was a major target in the war against organized crime waged by Robert Kennedy's Department of Justice. Had Giancana ever had anything on the president, he would certainly have

He offered young people the faith that individuals can make a difference to history. The Kennedy generation brought new ideas, hopes, vision, generosity and vitality to the national life.

exploited it to save his hide when the feds were hot on his trail. Instead, his future was round-the-clock FBI surveillance, federal indictments, and a year in prison.

A question remains about John Kennedy and women. His sexual waywardness does not constitute JFK's finest hour. But exaggeration is possible. Some think today that there was an unending procession of bimbos through Kennedy's White House and that the Washington press corps knew about it but covered up for him because newspapermen liked him and because, under the civilized rules of the day, a politician's private life was considered his own business.

Vague rumors about JFK and women did waft about Washington from time to time, but, as one who worked in the White House, I never saw anything untoward. Kennedy was a hardworking president, concentrating intently on the matters at hand. At no point in my experience did any preoccupation with women interfere with his conduct of the public business (apart from Caroline crawling under the presidential desk).

Lest this ignorance be attributed to the invincible innocence of a professor, let me call another witness, that hard-bitten reporter Ben Bradlee, then head of the *Newsweek* bureau in Washington, later the brilliant editor of the *Washington Post.* Bradlee was not only at the center of Washington newsgathering; he was also Kennedy's closest friend in the press. "It is now accepted history," Bradlee wrote in his 1995 memoir, *A Good Life,* "that Kennedy jumped casually from bed to bed with a wide variety of women. It was not accepted history then…[I was] unaware of this proclivity during his lifetime."

Who can really know about anyone else's sex life? Unless one of the partners talks, or compromising letters turn up, or a third person is in the bedroom (an unlikely circumstance), no one can be certain what may have gone on between consenting adults. All this does not prevent sensation-mongers writing with awesome certitude about the sex lives of famous people.

Nor can outsiders pronounce on the inwardness of a marriage. My impression, shared by others from the Kennedy White House, is that JFK, for all his adventures, always regarded Jacqueline with genuine affection and pride. Their marriage never seemed more solid than in the later months of 1963.

One sometimes hears the argument that recklessness in private life leads to recklessness in public life. But history shows no connection between private morals and public behavior. Martin Luther King, Jr., for example, had wayward sexual habits but was all the same a tremendous moral force for his people and for his nation. On the other hand, Pol Pot of Cambodia was apparently devoutly religious and a faithful family man. All he did was to murder hundreds of thousands of his countrymen. The adultery test has limitations as a predictor of official conduct.

In Kennedy's case, the argument that private recklessness leads to public recklessness is invoked to explain the Bay of Pigs and the CIA assassination plots against Castro. But these were initiatives of the Eisenhower administration, and no one has accused Ike of a reckless private life, at least since the Second World War.

In fact, Kennedy was a cautious president, notable for his capacity to refuse escalation. When the Bay of Pigs invasion appeared to be failing, though under pressure from the military and the CIA to send in American forces, Kennedy declined to do so—as he later declined escalation in the Berlin crisis of 1961 and the missile crisis of 1962.

The missile crisis was not only the most dangerous moment in the Cold War. It was the most dangerous moment in all human history. Never before in the annals of life on this planet have two contending powers possessed between them the technical capacity to blow up the world. The tapes of the debate within the American government-not available when I wrote *A Thousand Days,* their existence not even suspected—show Kennedy's cool determination to expel the missiles without going to war.

We know now that the Soviet forces in Cuba had tactical missiles equipped with nuclear warheads and the authority to use them in case of an American attack. Had Kennedy yielded to the pressure applied by the Joint Chiefs of Staff for an invasion, the result would probably have been nuclear war. Fortunately, after the Bay of Pigs, Kennedy had little regard for the JCS and their recommendations. Instead he steadily pursued—and successfully achieved—a diplomatic solution. "It quickly became clear," Khrushchev wrote in his memoirs, "he understood better than Eisenhower that an improvement in relations was the only rational course."

Then came Vietnam. Though Kennedy increased the number of American military advisers attached to the South Vietnamese army, he rejected every proposal to send in American combat units. "The last thing he wanted," said General Maxwell Taylor, chairman of the Joint Chiefs, "was to put in ground forces." Both Robert McNamara, his secretary of defense, and McGeorge Bundy, his national security adviser, said later that in their judgment Kennedy would never have Americanized the war-though they advised President Johnson to do exactly that and he, with deep misgivings, followed that advice, thinking that that was what Kennedy would have done.

Kennedy believed that in the end American influence in the world depended less on American arms than on American ideals. Undertakings like the Peace Corps and the Alliance for Progress were closest to his heart. And he believed too that Americans must live up to their own ideals. He regretted that he had to spend so much time on foreign policy; "each day," he said, "was a new crisis." He looked forward to a second term in which he could concentrate on domestic problems, especially in combating poverty, enlarging economic opportunity and promoting racial justice. Actually Kennedy in his thousand days compiled a pretty good record in domestic policy, as Professor Irving Bernstein showed in his book *Promises Kept: John F. Kennedy's New Frontier* (1991).

Kennedy came slowly to appreciate the intensity of black America's demand for full citizenship, and by 1963 he made himself, at distinct political cost, the leader of the movement for new civil rights legislation. "We are confronted," he said, "primarily with a moral issue. It is as old as the Scriptures and as clear as the American Constitution."

He made his share of mistakes. There was an excessive New Frontier faith in activism, a conviction that if there was a problem, there must be a solution, and let's do it now. But he never lost the capacity to learn from his mistakes. Each year he became a better president.

Most important was the impact Kennedy had on a new generation of Americans. His irreverence toward conventional ideas and institutions provoked a discharge of critical energy throughout American society. At Kennedy's behest, bright, idealistic, and capable young men and women, asking not what their country could do for them but what they could for their country, entered politics and public service. JFK liked to quote John Buchan: "Politics is still the greatest and the most honorable adventure." He offered young people the faith that individuals can make a difference to history. The Kennedy generation brought new ideas, hopes, vision, generosity and vitality to the national life.

John Fitzgerald Kennedy in his thousand days gave the country back to its own best self. And he taught the world that the process of rediscovering America was not over.

ARTHUR M. SCHLESINGER, JR.

FOREWORD

THIS WORK IS NOT a comprehensive history of the Kennedy Presidency. It is a personal memoir by one who served in the White House during the Kennedy years.

A personal memoir, at best, can offer only a partial view. The Presidency is such a complex institution that only the President himself can fully know his problems and his purposes. John Fitzgerald Kennedy had intended to write the history of his own administration. No one else will ever be able to achieve the central, the presidential, perspective on these years. Even the public official closest to Kennedy, then the Attorney General of the United States, looking at the White House Papers after his brother's death, was astonished at the variety of presidential issues he had not known about before.

A presidential associate, moreover, inevitably tends to overrate the significance of the things he does know about. Grace Tully, who was Franklin D. Roosevelt's personal secretary, acutely observed of the books written by the men around F.D.R., "None of them could know that for each minute they spent with the President he spent a hundred minutes by himself and a thousand more with scores of other people—to reject, improvise, weigh and match this against that until a decision was reached."* This book, for example, deals largely with foreign affairs and only occasionally records President Kennedy's intense feeling about his own country and his deep desire to improve the quality of life and opportunity in the United States. This was an animating purpose of his Presidency, but, as one only irregularly involved in these matters, I have less to say about them. Similarly others will have to describe in greater detail President Kennedy's relations with Congress and with party politics.

The presidential perspective on this administration is now tragically and irretrievably lost. But sometime in the future an historian, today perhaps a very young man, will read the volumes of reminiscence and analysis, immerse himself in the flood of papers in the Kennedy Library and attempt by the imaginative thrust of his craft to recover that perspective. He will not attain it; but he will do the best he can on the basis of the evidence and his own insight to reproduce the form and color and motion of the years as they unrolled before the occupant of the Oval Room. I hope that this and similar books published in the time between may advance his task.

A number of my colleagues in the Kennedy administration helped check and supplement my own recollections as I worked on this book, and I am deeply grateful for their assistance. But the reconstruction of past events is exceedingly difficult, if not impossible; and, when I have been confronted by diverging judgments and memories, I have had no choice but to consider the evidence as best I could and draw conclusions on my own responsibility. Therefore I am, as author, totally and exclusively accountable for the shape that incidents and people assume in this narrative. I do wish, however, to express special thanks to Nancy Riley Newhouse for valuable assistance on research and to Gretchen Stewart for devoted and unstinting help in every aspect of this undertaking.

This work is based on papers as well as on interviews and recollections. Every statement, I believe, has its warrant; but in order to protect confidential communications it has seemed better not to give a systematic indication of sources at this time. A fully footnoted manuscript will be deposited under seal in the Kennedy Library along with my own White House papers. After an appropriate interval these will be open to scholars.

Many of the quotations come from a journal I kept through these years. At the start of his administration President Kennedy said that he did not want his staff recording the daily discussions of the White House. Remarks tossed off gaily or irritably in conversation, he knew, looked very different in print. He mentioned Henry Morgenthau's solemn chronicling in his diaries of Franklin Roosevelt's jocosities during the gold-buying episode of 1933; and he wished no restraint on his own freedom of expression. Accordingly my White House notes for the first weeks were fragmentary. Then after the Bay of Pigs he said, "I hope you kept a full account of that." I said that I had understood he did not want us to keep full accounts of anything. He said, "No, go ahead. You can be damn sure that the CIA has its record and the Joint Chiefs theirs. We'd better make sure we have a record over here. So you go ahead." I did.

None of this, I fear, can come close to recapturing the exceptional qualities of John F. Kennedy as a man and as a President. But I hope it will suggest something of the way in which he quickened the heart and mind of the nation, inspired the young, met great crises, led our society to new possibilities of justice and our world to new possibilities of peace and left behind so glowing and imperishable a memory.

Washington, D. C. / February 4, 1965
ARTHUR M. SCHLESINGER, JR.

*Grace Tully, *FDR, My Boss* (New York, 1949), xi.

TABLE OF CONTENTS:

PROLOGUE: JANUARY 1961

IT ALL BEGAN IN THE COLD.

It had been cold all week in Washington. Then early Thursday afternoon the snow came. The winds blew in icy, stinging gusts and whipped the snow down the frigid streets. Washingtonians do not know how to drive in the snow: they slide and skid and spin their wheels and panic. By six o'clock traffic had stopped all over town. People abandoned their cars in snowdrifts and marched grimly into the gale, heads down, newspapers wrapped around necks and stuffed under coats. And still the snow fell and the winds blew.

At eight o'clock the young President-elect and his wife went to the Inaugural Concert at Constitution Hall. An hour later they left at the intermission to go on to the Inaugural Gala at the Armory. The limousine made its careful way through the blinding snow down the Mall. Bonfires had been lit along the path in a vain effort to keep the avenue clear. Great floodlights around the Washington Monument glittered through the white storm. It was a scene of eerie beauty. As stranded motorists cheered the presidential car, the President-elect told his friend William Walton, "Turn on the lights so they can see Jackie." With the light on inside the car, he settled back to read Jefferson's First Inaugural, which had been printed in the concert program. When he finished, he shook his head and said wryly, "Better than mine."

By midnight the city was choked with snow. Workmen labored to clear Pennsylvania Avenue for next day's parade. Soldiers used flame throwers to melt the frozen drifts

PRESIDENT ELECT JOHN F. KENNEDY AND JACQUELINE LEAVE THEIR HOME IN GEORGETOWN ON THE WAY TO THE INAUGURAL BALL.

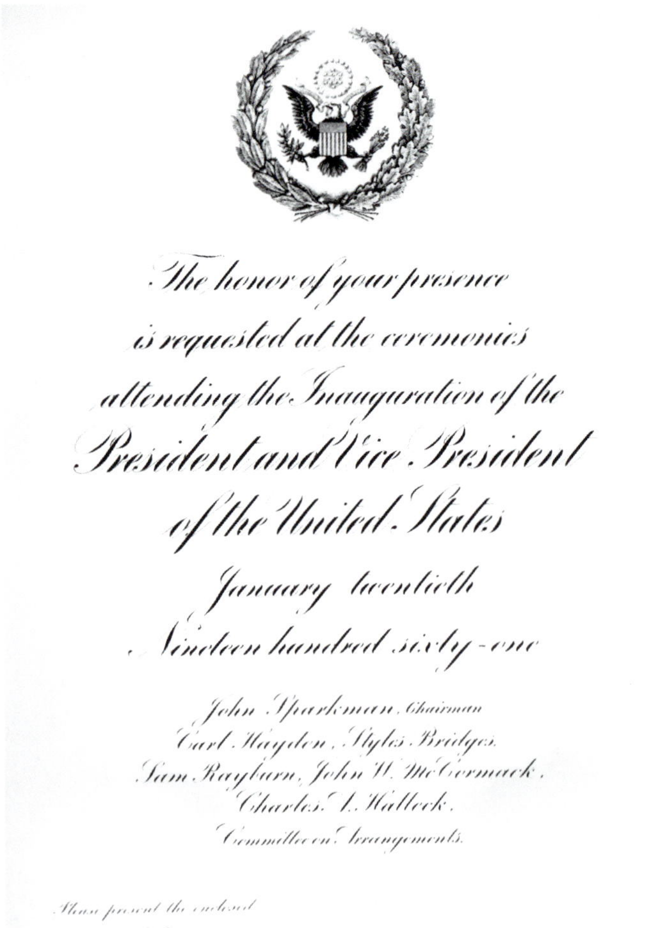

The honor of your presence
is requested at the ceremonies
attending the Inauguration of the
President and Vice President
of the United States
January twentieth
Nineteen hundred sixty-one

John Sparkman, Chairman
Carl Hayden, Styles Bridges,
Sam Rayburn, John W. McCormack,
Charles A. Halleck,
Committee on Arrangements.

Please present the enclosed

OFFICIAL INVITATION FOR THE JANUARY 20, 1961 INAUGURATION CEREMONIES.

RETIRING PRESIDENT DWIGHT D. EISENHOWER AND KENNEDY LEAVE THE WHITE HOUSE TO RIDE TOGETHER TO THE CAPITOL FOR THE INAUGURATION.

around the inaugural stand in the Capitol Plaza. At quarter to four in the morning, the President-elect returned to his house in Georgetown from a supper given him downtown by his father after the Gala. His wife, recuperating from the birth of their second child, had gone home hours earlier; but he found her awake, too excited to sleep, and they talked for a moment about the day that had passed and the day yet to come.

Toward dawn the snow began to stop. It covered houses and clung to trees and filled the windswept streets: the white city faintly shimmered in the pale sunrise. The President-elect arose at eight, read over the text of his inaugural address, pencil in hand, and then left to attend mass at a neighboring church. The crowd began to gather in the Capitol Plaza long before noon. At eleven the President-elect and his wife drank coffee with the retiring President and Vice-President and their wives in the Red Room of the White House. They talked formally and inconsequentially. In morning coats and top hats they entered limousines to drive along the snowy streets to the Capitol. The wife of the retiring President said, "Look at Ike in his top hat. He looks just like Paddy the Irishman."

The skies were now blue and cloudless, and the Plaza glistened in the sun, but the wind had not fallen and the temperature was barely twenty degrees above zero. The waiting crowd huddled and shivered. They enveloped themselves in sweaters and mufflers, blankets and sleeping bags. They stamped their feet to keep out the chill. They watched restlessly as the dignitaries slowly took their places on the platform. When the Vice President-elect entered, a man in a ten-gallon hat shouted, "All the way with L.B.J."; the Vice President-elect acknowledged the shout with a slight inclination of his head. Noon passed, and the crowd shuffled with impatience when the ceremony failed to begin. The President-elect, starting to come from the Capitol onto the platform, was instructed to wait. Then, at twenty minutes after twelve, he appeared, and the spectators warmed themselves with applause.

Now they listened with stoicism as the Cardinal boomed out an interminable invocation. They looked with envy as blue smoke thinly curled up from a short circuit in the electric wires underneath the lectern: where there was fire, there must be heat. The Chief of the Secret Service watched the smoke with apprehension, fearful that the whole inaugural stand might go up in flames. Three times he started to give the order to clear the stand, and three times he paused; then the smoke stopped. The Chief mused that his Service would be in for a lively era protecting the athletic and fearless new President.*

On the platform, the breath of the old poet congealed in the freezing air; and now, when he stepped forth to speak, the glare from the sun and snow blinded him. He read three lines from a manuscript:

Summoning artists to participate
In the august occasions of the state
Seems something artists ought to celebrate.

Then he stopped and said, "I'm not having a good light here at all. I can't see in this light." The Vice President-elect held out his hat to shield the old man's eyes; Robert Frost still could not see, could not conclude the poem:

It makes the prophet in us all presage
The glory of a next Augustan age
Of a power leading from its strength and pride,
Of young ambition eager to be tried,
Firm in our free beliefs without dismay,
In any game the nations want to play.
A golden age of poetry and power
Of which this noonday's the beginning hour.

Instead he said, "This was to have been a preface to a poem which I do not have to read," and from memory he recited "The Gift Outright"—"The land was ours before we were the land's"—changing the last line:

Such as we were we gave ourselves outright
(The deed of gift was many deeds of war)
To the land vaguely realizing westward,
But still unstoried, artless, unenhanced,
Such as she was, such as she will become.

* U. E. Baughman, *Secret Service Chief* (New York, 1962), 3, 12.

KENNEDY DELIVERING HIS INAUGURATION SPEECH.

At nine minutes before one the Chief Justice came forward to administer the oath. The President-elect, without hat or coat, the old Douay Bible of the Fitzgerald family open before him, gave his responses in firm tones. At last he began his inaugural address, his voice ringing out in the frosty air. "Let the word go forth from this time and place, to friend and foe alike, that the torch has been passed to a new generation of Americans—born in this century, tempered by war, disciplined by a hard and bitter peace, proud of our ancient heritage." And so he continued, striking notes of strength, conciliation and hope. "Let us begin anew," he said, "—remembering on both sides that civility is not a sign of weakness, and sincerity is always subject to proof. Let us never negotiate out of fear. But let us never fear to negotiate." The prospect would not be easy. "All this will not be finished in the first hundred days. Nor will it be finished in the first thousand days, nor in the life of this Administration, nor even perhaps in our lifetime on this planet. But let us begin." The burden of the "long twilight struggle" lay on this people and this generation. "And so, my fellow Americans: ask not what your country can do for you—ask what you can do for your country." (That morning, reading over his text, he had scratched out "will" and replaced it by "can.") He concluded: "My fellow citizens of the world: ask not what America will do for you, but what together we can do for the freedom of man."

The applause was strong and sustained. The President left the platform. His young wife joined him in the Capitol, whispered, "Oh, Jack, what a day," and softly touched his face. Then the inaugural parade marched through the freezing afternoon, and the thirty-fifth Presidentiad, as Walt Whitman would say, began.

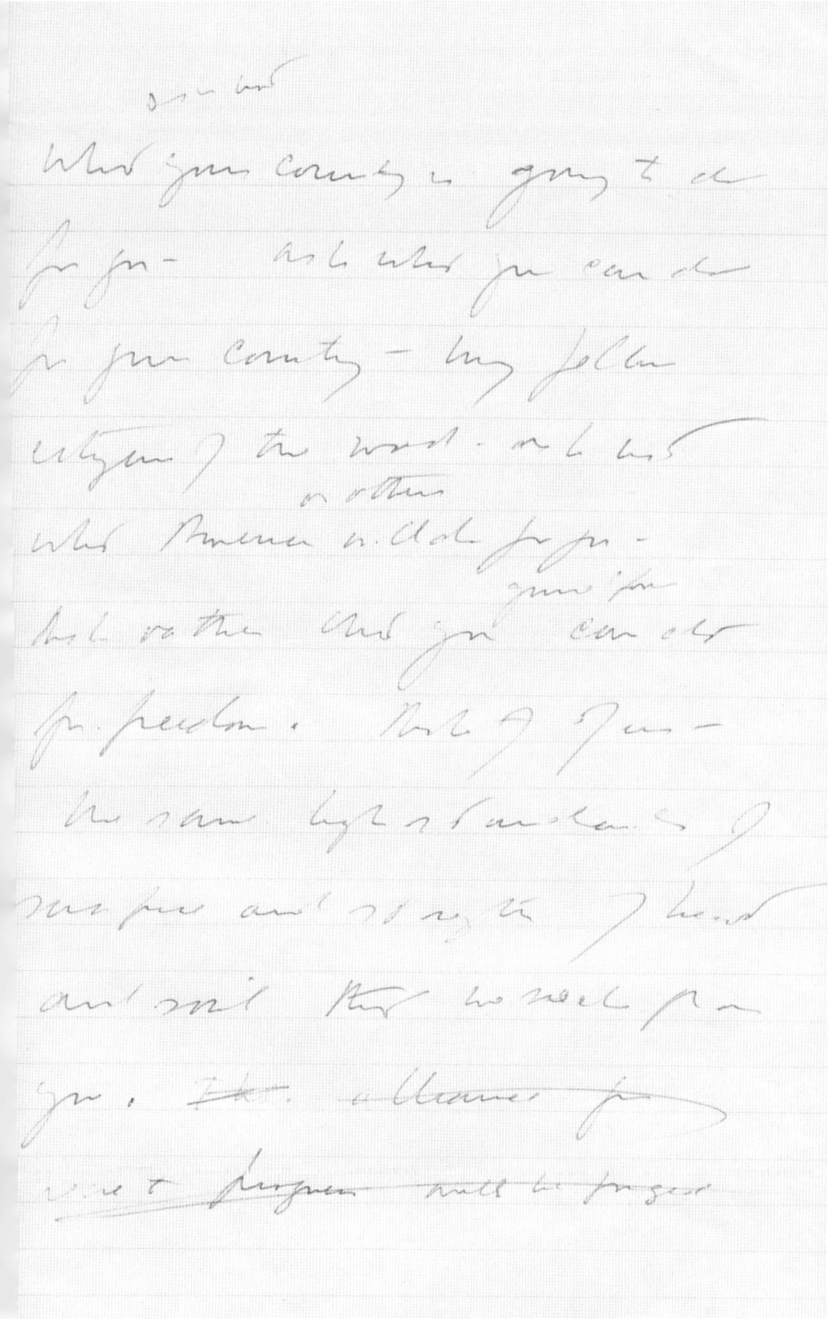

ABOVE LEFT: A PAGE FROM A DRAFT OF KENNEDY'S INAUGURATION SPEECH.

ABOVE RIGHT: KENNEDY'S MOTORCADE LEAVING THE STEPS OF THE CAPITOL AFTER THE INAUGURATION CEREMONIES.

BELOW: JACQUELINE WITH HER HUSBAND MOMENTS AFTER HE WAS SWORN IN AS THE 35TH PRESIDENT OF THE UNITED STATES.

I.
THE ROAD TO THE NOMINATION

LEFT: SENATOR KENNEDY MEETS UNDER THE MASSACHUSETTS STANDARD WITH MEMBERS OF THE STATE'S DELEGATION TO THE 1952 DEMOCRATIC NATIONAL CONVENTION.

RIGHT: GOVERNOR ADLAI STEVENSON POSES WITH TWO POLICE CAPTAINS AS HE LEAVES THE DEMOCRATIC NATIONAL CONVENTION IN CHICAGO ON JULY 26, 1952.

THE ELECTION OF Dwight D. Eisenhower to the Presidency in 1952 had signaled a change in the prevailing weather of American politics—a return, in effect, to Republican 'normalcy' after twenty years of Democratic activism. Yet, in losing the 1952 campaign, Adlai Stevenson had left an indelible imprint on the American mind. By giving the tradition of progressive idealism brilliant and exciting expression, he renewed, even in defeat, the vitality of American liberalism. "A whole new generation," said Edward M. Kennedy in later years, "was drawn to take an interest in public affairs when he came on the scene. They were led by him, taught by him and inspired by him."

By 1956 that new generation of Democrats was preparing to claim national recognition. John Fitzgerald Kennedy had been one of its first members to enter politics. Elected to the House of Representatives from Massachusetts after the war in 1946 and then to the Senate in 1952, he was now a contender for the second place on the national ticket. The vice-presidential contest at the Democratic convention that year brought him for the first time toward the center of the national consciousness—a brief fifty-four months before he took the presidential oath in Washington.

1. CHICAGO: 1956

Kennedy's father, Joseph P. Kennedy, was dubious about his son and the Vice-Presidency. He feared that the Democrats would lose in 1956 and a Catholic running mate would be blamed for the defeat. But the young administrative assistant whom Kennedy had taken on in 1953 at the suggestion of Senator Paul Douglas of Illinois, Theodore C. Sorensen of Nebraska, was all for going ahead. Without finally committing himself, Kennedy decided to let Sorensen test the wind. Through the spring of 1956 Sorensen talked to political leaders, wrote a persuasive memorandum designed to prove from the distribution of the Catholic vote that a Catholic would strengthen the ticket and worked unceasingly to line up support.

In the course of his missionary endeavors Sorensen got in touch with me. I had served on Stevenson's campaign staff in 1952 and, if he were renominated, would presumably do so again. Moreover, I had come to the view that, of the various vice-presidential possibilities, Kennedy would help Stevenson most. I also felt that putting a Catholic on the lower half of the ticket would be the most expeditious way to attenuate the taboo against a Catholic President which had too long

TED SORENSEN WHO WAS ALSO A KEY MEMBER OF KENNEDY'S 1960 CAMPAIGN AND LATER SERVED AS SPECIAL COUNCIL TO THE PRESIDENT.

disgraced American politics. Accordingly I had told Kennedy in the spring that I wanted to assist in any way I could consistent with my role in the Stevenson campaign. Sorensen came to our place at Wellfleet on Cape Cod early in July to discuss tactics at the convention.

Kennedy already had friends at the Stevenson headquarters in Chicago, but he had opposition within the party, especially from professional Catholic politicians and from the older generation of party leaders. Stevenson was troubled by the reaction of experienced pros. On the other hand, he wanted to give the new political generation prominence, and he considered Kennedy its most attractive spokesman. As the Democrats began to assemble in Chicago for the convention, he therefore decided to ask Kennedy to put his name in nomination.

The Stevenson staff had taken on itself to write drafts of all the nominating and seconding speeches in order to make sure that the proper points would be made. Kennedy characteristically rejected his draft, and he and Ted Sorensen set to work to produce a new one. I conducted these negotiations, and it was then that I first saw the Kennedy-Sorensen team in operation. There was no question which was the dominant partner, but there was no question either that in Sorensen Kennedy had found a remarkably intelligent, sensitive and faithful associate. Eventually the two labored together nearly till dawn on the speech. Kennedy nominated Stevenson the next evening, and Stevenson won on the first ballot. The vice-presidential nomination was ultimately thrown open to the convention, and Estes Kefauver was chosen.

The open-convention device left a wake of obscure resentments. Both Kennedy and Senator Hubert Humphrey of Minnesota had expected Stevenson's backing (though neither had solid ground for such hopes), and both now felt let down. Stevenson, in Kennedy's case, thought that, in asking him to make the nominating speech, he had already given a thirty-nine-year-old first-term Senator an unexampled opportunity to impress the convention and the nation and that Kennedy should appreciate this. Kennedy instead began to look on Stevenson as indecisive and elusive. Up to this time, the two men, without knowing each other well and divided by seventeen years, had had the friendliest feelings for each other. Now their relationship began to take on a slight tinge of mutual exasperation. Eisenhower's personal popularity, replenished by his success in ending the Korean War, proved invincible in the presidential contest, and in later years, however, Kennedy rejoiced that he had lost in Chicago. Had he won the nomination for Vice-President in 1956, he might never have won the nomination for President in 1960.

2. KENNEDY AND THE LIBERALS

Kennedy was having his problems with the liberal intellectuals. The Chicago convention had made him a national figure; and it was increasingly clear that the vice-presidential nomination would not satisfy him the next time around. In 1958 he came up for his second term in the Senate. His hope was to return to Washington by the largest possible vote in order to lay the basis for a presidential try two years later. His wife later remembered it as "the hardest campaign ever…just running, running." He won by 875,000 votes, the greatest margin up to that point in Massachusetts history.* Now his presidential campaign was starting in earnest.

Many liberal Democrats regarded him with suspicion. In part this went back to the days of Senator Joseph McCarthy in the early fifties. Kennedy at first had not taken the Wisconsin Senator very seriously. One might have hoped that Kennedy, another Irish Catholic Senator and a genuine war hero, would have seen himself in a particularly strong position to challenge McCarthyism. But there were perhaps deeper reasons for his lack of involvement. His family's relations with McCarthy were certainly an important factor. His father liked McCarthy and invited him once or twice to Hyannis Port. Moreover, Robert Kennedy worked for a time on the staff of the McCarthy Committee, though he soon found himself in disagreement with the Committee's procedures and resigned, returning later as counsel for the Democratic minority.

As for John Kennedy himself, McCarthyism simply did not strike him as one of 'his' issues. This diffidence was no doubt related to his exasperation with the ideological liberals

* His younger brother Edward exceeded this margin in 1964.

of the day and what he regarded as their emotional approach to public questions. Still, Kennedy's actual position was no better and no worse than that of most Democrats, including those more clearly in the liberal stream of things.

Kennedy's silence on McCarthy contrasted with Stevenson's eloquent defense of civil freedom; and, if Humphrey had been silent too, he had not made the mistake of writing a book called *Profiles in Courage.* Mrs. Roosevelt was the conscience of the liberal community, and her reproach carried force: "I feel that I would hesitate to place the difficult decisions that the next President will have to make with someone who understands what courage is and admires it, but has not quite the independence to have it."

Old New Dealers, moreover, cherished an ancient and ardent suspicion of Kennedy's father. And his candidacy touched uglier strains in the liberal syndrome, especially the susceptibility to anti-Catholicism. Most liberals, in addition, already had their hero in Stevenson and continued to hope that he might change his mind about not running in 1960. If Stevenson remained unavailable, then Humphrey, by temperament, record and rhetoric, better fitted liberal specifications than Kennedy. The Minnesota Senator was a man of exuberance, charm, courage and political skill, who had given unstintingly of himself to liberal causes, and his inexhaustible flow of language did not conceal his sharp intelligence and discriminating judgment. Kennedy seemed too cool and ambitious, too bored by the conditioned reflexes of stereotyped liberalism, too much a young man in a hurry. He did not respond in anticipated ways and phrases and wore no liberal heart on his sleeve.

SENATOR JOSEPH MCCARTHY PRESIDING AT A HEARING OF THE SENATE INVESTIGATIONS SUBCOMMITTEE ON MARCH 10, 1954.

6. KENNEDY AND CAMBRIDGE

To those who knew Kennedy in Massachusetts the liberal mistrust seemed unfair and unwarranted. My main interest in these years, like that of Kenneth Galbraith, was in having a liberal nominee in 1960, whether Kennedy, Humphrey or, if he became a candidate, Stevenson. Kennedy and Humphrey seemed likely to be the active contenders; and we feared that, if the rivalry between them turned into enmity, it might divide the liberals and permit a conservative to seize the prize.

Kennedy himself was now prepared to go some distance to propitiate the liberals. After 1956 he made a special effort with issues in the civil liberties field, such as getting rid of the loyalty oath in the National Defense Education Act, and he counted on the strong liberalism of his senatorial record to overcome doubts. He was unwilling, however, to engage in retrospective denunciations of McCarthy; it seemed to him undignified. This reluctance only confirmed his critics in their view that he lacked moral sensitivity.

Galbraith and I resolved to do what we could to combat the continuing mistrust. We declared our confidence in Kennedy's basic liberalism. We also tried to help recruit people for his growing brain trust, though we had little or nothing to do with its actual operations. One morning in mid-July 1959, as I was sitting in the sun at Wellfleet, Kennedy called from Hyannis Port to invite me for dinner that night. This was my first visit to the Kennedy compound; and, though I had met Jacqueline Kennedy several times since their marriage, it was really the first occasion for a leisurely chat with her. My wife was not able to come, and there were only the three of us. Jacqueline was reading *Remembrance of Things Past* when I arrived. In the course of the evening I realized that, underneath a veil of lovely inconsequence, she concealed tremendous awareness, an all-seeing eye and a ruthless judgment. As for Kennedy, our relations had hitherto been more political than personal; this was the freest, as well as the longest, talk I had ever had with him. I was struck by the impersonality of his attitudes and his readiness to see the views and interests of others. I was also a little surprised by the animation and humor of his assessment of people and situations. I now began to understand that the easy and casual wit, turned incisively and impartially on himself and his rivals, was one of his most beguiling qualities, as those who had known him longer had understood for years.

Kennedy was fairly optimistic over his presidential chances. He did not think that Humphrey could win the nomination. He supposed that Lyndon Johnson would edge out Symington, and that Johnson could not win either. Stevenson's sleeping candidacy he regarded as his greatest threat. He was inclined toward Humphrey or Governor Orville Freeman of Minnesota as his running mate. And he said that he would have to go into the primaries in order to maintain his momentum.

His greatest need, he thought, was to give his campaign identity—to distinguish his appeal from that of his rivals and suggest that he could bring the country something no one else could. He observed in this connection that he had been stimulated by a memorandum I had written called "The Shape of National Politics To Come." This memorandum had argued that the Eisenhower epoch, the period of passivity and acquiescence in our national life, was drawing to its natural end, and that a new time—a time of affirmation, progressivism and forward movement—impended. This thesis was an extension of the cyclical account of American politics which my father had set forth twenty years earlier in an essay called "Tides of National Politics." He had forecast in 1939 that the then dominant liberal impulse would taper off around 1947. The ensuing conservative period, if the rhythm held, could be expected to run its course about 1961–62.

Invoking this analysis, I had gone on to propose that the approaching liberal epoch would resemble the Progressive period of the turn of the century more than it would the New Deal. The New Deal had taken its special character from the fight against depression; but the Progressive revolt grew out of spiritual rather than economic discontent; and this seemed the situation in 1959. I hazarded the guess that "a revival of a new sense of the public interest will be central to the new period." Aspects of this argument—the belief that we stood on the threshold of a new political era, and that vigorous public leadership would be the essence of the next phase—evidently corresponded to things which Kennedy had for some time felt himself.

Kennedy's candor throughout the evening provoked candor. I asked him about the rumors that he had Addison's disease and was taking regular doses of cortisone for adrenal deficiency. He said that after the war fevers associated with malaria had produced a malfunctioning of the adrenal glands, but that this had been brought under control. He pointed out that he had none of the symptoms of Addison's disease—yellowed skin, black spots in the mouth, unusual vulnerability to infection. "No one who has the real Addison's disease should run for the Presidency, but I do not have it."

4. THE PRIMARIES AND STEVENSON

In the next weeks, Kennedy's campaign began to take shape. My Harvard classmate Theodore H. White has described it vividly in *The Making of the President: 1960;* and I can only add a few notes from the outside. With Humphrey's candidacy now definite and Symington's highly probable, there remained the enigmas of Stevenson and Johnson. Stevenson was seizing every opportunity to insist that he was not a candidate, though he was clearly the favorite of some politicians and many voters. As for Johnson, Kennedy told me in July 1959 that he had recently encountered the Majority Leader, who put out his hand, looked him straight in the eye and said, "As you know, John, I am not a candidate." Kennedy said, "He hasn't done this for nearly two months."

This seemed certain to change. Six months later, Philip L. Graham, the publisher of the *Washington Post* and a close friend of Johnson's, outlined the strategy. He predicted that Kennedy and Johnson would be the only candidates to come into the convention with sizable blocs of delegates—about 500 for Kennedy, perhaps 300 for Johnson. But Kennedy would not quite make it, and after one or two ballots Stevenson would emerge as the northern candidate. Then the convention would settle down to a struggle between Johnson and Stevenson. In this fight, the northern pros would go for Johnson partly because, Graham said, they disliked Stevenson and partly because they did not think he could be elected.

In March, Kennedy spoke with me about the campaign. As usual, he was objective and wryly humorous, candid about himself and impressively dispassionate in his judgment of others. He said that he expected to win in Wisconsin but that he hoped, if possible, to avoid a contest in West Virginia. He did not want to expend the energy or the money. In addition, West Virginia was 97 percent Protestant, and the religious issue was always a risk, though if Humphrey were determined on West Virginia, Kennedy was confident that he could beat him there. And even if he should lose in West Virginia, this would not bring Humphrey any closer to the nomination. He would knock out Kennedy, but the real victor would be a more conservative candidate, probably Symington. On the other hand, if Humphrey withdrew before West Virginia, he would be the logical man for Vice-President. Kennedy added that, if he himself won in West Virginia under present conditions, he would get the nomination on his own without owing anything to anyone. But if other leaders—

KENNEDY IN MILWAUKEE, WISCONSIN ON JANUARY 21, 1960 HAVING JUST ANNOUNCED HIS DECISION TO ENTER THE WISCONSIN PRESIDENTIAL PREFERENCE PRIMARY.

Humphrey, for example, and Stevenson—came out for him between Wisconsin and West Virginia, he would of course feel under certain obligations to them. He suggested that I talk to Humphrey and Stevenson and mention some of these considerations.

When I talked to Humphrey the next day, he simply said that he was committed to going into West Virginia, whether he won or lost in Wisconsin. As for the Vice-Presidency, he said emphatically, "I have no interest at all in the Vice-Presidency. I would not go on the ticket with Jack. I would not go on with Adlai. I would not go on with Lyndon or Stu or any one of them. If I am knocked out of this presidential fight, I am going back to Minnesota and do my damnedest to win re-election as Senator.

A few days later I talked to Stevenson. He said that he had given his word to all the candidates that he would remain neutral, that he planned to keep his word, and that his great concern was to have a united party. Kennedy did not give up on Stevenson, however, and, as the weeks passed, he became more and more the critical figure in the Kennedy calculations. Though Stevenson continued to maintain that he was not a candidate, his supporters, including Mrs. Roosevelt and Thomas Finletter of the New York liberals, were increasingly active, even working on strategy for the convention. A popular demand for Stevenson seemed to be rising steadily.

Relations between Stevenson and Kennedy, while nominally still friendly, had become uneasy. This was unfortunate because, in spite of differences in temperament and disparities in age, they had affinities in background and taste. A relaxed afternoon at Libertyville or Hyannis Port had very much the same mood and tempo—the same sort of spacious, tranquil country house; the same patrician ease of manners; the same sense of children and dogs in the background; the same kind of irrelevant European visitors; the same gay humor; the same style of gossip; the same free and wide-ranging conversation about a variety of subjects; the same quick transition from the serious to the frivolous. Moreover, the two men were in substantial agreement on the great issues of public policy.

And, in a sense, Stevenson had made Kennedy's rise possible. The Democratic party had undergone a transformation in its eight years in the wilderness. In the last days of Truman the party motto had been, "You never had it so good." The essence of the party appeal was not to demand exertions but to promise benefits. Stevenson changed all that. His lofty conception of politics, his conviction that affluence

SENATOR LYNDON B. JOHNSON CAMPAIGNING FOR PRESIDENT IN APRIL 1960.

was not enough for the good life, his impatience with liberal clichés, his contempt for conservative complacency, his summons to the young, his demand for new ideas, his respect for the people who had them, his belief that history afforded no easy answers, his call for strong public leadership—all this set the tone for a new era in Democratic politics. By 1960, the candidates for the Democratic nomination, and Kennedy most of all, were talking in the Stevenson idiom and stressing peril, uncertainty, sacrifice, purpose. More than either of them ever realized or admitted, Kennedy was emerging as the heir and executor of the Stevenson revolution.

But by 1960 it was too late for them ever really to know one another. Each felt that the other did not understand his problems. Each doubted whether the other appreciated what had been done for him—Stevenson by giving Kennedy his opportunities in the 1956 convention, Kennedy by campaigning in twenty-six states for Stevenson in the election. And rivalry now made the differences in temperament and age emotionally more important than the affinities. Certainly the contrast between Stevenson's diffidence and Kennedy's determination in the spring of 1960 heightened for each his misgivings about the other. And Stevenson, like all the political leaders of his generation, thought that Kennedy was a young man pushing too hard who should wait his turn.

Yet every day made Stevenson more crucial to Kennedy's hopes; and later in the spring he renewed his efforts to persuade Stevenson, if not to endorse him publicly, at least to assure him private support at some definite point before the convention.

Returning from the Oregon primaries, Kennedy stopped off to see Stevenson at Libertyville. Stevenson and Kennedy first discussed foreign policy. This was just after the Soviet Union had shot down the CIA's U-2 plane engaged in photographic reconnaissance over Russia, and the two men agreed in their assessment of what they regarded as a bungled administration response. Then they turned to the campaign. Kennedy reviewed his situation, state by state, pointing out how much Stevenson, with his strength in the Far West and the East, could help him. Stevenson replied that he wanted to be consistent and therefore could not declare for Kennedy now, but that he would not be a party to any stop-Kennedy movement, nor would he encourage the various draft-Stevenson movements.

Stevenson, who had met with Lyndon Johnson a few days before, then mentioned the importance of Johnson's cooperation if Kennedy were elected. Kennedy, who knew of the meeting, feared that Stevenson had been, as he later put it, "snowed" by Johnson into thinking that, if he stayed neutral, he would be Johnson's second choice. (Kennedy's conjecture was right. Johnson had said that he could not stand to be pushed around by a forty-two-year-old kid, and that he favored Adlai next to himself.) Kennedy told Stevenson, as he later described it to me, that there was only one way to treat Johnson; that was to beat him.

"The meeting [with Kennedy] was entirely satisfactory from my point of view," Stevenson wrote me later, "and I cannot say he seemed disappointed or surprised about my attitude." He added, "He seemed very self-confident and assured and much tougher and blunter than I remember him in the past." Kennedy also thought the talk pleasant but less satisfactory. He said later, "I guess there's nothing I can do except go out and collect as many votes as possible and hope that Stevenson will decide to come along."

5. AFTER WEST VIRGINIA

West Virginia had gone to the polls on May 10. That night, as the returns showed a stunning Kennedy victory, an impassioned debate took place in the Charleston hotel room of Hubert Humphrey. In the end, Humphrey was convinced that he could not get the nomination himself, that if he hung on to his delegates and stayed in the race he would only be serving the purposes of the stop-Kennedy movement and that the course of liberalism as well as personal dignity was to announce his withdrawal.

TOP: SENATOR HUBERT HUMPHREY CONCEDES THE WEST VIRGINIA PRESIDENTIAL PREFERENCE PRIMARY ELECTION TO KENNEDY ON MAY 10, 1960.

BOTTOM: KENNEDY RELAXES AT HOME ON MAY 11, 1960 AFTER HIS VICTORY OVER SENATOR HUBERT HUMPHREY IN WEST VIRGINIA.

As his key aides moved on to work in either the Kennedy or Johnson camps, Humphrey himself remained enigmatic about his preference. In the meantime, the U-2 incident was putting the contest in a new and grave setting. The collapse of the summit in Paris suddenly reminded the nation that the next President would have to deal with issues of nuclear war. Was the boyish Kennedy the man for this appalling responsibility? The supporters of Johnson began to talk about the need for a man of maturity and experience—a man "with a touch of gray in his hair." And, even more important, there ran through the party a convulsive movement toward the candidacy of Adlai Stevenson.

But Stevenson, when he came to Cambridge a week after Memorial Day, still insisted that he was not a candidate. I urged him once again to consider declaring for Kennedy. He said, "I don't preclude the possibility of coming out for Kennedy. But how am I going to do this without letting down Johnson and Symington, whom I have assured I would remain neutral, and Monroney, Gore, Joe Clark and a lot of others who have begged me to stay out of this?" Then he observed in a worried way that, if his support became necessary to put a liberal over, this might change things.

By this time, a group of liberals, including Rauh, Galbraith, Arthur J. Goldberg of the AFL-CIO, Gilbert Harrison of the *New Republic,* the historians Allan Nevins and Henry Steele Commager, the political scientist James MacGregor Burns, myself and half a dozen others were

"...We are convinced that Senator Kennedy's adherence to the progressive principles which we hold is strong and irrevocable. He has demonstrated the kind of firmness of purpose and toughness of mind that will make him a great world leader."

planning an endorsement of Kennedy. Word leaked in the newspapers forty-eight hours after Stevenson's visit. Stevenson had obviously been touched by the cries through the country for his nomination; and he could not but have been hurt by the defection of old friends like Galbraith (who, indeed, had come out for Kennedy some weeks before) and myself. But he never spoke a word of reproach, and our relations suffered no permanent damage.

Our statement, as drafted and redrafted by Commager and Rauh, finally appeared on June 17. "The purpose of this letter," it read, "is to urge, now that Senator Humphrey has withdrawn from the race and Mr. Stevenson continues to stand aside, that the liberals of America turn to Senator Kennedy for President.... We are convinced that Senator Kennedy's adherence to the progressive principles which we hold is strong and irrevocable. He has demonstrated the kind of firmness of purpose and toughness of mind that will make him a great world leader." On civil rights, "he has assured us that he favors pledging the Democratic Party to Congressional and Executive action in support of the Supreme Court's desegregation decisions and to whatever measures may prove necessary to make voting a reality for all citizens." As for Stevenson, "all of us supported Adlai Stevenson in 1952 and 1956 and hope that he will be a leading foreign affairs figure in any new Democratic Administration. But he insists he is not a candidate in 1960, and Senator Kennedy, a man of whom liberals can be proud, is an active candidate who has proved his appeal to men and women of all ranks and creeds."

The reaction from several leaders of the Stevenson movement was not unsympathetic. Other Stevensonians were less tolerant, however, and in the next few days I received a flood of bitter letters and telegrams.

A few days before the statement finally came out, my wife and I drove to the Cape with Galbraith for luncheon at Hyannis Port. It was a hot, overcast day, and we vainly sought cool breezes on the *Marlin,* the Kennedy power launch. Kennedy was looking forward to Los Angeles and the convention with apparent confidence. Johnson now seemed to him his serious opponent. He talked of Johnson with mingled admiration and despair, calling him the "riverboat gambler" and evoking a picture of the tall Texan in ruffles and a long black coat, a pistol by his side and aces up his sleeve, moving menacingly through the saloon of a Mississippi steamer.

On the Vice-Presidency, Kennedy seemed inclined toward Humphrey. He reported Arthur Goldberg as telling him that Humphrey would accept if he were Kennedy's definite choice. Humphrey would add more to the ticket than anyone else, Kennedy said, but he thought Hubert had campaigned irresponsibly in West Virginia, even though he had been under provocation (he had in mind Franklin Roosevelt Jr.'s attack on Humphrey's war record). He hoped he wouldn't have to spend the campaign explaining away extravagant statements Hubert might make about the Republicans.

On Stevenson he said, "One reason I admire him is that he is not a political whore like most of the others. Too many politicians will say anything when they think it will bring them votes or money.... You have to stick to what you believe."

Much of the talk concerned organization. Galbraith and I urged him to build his own staff and to avoid people like ourselves who had been identified with Stevenson. The civil rights question was much on his mind, and we discussed that at some length.

So the Democrats moved on toward Los Angeles. I had a final talk with Kennedy early in July after President Truman had denounced him for being young and others had denounced him for being sick. He said that he was glad that Truman had brought out the youth issue and that India Edwards, who had been vice-chairman of the Democratic

DEMOCRATIC CANDIDATES SENATOR STUART SYMINGTON OF MISSOURI, SENATOR JOHNSON OF TEXAS, SENATOR KENNEDY, AND SENATOR STEVENSON OF ILLINOIS POSE FOR A HANDSHAKE AT A RECEPTION IN BEVERLY HILLS, CALIFORNIA IN JULY 1960.

National Committee in Truman's day and was now supporting Johnson, had brought out the health issue; this gave him the opportunity to dispose of both matters before the convention. He spoke gratefully of Averell Harriman's rejoinder to the Truman attack and thought he would ask Harriman to second his nomination. "It will be useful for me to have someone who serves as a link to the Roosevelt and Truman administrations; also an older man. I don't want the convention to think that we're just a collection of angry young men." As for the Vice-Presidency, he still leaned toward Humphrey, though he said he had made no commitments because he wanted to preserve flexibility for the convention.

II.
TRIUMPH IN LOS ANGELES

ROBERT KENNEDY CAMPAIGNING FOR HIS BROTHER IN NEW YORK IN 1960.

AMERICAN POLITICS has an occasion to match every mood: ceremony, circus, farce, melodrama, tragedy. Nothing rolls them together more opulently than a presidential convention; nothing else offers all at once the whirl, the excitement, the gaiety, the intrigue and the anguish. But a convention is far too fluid and hysterical a phenomenon for exact history. Everything happens at once and everywhere, and everything changes too quickly. People talk too much, smoke too much, rush too much, and sleep too little. Fatigue tightens nerves and produces a susceptibility to rumor and panic. No one can see a convention whole. And no one can remember it with precision later, partly because it is so hard to reconstruct the sequence of events and partly because people always say and do things they wish to forget. At the time it is all a confusion; in retrospect it is all a blur.

Though I had attended and enjoyed every Democratic convention since 1948, I headed toward Los Angeles in July 1960 with distinct foreboding. I was vigorously in favor of Kennedy; but I retained strong personal ties to Stevenson who now, in the last days, evidently against his conscious will, was emerging as the candidate of a growing and impassioned movement that was becoming the center of emotion in L.A.

On Monday morning Galbraith and I attended the staff meeting at the Kennedy headquarters in Room 8314 of the Hotel Biltmore. About twenty-five people were present, most of whom were assigned to one or another of the state delegations. After a time Robert Kennedy, his coat off, his tie loose, climbed up on a chair to call the meeting to order. He gave detailed instructions about the demonstration to follow his brother's nomination. Then he discussed the platform, saying crisply: "I want to say a few words about civil rights. We have the best civil rights plank the Democratic party has ever had. I want you fellows to make it clear to your delegations that the Kennedy forces are unequivocally in favor of this plank and that we want it passed in the convention. Those of you who are dealing with southern delegations make it absolutely clear how we stand on civil rights. Don't fuzz it up. Tell the southern states that we hope they will see other reasons why we are united as Democrats and why they should support Kennedy, but don't let there be doubt anywhere as to how the Kennedy people stand on this." It was an impressive performance—in its efficiency, its incisiveness and, in an odd way, in its charm.

In the afternoon, Ken Galbraith and I called on Stevenson, who received us with entire friendliness. He still disclaimed interest in the nomination, but Stevenson enthusiasm was rising on every hand. Adlai himself, I think, had few illusions; but he did not wish to let his friends down, and with every passing hour they were becoming more importunate and optimistic. The prospect of his candidacy, moreover, was generating an extraordinary popular response, especially in Los Angeles, his birthplace and long a Stevenson citadel. The makeshift headquarters in the shabby Paramount Building was soon inundated with telegrams and volunteers. Already Stevenson pickets were gathering around the Sports Arena.

1. CHOOSING A PRESIDENT

One cannot speak with certitude about the motives and actions of politicians in that week of strain and clamor and heat, of vast distances and interminable taxi rides. My own impression is that the Johnson strategy was based on building up Stevenson against Kennedy. Nearly every vote cast for Stevenson, the Johnson people reasoned, would be a vote taken away from Kennedy. If Stevenson denied enough votes to Kennedy to prevent nomination on the first ballot, then the Kennedy strength, held together so precariously by momentum and muscle, might begin to crumble. This was,

KENNEDY ARRIVES IN LOS ANGELES FOR THE DEMOCRATIC NATIONAL CONVENTION ON JULY 9, 1960.

of course, the reason why the Kennedy people, who knew better than anyone the fragility of the combination they had so laboriously put together, were so determined to win on the first round.

There followed two frenetic days of politicking and maneuvering by all camps. The candidates presented themselves before various state delegations, while behind the scenes, their aides and staff monitored a constant flurry of rumor, and juggled the uncertain, shifting allegiances of countless key figures within the party. Hubert Humphrey's last-minute endorsement of Stevenson kicked the Kennedy team into an almost manic level of activity.

Then on to the Sports Arena, surrounded by lines of men and women chanting for Stevenson. The nominations began: Sam Rayburn for Johnson; Orville Freeman for Kennedy, gallantly improvising when the teleprompter went dead; then Eugene McCarthy, in much the best speech of the convention so far, for Stevenson. The Stevenson demonstration was sustained and riotous. After it had gone on for a long time, Governor Collins of Florida, the permanent chairman, ordered the lights turned off in the auditorium in an effort to bring the clamor to an end. There were a few moments of singular beauty—everything black except for spotlights stabbing into the vast darkness, flashing across the delegates and demonstrators on the floor. This was the last burst of defiance. The balloting began. By Washington, Kennedy had 710 votes; and, as Bobby had forecast, the rush began. In a moment Wyoming made him the nominee.

The hall cheered its choice with enthusiasm. But pools of bitterness remained. Many Stevensonians were unreconciled. The hope of the nation and the labor of a decade, as they saw it, had been crushed by a steamroller operated by tough and ruthless young men. The next morning I started to urge on Robert Kennedy the importance of doing something to conciliate the Stevenson people and to bring them into the campaign. He listened patiently for a moment, then put his hand on my knee and said, "Arthur, human nature requires that you allow us forty-eight hours. Adlai has given us a rough time over the last three days. In forty-eight hours, I will do anything you want, but right now I don't want to

* His younger brother Edward exceeded this margin in 1964.

hear anything about the Stevensonians. You must allow for human nature."

2. CHOOSING A VICE PRESIDENT

The next question was the Vice-Presidency. This obviously was not a choice Kennedy could sensibly make before the convention, if only for the reason that he might have to use the second place on the ticket, in the manner of Franklin Roosevelt in 1932, as a counter in his own fight for the presidential nomination. He had nevertheless set forth certain general specifications, saying that he wanted a running mate from another section of the country with particular background in the farm problem. His preference would be Hubert Humphrey or another midwestern liberal.

As the delegates assembled, there was inevitable speculation about the vice-presidential choice. On the weekend before the convention a group of party professionals agreed that, if Kennedy won the nomination, Johnson would add most to the ticket. Many of Kennedy's liberal supporters, myself among them, hoped it would be Humphrey. By Wednesday of convention week, however, Humphrey's endorsement of Stevenson made it obvious that, if the nomination went to a Minnesota liberal, it must go to Freeman.

As for the Kennedys, their drive for a strong civil rights plank suggested a continuing commitment to the strategy of no-compromise-with-southern-conservatism. Robert Kennedy and Ken O'Donnell repeated to liberal and labor leaders the candidate's assurance that the vice-presidential probability remained a "midwestern liberal"—a description implying Symington or Freeman and, by broad geographic construction, Senator Henry M. Jackson of Washington, and also loose enough to keep up the hopes of other governors and Senators west of the Mississippi whose support might be needed for the nomination.

Now that the presidential balloting was over, the vice-presidential speculation engulfed the town. Through Thursday morning and early afternoon we lived in a great swirl of rumors, many of them mentioning Symington. But Kennedy's intention remained impenetrable. In search of clues, I stopped by at Stevenson's hotel suite shortly after three o'clock. Bill Blair told me that Stevenson was taking a phone call in another room. In a few moments Adlai emerged, visibly startled. Philip Graham of the *Washington Post* had just told him, he said, that Kennedy had chosen Lyndon Johnson.

In Los Angeles Graham thus had an almost unique acces to all the key figures. On Monday, with the tide apparently running strongly for Kennedy, Graham and another longtime Johnson admirer, Joseph Alsop, decided that Kennedy must be persuaded to take Johnson as his running mate. At Alsop's urging, Graham accompanied him to Kennedy's suite, where they sent in a message requesting five minutes of his time. As Graham remembered the meeting, Kennedy immediately agreed—"so immediately," Graham later wrote, "as to leave me doubting the easy triumph." Graham therefore restated the argument, telling Kennedy he could not assume that Johnson would decline and he must make the offer compelling enough to win Johnson over. "Kennedy was decisive in saying that was his intention, pointing out that Johnson would help the ticket not only in the South but in important segments of the Party all over the country."

Graham was astonished that Kennedy should respond to Johnson at all, especially since Robert Kennedy had told him that Johnson would not be considered. He now passed the word on to Johnson, who dismissed it at once, saying impatiently that he expected the same message was going out to all the candidates.

3. FALLING INTO A DECISION

The week of the convention had been too tense and chancy to give Kennedy time for serious thought about the Vice-Presidency. Now the question could no longer be postponed. During the victory celebrations Wednesday night he observed a little wistfully how terrible it was to have only twenty-four hours in which to make so fateful a choice. But he came that night to a quiet decision to make the first offer to Johnson.

He decided to do this because he thought it imperative to restore relations with the Senate leader. Johnson was the man whose co-operation would be essential for the success of a Kennedy legislative program, and he was in addition the representative of the section of the country which regarded Kennedy with the greatest mistrust. News of the offer, Kennedy hoped, would reunite the Democrats, please the older generation of professionals, now so resentful of the 'angry young men' who had taken over their party, improve the ticket's chances in the South and lay the basis for future collaboration with Johnson. He was certain, on the basis of Johnson's multitudinous declarations and attitudes, that there was practically no chance that Johnson would accept. Very few people in Los Angeles that week imagined for an instant that Johnson would exchange the power of the majority leadership for the oblivion of the Vice-Presidency.

It is true that a week before Los Angeles, Johnson, reflecting that the only duty assigned by the Constitution to the Vice-President was that of presiding over the Senate, had said with feeling, "I wouldn't trade a vote for a gavel."

Yet there are reasons to suppose that the idea of the Vice-Presidency had lain for some time in the inner recesses of that infinitely complex and subtle mind. Indeed, in the winter and spring of 1960, he had striven to avoid trouble with Kennedy almost as if he wished to keep the vice-presidential option open. Thus he had shunned confrontations in the primaries, even though he had been under great pressure to enter West Virginia where his southern accent and Protestant faith might have made him a powerful contender. Only toward the end, carried away by the emotions of combat, had he risked personal clashes with the man who seemed most likely to win the nomination.

During the spring Johnson must have thought a good deal about his future if Kennedy and Nixon became the nominees. Whoever won the election, the post of Senate leader would be very different from what it had been under an indifferent and passive President like Eisenhower. Johnson could hardly expect to retain the power he had exerted with such relish and skill in the late fifties. Moreover, it was a taxing job, and he was tiring of it. And he could not but recall the fate of his predecessors, all of whom had become politically vulnerable at home as a result of their absorption in the responsibilities of Senate leadership.

Beyond this, Johnson had long wanted to be a national and not a sectional political figure. But this ambition had always been blocked by his identification with his Texas constituency. The Vice-Presidency had attracted him before as a way of escape from the purely regional role. Now he saw what might be a last chance to break out of the Texas trap and become a national leader.

He had, in addition, a deep sense of responsibility about the future of the South in the American political system. He used to lament the fact that so much southern political energy was diverted from constructive channels to the defense of the past, that a Senator with the manifest abilities of Russell, for example, had wasted his talent and energy in fighting for lost causes. If the Democratic party did not give a southerner a place on the ticket in 1960, it would drive the South even further back on itself and into self-pity, bitterness and futility. He may well have seen in the Vice-Presidency a means of leading the South back into the Democratic party and the national consensus.

Such considerations were doubtless in Johnson's mind when Kennedy arrived at his suite on Thursday morning, and the two men sat together on a couch in the living room of Johnson's suite.

To Kennedy's astonishment, Johnson showed every interest in the project. "I didn't offer the Vice-Presidency to him," Kennedy told a friend later. "I just held it out like this"—here he simulated taking an object out of his pocket and holding it close to his body—"and he grabbed at it."

Having indicated receptivity, Johnson went on to say that his own people—Lady Bird and Sam Rayburn in particular—did not want him to go on the ticket. Finally Johnson asked time to think the matter over. Kennedy left, saying, "I'll call you back in two or three hours."

4. THE NOMINATION OF LYNDON JOHNSON

Back again in his own suite, Kennedy now began to review the situation. The offer to Johnson and the appeal to Rayburn had been more effective than he had anticipated. Contrary to every expectation, Johnson evidently wanted the Vice-Presidency. Kennedy's problem now was whether this was the result he himself, as presidential nominee, wanted, and, if not, whether he could get out of it.

As he discussed the matter with his brother, they saw strong arguments for taking Johnson. He would probably help the ticket more than anyone else because he could bring with him states which Kennedy might not otherwise carry—Texas and possibly other states in the South. Even more important, as the Kennedys talked it over, a Kennedy administration would certainly have a greater prospect of success with Johnson as a collaborator in the executive branch than as a competitor on the Hill. And Johnson, as Kennedy had often acknowledged, was a man of force and decision to whom, in case anything happened, the government could be responsibly consigned.

On the other hand, the designation of Johnson would outrage the liberal wing of the party. While Kennedy, as a realist, had no doubt that he could ride out a liberal revolt, he did not like to make his first act as party leader a repudiation of his earlier assurances nor did he wish to begin his campaign amidst angry accusations of bad faith. And the question of how, if elected, he would work with his Vice-President also troubled him. The Senate leader was a proud and testy man, well known for his sensitivity and his egotism, unlikely to defer easily to a backbencher nine years his junior. He had already shown a strain of bitterness in the convention. Though the Kennedy-Johnson relationship had been affable in the past and even not without a certain affection, the rapport between the self-possessed New Englander, urbane and tough, and the emotional Texan, so expansive one minute, so vulnerable the next, had its distinct limitations.

KENNEDY CONSULTING ON MATTERS INCLUDING THE VICE PRESIDENCY WITH HIS BROTHER ROBERT, WHO ALSO SERVED AS CAMPAIGN MANAGER.

As he weighed these considerations in his mind, Kennedy began his own process of consultations. His own nomination was now a fact, but still there was no time to exhale. A new round of urgent meetings and phone calls began, as both Kennedy and Johnson sought clarity in this murky situation. Miscommunications during the next frenetic hours nearly derailed the process, but at the end of the day, Kennedy stood by his offer, and Johnson pledged his "total commitment" to play his role as part of the Kennedy team.

5. THE NEW FRONTIER

At the Sports Arena, however, the Kennedy team was in considerable disarray. The announcement had stunned the convention. Liberal Democrats were unbelieving and angry. The choice of Johnson was regarded as a betrayal. It seemed to confirm the campaign stereotypes of the Kennedys as power-hungry and ruthless. The word "double-cross" was used. Soon, however, emotions were subsiding everywhere. The balloting began and, before the roll call reached Michigan, John McCormack moved that Johnson be nominated by acclamation. A roar came up from the hall, mingling "ayes" and "nays," it seemed to me, in about equal proportions, but Governor Collins promptly declared that the vote had carried.

All emotions did not subside. That evening there was an air of depression at Joe Kennedy's house. Jack and Bobby were sitting gloomily around the swimming pool when their father appeared at the doorway, resplendent in a fancy smoking jacket, and said, "Don't worry, Jack. In two weeks everyone will be saying that this was the smartest thing you ever did." Johnson too found himself unaccountably depressed and thought for a moment that he had made the mistake of his life. He growled accusingly to his aides the next morning, "You talked me into this."

My own sense of outrage vanished in forty-eight hours. On Saturday morning I had a talk with Reinhold Niebuhr, who was a few miles away in Santa Barbara, and found him strongly in favor of Johnson's nomination. He pointed out that the Democratic party had pledged itself to the strongest civil rights plank in history. If, in addition, it had nominated a militant northern liberal for the Vice-Presidency, this could only have confirmed the South in its sense of isolation and persecution. But the nomination of a southern candidate who accepted the platform, including the civil rights plank, restored the Democrats as a national party and associated the South with the pursuit of national goals. I noted that weekend, "After reflection, I am reconciled to the Johnson nomination and believe that it may come to be seen as a master stroke.... I now think that on balance, from

LYNDON JOHNSON ACCEPTING THE VICE PRESIDENTIAL NOMINATION FROM THE DEMOCRATS IN LOS ANGELES. HIS WIFE, LADY BIRD, AND DAUGHTER, LUCI, ARE BESIDE HIM.

THE KENNEDY/JOHNSON TICKET.

the viewpoint both of winning the election and of governing the country, the decision was brave and wise."

And so we had our ticket. I dropped by Stevenson's suite on Friday morning and found him unruffled and witty, acting as if a great burden had been taken from his shoulders. Watching him, one sensed the difference between the old group and the new. Kennedy was in the school of Roosevelt. The thought of power obviously neither rattled nor dismayed him. He did not wish cups to pass from his lips. He displayed absolute assurance about his capacity to do the job; and he had a hard and sure instinct about how to get what he wanted. In Kennedy the will to command and the will to victory were visible and unbeatable. One watched the changing of the guard with a mixture of nostalgia and hope.

Late Friday afternoon, in the shadows of the setting sun, John F. Kennedy appeared before a crowd of eighty thousand people in the Los Angeles Coliseum to record his formal acceptance of the nomination. The speech began conventionally enough with tributes to his defeated rivals, who sat behind him in a circle on the platform. Next came the litany of historical allusions: "Richard I ... bold Henry II ... Richard Cromwell ... Pierce ... Fillmore ... Buchanan." Then, in a moment, the speech moved on to a new pitch of gravity and emphasis.

The American people expect more from us than cries of indignation and attack.... For the world is changing. The old era is ending. The old ways will not do.

Abroad, the balance of power is shifting. There are new and more terrible weapons, new and uncertain nations, new pressures of population and deprivation.... More energy is released by the awakening of these new nations than by the fission of the atom itself...

The world has been close to war before—but now man, who has survived all previous threats to his existence, has taken into his mortal hands the power to exterminate the entire species some seven times over.

Here at home, the changing face of the future is equally revolutionary. The New Deal and the Fair Deal were bold measures for their generations—but this is a new generation.... A technological revolution on the farm ... an urban-population revolution ... a peaceful revolution for human rights—demanding an end to racial discrimination in all parts of our community life ... a medical revolution ... a revolution of automation....

There has also been a change—a slippage—in our intellectual and moral strength. Seven lean years of drought and famine have withered the field of ideas. Blight has descended on our regulatory agencies.... Too many Americans have lost their way, their will and their sense of historic purpose. ...

It is time, in short, for a new generation of leadership—new men to cope with new problems and new opportunities. All over the world, particularly in the newer nations, young men are coming to power, men who are not bound by the traditions of the past, men who are not blinded by the old fears and hates and rivalries, young men who can cast off the old slogans and delusions and suspicions....

He was very tired; his delivery was uncertain and at times almost strident; but his conviction carried him along, and the crowd stirred in response to the words, as the sun continued to sink into the sea.

For I stand tonight facing west on what was once the last frontier. From the lands that stretch 3000 miles behind me, the pioneers of old gave up their safety, their comfort and sometimes their lives to build a new world here in the West.... Their motto was not "Every man for himself," but

SENATOR JOHN F. KENNEDY ACCEPTS THE DEMOCRATIC PARTY'S NOMINATION FOR PRESIDENT AT THE LOS ANGELES COLISEUM ON JULY 15, 1960.

"All for the common cause."…

Today some would say that those struggles are all over, that all the horizons have been explored, that all the battles have been won, that there is no longer an American frontier. But … the problems are not all solved and the battles are not all won, and we stand today on the edge of a new frontier—the frontier of the 1960s, a frontier of unknown opportunities and paths, a frontier of unfulfilled hopes and threats….

The new frontier of which I speak is not a set of promises—it is a set of challenges. It sums up not what I intend to *offer* the American people, but what I intend to *ask* of them…. It holds out the promise of more sacrifice instead of more security…. Beyond that frontier are uncharted areas of science and space, unsolved problems of peace and war, unconquered pockets of ignorance and prejudice, unanswered questions of poverty and surplus.

It would be easier to shrink back from that frontier, to look to the safe mediocrity of the past…. But I believe the times demand invention, innovation, imagination, decision. I am asking each of you to be new pioneers on that new frontier….

For the harsh facts of the matter are that we stand on this frontier at a turning point in history….

It has been a long road from that first snowy day in New Hampshire to this crowded convention city. Now begins another long journey….

The crowds cheered; they promised their help, their hand, their voice, their vote; then, in a few moments, they began to melt away into the hushed dusk. John Fitzgerald Kennedy's long journey had begun.

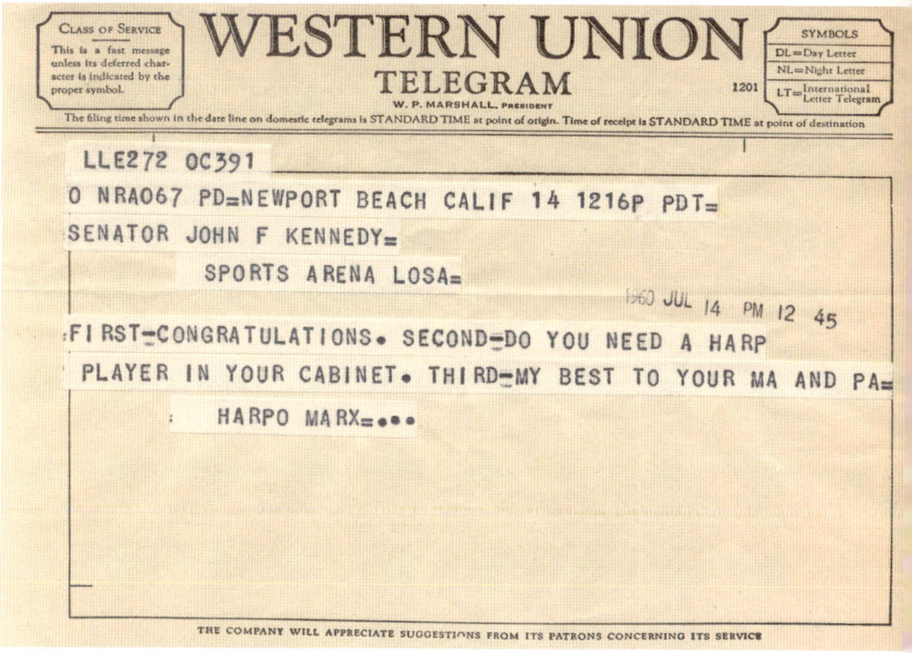

CLASS OF SERVICE
This is a fast message unless its deferred character is indicated by the proper symbol.

WESTERN UNION
TELEGRAM
W. P. MARSHALL, PRESIDENT

SYMBOLS
DL=Day Letter
NL=Night Letter
LT=International Letter Telegram

1201

The filing time shown in the date line on domestic telegrams is STANDARD TIME at point of origin. Time of receipt is STANDARD TIME at point of destination

LLE272 OC391
O NRA067 PD=NEWPORT BEACH CALIF 14 1216P PDT=
SENATOR JOHN F KENNEDY=
SPORTS ARENA LOSA=
1960 JUL 14 PM 12 45
FIRST=CONGRATULATIONS. SECOND=DO YOU NEED A HARP PLAYER IN YOUR CABINET. THIRD=MY BEST TO YOUR MA AND PA=
HARPO MARX=...

THE COMPANY WILL APPRECIATE SUGGESTIONS FROM ITS PATRONS CONCERNING ITS SERVICE

KENNEDY RECEIVED A TELEGRAM FROM HARPO MARX CONGRATULATING HIM ON THE NOMINATION.

III.
CAMPAIGN FOR THE PRESIDENCY

LEFT: JFK WITH JACQUELINE ON THE "MARLIN" AT HYANNIS PORT, MASSACHUSETTS JUST AFTER THE CONVENTION IN JULY, 1960.

RIGHT: RICHARD NIXON CAMPAIGNING WITH HIS WIFE, PAT.

EARLY IN AUGUST my wife and I were asked to luncheon at Hyannis Port. It was a shining summer Saturday, sunny, clear and still. But the once placid Cape Cod village had lost its wistful tranquillity. It looked more like a town under military occupation, or a place where dangerous criminals or wild beasts were at large. Everywhere were roadblocks, cordons of policemen, photographers with cameras slung over their shoulders, children selling souvenirs, tourists in flashy shirts and shorts waiting expectantly as if for a revelation. The atmosphere of a carnival or a hanging prevailed. The summer residents, proceeding frostily down the streets, were identifiable by their expressions of disapproval.

A stockade now half surrounded the Kennedy compound, and the approach was like crossing a frontier, with documents demanded every ten feet. Eventually we made our way past the tourists and the children and the roadblocks and approached the house.

1. OPENING MOVEMENTS

Conversation filled in the interstices of the afternoon. I had never seen Kennedy in better form—more relaxed, funny and free. He chatted a bit about healing the wounds of Los Angeles. He had had a successful visit from Lyndon Johnson, and he was full of enthusiasm for Orville Freeman and Mennen Williams. Humphrey's behavior still puzzled him: "Hubert was supposed to come out for me on that Tuesday. I have never understood what happened to him." Stevenson's visit, he thought, had gone all right. Adlai's political counsel, Kennedy said with some surprise, was shrewd and realistic, and his thinking on foreign policy generally congenial. Stevenson had pointed out that Kennedy, after his months of absorption in the campaign, would need to be brought promptly up to date on the main problems of foreign policy if elected; perhaps he should make provision now for a report to be delivered right after the election. Though Kennedy's mind was primarily on politics, he saw the point and immediately asked Stevenson to prepare the report himself. Stevenson had said nothing about his own future, so Kennedy had said nothing either; "however, I would not ask him to help me now if I did not think of him as playing a role in the future." Kennedy went on to remark a little sadly that he wished he had more rapport with Stevenson. He had rapport with Bill Blair, he noted, and Stevenson obviously had it with Jacqueline; but he always was conscious of strain when he and Stevenson were in direct contact. At one point, he asked, "If you were me, would you appoint Stevenson Secretary of State?" I said yes and explained why. He listened with apparent interest but without disclosing his own feelings.

He talked a good deal about Nixon, who had just been making imprudent statements in Honolulu. This pleased Kennedy; he said he was sure he could count on Nixon's capacity to make mistakes. But he was irritated over a rather striking column by Eric Sevareid in that morning's *Boston Globe.* Sevareid had argued that there were no real differences between the two candidates: "The 'managerial revolution' has come to politics and Nixon and Kennedy are its first completely packaged products." Both men, Sevareid said, were sharp, ambitious, opportunistic, devoid of strong convictions and deep passions, with no commitment except to personal advancement. The genius of these "tidy, buttoned-down men" was not that of the heroic leader but of the junior executive on the make. They represented the apotheosis of the Organization Man. The contention that Kennedy and Nixon were two peas from the same pod exasperated him. He said that this was the fashionable cliché of the campaign, and he obviously feared that it might have some impact. I think, moreover, that he felt personally insulted by it, for he considered that there was no one he resembled less than Nixon. He scorned the way Nixon opened his speeches with the "Pat and I" greeting and employed what one reporter called the "humble bit." "He has no taste," Kennedy said with contempt. On issues, he added with disarming candor, "Nixon is about as far advanced as I was ten years ago."

These were last interludes before the grinding labor of the election began. I had little to do with the inner workings of the campaign and can supplement Theodore H. White's account only by adding some notes on the relations between Kennedy and the liberals. There had been growing enthusiasm for Kennedy in the liberal community in the weeks from West Virginia to Los Angeles. Then the convention, the Stevenson uprising and the Johnson nomination stopped this movement in its tracks. The acceptance speech and the promulgation of the New Frontier revived it for the moment. But it ebbed again in the doldrums of the special session of Congress.

At the end of August the National Board of Americans for Democratic Action held a meeting to decide its position on the election. The leadership called for an all-out endorsement of the Kennedy-Johnson ticket; but the representatives of the local chapters, rising one after another to report the sentiments of their members, expressed quite different views. About half the chapters recommended no endorsement for the time being; the other half recommended endorsement but with marked tepidity (except for Massachusetts and one or two others) and only because of their fear of Nixon. In the end, the leadership prevailed on the Board to endorse Kennedy and "the national Democratic ticket," but it was a struggle. The ADA statement studiously omitted the fact that there was also a candidate for Vice-President. I wrote Kennedy after the meeting, "I was prepared for the apathy on the part of grass-roots liberals. I was not prepared for the depth of hostility which evidently exists."

A significant section of the traditional Democratic activists—the liberals, the reformers, the intellectuals: in general, the people who were in politics, not because it was their livelihood, but because they cared about issues—seemed immobilized. Adlai Stevenson had enlisted them in active Democratic affairs, and they were not prepared to forgive the man who had usurped his place. The influence of these issue-minded people far exceeded their numbers because they were crusaders of the party; they were the men and women who by Labor Day should have been arguing with their friends, writing letters to their papers, manning their local organizations, canvassing their neighborhoods, plastering their station wagons with Kennedy stickers and, in general, charging the campaign with emotion and zeal. Instead, many of them were sulking; and, worse, some who would have liked to help felt that the Kennedy people in the regular party organizations did not want them in the campaign.

Early in September, as part of his effort to meet this problem, Robert Kennedy asked me to go with James Doyle on a trip through areas of Stevenson popularity in California. Doyle and I did our best to explain to Stevenson supporters in Los Angeles, San Diego and Palo Alto why we thought Kennedy would make a great President. One sensed an awakening of interest in Kennedy, a new readiness to give him a chance; this appeared among the film people in Beverly Hills as well as among the academics at Stanford. Our trip had little effect, however, compared to what Stevenson himself did later.

Kennedy, who had not forgotten those lines of people surrounding the Sports Arena, asked Stevenson to spend as much time as he could in California. This Stevenson did in the next weeks, speaking with his customary grace and magnanimity. Murray Kempton preserved a glimpse of him during a Kennedy trip to Los Angeles. Introducing the young man who had beaten him to the crowds who loved him, Stevenson said, "Do you remember that in classical times when Cicero had finished speaking, the people said, 'How well he spoke'—but when Demosthenes had finished speaking, the people said, 'Let us march.'" So with characteristic style he accepted the succession. "Let us never forget,"

Kempton wrote, "that if a light still rises above this dreary land, it is because for so long and so lonely a time this man held it up."*

2. THE TIDE TURNS

While the Stevenson Democrats were coming to terms with the new order, Kennedy himself was beginning to hit his stride. On September 12, before the Greater Houston Ministerial Association, he knocked religion out of the campaign as an intellectually respectable issue; it would persist, of course, as a stream of rancor underground. And his own political purpose was gradually coming into focus. He was developing with emphasis, and more and more often with eloquence, his distinctive theme—the appeal to get the country moving again. On a hundred platforms, at airports and in armories, at state

TOP: CAMPAIGNING IN NEW YORK CITY IN FALL 1960.
BOTTOM: GREETING SUPPORTERS AT A DEMOCRATIC RALLY IN YONKERS, NEW YORK IN THE POURING RAIN.

* Murray Kempton, "L'Envoi," *New York Post,* November 2, 1960.

NIXON AND KENNEDY DURING A LIVE BROADCAST OF THEIR FOURTH PRESIDENTIAL DEBATE ON OCTOBER 21, 1960.

fairs and in war memorials and municipal auditoriums, before crowds baked in the sun or shivering in the autumn's early frost, from the interior valleys of California to the familiar town squares of New England, he was defining the issue, his voice twanging and rapid, his sentences punctuated by the staccato movement of the outthrust arm and the pointed finger, his argument so intent that his flow of discourse often smothered the bursts of applause.

By mid-September his intelligence and intensity were beginning to command the attention of the electorate—and then the debates began. In retrospect, September 26 was surely the turning point. My wife saw the first debate with Jacqueline at Hyannis Port. Marian told me later that Kennedy, calling Jacqueline after the broadcast, could not suppress his delight. Nixon's key issue—Kennedy's supposed youth and inexperience—had been eliminated from the campaign in one stroke.

When I went to San Francisco again in a few days, the atmosphere had changed. The liberals were now showing enthusiasm and commitment. A few days later Jacqueline called to say that her husband wanted Galbraith and me to come to New York to help in the preparation for the third debate on October 13. She also said he wanted new ideas and speeches.

Actually he was in no need of assistance. His speech and research operations were in excellent shape. Though Kennedy had no time now to do any writing, he was a confident and skilled improvisor who very often departed from or even abandoned his prepared manuscript—a practice which tried the warm affection of the newspapermen for him, since it required them to listen to every speech and, when he deviated from the text, to file a second story. As for the manuscripts themselves, they came mostly from two members of his senatorial staff, Ted Sorensen and a young Harvard Law School graduate and former Frankfurter law clerk, Richard N. Goodwin.

I had helped in a speech or two early in the campaign, especially the Liberal party speech in New York on September 14, and Ted had asked me to try my hand some more; but one knew from previous elections how impossible it was to prepare drafts from a distance. Kennedy agreed and remarked that in due course his people might start to grow tired and run out of ideas, in which case he might want to send for Galbraith and me. He noted, though, that there were public reactions to be taken into account—Nixon's refrain about the Democrats as "the party of Galbraith and Schlesinger and Bowles," as well as press stories about the Kennedy team collapsing and Stevenson's writers taking over. He said that, if I had anything I wanted to get to him, I should communicate through Jacqueline—a channel designed, I assume, to simplify his relations with his immediate staff.

Regarding Nixon, his attitude continued one of amused scorn. During the second debate, the studio, at Nixon's request, had been cooled to almost sixty degrees. Kennedy, trying out his chair, discovered that four lights were shining in his face as against one shining on Nixon. "When I saw all these lights, I decided that NBC had chosen its candidate." After the broadcast, he had gone over to shake hands with Nixon, and they had a moment or two of inconsequential chat. Then a photographer began to take a picture. Nixon, without altering the subject of his conversation or the tone of his voice, started waving his finger in Kennedy's face to give the impression that he was telling off Kennedy as he had told off Khrushchev. Kennedy described this episode with mixed incredulity and contempt. Some days later, he asked lightly, "Do you realize the responsibility I carry? I'm the only person standing between Nixon and the White House."

3. THE PEOPLE SPEAK

In mid-October, Kennedy felt that things were going well; as he put it, he had "everything made" except the religious issue, and this remained the great imponderable. He also expressed concern, however, about Cuba. Nixon, aided by Khrushchev's shoe-banging performance at the United Nations, was making inroads among suburban Catholics, to whom anti-communism made a strong appeal, denouncing Kennedy as "soft." As we discussed Cuba, Kennedy remarked that any measures against the Castro regime must of course be taken in concert with the other American republics.

After hearing this reasonable view, I was considerably surprised to read in the afternoon papers a militant Kennedy statement attacking the Republicans for their complacency before communism in Cuba and, while affirming the importance of "collective action," adding the ambiguous proposal: "We must attempt to strengthen the non-Batista democratic anti-Castro forces in exile, and in Cuba itself, who offer eventual hope of overthrowing Castro. Thus far these fighters for freedom have had virtually no support from our Government."

In fact, Kennedy had not seen this statement. Richard Goodwin, who had written it the evening before, had shown it to Sorensen and Salinger. They all agreed that this would be an effective riposte to Nixon's attacks on Kennedy's 'softness,' but, by the time they had finished discussing it, Kennedy himself had gone to bed. No one likes to awaken a sleeping candidate; and, since the staff thought the statement did no more than express compactly the things Kennedy had been saying about Cuba for several days, they decided to put it out without bothering him. (This had not happened before during the campaign, it did not happen again.) In all probability, Kennedy would have approved the text, though he told me later he would have changed the phrase "fighters for freedom" to "forces of freedom."

The statement produced an immediate uproar among his liberal and intellectual supporters. James B. Reston described it in the *New York Times* as Kennedy's first major blunder, and Walter Lippmann wrote a column of measured dismay. Kennedy thereafter dropped Cuba and concentrated for the rest of the campaign on his central themes.

It was late October, with events rushing toward their climax. A Georgia court sent Martin Luther King to jail on October 24. Harris Wofford of the campaign staff, who had been handling civil rights matters for Kennedy, told Sargent Shriver that Mrs. King was pregnant and in a state of near-hysteria and suggested that it might be good if Kennedy made a phone call of sympathy to her. Kennedy, responding with instinctive compassion, phoned Mrs. King at once.

KENNEDY LOOKS OVER HIS SPEECH BEFORE ADDRESSING A CROWD OF THOUSANDS AT THE COW PALACE AUDITORIUM IN SAN FRANCISCO, CALIFORNIA ON NOVEMBER 2, 1960.

Robert Kennedy put through a call to the Georgia judge asking that King be given bail. Before he did, he alerted Lyndon Johnson. Johnson said, "Tell Jack that we'll ride it through down here some way, and at least he's on the side of right." In the meantime, King's father told newspapermen that he never thought he could vote for a Catholic but that the call to his daughter-in-law had changed his mind. "Imagine Martin Luther King having a bigot for a father," Kennedy said—then added quizzically, "Well, we all have fathers, don't we?"

The call to Mrs. King was only one of a number of personal gestures revealing the grace and force of feeling which lay beneath the supposedly cool façade. By mid-October one began to feel that the real Kennedy was coming over.

"This race is a contest between the comfortable and the concerned, between those who believe that we should rest and lie at anchor and drift, and between those who want to move this country forward in the 1960s..."

CROWDS CHEER AND THROW CONFETTI AND PAPER STREAMERS AS KENNEDY'S CAR INCHES ALONG IN DOWNTOWN LOS ANGELES ON NOVEMBER 1, 1960.

No one could mistake him for Nixon any longer. Even the Stevensonians were responding to his wit and resolve. Young people in particular felt, in many cases for the first time, a connection with politics. Wildly cheering crowds surged around him as he crisscrossed the country. One has an unmistakable feeling when a campaign catches fire: it happened to Stevenson for a time in 1952 but not in 1956. It was plainly happening to Kennedy in the third week in October, 1960.

The surge continued for a number of days. Then, toward the end of the month, as mysteriously as it had begun, it started to wane. It was a strange, impalpable ebbing away. Reporters related it to events: the end of the debates, the intervention of Eisenhower. In retrospect one felt it had deeper roots—that it was almost as if the electorate were having sudden doubts whether it really wanted so intense a leader, so disturbing a challenge to the certitudes of their existence; it was as if the American people commenced to think that the adventure of Kennedy might be too much and that they had better fall back to the safe and familiar Nixon. Some close to Kennedy believed that, if the campaign had gone on three days more, he would have been beaten. The candidate himself knew the tide was shifting. When Nixon at the end went on television for a prolonged question-and-answer session, an aide told Kennedy that his opponent could be seen on a set in the next room. Utterly weary, Kennedy waved him away.

On election eve Kennedy, exhilarated by a return to home territory, spoke at the Boston Garden. A chapter of American history was spread out in the hall that evening—Kennedy, cool, poised, masterful, a son of Ireland and of Harvard, surrounded by a conventionally seedy Massachusetts state ticket, which he dutifully endorsed with breakneck speed and evident indifference, and confronting an audience of his supporters, from South Boston to Harvard Yard, shouting their hearts out: it was, as one reporter wrote, the young prince come home. He summed up the campaign: "This race is a contest between the comfortable and the concerned, between those who believe that we should rest and lie at anchor and drift, and between those who want to move this country forward in the 1960s.... War and peace, the progress of this country, the security of our people, the education of our children, jobs for men and women who want to work, the development of our resources—the symbolic feeling of a nation, the image the nation presents to the world, its power, prestige and direction—all ultimately will come to rest on the next President of the United States.... I do not run for the office of the Presidency after fourteen years in the Congress with any expectation that it is an empty or an easy job. I run for the Presidency of the United States because it is the center of action.... The kind of society we build, the kind of power we generate, the kind of enthusiasm that we incite, all this will tell whether, in the long run, darkness or light overtakes the world.... I ask you to join us tomorrow, and, most of all, I ask you to join us in all the tomorrows yet to come."

What one noticed most was the transformation of Kennedy himself—from the vigorous but still uncertain figure of early September to a supremely assured and powerful leader. His growth in the campaign conquered even the most skeptical. Mrs. Roosevelt said to me a few days after the election, "I don't think anyone in our politics since Franklin has had the same vital relationship with crowds. Franklin would sometimes begin a campaign weary and apathetic. But in the course of the campaign he would draw strength and vitality from his audiences and would end in better shape than he started. I feel that Senator Kennedy is much the same—that his intelligence and courage elicit emotions from his crowds which flow back to him and sustain and strengthen him."

On Tuesday the people by an alarmingly narrow margin in the popular vote chose John Fitzgerald Kennedy of Massachusetts as the thirty-fifth President of the United States.

IV.
KENNEDY ON THE EVE

THE KENNEDY CLAN. FROM LEFT: JFK, JEAN, ROSE, JOSEPH SR., PAT, RFK, EUNICE AND TED (BOTTOM).

MY FIRST KNOWLEDGE OF John F. Kennedy went back to undergraduate days at Harvard twenty-five years before. His older brother, Joseph P. Kennedy, Jr., was one of my classmates, a confident, gregarious young man with a rollicking personality that swept all before it. He seemed destined to be a man of power, though one did not feel in him the inward and reflective quality one later found in his brothers John and Robert. But I never knew him well. He was a brave man and died in the war.

His younger brother John arrived in Cambridge as a freshman when Joe and I were in our third year. In those days the freshman class put on a smoker each spring; and the Freshman Smoker of 1937 shamed the older classes with its prodigies of talent imported from Broadway and Hollywood. One learned that young Jack Kennedy was responsible for this triumph. Even upper-classmen were impressed. I saw him from time to time in the Yard but do not recall that I ever exchanged a word with him. Joe and I finished Harvard in 1938, Jack two years later.

My next memory of Jack Kennedy goes back to London in the summer of 1944 when, as buzz-bombs roared overhead, I read one day in *The New Yorker* John Hersey's quiet account of his adventures in the Pacific. In 1946 I heard that he had returned to Boston to run for Congress. In due course he won the Democratic nomination for the House of Representatives in the 11th district, which included Cambridge, and was elected. I saw him from time to time in these years before the Presidency, with increasing frequency toward the end of the fifties, though I was not one of his intimates, if indeed he had real intimates outside his family.

In these years I began to understand better the complexity of mind and emotion which underlay that contained and ironic exterior, but only a little better. Kennedy had to an exceptional degree the gift of friendship and, in consequence, a great diversity of friends; part of his gift was to give each the sense that he alone had a clue to the mystery. The friends came in layers—the Choate and Harvard friends, the friends from the Navy, the social friends from Palm Beach and Newport, the Irish friends, the senatorial friends, the intellectual friends—and each layer considered itself closest to the center. But Kennedy kept the layers apart and included and baffled them all. The ultimate reserve was a source of his fascination and his power.

JOHN F. KENNEDY AT SIX MONTHS.

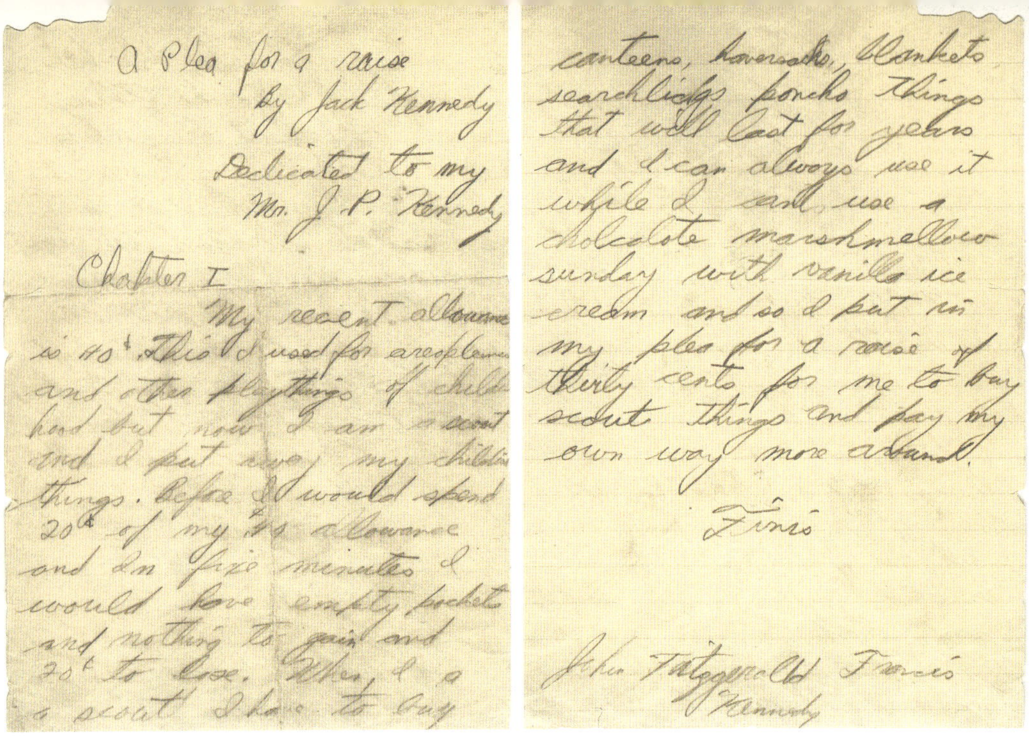

A Plea for a raise
By Jack Kennedy
Dedicated to my
Mr. J. P. Kennedy

Chapter I

My recent allowance is 40¢. This I used for areoplanes and other playthings of childhood but now I am a scout and I put away my childish things. Before I would spend 20¢ of my ¢40 allowance and In five minutes I would have empty pockets and nothing to gain and 20¢ to lose. When I a a scout I have to buy canteens, haversacks, blankets searchlidgs poncho things that will last for years and I can always use it while I cant use a cholcolate marshmellow sunday with vanilla ice cream and so I put in my plea for a raise of thirty cents for me to buy scout things and pay my own way more around.

Finis

John Fitzgerald Francis Kennedy

YOUNG JOHN'S PLEA TO HIS FATHER FOR A RAISE IN ALLOWANCE.

JOHN F. KENNEDY, AGE 8.

1. THE KENNEDY FAMILY

How had it all come about? Part of the answer, of course, lay in his upbringing. He was born into a family that was large, warm and spirited. There is no point in idealizing the Kennedys. Like any family, it had its share of tensions. Young Joe Kennedy, the oldest son, was bigger and stronger than the others; he was the leader of the children and occasionally, in discharging his role, something of a bully. No doubt Jack Kennedy was shoved around a good deal by his older brother. But, more than most families, the Kennedys were bound together by a love which gave all the children a fundamental confidence. With its subtle and disparate solidarity, the family nourished a capacity for competition, for individuality and for loyalty.

Little is more dangerous than to try to explain a man in terms of supposed ethnic traits. In most respects, Kennedy departed considerably from the Irish-American stereotype. He was reticent, patrician, bookish, urbane, yet the Irishness remained a vital element in his constitution. It came out in so many ways—in the quizzical wit, the eruptions of boisterous humor, the relish for politics, the love of language, the romantic sense of history, the admiration for physical daring, the toughness, the joy in living, the view of life as comedy and as tragedy.

And it gave him a particular slant on American society. Though the Kennedy family was well established politically and financially, it was still marginal socially in Brahmin Boston; and its folk memories were those of a time, not too far distant, when to be Irish was to be poor and have gates slammed in one's face. Joseph P. Kennedy, a man of driving ambition, was determined to reverse all that. Business success helped; it enabled him to open doors for them all their lives. But what was more important than money was the training he gave his children—a regimen of discipline tempered and transformed by affection.

Regarding money as a means and not as an end, Joe Kennedy forbade its discussion at the dinner table. Conversation turned, not on business, but on public affairs; no child could doubt the order of priority. The father confronted the children with large questions, encouraged them to have opinions of their own, demanded that their opinions make sense, wrote them endless letters when he was away (which was often), told them they had an obligation to take part in public life and instilled convictions of purpose and possibility. Young Jack kept up his side in the competitive world of the Kennedys. But for all his vitality he had both a frailness and a sensitivity which set him somewhat apart from the extroverted and gregarious family. He may even have been a little lonely at times. He passed a surprising amount of his childhood sick in bed—with diphtheria, scarlet fever, acute appendicitis and chronic stomach trouble. He was the only one in the family who liked to read; loneliness and sickness made him read all the more. He spent hours in his room absorbed in history and biography. History was full of heroes for him, and he reveled in the stately cadences of historical prose. His memory of what he read was photographic. Situations, scenes and quotations stuck in his mind for the rest of his life.

The interior life was a source of identity and of power. Already he was moving beyond his brother Joe, moving beyond his father, and developing distinctive standards and goals. The Kennedys were supposed never to finish second; but Jack could present a favorite quotation from Alan Seeger: "Whether I am on the winning or losing side is not the point with me. It is being on the side where my sympathies lie that matters." It used to be said that the older Kennedy 'made' his son Jack President and, if Joe, Jr., had only lived, would have 'made' him President first. I do not believe either of these things for a moment. I doubt whether young Joe, for all his charms and gifts, would have been President.

JOSEPH KENNEDY

And it was Jack Kennedy who, in the existential sense, first made himself and then made himself President. Out of some fierce, cool inner passion, he became a man in his own right who grew from but beyond the family in which he was born, which loved him so much and which he loved so much.

It is hard to judge how much his formal education mattered. He spent only one year at a Catholic school, Canterbury in Connecticut. He then went on to Choate, which he disliked heartily. Choate provided no intellectual excitement, and he finished only slightly above the middle of his class. His father sent him that summer to the London School of Economics, hoping to expose him to Harold Laski. Instead Kennedy exposed himself to jaundice and had to delay his entry into Princeton in the fall. Then a recurrence of jaundice knocked out the rest of his freshman year. With his Princeton friends advancing into the sophomore class, he yielded to his father's preference and shifted the next autumn to Harvard.

2. THE ENGLISH EXPERIENCE

For a time Kennedy continued in his prep-school mood. He organized the Freshman Smoker, ruptured a disk in his back playing football, made the swimming squad and the *Crimson,* kept apart from the greaseballs in the Harvard Student Union and concentrated desultorily in the field of government.

In the meantime, a summer in Europe between his first and second Harvard years exposed him to wider horizons. He spent a carefree two months wandering around the continent. His diary of the summer records a growing interest in public affairs. Later in the year his father became ambassador to Britain and Jack began spending his holidays whenever possible in London. This speeded his intellectual awakening. He was fascinated by English political society, with its casual combination of wit, knowledge and uncon-

* His younger brother Edward exceeded this margin in 1964.

TOP: YOUNG JOHN F. KENNEDY IN 1923 WITH MOTHER, ROSE. THE CHILDREN FROM LEFT ARE EUNICE, KATHLEEN, ROSEMARY, JOHN, AND JOSEPH, JR.
BOTTOM: KENNEDY, AGE 16, AT CHOATE SCHOOL IN WALLINGFORD, CONNECTICUT. KENNEDY IS FRONT ROW, SECOND FROM RIGHT.

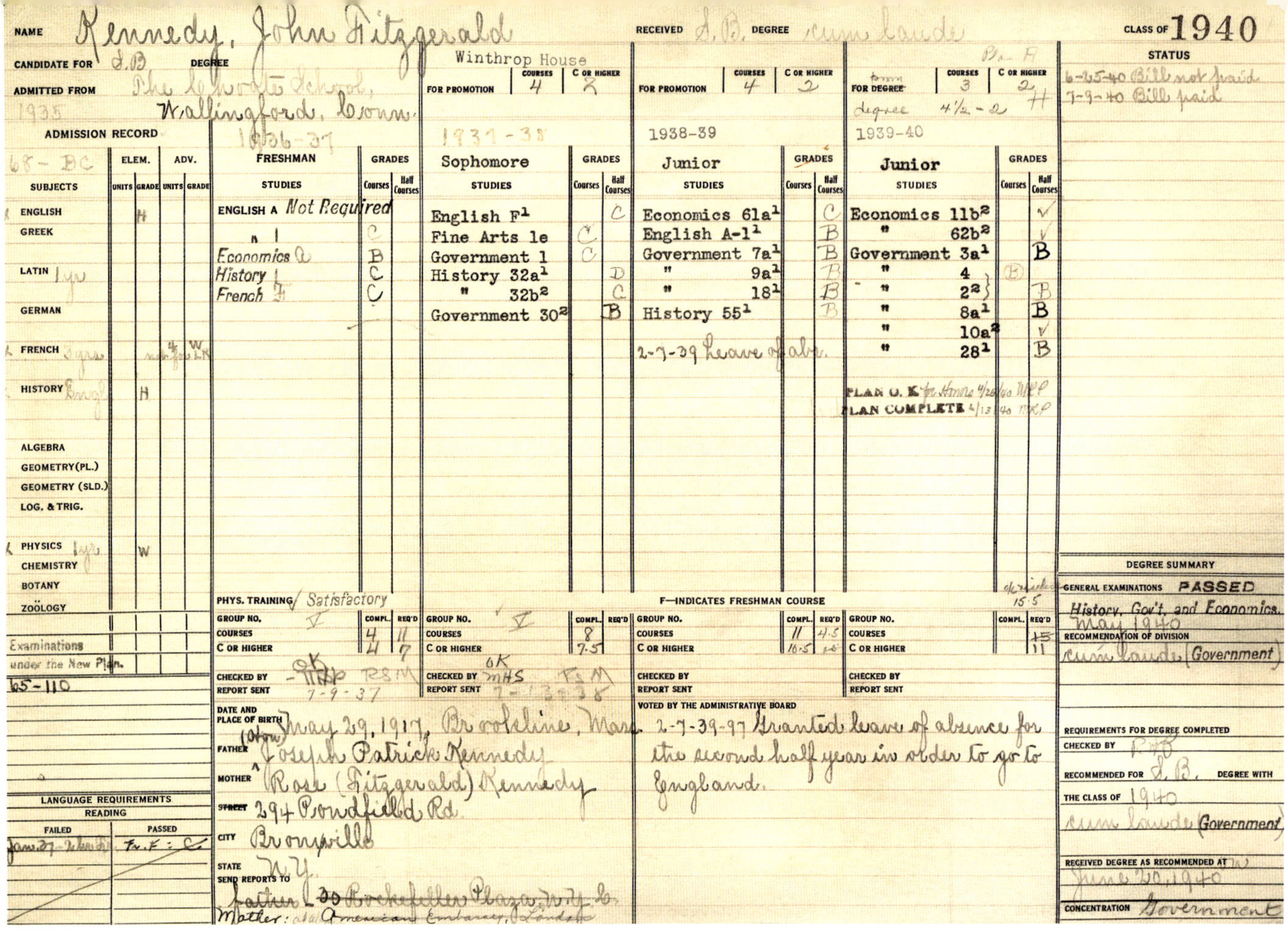
NAME Kennedy, John Fitzgerald RECEIVED S.B. DEGREE cum laude CLASS OF 1940

CANDIDATE FOR S.B. DEGREE Winthrop House STATUS

ADMITTED FROM The Choate School, Wallingford, Conn. 1935

6-25-40 Bill not paid
7-9-40 Bill paid

ADMISSION RECORD 68 - BC

	Freshman 1936-37	Grades	Sophomore 1937-38	Grades	Junior 1938-39	Grades	Junior 1939-40	Grades
For promotion	Courses 4	C or higher 2	Courses 4	C or higher 2	Courses 3	C or higher 2		
	English A Not Required		English F1	C	Economics 61a1	C	Economics 11b2	✓
	" 1	C	Fine Arts 1e	C	English A-11	B	" 62b2	✓
	Economics A	B	Government 1	C	Government 7a1	B	Government 3a1	B
	History	C	History 32a1	D	" 9a1	B	" 4	B
	French F	C	" 32b2	C	" 181	B	" 22	B
			Government 302	B	History 551	B	" 8a1	B
							" 10a2	✓
					2-7-39 Leave of abs.		" 281	B

PLAN O.K. / PLAN COMPLETE

PHYS. TRAINING Satisfactory

F—INDICATES FRESHMAN COURSE

DATE AND PLACE OF BIRTH May 29, 1917, Brookline, Mass.
FATHER Joseph Patrick Kennedy
MOTHER Rose (Fitzgerald) Kennedy
STREET 294 Pondfield Rd.
CITY Bronxville
STATE N.Y.
SEND REPORTS TO Father 30 Rockefeller Plaza, N.Y.C.
Mother: c/o American Embassy, London

VOTED BY THE ADMINISTRATIVE BOARD
2-7-39-97 Granted leave of absence for the second half year in order to go to England.

DEGREE SUMMARY
GENERAL EXAMINATIONS PASSED
History, Gov't. and Economics. May 1940
RECOMMENDATION OF DIVISION cum laude (Government)
REQUIREMENTS FOR DEGREE COMPLETED
RECOMMENDED FOR S.B. DEGREE WITH THE CLASS OF 1940 cum laude (Government)
RECEIVED DEGREE AS RECOMMENDED AT June 20, 1940
CONCENTRATION Government

JOHN FITZGERALD KENNEDY

Born May 29, 1917, in Brookline, Massachusetts. Prepared at The Choate School. Home Address: 294 Pondfield Road, Bronxville, New York. Winthrop House. *Crimson* (2–4); Chairman Smoker Committee (1); St. Paul's Catholic Club (1–4). Football (1), Junior Varsity (2); Swimming (1), Squad (2). Golf (1). House Hockey (3, 4); House Swimming (2); House Softball (4). Hasty Pudding-Institute of 1770; Spee Club. Permanent Class Committee. Field of Concentration: Government. Intended Vocation: Law.

TOP: KENNEDY'S HARVARD REPORT CARD.
BOTTOM: THE ENTRY FOR KENNEDY IN THE HARVARD UNIVERSITY YEARBOOK.

cern. The intelligent young Englishmen of his own age, like David Ormsby Gore, seemed more confident and sophisticated than his Harvard friends. He enjoyed the leisured weekends in the great country houses. It was history come alive for him, and it had a careless elegance he had not previously encountered.

London gave him a sense of the tone in which politics might be approached. It also gave him a rather appalling look at the way democracy responded to crisis. Kennedy was in and out of England in the months when Churchill was calling on his fellow countrymen with such slight effect to rouse themselves against the menace of Nazism. Harvard allowed him to spend the second term of the academic year of 1938–39 abroad, and he traveled through Eastern Europe to Russia, the Middle East and the Balkans, stopping in Berlin and Paris on his way back to Grosvenor Square. When he returned to Harvard in the fall of 1939, the question of British somnambulism before Hitler perplexed him more than ever. Professor Arthur Holcombe of the government department had already aroused an interest in the study of politics; and now, under the guidance of Professors Payson Wild and Bruce Hopper, he set to work on an honors essay analyzing British rearmament policy. After his graduation in 1940, the thesis was published.

Remembering that Churchill had called his collection of speeches *While England Slept,* Kennedy brashly called his own book *Why England Slept.* In retrospect, *Why England Slept* presents several points of interest. One is its tone—so aloof and clinical, so different from the Churchillian history he loved, so skeptical of the notion that the individual could affect events ("personalities," he wrote with regret about the American attitude toward history, "have always been more interesting to us than facts"). This detachment was all the more remarkable midst the flaring emotions of 1940. Though ostensibly writing to prepare America for its own crisis ("in studying the reasons why England slept, let us try to profit by them and save ourselves her anguish"), he remained agnostic about the choices confronting the American President. Kennedy did make the quiet suggestion that "a defeat of the Allies may simply be one more step towards the ultimate achievement—Germany over the world"; but, beyond this, and doubtless out of deference to his father's and older brother's isolationism, he stood aside in the book from the great debate between the isolationists and the interventionists. (At Harvard, however, he wrote to the *Crimson* criticizing the isolationist views of his fellow editors.)

3. THE WAR

As war came closer to America, Kennedy, having been rejected by the Army because of his back, succeeded in 1941 in persuading the Navy to let him in. After Pearl Harbor, he pulled every possible string to get sea duty, finally enrolling his father in the cause. In due course there followed the Pacific, PT-109, the Solomon Islands campaign, Talagi and Rendova, and the incredible few days in August 1943 when the Japanese destroyer *Amagiri* sliced his boat in half and plunged Kennedy and his crew into the waters of Ferguson Passage, now suddenly aflame with burning gasoline. Kennedy's calm bravery, his extraordinary feat in towing one of his crew to refuge by gripping the end of the life jacket belt in his teeth, his leadership, resourcefulness and cheer until rescue came—this was one of the authentic passages of heroism in the war, so well described in later accounts by John Hersey and Robert Donovan and so seldom mentioned by Kennedy himself.

The incident in the Solomons embodied two of Kennedy's deeper preoccupations—with courage and with death. He hated discussing these matters in the abstract, but they were nonetheless enduring themes of his life. Robert Kennedy tells us that courage was the virtue his brother most admired. In the first instance, this meant physical courage—the courage of men under enemy fire, of men silently suffering pain, the courage of the sailor and the mountain climber and of men who stared down mobs or soared into outer space. And, when he entered politics, it came to mean moral courage—the courage to which he later dedicated his *Profiles,* the courage of "a man who does what he must—in spite of personal consequences, in spite of obstacles and dangers and pressures," the courage which, he said, "is the basis of all human morality."

Courage—and death. The two are related, because courage, if it is more than reckless bravado, involves the exquisite understanding that death may be its price.

4. IN SEARCH OF SELF

Along with a deep sorrow over the battalions of wasted lives, the war left him with an intense concern about the prevention of such waste in the future. He went to San Francisco in June 1945 as a special writer for the Hearst press to watch the founding of the United Nations. For a young veteran, with stabbing memories of violence and death, it was in a way a disenchanting experience. But for a student of politics

LIEUTENANT KENNEDY, SKIPPER OF PT BOAT 109, IN THE SOUTH PACIFIC IN 1943.

it was an indispensable education. The hard fact was that nations were not prepared to yield their sovereignty to an international organization.

He had expected to become a writer; but the San Francisco experience may have helped persuade him that it was better to sit at the conference table than to wait outside with the press. His brother's death also changed things. The family assumption had been that Joe, who had made his political debut as a delegate at the 1940 Democratic convention (where he cast his vote, as pledged, against Franklin Roosevelt), would be the Kennedy to enter politics. Though Ambassador Kennedy did not, as myth later had it, automatically promote his second son into the slot now so sadly vacant, Jack, like many young veterans, felt the need of doing something to help the world for which so many friends had died. Politics perhaps attracted him less as a means of saving this world than of keeping it from getting

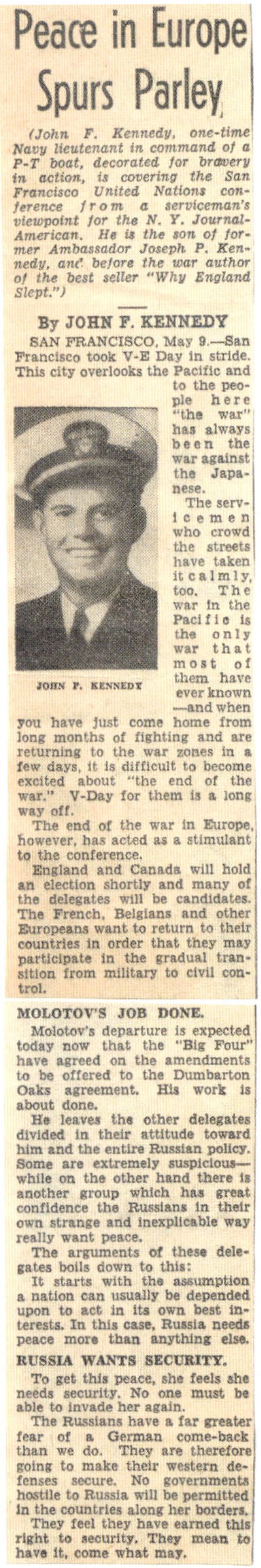

Peace in Europe Spurs Parley

(John F. Kennedy, one-time Navy lieutenant in command of a P-T boat, decorated for bravery in action, is covering the San Francisco United Nations conference from a serviceman's viewpoint for the N. Y. Journal-American. He is the son of former Ambassador Joseph P. Kennedy, and before the war author of the best seller "Why England Slept.")

By JOHN F. KENNEDY

SAN FRANCISCO, May 9.—San Francisco took V-E Day in stride. This city overlooks the Pacific and to the people here "the war" has always been the war against the Japanese.

JOHN F. KENNEDY

The servicemen who crowd the streets have taken it calmly, too. The war in the Pacific is the only war that most of them have ever known—and when you have just come home from long months of fighting and are returning to the war zones in a few days, it is difficult to become excited about "the end of the war." V-Day for them is a long way off.

The end of the war in Europe, however, has acted as a stimulant to the conference.

England and Canada will hold an election shortly and many of the delegates will be candidates. The French, Belgians and other Europeans want to return to their countries in order that they may participate in the gradual transition from military to civil control.

MOLOTOV'S JOB DONE.

Molotov's departure is expected today now that the "Big Four" have agreed on the amendments to be offered to the Dumbarton Oaks agreement. His work is about done.

He leaves the other delegates divided in their attitude toward him and the entire Russian policy. Some are extremely suspicious—while on the other hand there is another group which has great confidence the Russians in their own strange and inexplicable way really want peace.

The arguments of these delegates boils down to this:

It starts with the assumption a nation can usually be depended upon to act in its own best interests. In this case, Russia needs peace more than anything else.

RUSSIA WANTS SECURITY.

To get this peace, she feels she needs security. No one must be able to invade her again.

The Russians have a far greater fear of a German come-back than we do. They are therefore going to make their western defenses secure. No governments hostile to Russia will be permitted in the countries along her borders.

They feel they have earned this right to security. They mean to have it, come what may.

ABOVE: U.S. AMBASSADOR JOSEPH KENNEDY WITH SONS JOE JR. (LEFT) AND JOHN. THIS PHOTO WAS TAKEN IN 1938.
LEFT: AN ARTICLE BY KENNEDY, PUBLISHED IN MAY 1945 WHILE HE SERVED AS A SPECIAL WRITER FOR THE HEARST PRESS.

worse. In 1946 he returned to Boston to test the political air.

The return to Boston must have involved a form of what anthropologists call 'culture shock.' While born a Boston Irishman, he had never been a member of the Boston Irish community; and his life had carried him far away from his roots. Now, in the 11th Congressional District, he was back among his own people, yet not quite of them. He liked their toughness and their loyalty, but regretted their anti-intellectualism. Campaigning through the three-deckers of Charlestown and the North End, he fraternized for the first time with the men and women from whom the Kennedys and Fitzgeralds had sprung. In the dimly lit hall of one Charlestown tenement he encountered David Powers, a man of exceptional sweetness and fidelity, who beguiled him with his flow of stories, his knowledge of Irish Boston, and his capacity for affable relaxation. Kennedy, at first a little stiff and shy, soon began to relax himself, though, as the old Boston politician and raconteur Clem Norton (the model for Hennessy in Edwin O'Connor's *The Last Hurrah*) put it, he never quite acquired 'a street personality.'

Occasional meetings with Kennedy in the next years strengthened the impression of a skeptical mind, a laconic tongue, enormous personal charm, an agreeable disdain for the rituals of Massachusetts politics and a detachment from the pieties of American liberalism. He still looked exceedingly young (actually he was six months older than I), but he was plainly purposeful and his own master.

In 1949, for some reason which now escapes me, perhaps because it might be a first step toward the governorship, I urged him to run for mayor of Boston. He replied, "I am interested in my work here in the House, and feel that there is much good that I can do from here." He was right, of course, to avoid the mayoralty trap; but it was soon evident that he was considering possibilities beyond the House. By 1950 he was making regular weekend visits to Massachusetts, speaking in places remote from his own district. He was plainly preparing to run for senator or governor in 1952. Which it would be depended on whether Paul Dever, now governor, chose to seek re-election or to challenge the incumbent Senator Henry Cabot Lodge, Jr. Kennedy's preference for the Senate was clear. As he said one day, gesturing at the State House, "I hate to think of myself up in that corner office deciding on sewer contracts." When Dever announced in April that he planned to run again for the governorship, Kennedy promptly declared his candidacy for the Senate.

I was away from the state most of the fall, working on Adlai Stevenson's staff in Springfield, Illinois. When the Stevenson party was campaigning through Massachusetts in October, we were much impressed by the cool efficiency of the Kennedy operation and by Kennedy himself, slim, careless and purposeful against the sodden background of the old-time Boston politicians. He beat Lodge by 70,000 votes. In the gloom of Stevenson's defeat, his success was a consolation. Victory now sent him back to Washington as a junior member of the Democratic minority in the Senate.

War had been a hardening experience, and politics hardened him more. Massachusetts Democrats did not exist as a party in the usual sense of the word. They formed rather a collection of rival tongs, controlled by local chieftains and presided over by an impotent state committee. Kennedy carved out his own domain and pursued his own goals. He showed himself determined, unrelenting and profane, able to beat the pols on their own ground and in their own language.

With his instinct for compartmentalization, he did not often display this part of his life to friends in other layers. His closest associate in these enterprises was his brother Robert, who managed his campaign for the Senate in 1952. Though Robert Kennedy was also a Harvard man, the Cambridge liberals regarded him with marked distrust because of his association with the McCarthy Committee; nor were his expressed views on public policy reassuring.

In the 1956 campaign, Robert Kennedy joined the Stevenson party and accompanied the candidate in his trips around the country. He said very little, and no one quite knew what he was doing. (Actually he was learning how a national campaign should—or should not—be run.)

Next to his brother, Kennedy's chief lieutenant in Massachusetts was a Springfield public relations man, Lawrence O'Brien. O'Brien played a large role in organizing

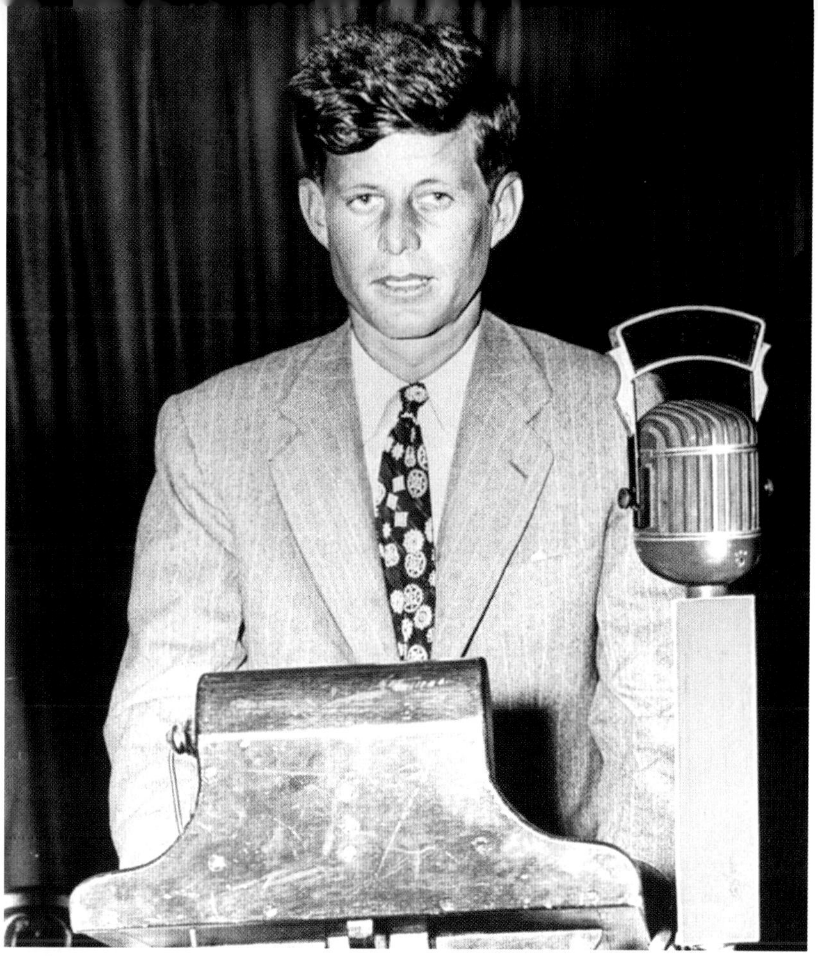

TOP: A YOUTHFUL KENNEDY CAMPAIGNING FOR CONGRESS IN 1946.
BOTTOM: SENATOR KENNEDY SEARCHING THE REAL ESTATE SECTION FOR A NEW HOME IN WASHINGTON D.C. UPON HIS ELECTION TO CONGRESS.

FRIENDS AND FAMILY SURROUND KENNEDY AND JACQUELINE AT THEIR WEDDING ON SEPTEMBER 12, 1953.

the 1952 campaign for the Senate and subsequently joined the senatorial staff. In 1956 the Kennedys engaged in a bitter fight with John McCormack for control of the Democratic State Committee. For that fracas Bobby added to the group a Harvard classmate and former football captain, Kenneth O'Donnell; in 1960 O'Donnell became John Kennedy's appointments secretary and a key figure in the campaign. O'Brien and O'Donnell were both astute, unruffled, soft-spoken and terse. They worked in perfect unison with the Kennedys, shared that common understanding which abbreviates communication to swift phrases and imperceptible changes in facial expression, and filled in a vital part of Kennedy's life. Dave Powers, less involved in politics, kept the whole group happy.

But the Irish Mafia did not possess Kennedy any more than anyone else did. They were his instruments in politics, as Ted Sorensen was his instrument on issues. He admired them all because he admired virtuosity in performance—"the ability," as he once put it, "to do things well, and to do them with precision and with modesty." The techniques by which people did things fascinated him, whether in politics or statecraft, writing or painting, sailing or touch football. He had an instinctive appreciation of excellence.

But, if there were several human excellences, faith in virtuosity per se could not be enough. Which would take precedence over the others? The Kennedy of these years was still undefined. He was a Harvard man, a naval hero, an Irishman, a politician, a *bon vivant,* a man of unusual intelligence, charm, wit and ambition, "debonair and brilliant and brave," but his deeper meaning was still in process of crystallization.

5. MARRIAGE

Then he met Jacqueline Bouvier and leaned across the asparagus at Charles Bartlett's house in Washington to ask her for a date. She was a girl of great beauty, at once wistful and luminous, and also of acute intelligence and exacting expectation. She was a Catholic, but from a securely established French-American family; childhood on Park Avenue and in East Hampton had exposed her to none of the social discrimination visited on the Boston Irish. Her father and mother were divorced, and she had grown up in a rather lonely way. Her loneliness and teachers she had encountered at Miss Porter's and Vassar had given her the capacity to care deeply about life, as the rest of her upbringing had given her the skill to disguise her caring. Her response to life was aesthetic rather than intellectual or moralistic. The intensity of this response attracted Kennedy and perhaps alarmed him; their courtship, Jacqueline said later, was "spasmodic." But they shared the gospel of excellence, and this, as well as more youthful emotions, bound them together.

Kennedy was a new experience for Jacqueline Bouvier. He pursued her with penetrating questions of a sort she had not heard before and, in self-defense, she began to ask questions back. One day she inquired how he would define himself. He said, "An idealist without illusions." And the week before they were married in September 1953 she asked him what he considered his best and worst qualities. He thought his best quality was curiosity, and his worst quality irritability. By irritability he meant impatience with the boring, the commonplace and the mediocre. And by curiosity he meant a good deal more than the purely intellectual trait; he meant that hunger for experience which caused him to demand that life be concentrated, vivid and full. "He lived at such a pace," Jacqueline Kennedy said later, "because he wished to know it all." It was all somehow connected with the precariousness of his health: this seemed to give his life its peculiar intensity, its determination to savor everything, its urgent sense that there was no time to waste.

The shadow had never left him. The shock of the collision with the Japanese destroyer in the Solomon Islands had torn his back, already weakened by the football injury at Harvard half a dozen years before. In his exhaustion after the rescue he came down with malaria. When he returned to the United States, he weighed 127 pounds and was in agony from sciatica. He had a lumbar disc operation at the Chelsea Naval Hospital, relieving the pressure on the nerve fibers. But his spine did not cease to torment him. "At least one half of the days that he spent on this earth," his brother has written, "were days of intense physical pain."

Then he was told that he had Addison's disease—a degeneration of the adrenal glands—and between 1946 and 1949 he went on a regimen of cortisone. One day when Joseph Alsop asked about the occasional greenness of his complexion, Kennedy replied matter-of-factly, "The doctors say I've got a sort of slow-motion leukemia, but they tell me I'll probably last until I'm forty-five. So I seldom think about it except when I have the shots." It developed later that he did not have Addison's disease in the classic sense—that is, as caused by tuberculosis of the adrenal glands—that he had not had tuberculosis in any form and that, with modern methods of treatment, his adrenal insufficiency, evidently induced by the physical strain of the long night of swimming and the subsequent malaria, presented no serious problem. He stopped the cortisone shots, though he continued to take corticosteroid tablets from time to time to assure the best possible protection against excessive physical stress or exertion. During these years, except when his back stopped him, he lived, between politics and athletics, a life of marked and exuberant physical activity.

Still the shadow did not leave him. In 1948 his beloved sister Kathleen was killed in a plane crash. In 1951, traveling in the Far East, he came down with a fever in Japan and was rushed to the military hospital in Okinawa. His temperature rose to more than 106 degrees, and they did not think he would live. He recovered, but then his back troubled him again. Jacqueline remembers him in their courtship as on crutches more often than not. By 1954 the pain became so incessant that he decided to try another operation—this time a lumbar fusion with a steel plate inserted in his spine. The surgeons were not sure it would help and warned it would be risky, but Kennedy, drained by the unceasing torment, said, "I don't care, I can't go on like this." If there were a reasonable chance, he was going to take it. The winter after the surgery was torture. The steel plate led to a staphylococcus infection. His condition grew worse. Last rites were pronounced, and death brushed him again. Finally a second operation removed the plate. He continued weak and in

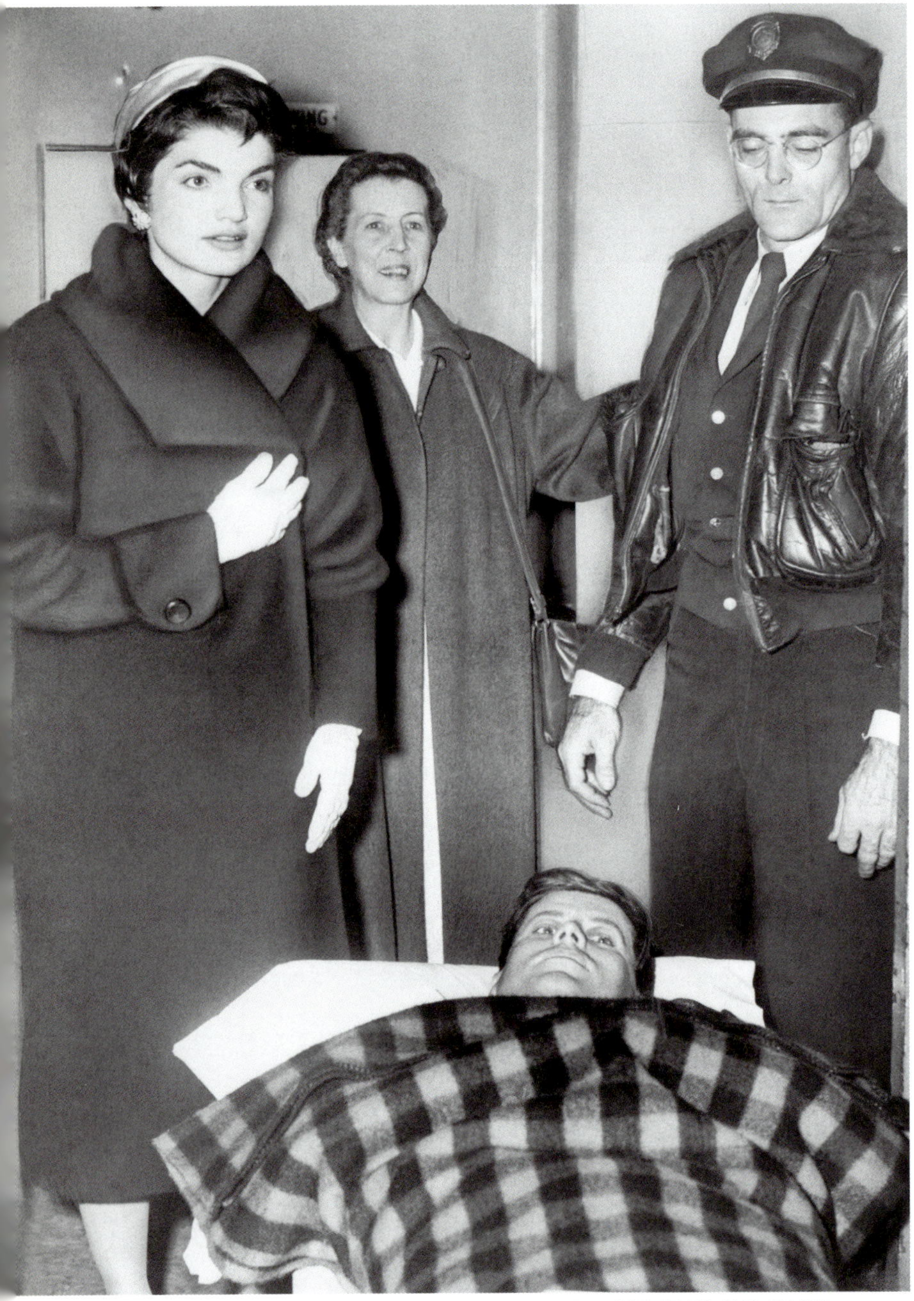

JACQUELINE LEAVING THE HOSPITAL WITH KENNEDY AFTER ONE OF HIS BACK SURGERIES.

pain, lying miserably in bed, turned by nurses at regular intervals from one side to the other. After a time, he started to walk, but, just as he was beginning, one of his crutches broke, he fell and was back in bed again.

The operations did not help. They left his back weaker than ever, and Kennedy later concluded without recrimination that they had been unnecessary. In the spring of 1955 he heard about Janet Travell, a New York physician who treated certain painful muscular conditions with Novocaine. He came to her deeply skeptical about doctors but more ready than ever to try anything. His infection had not healed; he now had anemia; and the pain was constant. Dr. Travell decided that what was causing the pain was not the spine itself or the discs but the old weakness in the back muscles leading to chronic spasm. Now her Novocaine relaxed the cramps in his spinal muscles and brought quick relief. But, when daily mechanical strain was a factor in spasm, Novocaine might have only a temporary effect. Then Dr. Travell discovered that his left leg was three-quarters of an inch shorter than his right—an obvious mechanical aggravation of the weakness along his spine, but, amazingly, unnoticed by doctors up to this point. Every step he had taken for years had caused a seesaw movement in his back and increased the strain on his spinal muscles. He procured shoes with a lift on the left foot and a lowered heel on the right. He also wore a small 'brace' or belt, and, finding relief in a rocking chair in Dr. Travell's office, acquired one for himself. Various nutritional supplements ended his anemia. Dr. Travell's treatment and gentle counsel changed his life. In a surprisingly short time, he regained his old vitality and strength.

Kennedy endured all this with total stoicism. Yet his ordeal no doubt accelerated his private crisis of identity. Like Roosevelt, he emerged better focused, more purposeful, more formidable. He conveyed a growing impression of weight and power.

6. POLITICS AND PRIVACY

"No congressional leader of the very first rank save James Madison has been elected Pres.," Kennedy wrote in a notebook he kept during his sickness, "—and apart from Polk, Garfield, McKinley & Truman no parliamentarians of the 2nd rank."

Being a Senator was another obstacle, like being a Catholic, but I suppose that for a man who had survived the Ferguson Passage form sheets were made to be ignored. In any case, he was not investing energy in the laborious process of infiltrating the inner ring of the Senate leadership. He preserved affable relations with the club, but he was not of them. He discharged his party duties with efficiency, indulged his own interests in matters like Indochina, Algeria and the electoral college, and wondered how to pursue larger goals. He had discussed the Vice-Presidency with his father as early as 1953; and after 1956 the Presidency itself no longer seemed so far away. When Joseph Alsop suggested to him in the summer of 1958 that the vice-presidential nomination was now his for the asking, Kennedy quickly replied, "Let's not talk so much about vice. I'm against vice, in all forms."

On issues he showed himself a practical and moderate liberal, who made quiet progress on questions of labor and social welfare without trying to force the pace faster than he thought the times permitted. These were his years of concentration on politics, and he soon showed the toughness, adroitness and intuition of a master. Yet while he considered politics—in another phrase he cherished from *Pilgrim's Way*—"the greatest and most honorable adventure," took pride in his political skills, delighted in political maneuver and combat and never forgot political effects for a single second, he stood apart, in some fundamental sense, from the political game. When David Ormsby Gore visited him in the hospital, Kennedy remarked that he was not sure he was cut out to be a politician; he saw the strength of opposing arguments too well; it would be easier if he had divine certitude that he was right.

Gradually there evolved a sense of his own identity as a political man, compounded of his growing mastery of the political arts and, even more, of his growing understanding that, for better or worse, his public self had to be faithful to his private self. This second point may sound like something less than a blinding revelation. But it takes many politicians a long time to acquire it. Some never do, always hoping to persuade the voters that they are different from what they are. "No man, for any considerable period," Hawthorne once wrote, "can wear one face to himself, and another to the multitude, without finally getting bewildered as to which may be the true." Kennedy was prepared to settle for his own face—and no doubt was encouraged to do so by his own cool evaluation of the alternatives. One day his father asked him why he wanted to take on the appalling burden of the Presidency. "These things have always been done by men," Kennedy said, "and they can be done by men now." As he looked around him, the others who yearned to assume the burden did not seem to him conspicuously better qualified than himself.

The process of internal definition went on in other ways, and Jacqueline Kennedy made her own contribution to it. She must at first have been overwhelmed by the life into which marriage plunged her. Politics had been for her corny old men shouting on the Fourth of July, at least until the advent of Stevenson; his was the first political voice to whom she listened. And, once in this new world, she found it hard to get used to the ground rules.

The teeming world of the Kennedys was another problem. Jacqueline had to fight to preserve her own identity in this family of active parents-in-law, athletic, teasing brothers-in-law, energetic, competent sisters-in-law. There often seemed no point in trying to compete in politics, any more than in touch football; and she sometimes carried her self-defense to inordinate extremes, as when she would pretend a total ignorance about politics or impose a social ban on politicians. Like all marriages, this one may have had its early strains. Their life together was almost nomadic, shuttling back and forth from Washington to Boston, from Newport to Palm Beach, living often with parents-in-law. They did not really have a house of their own until they had been married four years and their first child was born. Jacqueline often feared that she was a political liability and that everyone considered her a snob from Newport who had bouffant hair and French clothes and hated politics. Some of Kennedy's supporters did feel this way in 1960, but he never mentioned it to her and never asked her to change. He was never worried; he loved her as she was. More and more she embodied something of increasing value for him—a surcease from daily business, a standard of excellence, a symbol of privacy, a style of life.

This was partly because she proved able to extend his knowledge and sensibility. Whatever concerned her interested him, and often he would soon know more about it than she did. But perhaps her greatest influence was to confirm his feelings about the importance of living his life according to the values he honored most. He was determined not to let his public role stunt or stifle his inner existence.

Kennedy's determination to defend his privacy was crucial; for it permitted the inner self, so voracious for experience and for knowledge, so intent on reason and result, so admiring of grace and elegance, to ripen into free and confident maturity—and to renew and replenish the public self. By holding part of himself back from politics, he opened himself to fresh ideas and purpose. I do not mean to imply that he ever condescended to politics. His highest hope was to inspire the young with a lofty sense of the political mission. But politics was not the be-all and end-all; and because, with his wife's complicity, he declined to yield himself entirely to it, he was able to charge it with creativity.

7. THE KENNEDY MIND

Kennedy was called an intellectual very seldom before 1960 and very often thereafter—a phenomenon which deserves explanation.

One cannot be sure what an intellectual is; but let us define it as a person whose primary habitat is the realm of ideas. In this sense, exceedingly few political leaders are authentic intellectuals, because the primary habitat of the political leader is the world of power. Yet the world of power itself has its intellectual and anti-intellectual sides. Some political leaders find exhilaration in ideas and in the company of

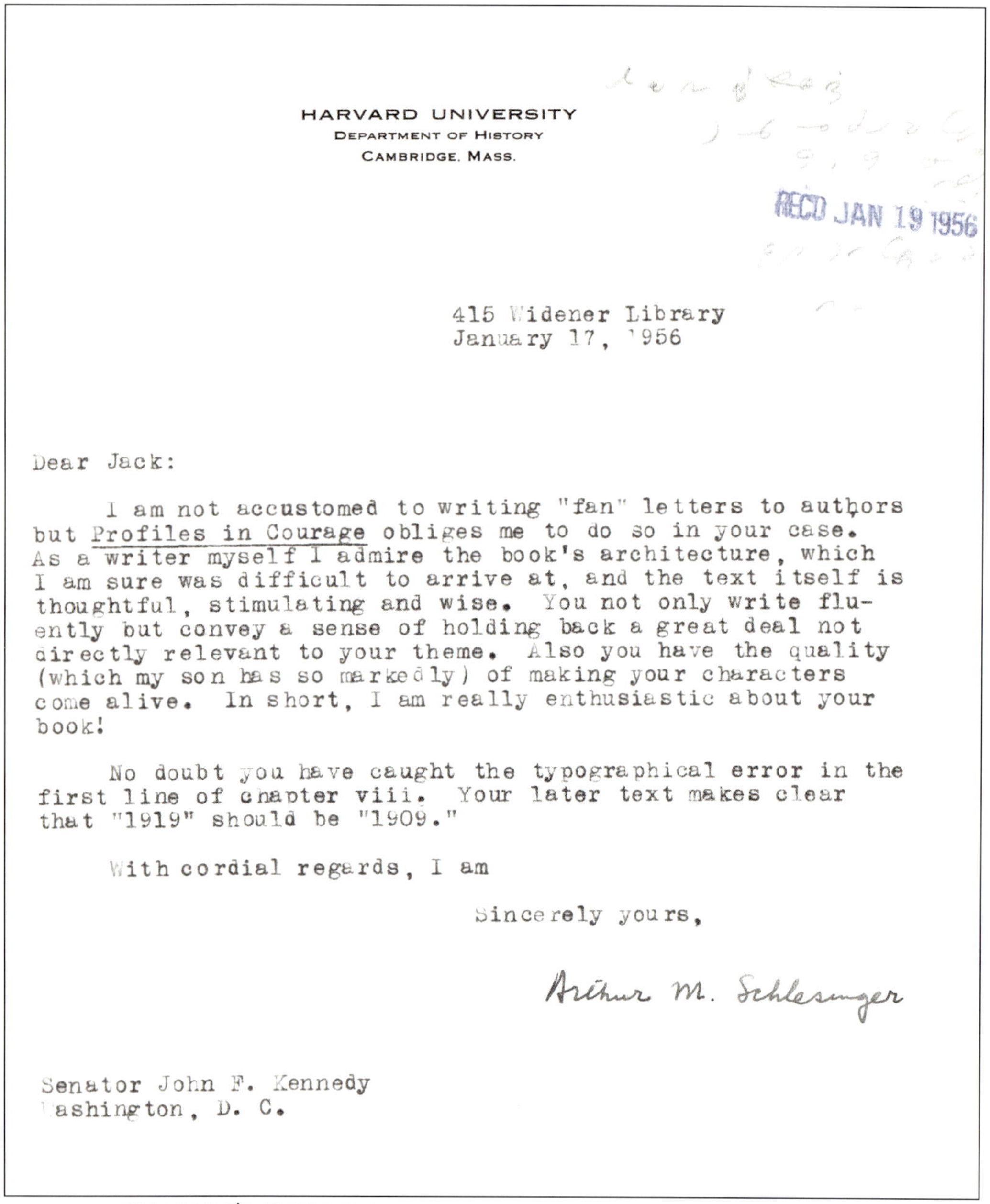

HARVARD UNIVERSITY
DEPARTMENT OF HISTORY
CAMBRIDGE, MASS.

RECD JAN 19 1956

415 Widener Library
January 17, 1956

Dear Jack:

I am not accustomed to writing "fan" letters to authors but Profiles in Courage obliges me to do so in your case. As a writer myself I admire the book's architecture, which I am sure was difficult to arrive at, and the text itself is thoughtful, stimulating and wise. You not only write fluently but convey a sense of holding back a great deal not directly relevant to your theme. Also you have the quality (which my son has so markedly) of making your characters come alive. In short, I am really enthusiastic about your book!

No doubt you have caught the typographical error in the first line of chapter viii. Your later text makes clear that "1919" should be "1909."

With cordial regards, I am

Sincerely yours,

Arthur M. Schlesinger

Senator John F. Kennedy
Washington, D. C.

THE AUTHOR'S COMPLIMENTARY LETTER TO KENNEDY REGARDING *PROFILES IN COURAGE*.

those whose trade it is to deal with them. Others are rendered uneasy by ideas and uncomfortable by intellectuals.

Kennedy belonged supremely to the first class. He was a man of action who could pass easily over to the realm of ideas and confront intellectuals with perfect confidence in his capacity to hold his own. His mind was not prophetic, impassioned, mystical, onto-logical, utopian or ideological. It was less exuberant than Theodore Roosevelt's, less scholarly than Wilson's, less adventurous than Franklin Roosevelt's. But it had its own salient qualities—it was objective, practical, ironic, skeptical, unfettered and insatiable.

It was marked first of all, as he had noted to Jacqueline, by inexhaustible curiosity. Kennedy always wanted to know how things worked. Vague answers never contented him. This curiosity was fed by conversation but even more by reading. His childhood consolation had become an adult compulsion. He was now a fanatical reader, 1200 words a minute, not only at the normal times and places but at meals, in the bathtub, sometimes even when walking. Dressing in the morning, he would prop open a book on his bureau and read while he put on his shirt and tied his necktie. He read mostly history and biography, American and English. Kennedy seldom read for distraction. He did not want to waste a single second. He read partly for information, partly for comparison, partly for insight, partly for the sheer joy of felicitous statement. He delighted particularly in quotations which distilled the essence of an argument.

There emerges from Kennedy's favorite literary passages the impression of a moderate and dispassionate mind, committed to the arts of government, persuaded of the inevitability of change but distrustful of comprehensive plans and grandiose abstractions, skeptical of excess but admiring of purpose, determined above all to be effective.

His intelligence was fundamentally secular, or so it seemed to me. Of course, this was not entirely true. As Mary McCarthy wrote in her *Memories of a Catholic Girlhood,* "If you are born and brought up a Catholic, you have absorbed a great deal of world history and the history of ideas before you are twelve, and it is like learning a language early; the effect is indelible." Though Kennedy spent only one year of his life in a Catholic school, he assimilated a good deal of the structure of the faith, encouraged probably by his mother and sisters. He often adopted the Catholic side in historical controversy, as in the case of Mary Queen of Scots; and he showed a certain weakness for Catholic words of art, like 'prudence,' and a certain aversion toward bad words for Catholics, like 'liberal.' Nor could one doubt his devotion to his Church or the occasional solace he found in mass.

Yet he remains, as John Cogley has suggested, the first President who was a Roman Catholic rather than the first Roman Catholic President. His attitude toward life showed

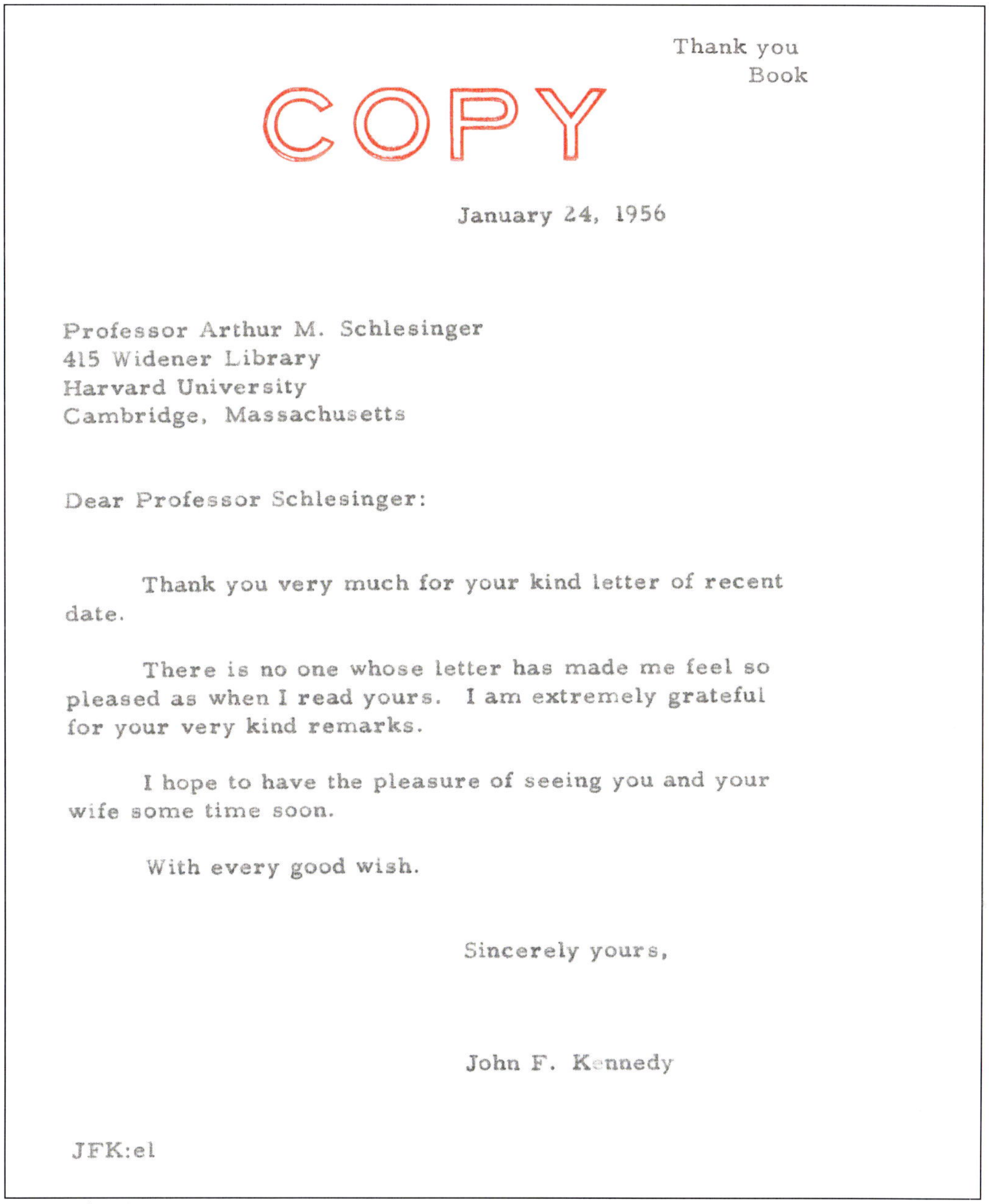

Thank you
Book

COPY

January 24, 1956

Professor Arthur M. Schlesinger
415 Widener Library
Harvard University
Cambridge, Massachusetts

Dear Professor Schlesinger:

Thank you very much for your kind letter of recent date.

There is no one whose letter has made me feel so pleased as when I read yours. I am extremely grateful for your very kind remarks.

I hope to have the pleasure of seeing you and your wife some time soon.

With every good wish.

Sincerely yours,

John F. Kennedy

JFK:el

KENNEDY'S CORDIAL REPLY.

no traces of the black-and-white moralism, the pietistic rhetoric, the clericalism, the anti-intellectualism, the prudery, the fear of Protestant society, which had historically characterized parts of the Irish Catholic community in America. On the other hand, he did not, like Eugene McCarthy, seek to rescue Catholic doctrine from fundamentalism and demonstrate its relevance to the modern world. Catholic intellectuals recognized his indifference to the scholastic tradition, and some disdained him for it.

His detachment from traditional American Catholicism was part of the set of detachments—detachment from middle-class parochialism, detachment from the business ethos, detachment from ritualistic liberalism—which gave his perceptions their peculiar coolness, freshness and freedom, and which also led those expecting commitments of a more familiar sort to condemn him as uncommitted. In fact, he was intensely committed to a vision of America and the world, and committed with equal intensity to the use of reason and power to achieve that vision. This became apparent after he was President; and this accounts in part for the sudden realization that, far from being just a young man in a hurry, a hustler for personal authority, a Processed Politician, he was, as politicians go, an intellectual and one so peculiarly modern that it took orthodox intellectuals a little time before they began to understand him.

Kennedy was in many respects an historian manqué. The historical mind can be analytical, or it can be romantic. The best historians are both, Kennedy among them. *Why England Slept,* with its emphasis on impersonal forces, expressed one side; *Profiles in Courage,* with its emphasis on heroes, expressed the other. But, even in his most romantic mood, Kennedy never adopted a good-guys vs. bad-guys theory of history. He had both the imagination and the objectivity which enabled him to see the point in lost causes, even in enemy fanaticisms.

He liked to quote Lincoln: "There are few things wholly evil or wholly good. Almost everything, especially of Government policy, is an inseparable compound of the two, so that our best judgment of the preponderance between them is continually demanded." When something had enough steam behind it to move people and make an impression on history, it must have some rational explanation, and Kennedy wanted to know what that rational explanation was. The response of the fifties that it was all a struggle between good and evil never satisfied him.

But it was not a case of *tout comprendre, tout pardonner.* Though he saw the human struggle, not as a moralist, but as an historian, even as an ironist, irony was never permitted to sever the nerve of action. His mind was forever critical; but his thinking always retained the cutting edge of decision. When he was told something, he wanted to know what he could do about it. He was pragmatic in the sense that he tested the meaning of a proposition by its consequences. The Kennedy years were not ideological, though they could perhaps be termed intellectual.

The historical mind is rarely ideological—and, when it becomes so, it is at the expense of history. Whether analytical or romantic, it is committed to existence, not to essence. Kennedy was bored by abstractions. He never took ideology very seriously, certainly not as a means of interpreting history and even not as part of the material of history.

Kennedy had an unusual capacity to weigh the complexities of judgment—in part because of the complexities of his own perceptions. The contrast in *Profiles* between the courage of compromise and the courage of principle expressed, for example, a tension deep within Kennedy—a tension between the circumspection of his political instinct and the radicalism of his intellectual impulse; so too the contrast between the historical determinism, the deprecation of the individual and the passive view of leadership implied in *Why England Slept* and the demand in *Profiles* that the politician be prepared, on the great occasions, to "meet the challenge of courage, whatever may be the sacrifices he faces if he follows his conscience." All this expressed the interior strain between Kennedy's sense of human limitation and his sense of hope, between his skepticism about man and his readiness to say, "Man can be as big as he wants. No problem of human destiny is beyond human beings."

All these things, coexisting within him, enabled others to find in him what qualities they wanted. They could choose one side of him or the other and claim him, according to taste, as a conservative, because of his sober sense of the frailty of man, the power of institutions and the frustrations of history, or as a progressive, because of his vigorous confidence in reason, action and the future. Yet within Kennedy himself these tensions achieved reunion and reconciliation. He saw history in its massive movements as shaped by forces beyond man's control. But he felt that there were still problems which man could resolve; and in any case, whether man could resolve these problems or not, the obligation was to carry on the struggle of existence. It was in essence, Richard Goodwin later suggested, the Greek view where the hero must poise himself against the gods and, even with knowledge of the futility of the fight, press on to the end of his life until he meets his tragic fate.

8. THE CONTEMPORARY MAN

After Kennedy's death, Adlai Stevenson called him the "contemporary man." His youth, his vitality, his profound modernity—these were final elements in his power and potentiality as he stood on the brink of the Presidency. For Kennedy was not only the first President to be born in the twentieth century. More than that, he was the first representative in the White House of a distinctive generation, the generation which was born during the First World War, came of age during the depression, fought in the Second World War and began its public career in the atomic age.

This was the first generation to grow up as the age of American innocence was coming to an end. The realities of the twentieth century which had shocked their fathers now wove the fabric of their own lives. Instead of reveling in being a lost generation, they set out in one mood or another to find, if not themselves, a still point in the turning world. The predicament was even worse for the generation which had been too young to fight the war, too young to recall the age of innocence, the generation which had experienced nothing but turbulence. So in the fifties some sought security at the expense of identity and became organization men. Others sought identity at the expense of security and became beatniks. Each course created only a partial man. There was need for a way of life, a way of autonomy, between past and present, the organization man and the anarchist, the square and the beat.

It was autonomy which this humane and self-sufficient man seemed to embody. Kennedy simply could not be reduced to the usual complex of sociological generalizations. He was Irish, Catholic, New England, Harvard, Navy, Palm Beach, Democrat and so on; but no classification contained him. He had wrought an individuality which carried him beyond the definitions of class and race, region and religion. He was a free man, not just in the sense of the cold-war cliché, but in the sense that he was, as much as man can be, self-determined and not the servant of forces outside him.

This sense of wholeness and freedom gave him an extraordinary appeal not only to his own generation but even more to those who came after, the children of turbulence. Recent history had washed away the easy consolations and the old formulas. Only a few things remained on which contemporary man could rely, and most were part of himself—family, friendship, courage, reason, jokes, power, patriotism. Kennedy demonstrated the possibility of the new self-reliance. As he had liberated himself from the past, so he had liberated himself from the need to rebel against the past. He could insist on standards, admire physical courage, attend his church, love his father while disagreeing with him, love his country without self-doubt or self-consciousness. Yet, while absorbing so much of the traditional code, his sensibility was acutely contemporaneous. He voiced the disquietude of the postwar generation—the mistrust of rhetoric, the disdain for pomposity, the impatience with the postures and pieties of other days, the resignation to disappointment. And he also voiced the new generation's longings—for fulfillment in experience, for the subordination of selfish impulses to higher ideals, for a link between past and future, for adventure and valor and honor. What was forbidden were poses, histrionics, the heart on the sleeve and the tongue on the cliché. What was required was a tough, nonchalant acceptance of the harsh present and an open mind toward the unknown future.

His 'coolness' was itself a new frontier. It meant freedom from the stereotyped responses of the past. It promised the deliverance of American idealism, buried deep in the national character but imprisoned by the knowingness and calculation of American society in the fifties. It held out to the young the possibility that they could become more than satisfied stockholders in a satisfied nation. It offered hope for spontaneity in a country drowning in its own passivity—passive because it had come to accept the theory of its own impotence.

V.
GATHERING OF THE FORCES

CAPE COD IS NEVER MORE POIGNANT than in the last still blue and gold of autumn. The November sun is luminous, the sky and sea are aquamarine, and the light is the light of Greece. It was one of those translucent days on the third day after election when my wife and I drove down from Cambridge to Hyannis Port for luncheon.

The frenzy of August had gone, though people stood in quiet clusters at each end of the Kennedy block on Irving Avenue. The compound itself was tranquil and secluded in the drowsy sunlight. The Kennedys were out for a stroll on the dunes. In a moment they returned, Jack in tweed jacket, sweater and slacks, hatless and tieless, swinging a cane and looking fit and jaunty, and Jacqueline, her hair slightly blown in the breeze, glowing in beauty from the walk. One could only think: What a wildly attractive young couple. It took another minute to remember that this was the President-elect of the United States and his wife.

Kennedy brandished a collection of memoranda on the issues of transition prepared, he said, by Clark Clifford and "Professor Neustadt of Columbia." These papers were "shrewd and helpful," he said, but the hardest problem of all would be "people"—finding the right men for the right jobs. He wished Galbraith and me to collect our Cambridge ideas and send them along to Sargent Shriver, whom he had asked to take charge of recruitment. He named four men he particularly wanted in important positions—Orville Freeman and Mennen Williams, Frank Coffin of Maine and George McGovern of South Dakota. He meant to build up the job of American Ambassador to NATO and wondered whether Thomas K. Finletter might be interested. He expressed concern over the downward turn in Latin America: would Adolf Berle be the man to undertake advance planning on hemisphere policy? (All these names, of course, were well calculated to appeal to a liberal guest.) He mentioned Stevenson only to say that he looked forward to receiving his foreign policy report. He solicited opinions about a variety of people without disclosing his intentions toward them.

The time passed lightly and quickly. The Kennedys were leaving in the afternoon for Palm Beach. After luncheon his father and mother came in while the President-elect and his wife went upstairs to change for the trip. The Ambassador talked beguilingly about present and past. In a few moments, the younger Kennedys reappeared, and we all waved them off to the airfield.

1. PLANNING FOR POWER

He was determined to be a strong President—and this meant for him, I believe, a President in the manner of Franklin Roosevelt. Kennedy was by no means an F.D.R. idolator. I think that he considered Roosevelt's policies, especially in foreign affairs, sometimes slapdash and sentimental. But he admired Roosevelt's ability to articulate the latent idealism of America, and he greatly envied Roosevelt's capacity to dominate a sprawling government filled with strong men eager to go into business on their own. He had mentioned to me a number of times the account of Roosevelt's fluid administrative methods in the last section of *The Coming of the New Deal.* The interregnum was now to provide a first test of Kennedy's own executive instincts and, in particular, of his skill in defending his personal authority against people striving, always for the best of motives, to contract his scope for choice.

The Twentieth Amendment left him only ten weeks to recover from the campaign, reassure his vanquished opponents, select the top officers of his administration and work out his legislative program.

Shortly after the convention, Kennedy asked Clark Clifford out to Georgetown for breakfast. Clifford, who had become an enormously successful Washington lawyer after his years with Truman, was a man of unusual ability and discretion, concealing a sharp and quick mind under a big-man-on-campus exterior. Kennedy had known him for a decade as a friend and also as a lawyer. He told clifford what was on his mind: "If I am elected, I don't want to wake up on the morning of November 9 and have to ask myself, 'What in the world do I do now?'" His own experience and that of his staff, he pointed out, had been on the legislative side. He needed someone to analyze the problems of taking over the executive branch, and he thought that Clifford, with his White House background, would be ideal. Clifford, impressed by Kennedy's foresight, promptly accepted the assignment. Kennedy did not mention the matter to him again before the election.

Clifford also discussed transition problems with an associate from Truman days, Richard Neustadt, a political scientist who had worked in the Bureau of the Budget and later as a Special Assistant in the White House before becoming a professor at Columbia. Neustadt shared Clifford's concern about the interregnum. By the time Clifford spoke to him, however, Neustadt had already been tapped by Senator Henry Jackson, the chairman of the Democratic National Committee to prepare a memorandum on the problems of change-over for the new President.

Neustadt completed "Organizing the Transition" by September 15. Three days later Jackson took him out to Georgetown to meet Kennedy. Kennedy, sitting in his garden, flipped through the twenty pages of the memorandum in his usual manner. He liked it at once, and it is easy to see why. The presentation was crisp and methodical, with a numbered list of specific problems and actions. It constantly stressed the importance of flexibility. The President's requirements for his personal staff, for example, *"cannot be fully understood, or met, until they have been experienced."* Kennedy told Neustadt to elaborate his argument in further memoranda. "When you finish," he said, "I want you to get the material back directly to me. I don't want you to send it to anybody else." Neustadt

PRESIDENT ELECT AND JACQUELINE WITH DAUGHTER, CAROLINE, IN THE GOLDEN LIGHT OF CAPE COD.

asked, "How do you want me to relate to Clark Clifford?" Kennedy replied quickly, "I don't want you to relate to Clark Clifford. I can't afford to confine myself to one set of advisers. If I did that, I would be on *their* leading strings."

Neustadt went back to Columbia and set to work. Toward the end of October he handed Kennedy a bundle of memoranda and said, "You don't have to say anything—here are the memoranda—don't bother with them till after the election." One memorandum listed priority actions from election to Thanksgiving. Another dealt with cabinet posts. Another was called "Staffing the President-Elect"; sensing Kennedy's affinities, Neustadt added to this appendixes discussing Roosevelt's approach to White House staffing and to the Bureau of the Budget. Half an hour later Kennedy bounded out of his compartment in search of Neustadt. Finding him, he said, "That Roosevelt stuff is fascinating." Neustadt said, "You're not supposed to read it now." Kennedy repeated, "It's fascinating."

The day after election, Clifford's memorandum was delivered to Hyannis Port. It was shorter and less detailed than the Neustadt series. Where Neustadt viewed the problem in its administrative and organizational context, Clifford viewed it more in its policy context. But in the main the two advisers reinforced each other all along the line, even, in the end, agreeing that Kennedy would do best to serve as his own chief of staff.

These were the memoranda which Kennedy flourished at luncheon in Hyannis Port. He ignored a good many of their recommendations; but the Clifford-Neustadt emphasis on molding the executive machinery to meet the needs of the President was exactly what Kennedy wanted. When Eisenhower proposed the day after the election that Kennedy designate a representative to serve as liaison with the outgoing administration, Kennedy immediately named Clifford.

2. NAVIGATING THE TRANSITION

Kennedy now had seventy-three days to go until inauguration. With all his resilience, the daily barnstorming in the general election added to the months of primary fights, had

ABOVE: DIRECTOR OF CIA, ALLEN DULLES, MEETING WITH KENNEDY IN PALM BEACH IN NOVEMBER 1960.

RIGHT: AN AERIAL VIEW OF JOE KENNEDY'S ESTATE IN PALM BEACH, FLORIDA. PALM BEACH PROVIDED QUIET RESPITE FOR KENNEDY AFTER THE ELECTION.

left him physically exhausted. In earlier times, a President-elect had four months to recover—and less to recover from. Palm Beach now promised him a badly needed respite.

He also had to begin his work of reassuring the losers—a task all the more essential because of the slimness of the victory. He started this even before he left Hyannis Port. On Wednesday night after the election he relaxed at dinner with several friends. The group fell into an animated discussion of what the President-elect should do first. One guest suggested that he fire J. Edgar Hoover of the Federal Bureau of Investigation, another that he fire Allen W. Dulles of the Central Intelligence Agency. Kennedy, listening with apparent interest, egged his friends on. When they opened their papers the next morning, they were therefore a little irritated to read a Kennedy announcement that Hoover and Dulles were staying in their jobs.

This was part of the strategy of reassurance. Hoover and Dulles were still national ikons in 1960. Since the political cost of discharging them would have been considerable, reappointment enabled Kennedy to get full credit with their admirers for something he had no real choice but to do anyway. The same motive led him, soon after he arrived in Florida, to make a well-publicized call on Nixon, who was conducting his own recuperation not far away in Key Biscayne. Someone asked him why in the world he was doing this; Eisenhower would never have dreamed of calling on Stevenson in 1952 or 1956. Kennedy replied realistically, "There are some things Democrats must do which Republicans don't have to do."

Early in December, Kennedy and Eisenhower had their first formal meeting. The President-elect prepared himself with great care, and the two men talked by themselves for seventy-five minutes before walking arm-in-arm into the Cabinet Room where Clifford and his Republican counterpart, General Wilton Persons, were waiting. Persons phoned Clifford later and reported that Eisenhower, who had previously called Kennedy a "young whippersnapper," was "overwhelmed by Senator Kennedy, his understanding of the world problems, the depth of his questions, his grasp of the issues and the keenness of his mind." The subsequent rapport between the two principals assisted the transition process.

3. CHOOSING THE CABINET: I

The question of "people" became more urgent every day. The Senate Committee on Post Office and Civil Service had thoughtfully produced a heavy green volume listing all the posts which the new President had the power to fill—the cabinet and agency heads, of course, plus about 1200 so-called Schedule C jobs, to which presidential appointees could name persons of their own choosing. For the next weeks the Green Book was the favorite reading on the New Frontier. It was known as the shopping list.

The White House staff was easy enough. Kennedy promptly announced Ted Sorensen as his Special Counsel and Pierre Salinger as his press man and made it clear that Ken O'Donnell, Lawrence O'Brien, Richard Goodwin, Myer Feldman and Ralph Dungan would all be Special Assistants. But beyond the White House lay the cabinet, and beyond the cabinet the long, hazy rank-on-rank of Green Book vacancies.

Kennedy's acquaintance had, indeed, certain limitations. He knew most national and many local politicians, Republican as well as Democratic; he knew a number of government officials; he knew Washington newspapermen; he knew labor leaders; and he knew a smattering of college professors, mostly from the Northeast. He had his chums from Harvard, the Navy, Massachusetts politics and Palm Beach. He knew, in addition, a miscellany of writers, theatrical figures and society people. On the other hand, he knew relatively few bankers, industrialists, leaders of the bar, university presidents, deans, foundation officials, generals, farmers, social workers, scientists or engineers. In particular, he was little acquainted in the New York financial and legal community—that arsenal of talent which had so long furnished a steady supply of always orthodox and often able people to Democratic as well as Republican administrations. This community was the heart of the American Establishment. Its household deities were Henry L. Stimson and Elihu Root; its present leaders, Robert A. Lovett and John J. McCloy; its front organizations, the Rockefeller, Ford and Carnegie foundations and the Council on Foreign Relations; its organs, the *New York Times* and *Foreign Affairs*.* Its politics were predominantly Republican; but it possessed what its admirers saw as a commitment to public service and its critics as an appetite for power which impelled its members to serve Presidents of whatever political faith. Roosevelt and Truman had drawn freely upon them, partly to avail themselves of Establishment competence, partly to win protective coloration for policies which, with liberals in front, would have provoked conservative opposition. It was never clear who was using whom; but, since it was never clear, each side continued to find advantages in the arrangement.

The New York Establishment had looked on Kennedy with some suspicion. This was mostly because of his father, whom it had long since blackballed as a maverick in finance and an isolationist in foreign policy. It was perhaps also because the younger Kennedy's main associations were with

* The term Establishment was revived by Henry Fairlie for use in England in a series for *The Spectator* in September–October 1955. Anyone who writes on the American Establishment must, of course, acknowledge his debt to our most brilliant and persevering practitioner of Establishment Studies, the devoted Hudson River scholar, Richard H. Rovere. All such inquiries begin with Dr. Rovere's pioneering monograph, *"The American Establishment,"* in The American Establishment (New York, 1962).

Democratic politicians and academic intellectuals, two groups the New York Establishment regarded with mistrust. Now that he was President, however, they were prepared to rally round; and, now that he was President, he was prepared to receive them. This too was part of the strategy of reassurance. It also might help solve the problem of people.

The chief agent in the negotiation was Lovett, a man of great subtlety, experience and charm. Lovett punctiliously informed Kennedy that he had voted for Nixon, apparently out of fear of J. K. Galbraith. After a couple of conversations, Kennedy found himself captivated by Lovett. No doubt Lovett's urbane realism was a relief from the liberal idealists, like myself, who were assailing the President-elect with virtuous opinions and nominations. Certainly Lovett opened a new sector of talent for him and exerted a quiet influence on his tastes in the next weeks.

The President-elect talked a good deal about cabinet problems when I saw him in Washington on December 1. "State, Treasury and Defense," he told me, "are giving me the most trouble. I'd like to have some new faces here, but all I get is the same old names. He had reached firm decisions on two Cabinet appointments—Governor Luther Hodges of North Carolina for Commerce and Governor Abraham Ribicoff of Connecticut for Health, Education and Welfare. Both appointments fitted into the pattern of reassurance. Hodges was an older man, nearly twenty years the President's senior, a southerner of geniality and presence; his designation would appeal to Congress and to the business community. Ribicoff, too, had been an attractive and prudent governor as well as a man to whom Kennedy was indebted for support in the pre-convention period.

Kennedy had also by this time substantially decided on two more appointments—Stewart Udall of Arizona as Secretary of the Interior, and Arthur Goldberg of Illinois as Secretary of Labor, if opposition within the labor movement, especially from the building trades, could be overridden. Both appointments were almost inevitable. Udall, young, brisk, literate and a Mormon, not only had a distinguished record in Congress as a defender of the nation's resources but had snatched the Arizona delegation away from Lyndon Johnson and turned it over to Kennedy before Los Angeles. Goldberg was a man of unquestioned ability and drive whom Kennedy had got to know well in the Senate fights over labor legislation in 1958 and 1959.

Our talk had begun at noon in his Senate office. We then drove out to Georgetown for a drink before luncheon. In due course Lovett arrived for lunch, and I took my leave. Actually, after this meeting with Lovett, Kennedy was well on his way to the solution of the Defense problem. During his talk with Clifford in New York, Lovett had mentioned Robert S. McNamara, a Michigan business executive, just a year older than Kennedy, who had been elected president of the Ford Motor Company the day after Kennedy had been elected President of the United States. During the Second World War, Lovett, then Assistant Secretary of War for Air, had brought to the Pentagon a team of management specialists from the Harvard Business School. McNamara, he told Clifford, was the prize of the lot, and the Kennedy people ought to consider him for either the Treasury or Defense.

PIERRE SALINGER, KENNEDY'S PRESS SECRETARY.

The look revealed that McNamara was, indeed, an exceptional figure. A Phi Beta Kappa graduate of the University of California in 1937, he had gone on to the Harvard Business School. He was already beginning to display quiet symptoms of heterodoxy. During the 1940 election, a poll of the Business School faculty produced a vote of 98 to 2 in favor of Willkie against Roosevelt. McNamara was one of the heretics. Ending the war as a lieutenant colonel in the Air Force, McNamara then joined Ford, rising steadily to the top. In Michigan, he continued to show wayward tendencies. He declined, for example, to live with other Ford executives in the suburb known derisively on the New Frontier as Fat Point, preferring the academic environment of Ann Arbor. He exhibited sympathy for such dubious organizations as the American Civil Liberties Union and the National Association for the Advancement of Colored People. He had been tremendously impressed by *Profiles in Courage,* and, though nominally a Republican, had voted for Kennedy and contributed money to his campaign.

Sargent Shriver, arriving in Detroit later that day, said that the President-elect had authorized him to offer McNamara an appointment either as Secretary of Defense or as Secretary of the Treasury. Nothing could have surprised McNamara more. He quickly declined the Treasury on the ground that he had had no experience in banking or fiscal affairs. As for Defense, such experience as he had had was fifteen years out of date and pre-nuclear. Moreover, he had only just begun his new job as president of Ford.

When McNamara repeated his arguments to the President-elect the next day, Kennedy replied drily that he was not aware of any school for either cabinet members or Presidents, and that he considered lack of experience no excuse. McNamara left under Kennedy's spell, thought about the matter some more, and, at their second meeting, ascertained that he would have a free hand in making appointments and accepted the post.

4. CHOOSING THE CABINET: II

The problem of the Treasury was still unresolved. Throughout the autumn Kennedy had heard a great deal about the balance of payments and the flight of gold from the country, and since the election he had heard very little else. A task force on national security headed by Paul Nitze reported to him that "all those whom we consulted in the New York business community" had put the gold drain at the top of their list of issues, and that friends in State and Treasury had told the task force that the problem was worse than publicly admitted. "The early appointment of a Secretary of the Treasury who enjoys high respect and confidence in the international financial world," the Nitze report declared, "would do more than anything else that your Committee can think of to consolidate confidence in the international payments position of the United States."

One name that came up repeatedly was Douglas Dillon, Under Secretary of State in the outgoing administration and the son of Clarence Dillon of Dillon, Read and Company.

Even some who accepted the Wall Street-acceptability thesis were dismayed at the prospect of installing a Republican in the economic high command of a Democratic administration. Admitting that the gold drain was a problem, they feared that a conservative Secretary would apply the conventional remedy—i.e., reduce public spending and increase the interest rate, even at the risk of deflation and unemployment. It seemed essential to have a Secretary committed to the use of fiscal and monetary policy to stimulate economic growth. Thus Senator Albert Gore of Tennessee contended to Kennedy on November 22 that the Treasury was the key to the success of his Presidency. "The present difficulties with balance of payments…are symptoms, really, of the failure of the present administration to keep the United States on the 'move.' …Why, then, should you consider for a fleeting moment for appointment to the key post of Treasury one whose chief claim to fame is that he has been a member of a team that failed its most important test? This applies not only to Mr. Dillon, who is an affable easy-goer, but to other conservative Republicans who have been mentioned." Such an appointment "would be a signal that you had given up the goals of a truly Democratic Administration."

We had similar apprehensions in Cambridge. Without knowing Dillon, we mistrusted him on principle as a presumed exponent of Republican economic policies. In addition, as an historian and therefore a conservative, I could recall no precedent for giving a vital cabinet post to a sub-cabinet official of a defeated administration, especially to an official who had contributed to Nixon's campaign and might well have been Nixon's nominee for the same job.

When I mentioned this to the President-elect in Washington on December 1, he remarked of Dillon, "Oh, I don't care about those things. All I want to know is: Is he able? and will he go along with the program?" Dillon was surprised to get a phone call from Salinger in late November saying that Kennedy wanted to come over to his house that evening. Pressing Dillon on the question of economic growth, Kennedy satisfied himself that he had found a man whom bankers would trust but who also would support expansionist policies. He therefore resolved to ignore the liberal protests and go ahead. Following a balancing principle, Kennedy prepared to give the other key economic posts—the directorship of the Bureau of the Budget and the chairmanship of the Council of Economic Advisers—to liberal Democrats.

Clark Clifford had already proposed David Bell, another of Harry Truman's young men in the White House, for the Budget. After serving as a Truman Special Assistant, Bell had worked in the Stevenson campaign in 1952, then spent some years in Pakistan running an economic mission for the

CHESTER BOWLES, HAVING JUST BEEN SWORN IN AS UNDER SECRETARY OF STATE.

Ford Foundation and had come to the Littauer School at Harvard in the late fifties. The audacity of Clifford's suggestion can be measured by the fact that the Cambridge group, admiring Bell's ability but wondering at his youth, had only dared suggest him as associate director.

For the chairmanship of the Council, the Harvard group, and doubtless many others, proposed Professor Walter Heller of the University of Minnesota. Kennedy's first thought was Paul Samuelson; but Samuelson could not be lured down from the Massachusetts Institute of Technology and, in any case, Kennedy was beginning to fear that he might be overdoing appointments from Cambridge. Hubert Humphrey had introduced Heller to him in Minnesota during the campaign. Kennedy, who had instantly subjected him to a cross-examination on economic policy, remembered him favorably and decided to go ahead. For the second place in the Council, Heller suggested James Tobin who, though he had a Harvard degree, had fortunately moved on to Yale and was thus not subject to the Cambridge ban. Tobin was a brilliant economic theorist; and, when Kennedy called him, he tried to set forth what he considered his lack of qualifications for the job, concluding, "I am afraid that I am only an ivory-tower economist." Kennedy replied, "That is the best kind. I am only an ivory-tower President." The deal was promptly consummated. For the third member, Heller wanted Kermit Gordon of Williams. Both appointments proved great successes; and Gordon, who quickly won Kennedy's esteem, eventually succeeded Bell at the Budget.

Two conundrums remained—State and Justice—and two uncertainties—Agriculture and Post Office. Nothing was giving Kennedy more trouble than State. The Democrat with the strongest claim was Adlai Stevenson, and Stevenson fully expected to be offered the job. But when the President-elect returned from Palm Beach in late November he told Stevenson that he had taken too many public positions on prickly issues and would in consequence be too 'controversial' for Congress; given the margin of the election, Kennedy said that he needed most of all a Secretary of State who could get along on Capitol Hill. In addition, Kennedy privately questioned Stevenson's capacity for decision and no doubt also did not want a Secretary of State with whom he feared he might not feel personally comfortable.

In talking to Stevenson, Kennedy went on to say that Stevenson had more international prestige than any other Democrat and, in Kennedy's view, could make his greatest contribution as Ambassador to the United Nations. Though this was a hard blow to Stevenson, he accepted it realistically, saying only that he could not take the UN assignment until he knew who the Secretary of State would be.

The political grounds which excluded Stevenson from the Secretaryship applied just as much, or more, in Kennedy's mind to Chester Bowles. But his political indebtedness to Bowles, who had been the first nationally known liberal to support him for the nomination and had served as a nominal 'foreign policy adviser' during the campaign, was very much greater. He therefore decided to make Bowles Under Secretary. The leading candidates for the top job were now David Bruce, Senator J. William Fulbright of Arkansas, and Dean Rusk of the Rockefeller Foundation.

Rusk, who was fifty-one years old, had a plausible background. He had been a Rhodes Scholar and a professor of government before the war. He had served with the Army in the Far East; and, after the war, he had gone to the State Department, heading the Office of United Nations Affairs and ending up as Assistant Secretary for Far Eastern Affairs. At the Rockefeller Foundation he had supervised programs of health, education and technical assistance in the under-developed countries. He was a Democrat (in fact, he had been chairman of the Stevenson-for-President Committee in

ONE OF THE FIRST MEETINGS WITH SECRETARY OF STATE DEAN RUSK (LEFT) AND SECRETARY OF DEFENSE ROBERT S. MCNAMARA.

Scarsdale in the spring of 1960). Lovett recommended him for the job as against Bruce or Fulbright. Acheson thought highly of him. Bowles, who was a trustee of the Rockefeller Foundation, spoke of him with enthusiasm. Robert Kennedy believed him the best solution. The Kennedy staff read all his speeches and articles they could find and discovered nothing which would cause trouble on the Hill. Kennedy himself was especially taken with parts of a piece Rusk had written for *Foreign Affairs* in the spring of 1960 entitled "The President." Here Rusk discussed the Presidency as the place from which leadership in foreign policy must flow and emphasized the President's responsibility "to influence and shape the course of events." (Actually, though the article showed a nice appreciation of the Presidency, it also contained another and somewhat contradictory argument that the President should *not* engage in foreign negotiations, above all at the summit, and should leave diplomacy to the diplomats.)

Kennedy was attracted by the clarity of Rusk's views, the quiet competence of his manner and the apparent solidity of his judgment. Accordingly he offered Rusk the Secretaryship the next day. The appointment was announced on December 12 with Bowles as Under Secretary and Stevenson, who knew and liked Rusk, as Ambassador to the United Nations.

THE CABINET POSES FOR PHOTOGRAPHERS IN JANUARY 26, 1961. FROM LEFT, POSTMASTER GENERAL EDWARD DAY; U.N. AMBASSADOR ADLAI STEVENSON; VICE PRESIDENT LYNDON B. JOHNSON; DEFENSE SECRETARY ROBERT MCNAMARA; AGRICULTURE SECRETARY ORVILLE FREEMAN; LABOR SECRETARY ARTHUR GOLDBERG; WELFARE SECRETARY ABRAHAM RIBICOFF, CENTER; COMMERCE SECRETARY LUTHER HODGES; ATTORNEY GENERAL ROBERT KENNEDY; SECRETARY OF STATE DEAN RUSK; PRESIDENT KENNEDY; TREASURY SECRETARY DOUGLAS DILLON; AND INTERIOR SECRETARY STEWARD UDALL.

The Department of Justice confronted Kennedy with a problem almost as difficult as State but for different reasons. The President-elect's father hoped that Robert Kennedy would become Attorney General. Bobby himself was reluctant. He felt that, after five years as counsel for the Senate Rackets Committee, he had been "chasing people" too long and wanted a different kind of assignment now. Also, he recalled an incident in the campaign when Nixon, passing through South Carolina, had tried to conceal the presence of Attorney General William Rogers on his plane, knowing how unpopular Rogers's civil rights activity had made him in the South. Bobby's view was that, if the new Attorney General were named Kennedy, this inevitable unpopularity would quickly spread to the President himself. Instead, he contemplated the possibility of becoming Under Secretary of Defense or perhaps Assistant Secretary for Inter-American Affairs in the State Department. His father argued forcibly, however, that Bobby obviously had to report directly to the President; if he were in a subordinate post, the position of the official who stood between himself and the President would be impossible. Since Bobby did not want to work in the White House, this left the cabinet. Nonetheless, after a time Bobby decided against Justice, thinking that he might return to Massachusetts and run for governor in 1962.

The President-elect, however, wanted his brother in Washington and also wanted an Attorney General in whom he could repose absolute trust. Though nearly all the advice to both brothers was against the idea, he called Bobby over for breakfast one morning and told him that he would have to take the job.

I had luncheon with Bobby in Washington the day before his appointment was announced. He seemed both rueful and fatalistic about his prospective eminence. The problem of assuring his brother a sufficiently diversified White House staff was much on his mind. Obviously, he said, the President needed to enlarge his staff beyond the men who had worked for him in the Senate and the campaign, able and loyal as they were. As we were chatting, he abruptly asked me what I intended to do for my country. I said that an ambassadorship and the Assistant Secretaryship of State in charge of cultural relations had been mentioned, but that neither prospect attracted me much. He then asked whether it would be agreeable if he suggested to his brother that I come down as a Special Assistant to the President and serve as a sort of roving reporter and trouble-shooter. I said I would be delighted.

Bobby's appointment left Agriculture and the Post Office untenanted. By this time, there was spreading unhappiness among the liberals over the failure of any of their particular favorites, except Arthur Goldberg, to make the cabinet.

Still, one policy position remained—Agriculture—and one strong liberal candidate—Orville Freeman. Actually Freeman did not much want Agriculture. He would have preferred to be Attorney General or even for some reason, Secretary of the Army. But as time passed, Kennedy decided that Freeman was the man. Freeman had a political base in the Middle West, even if he came from Minneapolis rather than from the farms; he was intelligent and brave; he had an ex-Marine's indomitability before insoluble problems.

Only the Post Office was left. Because the Pacific coast was conspicuously unrepresented in the cabinet, word went out to dig up a California businessman. Someone suggested J. Edward Day of Prudential Insurance. Day, a man of rollicking humor, had been Adlai Stevenson's Insurance Commissioner in Illinois before moving to the West. His credentials appeared good, and his rather hasty appointment on December 17 completed the Kennedy cabinet.

VI. PRELUDE TO THE NEW FRONTIER

THE WHITE HOUSE ADMINISTRATIVE STAFF TAKES A BREAK FROM THEIR BUSY DAY TO POSE WITH PRESIDENT KENNEDY.

THE CABINET WAS only the beginning. There remained those vital levers of power in the policy-making jobs just below the cabinet, and these the new President had to control if he meant to command the executive branch. This was the domain of the Green Book and of Schedule C; here, presumably, 1200 places waited to be filled.

He had given Sargent Shriver the job of spying out the land and carrying through the occupation. Though people were sometimes deceived by Shriver's unruffled courtesy and easy amiability into dismissing him as something of a Boy Scout, the President-elect had confidence in his energy and imagination—a confidence Shriver had justified in the campaign and justified again now. He assembled a small group, and the great talent hunt began.

SARGENT SHRIVER WAS GIVEN THE DIFFICULT TASK OF SCOUTING OUT THE REST OF THE WHITE HOUSE STAFF.

1. MANNING THE SHIP

Kennedy, as usual, did not propose to give anyone exclusive authority. He therefore charged Shriver to work with Lawrence O'Brien, Ralph Dungan and Richard Donahue, who represented the political interest in appointments. In a sense, the Shriver group began with the positions and looked for people qualified to fill them, and the O'Brien group began with the people and looked for positions they were qualified to fill; one concentrated on recruitment and the other on placement. But the Shriver group understood the importance of finding people who would be loyal to the administration, and the O'Brien group understood the importance of finding people who would do a good job, so there was not too much friction between them.

The proportions of the search turned out to be not so great as it had first looked. Of the 1200 Schedule C jobs, nearly four-fifths were presently filled from the career service, and about half the incumbents had competitive Civil Service status. Almost 500 of the Schedule C jobs, indeed, were not "policy-determining" at all but rather personal aides to policy makers—secretaries, chauffeurs, and the like. In the end, the Kennedy administration kept most of the career people, including even some on the sub-cabinet level. Nevertheless, a considerable number of vacancies remained.

To fill these, the Shriver group began to compile what they hopefully described as an index of excellence.

They worked night after night through November and December in offices provided by the Democratic National Committee, striving to make sure that all groups and regions were represented in their recommendations. They cast their net especially for women, for Negroes, for westerners. After a time, to be a Harvard graduate, a member of the Cambridge academic complex or an Irish Catholic was almost a handicap, surmountable only by offsetting evidence of spectacular excellence. As each cabinet member was appointed, a representative of the Shriver group provided him with a list of names carefully culled for his consideration. By mid-December, the first stage of the roundup was complete.

GEORGE BALL, UNDER SECRETARY FOR ECONOMIC AFFAIRS.

Shriver now left for a holiday in the West Indies. Ralph Dungan took over the talent hunt, later continuing it from the White House.

Each department presented special circumstances. By the time Rusk was offered the State Department, for example, several crucial appointments in the foreign field—Stevenson, Bowles, Williams—had already been made. The next important place was the Under Secretary for Economic Affairs; and here the leading candidate was William C. Foster, a liberal-minded Republican businessman who had held important jobs in the Truman administration. But the prospect of a Republican appointment in addition to Dillon and McNamara seemed excessive, especially when a well-qualified Democrat was available. The well-qualified Democrat was George W. Ball, the Washington lawyer and long-time friend of Adlai Stevenson's. Senator Fulbright, suggested to the President-elect that giving Republicans so many top posts in State, Treasury and Defense was manifestly unfair to Democrats who had worked hard for his election. He added that this policy would create the impression that the Democratic party lacked men of sufficient stature. The argument proved effective. Kennedy withdrew the offer to Foster and appointed Ball; he later made Foster director of the Arms Control and Disarmament Agency.

The Ball argument also applied to the case of Averell Harriman. Kennedy had not known Harriman well, but he appreciated his staunch support before the convention and recognized that Harriman's record and experience in foreign affairs were unmatched in the nation. Still, both the President-elect and his brother remembered Harriman most as a political leader in New York, where he had not always been at his best, and they feared that, at sixty-nine and slightly deaf, he was too old for active service.

When I lunched with him in New York on December 11, he was temperate and wise. He understood the need for caution in view of the closeness of the election but added that he hoped Kennedy would not appoint too many businessmen. Turning to his area of expertise, Harriman thought there might be an opportunity for fresh initiatives in the cold war; but he also feared that the Russians might try something risky somewhere in order to test Kennedy's will and response. Harriman had many admirers on the New Frontier. In time Kennedy, though still a little skeptical, yielded to their enthusiasm and decided to appoint him as the State Department's roving ambassador.

Staffing the rest of the State Department involved complicated negotiations among Kennedy, Rusk, Bowles and the Shriver office. Kennedy wanted McGeorge Bundy somewhere on the top level of the State Department; for a moment in early December he had even wondered whether he might be a possible Secretary. He also thought that Walt W. Rostow, with his force and fertility of thought, should be counselor and chairman of the Policy Planning Council. But Rusk for various reasons resisted both Bundy and Rostow. From the institutional interests of the Department, this was a grievous error. Kennedy promptly decided to take them into the White House, Bundy as Special Assistant for National Security Affairs and Rostow as his deputy. The result was to give the White House an infusion of energy on foreign affairs with which the State Department would never in the next three years (even after Rostow finally got the policy planning job) quite catch up.

Rusk did not have a consuming interest in personnel; and a letter just before Christmas from Ted Sorensen, listing twenty-three issues of policy, all of complexity and moment, on which the President wanted his immediate advice, gave him other things to do. Accordingly he relinquished to Bowles, as Under Secretary, the responsibility for filling the top posts. Bowles had considerable respect for the professionals and a particular desire to seek out able men in the lower ranks of the Foreign Service. At the same time, he also wanted to bring people from outside "unhampered by past loyalties" and committed to the New Frontier into the conduct of foreign relations. He canvassed the universities, the foundations, the press and politics and was more responsible than anyone else for the high quality of Kennedy's first wave of appointments in foreign affairs. Bowles was also the strong advocate of the appointment of Edward R. Murrow as head of the United States Information Agency.

In the case of Defense, McNamara organized the personnel effort himself. He came to Washington early in December, set up an office in the Ford suite at the Shoreham Hotel and began to pursue a staff by round-the-clock telephoning all over the country. Among his prominent appointments, McNamara selected Paul Nitze, a man of trenchant mind and wide experience, as Assistant Secretary for International Security Affairs, presiding over the intersection of defense and foreign policy.

Kennedy played a more direct role in filling the top positions in the Treasury with men of youth and vigor. When Dillon mentioned to Kennedy one day the lack of senior economists in the Treasury (most had left in the Eisenhower years), Kennedy suggested that he ask Seymour Harris to serve as economic adviser. Harris, with his versatility, his resourcefulness on policy matters, his deep commitment to the Kennedy program and his imperturbable good humor, played an invaluable role both in mobilizing economic advice for the Treasury and in tranquilizing relations between the Treasury and the Council of Economic Advisers.

MCGEORGE BUNDY, WHOM THE PRESIDENT APPOINTED SPECIAL ASSISTANT FOR NATIONAL SECURITY AFFAIRS, SHOWN IN 1955 IN HIS HARVARD UNIVERSITY PHOTO.

And so, one after another, the departments began to acquire their new leaders. Robert Kennedy assembled a crack group from law schools and law offices to man the Department of Justice. Udall similarly worked out his own appointments for Interior. Hodges and Klotz produced the list for Commerce. Goldberg and Ribicoff consulted closely with Ralph Dungan in staffing Labor and Health, Education and Welfare. As the day of inauguration drew near, the Kennedy administration was beginning to take shape.

2. DRAFTING THE PROGRAM

While Kennedy was choosing the members of his administration, he was engaged in still another, and quite separate, effort to chart the main directions of policy. For this purpose, he set up a series of task forces in both domestic and foreign affairs.

The task force idea was hardly new in the Kennedy operation; Ted Sorensen had experimented with one variation or another in the pre-convention period. But the post-election task forces began with Stevenson's July proposal for a foreign policy report to be submitted early in the interregnum. A week after he told Stevenson to go ahead, Kennedy

Out of the task force experience there came—for the President-elect and for those close to him—a freshened sense of programs, of priorities and of people.

asked Stuart Symington to head a task force on the organization of the defense establishment. Then at the end of August he announced a committee to deal with national security policy.

Before the election, Kennedy appointed four more task forces—on natural resources, wheat, cotton and the use of the agricultural surplus abroad. Meanwhile, Stevenson found himself more involved in the campaign than he had expected—he ended by delivering eighty-four speeches—and he therefore asked George Ball to work with him on his report. On November 14, John Sharon delivered the report to Kennedy in Palm Beach.

The report revolved in the main around Europe and reflected to a considerable degree Ball's preoccupations with NATO and with Atlantic trade policies. Within its limits, it was an exceedingly able statement. Part I listed questions requiring immediate attention—the gold drain, the postponement of the discussions of the NATO deterrent, new initiatives in disarmament, assurances on Berlin, support of the Organization for Economic Cooperation and Development. Part II proposed long-term policies in the field of trade, economic development, NATO nuclear cooperation and arms control. Of particular interest was Ball's idea for a comprehensive economic bill which would combine new aid proposals with the delegation to the President of five-year authority to reduce tariffs by 50 per cent across the board. Appendixes dealt with the problems of China, sub-Saharan Africa and the organization of the State Department. The memorandum concluded by recommending the formation of further task forces to deal with Latin America and Africa.

Kennedy promptly read Part I, throwing questions at Sharon as he turned the pages: How many presidential appointments would he have in State? Would Stevenson prepare a list of people whom he thought qualified for key positions? How should the proposed peace or disarmament agency be set up? Were there Republicans who might be considered as head of this agency? What was the OECD doing—that is the kind of thing he had not been able to keep up with during the campaign? What about Cuba? How effective was the embargo? Would there be any chance of a 'rapprochement' with Castro after January 20? What about the problem of State Department allowances for ambassadors? When he finished Part I, Kennedy closed the volume and said, "Very good. Terrific. This is excellent. Just what I needed."

In the next few days, Ball and Sharon prepared answers to Kennedy's supplementary questions. In the meantime, the President-elect received the Nitze report on national security policy. This report provided an incisive analysis of the case for a more diversified defense posture. It then offered useful discussions of the relationship between defense policy and disarmament and of the balance-of-payments problem before concluding with some sketchy paragraphs on foreign policy. The two reports evidently convinced the President-elect that the task force approach would help in the interregnum. He told Sorensen to mobilize a broad range of domestic policy task forces, and on November 18 dictated a letter to Sharon proposing a list of further task forces for foreign policy.

He concluded by saying that he was sending copies of this letter to Nitze, Bowles and Rostow. "I think it would be helpful if you four could communicate and arrange for the organization of these groups. I will rely on you, John, to be in touch with everyone."

This letter expressed Kennedy's preliminary thoughts, and in the end he did not send it (by accident, however, a copy went to Bowles). On reflection he evidently decided that a four-headed directorate was too much. Instead, he called Sharon on November 23 and told him to set up task forces for Latin America, Africa, USIA and foreign economic policy. Sorensen gracefully called Sharon and arranged to turn over all the foreign policy groups except three which were already at work—Latin America, India and the overseas food program.

The task forces now shot forward in all directions. In addition to the seven set up during the campaign, nineteen more were at work by mid-December—eleven in foreign policy and eight in domestic policy. Three further domestic policy groups were added in January. Sharon and Sorensen recruited what they regarded as the best talent in the country. By inauguration twenty-four of the twenty-nine groups had turned in their reports.

Kennedy did not read every word of every report, but he looked at them all and studied some with care. Though he sent most along to the cabinet or agency head who would become responsible after January 20, he clearly considered the task force effort as above all a service for himself. Thus, when he appointed Rusk, he had Sorensen pass on word to Sharon that "although he had designated a Secretary of State, those working on the foreign policy task forces were to understand that they had been commissioned by the President-elect and that their reports and recommendations were to be channeled directly to him for consultation with the Secretary of State."

The documents varied in length and quality—the ones on Africa, foreign economic policy and regulatory agencies, for example, were small books; but, in sum, they represented an extraordinary canvass of vital issues by some of the nation's best specialists. The task force effort also equipped Kennedy with an instrument which he could use on special occasions during the transition; thus Ball and Sharon prepared the briefing papers which helped Kennedy to dazzle Eisenhower during their December meeting. It exposed him to people whom he might want in his administration and whom he had not met in the campaign. It encouraged his old staff to accept the necessity of enlarging his circle of advisers. It gave the men of the New Frontier an opportunity to work together in hammering out new policies. Out of the task force experience there came—for the President-elect and for those close to him—a freshened sense of programs, of priorities and of people.

CAROLINE KENNEDY, AGE 3, KISSES HER NEW BABY BROTHER JOHN F. KENNEDY, JR. PALM BEACH, 1961.

3. PREPARING FOR THE DAY

So the transition proceeded, with Kennedy presiding benignly over this diversity of activities and making sure that every thread was securely in his own hands. His second child, John, Jr., had been born at the end of November. The birth was difficult, and Jacqueline was making a slow recovery. This meant that she had to stay in Palm Beach, and it meant too that the President-elect spent as much time as he could there in the days between the election and the inauguration. The time passed placidly in Florida, punctuated by visitations from political dignitaries, press conferences (with Caroline teetering into the room in her mother's shoes), meetings with the new cabinet members and with the staff, swimming and golf.

On January 9, Kennedy came to Cambridge to address the Massachusetts Legislature and attend a meeting of the

THE AUTHOR AS HE EMBARKS UPON HIS POSITION AS SPECIAL ASSISTANT TO PRESIDENT KENNEDY.

ONE OF SEVERAL SUCCESSFUL MEETINGS BETWEEN EISENHOWER AND KENNEDY DURING THE INTERREGNUM

Harvard Board of Overseers. After luncheon he set up headquarters in my house on Irving Street. It was a gray, chilly day, but a good many spectators stood outside to catch a glimpse of the President-elect. He received a stream of visitors through the afternoon. McGeorge Bundy rode over on his bicycle to complete the arrangements which would bring him to the White House as Special Assistant for National Security Affairs. Abram Chayes agreed to go to Washington as Legal Adviser to the State Department. Jerome B. Wiesner discussed his assignment as Science Adviser.

At some point between interviews the President-elect turned to me, mentioned my conversation with Bobby in December and asked whether I was ready to work at the White House. I said, "I am not sure what I would be doing as Special Assistant, but, if you think I can help, I would like very much to come." He said, "Well, I am not sure what I will be doing as President either, but I am sure there will be enough at the White House to keep us both busy."

He went south that evening and in the next few days began work on his inaugural address. Morning after morning, puffing a small cigar, a yellow, legal-sized pad of paper on his knees, he worked away, scribbling a few lines, crossing out others and then putting the sheets of paper on his already overflowing desk. Many people submitted suggestions, and Ted Sorensen gave his usual brilliant and loyal cooperation. Kennedy's hope was to strike a series of distinctive notes—to express the spirit of the postwar generation in politics, to summon America to new exertions and new initiatives, to summon the world to a new mood beyond the clichés of the cold war. As time passed, the speech took form. Then one day the President-elect stuffed the papers into his battered black briefcase and went north into the cold and snow.

On January 19 Kennedy held a final meeting with Eisenhower. They talked alone and then met with their advisers in the Cabinet Room. The discussion concentrated on points of crisis, and especially on the mounting difficulties in Laos. Eisenhower said that he had hoped that the South-East Asia Treaty Organization would take charge of the "controversy" but that the British and French did not want SEATO to act. He added that Laos was the key to all Southeast Asia. If the communists took Laos, they would bring "unbelievable pressure" on Thailand, Cambodia and South Vietnam. Laos, he said with solemnity, was so important that, if it reached the point where we could not persuade others to act with us, then he would be willing, "as a last desperate hope, to intervene unilaterally."

Kennedy, listening quietly, finally asked how long it would take to put an American division into Laos. Secretary Gates replied: twelve to seventeen days from the United

States, less if we used troops already in the Pacific. Gates went on to say that he was "exceedingly sanguine" about American capabilities for limited war; our forces were fully adequate to meet "any foreseeable test." Then he added that, while the United States was in excellent shape to meet one "limited war situation," it could not of course meet two limited war "situations" going on at the same time.

Secretary of the Treasury Anderson spoke about the balance-of-payments crisis. The erosion of the gold position, he said, was continuing unabated; measures had to be found to reverse the present trend.

The *tour d'horizon* reached Cuba. On November 18 Kennedy had learned for the first time from Allen Dulles and Richard Bissell of CIA that on March 17, 1960, the Eisenhower administration had decided to equip and drill Cuban exiles for possible action against the Castro regime. The outgoing President now said that it was "the policy of this government" to aid anti-Castro guerrilla forces "to the utmost." At present, "we are helping train anti-Castro forces in Guatemala." Eisenhower recommended that "this effort be continued and accelerated."

Twenty-four hours later, as he took the presidential oath in the freezing cold of Capitol Plaza, these became John F. Kennedy's problems.

VII. LATIN AMERICAN JOURNEY

THE KENNEDY PRESIDENCY BEGAN with incomparable dash. The young President, the old poet, the splendid speech, the triumphant parade, the brilliant sky and the shining snow: it was one of the most glorious of inaugurals. And the new President himself obviously savored every moment of it. He slept tranquilly in Lincoln's bed and woke very early the next morning. The sun streamed through the windows while he dressed and contemplated the prospects of the day. Soon he was off with springy step to the presidential office in the West Wing. He sat on the presidential chair, tried out the buttons on his desk, summoning Evelyn Lincoln from one adjacent office and Ken O'Donnell from the other, asked Dave Powers where his mail was and explored the West Wing, seeking out the offices of his staff. He called Ted Reardon, who had been with him since his first days on the Hill, and, mentioning a problem, said, "Phone so-and-so, and tell him the Senator says that he wants it such-and-such a way." Then, remembering that he was Senator no longer, they both laughed, and Kennedy said, "Do you think the country is ready for us yet?"

President Truman stopped by to pay his respects; it was his first visit to the White House since he had left it himself eight years before. After a few moments, Kennedy took him back to the Mansion to make a call on Jacqueline. They had a gay talk, the old and the new Presidents and the young wife. Later Kennedy brought Robert Frost over for another talk. It was a happy day.

He turned to his new responsibilities with zest. He issued his first executive order, doubling the rations of surplus food provided by the federal government to four million needy people across the nation; this was a response to his memories of West Virginia and the pitiful food rations doled out to the unemployed miners and their families. And he plunged into the great questions of foreign policy. The afternoon before he had received a message from Moscow, signed N. Khrushchev and L. Brezhnev, expressing the hope that "by our own joint efforts we shall succeed in achieving a fundamental improvement in relations between our countries and a normalization of the whole international situation." Kennedy now replied that he was "ready and anxious to cooperate with all who are prepared to join in genuine dedication to the assurance of a peaceful and more fruitful life for all mankind." This message, a piece of State Department boiler plate, expressed the quality neither of the President's hope nor of his concern. For, at the very moment when Khrushchev and Brezhnev were sending their good wishes, the situation was growing worse in Laos. The central committee of the Chinese Communist Party was putting out a statement affirming its solidarity with the Soviet Union and naming the United States as the great enemy of the workers of the world. And the band of Cuban exiles were training on a plantation in Guatemala.

1. FOOD FOR PEACE

Arriving in Washington on January 30th, I was assigned the office in the East Wing, where James F. Byrnes had held forth twenty years before as the director of the Office of War Mobilization. I was also given an extraordinarily able and reliable secretary, Gretchen Stewart, who had served in the White House since the days of Truman.*

A few minutes later I went to Capitol Hill with a number of my new colleagues to hear the President deliver his first State of the Union message. Kennedy described his inheritance in grim terms—recession in the economy, deficit in the balance of payments, deficiencies in housing, education and medical care, imbalance in the posture of defense, trouble in Laos, the Congo and Latin America—and then, with heartening eloquence, called for action to stimulate economic

* And to whom I must express deep gratitude for her unstinted assistance during the writing of this book.

recovery, to protect the dollar, to improve the national household, to diversify the means of defense and to establish an alliance for progress in the hemisphere, a Food for Peace program and a Peace Corps. "Life in 1961 will not be easy," he concluded. "Wishing it, predicting it, even asking for it, will not make it so. There will be further setbacks before the tide is turned. But turn it we must. The hopes of all mankind rest upon us." We stood along the back wall in the chamber of the House, welcoming the applause as our President set forth his proposals, and then went back to the White House, exhilarated by the sense of taking part in a great new national adventure.

What precisely my own part would be was not, however, clear. The first days in the White House, as a Special Assistant without a special assignment, were uncertain and confusing. Then at the end of the week the President told me that George McGovern, now director of the Food for Peace program, was going to Latin America to discuss food problems with the governments of Argentina and Brazil. As this would be, he said, the first mission of his administration to Latin America, he wanted to demonstrate his personal concern with hemisphere problems by sending along someone from the White House. Knowing my interest in Latin America, he wondered whether I was not the person to go. Moreover, the Latin American intellectual community had the idea that the United States was a reactionary and materialistic nation; maybe my presence in the mission might persuade somebody that things had changed in Washington. He would be particularly interested, he emphasized, in anything that could be discreetly learned about attitudes toward Castro.

The Food for Peace idea went back to the Agricultural Trade Development and Assistance Act of 1954, better known as Public Law 480. This measure had been passed to ease the problems created by mounting farm surpluses and storage charges after the Korean War; and the Eisenhower administration had carried it out basically as a program for the disposal of unwanted American surpluses abroad. Though a good deal of food and fiber went to the new nations in these years, the surplus-disposal philosophy had seriously limited the effectiveness of the program both as an aid to

PRESIDENT JOHN F. KENNEDY WITH A CLEAN DESK ON HIS FIRST DAY OF WORK, JANUARY 21, 1961.

SWEARING IN GEORGE MCGOVERN (RIGHT), DIRECTOR, FOOD FOR PEACE.

development and as an instrument of national policy. Some foreign countries mistrusted PL 480 as a disguised dumping operation; others acted as if they were doing the United States a favor by relieving the American economy of the embarrassment of surpluses.

In the late fifties, liberal Democrats in Congress—especially McGovern in the House and Hubert Humphrey in the Senate—began to agitate for a reconstruction of the program. This was one aspect of farm policy to which Kennedy was immediately and whole-heartedly responsive.

In October Kennedy had appointed a task force to study new ways of using American agricultural abundance overseas. The report condemned "the conception, the philosophy and the nomenclature of 'surplus disposal.'" Instead of sending overseas whatever happened to be in surplus in the United States, it envisaged the use of American agricultural abundance to meet specific wants abroad both of nutrition and of development. This could mean shifts in domestic production from wheat and corn into oils and fats and protein foods; it could mean the use of food to generate local currency for productive investment and to check the inflation of food prices which might otherwise result from development projects; it could mean the use of food as capital through direct payment in kind to labor working on dams, roads, ports or similar projects.

Kennedy in his second executive order put the program within the Executive Office of the President and named McGovern as director (after Robert Kennedy had objected to the title coordinator on the ground that it would mean nothing in South Dakota, McGovern's home state). McGovern went swiftly to work. Though both Agriculture and State coveted the program, McGovern argued that it should have a public identity of its own and established himself in a vacant suite in the Executive Office Building before State or Agriculture knew what was happening. To further the cause of giving Food for Peace a separate identity, he sent the President a memorandum urging that Food for Peace missions be dispatched right away to Latin America, Asia and Africa—a proposal about which he heard nothing until the Latin American mission turned up as a recommendation in the State of the Union message. As McGovern prepared for his trip, he received one day a phone call from Kennedy saying that he wanted Arthur Schlesinger to go along "to look into some things for me."

2. THE LATIN AMERICAN DILEMMA

My interest in Latin America was of long standing. It had begun twenty years earlier in the Office of Strategic Services where I followed Latin American affairs closely. This immersion in hemisphere affairs called my attention to the conspicuous omission of Roosevelt's Good Neighbor policy. Roosevelt had, of course, wrought a revolution in hemisphere relations. His affirmation of 'nonintervention' and of the juridical equality of the American republics, as well as his sponsorship of the New Deal at home, had disposed Latin America for the first time to trust United States leadership. The evident concern of Roosevelt, Cordell Hull, Sumner Welles, Adolf Berle and others had created bonds of confidence—almost of affection—unprecedented in the history of the hemisphere. Yet, though Latin Americans trusted Roosevelt, among other reasons, as the champion of democratic reform, the Good Neighbor policy did not, as such, call for an extension of the New Deal to the hemisphere.

After the war, the United States government, preoccupied

first with the recovery of Europe and then with the Korean War, forgot Latin America—a bipartisan error pursued with equal fidelity by the Truman and Eisenhower administrations. Between 1945 and 1960 the single country of Yugoslavia—a communist country at that—received more money from the United States than all the Latin American countries put together.

I was among those who watched these developments with increasing concern. In 1946 I wrote in a piece for *Fortune:* "All across Latin America the ancient oligarchies—landholders, Church, and Army—are losing their grip. There is a groundswell of inarticulate mass dissatisfaction on the part of peons, Indians, miners, plantation workers, factory hands, classes held down past all endurance and now approaching a state of revolt." What should United States policy be? "Many facets of the complex South American problem," the article suggested, "are not accessible to U.S. policy. One facet is accessible—the economic."

In 1950 the Inter-American Association for Democracy and Freedom invited a number of politicians and intellectuals from North and South America to a conference in Havana. It was then that I first met José Figueres of Costa Rica, who two years before had repelled the first serious communist attempt to seize a Latin American government. I also met eminent figures exiled by their own countries, notably Rómulo Betancourt and Raúl Leoni of Venezuela and Juan Bosch of the Dominican Republic. Eduardo Frei and Salvador Allende, who fourteen years later would compete for the presidency of Chile, were there; so too was German Arciniegas, the Colombian historian, and Aprista leaders from Peru. Though memories of Yanqui imperialism had not died, these Latin American democrats had by no means given up on the United States. They cherished the hope that the Good Neighbor policy of Franklin Roosevelt would someday revive and that the influence of the United States would go to the support of progressive democracy in Latin America. A few years later I spent some time with Adolf Berle in Costa Rica as a guest of President Figueres, an experience which further strengthened my faith in a progressive democratic solution in the hemisphere.

This view found little support in the United States in the fifties. The stimulus to raw material prices provided first by the Second World War and later by the Korean War made it easy to argue that Latin America had no basic economic problems. The Eisenhower administration was thus able to relax in the comfortable doctrine that private investment by itself would bring about development in Latin America, as they supposed it had done in the United States; that government aid should be confined to military and technical assistance; and that the way to enable private investment to do its job was to back governments which would foster a 'favorable' investment climate by leaving private business alone, guaranteeing investors, especially foreign investors, full and unrestricted returns and insuring monetary stability. This meant, of course, right-wing governments.

The theory of development as an act of immaculate private conception was founded, among other things, on a considerable ignorance of the history of economic development in the United States itself. In the first half-century of our own history government had played a relatively active role in building the turnpikes, canals, harbors, railroads and schools which made subsequent economic expansion possible. When what economists unhappily term 'social overhead capital' or 'infrastructure' is the great need, public investment becomes a necessity, since private capital will not go into these areas of low return.

The policy of the fifties not only violated our own national practice; it was also manifestly inadequate to the problems of Latin America, and it reinforced the cherished Latin conviction that the essence of the United States purpose was economic imperialism. Its result had been to place our position in extreme jeopardy throughout the hemisphere. And the rise of Fidel Castro in Cuba was transforming a failure of policy into a threat to security. This was the situation which the President feared and into which he was now asking McGovern and me to look.

3. HEMISPHERE RECONNAISSANCE: I

We left Idlewild Airport in New York on the evening of February 12. Our mission began in Buenos Aires. Though President Arturo Frondizi had been elected as a nationalist and a radical, his administration had become increasingly pro-United States in its foreign policy and pro-laissez faire in its domestic policy. The change in foreign policy was especially striking. Historically Argentina had resisted United States leadership in the hemisphere, always seeking to play off Europe—whether Great Britain, the League of Nations or even Nazi Germany—against Washington's attempts to promote an inter-American system. But the days when Argentina could aspire to an independent role were over. In recent years Brazil had so far outdistanced her in every respect that no realistic Argentine could any longer suppose that his country was competing with Washington for dominance in the hemisphere. Frondizi, relieved of this traditional antagonism, was the most pro-American president in Argentine history.

Frondizi was skeptical about Food for Peace and, indeed, about 'social investment' in general. This was a common

Latin reaction to the program launched in 1960 at Bogotá providing for a Social Progress Fund and increased investment in housing, education and other forms of welfare. Frondizi argued that development required hard capital investment in heavy industry; if this were done, the new wealth produced would take care of the social problems. A continent-wide program of basic economic growth, he said, was the only way to save the hemisphere from communism.

This observation gave me the opportunity to pursue my mission for the President and raise the question of Castro. Frondizi indicated that he regarded the Cuban regime as essentially communist but added: "Castro is not the fundamental question. The elimination of Castro will not solve the underlying problem. What is required is an attack on the conditions which produced him. If he is eliminated and these conditions are left unchanged, new Castros will arise all over the continent." We agreed but tried to point out that social and economic reform, however desirable, would not counter the existing threat which Castro posed to hemisphere unity. What kind of measures against Castro, we asked, was the Organization of American States likely to support? He became exceedingly obscure, saying at last that it would be hard for the OAS to act because a number of nations—Mexico, Peru, Colombia, Brazil—would hesitate to endorse anti-Castro measures for fear of domestic political repercussions. He gave no hint as to what Argentina might do, though we knew, of course, that Argentina had declined to go all the way with the OAS sanctions against the Trujillo dictatorship in the Dominican Republic. In general his position was that little could be done about Castro except to press for long-range development.

Buenos Aires itself was depressing. In general, the government appeared weary and lacking in imagination or energy. When we went on to Brazil, the contrast was spectacular. Under Juscelino Kubitschek, the retiring president, the sheer momentum of growth had charged the nation with a certain economic dynamism. That growth could hardly have been more vagrant, disorderly and undisciplined; a Brazilian economist described Kubitschek to us as "the playboy of economic development." Yet Brazil, while defying the orthodoxies of public finance and defrauding the International Monetary Fund, could show as a result not only inordinate inflation and inordinate graft but a solid increase in its industrial base and national output. Wild as it all was, it somehow seemed better than the stagnation of Argentina; but one wondered whether a middle course might not be possible.

The hope was that the new president, Janio Quadros, would provide this middle way. He had been a tough administrator as governor of the state of São Paulo, and his inaugural address of a few days before displayed a clear understanding of the fiscal mess he had inherited from Kubitschek. The atmosphere in the new government was bracing and hopeful. Our Food for Peace discussions elicited a concrete response. Following a day of talks in Rio, we went on to Brasília to see Quadros.

Quadros greeted us cordially—we were the first foreign delegation he had received since his inauguration—and showed a lively interest in the new administration in Washington. We had decided not to raise the question of Cuba because Adolf Berle was due to see him in a few days. About Brazil, Quadros said that the financial situation was desperate and that he planned to set forth the facts as bluntly as possible in order to prepare the nation for drastic remedies. He talked well, but with a certain elusiveness. I cannot claim to have detected the instability which would later produce his dramatic resignation.

From Brasília we flew to Recife in Brazil's desolate northeast. Here we met Celso Furtado, a young economist who was now head of SUDENE, the federal commission for the development of the northeast. We drove with him through the humid area along the coast, devoted largely to sugar cultivation. Then we headed toward the semi-arid land in the interior. I had never seen such an area of despair—one bleak, stagnant village after another, dark mud huts, children with spindle legs and swollen bellies, practically no old people (Furtado noted that life expectancy, for those who survived their first year, was twenty-nine years). Furtado was realistic in his assessment of possibilities. Seeing no present hope of doing anything in the semi-arid zone, he was concentrating on the sugar lands. An emergency food program, he said, would do no good; it might even disturb the existing dietary balance which kept the people marginally alive. "Real development," he said, "means giving man the possibility of being happy in his work. These people hate their work. They are too weak anyway to work very long. If you give them food and do nothing to change their way of life, they will only work less." McGovern and I were both appalled by the magnitude of the problem and impressed by the initiatives which Brazil had already taken. We carried the cause of northeast Brazil with us back to Washington.

4. HEMISPHERE RECONNAISSANCE: II

McGovern now returned to the United States, while I went on to Peru to complete my presidential mission in the company of a Food for Peace technical group bound for Bolivia.

The process of revolution in Bolivia, which had begun

haltingly with the MNR uprising of 1943, had reached its climax when the MNR returned to power in 1952 and, during the presidency of Victor Paz Estenssoro, carried through one of the few genuine social transformations in Latin America's long history of political upheaval. Despite the nationalization of the tin mines and other offenses against free enterprise, the Eisenhower administration exempted Bolivia from its Latin American canons and actually gave it more grant aid than any other country in the hemisphere—about $150 million. This aid, however, had produced little in the way of economic stimulus or other visible result. Paz Estenssoro, whose second term as president had recently begun, was now struggling to get his poor and isolated nation moving again.

An intelligent and harassed man, Paz began by setting forth the general case for revolution with fluency and candor. The great need in Latin America, he said, was to incorporate the poor people into both the money economy and the political society. But too much of Latin America lingered in a quasi-feudal state, with the very poor, and especially the Indians, living under the domination of a landed oligarchy which thought it was ruling by divine right. The longer the oligarchs resisted change, Paz said, the more violent revolution would be when it came. Peru and Ecuador, he added, were particularly near the point of social explosion.

"There is much poverty in my country," Paz said "The communists have made themselves the advocates of the just demands of the workers and peasants. That makes it hard for us to oppose them without seeming to oppose what we regard as a just social program." But he gloomily admitted that they might try to take over Bolivia as they had taken over Cuba; ever since the Castro revolution, he added, the communists had proved especially successful in winning adherents and forcing issues.

I seized the opportunity to put the President's question. Paz replied without hesitation, "Castro must be eliminated." I wondered how this might be done. He said that first the economic screws must be tightened against him; then an educational campaign must inform the hemisphere of the true character of the Castro regime; then—but at this point he muttered something about the OAS and trailed off into vagueness. His attitude could be described, I think, as composed in equal parts of a strong fear of Castro, a fervent hope that the United States would rid the hemisphere of him and a profound disinclination to identify himself, except in the most marginal way, with anti-Castro action.

When I returned to Lima, I found Victor Haya de la Torre, the leader of the APRA party, even more outspoken in his condemnation of Castro. He regarded the Castro regime as the great threat to progressive democracy in the Americas and felt that the OAS might consider invoking the Rio Treaty of 1947 against aggression in the hemisphere. Haya spoke with great warmth about Kennedy and the references to an alliance for progress in his State of the Union message. The new American President, he said, had an unexampled opportunity to lift the hemisphere to new levels of unity. The Good Neighbor policy had been all right for its day, but, though benevolent, it had been unilateral. What the Latin American republics sought from the United States was a genuine coordination of hemisphere policy through consultation and especially through a willingness to create a hemisphere pool of ideas. Now that Washington had abandoned imperialism, relations between the United States and Latin America were largely a "question of style."

My last stop was Caracas. I had not met Betancourt since Havana more than a decade before. He was far the most impressive of the Latin American leaders. Tough and good-humored, he conveyed an impression of strength, authority and inextinguishable vitality. Our talk during eight hours ranged widely. He inquired about the new administration in Washington, mentioning the hope that President Kennedy had already excited through the continent. When I brought up Castro, he repeated a remark Quadros had made to him after visiting Cuba: "Those people have no aim, no purpose, no doctrine, no ideology. It is government by epilepsy." Betancourt himself, however, had no doubt of the Castro regime's ideological drift. The personalism of Latin American politics, he said, was a great source of weakness. Without strong democratic parties, like Acción Democrática, the temptation to rely on the disciplined organization of the communists was hard for a man like Castro—even possibly for one like Quadros—to resist. As for a hemisphere policy toward Castro, Betancourt argued that if the OAS first took action against Trujillo it would be easier to unite the American republics against Castro. Beyond this, it was necessary to use all the resources of progressive democracy to combat poverty, illiteracy and injustice.

VIII. THE ALLIANCE FOR PROGRESS

IN A FAMOUS QUOTATION of 1952 German Arciniegas spoke of two Latin Americas: the visible and the invisible. The visible Latin America was the Yanqui's Latin America of presidents, chancelleries, generals, embassies, business houses, law offices, *estancias* and *haciendas*. The other, the "mute, repressed" Latin America, was a "vast reservoir of revolution.... Nobody knows exactly what these 150 million silent men and women think, feel, dream or await in the depths of their being."

By 1961 there were a good deal more than 150 million people; they were no longer silent; and the whole hemisphere was seeming to move in response to their inchoate stirrings. When I came back to Washington in early March, it was with the conviction, more urgent now than ever, that the struggle of the invisible Latin America to join the twentieth century was confronting the United States with a crisis—one which, if ignored, might end by transforming the southern half of the hemisphere into a boiling and angry China, but which, if approached in a strong and comprehensive way, might still not be beyond our power to affect.

1. EVOLUTION OF A POLICY

Here was a continent of 200 million souls, at least two-fifths of whom were under fifteen years of age, nearly 50 percent of whom were illiterate, 30 percent of whom would die before their fortieth year—a population multiplying faster than any other in the world—where 2 percent of the people owned 50 percent of the wealth and 70 percent lived in abject poverty; yet here also was a part of the west, permeated and tantalized by democratic ideals of freedom and progress, where the existence of a common ethical and political in-heritance might create possibilities of partnership and action which did not exist in Asia or Africa.

Here was a world at once fascinating and appalling in its internal contrasts, where a highly polished nineteenth century civilization coexisted with unimaginable primitivism and squalor, and where a surging passion for modernization now threatened to sweep both aside. Here were free republics with meager traditions of stability or continuity—where, indeed, ninety-three illegal changes of regime had taken place in the last thirty years—but with deep pride in their more than a century of independence. Here was half of the western hemisphere, which, if it turned against the United States, would mock our leadership before the world and create a hard and lasting threat to our national security, but which, if we could work effectively with its people, might provide the world a model in the processes of democratic development.

The old order in Latin America was obviously breaking up. There was no longer any question of preserving the status quo. The only question now was the shape of the future. Here was Fidel Castro, the passionate leader of the Cuban Revolution, behind him the inarticulate woes of generations, and behind him too the thrust of communism from beyond the hemisphere; and here was the new young President of the United States, whose accession to power had already awakened fresh hope in the Americas, and behind him the uneven and uncoordinated energies of reasonable men and of indigenous Latin democracy. Which road into the future? My talks with Betancourt, Haya de la Torre, Paz Estenssoro and others had given me the strong impression that the democratic left in Latin America had turned decisively against Castro and that he would increasingly appear as the symbol not of social revolution but of Soviet penetration. Nonetheless, if the United States were not ready to offer an affirmative program for democratic modernization, new Castros would undoubtedly rise across the continent. This was the nature of the crisis.

President Kennedy knew all this, of course; and, when I reported to him, he proceeded, in the manner that was so characteristic, to ask a series of rapid and specific questions: which countries and social groups gave Castro most support? how capable was Castro of setting off simultaneous and prearranged violence in a number of countries? naturally we sympathized with the leaders of the democratic left, but how really effective in fact were they? what were my impressions of Frondizi, of Quadros, of Betancourt? what about our own ambassadors? how prepared were our embassies to handle a massive aid program? He had no illusions about the difficulty of maintaining the position of the United States in the midst of a social revolution in Latin America, but, as revolution seemed inevitable, he clearly believed we had no choice but to do our best, partly because the loss of Latin America would damage our own security but even more because we had a particular, almost familial, responsibility to help these peoples in their battle for democracy.

I put my answers to these and other questions in a memorandum on the dilemmas of modernization in the hemisphere. The modernization of Latin America, I suggested, was basically a task for Latin Americans, though the United States could make a significant, and possibly decisive, contribution to its fulfillment. But no one should underrate the size of the problem. The memorandum emphasized the following points:

1. Because population has been growing faster than output in recent years, Latin America has begun to lose ground in the struggle for development.
2. The Soviet Union, in association with Cuba, is exploiting the situation and providing the U.S. with unprecedentedly serious competition.
3. Time is running out for the parties of the middle-class revolution.... The democratic parties...have thus far failed to deliver the goods to the satisfaction of the younger and more impatient members of the middle and working classes.
4. Latin America is waiting expectantly for new initiatives in Washington.... The Inaugural Address evoked particular admiration. People are looking on J.F.K. as a reincarnation of F.D.R. To a surprising degree, the slate has been wiped clean of past neglect and error. The atmosphere is set for miracles. There is consequently real danger that the intensity of present expectations may lead to future disappointments.

My report only added one more document to the intensive review of Latin American policy which was already under way.

2. ORIGINS OF THE ALLIANCE

Kennedy's Latin American interest went back to a tour of South America twenty years earlier. During most of the fifties he had shared the common Washington preference for the problems of Asia until the ferment at the end of the decade—and especially Vice-President Nixon's disastrous trip—renewed his interest in the western hemisphere. Obviously, if the Vice-President were stoned and spat upon in South America, even if one allowed for Nixon's capacity to arouse personal animosity, the position of the United States had declined a good deal since Good Neighbor days. In a speech in Puerto Rico at the end of 1958, a few days before Fidel Castro entered Havana, Kennedy urged that Latin America be given a new priority in United States foreign policy. He warned against the illusion prevalent in North American discussions "that all Latin American agitation is Communist-inspired—that every anti-American voice

FIDEL CASTRO VISITING WASHINGTON, D.C. ON MAY 15, 1959.

is the voice of Moscow—and that most citizens of Latin America share our dedication to an anti-Communist crusade to save what we call free enterprise." And he endorsed a number of specific proposals, including the Inter-American Bank, commodity agreements, loans to encourage land reform and the enlargement of programs of cultural and educational exchange.

Critics of the Eisenhower Latin American policy had been making such points for some time. Perhaps the most influential was Adolf Berle, who, after playing a role in the creation of the Good Neighbor policy, had served Roosevelt as Assistant Secretary of State and as ambassador to Brazil. More than anyone else, Berle provided the link between the Good Neighbor policy and the Alliance for Progress. If Good Neighborism did not mean a set of democratic ideas, it would be no more than a policy of sanctifying economic stagnation and political tyranny—a result that would injure the moral position of the United States without furnishing strategic security.

These ideas, in Berle's view, implied not only guarantees against aggression, whether from within the hemisphere or without, but the assurance of basic rights, including the freedoms of expression and political opposition, and the commitment to an economic program which would raise mass living standards. Only these positive elements could create a genuine inter-Americanism based on a community of confidence, not just among governments (which was what nonintervention achieved), but among peoples.

This evolution of the Good Neighbor policy, Berle well understood, required the emergence in Latin America of political leaders and parties committed to democratic objectives. During the forties and fifties, when the State Department was ignoring or harassing Latin American democrats, Berle made it his business to keep in close touch with men like Betancourt and Figueres. In this effort, he worked closely with Luis Muñoz Marín, the remarkable governor of Puerto Rico. Together they developed a network of unofficial relationships with the *partidos populares* of Latin America. Kennedy, whose friendship with Muñoz began with the Puerto Rican trip of 1958, fell heir to these ideas and relationships.

Kennedy's man on Latin America was Richard Goodwin. Goodwin's friendship with Karl Meyer, who wrote editorials on Latin America for the *Washington Post,* had given him an acquaintance with hemisphere problems and personalities even before he met Kennedy. During the campaign the candidate repeatedly cited Latin America as a signal Republican failure in foreign affairs. When the time approached for a full-dress exposition of Kennedy's own Latin American views, Goodwin was charged with preparing a draft, and helped formulate the phrase "Alliance for Progress."

3. THE LATIN AMERICAN TASK FORCE

Kennedy gave the Latin American speech in October in front of the county courthouse in Tampa, Florida. Finding himself before a restless outdoor crowd, he did not deliver all the prepared text; but when he finished, he told Goodwin that he considered it a most important speech and wanted it released in full as a statement. The speech reached its climax when Kennedy declared his belief "in a Western Hemisphere where all people—the Americans of the South and the Americans of the North—the United States and the nations of Latin America—are joined together in an alliance for progress—*alianza para progreso.*" (In the interest of euphony, Goodwin had excised "el" from the phrase; eventually the grammarians of USIA insisted on its restoration.) The *Alianza* would mean, Kennedy said, "a great common effort to develop the resources of the entire hemisphere, strengthen the forces of democracy, and widen the vocational and educational opportunities of every person in all the Americas." It would also mean "constant consultation" with Latin American nations on hemisphere and world problems.

More specifically, the Alliance would involve a number of departures in United States policy:

- *"unequivocal support to democracy" and opposition to dictatorship*
- *provision of "long-term development funds, essential to a growing economy"*
- *stabilization of "the prices of the principal commodity exports"*
- *aid to "programs of land reform"*
- *stimulus to private investment and encouragement to private business "to immerse themselves in the life of the country ... through mixing capital with local capital, training local inhabitants for skilled jobs, and making maximum use of local labor"*
- *expansion of technical assistance programs*
- *enlargement of information and student exchange programs*
- *an arms control agreement for the hemisphere*
- *strengthening the OAS*
- *the appointment of ambassadors who understood and cared about the problems of Latin America.*

The Tampa speech summed up Kennedy's thinking on Latin America before the election. But he himself did not feel that the speech had gone nearly far enough; and his letter of November 18, 1960, to John Sharon had expressed his sense of urgency about the need for dramatic new recommendations. In the meantime, Goodwin had begun the work of setting up a Latin American task force. Berle agreed to serve as chairman.

The task force submitted its report early in 1961. The problem, it said, was "to divorce the inevitable and necessary

Latin American social transformation from connection with and prevent its capture by overseas Communist power politics." The communist objective was obviously "to convert the Latin American social revolution into a Marxist attack on the United States itself." The report gave a somber picture of the communist threat, which, it concluded, "resembles, but is more dangerous than, the Nazi-Fascist threat of the Franklin Roosevelt period and demands an even bolder and more imaginative response."

The task force emphasized the danger of armed rebellion and guerrilla warfare in the Caribbean and Andean countries. Since "good wishes and economic plans do not stop bullets or hand grenades or armed bands," the United States must be prepared to offer the military support necessary to defend, for example, the Betancourt regime in Venezuela. But military action alone could not stop communism. Democracy was weak in Latin America in part because the United States "has stated no clear philosophy of its own, and has no effective machinery to disseminate such a philosophy." It was useless to try to "stabilize the dying reactionary situations." A first task of the new administration must be to formulate a positive democratic philosophy; and, since the United States role could only be supplementary, particular effort must go to working with the indigenous democracy of Latin America. Political movements desiring social transformation and intensified cooperation with the United States "should be known to have the good-will and support of the United States, just as every Communist group in Latin America is known to have the support of Moscow or of Peiping." To accomplish this, the report proposed the formation of "a coordinating center for a Latin American democratic-progressive front."

Within the State Department, the principal officer in charge of relations with Latin America should have the rank of Under Secretary. In the economic field, Washington must offer "a long-range economic plan for the whole hemisphere." While private enterprise "has a major part to play," the United States should give greater relative emphasis to indigenous as against foreign capital and end its "doctrinaire opposition" to loans to state enterprises. The hemisphere is large enough "to have diverse social systems in different countries.... Our economic policy and aid need not be limited to countries in which private enterprise is the sole or predominant instrument of development." The government should make clear that private enterprise "is not the determining principle or sole objective of American policy."

The report also offered specific suggestions about emergency situations. Its significance, however, lay in the new elements it brought into official thinking. It saw the communist threat as requiring not just a military response, as the Pentagon believed, or just an economic response, as some Latin Americans believed, but a combination of both. Besides military containment, it urged the systematic and semiofficial promotion of democratic political parties and a new stress on economic development through country development plans. If the recommendations were accepted, the goal of the United States would be not just the limited program of social development envisaged at Bogotá but a long-term program of national and continental development, shielded against communist disruption and aimed at leading the whole hemisphere to self-sustaining economic growth and democratic political institutions.

4. BIRTH THROES OF THE ALLIANCE

This view did not prevail in all parts of the executive branch. A preference for right-wing governments had been implicit in the policy of the early Eisenhower years; and the evolution of the Castro regime in Cuba had persuaded some, especially in the armed services, that the right-wing alternative should now become the explicit object of United States policy. The Cuban experience, it was argued, proved that the United States could never retain control of a Latin American revolution, no matter how plausible it might seem in its first stages. As for attempts to avert revolution through pressure for reform, this would only alienate those who held the real power—the oligarchy (more favorably known as the 'producing classes' or 'those commanding capital resources') and the military—and open the door to incompetent liberals who would bring about inflation, disinvestment, capital flight and social indiscipline and would finally be shoved aside by the communists. The conclusion was that we should oppose revolution and reform in Latin America and concentrate on helping our 'tested friends'—those who gave us economic privileges, military facilities and votes in the United Nations and who could be relied on to suppress local communists, tax and land reformers, and other malcontents and demagogues.

In Washington the case for the right-wing alternative seemed to proceed less from thoughtful analysis of the conditions of growth than from unthinking satisfaction with the existing social order. During the Second World War the United States armed services began to become acquainted with Latin America. Our officers naturally associated with members of the oligarchy, who spoke English and invited them to parties, and they naturally developed a fellow feeling for their brother officers south of the border. After the war, came a program of arms exports to Latin American countries. This program was re-inforced by the Pentagon's chronic need to dispose of obsolescent weapons and thereby acquire credits against which new ones could be purchased.

In these years the United States military fell into the habit of conducting their own direct relations with their Latin American counterparts, training them in United States staff schools, sending them on tours of United States military installations, welcoming their arms missions in Washington, showing them the latest available (i.e., most recently obsolescent) 'hardware' and engaging in elaborate return visits of their own—all with minimal notice to the Department of State and minimal coordination with the country's foreign policy objectives.

All this had political and economic side effects. United States military aid obviously gave the recipient governments prestige and their military forces power. The service attachés in United States embassies often disagreed with the policies of the Department of State and on occasion communicated the impression that Washington would not really object to actions the local American ambassador might be trying to stop. For their part, democratic Latin American leaders began to use the United States arms program as a means of warding off right-wing coups, appeasing their own military and purchasing time for social reform.

By 1961 the special interests of the military were threatening to distort United States policy much as the special interests of business had distorted policy thirty-five years earlier. Still, even in the Eisenhower administration, the counterrevolutionary case had been a minority view, and in the new administration it had even less hope. Nonetheless, pressure for a revival of the policy stirred beneath the surface. The chief voice of the counterrevolutionary line within the government was Admiral Arleigh Burke, who represented the Navy on the Joint Chiefs, who took every opportunity to advocate full support for all anti-communist regimes, whatever their internal character. For men of Burke's persuasion, talk of an alliance for progress could only seem bleeding-heart, do-good globaloney.

It was here that Adolf Berle made an essential contribution. For Berle, with all his ardor for democracy and development, comprehended also, in another part of his nature, the shadowy world of intrigue, conspiracy and violence. He had an extensive knowledge of communist movements and a vivid apprehension of communist dangers. He was therefore able to give the new social initiatives an edge of 'toughness' which, while it was kept strictly separate from the Alliance for Progress, was still able to protect the idea of the Alliance from those for whom anti-communism was the only issue (as well as in time protect the operations of the Alliance from the communists who sought to destroy it).

But the revolutionary point remained primary. For Kennedy fully understood—this was, indeed, the mainspring of all his thinking about Latin America—that, with all its pretensions to realism, the militant anti-revolutionary line represented the policy most likely to strengthen the communists and lose the hemisphere. He believed that, to maintain contact with a continent seized by the course of revolutionary change, a policy of social idealism was the only true realism for the United States.

5. THE ALLIANCE LAUNCHED

Berle, believing on principle that the top State Department man on hemisphere affairs should have the rank of Under Secretary, was unwilling to accept the post of Assistant Secretary for Inter-American Affairs. Instead Thomas Mann, whom Dillon had transferred to the hemisphere job in August 1960, stayed on in the new administration, and Berle took a somewhat ambiguous appointment as special adviser on Latin American affairs and chairman of a new and now official Latin American Task Force. This was not an altogether satisfactory arrangement. While Berle knew the State Department well, he had always been something of a loner, and the Foreign Service regarded him with ancient suspicion. But Mann was a good bureaucrat and ready enough to go along.

Berle and Mann convened the reconstituted Task Force in February. On February 16, Berle again defined the issue—"to develop policies and programs which would channel the revolution now going on in Latin America in the proper direction and to prevent it from being taken over by the Sino-Soviet bloc." The situation in Latin America, he suggested, resembled that of western Europe in 1947. The Communists had failed then because the Marshall Plan restored western Europe economically while their own opposition to European recovery discredited communism politically. The need now was to confront the Latin American communists with a similar dilemma by offering, so to speak, a moral equivalent of the Marshall Plan, but of course a plan for the development of a continent held down by ignorance and poverty rather than for the reconstruction of a continent rich in managerial and labor skills. The Task Force concluded by recommending that the President deliver a major address on Latin American policy in the near future.

In the next week, Dick Goodwin began the White House review of Latin American policy in preparation for the presidential speech. He summoned representatives from all agencies having anything to do with Latin America and asked that each agency submit its recommendations within a week.

He also consulted with Latin Americans in Washington. On March 8 a document of particular interest came in from

A RECEPTIVE AUDIENCE OF LATIN AMERICAN DIPLOMATS LISTEN AS KENNEDY DESCRIBES THE ALLIANCE FOR PROGRESS.

the group of Latin American economists who had been foremost in the fight for development. "Latin America," the memorandum began, "is in a state of crisis. Deep-running currents are bringing about great changes in the economic and social structure. "The responsibility for such changes," the memorandum emphasized, "lies with Latin America," but international cooperation was imperative if they were to come about in a democratic way. Such international interest had to be free from any suspicion of economic imperialism. Nor could it be supposed that the free play of economic forces alone would bring about the required structural change. "Vigorous state action" was necessary; and it would not be easy "to overcome the resistance of private groups without disturbances."

Goodwin's task now was to reduce the jumble of recommendations to a coherent policy. He finally sought refuge in his house in Georgetown, emerging a day or so later with a draft, which was reviewed by Sorensen, Rusk, and ultimately, the President. On March 13 the Latin American diplomatic corps assembled in the East Room of the White House. One hundred thirty-nine years earlier that week the United States had urged the recognition of the Latin republics fighting for independence against Spain. Kennedy noted that the revolution which had begun in Philadelphia in 1776 and Caracas in 1811 was not yet finished; "for our unfulfilled task is to demonstrate to the entire world that man's unsatisfied aspiration for economic progress and social justice can best be achieved by free men working within a framework of democratic institutions." Now was the time, Kennedy said, to turn away from the failures of the past to a future "full of peril, but bright with hope."

> *I have called on all people of the hemisphere to join in a new Alliance for Progress*—Alianza para Progreso—*a vast cooperative effort, unparalleled in magnitude and nobility of purpose, to satisfy the basic needs of the American people for homes, work and land, health and schools*—techo, trabajo y tierra, salud y escuela.

He pronounced the Spanish manfully, but with a distinct New England intonation.

He went on to outline the program, stressing the need for self-help, for national planning, for regional markets, for commodity stabilization and for hemisphere cooperation in education, technical training and research. He emphasized that "to complete the revolution of the Americas ... political freedom must accompany material progress ... *progreso si, tirania no!*" The task was to create an American civilization "where, within the rich diversity of its own traditions, each nation is free to follow its own path towards progress." His peroration was thrilling:

> *Let us once again transform the American continent into a vast crucible of revolutionary ideas and efforts—a tribute to the power of the creative energies of free men and women—an example to all the world that liberty and progress walk hand in hand.*

It was an extraordinary occasion. The people in the East Room came suddenly alive as the young President spoke his words of idealism and purpose. There was strong applause. Goodwin and I circulated among the group as it dispersed. One found still a measure of doubt and cynicism, but most people were deeply moved. The Venezuelan Ambassador took my arm and said urgently, "We have not heard such words since Franklin Roosevelt." The future of the hemisphere did seem bright with hope.

IX. THE HOUR OF EUPHORIA

EVELYN LINCOLN.

THE FUTURE EVERYWHERE, INDEED, seemed bright with hope. By the time I came back from Latin America in early March, the New Frontier was in full swing. The capital city, somnolent in the Eisenhower years, had come suddenly alive. The air had been stale and oppressive; now fresh winds were blowing. There was the excitement which comes from an injection of new men and new ideas, the release of energy which occurs when men with ideas have a chance to put them into practice. Not since the New Deal more than a quarter of a century before had there been such an invasion of bright young men. Not since Franklin Roosevelt had there been a President who so plainly delighted in innovation and leadership.

Before I went to South America, there had been a White House reception for presidential appointees. We had all wandered around the East Room in an intoxication of pleasure and incredulity. One's life seemed almost to pass in review as one encountered Harvard classmates, wartime associates, faces seen after the war in ADA conventions, workers in Stevenson campaigns, academic colleagues, all united in a surge of hope and possibility. The President himself appeared to share the mood, though in his case it was a response to possibilities rather than to facts. He already had his gallery of anxieties—the sliding situation in Southeast Asia, the gold drain, the stagnation of the economy, the Cuban exiles in Guatemala. Yet anxiety did not disturb his easy composure, and he watched the exhilaration around him with pleasure, even if a skeptical smile played on his lips as he considered its more naïve manifestations.

Now, when I returned to Washington a month later, the New Frontier was hard at work. The pace was frenetic. Everyone came early and stayed late. I soon found myself arriving in the East Wing by eight or eight-thirty in the morning and remaining until seven-thirty or eight at night. Telephones rang incessantly. Meetings were continuous. The evenings too were lively and full. The glow of the White House was lighting up the whole city. Washington seemed engaged in a collective effort to make itself brighter, gayer, more intellectual, more resolute. It was a golden interlude.

1. THE WHITE HOUSE STAFF

Within the White House itself, things were beginning to settle into a pattern. Evelyn Lincoln and Ken O'Donnell guarded the two entrances into the presidential office. Pierre Salinger entertained the press with jocular daily briefings. Larry O'Brien, having won the critical fight to enlarge the House Rules Committee, was now deploying his people all over the Hill in support of the presidential program. Myer Feldman and Lee White were working on legislation and messages. Ralph Dungan was conducting the last stages of the talent hunt and supervising questions of government reorganization. Dick Goodwin was handling Latin America and a dozen other problems. Fred Dutton was Secretary of the Cabinet and dealt with many questions of politics and program.

It was already apparent that the key men around the President, so far as policy was concerned, were Theodore Sorensen and McGeorge Bundy. There had been predictions of conflict between the two. Sorensen, it was supposed, having had a monopoly of Kennedy for so long, would not easily relinquish him to other hands. I myself had been warned that, in entering the White House, I would be plunging into a ruthless scramble for access and power. But this did not seem to be taking place—and, indeed, the Kennedy

White House remained to the end remarkably free of the rancor which has so often welled up in presidential households. One reason for this was that staff members had more than enough to do and therefore not much time for resentment or feuding. Another was that the President handled the situation with effortless skill, avoiding collective confrontations, such as staff meetings where everyone might find out what everyone else was up to. He tactfully kept the relations with his aides on a bilateral basis.

Sorensen and Bundy themselves were aware of the dangers and behaved with poise and amiability. I had known Ted for some years but never well; it was hard to know him well. Self-sufficient, taut and purposeful, he was a man of brilliant intellectual gifts, jealously devoted to the President and rather indifferent to personal relations beyond his own family.

Contrary to the predictions, Sorensen accepted the new situation in the White House with imperturbable grace. The legislative program, domestic policy and speeches became his unchallenged domain; and speeches, of course, assured him an entry into foreign policy at the critical points. No one at the White House worked harder or more carefully; Kennedy relied on no one more. For his part, McGeorge Bundy treated Sorensen and his relationship with Kennedy with invariable consideration. Bundy possessed dazzling clarity and speed of mind—Kennedy told friends that, next to David Ormsby Gore, Bundy was the brightest man he had ever known—as well as great distinction of manner and unlimited self-confidence. One felt that he was forever sustained by those two qualities so indispensable for success in government—a deep commitment to the public service and a large instinct for power.

Mac was presently engaged in dismantling the elaborate national security apparatus built up by the Eisenhower administration. The National Security Council had become a ponderous system of boards, staffs and interdepartmental committees through which national security policy was supposed to rise to the top, but usually resulted in what Dean Acheson called "agreement by exhaustion." After the inauguration, Bundy promptly slaughtered committees right and left and collapsed what was left of the inherited apparatus into a compact and flexible National Security Council staff. With Walt Rostow as his deputy and Bromley Smith, a remarkable civil servant, as the NSC's secretary, he was shaping a supple instrument to meet the new President's distinctive needs.

2. THE SPIRIT OF THE NEW FRONTIER

The excitement in the White House infected the whole executive branch. A new breed had come to town, and the New Frontiersmen carried a thrust of action and purpose wherever they went. It is hard to generalize about so varied and exuberant a group; but it can be said that many shared a number of characteristics.

KEN O'DONNELL.

For one thing, like the New Dealers a quarter century earlier, they brought with them the ideas of national reconstruction and reform which had been germinating under the surface of a decade of inaction. They had stood by too long while a complaisant government had ignored the needs and potentialities of the nation—a nation whose economy was slowing down and whose population was overrunning its public facilities and services; a nation where the victims of racism and poverty lived on in sullen misery and the ideals held out by the leaders to the people were parochial and mediocre. Now the New Frontiersmen swarmed in from state governments, the universities, the foundations, the newspapers, determined to complete the unfinished business of American society. Like Rexford G. Tugwell in another age, they proposed to roll up their sleeves and make America over.

For another, they aspired, like their President, to the world of ideas as well as to the world of power. They had mostly gone to college during the intellectual ferment of the thirties. Not all by any means (despite the newspapers and the jokes) had gone to Harvard, but a good many had. Certainly there were Rhodes Scholars on every side. Many of the New Frontiersmen had been college professors. Jean Monnet said, of the New Frontier, "The thing I note most is that the conversation is recommencing. You cannot have serious government without collective discussion. I have missed that in Washington in recent years."

Another thing that defined the New Frontiersmen was the fact that many had fought in the war. Kennedy and McGovern were not the only heroes in the new Washington. Throughout the administration were men who had distinguished themselves in combat in Europe and the Pacific. The war experience helped give the New Frontier generation its casual and laconic tone, its grim, puncturing humor and its mistrust of evangelism. The mood of the new Washington was more to do things because they were rational and necessary than because they were just and right.

The New Frontiersmen had another common characteristic: versatility. They would try anything. Most had some profession or skill to which they could always return; but ordinarily they used it as a springboard for general meddling. Kenneth Galbraith was an economist who, as ambassador to India, reviewed novels for *The New Yorker* and wrote a series of pseudonymous satiric skits for *Esquire*. Bill Walton was a newspaperman turned abstract painter. This was especially true in the White House itself. Where Eisenhower had wanted a staff with clearly defined functions, Kennedy resisted pressures toward specialization; he wanted a group of all-purpose men to whom he could toss anything. It seemed to me that in many ways Dick Goodwin, though younger than the average, was the archetypal New Frontiersman. His two years in the Army had been too late for the war, even too late for Korea: But he was the supreme generalist who could turn from Latin America to saving the Nile monuments at Abu Simbel, from civil rights to planning the White House dinner for the Nobel Prize winners, from composing a parody of Norman Mailer to drafting a piece of legislation, from lunching with a Supreme Court Justice to dining with Jean Seberg—and at the same time retain an unquenchable spirit of sardonic liberalism and an unceasing drive to get things done.

Not everyone liked the new people. Washington never had. "A plague of young lawyers settled on Washington," one observer had said of the New Dealers. Old-timers felt the same resentments in March 1961. One could not deny a sense of New Frontier autointoxication; one felt it oneself. The pleasures of power, so long untasted, were now being happily devoured—the chauffeur-driven limousines, the special telephones, the top secret documents, the personal aides, the meetings in the Cabinet Room, the calls from the President. Merriman Smith, who had seen many administrations come and go, wrote about what he called the New People: "hot-eyed, curious but unconcerned with protocol, and yeasty with shocking ideas ... they also have their moments of shortsightedness, bias, prejudice and needlessly argumentative verbosity." The verbosity, I have suggested, was marked only in comparison with the muteness of the Eisenhower days; but the rest was true enough, especially in these first heady weeks.

The currents of vitality radiated out of the White House, flowed through the government and created a sense of vast possibility. The very idea of the new President taking command as tranquilly and naturally as if his whole life had prepared him for it could not but stimulate a flood of buoyant optimism. The Presidency was suddenly the center of action: in the first three months, thirty-nine messages and letters to Congress calling for legislation, ten prominent foreign visitors (including Macmillan, Adenauer and Nkrumah), nine press conferences, new leadership in the regulatory agencies and such dramatic beginnings as the Alliance for Progress and the Peace Corps. Above all, Kennedy held out such promise of hope. Intelligence at last was being applied to public affairs. Euphoria reigned; we thought for a moment that the world was plastic and the future unlimited.

Yet I don't suppose we really thought this. At bottom we knew how intractable the world was—the poverty and disorder of Latin America, the insoluble conflict in Laos, the bitter war in Vietnam, the murky turbulence of Africa, the problems of discrimination and unemployment in our own country, the continuing hostility of Russia and China. The President knew better than anyone how hard his life was to be. Though he incited the euphoria, he did so involuntarily, for he did not share it himself.

Perhaps the sense of possibility had its gayest image in a party the Kennedys gave for the Radziwills in the middle of March. Eighty guests sat around small tables in the Blue Room, and there was dancing till three in the morning. Never had girls seemed so pretty, tunes so melodious, an evening so blithe and unconstrained. The President, who rarely danced, moved from one group to another, a glass of champagne in his hand (the same glass most of the evening—he rarely drank either), while the music played lightly on. The glitter of that night remained in slightly ironic memory for a long time.

3. THE SHADOW OF CASTRO

In the meantime, the Central Intelligence Agency was training 1200 Cuban exiles at a coffee *finca* high in the Sierra Madre mountains on the Pacific coast of Guatemala, and Kennedy was confronting the first drastic decision of his administration.

The circumstances which brought these Cubans to alien shores and desperate designs were mixed. In the main, they had not been adherents of Fulgencio Batista. Some had fought with Fidel Castro in the Sierra Maestra, many more had welcomed Castro's entry into Havana. They were less opponents than casualties of the Cuban Revolution.

Much has been written about that revolution, its origins and its objectives. Jean-Paul Sartre and C. Wright Mills, who visited Cuba in 1959–60, later proclaimed that the revolution was a peasant uprising, caused by conditions of intolerable poverty and despair in a wretchedly underdeveloped country. In fact, as more careful writers like Theodore Draper and Hugh Thomas have pointed out, Cuba was hardly in so hopeless a shape. It was, indeed, the perfect test of the Eisenhower theory that unhampered private investment was Latin America's road to salvation. It stood fourth among Latin American nations in per capita income, fifth in manufacturing, first in per capita distribution of automobiles and radios. It ranked near the top in education, literacy, social services and urbanization. These aggregate statistics, however, concealed shocking disparities in the distribution of wealth, especially as between city and countryside and between white and Negro. There was enough wealth about to reveal to all how agreeable wealth might be. The statistics also—along with the popularity of Havana cigars—concealed the extent to which the Cuban economy depended on a single industry, sugar, which not only was at the mercy of world markets but was itself then in a state of decline. Still, if Cuba had serious economic problems and, compared to the United

KENNETH GALBRAITH IN APRIL 1961, SHORTLY AFTER BEING APPOINTED U.S. AMBASSADOR TO INDIA.

States, a low standard of living, it was quite well off compared to Haiti or Bolivia. The immediate motives behind the revolution were as much political as economic, and the revolutionaries themselves were members of the middle class rather than peasants or workers.

By the late 1950s a feeling was spreading through the intellectual community and the professional and even business classes that life was becoming intolerable—the sugar industry was deteriorating, the educational system was decaying, illiteracy was increasing, and Batista was keeping himself in power only by a mounting use of repression, corruption and violence.

This feeling of political and social disgust produced a passion for change. In its origins, the Cuban Revolution was led by professional men and intellectuals (like the Castro brothers and Ernesto Guevara, the Argentine physician) and subsidized by businessmen and landowners. The avowed aim was to establish a regime pledged to carry out the liberal constitution of 1940, which provided for free elections, civil liberties and agrarian diversification and reform. This aim enlisted wide backing throughout the country. At the start of 1957 Castro had been the leader of a beleaguered band of a dozen men hiding out in the hills; at the end of 1958 he entered Havana in triumph. He did this, not because he defeated Batista's 40,000 soldiers on the battlefield—at the moment of victory, his own force numbered less than two thousand men—but because of the withdrawal of support from Batista's government on the part of most of the people

RAUL CASTRO (LEFT), YOUNGER BROTHER OF FIDEL AND ERNESTO "CHE" GUEVARA IN THEIR SIERRA DE CRISTAL MOUNTAIN STRONGHOLD SOUTH OF HAVANA, CUBA. PHOTO TAKEN IN JUNE, 1958.

and most of the army. The Havana underground, brilliantly organized by a radical young engineer named Manuel Ray, completed the work Castro had begun in the Sierra Maestra.

To what extent did Castro at this point conceal secret communist purposes? He later said that he hid radical views in order to hold the anti-Batista coalition together, and this was probably true. But, though a radical, there is no conclusive evidence that he was then a Communist or even a Marxist-Leninist. Some time in 1958 the Communists began quietly to cooperate with Castro's 26th of July Movement. When Castro came to Havana in January 1959, the Communists were firmly installed as part of the coalition behind him. The next months were critical. Fidel was accustomed to running a guerrilla band, not a government. He had slogans but no program. He was an exciting figure, but a personal following was no substitute for an organization. In the clamor and confusion, one group stood out as experienced, disciplined, effective, possessed of both revolutionary ideas and the capacity to execute them. This was the Communist Party. Fidel's younger brother Raúl and Guevara, who had long had close relations with the Communists, no doubt helped move Fidel in this direction. Now that he had won his power, the Communists offered him the means of keeping it and using it.

The next months brought widespread and largely beneficial social cleansing and reform. Castro spoke eloquently about a "humanist" revolution which would avoid the errors of both capitalism and communism. But all the while the Communists were filling every available vacuum, until the revolution had become in large measure their own. It cannot be said that there was a fight between the Marxist and democratic wings of the revolution, because the democrats allowed themselves to be picked off one by one. Nor can it be said that the fusion of the Communist Party and the Castro Revolution was ever complete. Though Fidel came to boast of his Marxism-Leninism, he himself never joined the Communist Party. As the revolution careened along, the Communists may even at times have served as a restraining force, especially in foreign affairs. Yet, despite the jostling for position between Communists and *Fidelistas,* the year 1959 saw the clear commitment of Castro's revolution to the establishment of a Marxist dictatorship in Cuba and the service of Soviet foreign policy in the world—a commitment so incompatible with the expressed purposes of the revolution as surely to justify the word betrayal.

4. WHO LOST CUBA?

Was all this inevitable? Or was it the result of mistaken United States policy which left Castro no alternative? No legend is more enduring than the notion that Washington 'forced' Cuba into the arms of Moscow. In fact, the revolution was very popular in the United States in the early months of 1959. Even the Eisenhower administration hoped for a while they could do something with Castro. When Batista fled the country, Washington gave the revolutionary government prompt recognition. When Castro reached Washington in April, the State Department set up meetings with the economic members of his delegation to discuss an aid program.

But Castro had instructed these officials, to their astonishment, not to raise the question of assistance. As early as the spring of 1959, Castro seems to have decided to cast the United States in the role of enemy of the revolution. The hostility of Washington would provide the all-purpose excuse to cancel elections, eliminate political opposition and tighten internal controls. It is notable that Castro himself never then or later used the argument so dear to Castro sympathizers outside Cuba that rejection in Washington drove him to Moscow. Che Guevara denied in 1964 that Castro could ever possibly have been seduced by American blandishments.

Castro's evident pleasure in shooting *Batistianos* after circus-like trials shocked opinion in the United States; this reaction, in contrast to the earlier North American ennui over Batista's terror, shocked Cubans. The State Department grew obsessed with the problem of getting American citizens proper indemnification for expropriated land and business; Havana construed this as the anticipated enmity of American business to Cuban reform. Washington became disturbed over Castro's nonstop anti-Yanqui orations; Havana complained about exile bombing raids apparently launched from private airfields in Florida. These recriminations only confirmed Castro in a course set for other reasons.

Relations between the two countries degenerated, but Washington still declined to use the weapons of economic pressure which lay so easily at hand. It was not until July 1960, long after Castro had effected the substantial communization of the government, army and labor movement and had negotiated economic agreements with Russia and China, that the United States took public retaliatory action of a major sort. The suspension of the balance of Cuba's 1960 sugar quota (that same quota which Guevara had already denounced in March as "economic slavery") was the conclusion, and not the cause, of Castro's hostility. Or rather it was not quite the conclusion. Washington did not finally break off diplomatic relations until January 3, 1961, and then because of Castro's scornful demand that the staff of the Havana Embassy be reduced to eleven people in forty-eight hours.

Once Castro had taken power, it is hard to see that any different United States policy, short of invasion, could have averted the capture of the revolution. The policy of the Eisenhower administration lacked both imagination and consistency, but it was certainly not one of purposeful hostility. Castro took the revolution east for his own reasons. In doing so, he drove many Cubans who had opposed Batista and still held to the original principles of the revolution from their homeland. Some of these men were now drilling on the coffee plantation in Guatemala.

The perversion of the Cuban Revolution was evident enough to leaders of the democratic left in Latin America, like Betancourt, Figueres and Haya de la Torre. It was less evident, however, to left-wing intellectuals in North America and Europe. In spite of a score of disillusionments in Russia, eastern Europe and China—so many eggs broken and so few omelettes—many still cherished the hope that sometime, somewhere, revolution would at last achieve the dream of a truly just and joyous society. Among the pilgrims Cuba for a moment rekindled emotions which had not burned with such purity since the Spanish Civil War.

And it was true that revolutionary Cuba had a reckless and anarchic verve unknown in any other communist state, that it had abolished corruption, that it was educating and inspiring its people, that it had exuberantly reclaimed a national identity, that it was traduced and slandered in the foreign press—and these truths blotted out harsher truths and subtler corruptions. As Castro's dictatorship within Cuba was a fact, so too was the faith men of good will outside Cuba vested in him.

5. CASTRO AND KENNEDY

Cuba was not a new issue for Kennedy, nor had his view of Fidel Castro been wholly negative. Early in 1960, writing of the "wild, angry, passionate course" of the Cuban Revolution in *The Strategy of Peace,* he described Castro as "part of the

FULGENCIO BATISTA SURROUNDED BY CUBAN SOLDIERS IN 1954.

legacy of Bolivar," part too "of the frustration of that earlier revolution which won its war against Spain but left largely untouched the indigenous feudal order." He had no doubt, as he said later in the year, that "the brutal, bloody, and despotic dictatorship of Fulgencio Batista" had invited its own downfall; and he freely declared his sympathy with the motives behind the revolution and with its expressed objectives. He even raised the question in *The Strategy of Peace* whether Castro might not have taken "a more rational course" had the United States government not backed Batista "so long and so uncritically" and had it given Castro a warmer welcome on his trip to Washington. But he had no question now that Castro had "betrayed the ideals of the Cuban revolution" and transformed Cuba "into a hostile and militant Communist satellite."

He made his most extended statement in a speech at Cincinnati in early October. He began by appearing to adopt the thesis that the State Department should have listened to its pro-Batista ambassadors and recognized the revolution as a communist conspiracy from the outset. This differed markedly from his interpretation in *The Strategy of Peace*. Doubtless it was campaign oratory.

The more substantial part of the Cincinnati speech—and the part which I believe more faithfully reflected Kennedy's views—condemned the Eisenhower policy toward Cuba on quite different grounds. In the years before Castro, Kennedy charged, the administration had declined "to help Cuba meet its desperate need for economic progress"; it had employed "the influence of our Government to advance the interests and increase the profits of the private American companies, which dominated the island's economy"; and it had given "stature and support to one of the most bloody and repressive dictatorships in the long history of Latin America." He concluded: "While we were allowing Batista to place us on the side of tyranny, we did nothing to persuade the people of Cuba and Latin America that we wanted to be on the side of freedom."

What could be done about Castro now? Kennedy had told me at Hyannis Port, "We can't do anything except through the OAS, and most of the members of the OAS don't want to do anything at all. Our best hope is to stop the spread of Castro's influence by helping genuine democracy elsewhere in the continent." This also was his theme in Cincinnati: "For the present, Cuba is gone. ...For the present no magic formula will bring it back." Only by extending "the hand of American friendship in a common effort to wipe out the poverty and discontent and hopelessness on which communism feeds—only then will we drive back tyranny until it ultimately perishes in the streets of Havana."

Immediately after the election, his concern was with an affirmative program for Latin America rather than with Cuba. On November 14 he asked John Sharon for estimates of the effectiveness of the trade embargo against Cuba and of the possibilities of a rapprochement. Four days later Dulles and Richard Bissell of CIA informed him for the first time about the Guatemalan project.

6. PLANNING IN THE SHADOWS

The Eisenhower decision of March 17, 1960, had two main parts. On the political side, it directed the CIA to bring together a broad range of Cuban exiles, with *Batistianos* and Communists specifically excluded, into unified political opposition to the Castro regime. On the military side, it directed the CIA to recruit and train a Cuban force capable of guerrilla action against that regime.

When Nixon first proposed the use of exiles against Castro in the spring of 1959, United States action would have inevitably been pro-Batista; only *Batistianos* were then available. A year later the situation had improved. Thousands of disenchanted Cubans who had disliked Batista and at first welcomed the revolution were now streaming into Florida and Central America, some flying boldly out on commercial airlines, others stealing onto small boats and disappearing into the Caribbean night. Many were lawyers, doctors and businessmen, accustomed to political expression. By the end of 1959 Miami was alive with anti-Castro political activity of an unorganized and feckless sort. Every time two or three refugees gathered together a new *unión* or *movimiento* was likely to emerge.

The political leaders of this second migration were men who had served neither Batista nor Castro. They were characteristically identified with the old Cuba of the traditional parties, of progressive intent and ineffectual performance. Some were decent men; others were racketeers who had found politics a lucrative way of life. They wanted the restoration of political 'democracy' as they had known it before Batista, but they saw no need for far-reaching social change. Their objectives were compatible with the interests of North American investors and with the prejudices of the Eisenhower administration.

The CIA turned first to such men when it began to organize the political front in the early months of 1960. In June five leading groups were cajoled into forming the Frente Revolucionario Democrático. Three of the five members of the new committee represented pre-Batista Cuba; Manuel Antonio de Varona, who had been prime minister under Prío Socarrás, was typical. Varona promptly declared that the post-Castro government would restore properties seized by the Castro regime to their United States and Cuban owners. The other two members of the Frente had briefly served the revolutionary government. Dr. Justo Carrillo, an honorable man of liberal views, had been president of the Bank for Industrial and Agricultural Development under both Prío and Castro and had taken part in a plot to overthrow Batista in 1956. The fifth member, a young lieutenant named Manuel Artime, had joined Castro at the end of 1958 and later worked for Castro's National Institute of Agrarian Reform. Soon after he broke with the regime in November 1959, the CIA brought him out of Cuba. His youth, his military experience, his political inexperience and his personal tractability all recommended him to the CIA field operatives. He became their man on the Frente and soon the only Cuban link between CIA's political and military operations.

The Frente was appropriately named: it was a front and nothing more. While its members talked among themselves, CIA was engaged in a recruiting drive among Cuban refugees in Florida and Central America. It had also persuaded President Ydígoras of Guatemala to permit the establishment of a secret training camp and air base in the Guatemalan mountains. By midsummer the Cubans began to arrive.

The first CIA plan was to form small groups designed to slip into Cuba and establish active centers of resistance. Arms and supplies flown in from outside would enable these bands to enlarge their operations until, like Castro himself, they could enlist enough popular support to challenge the regime. It is true that several hundred guerrillas were presently hiding out in the Escambray Mountains and that Manuel Ray was reactivating his underground in the cities;

but the CIA found it hard to make contact with the Cuban resistance. Efforts to parachute supplies into the Escambray were not very successful. The CIA people feared that the guerrilla bands had been penetrated by Castro's agents. Certainly Castro, who knew all the tricks himself, was a master at counterguerrilla action. Moreover, his army was being strengthened by Soviet equipment, and his control was tightening over the civilian population: all this made him a far more formidable opponent than the Batista of 1958. For these reasons, as the Escambray resistance began to fade out, CIA now reconsidered its original plan.

The men of Washington were moving on to a new and drastically different conception: the idea of a direct assault on Castro by landing a force of exiles on the Cuban coast. Since amphibious operations required air cover, it seemed reasonable to equip the prospective invaders with a few B-26 planes left over from the Second World War. By the time of the United States election in 1960, the CIA conception had definitely shifted from guerrilla infiltration to a beachhead assault. The guerrilla exercises came to a virtual stop, and a new United States team came in to train the Cubans, now numbering almost 500 men, along conventional lines as a pocket army, complete with artillery and air support.

7. AGENTS AND PATIENTS

In the meantime, a new wave of refugees had begun to arrive in Florida. This third migration was led by men who had done more than passively applaud the revolution. They characteristically had conspired against Batista, fought with Castro and served in the revolutionary government. They opposed Castro not for having brought about a social revolution but for having delivered it to the Communists. They sought not to reverse the revolution but to redeem it. Their inspiration was Huber Matos, now in Castro's jail. Their strongest figure was Manuel Ray, who, after resigning from Castro's government, formed the *Movimiento Revolucionario del Pueblo* (MRP) and spent most of 1960 in Cuba organizing an underground against Castro, as he had done two years before against Batista. The men of this third migration tended to be politically radical and nationalist, personally proud and defiant.

In November Ray himself escaped from Cuba and made his way to Miami. He brought a new thesis to which he hoped the new American government might be responsive: that Castro had to be overthrown from within, that the Cuban people must be the means, and that an uprising would succeed only if its clear purpose was to rescue the revolution from the Communists and resume the revolutionary task of building a new and progressive Cuba. Ray's arrival confronted the CIA with a difficult problem.

It is sometimes essential for a state, even for a democratic state, to undertake clandestine operations, as I learned in OSS during the Second World War. But, when such operations are undertaken, it is important never to forget that the relationship between an intelligence agency and its instruments tends to be a corrupting one.

The relationship is degrading for recruited exiles, for example, and demoralizing for the agent. CIA's main contact with the exile leaders was a ubiquitous operative who went under the name of Frank Bender. He knew little Spanish and even less about Latin America, but he had money and authority, and he fell easily into habits of command. His power appears to have gone to his head; he liked to say that he was carrying the counterrevolution around in his checkbook. The older exiles disliked and feared him, but they felt they had no choice but to obey him.

Ray and his people proved different. When Bender told him to bring the MRP into the Frente, he refused. His personality, his politics and his advocacy of the underground thesis posed a threat both to the status of the more conservative exiles and to the control of the CIA. Accordingly the older exiles and the Agency were ready to collaborate in an attempt to discredit him.

But the arbitrary CIA control was beginning to cause resentment even within the Frente itself. Bender, finding it inconvenient to deal with five men, insisted that the Frente appoint a coordinator. When Tony Varona was chosen in September, other members became bitter or suspicious of the CIA. Requests by the Frente to visit the training camp in Guatemala were turned down.

By November 1960 the CIA operation had taken on a life of its own. The agents in the field were shaping it to meet their own needs. In favoring the 'reliable' exiles—those who would take orders—they were conceivably endangering the whole project; for the men most capable of rallying popular support within Cuba against the Castro regime were bound to be more independent, more principled and more radical than the manageable types whom the intelligence agency preferred for operational reasons. As for the nominal Cuban leadership in the Frente, it was growing uneasily aware that it lacked authority; that, as it accepted its instructions and its cash from Bender and his associates, it lacked dignity; that it did not even know what was going on.

Meanwhile in the camps of Guatemala the Cubans were turning with enthusiasm from the idea of a guerrilla operation to the idea of an amphibious invasion. The new training and the new weapons filled them with sudden hope. Their American officers—or so the Cubans later told Haynes Johnson—assured them that they were only one of many

MANUEL RAY IN 1959.

such groups, one-tenth of the force, and that they would have all the support they needed.* Supposing that everyone they had left behind hated Castro as much as they did, they genuinely believed that a mass landing on the Cuban beaches might set off a general revolt. The CIA and Army officers, knowing less about Cuba, were even more sanguine. Once possessed of this dream, neither the Cubans nor their American colleagues were disposed to retreat to the more modest idea of a guerrilla infiltration. As for demobilizing the operation, this would have been unthinkable. This was the way matters stood when John F. Kennedy learned of the project on November 17, 1960.

* Haynes Johnson, *The Bay of Pigs* (New York, 1964, [Dell edition]), 56.

X.
THE BAY OF PIGS

ON NOVEMBER 29, 1960, twelve days after he had heard about the Cuban project, the President-elect received from Allen Dulles a detailed briefing on CIA's new military conception. Kennedy listened with attention, then told Dulles to carry the work forward. The response was sufficiently affirmative for Dulles to take it as an instruction to expedite the project.

Dulles understood, however, that interest did not mean commitment. All Kennedy wanted at this point was to have the option of an exile attack on the Castro regime. He did not yet realize how contingency planning could generate its own momentum and create its own reality.

1. CONFUSION IN THE INTERREGNUM

In the next weeks government floated as in a void. Neither the outgoing nor the incoming administrations wanted to make fundamental decisions, and most matters continued to move along existing tracks. Early in December the new CIA plan went in a routine way before the Special Group, the secret interdepartmental committee charged with the supervision of special operations. The lieutenant colonel in command of the training in Guatemala came along to offer his personal testimony about the Cuban Brigade.

The plan was taking definite shape. Its sponsors said little now about the old ideas of guerrilla infiltration or multiple landings except as diversionary tactics. Instead they envisaged 600 to 750 Cubans coming ashore in a body at a point still to be chosen along the southern coast of Cuba. Air strikes from Nicaragua in advance of the attack would knock out Castro's air force. These strikes, along with supply flights, would continue during the landing. The invaders would also have artillery. The mission would be to seize and hold an area sufficiently large to attract anti-Castro activists, induce defections in Castro's militia and set off a general uprising behind the lines. As for the Brigade itself, the lieutenant colonel assured the Special Group that his charges were men of unusual intelligence and 'motivation' and that their morale was superb. They would have no trouble, he said, in taking care of much larger numbers of Cuban militia.

The Special Group itself was infected with interregnum uncertainties. Not wishing to anticipate the new administration, it did not formally approve the new scheme or even subject it to very severe scrutiny. Instead, it encouraged the CIA to press on with the training in Guatemala and start work on operational planning in Washington.

The original plan for a clandestine infiltration would have allowed the United States to disown, if necessary, any involvement in the operation. But the new plan called for an expeditionary force of size, scope and visibility; and it proposed to pit that force in pitched battle against defending armies of vastly superior numbers. Could the United States convincingly deny complicity in an expedition well trained and equipped to conduct an amphibious invasion? And, if it could not escape accountability, could it afford to let such an expedition fail? In short, if the United States kept its role small enough to conceal its responsibility, the operation might not have a fair chance of success; while if it made its role large enough to give the operation a fair chance of success, the responsibility could not be plausibly disclaimed in case of failure. Washington might then face the choice between the political humiliation of defeat and the commitment of United States troops to ensure victory.

There was reason to suppose that the CIA ground rule had already been stretched to the point of no return. The Guatemala base was no longer much of a secret. By December a number of North American papers were writing about mysterious happenings in Guatemala. The publicity might well have raised the question whether the old ground rule was compatible with the new plan; but no one in the interregnum seemed to feel final responsibility, and so matters drifted along. In January the Joint Chiefs of Staff began for the first time to get into the act, tacitly questioning the ban on United States participation in military operations and discussing.

The hiatus in Washington gave the CIA operatives in the field a free hand. Since the force in Guatemala was still too small for the new plan, recruitment now had the urgent priority. The political criteria laid down by the CIA in Washington and demanded by most members of the Frente were abandoned in the rush. Bender gave particular authority to a dubious figure in Miami named Joaquin Sanjenis, and Sanjenis favored men of the Cuban right.

The influx of new recruits created problems in the training camp. Men who had taken part in the revolution had a natural hatred of officers who had served Batista. The American advisers, preferred men who had professional military experience (like Pepe San Román) and could be relied on to follow orders. It is true that most of the *Bastistianos* were so called because they had once been in Batista's army, not because they now wanted to return Batista to power. But this did not make the Cubans selected by the United States advisers to command the Brigade any more popular with the rank and file.

In spite of the optimistic reports rendered to CIA in Washington about the splendid morale in the camp, discontent increased. In January it broke out into mutiny. Almost half of the now more than 500 Cubans in the camp resigned. When they were promised a visit from the Frente, most agreed to rejoin the Brigade, but a few still held out. In one of the unhappier passages in this whole unhappy story, the CIA operatives arrested a dozen of the ringleaders and held them prisoner under stark conditions deep in the jungle of northern Guatemala.

The CIA now decided to bring in Artime, the most amenable member of the Frente, as one of the military commanders. In the end only two other members of the Frente visited the camp—Tony Varona and Antonio Maceo; the CIA successfully discouraged Justo Carrillo as too friendly to the mutineers. When Varona arrived, he cheered the rebels by a speech to the Brigade critical of the intervention by the United States advisers. Then, after a private conference with the senior American officer, Varona capitulated. In a second speech the next day he wholeheartedly endorsed the American choices for the leadership of the Brigade. The CIA was now in complete command.

This episode had scant impact on Washington. If it was ever reported to the new President, it must have been greatly minimized. The impression given at the White House meetings in March was that life in the Brigade could not be happier.

In the meantime, the CIA planners in Washington had settled on the town of Trinidad as the point of invasion. Trinidad, they pointed out, had the advantages of a harbor, a defensible beach-head, remoteness from Castro's main army and easy access to the Escambray Mountains. They proposed a heavy and concentrated amphibious assault, to take place at dawn and to be supported by paratroop drops on the hills behind the town and by simultaneous (though not advance) strikes against the Cuba air force. Once the landing force had established itself on the beaches, it could expect to rally support from the townspeople and overpower the local militia.

As the expeditionary force enlarged its hold, the CIA men argued, now introducing a new idea, a provisional government could be flown in; and, if the invaders could sustain themselves for ten days or two weeks, this government could receive recognition as the government of Cuba. Once this was done, the new government could request United States aid, though this aid was carefully defined as "logistic" and therefore presumably excluded military intervention. The CIA planners envisaged a continuous build-up and enlargement of the perimeter around the beachhead over a long period, rather like Anzio in 1944. The scheme envisaged victory by attrition rather than by rebellion and no longer assigned a significant immediate role to the internal resistance. As the invaders strengthened their position, this, along with their command of the skies and the acceptance of the new government by other American republics, would produce a steady withdrawal of civil support from Castro and his eventual collapse. And, if by any chance the attack failed, Trinidad was near enough the Escambray for the invaders to disappear into the hills.

KENNEDY MEETS WITH THE JOINT CHIEFS IN JANUARY 1961. FROM LEFT: GEN. DAVID M. SHOUP; GEN. THOMAS D. WHITE; GEN. LYMAN LEMNITZER; JFK; ADM. ARLEIGH A. BURKE; GEN. G.H. DECKER.

About this time the snow began to fall, and John F. Kennedy took his oath as President of the United States.

2. KENNEDY AND HIS CUBAN INHERITANCE

The Eisenhower administration thus bequeathed the new President a force of Cuban exiles under American training in Guatemala, a committee of Cuban politicians under American control in Florida and a plan to employ the exiles in an invasion of their homeland and to install the committee on Cuban soil as the provisional government of a free Cuba.

On January 22, two days after the inauguration, Allen Dulles and General Lemnitzer exposed the project to leading members of the new administration. Six days later President Kennedy instructed the Defense Department to take a hard look at CIA's military conception and the State Department to prepare a program for the isolation and containment of Cuba through the OAS. In the meantime, CIA was to continue what it had been doing. The ground rule against overt United States participation was still to prevail.

The Joint Chiefs, after brooding over CIA's Trinidad plan for a week, pronounced favorably on the chances of initial military success. The JCS evaluation was, however, a peculiar and ambiguous document. At one point it said categorically, in what would seem an implicit rejection of the Anzio model, that ultimate success would depend on either a sizable uprising inside the island or sizable support from outside. Then later, without restating these alternative conditions for victory, the document concluded that the existing plan, if executed in time, stood a "fair" chance of ultimate success. Even if it did not immediately attain all its goals, the JCS remarked philosophically, it would still contribute to the eventual overthrow of the regime.

There was plainly a logical gap between the statement that the plan would work if one or another condition were fulfilled and the statement that the plan would work anyway. One cannot know whether this gap resulted from sloppiness in analysis or from a conviction, conscious or unconscious, that once the invasion were launched, either internal uprising or external support would follow, and, if not the first, then the second—that, in short, once the United States government embarked on this enterprise, it could not risk the disaster of failure. Certainly this conviction permeated the thinking of the exiles themselves as well as of the United States officers in Guatemala. Since some, at least, of the Joint Chiefs had always been skeptical of the CIA ground rule, that conviction may well have lurked in the back of their minds too.

In a new report in early March, the Chiefs dropped the point about external support and hinged victory on the capacity of the assault to produce anti-Castro action behind the lines. From the viewpoint of the Joint Chiefs, then, the Cuban resistance was indispensable to success. They could see no other way—short of United States intervention—by which an invasion force of a thousand Cubans, no matter how well trained and equipped nor how stout their morale, could conceivably overcome the 200,000 men of Castro's army and militia.

The pace of events was quickening. Guatemalan president Ydígoras requested that the Cuban Brigade depart his country by the end of April. For its part, the CIA reported that the Cubans themselves were clamoring to move; the spirit of the Brigade had reached its peak, and further postponement would risk demoralization. Moreover, the rainy season was about to begin, the ground would turn into volcanic mud, and training would have to stop. And there was another potent reason for going ahead: Castro, the CIA said, was about to receive jet airplanes from the Soviet Union along with Cuban pilots trained in Czechoslovakia to fly them; once the MIGs arrived, an amphibious landing would turn into a slaughter. After June 1, it would take the United States Marines and Air Force to overthrow Castro. If a purely Cuban invasion were ever to take place, it had to take place in the next few weeks.

By mid-March the President was confronted, in effect, with a now-or-never choice.

3. CUBA IN THE CABINET ROOM

On March 11, about a week after my return from Latin America, I was summoned to a meeting with the President in the Cabinet Room. An intimidating group sat around the table—the Secretary of State, the Secretary of Defense, the director of the Central Intelligence Agency, three Joint Chiefs resplendent in uniforms and decorations, the Assistant Secretary of State for Inter-American Affairs, the chairman of the Latin American Task Force and appropriate assistants and bottle-washers.

I had first heard of the Cuban operation in early February; indeed, the day before leaving for Buenos Aires I had sent the President a memorandum about it. The idea sounded plausible enough, the memorandum suggested, if one excluded everything but Cuba itself; but, as soon as the focus was enlarged to include the rest of the hemisphere and the rest of the world, arguments *against* the decision gained strength. Above all, "this would be your first dramatic foreign policy initiative. At one stroke you would dissipate all the extraordinary good will which has been rising toward the

MCNAMARA, JOHNSON AND KENNEDY IN A MEETING ON MARCH 16, 1961, ONE MONTH BEFORE THE BAY OF PIGS INVASION.

new Administration through the world. It would fix a malevolent image of the new Administration in the minds of millions."

It was apparent now a month later that matters were still very much in flux. No final decision had yet been taken on whether the invasion should go forward at all and, if so, whether Trinidad should be the landing point. It fell to Allen Dulles and Richard M. Bissell, Jr., as the originators of the project to make the main arguments for action.

Both Dulles and Bissell were at a disadvantage in having to persude a skeptical new administration about the virtues of a proposal nurtured in the hospitable bosom of a previous government—a proposal on which they had personally worked for a long time and in which their organization had a heavy vested interest. This cast them in the role less of analysts than of advocates, and it led them to accept progressive modifications so long as the expedition in some form remained; perhaps they too unconsciously supposed that, once the operation began to unfold, it would not be permitted to fail.

The determination to keep the scheme alive sprang in part, I believe, from the embarrassments of calling it off. The Cubans themselves were determined to go back to their homeland, and they might well forcibly resist efforts to take away their arms and equipment. Moreover, even if the Brigade were successfully disbanded, its members would disperse, disappointed and resentful all over Latin America. This could only result, Dulles kept emphasizing, in discrediting Washington, disheartening Latin American opponents of Castro and encouraging the *Fidelistas* in their attack on democratic regimes. For all these reasons, CIA argued, instead of turning the Cubans loose, we must find some means for putting them back into Cuba "on their own."

The contingency had thus become a reality: having created the Brigade as an option, the CIA now presented its use against Cuba as a necessity. Kennedy tentatively agreed that the simplest thing, after all, might be to let the Cubans go where they yearned to go—to Cuba. Then he tried to turn the meeting toward a consideration of how this could be done with the least political risk. The first step was to form a more liberal and representative exile organization, and this the President directed should be done as soon as possible. The President concluded the meeting by defining the issue with his usual crispness. The trouble with the operation, he said, was that the smaller the political risk, the greater the military risk, and vice versa. The problem was to see whether the two risks could be brought into reasonable balance.

For the next three days the CIA planners canvassed alternative landing sites, coming up with three new possibilities, of which the most likely was about 100 miles west of Trinidad in the Zapata area around Cochinos Bay—the Bay of Pigs. The Joint Chiefs, examining these recommendations on March 14, agreed that Zapata, with its airstrip and the natural defense provided by its swamps, seemed the best of the three but added softly that they still preferred Trinidad. When we met again in the Cabinet Room on March 15, Bissell outlined the Zapata plan. The President authorized CIA to continue on the assumption that the invasion would occur. But he repeated his decision against any form of United States military intervention and added carefully and categorically that he was reserving his final decision on the plan itself. The expedition, he said, must be laid on in a way which would make it possible for him to call it off as late as twenty-four hours before D-day.

4. THE CUBAN REVOLUTIONARY COUNCIL

In the meantime, the CIA had been carrying out Kennedy's instruction to bring representatives of the new Cuba into the Frente. Bender, reversing his earlier position, told the Frente that it must come to an agreement with Manuel Ray and his MRP. But, though Bender changed his line, he did not change his manner, nor were the more conservative members of the Frente themselves eager to embrace *Fidelismo sin Fidel.* Representatives of the Frente and the MRP engaged in complex and acrimonious negotiations. After persistent CIA pressure persuaded the negotiators to return to their groups with a draft agreement, the Frente rejected the common program as too radical.

The CIA now decided on direct intervention. On March 18 at the Skyways Motel in Miami a CIA operative—not Bender, whom the CIA belatedly concluded was not the man for the job—told the Frente that the two groups must unite, that they must together choose a provisional president for Cuba, and that if these things were not done right away, the whole project would be called off. The Frente finally caved in and reluctantly submitted a list of six possibilities for the presidency. For its part, the MRP was no happier about this coerced alliance. Ray and his people liked neither the CIA control nor the idea of an invasion, but, supposing that United States backing guaranteed success, they wanted both to defend the interests of the Cuban underground and to assure their own part in a post-Castro future. Accepting the list, they chose Dr. Miró Cardona as provisional president. Miró, a lawyer and professor at the University of Havana, had been a noted leader in the civil opposition to Batista. He had inspired many students to work for the revolution, and Castro made him the first prime minister of the revolutionary regime, though Miró did not last long in the government.

On March 22 Varona for the Frente and Ray for the MRP signed an agreement conferring on Miró Cardona authority to organize the Cuban Revolutionary Council. The document also pledged the Council to give "maximum priority" to the resistance inside Cuba, declared that no one who "held an objectionably responsible position with the criminal dictatorship of Batista" was to be admitted into any armed forces organized outside Cuba and said hopefully that the military command of such forces must pledge "their full deference" to the Council's authority. Miró then held a press conference to announce the formation of the Council as the basis for a provisional government of Cuba once it had gained "a piece of Cuban soil." The CIA asked Miró to ratify the selection of Artime as commander of the Brigade. When he did so, Ray, Varona and Carrillo all protested; but Miró wearily explained that he had no alternative: this was what the Americans wanted, and the Americans would make the invasion a success.

While this reorganization was going on, I learned that my assignment was to help clarify the new political objectives by preparing a White Paper on Cuba. The President told me that, *if* the invasion took place (the emphasis was his own), he wanted everyone in the hemisphere to know that its intent was not to bring back the old order in Cuba. "Our objection isn't to the Cuban Revolution," he said; "it is to the fact that Castro has turned it over to the communists."

Setting to work, I buried myself under a mass of papers and came up with a draft in a few days. The paper sought to explain, with documentation, the United States attitude toward the Cuban Revolution and the Castro regime. The thesis was that the first had been betrayed by the second, and that the result offered "a clear and present danger to the authentic and autonomous revolution of the Americas." It endorsed the original aims of the Cuban Revolution and said concluded:

We call once again on the Castro regime to sever its links with the international Communist movement, to return to the original purposes which brought so many gallant men together in the Sierra Maestra and to restore the integrity of the Cuban Revolution.

If this call is unheeded, we are confident that the Cuban people, with their passion for liberty, will continue to strive for a free Cuba.

After departmental review, the document went to the President over the weekend, and we discussed it on the following Tuesday, March 28. As we finished, I said, "What do you think about this damned invasion?" He said wryly, "I think about it as little as possible." But it was clear, as we talked, that he had of course been thinking about it a good deal. In his judgment, the critical point—the weak part of the case for going ahead—lay in the theory that the landings would touch off a mass insurrection against the regime.

We all in the White House considered uprisings behind the lines essential to the success of the operation; so too did the Joint Chiefs of Staff; and so, we thought, did the CIA. Later, it became clear that the CIA invasion would win by attrition rather than by rebellion. No one expected the invasion to galvanize the unarmed and unorganized into rising against Castro at the moment of disembarkation. But the invasion plan, as understood by the President and the Joint Chiefs, did assume that the successful *occupation* of an enlarged beachhead area would rather soon incite *organized* uprisings by *armed* members of the Cuban resistance. Dulles and Bissell claimed that the Brigade, once established on the island, could expect the active support of, at the very least, a quarter of the Cuban people.

There were about CIA's estimates. He said that, though anti-Castro sentiment had markedly increased since his last visit the year before, Castro still roused intense enthusiasm and faith, especially among the young and among those who had benefited from the social changes of the revolution. These two groups constituted a considerable part of the population. Even a sizable middle group, now disillusioned about Castro, would not be likely to respond with enthusiasm to an invasion backed by the United States because we were so thoroughly identified in their minds with Batista. As much as many Cubans detested the present situation, they still preferred it to a restoration of the old order.

5. APPROACH TO A DECISION

The meetings in the Cabinet Room were now taking place every three or four days. The President, it seemed to me, was growing steadily more skeptical as his hard questioning exposed one problem after another in the plans. Moreover, the situation in Laos was at a point of crisis. Kennedy feared that, if the Cuban invasion went forward, it might prejudice chances of agreement with the Soviet Union over Laos. Laos and Cuba were tied up with each other, though it was hard to know how one would affect the other.

Dulles and Bissell, convinced that if the Cubans were ever to be sent against Castro they had to go now, sure that the Brigade could accomplish its mission and nagged by the disposal problem, now redoubled their efforts at persuasion. CIA concentrated particularly in the meetings on trying to show that, even if the expedition failed, the cost would not be excessive. Obviously no one could believe any longer that the adventure would not be attributed to the United States but somehow the idea took hold around the cabinet table that this would not much matter so long as United States soldiers did not take part in the actual fighting.

Moreover, if worst came to worst and the invaders were beaten on the beaches, then, Dulles and Bissell said, they could easily "melt away" into the mountains. But the CIA exposition was less than candid both in implying that the Brigade had undergone guerrilla training and in suggesting the existence of an easy escape hatch. I don't think we fully realized that the Escambray Mountains lay eighty miles from the Bay of Pigs, across a hopeless tangle of swamps and jungles. And no one knew (until Haynes Johnson interviewed the survivors) that the CIA agents in Guatemala were saying nothing to the Cubans about this last resort of flight to the hills, apparently fearing to lower their morale.

Our meetings were taking place in a curious atmosphere of assumed consensus. The CIA representatives dominated the discussion. The Joint Chiefs seemed to be going contentedly along. Their collaboration with CIA in refining the scheme gave the White House the impression of their whole-hearted support. Robert McNamara, who was absorbed in the endless task of trying to seize control of the Pentagon, accepted the judgment of the Chiefs on the military aspects of the plan, understood the CIA to be saying that invasion would shortly produce a revolt against Castro and supposed in any case that the new administration was following a well-established policy developed by its predecessors. Dean Rusk listened inscrutably through the discussions, confining himself to gentle warnings about possible excesses. Chester Bowles gave Rusk a strong memorandum opposing the invasion and asked to be permitted, if Rusk disagreed, to carry the case to the President. Rusk reassured Bowles, leaving him with the impression that the project was being whittled down into a guerrilla infiltration, and filed the memorandum away.

In the meantime, Senator Fulbright had grown increasingly concerned over the newspaper stories forecasting an invasion, and wrote a memorandum which he gave Kennedy.

There were two possible policies toward Cuba, Fulbright argued: overthrow, or toleration and isolation. The first would violate the spirit and probably the letter of the OAS charter, hemisphere treaties and our own federal legislation. If successful, it "would be denounced from the Rio Grande to Patagonia as an example of imperialism." It would cause trouble in the United Nations. It would commit us to the heavy responsibility of making a success of post-Castro Cuba. If it seemed to be failing, we might be tempted to use our own armed force; and if we did this, "even under the paper cover of legitimacy, we would have undone the work of thirty years in trying to live down earlier interventions."

> To give this activity even covert support is of a piece with the hypocrisy and cynicism for which the United States is constantly denouncing the Soviet Union in the United Nations and elsewhere. This point will not be lost on the rest of the world—nor on our own consciences.

Instead, Fulbright urged a policy of containment. The Alliance for Progress provided a solid basis for insulating the rest of the hemisphere from Castro. As for the Cuban exiles, an imaginative approach could find a more productive use of their talents than invading their homeland. Remember always, Fulbright concluded, "The Castro regime is a thorn in the flesh; but it is not a dagger in the heart."

It was a brilliant memorandum. Yet the President returned from Palm Beach more militant than when he had left. But he did ask Fulbright to attend the climactic meeting on April 4. This meeting was held at the State Department in a small conference room beside Rusk's office. After the usual routine—persuasive expositions by the CIA, mild disclaimers by Rusk and penetrating questions by the President—Kennedy started asking people around the table what they thought. Fulbright, speaking in an emphatic and incredulous way, denounced the whole idea. The operation, he said, was wildly out of proportion to the threat. It would compromise our moral position in the world and make it impossible for us to protest treaty violations by the Communists. He gave a brave, old-fashioned American speech, honorable, sensible and strong; and he left everyone in the room, except me and perhaps the President, wholly unmoved.

Kennedy continued around the table. McNamara said that he favored the operation. Mann said that he would have opposed it at the start, but, now that it had gone so far, it should be carried through. Berle wanted the men to be put into Cuba but did not insist on a major production. Kennedy once again wanted to know what could be done in the way of quiet infiltration as against the beachhead assault. The meeting fell into discussion before the round of the table was completed. Soon it broke up.

6. A PERSONAL NOTE

As we were leaving the room, the President called me back and asked for my opinion. I said that I was against the operation and tried to explain why. Listening, he nodded his head once or twice but said little. My explanation seemed to me hurried and disorderly, so the next morning I went to the office at six-thirty and wrote down my views in time to put them on the President's desk before his day began.

I was clear in my mind that the invasion was a terrible idea. This was not because the notion of sponsoring an exile attempt to overthrow Castro seemed intolerable in itself. As my memorandum said, "If we could achieve this by a swift, surgical stroke, I would be for it." The rigid nonintervention argument had never deeply impressed me. The United States had a proud tradition of supporting refugees against tyranny in their homelands. Moreover, in a world shadowed by communism, the pure theory of nonintervention had even less force.

Nor did I object to the operation because of its possible impact on Moscow. My guess was that the Soviet Union regarded Cuba as our special domain and was surprised that we had not taken action long since to rid ourselves of Castro on the model of their own intervention in Hungary. (I was probably wrong here in not allowing for the possibility of Soviet reprisals against West Berlin.) Nor did the impact on Latin America unduly disturb me. I had reported to the President after my Latin American trip, "Action against Castro would unquestionably produce a calculated sequence of riots, demonstrations, etc., in the post-Lumumba manner; but I do not believe that such chain reaction would convulse the hemisphere, as it might have a year ago, especially if the action were taken in the name of the authentic July 26 revolution." Nor could I well question the military premise advanced by CIA and endorsed by the Joint Chiefs that the Brigade would be able to establish itself on the shores of Cuba.

My opposition (expressed in this memorandum of April 5 and a second one five days later) was founded rather on the implausibility of its two political premises: that, if only Cubans took part, the United States could dissociate itself from the consequences; and that, if the beachhead could be held for a

More than once I left the meetings in the Cabinet Room fearful that only two of the regulars present were against the operation; but, since I thought the President was the other, I kept hoping that he would avail himself of his own escape clause and cancel the plan.

few days and enlarged, there would be defections from the militia and uprisings behind the lines. The memorandum proposed two counter-considerations as fundamental:

a) *No matter how "Cuban" the equipment and personnel, the U.S. will be held accountable for the operation, and our prestige will be committed to its success.*

And, because there was no convincing evidence that the invasion would touch off a mass insurrection:

b) *Since the Castro regime is presumably too strong to be toppled by a single landing, the operation will turn into a protracted civil conflict.*

If the military estimate was correct that the Brigade could secure its foothold in Cuba, the danger would be "that, if the rebellion appears to be failing, the rebels will call for U.S. armed help; that members of Congress will take up the cry; and that pressures will build up which will make it politically hard to resist the demand to send in the Marines."

Nor would sending in the Marines solve the problem, because the *Fidelistas* could be counted on to fight to the end, retreating, if necessary, to the Sierre Maestra. If the threat to our security were direct and demonstrable, then "the controlled use of force for limited objectives might well enhance respect for the United States." But a great many people around the globe, beginning with the chairman of our own Senate Foreign Relations Committee, "simply do not at this moment see that Cuba presents so grave and compelling a threat to our national security as to justify a course of action which much of the world will interpret as calculated aggression against a small nation in defiance both of treaty obligations and of the international standards as we have repeatedly asserted against the Communist world." Seeing no justification for intervention, other nations would sympathize with David rather than Goliath. A prolonged civil war in Cuba between the Castro regime and an exile army backed by the United States, the memorandum went on, would open us to damaging attack in the United Nations and elsewhere around the globe. The Russians would enlist volunteers in José Martí and probably even Abraham Lincoln Brigades and seek to convert the conflict into another Spanish Civil War.

More than that, a course of bullying intervention would destroy the new image of the United States—"the image of intelligence, reasonableness and honest firmness which has had such an extraordinary effect in changing world opinion about the U.S. and increasing world confidence in U.S. methods and purposes.... It is this reawakening world faith in America which is at stake in the Cuban operation." What this stately language meant was that the operation might recklessly expend one of our greatest national assets—John F. Kennedy himself. Nothing had been more depressing in the whole series of meetings than to watch a collection of officials, some of them holdovers from the previous administration, contentedly prepare to sacrifice the world's growing faith in the new American President in order to defend interests and pursue objectives of their own.

The first memorandum concluded by doubting the CIA thesis that time was on the side of Castro and arguing that the risks of the operation outweighed the risks of abandonment; the second by proposing ways to counter the communist political attack.

7. THE PRESIDENT'S DECISION

More than once I left the meetings in the Cabinet Room fearful that only two of the regulars present were against the operation; but, since I thought the President was the other, I kept hoping that he would avail himself of his own escape clause and cancel the plan. But he too began to become a prisoner of events. After another meeting on April 6, I noted: "We seem now destined to go ahead on a quasi-minimum basis—a large-scale infiltration (hopefully) rather than an invasion." This change reflected the now buoyant CIA emphasis on the ease of escaping from the beaches into the hills. By this time we were offered a sort of all-purpose operation guaranteed to work, win or lose. If it failed of its maximum hope—a mass uprising leading to the overthrow of the regime—it would at least attain its minimum objective—supply and reinforcement for the guerrillas already on the island.

Probably by that Saturday morning the President had already made up his mind. Why had he decided to go ahead? So far as the operation itself was concerned, he felt, as he told me that afternoon, that he had successfully pared it down from a grandiose amphibious assault to a mass infiltration. Accepting the CIA assurances about the escape hatch, he supposed that the cost, both military and political, of failure was now reduced to a tolerable level. He added, "If we have to get rid of these 800 men, it is much better to dump them in Cuba than in the United States, especially if that is where they want to go"—a remark which suggested how much Dulles's insistence on the disposal problem had influenced the decision, as well as how greatly Kennedy was himself moved by the commitment of the Cuban patriots. He was particularly impressed by the fact that three members of the Cuban Revolutionary Council had sons in the Brigade; the exile leaders themselves obviously believed that the expedition would succeed. As the decision presented itself to him, he had to choose whether to disband a group of brave and idealistic Cubans, already trained and equipped, who wanted very much to return to Cuba on their own, or to permit them to go ahead. The President saw no obligation to protect the Castro regime from democratic Cubans and decided that, if the Cubans wished to make the try on the categorical understanding that there would be no direct United States military support, he would help them do so. If the expedition succeeded, the overthrow of Castro would greatly strengthen democratic prospects in the hemisphere; if he called it off, he would forever be haunted by the feeling that his scruples had preserved Castro in power.

More generally, the decision resulted from the fact that he had been in office only seventy-seven days. He had not had the time or opportunity to test the inherited instrumentalities of government. He could not know which of his advisers were competent and which were not. For their part, they did not know him or each other well enough to raise hard questions with force and candor. Moreover, the massed and caparisoned authority of his senior officials in the realm of foreign policy and defense was unanimous for going ahead. Had one senior adviser opposed the adventure, I believe that Kennedy would have canceled it. Not one spoke against it.

One further factor no doubt influenced him: the enormous confidence in his own luck. Everything had broken right for him since 1956. He had won the nomination and the election against all the odds in the book. Everyone around him thought he had the Midas touch and could not lose. Despite himself, even this dispassionate and skeptical man may have been affected by the soaring euphoria of the new day.

8. THE POLITICS OF CLANDESTINITY

And so we were going ahead. If this were so, the next thing was to do what could be done to minimize the damage. It was evident that the political and diplomatic planning was far less advanced than the military planning. And it was evident too that, if the invasion was to win support within Cuba, its sponsor, the Cuban Revolutionary Council, must appear not a counterrevolutionary but a revolutionary movement, offering Cuba not a restoration but a liberation.

The formation of the Council on March 22 was only a first halting step. A few days later Tracy Barnes of CIA sent me the first draft of a proposed Council manifesto and we discussed how to go about strengthening it. After some thought, we asked two Latin American specialists from Harvard to suggest guiding principles for a sensible and progressive platform.

In the meantime, Berle, Philip Bonsal and I held a conference with Miró Cardona. Our purpose was to persuade him to give the Council's program social and economic content. We pointed out that the Council draft was filled with impassioned appeals to the foreign investor, the private banker, the dispossessed property owner, but had very little to say to the worker, the farmer or the Negro. I remarked at one point, "It would be foolish if the Cuban Revolutionary Council turns out to be to the right of the New Frontier." We suggested that the Council must reassure the Cubans that it had no intention of destroying the social and economic gains of the last two years.

Miró threw his hands in the air, heartily agreed, and said that we must understand the situation in Miami: whenever he delivered a speech about social justice, half the audience went away convinced that he was a communist. This gave us the opportunity to make a second point—that the Council should move to New York. This would take it away from the feverish atmosphere of Miami, dominated by Cubans of the right, and put it in a better position to present the exile case to the United Nations. Again Miró acquiesced.

CUBAN RECRUITS EAGER TO FIGHT AGAINST CASTRO LINE UP FOR THEIR PHYSICALS IN MIAMI, FLORIDA IN APRIL 1961.

In Miami the recruitment effort had reached its last frantic phase. By now all pretense of discretion was gone. Talk was unrestrained in the motels and bars, and now even in the press. The Council meanwhile transferred its operations to the Hotel Lexington in New York. The members of the Council knew that a climax was imminent even if they did not know how, when or where. As decent men, burning with love for their country, they were eager to do anything to free their homeland. This generated an understandable readiness to subordinate the interests of the United States to those of a free Cuba; and, however understandable this was from a Cuban viewpoint, it presented dangers to the United States—above all, the danger of losing control over our own policy and being pulled by political suction into a greater degree of intervention than we intended. The first protection against step-by-step involvement, I suggested to the President in a memorandum on April 10, would be "to convince the Cuban leaders that in no foreseeable circumstances will we send in U.S. troops ....We must tell the Revolutionary Council that it cannot expect immediate U.S. recognition; that recognition will come only when they have a better than 50-50 chance of winning under their own steam; that this is a fight which Cubans will have in essence to win for themselves."

Kennedy understood this better than anybody and needed no prodding. Two days later he seized the occasion to say in a press conference: "There will not be, under any conditions, an intervention in Cuba by the United States Armed Forces. ... The basic issue in Cuba is not one between the United States and Cuba. It is between the Cubans themselves. I intend to see that we adhere to that principle and as I understand it this administration's attitude is so understood and shared by the anti-Castro exiles from Cuba in this country." That afternoon in another meeting in the Cabinet

Room he again emphasized the importance of making the operation into an entirely Cuban affair. He inquired sharply whether the Revolutionary Council fully grasped that the provisional government would not receive United States recognition until it was fully established, and that in no case would there be overt military intervention. Lest there be any misunderstanding, he said, he was instructing Berle and Schlesinger to go to New York and make this clear to Miró Cardona. These points, of course, simply recorded the assumptions on which the CIA and the Joint Chiefs had drawn up their invasion plan and predicted its success; and, as they sat around the table, they did not protest now.

9. ON THE BRINK

The next day several of us met with Miró in New York. He was much irritated because CIA had not cut him in on the invasion. His particular concern, however, was with the question of United States military support. He displayed resistance and incredulity at the statement that no United States troops would be used. Miró, a driven man, probably heard what he desperately wanted to hear. He went on to tell us that, if the provisional government was established and things then began to go badly, he planned to call for help from all the nations of the hemisphere—including the United States. He said with solemnity, "This help must come." For, if the operation should fail, the American government would have suffered a severe defeat on its very doorstep, communism would be consolidated in Cuba, and Castro would move on to destroy the whole inter-American system. "You must understand what will happen to your own interests if we lose. You must commit yourselves to full support of our efforts."

I returned to Washington considerably depressed. Whatever Miró was told, it was evident he simply would not believe he could not count on United States military support. "He is a serious person," I reported to the President the next morning, "and will not be easily moved from his present position. Nonetheless I think a very tough effort should be made to get him to accept the President's press conference statement . . . as the basis for his future relations with the United States." The President promptly picked up the phone called Dick Bissell and told him that Miró must understand that either he agrees to proceed on the basis of no United States military intervention or else the whole expedition would be called off. Bissell sent Tracy Barnes to New York that day to stress the point. Though Barnes got a formal assent, he too returned to Washington doubtful whether Miró really believed him.*

Later that evening, as we returned from a meeting of the Pan American Union, where Kennedy had spoken about the Alliance for Progress, he stopped the car just inside the White House grounds and proposed a walk down to the pond to see Caroline's ducks. Caroline, who came running out of nowhere, joined us for a leisurely fifteen-minute stroll in the spring sun. It was a last peaceful moment before the storm broke.

*Later in the day the President returned to me my *aide-mémoire* on the Miró conversation with the scrawled notation: "I informed Bissell that he should have Cardona told that the operation would be cancelled immediately unless Cardona made the decision to go ahead with full understanding of the limitations on U.S. support."

XI.
ORDEAL BY FIRE

CASTRO IN HAVANA, APRIL 16, 1961, SPEAKS OUT AND BLAMES THE UNITED STATES FOR THE DAWN AIR RAIDS ON CUBA THE DAY BEFORE. HE TERMS THE ATTACKS "CUBA'S PEARL HARBOR."

EVENTS WERE RUSHING toward climax. D-day was set for April 17. In Guatemala the Cuban Brigade, now grown to almost 1400 men, waited with growing impatience. A veteran Marine colonel arrived to make a final inspection as the force prepared to leave its base. The day after the President had publicly excluded United States military intervention, Washington sent an urgent request for the colonel's evaluation of the Brigade and its capabilities. The reply came back in unequivocal language:

> *My observations have increased my confidence in the ability of this force to accomplish not only initial combat missions, but also the ultimate objective, the overthrow of Castro. The Brigade and battalion commanders now know all details of the plan and are enthusiastic. These officers are young, vigorous, intelligent and motivated by a fanatical urge to begin battle....*
> *They say they know their own people and believe that after they have inflicted one serious defeat upon the opposition forces, the latter will melt away from Castro, whom they have no wish to support. They say it is a Cuban tradition to join a winner and they have supreme confidence they will win against whatever Castro has to offer.*
> *I share their confidence.*

This message reached the White House on April 14 shortly before the hour of what is known in Pentagonese as the 'no-go' decision on preliminary operations. The fervent testimonial confirmed the President in his intention to let the expedition go ahead.

1. PRELUDE TO TRAGEDY

But I doubt whether anyone in Washington really knew what was taking place in Guatemala. The top CIA officials—Dulles, Bissell, Barnes—were civilized and responsible men; but the CIA operatives in the field and their military colleagues were a different breed, if, at least, the Cubans themselves are to be believed. As zero hour approached, the American advisers told them again (or so they later informed Haynes Johnson) that their Brigade would not be the only unit in the invasion. They received the impression that after seventy-two hours they could count on United States military and air support. At one point, according to Pepe San Román, the chief United States adviser even talked darkly of efforts in Washington to cancel the operation and said that, if a stop order came through, "you come here and make some kind of show, as if you were putting us, the advisors, in prison, and you go ahead with the program as we have talked about it, and we will give you the whole plan, even if we are your prisoners." He went on to hint that this was the desire of his superiors.* (Actually the United States Navy had been briefed to intercept and turn back the invasion in case of a last-minute decision against it.)

As for the Cubans themselves, their spirit was high. Many of the new recruits, however, had been at the base only a few days. Some had not even fired a gun. Of the 1400 men, only about 135 were soldiers. On April 10 the Brigade began to move by truck from the Guatemalan base to the point of embarkation at Puerto Cabezas in Nicaragua. By April 13 the men were beginning to board the boats. On April 14 the United States advisers finally disclosed the invasion plan—the seizure of three beaches along forty miles of the Cuban shore in the Bay of Pigs area, with paratroops dropping inland to control the roads crossing the swamps to the sea. Castro's air force, the advisers said, would be neutralized in advance, and five hundred guerrillas were waiting nearby to join the fight. The Brigade's mission was to hold the beach for three days, after which, as the chief American adviser put it, "you will be so strong, you will be getting so many people to your side, that you won't want to wait for us. You will go straight ahead. You will put your hands out, turn left, and go straight into Havana."** The Cubans, still regarding the Americans with veneration and not used to locker-room pep talks, left the briefing in a state of exaltation.

As the flotilla of seven small ships waited off Puerto Cabezas on the late afternoon of April 14, Luis Somoza, the

* Haynes Johnson, *The Bay of Pigs* (New York, 1964 [Dell edition]), 73–74.
** Johnson, *The Bay of Pigs*, 83.

AN ARIEL VIEW OF GLEN ORA, THE PRESIDENT'S VIRGINIA RETREAT.

dictator of Nicaragua, appeared at the dock, his face powdered, bodyguards in his wake. He shouted boldly, "Bring me a couple of hairs from Castro's beard," and waved the patriots farewell. The members of the Brigade trailed their vivid battalion scarves in the wind, and the boats, tinted by the red light of the dying sun, set out for Cuba.

The neutralization of Castro's air force was to be brought about by air strikes from Nicaraguan bases before the landings to be carried out by Cuban pilots pretending to be defectors from Castro's air force. After an interval to permit U-2 overflights and photographic assessment of the damage, a second strike would follow at dawn on D-day morning.

As the ships made their slow way toward Cuba, eight B-26s took off from Puerto Cabezas in the night. At dawn on Saturday morning they zoomed down on three main Cuban airfields. CIA had estimated Castro's air strength at about fifteen B-26s and ten Sea Furies; there were also four T-33 jet trainers, but these did not figure significantly in either CIA's or, what is worse, the Joint Chiefs' calculations. The Cuban air force, according to the CIA estimate, was "entirely disorganized," its planes "for the most part obsolete and inoperative," its combat efficiency "almost non-existent."

The pilots returned to Nicaragua with optimistic claims of widespread damage. The overflights the next day, however, showed only five aircraft definitely destroyed. And not all the attacking planes made it back to the base. One developed engine trouble, and its pilot headed for Florida, finally making an emergency landing in Key West. In the meantime, a ninth B-26 had flown straight from Nicaragua to Miami to put the cover plan into operation. The pilot on landing announced himself as a Castro defector who had just bombed the airfields. The unscheduled arrival of the second plane at Key West complicated things somewhat; and the appearance at Jacksonville the day before of a perfectly genuine Castro defector in a Cuban plane compounded the confusion.

In New York Adlai Stevenson was getting ready for a long-delayed debate in the United Nations General Assembly over a Cuban charge of aggressive intentions on the part of the United States. Kennedy, who had been much concerned about the UN aspect of the Cuban operation, told the group in the Cabinet Room that he wished Stevenson to be fully informed, and that nothing said at the UN should be less than the truth, even if it could not be the full truth.

In preparation for the debate, Tracy Barnes and I had held a long talk with Stevenson on April 8. But our briefing, which was probably unduly vague, left Stevenson with the impression that no action would take place during the UN discussion of the Cuban item. Afterward, Stevenson made it clear that he wholly disapproved of the plan, regretted that he had been given no opportunity to comment on it and believed that it would cause infinite trouble. But, if it was national policy, he was prepared to make out the best possible case.

After the Saturday air strike, word was passed to Stevenson that it was the work of genuine defectors, and Cleveland passed this information on to Stevenson. A few moments later Stevenson told the UN: "These two planes, to the best of our knowledge, were Castro's own air force planes and, according to the pilots, they took off from Castro's own air force fields." As Stevenson spoke, someone handed him a piece of press ticker containing what appeared to be corroborative detail, and Stevenson read further parts of the CIA cover story into the record.

The President had meanwhile gone off to his Virginia retreat at Glen Ora early Saturday afternoon; had he remained, contrary to custom, in Washington, the press would have presumed that something was up. At Sunday noon, the last 'no-go' point, he authorized the expedition to proceed to the beaches. But in Washington newspapermen were starting to call the State Department and ask penetrating questions about the fugitive B-26s in Key West and Miami. It was evident that the CIA cover story was cracking, that Stevenson had been permitted to misinform the UN and that the international repercussions might be extensive. Stevenson was understandably indignant. Rusk, remorseful at the position into which State had thrust its UN ambassador, now resolved that the Cuban adventure should not be permitted further to jeopardize the larger interests of United States foreign policy.

In particular, the collapse of the cover story brought the question of the second air strike into new focus. The President and the Secretary understood this strike as one which would take place simultaneously with the landings and have the appearance of coming from the airstrip on the beach. It had slid by in the briefings, everyone assuming that it would be masked by the cover story. But there could be no easy attribution to defectors now. Nor did the fact that the planes were B-26s flown by Cuban pilots save the situation; despite the great to-do about 'Cubanizing' the operation, they would still be United States planes in the eyes of the UN. Rusk, after his talks with Stevenson, concluded that a second Nicaraguan strike would put the United States in an untenable position internationally and that no further strikes should be launched until the planes could fly (or appear to fly) from the beachhead. Bundy agreed, and they called the President at Glen Ora.

It was now late Sunday afternoon. When Rusk said that the projected strike was one which could only appear to come from Nicaragua, Kennedy said, "I'm not signed on to this"; the strike he knew about was the one coming ostensibly from the beachhead. After a long conversation, the President directed that the strike be canceled. When he put down the phone, he sat on in silence for a moment, shook his head and began to pace the room in evident concern, worried perhaps less about this decision than about the confusion in the planning; what would go wrong next? Those with him at Glen Ora had rarely seen him so low.

By the next dawn, the expeditionary force was at its stations off the Bay of Pigs, and frogmen were beginning to mark the invasion points on shore. The first frogman on each beach was, in spite of Kennedy's order, an American.

2. FIASCO

The frogmen almost immediately encountered a militia patrol, rifle fire shattered the silence, and hope of tactical surprise was gone. On the ships the Cubans watched wild flashes of lights on shore and then began with uncertain hearts to clamber into landing craft. Some of the small boats, as they made their way through black waters, ran against coral reefs, not mentioned in the briefing, and foundered, the men swimming to other boats or toward land. Gradually the invaders gathered on the beaches and pushed inland. After daybreak paratroops dropped from the skies and seized interior points.

Castro's air force, alerted by the first clash, reacted with unexpected vigor against both the ships and the men on the beaches. At nine-thirty in the morning, a Sea Fury sank the ship carrying the ammunition reserve for the next ten days and most of the communications equipment: an inexplicable concentration of treasure in a single hull. Other ships

suffered damage, and the rest of the flotilla put out to sea. The Brigade's slow-moving B-26s flew defensive missions over the beachhead, but Castro's forgotten T-33s, fast jet trainers armed with 50-calibre machine guns, shot four of them down. The fighting went on through a hot, clear day, the invaders digging in behind their tanks, bazookas and mortars, while Castro's forces, unable to cross the swamps, massed to move down the highways toward the beaches.

In Havana Castro's police arrested two hundred thousand people, herding them into theaters and auditoriums. Through the island anyone suspected of underground connections was taken into custody. In New York the Cuban Revolutionary Council had become mysteriously inaccessible, for Miró had privately agreed with the CIA that the Council should go into hiding. By Sunday night they were installed in a house in the Opa-Locka airport to await transfer to the beachhead and establishment as the provisional government of a free Cuba. The next morning, as they listened to the radio, they were stunned to hear an announcement "from the Cuban Revolutionary Council" that the invasion had begun. Unknown to them, the CIA Lem Jones, was putting out press releases in the name of the Council.

In Washington President Kennedy arrived back by helicopter from Glen Ora early Monday morning. Dean Rusk

TOP: LARGE ARTILLERY IS FIRED ON THE REBELS AS THEY INVADE A BEACHHEAD IN CUBA ON THE MORNING OF APRIL 17.

BOTTOM: FIDEL CASTRO SITS INSIDE A TANK NEAR PLAYA GIRON, CUBA DURING THE BAY OF PIGS INVASION.

RIGHT: INVADERS CAPTURED BY CASTRO'S FORCES ARE MARCHED TO PRISON FROM TEMPORARY QUARTERS ON GIRON BEACH.

told a press conference later that morning, "The American people are entitled to know whether we are intervening in Cuba or intend to do so in the future. The answer to that question is no. What happens in Cuba is for the Cuban people to decide." An angry diplomatic note came in from Khrushchev, denouncing the invasion and pledging "all necessary assistance" to Castro. During the day the news from the beaches was confused and fragmentary as a result of the loss of communications facilities; but Washington could still remain hopeful.

By early Tuesday it was clear that the invasion was in trouble. An attempt to knock out Castro's planes by a B-26 raid that morning had been frustrated by heavy haze over the airfield. I noted later that day: "The T-33s turned out to be far more effective than any of us had been led to suppose. This created havoc.... In addition, Castro tanks reached the beachhead sooner than had been expected. And the landings failed to set off mass uprisings behind the lines."

Kennedy seemed deeply concerned about the members of the Brigade. They were brave men and patriots; he had put them on the beachhead; and he wanted to save as many as he could. But he did not propose to send in the Marines. Some people, he noted, were arguing that failure would cause irreparable harm, that we had no choice now but to commit United States forces. Kennedy disagreed. Defeat, he said, would be an incident, not a disaster. The test had always been whether the Cuban people would back a revolt against Castro. If they wouldn't, the United States could not by invasion impose a new regime on them. But would not United States prestige suffer if we let the rebellion flicker out? "What is prestige?" Kennedy asked. "Is it the shadow of power or the substance of power? We are going to work on the substance of power. No doubt we will be kicked in the can for the next couple of weeks, but that won't affect the main business."

That afternoon we met in the Cabinet Room to consider a reply to Khrushchev. Rusk and Bundy were there, with some new faces—Charles E. Bohlen and Foy Kohler, the Soviet experts, and Harlan Cleveland to cover the United Nations. Bohlen wrote the original draft, and the President amended it to his satisfaction. "I believe, Mr. Chairman," the message finally said, "that you should recognize that free peoples in all parts of the world do not accept the claim of historical inevitability for communist revolution. What your Government believes is its own business; what it does in the world is the world's business. The great revolution in the history of man, past, present and future, is the revolution of those determined to be free."

It was a long and grim day—the longest and grimmest the New Frontier had known. The reports from Cuba continued sketchy, but whatever news there was was bad. Hour after hour, hope steadily drained away. By late afternoon we learned that twenty thousand government troops with artillery and tanks were moving toward the water to encircle the invaders. Yet the Brigade fought on, its leaders still sustained by the dream of United States intervention—a dream stimulated, they later said, by assurances from Americans in the ships offshore.* We could not rid our minds of the thought of those brave men, running short of ammunition, without adequate air cover, dying on Cuban beaches before Soviet tanks. That morning, when CIA had assured San Román he would be taken off the beach, the Brigade commander replied: "I will not be evacuated. We will fight to the end here if we have to."

Around one in the morning, as I was getting into bed, the phone rang. It was Mac Bundy. He said, "I am in the President's office, and he would like to have you come down here as soon as possible." When I arrived, I found the President, the Vice-President, Rusk, McNamara, Lemnitzer and Burke, along with Bissell, Bundy and Walt Rostow. They were gloomily reading dispatches from the beachhead. Mac said to me as I entered: "We have no real news, but we fear that things are going badly. In any case, the Revolutionary Council is very upset. Some of its members are threatening

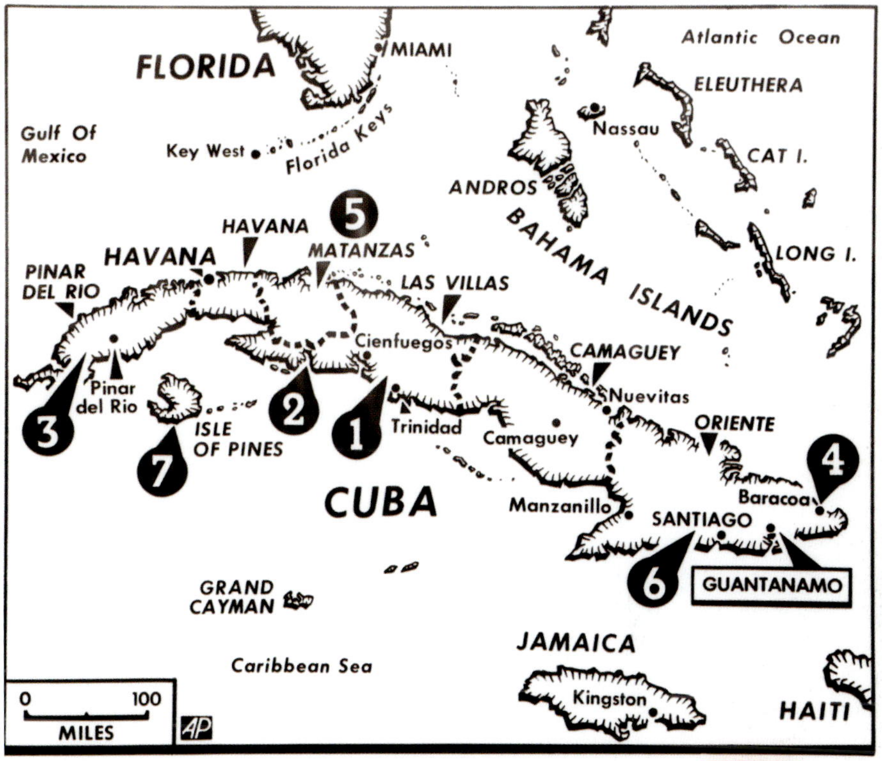

AN APRIL 17 MAP SHOWING THE LOCATIONS OF INVADING FORCES ON CUBA'S BEACHES.

*Johnson, *The Bay of Pigs*, 139.

ANXIOUS MEMBERS OF THE CUBAN COLONY IN MIAMI LISTEN TO A RADIO SET UP ON THE SIDEWALK FOR NEWS OF THE PROGRESS OF THE INVASION.

extreme action. The President wants Berle to go down and talk with them. If we can't find Berle, he wants you."

In a moment the President took charge. He was objective and trenchant in his questions; but absence of information made decision difficult. Finally the President decided to authorize a flight of six unmarked jets from the *Essex* over the Bay of Pigs for the hour after dawn Wednesday morning. Their mission would be to cover a B-26 attack from Nicaragua. (In Puerto Cabezas, the Cuban pilots were in a state of exhaustion from 48 hours of nearly continuous runs over the beachhead. A few now declined to go out on what seemed a suicide mission. Some American civilian pilots, under contract to the CIA, agreed, however, to fly sorties. Both the B-26s and the Navy jets started out later that night, but through one more mix-up in this doomed adventure—this one as elementary as a mix-up between the Nicaraguan and Cuban time zones—the B-26s arrived over the beachhead an hour ahead of their jet support. Without cover, the B-26s ran into sharp enemy fire, and four Americans were killed.)

In a short while Berle arrived. The President then turned to the problem of the Revolutionary Council. "One member is threatening suicide," he said. "Others want to be put on the beachhead. All are furious with CIA. They do not know how dismal things are. You must go down and talk to them." Berle said, "Yes," then added wryly, "I can think of happier missions." As the meeting broke up around two in the morning, Kennedy called me over and said, "You ought to go with Berle." Later that night, when the group had left his office, the President walked alone in the desolate silence of the White House garden.

3. MISSION TO MIAMI

A military plane was waiting when Berle and I arrived at National Airport. In a few minutes we were heading south. The next morning, we found ourselves in front of a nondescript frame house, guarded by young GIs, on the deserted airbase of Opa-Locka. As we stumbled onto the sunporch, a young man lying asleep on a cot stirred uneasily and got up. It was, I soon discovered, Manuel Ray.

Our arrival brought the house to life. In a few moments we were all seated around a plain wooden table. The members of the Council wore khaki fatigues: Miró Cardona, with a son on the beachhead; Tony Varona, with a son, two brothers and two nephews; Antonio Maceo, with a son; Ray; Justo Carrillo; and Carlos Hevia. Bender and two CIA people joined the group.

Miró Cardona looked ten years older than the man with whom Berle and I had lunched at the Century a short week before. He spoke to us with deep earnestness. It was, he said, a life-and-death struggle and not too late to turn the tide. He talked of sending in more contract fliers. In any case, he said, the only excuse the Revolutionary Council could now offer the people of Cuba was to be permitted to die with the men on the beaches. "It is this," he said with immense gravity, "which I request, this which I beg."

Miró was followed by Varona. Where Miró was melancholy, Varona was intense, florid and truculent. Offering a violent indictment of CIA. CIA, he said, had not consulted with the Council nor coordinated with resistance groups inside Cuba. All it had done was to land 1400 men at the worst possible place. Why no uprisings behind the lines? Varona said vehemently that he had inspected the camps in Guatemala; that the CIA had deceived him; that on returning to Miami he had urged the sons of his friends to enlist. It was evident that he had condemned these young men, the flower of their generation, to a wretched death.

What could be done now? Evacuation was impossible. The only possible course, Varona said, was to put United States planes into the battle and, if this was not enough, to send the Marines. After all, Castro had Soviet planes, Soviet tanks, Soviet technicians. Why could not the United States do as much for its friends? The Americans, he said grimly, could not hope to escape responsibility.

Justo Carrillo spoke next. He said soberly that confidence in the United States depended on its capacity to fulfill its democratic professions. Kennedy's social and economic program—the Alliance for Progress and the Cuban White Paper—were right, but he had not yet developed the military foundations for his new course. He had revised State Department policy, but he had not yet succeeded in revising CIA policy. Maceo added that the struggle in Cuba was not between two groups of Cubans but between two ways of life; failure on the beaches would mean a world-wide defeat for democracy. If Castro could successfully defy the United States, more and more of Latin America would move into his orbit.

Manuel Ray was next—soft-spoken, direct, non-rhetorical and exceedingly impressive. His group, he said, had argued that the proper strategy was internal insurrection, not external invasion. He had tried in vain to interest the CIA in this approach. "We could get no support for our proposal."

"We have been brought here," Ray went on, "without any knowledge of the operations.... We have the feeling of being in a vacuum.... The Council has no power. Action is taken in our name without our control, without our clearance and even without our knowledge. We are unable to talk to the men on the beaches, to our people in the underground or to our friends throughout Latin America. Our conclusion is that we should abandon the pretense of command, go to Cuba and fight as soldiers. Let those who really run things begin to assume the responsibility." He ended by saying that, in the faith that President Kennedy would not desert them, they would stay with him and his decisions to the end.

Varona read a list of requests: immediate transportation to the beachhead; immediate air strikes; immediate reinforcements. "Someone placed us in this position—that person will have to get us out of it." He denounced the surveillance under which they were kept. "We don't know whether we are your allies or your prisoners." At noon today, he said, he was planning to leave the house despite the armed guards, go to Miami and hold a press conference. "Let them shoot me down if they dare." He asked to be sent forthwith on a Catalina to the beachhead. Ray spoke up and said that he felt he should be dropped into Havana. The others after some talk seemed ready to settle for the command post in Nicaragua.

Berle and I were much moved by the power and bitterness of the protests. Our first thought was to get them all to Nicaragua. But, when we returned to the hangar and called Washington, we were informed that the operation was substantially over. The only signal from the beach was a wail of SOS's. When we asked about evacuation, we were told that the time had passed even for that.

Our hearts sank as we walked out for a moment into the dazzling sun. How could we notify the Cubans that there was

CUBAN REFUGEES PRAY FOR THE SUCCESS OF THE BAY OF PIGS INVASION AT A RALLY IN DOWNTOWN MIAMI ON APRIL 19.

no hope, that their sons were abandoned for captivity or death—and at the same time dissuade them from public denunciation of the CIA and the United States government? It was clear that only Kennedy could save this situation.

I immediately called the White House, and Evelyn Lincoln put me through to the President's office. Dean Rusk, who answered the phone, agreed that the Council should be brought to Washington, though he seemed uncertain whether they should see the President. Before we finally took off for Washington, I called the President to explain why we hoped he would see the Council himself. He said immediately that he wanted us to bring them to the White House as soon as we arrived. After a funereal trip north, the Council waited in the Cabinet Room, while Berle and I went in to see the

President. Kennedy, exceptionally drawn and tired, was, as usual, self-possessed. We told him about the situation at Opa-Locka: the Council under virtual house arrest, the intensity of their resentment, the probability of public denunciations. He expressed shock at the Council's detention; CIA, he said, had told him nothing of this.

In a few moments the Cubans entered. They sat down on the two couches facing each other in front of the fireplace, with the President in his rocking chair. A naval aide, gave a report, precise and bleak, on the beachhead. Then Kennedy, speaking slowly and thoughtfully, declared his sorrow over the events of the last forty-eight hours. He explained why he had decided against intervention and why he had supposed that the operation might succeed on its own. Here he paused to read the message from the Marine colonel describing the training and condition of the Brigade. The struggle against communism, he said, had many fronts; leadership in that struggle imposed many responsibilities. The United States had to consider the balance of affairs all around the world. But, however tragic this episode, no one could doubt our commitment to the eventual freedom of Cuba. He added that he had himself fought in a war, that he had seen brave men die, that he had lost a brother, and that he shared their grief and their despair.

Miró and other members of the Council said a few words. After hearing Kennedy, they were far more subdued than in the morning. Discussion continued till six o'clock, when the President had a conference with congressional leaders. As the Cubans prepared to leave, he said, "I want you all to understand that, as soon as you leave the White House, you are all free men—free to go wherever you want, free to say anything you want, free to talk to anyone you want." I had never seen the President more impressive. In spite of themselves, his visitors were deeply moved. Then he asked me to take them back to the family quarters and await him there. There on the second floor of the Mansion, we had tea and sandwiches. After a time Kennedy rejoined us. The talk was about a rescue program for the survivors. United States destroyers, with air cover and orders to fire if fired upon, were already searching the waters off the coast; Kennedy was prepared to run more risks to take the men off the beaches than to put them there.

Later that night the CIA front man issued a final bulletin in the name of the Council. "The recent landings in Cuba," the release said, "have been constantly though inaccurately described as an invasion. It was, in fact, a landing of supplies and support for our patriots who have been fighting in Cuba for months.... The major portion of our landing party [has reached] the Escambray mountains."

The routine of Washington life is implacable. The prime minister of Greece was visiting the capital that week, and the Kennedys had to go to a dinner at the Greek Embassy. Once again, the President concealed anguish under a mask of courtesy and composure. So many regrets must have flowed through his mind during these bitter hours—the advice so authoritatively rendered and so respectfully accepted, the unexamined assumptions and the misconceived plans, the blow to the bright hopes of the new administration, the problems at home and abroad; but most of all, I think, it was the vision of the men on the beaches, who had gone off with such splendid expectations, who had fought so bravely and who now would be shot down like dogs or carted off to Castro's prisons. This vision haunted him that week and many weeks and months to come.

4. THE LAST ACT

Thursday, April 20, was the ninetieth day of the Kennedy administration. The gay expectations of the Hundred Days were irrevocably over, the hour of euphoria past. Through the country and the world the debacle was producing astonishment and disillusion.

At home the shock of defeat somewhat muted the voices of criticism. Some on the right, though fewer than one might have expected, were talking about sending in the Marines. But some on the left, more than one might have thought, now saw full vindication of their pre-election doubts about Kennedy. A number of these impassioned liberals convinced themselves that the cult of toughness, the determination to win at any cost or something else they supposed to characterize Kennedy, would now lead him to throw the book at Castro—though why he should do on Thursday what he had declined to do on Tuesday was not clear. Protest meetings erupted on a dozen campuses. A Fair Play for Cuba rally at Union Square in New York on April 21 drew three thousand people. Five literary magazines and Norman Mailer staged a demonstration. Pickets demonstrated in front of the White House.

Most Americans of course rallied to their President in the moment of national crisis. Still even many of these had their first harsh doubts about the new administration. The nation was in a state of shock, and no one understood more acutely than Kennedy himself the need to restore perspective. His first problem on Thursday was to contain the political consequences of the debacle. He moved now with sure instinct and remarkable dexterity, showing, as he had shown nearly twenty years earlier in the Solomons, the strength to accept disaster, omit recrimination and pitch in to bring the situation back. The war generation, having survived catastrophe, knew that it was not finality.

The President's concern was to head off any outcry within the United States for violent retaliation against Castro, to reassure the democratic world about the prudence of Washington and at the same time to dissuade the communists from regarding restraint as evidence of weakness. He had not wavered at any point in his determination not to commit American troops; if the United States moved against Cuba, Khrushchev might seize this as a pretext for moving against West Berlin. Even his deep concern over the men on the beaches led him to nothing further than a rescue mission. A speech that day to the American Society of Newspaper Editors at the Statler Hilton offered the opportunity to explain the policy of restraint and to divert the demand for action against Castro into a general strengthening of American purpose.

Unilateral intervention, he told the editors, would have violated our traditions and international obligations. "But let the record show," he added, "that our restraint is not inexhaustible. Should it ever appear that the inter-American doctrine of non-interference merely conceals or excuses a policy of non-action—if the nations of this Hemisphere should fail to meet their commitments against outside Communist penetration—then I want it clearly understood that this Government will not hesitate in meeting its primary obligations which are to the security of our Nation!"

Having uttered this obscure but emphatic warning, he went on to define the lesson of the episode. Communism, he said, was now less interested in arms as the means of direct aggression than "as the shield behind which subversion, infiltration, and a host of other tactics steadily advance, picking off vulnerable areas one by one in situations which do not permit our own armed intervention." This "new and deeper struggle," Kennedy said, was taking place every day, without fanfare, in villages and markets and classrooms all over the globe. It called for new concepts, new tools, a new sense of urgency. "Too long we have fixed our eyes on traditional military needs, on armies prepared to cross borders, on missiles poised for flight. Now it should be clear that this is no longer enough—that our security may be lost piece by piece, country by country, without the firing of a single missile or the crossing of a single border."

He concluded: "We intend to reexamine and reorient our forces of all kinds—our tactics and our institutions here in this community." I was never quite clear what this last phrase meant, unless it referred to the CIA and the Joint Chiefs; but once again obscurity probably helped the impact of the speech. Certainly the occasion reestablished him in a fighting stance without committing him to reckless action.

The next step was to secure the administration against partisan attack. The Republicans, of course, were a little inhibited by their own role in conceiving the operation; but Kennedy took no chances. Later that day he called in Richard Nixon, and by the weekend he had talked to Eisenhower, Nelson Rockefeller and Barry Goldwater. Harry S Truman, being a Democrat, required only the attention of the Vice-President.

As part of the strategy of protection, he moved to stop the gathering speculation over responsibility for the project. By Friday, the morning papers were filled with what purported to be 'inside' stories about the Cuba decision. An impulse for self-preservation was evidently tempting some of the participants in those meetings in the Cabinet Room to put out versions of the episode ascribing the debacle to everyone but themselves.

In a press conference that morning, the President dismissed the inside stories: "There's an old saying that victory has a hundred fathers and defeat is an orphan." (I later asked him where he had come upon this felicitous observation. He looked surprised and said vaguely, "Oh, I don't know; it's just an old saying."*) He then told the newspapermen: "I'm the responsible officer of the Government." He repeated this more fiercely in a White House statement the next Monday: "President Kennedy has stated from the beginning that as President he bears sole responsibility.... He has stated it on all occasions and he restates it now.... The President is strongly opposed to anyone within or without the administration attempting to shift the responsibility."

Reactions abroad proved more intense than at home. In Latin America demonstrations were brief, communist-inspired and not very serious; but in Western Europe there was widespread disenchantment. In the brief time from the Inaugural to the Bay of Pigs, Kennedy had come to seem the last hope of the west—a brilliant and exciting hope. He had conveyed an impression of United States foreign policy as mature, controlled, responsible and, above all, intelligent. Western Europe in return had made a heavy political and emotional investment in him. Now he suddenly seemed revealed as a mere continuator of the Eisenhower-Dulles past. The New Frontier looked like a collection not only of imperialists but of ineffectual imperialists—and, what was worst of all, of stupid, ineffectual imperialists. Yet, at the same time, it was clear that the fund of goodwill toward Kennedy, though somewhat dissipated, was far from destroyed, even on the democratic left.

Kennedy commented wryly on the discrepancy between the European and American reactions. If he had been a

*Emily Morison Beck, the editor of the new edition of Bartlett's *Familiar Quotations*, informs me that she knows of no previous use of this "old saying."

British prime minister, he remarked, he would have been thrown out of office; but in the United States failure had increased his charm: "if I had gone further, they would have liked me even more." At this point, Evelyn Lincoln brought in an advance on the new Gallup poll, showing an unprecedented 82 percent behind the administration. Kennedy tossed it aside and said, "It's just like Eisenhower. The worse I do, the more popular I get."

5. AFTERMATH

Afterward Kennedy would sometimes recur incredulously to the Bay of Pigs, wondering how a rational and responsible government could ever have become involved in so ill-starred an adventure. What caused the disaster? Too much comment on the Bay of Pigs has fallen into the fallacy of Douglas Southall Freeman, who once wrote a long chapter analyzing the reasons for Lee's defeat at Gettysburg without mentioning the interesting fact that the Union Army was there too. For the reality was that Fidel Castro turned out to be a far more formidable foe and in command of a far better organized regime than anyone had supposed.

One reason Washington miscalculated Castro, of course, was a series of failures in our own intelligence. We regarded him as an hysteric. We dismissed his air force and forgot his T-33s. We thought that his troops might defect. We supposed that, although warned by advance air strikes, he would do nothing to neutralize the Cuban underground (either that, or we supposed that the underground, without alert or assistance from us, would find means to protect itself and eventually rise against the regime). And there were tactical errors. We chose an invasion site without a way of escape, and we did not in any case tell the Brigade of the guerrilla option. We put too much precious ammunition and communications equipment in a single ship. We did not give the Brigade enough pilots to keep its planes in continuous action. On the other hand, if one renounced the fall-back plan of flight to the hills, the invasion site was well chosen and easily defensible. The men of the Brigade fought with great bravery against superior force and inflicted far more casualities than they received.

Subsequent controversy has settled on the cancellation of the second air strike as the turning point.* In retrospect, it is hard to see why, the first strike already having taken place, a second would have made things so much worse at the United Nations or elsewhere. Kennedy came later to feel that the cancellation of the second strike was an error. But he did not regard it as a decisive error. The second air strike might have protracted the stand on the beachhead from three days to ten; it might have permitted the establishment of the provisional government; it might have made possible the eventual evacuation of the invading force. There is certainly nothing to suggest that it could possibly have led to the overthrow of the regime on the terms which Kennedy laid down from the start—that is, without United States armed intervention.

The expedition was also misconceived technically. If it was to be a covert operation for which we could plausibly disclaim responsibility, it should have been, at most, a guerrilla infiltration. Once it grew into a conventional amphibious invasion, it was clearly beyond the limits of disownability. Unless we were prepared to back it to the hilt, it should have been abandoned. The President had insisted that the political and military risks be brought into balance: given the nature of the operation, this was impossible, and someone should have said so.

All of us, the President most of all, went through this sequence of thoughts again and again in the months to come. The President reserved his innermost thoughts and, in the end, blamed only himself. But he was a human being and not totally free of resentment. He would say at times, "My God, the bunch of advisers we inherited.... Can you imagine being President and leaving behind someone like all those people there?" My impression is that, among these advisers, the Joint Chiefs had disappointed him most for their cursory review of the military plans. About Dulles and Bissell he said little. I think he had made up his mind at once that, when things settled down, they would have to go.

But it was not Kennedy's way to waste energy in repining. He continued the task of political recovery. A Gallup poll early in May showed that 65 percent of the respondents agreed with his opposition to military intervention; only 24 percent said that the Marines should be sent to Cuba. Though he was genuinely concerned about the threat of subversive warfare, he was basically philosophical about the impact of the Bay of Pigs itself. He saw it as an episode, not as a cataclysm; and he was sure that the hope and confidence generated by the rest of the ninety days were entirely sufficient to absorb this error, if it were not repeated. He set quietly to work to make sure that nothing like the Bay of Pigs could happen to him again.

The first lesson was never to rely on the experts. He now knew that he would have to broaden the range of his advice, make greater use of generalists in whom he had personal confidence and remake every great decision in his own terms—

*Mythologists have even talked about a supposed presidential decision to "withdraw United States air cover." There was never, of course, any plan for United States air cover, and no air cover for the landing forces was withdrawn.

as, indeed, he had done with the other decisions of the ninety days. He understood too that the prestige of the presidential office had been lightly regarded by men whose primary loyalty was not to him or his administration. Thereafter he took care to make sure that the presidential interest would be represented in the large decisions. He turned from the people he had inherited in government to the people he had brought in himself—the people he had worked with longest, knew best and trusted most. Neither Robert Kennedy nor Ted Sorensen had taken part in the meetings in the Cabinet Room; both were at his right hand at every subsequent moment of crisis for the rest of his Presidency. He charged Dick Goodwin with responsibility for the next steps in policy toward Cuba and the exiles. He chose Maxwell Taylor as his personal adviser on military affairs until the time came when he could make him Chief of Staff.

And he took a new view of the White House staff. While Bundy and I had not performed with distintion, he had not used us as he would use his White House people later; he had not, for example, called us in for a staff discussion of Cuba, away from the inhibiting presence of the grandees in the Cabinet Room. In the future, he made sure that he had the unfettered and confidential advice of his own people. For our part, we resolved to be less acquiescent the next time. The Bay of Pigs gave us a license for the impolite inquiry and the rude comment. In addition, Bundy was moved over from the Executive Office Building to the West Wing of the White House and given new authority as a coordinator of security affairs within the White House. He instituted regular morning meetings for his National Security Council staff, to which he invited other members of the White House group involved in foreign affairs—Goodwin, Dungan and myself—as well as representatives from State, Defense, CIA and USIA. This valuable innovation provided the White House a point of information and control below the top and strengthened Bundy's services to Kennedy. All this helped the President to tighten his personal hold on the sprawling mystery of government. This was in the course of happening anyway, as Kennedy worked to establish control over his administration; it was in line with his theory of the Presidency; but the Bay of Pigs made it happen quickly.

The impact of the failure shook up the national security machinery. It taught every adviser something about the President, the other advisers, himself and his own department. It was a horribly expensive lesson; but it was well learned. In later months the President's father would tell him that, in its perverse way, the Bay of Pigs was not a misfortune but a benefit. I doubt whether the President ever fully believed this; the thought of the men of the Brigade suffering in Cuban prisons prevented easy consolation. But no one can doubt that failure in Cuba in 1961 contributed to success in Cuba in 1962.

KENNEDY AND EISENHOWER WALK WITH HEADS BOWED ALONG A PATH AT CAMP DAVID. THEY MET IN LATE APRIL TO DISCUSS THE BAY OF PIGS INVASION.

XII. NEW DEPARTURES

ARIEL VIEW OF THE WHITE HOUSE IN THE SPRING OF 1961.

THE INITIATION had been harsh; but then no one had expected the Presidency to be easy. And, though geography gave the Cuban problem a certain intimacy and intensity, it remained a side issue. The great challenge lay not in Havana but in Moscow. The supreme test lay in Kennedy's capacity to deal not with Fidel Castro but with N. S. Khrushchev.

Kennedy approached the Soviet Union without illusion about the character of Russian polity and purpose but also with considerable weariness over the rhetoric of the cold war. The John Foster Dulles contrast between the God-anointed apostles of free enterprise and the regimented hordes of atheistic communism bored him. Seeing the world as an historian rather than as a moralist, he could not utter without embarrassment the self-serving platitudes about the total virtue of one side and the total evil of the other. In 1958 he had called on Americans to renounce the proposition that "we should enter every military conflict as a moral crusade requiring the unconditional surrender of the enemy." The stereotypes of the fifties, he thought, were not only self-serving, but, worse, they simply did not provide a useful way of thinking about international affairs.

With his historian's perspective, he was disposed to view the conflict in national rather than ideological terms. While he recognized that ideology gave Moscow a potent international weapon, especially in the developing world, he was sure that the Soviet leaders would always use it in their own national interest. He cared less about the clash of abstractions than about the practical problem of living on the same planet with a great and powerful despotism, ambitious enough to seize all it could but sober enough not to wish to blow up the world.

He was an American, holding that a free democracy was the best form of government, and he was ready to go to war, if necessary, to save democracy from extinction. But he saw not a final battle between democratic good and communist evil but an obscure and intricate drama, where men, institutions and ideals, all bedeviled by the sin of self-righteousness, threatened to rush humanity to the edge of destruction, and where salvation lay in man's liberation from myth, stereotype and fanaticism. The cold war was a reality and would remain so as long as the Communists refused to acknowledge the permanence of the non-communist world. But he was determined to take the hysteria out of the cold war and get down to the business at hand.

1. FIRST APPROACHES

The new administration had the benefit of considerable discussion of foreign affairs during the Democratic party's interlude in the opposition. Much of this discussion had taken place in the Democratic Advisory Council, and in the course of the decade two divergent schools had emerged. Both opposed the main aspects of the Dulles policy—its exclusive reliance on nuclear power, its faith in military pacts, its intolerance of neutrals and its conception of diplomacy as a sub-branch of theology. But beyond this common ground they disagreed somewhat in diagnosis and prescription.

Dean Acheson led one school, very often with the support of Paul Nitze and one or two others. Acheson's ideas had grown out of his own brilliant period as Secretary of State, when the Soviet Union first became a nuclear power, a disorganized western Europe lay under the Soviet guns and the communists were attempting direct aggression in Korea. Those years had demanded, above all, a revival of military will and power in the west. Now, a decade later, Acheson took the view that, in spite of the death of Stalin, very little had changed in the Soviet Union. The communist purpose of world domination through the threat of military showdown seemed to him unalterable; and he was increasingly concerned lest the United States allow itself to be diverted from the main battleground of Europe into sentimental crusades against colonialism and hopeless efforts to democratize the underdeveloped world.

Actually most of his colleagues on the Foreign Policy Committee of the Democratic Advisory Council differed a good deal. The other school was led by Adlai Stevenson and included Averell Harriman, George Kennan, Chester Bowles, Thomas K. Finletter, Mennen Williams, J. K. Galbraith and Ben Cohen as well as Senators like J. William Fulbright and Mike Mansfield. These men believed that the world had indeed changed since 1950, that the conflict between Russia and China was real, that the military threat to western Europe had receded, that the underdeveloped world was the new battleground and that military measures had to be supplemented if not superseded by vigorous political and economic programs. In short, the policy of 1949–52, however sound at the time, was no longer adequate; a changing world called for flexibility and initiative.

Though Kennedy had, in the main, stayed aloof from the DAC debates, he was clearly aligned with the Stevenson-Harriman-Bowles position. A sharp critic of the tendency to suppose that all problems had military solutions, he was a strong advocate of economic assistance to the uncommitted world. His reactions in 1960 to the shooting down of the U-2 over the Soviet Union and to the Quemoy-Matsu issue showed his dislike for rigid interpretations of the cold war. He did not suppose that the United States had it within its power to work overnight changes in the Soviet Union; but he did not suppose either that the Soviet Union was fixed forever in its present mold. He therefore favored a policy of reasoned firmness accompanied by a determination to explore all possibilities of reasonable accommodation.

The Soviet Union watched the arrival of the new administration with marked interest. Khrushchev, who had given up on Eisenhower after the U-2 incident and the collapse of the Paris summit in May 1960, seized several opportunities to semaphore his hopes for Kennedy. Walt Rostow and Jerome B. Wiesner, who were among the Americans at the Moscow meeting on disarmament in December, returned with the feeling that the Russians might be prepared for action in arms control, though they also warned the President-elect that the Kremlin would give no ground on Berlin and would press its advantages in the underdeveloped world. Later Khrushchev's warm congratulatory message to Kennedy at the inaugural and his release of two American pilots shot down over the Arctic, reinforced the sense that Moscow desired, in the phrase of the moment, a reduction of tensions.

Yet the Soviet Union, as usual, was pursuing a double policy; and Khrushchev disclosed its other face in an elaborate speech in Moscow on January 6. This speech made a conspicuous impression on the new President, who took it as an authoritative exposition of Soviet intentions, discussed it with his staff and read excerpts from it aloud to the National Security Council.

Moscow had its own euphoria in January 1961, and the Khrushchev speech gave it truculent expression. The Soviet leader undoubtedly felt then and for the rest of the year, as he could never feel again, that communism was riding the crest of history. Since the death of Stalin, the end of the Korean War and the relaxation of the western rearmament drive, one event after another had strengthened the conviction of inevitable victory. The Soviet rate of industrial growth had been considerably higher than that of the United States. Success in developing the hydrogen bomb and surpassing America in long-range missiles gave the Soviet leaders confidence in their own technological prowess as well as assurance against foreign attack. At the same time, the revolutionary ferment in the underdeveloped countries from Vietnam to Cuba seemed to foreshadow the humiliation of the 'imperialist' powers and the passage of the third world into the communist camp. Now, Krushchev's oration sounded a brutal joy over a world where democracy was everywhere on the retreat and communism everywhere on the march.

He began by saying that "analysis of the world situation as it appeared at the beginning of the sixties" showed a state of affairs which "greatly exceeded the boldest and most optimistic predictions and expectations." History and communism were inseparable partners: "there is no longer any force in the world capable of barring the road to socialism." He then reviewed the possible ways to triumph. World wars and "local wars" he categorically rejected as leading directly or progressively to nuclear holocaust. "Wars of liberation or popular uprisings" were quite another matter. He defined "national-liberation wars" as those "which began as uprisings of colonial peoples against their oppressors [and] developed into guerrilla wars." "...The Communists support just wars of this kind wholeheartedly and without reservation and they march in the van of the peoples fighting for liberation." He named Cuba, Vietnam and Algeria as examples and added that the "multiplying of the forces of the national-liberation movement" in recent years stemmed largely from the opening of the new front against American imperialism in Latin America. As for "peaceful coexistence," this was, "so far as its social content is concerned, a form of intense economic, political and ideological struggle between the proletariat and the aggressive forces of imperialism in the world arena."

In a significant aside Khrushchev brought up Berlin. "The positions of the U.S.A., Britain and France have proved to be especially vulnerable in West Berlin," he said. "These powers ... cannot fail to realize that sooner or later the occupation regime in that city must be ended. It is necessary to go ahead with bringing the aggressive-minded imperialists to their senses, and compelling them to reckon with the real situation. And should they balk, then we will take resolute measures, we will sign a peace treaty with the German Democratic Republic."

Kennedy, reading the speech, accepted Khrushchev's rejection of nuclear war as honest enough; any other position in the President's view would have been mad. But the bellicose confidence which surged through the rest of the speech and especially the declared faith in victory through rebellion, subversion and guerrilla warfare alarmed Kennedy more than Moscow's amiable signals assuaged him. The references to Russia and China in his State of the Union message constituted Kennedy's response. "We must never be lulled," he said, "into believing that either power has yielded its ambitions for world domination—ambitions which they forcefully restated only a short time ago. On the contrary, our task is to convince them that aggression and subversion will not be profitable routes to pursue these ends." He added: "Open and peaceful competition—for prestige, for markets, for scientific achievement, even for men's minds—is something else again. For if Freedom and Communism were to compete for man's allegiance in a world at peace, I would look to the future with ever increasing confidence."

He designed these last words to help bring things into proportion. For the Khrushchev speech, though sufficiently tough, confined its bellicosity in the main to the underdeveloped world; and here, as Kennedy understood, the Russians were confronted by opportunities which they could not easily resist. Discussing the speech one day with Lippmann, Kennedy observed that, while Khrushchev sounded like a committed revolutionist, he would not press revolution to the point where it might threaten nuclear war. Kennedy consequently persevered in his task of de-emotionalizing the cold war at home.

Ambassador Thompson came home from Moscow in February, and Kennedy soon summoned him along with three former ambassadors to Russia—Harriman, Bohlen and George Kennan—for an extended discussion at the White House of Soviet problems. The new President, saying little himself, threw out questions to stimulate the experts. Finally he wondered aloud whether he should not consider a meeting with Khrushchev. The experts agreed that a face-to-face talk might be a good idea. Thompson carried back to Moscow a presidential letter suggesting a rendezvous in the late spring at Vienna or Stockholm. The Soviet leader, though showing no inclination to yield on issues, appeared pleased at the prospect of a meeting.

But already hopes for better relations were beginning to fade. One could have expected Moscow to continue its support for what it considered a national-liberation war in Laos, but the bleak Russian reaction to the new test ban proposals in Geneva was unexpected. When Ambassador Arthur H. Dean set forth the revised Anglo-American position in March, the Soviet representative, instead of welcoming an obvious attempt to resolve outstanding differences, responded by withdrawing Soviet assent to points already agreed upon and by introducing an unacceptable new proposal—that the organization policing the ban be directed by a tripartite board, representing the Soviet Union, the democracies and the neutrals, and required to act in unanimity. The troika doctrine meant, in effect, a Soviet veto on the verification process. It would have made the ban a farce, and the proposal ended any immediate prospect of agreement.

2. STATE OF THE NATION'S DEFENSE

The policy of probing around the edges would work in any case, Kennedy believed, only so long as the United States preserved its capacity to hold firm. This meant the existence of military power sufficient to restrain the Soviet Union from aggression. The next problem then was the condition of American defenses and the purpose of American strategy. In the years when the United States had a nuclear monopoly, the problem of American strategy did not at first appear very complicated. The atomic bomb and the Strategic Air Command were supposed to insure military supremacy; and, so long as they were adequately nourished, the rest of the military establishment did not much matter. But once the Soviet Union achieved its first nuclear explosion in 1949, the United States had to face a world where its adversary had the terrible new weapons too. This event accelerated a re-examination of strategy already under way within the Truman administration. Led by Paul Nitze, who was then head of policy planning in the State Department, this process resulted in the adoption by the National Security Council in 1950 of a paper known familiarly thereafter as NSC 68. This paper predicted that by 1954 the Soviet Union would have the capacity to launch a nuclear attack on the United States, that this would sufficiently offset American nuclear power to free the Communists for a variety of types of aggression, and that to discourage sub-nuclear forms of aggression the United States must not only continue to build its nuclear strength but must greatly expand its ability to fight non-nuclear wars.

Through the same winter of 1949–50, a number of members of the Harvard and Massachusetts Institute of Technology faculties had been independently discussing the same issues in regular Sunday-morning meetings. The sessions had taken place at the initiative of two MIT scientists, Jerrold R. Zacharias

JOHN FOSTER DULLES.

and Jerome B. Wiesner, who had been involved in weapons problems since the Second World War. What made this more than an academic exercise eleven years later was the fact that, among the members, Wiesner was now Science Adviser to President Kennedy, McGeorge Bundy was now Special Assistant on National Security Affairs and Carl Kaysen was Bundy's deputy for military and strategic matters. Kenneth Galbraith, Seymour Harris and I were also in the group, though this mattered less for the defense policy of the Kennedy administration.

In 1950, it was a dark and fascinating education for the nonscientists; and it resulted in a statement which appeared in the *New York Times* on May 1 of that year. "We believe," the eighteen signers wrote, "that our present strategic position is founded on a misplaced faith in atomic weapons and strategic bombing." This strategy, the statement said, provided the United States with no effective answer to limited aggression except the wholly disproportionate answer of atomic war. As a result, it invited Moscow to use the weapons of "guerrilla warfare and internal revolt in marginal areas in the confidence that such local activity would incur only local risks." In addition, continuing reliance on the bomb indicated to the world that American strategy was based on "the principle of mass destruction of human life," an idea which would lead to a misconstruction of American motives and resentment of American power. And, to the extent that the United States placed reliance on the bomb, an agreement restricting the use of atomic weapons would, in effect, constitute unilateral disarmament; only as we liberated our strategy from its bondage to atomic weapons could we press for international controls. In place of the atom-oriented, all-or-nothing strategy, the signers urged the strengthening of the ground Army, tactical air, air transport, and various specialized forces. "The United States," the statement concluded, "can ill afford a strategy ... which might doom it to the fearful choice between worldwide mass destruction, on the one hand, and outright military defeat, on the other."

The point became grimly evident with the outbreak of the Korean War a few weeks later; it seemed almost as if the Soviet leaders had reached the same conclusion as the drafters of NSC 68 and the Harvard-MIT group. Our unbalanced defense quite possibly persuaded the Kremlin that it could risk countenancing (or inciting) satellite aggression in an area like Korea, where the assault would be too serious for the conventional forces of the United States and not serious enough for nuclear war.

Then the end of the Korean War produced another spasm of reappraisal—this time by an administration dedicated to the thesis that the foundation of military strength was economic strength and the foundation of economic strength a balanced budget. Since preparation for conventional war cost more than nuclear arms and, if a choice had to be made, contributed less to the nation's security, the Eisenhower administration reverted to the thesis of the Truman administration in the carefree days of the American atomic monopoly and decided to place predominant reliance once again on nuclear weapons.

John Foster Dulles summed up the new policy when he propounded the doctrine of massive retaliation, declaring that the United States had abandoned the "traditional" policy of "meeting aggression by direct and local opposition" and would depend in the future "primarily upon a great capacity to retaliate, instantly, by means and at places of our choosing." This seemed to mean that the United States intended to counter local aggression, not by limited war, but by nuclear strikes against the Soviet Union or China. The threat of massive retaliation may not have terrified the Russians and Chinese, but it did terrify a good many Americans. For the United States no longer enjoyed its atomic monopoly; this was not the world of 1948. As our strategy, in Pentagonese, 'lost credibility,' it might well embolden the communists to new experiments in piecemeal aggression. This was the strong view taken by the service whose mission, money and traditions were most threatened by the new doctrine—the Army.

In the meantime critics outside the government were also emphasizing the dangers of the all-or-nothing policy. In 1958 Kennedy summed up the case in the Senate. The commitment to massive retaliation, he said, was producing a Maginotline mentality—a "dependence upon a strategy which may collapse or may never be used, but which meanwhile prevents the consideration of any alternative." The most likely threat, he said, was, not nuclear attack, but "Sputnik diplomacy, limited brushfire wars, indirect non-overt aggression, intimidation and subversion, internal revolution ... a thrust more difficult to interpret and oppose, yet inevitably ending in our isolation, submission, or destruction." Though the capacity for massive retaliation, he declared a year later, provided the only answer to the threat of nuclear war, "it is not the only answer to all threats of Communist aggression." "We have been driving ourselves into a corner," Kennedy said, "where the only choice is all or nothing at all, world devastation or submission." The way out was to enlarge the range of choice by

JEROME B. WEISNER.

strengthening and modernizing the nation's ability to wage non-nuclear war.

McNamara, as Secretary of Defense in the Kennedy administration, thus inherited a clear-cut strategic perspective—one which, it should be added, he firmly embraced on its merits—when he turned his appraising eye on the state of the national defenses.

3. THE OCCUPATION OF THE PENTAGON

McNamara brought striking gifts to his new responsibility—an inquiring and incisive mind, a limitless capacity for work and a personality which lacked pretense and detested it in others. But, more than this, he brought new techniques of large-scale management. McNamara appeared at a moment of intellectual and administrative crisis in defense affairs. The military establishment had now grown into a small empire. A third of the states in the United Nations had smaller populations than the American Department of Defense, and only a few had larger budgets. Defense operated enormous complexes of transport, communications, procurement, maintenance and distribution as well as of tanks, ships, planes and men. It made a multiplicity of fateful choices in the determination of strategy, the selection of weapons systems, the design of forces and the level of expenditure. Its decisions affected everything from the economy of San Diego to the destiny of mankind.

It had been, however, an empire without an emperor. Generals, admirals, scientists, administrators and Secretaries of Defense all had tried in vain to catch hold of the defense process as it hurtled along. By now it had acquired a dreadful momentum of its own; its direction, such as it was, was determined by a bewildering mixture of internal intrigues and extraneous pressures; and it was producing a set of unanticipated side effects on domestic and foreign policy. After eight years in the White House, even Eisenhower came to feel that something was wrong and issued his unexpected warning against "the acquisition of unwarranted influence, whether sought or unsought, by the military-industrial complex." Still, the military-industrial complex was more a consequence than a cause of the problem. The cause lay in the feebleness of civilian control of the military establishment; and this feebleness was the result in great part of the absence of rational understanding and hence of rational direction.

While technology and science were creating the problem, they were also creating a hope for its solution, or at least for its mitigation. The Second World War had made the scientist a partner, if for a time a suspect and scorned partner, in the enterprise of defense; the nuclear age made the association irrevocable. For better or worse, a new generation of military intellectuals was revolutionizing what had once been the art of strategy. The essence of their effort was the application of systematic quantitative analysis to strategic decisions. Operations research, as it was called, had begun during the Second World War, and was quick to demonstrate that there could be a variety of ways to achieve a desired end, and this both speeded the pace of innovation and left the military even further behind.

The Rand ("*r*esearch *and* *d*evelopment") Corporation, established by the Air Force in California after the war, provided the model of the new military-intellectual establishment. Scientists and economists invented new techniques of systems analysis, linear and dynamic programming and game theory, devising ingenious tools by which to formulate problems, break them down, distinguish alternatives, establish their quantitative equivalents, compare the effects of different decisions and seek the most favorable results in situations characterized by a great mass of variables. The electronic computer became an indispensable part of the machinery of national strategy. The strategy intellectuals did not claim infallibility for their black arts, knowing that some intangibles would always defy rigorous, quantitative analysis. Yet these techniques gave civil government the means of subjecting the anarchy of defense to a measure of order.

McNamara had been fascinated by the intellectual problem of administering large organizations since his days as a student and teacher of statistical control in the Harvard Business School and his experience as a junior officer in the

Pentagon during the war. The quest for control required in his judgment two things: the use of analysis to force alternative programs to the surface and the definition of the 'options' in quantitative terms in order to facilitate choice. He had no illusions about the difficulties of his quest. The Department had already balked, thwarted, exposed and broken a succession of able men imprudent enough to accept appointment as Secretary. "This place is a jungle—a jungle," McNamara himself cried in his first weeks. But nothing had ever defeated him yet; and he believed that the only way the Secretary could achieve control was through a new theory of the job—conceiving his responsibility not as that of a judge, reviewing and reconciling recommendations made to him by the services, but of an executive, aggressively questioning, goading, demanding and leading. The emergence during the fifties of the scientific-technological elite now gave him the men with whom to begin the reconquest of the Pentagon. The computer was his ally in making options precise.

Khrushchev's January speech made emphatic the point often expressed by Eisenhower during his Presidency—the impossibility of total nuclear war as an instrument of rational policy. Kennedy now charged McNamara with the problem of devising strategies to deal with a world in which total nuclear war was no longer conceivable. This called for a shift from massive retaliation to a capability for controlled and flexible response, graduated to meet a variety of levels and forms of aggression.

The legacy of armed force bequeathed by the Eisenhower administration followed from the belief that the all-out nuclear response was all that mattered. McNamara found a total of fourteen Army divisions, of which only eleven were ready for combat. Of the eleven, only three were deployed in the United States. Kennedy was appalled to discover a few weeks after the inauguration that, if he sent 10,000 men to southeast Asia, he would deplete the strategic reserve and have virtually nothing left for emergencies elsewhere. Indeed, the United States could not even have invaded Cuba after the Bay of Pigs without drawing troops from other parts of the world and thereby inviting communist moves on other fronts. Equipment was so low that, when Kennedy inspected the 82nd Airborne at Fort Bragg in October, the division had to borrow men and material to bring itself up to complement. The Army could hardly fight longer than a few weeks before running short on ammunition, nor was new production set to remedy the deficiencies. Tactical air power was also grievously weak. When McNamara demanded a demonstration of tactical air support of ground troops, the Air Force actually had to borrow certain types of ordnance from the Navy.

Even the nuclear striking power hardly constituted an invulnerable deterrent. The Strategic Air Command was almost entirely concentrated on about sixty bases, of which only a few were 'hardened' (i.e., capable of surviving nuclear attack) and only a third were on alert. They were, in other words, highly vulnerable to a surprise missile strike.

4. THE RECONSTRUCTION OF NATIONAL STRATEGY

These discoveries shocked McNamara. The United States, for all its splendid capacity to blow up the world, had, it was obvious, an entirely inadequate amount of what McNamara called "usable power"—military force capable of serving reasonable ends. The President, who was perhaps less surprised, directed him to begin the work of building a military establishment versatile enough to meet the full spectrum of possible threats from guerrilla infiltration to nuclear holocaust. Only such a force, Kennedy believed, could give his foreign policy a solid foundation and liberate diplomacy from the constraints imposed by a rigid military strategy.

As McNamara began his review, one fear which had affected the polemics, though not the essence, of the party debate on defense policy now dropped out of the picture. The idea of a 'missile gap' had been first set forth publicly by Eisenhower's second Secretary of Defense, Neil McElroy, who forecast in 1959 that the Soviet Union would probably have a 3–1 superiority in intercontinental ballistic missiles by the early sixties. This estimate rested on the best intelligence then available and was shared by various military experts, who conveyed it to Stuart Symington, Kennedy and other Senators. By 1960 it was a staple of Democratic oratory. But new intelligence methods and sources cast doubt on the estimate in the winter of 1960–61; Jerome Wiesner had long been skeptical, and in February McNamara, in a candid background talk to newspapermen, was ready to dismiss the gap as an illusion.

On March 1, McNamara mounted his first major assault on the Pentagon, firing a fusillade of ninety-six questions, each aimed at a specific area, directed to a specific man and requiring a specific answer by a specific time. He wanted to know what the military were doing, why they thought they were doing it and whether there was not a more economical and efficient way of achieving the same result. No one had asked such questions before.

By March 28 the review had advanced sufficiently for Kennedy to send a special message asking Congress for an additional $650 million for the defense budget. He then proposed a series of measures to improve the national ability to deter or restrict limited wars, including the expansion of guerrilla warfare units, as well as other measures to improve

ROBERT MCNAMARA TAKING QUESTIONS AT A MAY 26, 1961 PRESS CONFERENCE.

and protect the strategic deterrent and defenses. A third message "on urgent national needs," delivered in late May, a month after the Bay of Pigs and responding to Soviet success in space—Yuri Gagarin's orbital flight around the planet in early April—called for a vastly enlarged effort in space, including landing a man on the moon by 1970. Kennedy also requested "a further reinforcement of our own capacity to deter or resist non-nuclear aggression"—greater modernization of conventional forces, greater mobility and more training in paramilitary warfare. The work of reconstructing American defense strategy had only begun. Difficult problems of doctrine remained—the proper composition and function of the nuclear deterrent, for example. Difficult problems of command and control were yet to be solved. Morale in the Pentagon itself was also shaken by the new approach.

Within the White House McNamara's directness, intelligence and decisiveness immediately won the complete and lasting confidence of the President. The Secretary also quickly achieved an effective relationship with Jerome Wiesner who had fought hard through the fifties to improve the state of American defense and whose work on the Gaither committee of 1957 had prepared the ground for McNamara's reconstruction of strategy now. McGeorge Bundy also kept an alert eye on the evolution of defense policy; and both Bundy's and Wiesner's hands were strengthened when Carl Kaysen, a Harvard economist who united cogency as a debater and intrepidity as an operator, joined the National Security Council staff.

XIII. LEGACY IN SOUTHEAST ASIA

THE REORGANIZATION OF national defense was not merely a theoretical issue. For the communist challenge was already taking acute form in Southeast Asia. Communist guerrillas—the Viet Cong in South Vietnam, the Pathet Lao in Laos—were conducting savage and elusive warfare against pro-western regimes. When Kennedy had met with Eisenhower just before the inauguration, they spent more time talking about Laos than anything else. The situation in Vietnam was almost as bad. On February 2, Walt Rostow gave the President a memorandum about Vietnam written by Brigadier General Edward Lansdale, an imaginative officer who had worked with Magsaysay in ending the guerrilla action of the Hukbalahaps in the Philippines. Kennedy read it in Rostow's presence and said, "This is the worst yet." Then he added, "You know, Ike never briefed me about Vietnam."

1. KENNEDY AND SOUTHEAST ASIA

He was not unfamiliar with the territory. He had gone to Southeast Asia in 1951 when Laos, Cambodia and Vietnam were all part of French Indochina. In Saigon he discovered an acquaintance in the counselor of the American legation—a Foreign Service officer named Edward Gullion who had briefed him in the past on foreign policy. At the time, the official United States line was uncritical support for the French in their struggle against the Vietnamese nationalists. Kennedy had asked sharply why the Vietnamese should be expected to fight to keep their country part of France.

"In Indochina," Kennedy said on his return to Washington, "we have allied ourselves to the desperate effort of a French regime to hang on to the remnants of empire.... To check the southern drive of communism makes sense but not only through reliance on the force of arms. The task is rather to build strong native non-Communist sentiment within these areas and rely on that as a spearhead of defense rather than upon the legions of General de Lattre. To go this apart from and in defiance of innately nationalistic aims spells foredoomed failure." The trip gave Kennedy both a new sympathy for the problems of Asia and a new understanding of the power of nationalism in the underdeveloped world.

By early 1954 the French, who had persisted in their effort to fight a European war in the jungle, found themselves under siege in the fortress of Dien Bien Phu. When the French commander at Dien Bien Phu pleaded for American support, Dulles, forgetting massive retaliation, proposed an allied air strike at Dien Bien Phu to Sir Anthony Eden the British Foreign Minister. "I am fairly hardened to crises," Eden, wrote later, "but I went to bed that night a troubled man. I did not believe that anything less than intervention on a Korean scale, if that, would have any effect in Indochina." In Washington Vice-President Nixon suggested the possibility of "putting American boys in."

On April 6 Kennedy observed in the Senate that, if the American people were to go to war for the fourth time in the century, "particularly a war which we now realize would threaten the survival of civilization," they had a right to inquire in detail into the nature of the struggle and the possible alternatives. He cited a garland of optimistic statements about Indochina and contrasted this gush of official optimism with the grim actuality. "I am frankly of the belief," Kennedy said, "that no amount of American military assistance in Indochina can conquer...'an enemy of the people' which has the sympathy and covert support of the people.... For the United States to intervene unilaterally and to send troops into the most difficult terrain in the world, with the Chinese able to pour in unlimited manpower, would mean that we would face a situation which would be far more difficult than even that we encountered in Korea." He saw no hope for Indochina until the French granted the Vietnamese their independence.

The opposition of the congressional leaders, of General

Ridgway, of the British and eventually of President Eisenhower himself forced Dulles to drop the plan of intervention. "I trust," Kennedy said later, "the United States has learned that it cannot ignore the moral and ideological principles at the root of today's struggles." The French abandoned the fight after the surrender of Dien Bien Phu; and negotiations in Geneva, in which the United States ostentatiously took no part, soon resulted in an agreement to divide Vietnam at the 17th parallel and to ratify the independence of Laos and Cambodia.

Diem returned to Saigon in June as prime minister and within eighteen months was president. The French were skeptical about Diem, nor was he precisely, as Justice Douglas suggested, "revered" by the Vietnamese people. But he was remembered and respected as one of the first Indochinese nationalists. The United States now offered his government substantial economic assistance, and for the next few years South Vietnam enjoyed a significant measure of growth and reform. Then in the late fifties the guerrilla war began again. In spite of his economic successes, Diem, a man of austere and authoritarian temperament who preferred to govern through his immediate family, had failed to develop a solid basis of popular support. By 1961 the Viet Cong guerrillas, backed by Ho Chi Minh's Viet Minh in the north, roamed through large areas of the countryside, sometimes very near Saigon itself, murdering local officials, harassing government troops and placing the Diem regime in jeopardy.

2. THE DILEMMA OF LAOS

Propects in South Vietnam, however, were favorable compared to those in Laos. This curious land of perhaps two million inhabitants—no one knew how many—lay between Vietnam and Thailand along the east bank of the Mekong River and wandered into mountains farther to the north. It was a state by diplomatic courtesy. Though a royal family sat in Luang Prabang, the Lao, a relaxed and lackadaisical people, lacked the nationalist frenzy; and the hill tribes, untouched by the revolution of rising expectations, hardly knew that they lived in a new nation or cared who their rulers might be. As Buddhists, the Lao favored contemplation and disliked killing. Their ambition was to be let alone to enjoy themselves. Politics was reserved for a small elite, largely related to each other, who had begun a movement for independence at the end of the Second World War. When the French came back in 1946, some of these went into exile. Most returned in 1949, except for Prince Souphanouvong who joined Ho Chi Minh in North Vietnam and formed the Pathet Lao ("Land of the Lao") to free Laos from the imperialists. His half brother Prince Souvanna Phouma soon became head of the regular government at Vientiane. In 1953 the Pathet Lao, with Viet Minh support, occupied two provinces in northeastern Laos. The Geneva Agreement now called for a ceasefire and for the reintegration of the Pathet Lao into what was optimistically termed the 'national community.' Provisions against foreign military aid and bases, even though qualified to permit exceptions for purposes of defense, implied a desire to keep Laos out of the cold war—a policy explicitly avowed by Prince Souvanna as prime minister.

But the Laotian ambition for a quiet life was to be further disturbed. For Laos had an evident strategic importance. If the Communists gained possession of the Mekong valley, they could materially intensify their pressure against South Vietnam and Thailand. If Laos was not precisely a dagger pointed at the heart of Kansas, it was very plainly a gateway to Southeast Asia. As the French prepared to depart, Dulles performed his usual incantations and devised a new military pact—the Southeast Asia Treaty Organization (SEATO)—including three Asian states (Thailand, Pakistan and the Philippines) with the United States, Britain, France, Australia and New Zealand. A special protocol extended the protecting arm of the organization around South Vietnam, Cambodia and Laos. The Dulles plan for military containment required Laos to become a 'bulwark against communism' and a 'bastion of freedom.' As part of this program, Laos was expected to build an army of 25,000 men—a State Department idea which the Defense Department had originally opposed as ridiculous.

In pursuit of this dream, the United States flooded the wild and primitive land with nearly $300 million by the end of

COMMUNIST TROOPS DURING A MILITARY EXERCISE IN LAOS IN 1959.

1960. This amounted to $150 for every inhabitant—more aid per capita than any other country and almost double the previous per capita income of the Laotians. It was a misbegotten investment. Laos simply did not have the national or social structure to absorb the remorseless flood of American bounty. Instead of lifting living standards or even producing military force, aid led to unimaginable bribery, graft, currency manipulation and waste. Expensive motor cars thronged the dusty streets of Vientiane. As money flowed into Vientiane, the gap widened between the capital and the countryside. The Pathet Lao, speaking out for virtue and the people, gathered strength in the villages. Prince Souvanna Phouma, seeking the reintegration of the dissidents, conducted long talks with his half brother. In November 1957 they finally negotiated the Vientiane Agreements providing for a neutral Laos under a coalition government. The Pathet Lao were to be incorporated in the army and the cabinet, Souphanouvong himself becoming Minister of Economic Planning.

The Eisenhower administration watched the developments within its bastion with alarm. In 1958 Washington decided to install a reliably pro-western regime. CIA spooks put in their appearance, set up a Committee for the Defense of the National Interests (CDNI) and brought back from France as its chief an energetic, ambitious and devious officer named Phoumi Nosavan. Prince Souvanna, who had shown himself an honest and respected if impulsive leader, was forced out of office; a veteran politician named Phoui Sananikoune took his place. In 1959 the State Department backed Phoui, but the CIA preferred Phoumi. In time, Phoui was overthrown, and Phoumi now was in control. Prince Souphanouvong was in jail (from which, after winning over his guards, he soon escaped to the north). The Pathet Lao took to the hills and resumed the civil war.

During early 1960 Phoumi dominated non-communist Laos. Recognizing that Defense and CIA were committed to him, he felt free to ignore their advice. In August a new figure entered the drama. Kong Le, a young paratroop captain, was a simple man, without ambition for himself, who wanted to end domestic corruption and foreign intervention and bring peace to his people. One day when most of the government was out of town he seized power and asked Prince Souvanna to form a new government. Souvanna's aim as ever was to establish a neutralist regime; and he sought a coalition with the right in order to bargain with the Pathet Lao. Winthrop Brown, who had recently arrived in Vientiane as American Ambassador, supported the idea of bringing Souvanna and Phoumi together. The proper strategy, as he saw it, was to associate the neutralists and the anti-communists in the defense of a neutral Laos against the Pathet Lao. A united embassy, including CIA, followed Brown in recommending that Washington accept the coalition. But Kong Le opposed the inclusion of Phoumi; and Phoumi himself began to play for United States backing. For its part, the Bureau of Far Eastern Affairs in Washington considered Kong Le a probable communist and looked with great dubiety on the neutralist solution.

As for the Defense Department, it was all for Phoumi. Possibly with encouragement from Defense and CIA men in the field, Phoumi took the Royal Laotian Army to Svannakhet in September, proclaimed a new government and denounced Souvanna. The Phoumi regime became the recipient of American military aid, while the Souvanna government in Vientiane continued to receive economic aid. Ambassador Brown still worked to bring them together, but the military support convinced Phoumi that, if he only held out, Washington would put him in power.

At the working level in Washington doubts were beginning to rise. Some people in State thought that a 'military' (i.e., Phoumi) solution would work only if in the end we were ready to send in American troops. If we were not ready to do this, then should we not try for a 'political' (i.e., Souvanna) solution? Defense backed away from the idea of American troops but not from Phoumi. The Eisenhower team concept required that State's instructions be cleared through Defense, which led to long delays and sometimes contradictory instructions. The British and French favored Souvanna and did not want SEATO involved in a fight to put Phoumi in power. President Diem in Vietnam and Marshal Sarit in Thailand favored Phoumi lest neutralization threaten their own lands; Sarit even imposed a blockade on goods to Vientiane.

In October Eisenhower dispatched J. Graham Parsons to Laos in a strange effort to put intense pressure on Souvanna to forsake neutralism, accept Phoumi and make Laos a bastion of freedom again. Souvanna's lack of enthusiasm about these suggestions confirmed Washington's mistrust of him. Soon, sensing that Washington was preparing to dump him, Souvanna turned to the Russians, who established an embassy in Vientiane and instituted an airlift from Hanoi—first rice and oil; later guns.

In December, a few weeks after the election, Phoumi marched on Vientiane and with plans drawn up by his American advisers won the only military victory of his life. Souvanna fled to Cambodia and soon after came to terms with Souphanouvong, while Kong Le and his troops, leaving

KENNEDY MEETS WITH THE U.S. AMBASSADOR TO LAOS, LEONARD UNGER.

Vientiane in American trucks loaded with American supplies, joined up with the Pathet Lao in the field. Moscow and Peking continued to recognize the Souvanna regime as the true government of Laos. Winthrop Brown's hope of uniting the neutralists and the right against the communists had been thwarted. Instead, the Eisenhower administration, by rejecting the neutralist alternative, had driven the neutralists into reluctant alliance with the communists and provoked (and in many eyes legitimatized) open Soviet aid to the Pathet Lao. And all this was done without serious consultation with the incoming administration which would shortly inherit the problem.

The British, alarmed by this result, now bestirred themselves, sending a note to the Soviet Union in early January 1961 urging a revival of the International Control Commission in Laos. The State Department said publicly that the United States "had no desire to establish a western military position in Laos" and expressed readiness to accept a revived ICC if the Laotians wanted it. In the meantime, in Laos itself the civil war had succumbed to the national indolence.

3. THE RIDDLE OF INTERVENTION

The new President had a clear historical view of Laos. He thought that this was not a land "worthy of engaging the attention of great powers," that the effort to transform it into a pro-western redoubt had been ridiculous and that neutralization was the correct policy. But he knew that the matter was not that simple any longer. For the effort had been made, American prestige was deeply involved, and extrication would not be easy. To strive now for neutralization it was essential to convince the Pathet Lao that they could not win and to dissuade the Russians from further military assistance. In view of the pacifist inclinations of the Royal Laotian Army, moreover, it would be hard to induce the Pathet Lao to call off the war. And Phoumi himself, still receiving American military assistance, supposed that Washington would back his regime to the end. This made him more defiant and unmanageable than ever. One American official observed that he was behaving like a kid out of *West Side Story*.

In his first press conference Kennedy announced his hope for the establishment of Laos as "a peaceful country—an independent country not dominated by either side." This policy became an engrossing personal concern. In the first two months of his administration he probably spent more time on Laos than on anything else. Determined to lift the problem out of the slow-moving machinery of government, he established a Laos task force and sent word to the first meeting that he wanted daily reports on its progress. The change in Washington was instantly reflected in the instructions to the field. Instead of the confused and murky cables of a short while before, the embassy received straight orders and clear answers.

In early February Phoumi set out on a new campaign but his Royal Laotian Army retreated after a series of minor skirmishes. This fiasco confirmed Kennedy's impression of Phoumi's singular incompetence. He now decided that Laos must have a coalition of the sort that Eisenhower's State Department had vetoed six months before. In early March the Pathet Lao were ready to take the offensive. The Royal Laotian Army began a circumspect withdrawal, and the Mekong valley itself was threatened. The Pathet Lao attack put the crisis in bleak outline. The peace plan had failed, the pro-western Laotians were in retreat, the Russians were increasing their military support, the British and French were indifferent to everything except the thought of their own involvement, and the idea of an independent Laos seemed doomed.

There still remained the thin hope that the Russian interest sprang less from a desire to get in themselves than

PHOUMI NOSAVAN HEADED UP THE ROYAL LAOATION ARMY WITH BACKING FROM U.S. DEFENSE DEPARTMENT AND THE CIA.

THE THREE MAPS OF LAOS USED BY KENNEDY AT HIS PRESS CONFERENCE ON MARCH 23, 1961.

to keep the Chinese out and that they might eventually accept the policy of neutralization. But, as the Pathet Lao moved forward, it became a question whether Moscow could turn the local boys off even if it wanted to. In any case, the United States had no choice but to stiffen its position, whether in preparation for negotiation or for resistance. Dean Rusk made one more attempt to convince Andrei Gromyko, the Soviet Foreign Minister, of America's earnest desire for neutralization. Gromyko gave no ground, but Rusk may have got through better than he thought at the time. On March 20 Kennedy scheduled a National Security Council meeting on the problem.

The National Security Council discussed the possibility of moving a small number of American troops into the Mekong valley not to fight the Pathet Lao but to deter them by their presence and provide a bargaining counter for an international conference. The President himself was reluctant to order a limited troop movement into the Mekong. He knew how weak the conventional strength of the United States was, and, with Cuba in the wings, troubles in Vietnam and the Congo and the ever-present problem of Berlin, he did not wish to tie up armed force indefinitely in Laos. Moreover, the diplomatic road was not finally blocked. The British with Kennedy's strong approval were about to reintroduce the ICC plan along with a proposal for a conference in Geneva to be called after verification of a cease-fire in Laos.

Neither the meeting on March 20 nor another session the next day reached a decision. Kennedy's objective remained a political settlement. True, if the Russians remained intransigent, he might have to take the next step—a limited commitment of troops along the Mekong; and this might lead to further steps. But, unless the Russians believed that he was ready to go down this road, there would be no incentive for them to accept a political solution. As for the American people, Kennedy saw contradictions in their feelings between the desire to 'get tough' with the communists and the disinclination to get involved in another Asian war; still, if the worst came, he was confident that they would support intervention.

The problem now, in Kennedy's judgment, was to make Moscow understand the choice it confronted: cease-fire and neutralization on the one hand; American intervention on the other. On March 23 his press conference took place against the unusual background of three maps of Laos illustrating the progress of communist encroachment. The Soviet Union, he said, had flown more than 1000 sorties into the battle area since December. There could be no peaceful

solution without "a cessation of the present armed attacks by externally supported Communists." If the attacks do not stop, "those who support a genuinely neutral Laos will have to consider their response." As for the United States, no one should doubt its objective. "If in the past there has been any possible ground for misunderstanding of our desire for a truly neutral Laos, there should be none now." Nor should anyone doubt our resolution. "The security of all of southeast Asia will be endangered if Laos loses its neutral independence. Its own safety runs with the safety of us all—in real neutrality observed by all.... I know that every American will want his country to honor its obligations to the point that freedom and security of the free world and ourselves may be achieved."

His tone was grave; and he backed it up with military and diplomatic action, moving naval and ground forces into the area, and gaining assurances or support from other nations. In Washington the President saw Gromyko at the White House, took him to a bench in the Rose Garden and, observing that too many wars had arisen from miscalculation, said that Moscow must not misjudge the American determination to stop aggression in Southeast Asia. The sense of acute tension over Laos appeared to be subsiding. For his part Khrushchev had no desire to send Russian troops to fight in the jungles of Laos and even less to set off a nuclear war. Moreover, he could console himself, and hopefully the Pathet Lao, with the thought which had already occurred to Kennedy and which Khrushchev put to Llewellyn Thompson in an expansive moment: "Why take risks over Laos? It will fall into our laps like a ripe apple." After weighing these various factors, Khrushchev on April 1 expressed readiness in principle to consider the British proposal.

4. THE HUNDREDTH DAY

Kennedy had won his first objective. But Khrushchev was at first unwilling to call for a cease-fire as the condition of an international conference. For more than three weeks the British and the Russians debated this point. It is not clear whether Khrushchev was stalling because he wanted time to explain his policy to the Pathet Lao and the Chinese or because he wanted to give the neutralist and communist forces the chance to occupy as much of Laos as they could: probably for both reasons.

The fighting in these weeks made it more clear than ever that a cease-fire would mean little if Laos lacked a government strong and stable enough to deal with the Pathet Lao. Kennedy had come early to doubt the briefings he received about the virtues of General Phoumi. In February, David Ormsby Gore, now a Member of Parliament and an Under Secretary of State in the Foreign Office, stopped by in Washington and, speaking with the bluntness of an old friend, offered a caustic picture of American policy in Laos. The United States, he said, had done its best to destroy Souvanna Phouma, who represented the best hope of a non-communist Laos, and instead was backing a crooked, right-wing gang; the impression of Washington always rushing about to prop up corrupt dictators in Asia could not have happy consequences.

Then late in March Averell Harriman, on his first assignment as roving ambassador, arranged to see Souvanna Phouma in New Delhi. Souvanna said that the people of Laos did not wish to be communist and that Laos could be saved from communism, but that time was running out. He proposed the establishment of a coalition government, including the Pathet Lao, and the guarantee of Laotian neutrality by the fourteen-nation conference. He felt that, with the support of 90 percent of the people, he had the authority to unite his country. Harriman was favorably impressed, and Washington, or at the least the White House, found Averell's testimony weighty. The President concluded that Washington ought to take a new look at Souvanna, and the prince was encouraged to add the United States to his world tour.

Souvanna scheduled his Washington visit for April 19–20 but then canceled it when Rusk said he had a speaking engagement in Georgia and could not receive him. Snubbed again, as he thought, Souvanna returned to Moscow.

In the end Rusk did not keep his Georgia engagement, for this was the week of the Bay of Pigs. On Thursday, April 20, Kennedy, determined not to permit restraint in Cuba to be construed as irresolution everywhere, transformed the corps of American military advisers in Laos, who up to this point had wandered about in civilian clothes, into a Military Assistance and Advisory Group, authorizing them to put on uniforms and accompany the Laotian troops.

On April 24 the Russians finally agreed on the cease-fire appeal. The next day the Laotian government gratefully accepted the call. So did Souvanna, still on his travels, and even Souphanouvong. But fighting did not cease; and, according to reports reaching Washington on Wednesday, April 26, the Pathet Lao were attacking in force, as if to overrun the country before the cease-fire could take effect. On Thursday the National Security Council held a long and confused session. Walt Rostow has told me that it was the worst White House meeting he attended in the entire Kennedy administration.

Rostow and the Laos task force, supported by Harriman who was now on a trip of inspection in Laos, still urged a limited commitment of American troops to the Mekong valley. But the Joint Chiefs, chastened by the Bay of Pigs, declined to guarantee the success of the military operation, even with the 60,000 men they had recommended a month before. The participants in the meeting found it hard to make out what the Chiefs were trying to say. The military proved no more satisfactory in explaining the proposals they were prepared to make. The President was appalled at the sketchy nature of American military planning for Laos—the lack of detail and the unanswered questions.

For all their differences, the military left a predominant impression that they did not want ground troops at all unless they could send at least 140,000 men equipped with tactical nuclear weapons. By now the Pentagon was developing what would become its standard line in Southeast Asia—unrelenting opposition to limited intervention except on the impossible condition that the President agree in advance to every further step they deemed sequential, including, on occasion, nuclear bombing of Hanoi and even Peking. The Chiefs had their own way of reacting to the Cuban fiasco. It soon began to look to the White House as if they were taking care to build a record which would permit them to say that, whatever the President did, he acted against their advice. This had not yet been identified as a tactic, however, and in April 1961 their opposition to limited intervention had a powerful effect. The President encountered equally formidable opposition from congressional leaders. And there always remained the difficulty of justifying intervention against communism in Laos while rejecting it against communism in Cuba. But the President was determined to avert total collapse. He had, I believe, been prepared to undertake limited intervention in Laos before the Bay of Pigs, and he did not altogether exclude it now. Once again he ordered troops on the alert.

The Russians knew about the preparations, and they appeared to have their effect. On May 1 representatives of the warring factions negotiated a cease-fire. The International Control Commission arrived on the scene and reported on May 11 "a general and obvious discontinuance of hostilities." The next day the conference opened at Geneva to lay down the conditions for a neutralized Laos. April 30 marked the hundredth day of the Kennedy administration. Either Cuba or Laos by itself would have constituted a sufficient initiation into the horrors of the Presidency; but Kennedy endured both with customary composure.

This was a first experiment in Kennedy diplomacy under pressure, and it was marked by restraint of manner, toughness of intention and care to leave the adversary a way of escape without loss of face. Khrushchev, for his part, found himself involved with a group of local communist militants whose actions he could not entirely control and whose allegiance he sought in the struggle for the international communist movement. But he did not want war, and, once he believed that Kennedy would fight if pushed too far, he retreated to negotiation, confident that history would eventually deliver what opposition had temporarily denied. In retrospect, the Laos crisis of 1961 seems in some ways a dress rehearsal for the Cuban missile crisis of 1962.

5. COUNTERINSURGENCY

One quick effect of the Laos crisis was to lead the President to take up an old preoccupation from Senate days, now made more urgent by Khrushchev's January speech—the problem of countering guerrilla attack. If what he liked to call "the subterranean war" were to be the major form of communist aggression so long as the United States retained nuclear supremacy, then the Army must learn how to meet the guerrilla threat. The Philippines, Malaya and Greece showed that guerrilla warfare could be stopped, but not by close-order drill. In the next weeks and months he made anti-guerrilla instruction a personal project.

He asked General Clifton, his military aide, to bring in the Army's standard anti-guerrilla equipment, examined it with sorrow and ordered Army research and development to do better. Most important of all, he instructed the Special Warfare Center at Fort Bragg to expand its mission, which had hitherto been largely the training of cadres for action behind the lines in case of a third world war, in order to confront the existing challenge of guerrilla warfare in the jungles and hills of underdeveloped countries. Over the opposition of the Army bureaucracy, which abhorred separate elite commands on principle, he reinstated the SF green beret as the symbol of the new force.

With the President's detailed support, Major General William P. Yarborough made the Special Warfare Center into a vigorous and ingenious seminary in the new methods. Other centers were set up in Panama, Okinawa, Vietnam and West Germany. Eventually Foreign Service officers were even put through courses, sometimes of dubious value, in counterinsurgency methods. By the autumn of 1961 a Counter-Insurgency Committee under General Taylor set itself to developing the nation's capability for unconventional warfare.

There was, to be sure, a faddish aspect to this enthusiasm. Some of its advocates acted as if the delicate arts of blacking one's face and catching sentries by the throat in the night could by themselves eliminate the guerrilla threat. The President was under no such illusion. He insisted that the Special Forces be schooled in sanitation, teaching, bridge-building, medical care and the need for economic progress. I do not think he ever forgot Mao's warning that guerrilla action must fail "if its political objectives do not coincide with the aspirations of the people and their sympathy, cooperation and assistance cannot be gained." The problem of applying this maxim to Southeast Asia never ceased to trouble him.

XIV.
ENCOUNTER IN EUROPE

THE ONLY THING that really surprised us when we got into office," the President said late in May "was that things were just as bad as we had been saying they were; otherwise we have been enjoying it very much." The fragrant spring of 1961 found him, in spite of the trials of the first winter, in a cheerful mood. He had survived the crises of Cuba and of Laos. He had begun a reorganization of government which would enable him to meet crisis better in the future. He had watched Captain Alan Shepard improve the American position in space by rocketing 115 miles into the upper atmosphere. He was planning a trip to France to see General de Gaulle. And on May 12, he had received an unexpected reply from N. S. Khrushchev to his letter of February 22, reopening the question, presumed dead after the Bay of Pigs, of a meeting in Vienna in early June.

One event marred his buoyancy. In mid-May he went to Canada to return the visit that Prime Minister John Diefenbaker had paid him in Washington in February. At one point the President took part in a tree-planting ceremony in front of Government House. Forgetting to bend his knees and keep the shovel close to his body, he stood erect, held the shovel at arm's length and turned a few spadefuls of soil. A premonitory twinge deepened after a few hours into an acute and nagging ache. He had wrenched his back, severely straining the muscles so carefully restored in the years since he had first gone to Dr. Travell. The pain did not leave him for more than six months, and in the weeks of travel immediately ahead it was often sharp and exhausting.

1. BACKGROUND IN BERLIN

What had led Khruschev to renew the idea of a meeting with Kennedy? His letter, though noting his objections to the Bay of Pigs, reciprocated Kennedy's February hope for better relations and named Laos, disarmament and Germany as leading topics for an exchange of views. No doubt, like Kennedy, Khrushchev was curious about his adversary and eager to take his measure. No doubt too the Bay of Pigs had left him with an impression of the American President as an irresolute young man, incapable of the sort of drastic action Khrushchev himself had undertaken in Hungary; if this were so, then the Russian leader might hope to bully him in direct encounter as he had bullied so many other heads of state. More specifically, the occasion would give him a chance to resume the campaign, begun by Stalin thirteen years before, to drive the west out of Berlin.

For Khrushchev, the German question had become increasingly exasperating. In his speech of January 6, he had declared the allied position "especially vulnerable" in West Berlin, adding ominously that, if the democracies did not come to their senses and make the required adjustments, the Soviet Union would sign a peace treaty with the communist state of East Germany—an act which, in Khrushchev's view, would terminate the legal basis for the western presence in Berlin. That basis rested on the wartime agreements which divided Germany into four zones and established four-power control of the German capital. In 1945 these arrangements were intended only to tide things over until the wartime allies negotiated a final peace settlement with a post-Hitler German regime. But, as that hope perished with the spread of the cold war, the democratic allies and the Soviet Union began to convert their zones into separate German states—the Federal Republic in the west and the so-called Democratic Republic in the east. Only Berlin itself, though split into west and east sectors, retained four-power status. Situated in the midst of the Soviet zone, West Berlin, with its independent administration and its allied garrison, was now the last democratic outpost on the communist side of the Iron Curtain.

LEFT: KENNEDY WATCHES THE LAUNCH OF ALAN SHEPARD, THE FIRST MAN TO ORBIT THE EARTH, ON MAY 5, 1961. WITH HIM ARE THE FIRST LADY AND THE VICE PRESIDENT. THE AUTHOR CAN BE SEEN IN THE BACKGROUND WITH THE BOW TIE.

From an early point the Soviet Union had regarded the western presence in Berlin as intolerable. Khrushchev described West Berlin, according to mood, as a bone in the throat or a cancerous tumor. A few months after the first sputnik sailed through the skies, he took advantage of the changing balance of nuclear force to resume Stalin's 1948 campaign. This culminated in November 1958 in demands that the allied occupation end and West Berlin be made a demilitarized 'free city.' If the west did not accept the Soviet plan within six months, Khrushchev said, Russia would sign its own peace treaty with the Democratic Republic.

A number of motives evidently lay behind Khrushchev's action. Europe constituted the single anomaly in the picture which gave the Soviet leaders such satisfaction everywhere else they looked. In Asia, in Africa, in Latin America, in industrial growth, in space, communism was on the offensive. But in Europe communism had been in retreat ever since the late forties—from the time of the Marshall Plan and the organization of NATO. Not only had Western Europe recovered its economic and political vitality, but communist Eastern Europe had been shaken recurrently by revolts against Moscow—Yugoslavia in 1948, East Germany in 1953, Hungary in 1956. At the very least, Berlin offered the opportunity to consolidate the communist position in East Germany and legitimatize the existing territorial division of Europe. If Khrushchev could force the west to grant East Germany legal recognition, he would not only secure the status quo throughout Eastern Europe but would demoralize the West German government in Bonn, disrupt NATO, stop the momentum of western unification and regain the European offensive. And, if he attained his maximum objective and drove the allies out of Berlin, he would subject the west to a humiliation which would weaken it all around the globe and complete the alteration of the world balance of power.

The western leaders for their part found the 'free city' proposal unacceptable. Its practical effect would have been to place West Berlin at the mercy of East Germany and the Soviet Union. When Khrushchev made his American trip in 1959, Eisenhower therefore avoided the 'free city' idea. But he did accept the Soviet description of the Berlin situation as "abnormal" (as indeed it was, though it was not discreet to say so); and his administration soon laid certain concessions on the negotiating table, including limitations on the size of the western garrison as well as on democratic propaganda and intelligence activities. Khrushchev meanwhile postponed his six-month deadline.

As a Senator, Kennedy had repeatedly emphasized the gravity of the stakes in Berlin. In July 1960 he predicted on "Meet the Press" that by the next January or February Khrushchev would "face the next President of the United States with a very difficult decision, perhaps even an ultimatum on Berlin." He added: "We should make it very clear that we are not going to concede our position on Berlin, that we are going to meet our commitment to defend the liberty of the people of West Berlin, and that if Mr. Khrushchev pushes it to the ultimate, we are prepared to meet our obligation."

In the months after the U-2 incident and the collapse of the Paris summit, the Berlin problem seemed to subside. But it is evident that by 1961 local considerations in East Germany were giving Khrushchev an almost desperate feeling that he had to do something. He was, or claimed to be, afraid that West Germany was about to acquire nuclear weapons; and, as he told Walter Lippmann in the spring, he wanted to fix the status of Berlin and the two Germanys before Bonn, emboldened by possession of the bomb, could take advantage of the unsettled demarcation line to move against East Germany. Even worse was the rising stream of refugees fleeing from East Germany, now on the order of four thousand a week. The contrast between the glum and tacky despotism of East Berlin and the exuberant prosperity of West Berlin, with its gleaming new buildings, blazing lights and spirited intellectual life, was too much; and the resulting exodus not only made propaganda about the superiority of communism look foolish but was fast draining East Germany of the professionals and technicians so vital to its future. Indeed, the total population of East Germany declined by nearly two million between 1949 and mid-1961. If Khrushchev now moved against West Berlin, he could still hope to inflict a worldwide political and moral defeat on the democracies, and, even if he did not do this, he could at least stop the flight to the west and stabilize the territorial status quo in Europe.

He may conceivably too have had some genuine fears about the new American administration. Kennedy himself, with characteristic detachment, used to wonder later what had gone wrong in the spring of 1961. He thought at times that the March and May messages calling for an increased American defense effort might have sounded too threatening. It is possible that the acceleration of the Minuteman and Polaris programs had unintended effects in Moscow and that the Soviet leaders now saw no choice but to match the American build-up. In addition, Harriman in his March debut as roving ambassador had said that "all discussions in Berlin must begin from the start." This was a move to disengage Kennedy from the concessions the Eisenhower administration had made in 1959 and even more from the ones we had been informed Eisenhower

PRESIDENT JOHN F. KENNEDY AND PRESIDENT CHARLES DE GUALLE RIDE IN AN OPEN CAR THROUGH PLACE DE LA CONCORDE IN PARIS UPON KENNEDY'S ARRIVAL ON MAY 31, 1961.

was ready to make at the 1960 summit meeting in Paris; but Moscow no doubt read it as a hardening of American policy. Yet at the same time the Soviet signals were not, seen from Washington, very encouraging. Khrushchev's truculent speech of January preceded Kennedy's defense messages by many weeks; and his decision to move against West Berlin had ample explanation in his own problems and ambitions.

As for the President, he saw no sense in meeting Khrushchev unless something of substance was likely to result. When the Attorney General made this point to the Soviet Ambassador, he was given to understand that progress was entirely conceivable on Laos and on the test ban. Beyond these specific problems, the President was attracted by the meeting as offering an opportunity to define the framework for future American-Soviet relations. Kennedy saw the world as in a state of uncontrollable change, rushing in directions no one could foresee. The equilibrium of force, he believed, was now roughly in balance between the United States and the Soviet Union—if not in the sense of numerical parity, at least in the sense that neither could hope to destroy the other and emerge unscathed; and the overriding need, he felt, was to prevent direct confrontations between Russian and American power in the chaotic time ahead. He intended to propose, in effect, a standstill in the cold war so that neither great nuclear state, in the inevitable competition around the planet, would find itself committed to actions which would risk its essential security, threaten the existing balance of force or endanger world peace. In particular, if, as Ambassador Thompson's dispatches forecast, Khrushchev meant to get tough over Berlin, Kennedy wished to make clear, in a favorite Washington phrase that spring, that Khrushchev must not crowd him too much. With such thoughts in mind, Kennedy prepared to leave for Europe.

KENNEDY AND JACQUELINE ON THEIR FIRST EVENING IN PARIS.

2. INTERLUDE IN PARIS

General de Gaulle met the Kennedys at Orly and escorted them to their apartments at the Quai d'Orsay. Parisians lined the streets to admire the young couple and cheer the motorcade. As the presidential car moved through the Latin Quarter, American students enthusiastically waved a Harvard banner. On arrival Kennedy took a steaming bath to ease the pain of his back. Then he was almost immediately on his way again for his opening talk with the General.

Wasting little time in preliminaries, Kennedy cited Khrushchev's warnings to Thompson about Berlin. The problem, Kennedy said, was whether Khrushchev really believed in the firmness of the west; even President de Gaulle himself had recently questioned whether the United States was ready to defend Paris at the risk of the obliteration of New York. De Gaulle remarked that the west simply could not retreat; it could not withdraw its troops or accept obstacles to access or permit a change in the status of West Berlin. Make it clear, he advised Kennedy, that it was the Russians, and not the west, who sought a change; we were not asking for anything. The allies could not stop Khrushchev from signing whatever he wanted with East Germany, but no internal communist document could alter the status of Berlin. If Khrushchev wanted war, he must understand that he would have it at the first moment he used force against us. De Gaulle added that the West could not win a military victory in Berlin; Khrushchev must be made to recognize that fighting around Berlin would mean a general war. The General insisted again that this was the last thing Khrushchev wanted.

After luncheon Kennedy returned to the problem of how to convince the Russians that the west was in earnest.

The existing allied military plans, seemed to him inadequate. We must make our policy clear by action, Kennedy said, and Khrushchev must understand that, if necessary, we would go to nuclear war. De Gaulle, responding, put special emphasis on preparing for a new western airlift; after all, there could be no ambiguity when a plane was shot down. He also noted that Russia needed western trade and might be vulnerable to economic retaliation. The western position in Berlin, he said, was not so weak as people thought.

Kennedy turned the conversation to Laos. De Gaulle strongly supported the idea of a neutral coalition under Souvanna Phouma. In no case would the French dream of military intervention; but, when Kennedy argued that the threat of western intervention might be necessary to bring the communists to an agreement, de Gaulle said that he would not oppose the United States publicly. They talked for a moment about the tension between Peking and Moscow. Kennedy expressed doubts that the split would become acute until the west was forced out of the area; the rivalry between Caesar and Pompey, he recalled, came into the open only after they subdued their common enemies. Then they touched briefly on Africa, and de Gaulle reaffirmed French opposition to UN operations in the Congo.

As they prepared to break up, de Gaulle paused, charmingly cited the prerogatives of age and ventured to suggest that the President not pay too much attention to his advisers or give too much respect to the policies he had inherited. In the last analysis, the General said, what counted for every man was himself and his own judgment. He was expounding, of course, the Gaullist philosophy of leadership. His counsel, after the Bay of Pigs, fell on receptive ears.

The next morning the talks ranged from Latin America to Africa, dealing particularly with Angola, where Portugal was clinging to rigid colonial policies in the face of the native demand for self-government. After luncheon on June 1 Kennedy moved into trickier country and raised the problem of NATO. De Gaulle in a flow of felicitous exposition said that NATO was two things: an alliance and an organization in its present form had outlived its time. Its essence had been the defense of Europe by American nuclear weapons; its occasion, the weakness of the Western European states; its result, the integration under American leadership of European contributions to the American defense of Europe. But the world had changed. Washington no longer possessed its nuclear monopoly, and this fact reduced the value of the American nuclear sword. Moreover, America had commitments in all parts of the world. And in Europe the revival of national pride, especially in France, meant that integrated defense under American command was no longer

KENNEDY AND DE GAULLE STEP OUT AFTER TAKING A MEETING IN PARIS.

acceptable. The recent revolt of French generals against their government, de Gaulle said, was perhaps a result of the denationalization of defense; the generals, feeling no responsibility for the protection of France, felt no loyalty to the government of France. And the absence of national defense, he argued, weakened the alliance because only national motives could rally the full support of a population in a prolonged war. While France would do nothing to disrupt the existing organization during the Berlin crisis, the President must understand that it sought a different organization for the future. Since no one could be confident any longer that the United States would use nuclear weapons first, the future security of Europe had to be assured by European countries, not without the United States but not exclusively through the United States.

Kennedy responded with equal bluntness. For the United States, he said, the defense of Europe and of America was the same. American troops were stationed in Europe to remind Moscow that an attack on Europe automatically constituted an attack on America. If the Soviet Union threatened to overrun Western Europe, the United States was prepared to respond with nuclear weapons. The advantages were so great to the side which used nuclear weapons first, Kennedy emphasized, that the United States could not afford to hold

THE PRESIDENT AND FIRST LADY ON THEIR WAY TO A STATE DINNER IN THE HALL OF MIRRORS IN VERSAILLES.

back its nuclear arm even if the Russians used only conventional forces. If the European states built separate defense establishments, he added, this would create new problems; those states which had no nuclear weapons would be forced toward resentment and neutralism.

De Gaulle commented that all this would be fine if the Russians really believed that America would use its nuclear weapons in defense of other states; but he doubted whether Moscow did; he even doubted whether the Americans believed it. No state could be expected to place atomic weapons at the disposal of another state. That is why he did not ask the United States for atomic weapons or even for assistance in developing French atomic power. The United States, in his judgment, would use nuclear weapons only when its own territory was directly threatened; and why not? This was the way states behaved. France or Russia would do no differently. If Kennedy said that Americans regarded Europe and the United States as the same, "since you say so, Mr. President, I believe you," but could anyone be really certain? If he sat in Kennedy's place, de Gaulle said, he would not be certain himself when or where he intended to use these weapons. After all, had not the United States already raised the threshold—that is, postponed the point at which nuclear weapons were scheduled to come into play?

Kennedy explained that raising the threshold meant only making sure that local clashes would not lead to nuclear war; it meant not a decrease in commitment but an increase in control. Obviously any attack which challenged NATO would rise above the threshold. The General must understand that the United States, though isolationist as late as the Second World War, had changed. The American response to aggression in Korea should reassure our allies. Only as we strengthened confidence among ourselves could we convince Moscow that we would stand firm in Berlin.

At this point they adjourned; and that evening de Gaulle threw a dazzling dinner in the Hall of Mirrors at Versailles.

Jacqueline, fresh from a fascinating day with Malraux at the Jeu de Paume and Malmaison, glittered in a Givenchy gown.

On Friday morning, June 2, Kennedy and de Gaulle, still alone with their interpreters, held their fifth meeting. Kennedy, feeling de Gaulle out some more on the alliance, mentioned the possibility of giving NATO increased control of nuclear weapons. De Gaulle replied that such nominal transfer would not constitute the defense of Europe by Europeans, nor would it answer the question: when would nuclear weapons be used? The need therefore remained for Europe to organize its own defense, in association with the United States, of course, but under its own responsibility. Kennedy reiterated his assurance that either a massive conventional attack or the threat of a nuclear attack would produce a nuclear strike against the Soviet Union. De Gaulle remained dubious.

Later in the morning de Gaulle summed up the talks with customary elegance. At the end he said how pleased he had been to meet the President and to perceive his great future. The atmosphere of the talks had been excellent; never had the common destinies of the two nations been closer. The Franco-American alliance was fundamental to France; all the rest was machinery. Kennedy responded that his most vivid impression of France had been not even the magnificence of Versailles but the force and vitality of the French people.

The conversations had been candid and searching, and both were pleased with them. The meeting was of course pervaded by the contrast between the imperturbable nationalist, serenely certain that the classical state was the permanent and irreducible unit of international life, conducting a policy of national grandeur and expecting other leaders, if they had any sense, to do likewise; and the reasoned pragmatist, convinced that the world was changing and forever interested in testing out new patterns and possibilities. But the philosophical clash was muted. The General had begun with a benignly avuncular attitude toward a young man not even born until Captain de Gaulle had fought three years on the western front in the First World War. The French leader came away with the impression of the American President as *un homme sérieux,* fully aware of the weight of the responsibilities he had accepted and fully capable of meeting them.

As for Kennedy, he had long been fascinated by the idea of de Gaulle—this great and gloomy figure, pitting himself against the probabilities of history and then recording the results in such eloquent and fastidious prose. The Paris meeting increased his understanding of the clarity and tenacity, though not yet of the ferocity, of de Gaulle's vision of Europe and the world.

3. DISUNION IN VIENNA

And so on to Austria, the great plane touching down at the Vienna airport on a gray and rainy Saturday morning. The presidential party motored through crowded streets to the American Embassy. Khrushchev had arrived the day before, and the talks were scheduled to begin almost at once. Striking immediately a note at once jovial and edged, Khrushchev engaged the President in some light badinage.

Kennedy now expressed his hope that the meeting would lead to a better understanding of common problems. To his mind, the question was how two great nations, with different social systems, confronting each other across the world, could avoid head-on collision in an era of great change. Khrushchev went instantly on the offensive. The Soviet Union, he said, had tried for a long time to develop friendly relations with the United States. But it refused to do so at the expense of other peoples because agreements of this sort would not bring peace. America must understand that communism has won its right to grow and develop. The premise of John Foster Dulles's policy had been the liquidation of communism; this philosophy could never lead to good relations. He would not hope to persuade the President of the merits of communism, Khrushchev said, any more than he expected the President to waste time trying to convert him to capitalism. But *de facto* recognition of the existence of communism was indispensable.

Kennedy observed courteously that Americans were impressed by the economic achievement of the Soviet Union; it was a source of satisfaction to the whole world. But, as he saw the problem, it was not that the democracies were trying to eliminate communism in areas under communist control, but that the communists were trying to eliminate free systems in areas associated with the west. Khrushchev brusquely rejected this. It was impossible, he said, for the Soviet Union to implant its policy in other states. All the Soviet Union claimed was that communism would triumph; this was not propaganda but a scientific analysis of social development. Communism was superseding capitalism today as capitalism had superseded feudalism in the past. Changes in social systems were bound to come, but they would be brought about only by the will of the people themselves. The Communists believed in their systems, as the President believed in his. In any event, this was a matter for debate, not for war. The Soviet desire for general and complete disarmament proved its intention not to resort to arms.

The great need, Kennedy commented, was for each side to understand the other's views. The American position was that people should have freedom of choice. When communist minorities seized control against the popular will, the

ARRIVING IN VIENNA, AUSTRIA ON JUNE 3, 1961.

Chairman regarded this as historical inevitability; we did not, and this brought our two nations into conflict.

This led Khrushchev into a sententious discourse on intellectual freedom. History must be the judge, he said, in a competition of ideas. If capitalism could insure a better life, it would win. If not, communism would win; but this would be a victory of ideas, not of arms.

To this Kennedy responded that the two powers shared the obligation to conduct the competition of ideas without involving vital national interests. Khrushchev said sharply that he hoped he had misunderstood this remark. Did the President hold the Soviet Union responsible for the development of communist ideas? Did he mean that communism should exist only in countries already communist and that, if it developed elsewhere, the United States would be in conflict with the Soviet Union? This view was incorrect; and, if that was really the way the United States thought, conflict could not be avoided. Ideas did not belong to one nation. Once born, they grew. No immunization was possible against them. The only rule was that they should not be propagated by arms nor by intervention in the internal affairs of other countries. He could guarantee that the Soviet Union would never impose ideas by war. Kennedy repeated that Khrushchev must understand the American views; if our two nations failed to preserve the peace, the whole world would be the loser. "My ambition," Kennedy said, "is to secure peace." The greatest danger was the miscalculation by one power of the interests and policy of another.

The word "miscalculation" irritated Khrushchev. The Soviet Union was going to defend its vital interests, whether or not the United States regarded such acts as miscalculations; it did not want war, but it would not be intimidated either. Of course war would be fatal; both sides would lose equally and be punished equally. But the west should put the word "miscalculation" into cold storage, for its use did not impress the Soviet Union at all.

By "miscalculation," Kennedy patiently explained, he meant the difficulty of predicting what any country might do next. The United States itself had made misjudgments, as when it failed to foresee Chinese intervention in the Korean War. The purpose of the meeting, as he saw it, was to introduce precision into each side's assessments and thereby minimize the risks of misjudgment. Khrushchev, retreating to jolliness, commented that, if the meeting succeeded, the expenses of bringing it about would be well justified. If it failed, not only would the money be wasted but the hopes of the people of the world would be betrayed.

It was time for lunch. The conversation had been civil but tough. Khrushchev had not given way before Kennedy's reasonableness, nor Kennedy before Khrushchev's intransigence.

Kennedy and Khrushchev strolled in the garden for a moment after luncheon. Then they resumed the discussion. Kennedy restated his thesis: change was inevitable, but war would be catastrophic in the nuclear age; both sides must therefore take care to avoid situations which might lead to war. As for miscalculation, every leader had to make judgments; he himself had miscalculated about the Bay of Pigs. He had to estimate what the Soviet Union would do, just as Khrushchev had to estimate about the United States. If we could only reduce the margin of uncertainty in such calculations, then our two nations might survive the period of competition without nuclear war.

All right, said Khruschev, but how could we work anything out when the United States regarded revolution anywhere as the result of communist machinations? It was really the United States which caused revolution by backing reactionary governments: look at Iran, look at Cuba. This, Kennedy protested, was not the issue. The issue was the disruption of the existing equilibrium of power. The Castro regime was objectionable, not because it expelled American monopolies, but because it offered communism a base in the western hemisphere. The Soviet Union, he said pointedly, did not tolerate hostile governments in its own areas of vital interest; what would Khrushchev do, for example, if a pro-American government were established in Warsaw? The United States did not object to the Marxist governments of Guinea or Mali. If governments ruled in the interest of wealthy minorities, of course they were doomed; but social changes must take place peacefully and must not involve the prestige or commitments of America and Russia or upset the balance of world power.

He now brought up Laos. Past American policy there had not always been wise. The solution was to let a neutral and independent Laos decide its own future; and the problem was to make the cease-fire work by setting up a mechanism for its verification. Khrushchev, displaying no great interest in Laos, preferred to revert to the question of reactionary regimes. Our two sides differed, he said, in our understanding of what popular or anti-popular movements were. We should both agree not to interfere and to leave it to the people of the country. The worst thing for the United States to do, he warned, was to start guerrilla warfare against regimes it did not like; no undertaking was more hopeless than guerrilla action instigated from outside and not supported by the people. He did not know, Khrushchev went on, whether the balance of power was exact, but no matter; each side had enough power to destroy the other. That was why there should be no interference. But the United States supported colonial powers, as in Africa, and then was surprised when the people turned against it. Kennedy pointed out that the United States had in fact backed liberation movements in Africa and hoped that the number of independent African states would increase. Khrushchev replied with scorn that the American policy was uneven, its voice timid. It might endorse anti-colonialism for tactical reasons, but its heart was with the colonialists. Why not adopt the Soviet policy of tolerance and noninterference?

Kennedy brought up Khrushchev's pledge to support wars of national liberation in his speech of January 6. Was this noninterference? Obviously both nations were helping groups in other countries. The problem, while we backed our respective movements, was not to clash ourselves. Khrushchev vigorously defended his speech. If subject peoples, promised independence by the United Nations, were still denied their rights, how long were they expected to wait? Wars of national liberation, he said, were "sacred" wars, and the Soviet was certainly going to support them. America itself had rebelled in this manner against Britain. Now it opposed other peoples who followed their example. The Tsars had denied the revolutionary American republic recognition for twenty-six years as an illegitimate regime. Now America refused to recognize China; "things have changed, haven't they?" The realistic policy for the United States would be to recognize China and admit it to the United Nations. Of course, this could not be done so long as Chiang Kai-shek held his position, whether in Taiwan or the UN. If he were in Mao's place, Khrushchev added, he would probably have attacked Taiwan long ago.

Kennedy made once again the point about preserving the existing balance of power. The entry of additional nations into the communist camp, the loss of Taiwan—such developments would alter the equilibrium. But Khrushchev energetically rejected this conception. If some African country were to go communist, he said, it might add a few drops to the bucket of communist power, were the balance of power conceived as a bucket on each side. But it would also be an expression of the popular will; and any attempt to stop it from outside would bring about a chain reaction and possibly war.

Kennedy responded with equal force that, so far as Washington was concerned, countries with varied social systems could pursue independent policies, like India, Burma, Yugoslavia. But changes which altered the balance of world power were different; perhaps the Russians might agree if, for example, Poland should join the west. No doubt America supported some governments which did not represent the will of the people; but could the Chairman be certain about the result if the Poles were given a chance to express their

SOVIET PREMIER NIKITA KHRUSHCHEV AND KENNEDY SIT DOWN FOR THEIR FIRST DAY OF TALKS IN VIENNA.

free choice? He felt it time, Kennedy added, to discuss Laos and the test ban in detail.

Khrushchev affected outrage over Kennedy's reference to Poland, and added that preserving the existing balance were the premise of American policy, he must doubt whether the United States really wanted peaceful coexistence or was seeking a pretext for war. Kennedy, perhaps with a growing sense of the futility of the ideological dispute, now tried again to persuade his antagonist to focus on Laos. This time Khrushchev acquiesced. After some talk, both said they might influence their clients in Laos to cooperate with the International Control Commission in policing the cease-fire.

They broke up at quarter to seven. It had been a rough day. Kennedy was impressed by Khrushchev's vitality, his debating skill and his brutal candor, depressed by the blank wall of dogma.

4. PRELUDE TO BERLIN

Kennedy and Khrushchev would both have said that they wanted to preserve the status quo. But they had incompatible conceptions of what the status quo meant.

For Kennedy the status quo was the existing balance of international force. This did not at all mean that he wanted to freeze the world in its social mold. On the contrary, he believed internal political and institutional change to be both inevitable and desirable. But his hope was that it would take place without transferring power from one bloc to the other and therefore without making either side feel threatened and constrained to resist change by force.

For Khrushchev, on the other hand, the status quo was something very different: it was in essence the communist revolution in progress (as he hoped) across the world. From this perspective Kennedy's conception of a global standstill was an attempt not to support but to alter the status quo; it was an attack on the revolutionary process itself.*

Khrushchev's response left no doubt about the joker in the Soviet doctrine of coexistence: the idea of a dynamic status quo meant simply that the democracies had no right to intervene in the communist world, while the communists had every right to intervene in the democratic world. But Kennedy nevertheless felt that the offer of a standstill was worth the effort. Where he perhaps erred was in beginning by engaging Khrushchev in abstract discussion. Ideological debate was bound to be fruitless; Khrushchev was not likely to forswear the faith of a lifetime. Moreover, Khrushchev was a veteran dialectician.

That night the Austrians gave their guests a state dinner at the Schönbrunn Palace. Khrushchev, in a clowning mood, turned a heavy, waggish charm on Mrs. Kennedy; it was one gag after another, like sitting next to Abbott and Costello. When I asked the President later what Khrushchev was like, he described him as a combination of external jocosity and "internal rage."

They resumed their talks the next morning. The President began by saying that, if they couldn't agree on everything, at least they might be able to agree on Laos. Here after all was a land without strategic importance to either side but in which the United States had treaty commitments. America wanted to reduce its involvement in Laos, Kennedy said, and he hoped the Soviet Union would wish to do the same. Laos was not important enough to entangle two great nations.

Khrushchev responded that the Soviet Union had no desire to assume responsibilities in remote geographical areas. It was in Laos only at the request of Souvanna Phouma and the legitimate government. What business did the United States have claiming special rights in Laos? If America really wanted to normalize the situation and avoid confrontations, it must renounce its claim to special rights.

Kennedy responded that the commitments had been made before he became President; why they were undertaken was not an issue here. Whatever had happened in the past, the issue now was to decrease commitments on both sides

AFTER LUNCHEON ON THEIR FIRST DAY OF TALKS, THE TWO LEADERS WALK IN THE GARDEN. STANDING AT LEFT IS SECRETARY OF STATE, DEAN RUSK.

and get a neutral and independent Laos. Khrushchev doubted whether these commitments were altogether a legacy. As for the Soviet Union, it would guarantee to exert every effort to influence the Laotian forces to establish a truly neutral government. We should lock our foreign ministers into a room and tell them to find a solution. Kennedy said that he had been reluctant to send in the Marines. All this could be avoided if there were a genuine cease-fire. Khrushchev agreed to make the cease-fire a priority matter. The two men thus completed the one piece of business transacted at Vienna.

The next question was the test ban. There were two issues here, Khrushchev began: the number of suspicious events to be inspected, and the organization of the machinery of inspection. As for the first, the Soviet Union considered three inspections a year sufficient; any more would constitute espionage. As for the control mechanism, the only fair way was to establish a body made up of representatives of the three world groups—the Communists, the neutrals and the western states—empowered to adopt only decisions agreed upon by all. The work of other international organizations, Khrushchev added, should be organized along similar lines. In any case, Khrushchev continued, the test ban had little importance by itself; it must be linked with the general and complete disarmament. If the West would accept the Soviet disarmament plan, then the Soviet Union would drop the

* I am grateful to Senator Benton for letting me see the memorandum of his interview with Chairman Khrushchev on May 28, 1964.

troika and the requirement for unanimity and agree to any controls. Let the disarmament negotiations include the test ban. If we pushed ahead, we could have general and complete disarmament in two years.

Kennedy asked whether Khrushchev really thought it impossible to find any person neutral between the United States and the Soviet Union. Khrushchev replied that he did. But the *troika,* Kennedy said, meant a veto over the inspection process; how could either he or Khrushchev assure his people that no secret testing was going on in the other nation?

To Khrushchev's deprecation of the test ban Kennedy responded that, while by itself it would not lessen the number or the production of nuclear weapons, it would make their spread to new countries less likely. Without a test ban, there would be ten or fifteen nuclear powers in a few years. Surely the Soviet Union must balance the risks of espionage against the risks of proliferation. Khrushchev conceded the logic of this but pointed out that, while the test ban discussions were going on in Geneva, France was carrying its nuclear program forward. Unless the test ban were part of general disarmament, other countries would follow the example of France.

Kennedy replied that general disarmament was exceedingly complex and difficult: why not start with the easy question? They discussed the Soviet disarmament plan for a moment, and Khrushchev made it clear that he did not want to begin with the test ban even as part of the larger effort. Kennedy said again that the test ban, if not the most important measure, was at least a very significant start. Khrushchev

KHRUSHCHEV ENTERTAINS MRS. KENNEDY AT THE BANQUET.

said tersely that the Soviet Union would agree only subject to the *troika.* The conversation, Kennedy said, was now back to where they had started.

After this unsatisfactory discussion, they turned to Berlin. Here Khrushchev, while still stopping short of bluster, displayed his greatest animation and intensity. The German situation, he said, was intolerable. It was sixteen years after the end of the war, and there was still no peace settlement. He wanted to reach agreement with the west on a treaty, Khrushchev said; but, if the United States refused, the Soviet Union would sign the treaty alone. This act would end the state of war and cancel all existing commitments, including occupation rights, administrative institutions and rights of access. The treaty would establish a free city of West Berlin. There would be no interference with its internal affairs or its communications, though agreement on access would have to be reached with the Democratic Republic. Western troops would be acceptable in West Berlin under certain conditions—and, of course, with Soviet troops too.

Kennedy, thanking him for putting the case so frankly, came back with equal frankness. This discussion, he said, raised not only legal questions but practical facts which affect American security. They were not talking about Laos any longer; Berlin was of primary and vital concern to the United States. We were not in Berlin on anyone's sufferance. We fought our way there, and our continuing presence rested on contractual rights. If we allowed ourselves to be expelled, American pledges and commitments would ever after be regarded as scraps of paper. Moreover, if we abandoned West Berlin, it would mean the abandonment of Western Europe, which America had deemed essential to its security in two wars. If Khrushchev agreed that the equilibrium of world power was more or less in balance, he must understand the consequences of his demand. America, Kennedy said, would not accept an ultimatum.

Khrushchev said that he understood this to mean the United States did not want a treaty. Misinterpreting Kennedy again, he declared that the invocation of national security could mean that Americans would wish to go on to Moscow too, since that would improve their strategic position. Kennedy responded sharply that the Americans did not wish to go anywhere, just to stay where they were. No doubt the current situation in Berlin was not satisfactory; but conditions were unsatisfactory all over, and this was not the time to upset the world balance of power.

Khrushchev regretted that Kennedy did not get his point. All he wanted to do was to tranquilize the situation in the most dangerous spot in the world. The Soviet Union wanted to perform an operation—to excise this thorn, this ulcer—without prejudicing interests on either side. The treaty would not change boundaries; it would formalize them. It would only impede those, like Hitler's generals now in NATO, who still wanted *Lebensraum* to the Urals. No force in the world could stop the Soviet Union from signing the treaty; no further delay was necessary or possible. And thereafter any infringement of the sovereignty of East Germany would be regarded as open aggression with all its consequences.

Kennedy said that the United States opposed any military buildup in West Germany which might threaten the Soviet Union. But Khrushchev's proposal would bring about a basic change in the world situation overnight. This was a most serious challenge. He had not come to Vienna for this; he had come in the hope of improving relations. The United States could not accept the abrogation by one nation of the four-nation agreement.

Khrushchev waved this aside. Why did the United States want Berlin? To unleash a war? Berlin had no military significance. After a treaty, West Berlin would be accessible to all countries with which it wished ties; the United States and the Soviet Union could develop guarantees jointly or call in the UN. But, if the United States tried to maintain its present position after a treaty, this would violate the sovereignty of East Germany and of the communist camp as a whole. Once the Berlin question was out of the way, the road would be clear for an improvement of relations. In any case, the Soviet Union intended to sign the treaty by the end of 1961. If America wanted war over Berlin, there was nothing the Soviet Union could do about it. Maybe he should sign the treaty right away and get it over; that is what the Pentagon had wanted. But madmen who sought war ought to be put in strait jackets.

It was not quite a tirade; it was too controlled and hard and therefore the more menacing. Kennedy replied that the United States did not wish to precipitate a crisis. The Soviet Union was doing so by threatening unilateral changes in the existing situation. Was this the way to achieve peace? If the United States surrendered to the Soviet demand, it would not be regarded as a serious country any longer.

Khrushchev became even harsher. The Soviet Union, he said, would never under any conditions accept American rights in West Berlin after the treaty. After all, the United States itself had signed a unilateral peace treaty with Japan. The Soviet Union was determined to go ahead, and responsibility for subsequent violations of East German sovereignty would be heavy.

Kennedy replied that the United States did not wish to deprive the Soviet Union of its ties in Eastern Europe and would not submit to the loss of its own ties in Western

Europe. He had not assumed office to accept arrangements totally inimical to American interests.

After luncheon, Kennedy, making a final effort, asked to talk with Khrushchev alone. Accompanied only by interpreters, they sat together for a last conversation. The President began by expressing hope that in the interest of relations between their two countries the Chairman would not present him with a crisis so deeply involving the American national interest as Berlin. Of course any decision Khrushchev wanted to make about the Democratic Republic was his own. But change was taking place everywhere in the world, and no one could predict its end. At such a time, all decisions had to be carefully considered.

Khrushchev returned unrelentingly to the attack. The United States, he said, wanted to humiliate the Soviet Union. If the President insisted on occupation rights after a treaty and if East German borders were violated, whether by land, sea or air, force would be met by force. The United States should prepare itself for this, and the Soviet Union would do the same.

"I want peace," said Khrushchev, "but, if you want war, that is your problem."

Kennedy said, "It is you, and not I, who wants to force a change."

Khrushchev said again that it was up to the United States to decide on peace or war. The Soviet Union had no choice but to accept the challenge. It must, and it would, respond. The treaty decision was irrevocable. He would sign in December.

Kennedy, parting, said, "It will be a cold winter."

5. AFTERMATH IN LONDON

As Kennedy, carrying Khrushchev's *aide-mémoires* on Berlin and the test ban, left Vienna to see Harold Macmillan in England, he told a friend in the press that "somber" would be a good word for the meetings. For all the poise and command he displayed in the talks, the experience deeply disturbed him. Kennedy had never encountered any leader with whom he could not exchange ideas—anyone so impervious to reasoned argument or so apparently indifferent to the prospective obliteration of mankind. He himself had indicated flexibility and admitted error, but Khrushchev had remained unmoved and immovable. Apart from Laos, about which Khrushchev evidently cared little, there was no area of accommodation. The test ban seemed dead. Berlin held the threat, if not the certitude, of war. Filled with foreboding, the President flew on to London. It was a silent and gloomy trip. Arriving at London Airport, on Sunday afternoon, the presidential party drove into the city as a great disarmament rally in Trafalgar Square was beginning to disperse. The streets along the way were filled with black banners marked in white letters BAN THE BOMB.

The pretext for the stop was the christening of Lee Bouvier Radziwill's new baby. But the essential reason was the talk with Macmillan. The two men had met twice since the inauguration. In June their relationship was still tentative.

On Monday morning, June 5, Kennedy, tense and tired, went to 10 Downing Street. A formal conference, with each principal flanked by advisers, had been scheduled. But Macmillan said, with the usual weary fling of his hand, "Let's not have a meeting—the Foreign Office and all that. Why not have a peaceful drink and chat by ourselves?" Kennedy seemed grateful and relieved, and the two men settled down for a talk. The President described his grim impressions of Khrushchev. He and Macmillan then agreed that western proposals for negotiation over Berlin would be taken in Moscow as a sign of weakness unless the situation grew so much worse that there seemed imminent danger of war. Military planning on Berlin had to be stepped up. They would have to decide what the west should do in a series of contingencies.

Their talk, though brief, marked the real beginning of what became Kennedy's closest personal relationship with a foreign leader. Macmillan had a sharp, disillusioned mind, a vivid sense of history and a strong desire to accomplish certain objectives during his term in office. Possessed of a genuine horror of nuclear war, he was determined to press for a test ban and to search without cease for a *détente* with the Soviet Union. To this general purpose he added two other themes: the desire to bring Britian into Europe, and the hope of reconstructing the international monetary system.

On nearly all these points he and Kennedy made easy contact. More than that, they soon discovered, despite the differences in age, a considerable temperamental rapport. Kennedy, with his own fondness for the British political style, liked Macmillan's patrician approach to politics, his impatience with official ritual, his insouciance about the professionals, his pose of nonchalance even when most deeply committed. Macmillan, for his part, responded to Kennedy's courage, his ability to see events unfolding against the vast canvas of history, his contempt for cliché, his unfailing sense of the ridiculous. They found the same things funny and the same things serious. "It was the gay things that linked us together," Macmillan once told me, "and made it possible for us to talk about the terrible things." They soon discovered that they could match each other's transitions from gravity to mischief and communicate as in shorthand. It was as if they had known each other all their lives.

Refreshed by the stopover in London, Kennedy came

PRESIDENT AND MRS. KENNEDY ARRIVE AT THE HOME OF MRS. KENNEDY'S SISTER, PRINCESS LEE RADZIWILL IN BUCKINGHAM PALACE ON JUNE 4, 1961. HERE THEY GREET PRIME MINISTER HAROLD MACMILLAN AND LADY DOROTHY MACMILLAN.

back to Washington. Whatever the disappointments of Vienna or the stabbing pain in his spine, he seemed, after forty-eight hours, philosophical about the meeting. He knew how Khrushchev thought and where he stood, and that was invaluable. I think also that he felt he had tested himself and had proven more than equal to the test. The talks with Macmillan and de Gaulle had strengthened his confidence in his ability to rally the west. War was a danger but not an inevitability. Kennedy and Khrushchev each came away from Vienna with greater respect for the mind and nerve of his adversary. Having survived their personal confrontation and defined the impassable difference over Berlin, they now faced their first battle of wills.

XV. TRIAL IN BERLIN

PRESIDENT KENNEDY MEETING WITH WILLY BRANDT, MAYOR OF BERLIN, ON MARCH 13, 1961.

OFTEN DURING THE YEAR, the President set forth his conception of the American stake in Berlin. I think, however, the analysis I heard him make in the autumn carried particular cogency. Kennedy stripped the case of the legalistic and moralistic arguments so cherished in the west and placed it in terms of geopolitical realism which he hoped would be understood in Moscow.

"We do not accept the idea that the Soviet Union is in danger from West Germany," Kennedy replied. "West Germany is in an acutely vulnerable strategic situation. We have been successful in tying West Germany into Western Europe through NATO, the Common Market and so on. We want nothing to happen over Berlin which would weaken the ties of West Germany to Western Europe and set West Germany off on a nationalistic and independent course. It is in this possibility that the real danger lies of Germany setting off another war."

As we see Soviet policy in Berlin, the President continued, "it is designed to neutralize West Germany as a first step in the neutralization of Western Europe. That is what makes the present situation so dangerous. West Germany is the key as to whether Western Europe will be free." The pressure on West Berlin was the first move in a Soviet effort to break up NATO "if we don't meet our commitments in Berlin, it will mean the destruction of NATO and a dangerous situation for the whole world. All Europe is at stake in West Berlin."

1. THE BERLIN DEBATE

The administration had begun to consider its Berlin policy well before the President went to Vienna. In March Kennedy had invited Dean Acheson to undertake special studies of the problems of NATO and Germany. Acheson said if the Soviet Union planned to force the Berlin issue this year. He did not believe that Berlin could be satisfactorily settled apart from the larger question of Germany; and he saw no prospect of any agreement on either Berlin or Germany compatible with the interests of the west. Therefore, when Khrushchev moved to cut off West Berlin, the allies must instantly demonstrate their determination to stand up to the Soviet challenge. Skipping over possibilities of diplomatic or economic response, Acheson crisply offered a formidable catalogue of military countermeasures, concluding tentatively in favor of sending a division down the *Autobahn*. This, he hoped, would make clear that western interest in preserving access was greater than Russian interest in blocking access. If the Russians repulsed the probe, then at least the West would know where it stood, and it could rally and rearm as it did during the Korean War.

Acheson's basic thesis, which he developed in a long and powerful paper delivered to the President three weeks after Vienna, was that West Berlin was not a problem but a pretext. Khrushchev's object, as Acheson saw it, was not to rectify a local situation but to test the general American will to resist; his hope was that, by making us back down on a sacred commitment, he could shatter our world power and influence. This was a simple conflict of wills, and, until it was resolved, any effort to negotiate the Berlin issue per se would be fatal. Since there was nothing to negotiate, willingness on our part to go to the conference table would be taken in Moscow as evidence of weakness and make the crisis so much the worse.

Khrushchev had only dared precipitate the crisis, Acheson continued, because his fear of nuclear war had declined. Our problem was to convince him that this complacency was misplaced and that we would, in fact, go to nuclear war rather than abandon the status quo. This called for the build-up—prompt, serious and quiet—of both our conventional and nuclear forces. If Khrushchev signed his treaty with East Germany, we should not quibble about this or about changes in access procedures. But, the moment there was interruption of access itself, we must act: first an airlift—and then, if that could not be sustained against Soviet counter-measures, a ground probe in force too large to be stopped by East German troops alone. There was a substantial chance, Acheson said, that the necessary military preparations would by themselves cause Khrushchev to alter his purpose; but he added frankly that there was also a substantial possibility that nuclear war might result.

Though the preamble of the paper expressed categorical opposition to any form of negotiation, the paper itself was slightly less intransigent. If Khrushchev were to change his mind, Acheson was willing to offer a formula to cover his retreat through negotiations launched after the military build-up and before the signing of the treaty with East Germany. He even sketched the outlines of a settlement. But this section had somewhat the air of an afterthought. For Acheson the test of will seemed almost an end in itself rather than a means to a political end. And the thrust of Acheson's rhetoric, and especially of his brilliant and imperious oral presentations, helped fix the debate for a time in terms of a clear-cut choice between negotiation and a military showdown.

The Acheson case followed logically from his conviction that the Soviet Union had unlimited objectives in raising the Berlin question. But others in the government, especially some who knew the Soviet Union best, like Ambassadors Thompson and Harriman, believed that, on the contrary, Khrushchev's objectives might well be limited. Thompson argued after Vienna that the predominant Soviet motive was the desire to improve the communist position in Eastern Europe rather than to achieve the world-wide political humiliation of the United States. While Thompson favored the policy of quiet military build-up, he also argued that the west must begin a diplomatic offensive.

These questions were before the newly established Berlin Task Force; but this body temporarily put them aside in order to spend most of June and a good part of July composing an answer to the *aide-mémoire* on Berlin which Khrushchev had given Kennedy in Vienna.

No one in the White House, least of all the President, would ever understand why this not very exacting assignment proved so difficult. Week followed week with no word from the Department, and the President's exasperation grew. When a draft finally came over in mid-July, nearly six weeks after Vienna, it was a tired and turgid rehash of documents left over from the Berlin crisis of 1958–59. By this time it was too late to do anything but put the paper out, which the White House did, though after attaching a more cogent summary of its own.

Meanwhile, opposition to the bleak choices of the Acheson program was mounting. Influential Senators were critical. The British were unhappy. And in the White House Carl Kaysen, Henry Kissinger, who was in Washington regularly that summer as a consultant, and I, very much on the fringes, all wanted a more aggressive canvass of diplomatic possibilities. The first phase of the Berlin debate was under way.

Looking back, one can now see that the early terms of the debate were artificial. On the one hand, Acheson, for all his insistence on military confrontations, was not so implacable a foe of negotiation. On the other, some of us who argued that a diplomatic approach should accompany the military build-up unquestionably had illusions as to what negotiation might accomplish. Acheson was probably right in suggesting that the preservation of the status quo was the goal we should seek. Where the debate had value was in determining how best to pursue this goal. Those of us who talked about supplementing the build-up with negotiation had hold, however dimly, of one truth: that insistence on a military showdown, accompanied by the rejection of diplomacy and, in early July, by talk of war mobilization under a proclamation of national emergency, contained the risk of pushing the crisis beyond the point of no return.

2. THE CRISIS GROWS

Khrushchev's testy television report on Vienna in mid-June was soon followed by appropriately belligerent remarks by Walter Ulbricht, the Chairman of the East German Council of State. Ulbricht complained of the flow of refugees to West Berlin and forecast new restrictions, allegedly in the interests of safety, on planes flying along the air corridors from the west. Then early in July Khrushchev himself, citing Kennedy's call for a larger American defense effort, announced a suspension of the partial demobilization of the Red Army and a one-third increase in Soviet military spending.

In early July, Abram Chayes, Carl Kaysen and I got together to express a collective concern that the Acheson paper was shaping policy along restrictive and potentially dangerous lines. It all reminded me uncomfortably of the prelude to the Bay of Pigs; and, stimulated by this conversation, I set down my misgivings in a memorandum to the President the next morning.

The Cuban fiasco, the memorandum suggested, had resulted in large part from the "excessive concentration [in our advance planning] on military and operational problems and the wholly inadequate consideration of political issues. This error seems likely to be repeated here." The Acheson paper was excellent in analyzing the issues of last resort; it told us what we could fall back on when other alternatives were used up. But, if it were permitted to define our Berlin choices, there could be no systematic effort to bring these alternatives to the surface.

The memorandum questioned whether the military contingency envisaged by Acheson was the most probable way the situation would develop, and concluded by mentioning another Cuban resemblance—the tendency to define the issue, "to put it crudely, as: Are you chicken or not?"

As we finished, I handed the President the memorandum, saying that he might want to look at it on his way to Hyannis Port, where he had scheduled a meeting on Berlin the next day with Rusk, McNamara and General Taylor. His response was immediate. Agreeing that Acheson's paper was far too narrowly directed to military problems, he said with emphasis that Berlin planning had to be brought back into balance. Then he asked me to prepare an unsigned memorandum about the unexplored issues in the Berlin problem which he might use in his talks at the Cape. By furious effort, Chayes, Kissinger and I got the paper to Hyannis Port in time.

The memorandum first identified certain issues omitted in the Acheson paper:

1. What political moves do we make until the crisis develops? If we sit silent, or confine ourselves to rebutting Soviet contentions (cf. the draft reply to the *aide-mémoire*), we permit Khrushchev to establish the framework of discussion. As we do this, we in effect invite him to demand from us a definition of the guarantees we would find acceptable. This, of course, casts the U.S. as rigid and unreasonable and puts us on the political defensive.
2. The paper indicates no relationship between the proposed military action and larger political objectives. It defines an immediate *casus belli;* but it does not state any political objective other than present access procedures for which we are prepared to incinerate the world. It is essential to elaborate the cause for which we are prepared to go to nuclear war. Where do we want to come out if we win the test of wills? German unification, for example: what is our real intention with regard to this traditional objective?
3. The paper covers only one eventuality—that is, the Communist interruption of military access to West Berlin. Actually there is a whole spectrum of harassments, of which a full-scale blockade may well be one of the least likely.
4. The paper hinges on our willingness to face nuclear war. But this option is undefined. Before you are asked to make the decision to go to nuclear war, you are entitled to know what concretely nuclear war is likely to mean. The Pentagon should be required to make an analysis of the possible levels and implications of nuclear warfare and the possible gradations of our own nuclear response.
5. The paper does not define the problem of the relationship of the proposed strategy to the Alliance. What happens if our allies decline to go along? Which of them, for example, will go along with the ground probe? Even de Gaulle has indicated his opposition to sending a column through. What about the United Nations? Whatever happens, this issue will go into the UN. For better or for worse, we have to have a convincing UN position.

We concluded by recommending that the President tell the State Department to explore negotiating alternatives and ask Acheson to supply the missing political dimension in his argument.

While we were agitating the political side, McGeorge Bundy and Kissinger were bringing the President comparable questions about the state of military planning. Bundy now commented on the dangerous rigidity of the strategic war plan, pointing out that it called in essence for an all-out nuclear strike against the Soviet Union and left the President little choice as to how he would face his moment of thermonuclear truth.

At the Hyannis Port meeting on July 8 the President made his dissatisfaction with the state of planning abundantly clear. On the diplomatic side, he decided to ask Acheson to try his hand at a "political program" for Berlin and instructed Rusk to produce a negotiating prospectus. On the military side, he asked McNamara for a plan which would permit non-nuclear resistance on a scale sufficient both to indicate our determination and to provide the communists time for second thoughts and negotiation before everything billowed up in nuclear war. The State and Defense papers were to be delivered within ten days.

It did not, of course, prove that easy to reshape policy, but the meeting laid out the lines of battle within the American government for the rest of the summer. At first, Kennedy gained little ground. When the National Security Council met on Berlin on July 13, Rusk reaffirmed the Acheson argument that we should not negotiate until the crisis became more acute. And Acheson himself, supported by Lyndon Johnson, now argued strongly for a proclamation of national emergency. Only a response of this order, Acheson argued, could deter Khrushchev from irretrievable steps and make the American people understand the full gravity of the crisis.

The proclamation of national emergency encountered a number of objections. Rusk felt that it would have the flavor of mobilization and quoted back at Acheson his own original caution that the build-up take place in low key. McNamara also was skeptical. Kissinger argued that the Soviet Union would be more impressed by a broad and sustained improvement in American military readiness than by a single dramatic gesture, especially one which made us appear "unnecessarily bellicose,

THE JULY 8 MEETING IN HYANNIS PORT. PRESIDENT KENNEDY (LEFT) CONFERS WITH ROBERT MCNAMARA, DEAN RUSK, AND GENERAL MAXWELL TAYLOR ABOARD THE "MARLIN."

perhaps even hysterical." Moreover, if we declared the emergency now, we used up a measure which would be more effective if taken as a response to clear-cut Soviet provocation. Ted Sorensen pointed out that the declaration of national emergency might well "engage Khrushchev's prestige to a point where he felt he could not back down from a showdown, and provoke further or faster action on his part in stepping up the arms race." It would also, Sorensen feared, "arouse those at home and abroad who are fearful of 'rash' and 'trigger-happy' actions by the United States."

3. THE PRESIDENTIAL STRATEGY

The President was meanwhile fighting his way through the thicket of debate to his own conclusions. Cuba and Laos had been side issues. But Berlin threatened a war which might destroy civilization, and he thought about little else that summer. A once-and-for-all peace seemed equally unlikely. But he still hoped to arrive at a point where both the Soviet Union and the United States would accept the premise that the only alternatives were authentic negotiation or mutual annihilation. What worried him was that Khrushchev might interpret his reluctance to wage nuclear war as a symptom of an American loss of nerve. Some day, he said, the time might come when he would have to run the supreme risk to convince Khrushchev that conciliation did not mean humiliation.

This meant that the United States would not give way and, if the Soviet Union persisted in its determination to destroy the freedom of West Berlin, we would be prepared to go to war, even to nuclear war. But, while Kennedy wanted to make this resolve absolutely clear to Moscow, he wanted to make it equally clear that we were not, as he once put it to me, "warmad." He did not wish to drive the crisis beyond the point of no return; and therefore, while reiterating our refusal to retreat, he rejected the program of national mobilization and sought the beginnings of careful negotiation. On the night of July 25 television cables were installed in the presidential office, and the President made his report to the people.

"We cannot and will not permit the Communists," Kennedy said, "to drive us out of Berlin, either gradually or by force." To be ready for any contingency, he would seek an additional $3.25 billion for the defense budget, call up certain reserve and National Guard units, procure new weapons and enlarge the program of civil defense. But, if our military posture had to be defensive, "our diplomatic posture need not be.... We do not intend to leave it to others to choose and monopolize the forum and the framework of discussion. We do not intend to abandon our duty to mankind to seek a peaceful solution." We recognize, Kennedy said, the historical Russian concern about Central and Eastern Europe, and "we are willing to consider any arrangement or treaty in Germany consistent with the maintenance of peace and freedom, and with the legitimate security interests of all nations." We were determined to search for peace "in formal or informal meetings. We do not want military considerations to dominate the thinking of either East or West.... In the thermonuclear age, any misjudgment on either side about the intentions of the other could rain more devastation in several hours than has been wrought in all the wars of human history."

The White House group rejoiced at the speech. But for some reason the press, playing up the military points and almost ignoring the passages about negotiation, made it appear a triumph for the hard line. In Russia Khrushchev read it, or affected to read it, in the same way. The next day he told John J. McCloy emotionally that the United States had declared preliminary war on the Soviet Union. It had presented an ultimatum and clearly intended hostilities. This confirmed, Khrushchev said, the thesis of his January speech that the capitalist world had lost confidence in its capacity to triumph by peaceful means. However, Khrushchev concluded, he still believed in the President's good sense. After thunderstorms, people cooled off, thought problems over and resumed human shape.

The storms were apparently not quite over when Khrushchev replied in a televised broadcast on August 7. Though his tone was considerably higher-pitched than Kennedy's, the two speeches none the less bore curious resemblances of the sort which led the President later to invoke the mirror metaphor in discussing Soviet pronouncements. Like Kennedy, Khrushchev was unyielding on his basic position. Like Kennedy, he talked about calling up reservists. Like Kennedy, he mused about the perils of nuclear war. Like Kennedy, he asked his adversaries to meet round the conference table, clear the atmosphere, "rely on reason and not on the power of thermonuclear weapons."

And so the crisis grew in the first weeks of August. Kennedy, having launched his military build-up, now tried to set his diplomatic offensive in motion. He had been pressing the State Department to prepare negotiating positions ever since the Hyannis Port meeting, but it was uphill work. Now Acheson suggested that the western foreign ministers be called together at the end of August to concert a stand. As for the content of our negotiating position, Acheson offered in effect a dressed-up version of the status quo.

Early in August, Rusk went to Paris to work out a negotiating strategy with his three western counterparts. The hope was to find enough agreement to justify inviting the Soviet Union to a four-power conference. The British wanted this, and the West Germans were more receptive than anticipated. But the Americans still had no solid position to propose, and the French remained flatly hostile to the whole idea. The Paris gathering consequently broke up without result. One wonders whether, if it had produced an invitation to Moscow to discuss the crisis, the Russians would have dared carry through the drastic action they were preparing for the next weekend.

4. THE WALL

For the Berlin crisis was having its most spectacular effect in East Germany itself. The refugee exodus was growing every day; over thirty thousand fled to West Berlin in July alone. Toward the end of the month the East German regime imposed new measures intended to restrict the flight, but the effect was only to increase it. Escape was fast becoming an obsession.

Early in August the President observed that Khrushchev would have to do something internally to re-establish control over the situation—and that, if he did, we would not be able to do a thing about it. Eastern Europe was a vital interest for Khrushchev, and he could not stand by and let it trickle away. But it was not a vital interest for the United States. "I can get the alliance to move if he tries to do anything about West Berlin but not if he just does something about East Berlin."

On August 13, a few minutes after midnight, East German troops and police occupied most of the crossing-points on the East Berlin side of the dividing line, tore up the streets and installed road-blocks and barbed-wire barricades. Despite the presidential and other anticipations, the action caught the State Department and the CIA by surprise; evidently the test-of-will thesis had diverted attention too long from the local problems of East Germany. And it was at first hard to decide what the action meant. For—contrary to the later impression that on August 13 the East Germans built over-night a great wall, which the allies, if they had had any guts, should have promptly bulldozed down—a number of crossing-points remained open, the construction of a concrete wall did not begin till August 17, and movement between the sectors continued for several days after that. For all Washington could tell on the thirteenth, the intention might have been to control rather than to end the refugee flow; and this hardly was a reason for invading the eastern sector and thereby inviting retaliation and risking war.

Yet the possibility remained that the intention might be far more sinister: that the Wall might represent the unfolding of an unalterable Soviet plan, based on a conviction of American irresolution, to drive the west out of Berlin. Kennedy, remarking that there was one chance out of five of a nuclear exchange, instantly mobilized the resources of government. These were grim days and nights. The Berlin Task Force went into continuous session, reaching the somewhat impotent conclusion that accelerating the military build-up in the United States was the most effective response. The Task Force also drafted a formal protest. But it took four days—four interminable days so far as West Berlin was concerned—before the protest was delivered in Moscow.

LEFT: RESDIENTS OF EAST GERMANY PEER OVER ONE OF THE EARLIEST VERSIONS OF THE BERLIN WALL.
RIGHT: AN EAST GERMAN SOLDIER KEEPING GUARD.

The apparent American passivity not unnaturally alarmed the West Berliners; and on August 16 Mayor Willy Brandt wrote Kennedy condemning the feeble western reaction and proposing a series of more stringent responses. Brandt's letter, reinforced by cables from our Minister in Berlin, made it clear that some American reaction more specific than the general military build-up was necessary to sustain the morale of West Berlin. Kennedy therefore decided to send Vice-President Johnson to carry his answer to Brandt and at the same time to signify to the Russians that Berlin was an ultimate American commitment. He also ordered a battle group of 1500 men to move from West Germany to West Berlin.

Adenauer in the meantime, except for political speeches in preparation for the September election, was relatively quiet. He did not even visit West Berlin, and, however bold he became as the situation receded, he did not at the time propose ary form of direct action against the Wall. While he did write Kennedy on August 29 declaring that acquiescence in future acts of communist force in the manner of August 13 would be "out of the question," he did not record even at this point basic disagreement with western policy toward the Wall. In subsequent messages to Kennedy, both Adenauer and Brandt urged the west to move more speedily toward negotiations with the Soviet Union.

Though Johnson is said to have felt a little gloomy over the prospect of going to West Berlin, he performed his mission superbly. Johnson delivered an inspiring speech with genuine and convincing emotion. There was a weekend of anxiety in Washington while the 1st Battle Group, 8th Infantry, rolled down the *Autobahn* to West Berlin. However, the column proceeded without interference, and the Vice-President greeted the troops when they arrived. Johnson returned deeply moved to Washington. His visit was a turning point in relieving Berlin's crisis of confidence.

The Wall remained, a shabby obscenity straggling across the face of the city. In retrospect it seems to have been a defensive rather than an aggressive action. It represented a solution, at considerable political cost, of the problem which, more perhaps than anything else, had led Khrushchev to reopen the Berlin question earlier in the year. By stanching the blood-flow from East Germany, the Wall secured the most immediate Soviet interest in Berlin. Kennedy's determination to rebuild the military power of the west had shown Khruschev that he could not obtain his maximum objectives by bluff. Now the Wall, by achieving his minimum objective, released him from the necessity of forcing the issue to a showdown.

5. THE CRISIS FADES AWAY

This was not, however, fully perceived at the time. It is hard now to recall the forebodings of the late summer of 1961, to evoke again the pessimism that shrouded the government.

These were strange, moody days. Khrushchev told Drew Pearson of his admiration for John Foster Dulles, and this seemed to portend new Soviet experiments in brinksmanship. The Wall was followed on August 24 by an angry Soviet note accusing the west of using the air corridors to import "revanchists, extremists, saboteurs and spies" into Berlin and on August 30 by the Soviet resumption of nuclear testing (in the face of Khrushchev's statement to Kennedy at Vienna that he would not test until we did). When Rusk commented to the President on September 5 that Moscow was showing little interest in negotiation, Kennedy replied grimly, "It isn't time yet. It's too early. They are bent on scaring the world to death before they begin negotiating, and they haven't quite brought the pot to boil. Not enough people are frightened."

Given this apparent Soviet desperation, the White House group regarded it as more urgent than ever to speed the military build-up and at the same time to exhaust every diplomatic recourse before Armageddon. On August 14, the day after the first crossing-points were closed, Bundy reported to the President unanimity in his immediate staff for the view that we should take a clear initiative for negotiation within the next week or ten days.

In a few days Rusk announced that negotiation with the Soviet Union would definitely take place after the General Assembly convened in mid-September. The problem remained of producing a western, or even an American, position. Some of us at the White House clung to the hope of a real negotiation which might lead, we thought, if at the price of hard bargaining with Bonn, to a new status for West Berlin, new guarantees of western presence and access and perhaps a general arrangement for central European security. The President was sure that the traditional western plan was the wrong framework for negotiations and wanted something new. The reunification of Germany seemed to him an unrealistic negotiating objective. But at the same time he had no wish to perpetuate the idea of a divided Germany by recognizing East Germany. Nor did Soviet assurances of fresh guarantees of western presence and access impress him. "The Soviet Union," he said, "is asking us to make concessions in exchange for which they will give us again what we already have. And these concessions, in addition, would insure that West Germany goes nationalistic and becomes a danger to the peace. This is no bargain. We would be buying the same horse twice."

He lost no opportunity to signal his attitude to Moscow. James Wechsler, who had come away from his talk with Kennedy moved by the earnestness with which the President discussed the nuclear peril, proposed in late September that he write a column about Kennedy's thoughts on war and peace and challenge the Soviet press to republish it. Pierre Salinger thought this a good idea, and the President personally approved the Wechsler text. Wechsler wrote that nothing in the President's view was non-negotiable except the dignity of free men: "I have no trace of doubt about the authenticity and depth of his desire for rational settlements in a world that has trembled on the brink so long. Russian papers, please copy." Considerably to our surprise the Russian papers did copy in a few days, including even the suggestion that Khrushchev was a madman if he considered Kennedy a Wall Street imperialist.

There were many ways to initiate a dialogue; and in the end the substance of negotiations turned out to matter a good deal less than the willingness to negotiate. It was this which gave Khrushchev the pretext he needed for retreat, once he had stopped the refugee flight to the West. Khrushchev reported to Congress of the Soviet Communist Party on October 17 that "the western powers were showing some understanding of the situation, and were inclined to seek a solution to the German problem and the issue of West Berlin." If this were so, "we shall not insist on signing a peace treaty absolutely before December 31, 1961." The crisis was suddenly over.

6. CODA

Four months later I visited West Berlin with Robert and Ethel Kennedy. We arrived on Washington's Birthday, a freezing,

TOP: ATTORNEY GENERAL ROBERT F. KENNEDY WAVES TO EAST GERMAN SOLDIERS ON HIS FEBRUARY 24, 1962 VISIT TO CHECKPOINT CHARLIE. HIS WIFE, ETHEL, STANDS BESIDE HIM.

BOTTOM: ROBERT KENNEDY, FOLLOWED BY MAYOR BRANDT, CLIMBS A LADDER TO A PLATFORM GIVING A VIEW OVER THE WALL.

blowy, snowy day. Thousands of people endured the chill along the streets into West Berlin to welcome President Kennedy's brother. They waved, they shouted, some wept. Over a hundred thousand stood in the square before the *Rathaus* where Bobby, shivering in the bitter cold, gave an impromptu speech. When balloons bearing red flags floated over from the eastern sector, he said, "The Communists will let the balloons through, but they won't let their people come through," and the crowd mingled defiance and anguish in an animal roar. That night and the next morning, the Attorney General again spoke passionately and honestly, condemning the Wall as an atrocity, but making it clear that no miracle was going to suddenly bring it down. It was clear that the West Germans appreciated both his warmth and his candor.

Finally we made a tour of the Wall. It was more barbaric and sinister than one could have imagined—the crude, gray concrete blocks, the bricked-in windows of apartment houses along the sector line, the vicious tank traps, the tall picket fences erected to prevent East Berliners from even waving to relatives or friends in West Berlin, the plain white crosses marking places where people had jumped to their death and beside which Robert Kennedy now laid flowers.

Trouble was by no means at an end. Though Khrushchev had once again forsworn his deadline and permitted the situation (with the exception of the Wall) to revert to the status quo, he continued to consider West Berlin the exposed western foot and planned from time to time to stamp on the corns. The year after Vienna saw sporadic and unpredictable harassments of a more or less petty sort presumably designed to test western reactions and, with luck, to nibble at western rights. Worse, the Wall itself remained a haunting relic of the crisis and became, from time to time, the occasion for new tragedy, as in August 1962, when the East German police shot down a young man trying to flee to the west and left him to perish in agony in the full view of West Berlin.

The Berlin crisis of 1961 represented a further step beyond Laos in the education of the President in the controlled employment of force for the service of peace. One never knows, of course, what would have happened if Kennedy had ordered full mobilization, or if he had rushed straight to negotiation; but either extreme might well have invited Soviet miscalculation and ended in war. Instead he applied power and diplomacy in a combination and sequence which enabled him to guard the vital interests of the west and hold off the holocaust. The weeks from Vienna to the 22nd Party Congress had nevertheless been cruel and disheartening. The Berlin crisis, along with the Soviet resumption of nuclear tests, left the President no alternative but to forgo his pursuit of a standstill and harden his policy and purpose.

SOVIET FOREIGN MINISTER ANDREI GROMYKO MEETS WITH KENNEDY TO DISCUSS THE BERLIN CRISIS ON OCTOBER 6, 1961.

As for the negotiations which had seemed so urgent in the early autumn of 1961, they lost their priority after Khrushchev dropped his deadline and descended from the heads of state to the foreign office bureaucracies. In early 1962 each side tabled its set of proposals in a succession of Rusk-Gromyko talks. It seemed probable that Khrushchev realized after the summer of 1961 that he could not expel the west within the existing equilibrium of military force. But he still cherished his dream of a communist Berlin, and this no doubt led him to ponder in 1962 how he might revise the military equilibrium to permit the renewal of his campaign under a balance of power more favorable to the Soviet Union.

It would take still another and more terrible crisis—the moment of supreme risk which Kennedy had predicted to James Wechsler—before Khrushchev was willing to abandon the politics of intimidation and before Kennedy, two long years after Vienna, was able to pick up the threads of his policy and try again to lead the world beyond the cold war.

XVI.
THE RECONSTRUCTION OF DIPLOMACY

THE FRUSTRATIONS of the summer over Berlin brought the President's discontent with his Department of State to a climax. One muddle after another left Kennedy with little doubt that the State Department was not yet an instrumentality fully and promptly responsive to presidential purpose.

He well understood the difficulty of converting a tradition-ridden bureaucracy into a mechanism for swift information and decision. But resistance was no less great in Defense, where McNamara was plainly making progress in annexing the Pentagon to the United States government. Other departments provided quick answers to presidential questions and quick action on presidential orders. It was a constant puzzle to Kennedy that the State Department remained so formless and impenetrable. He would say, "Damn it, Bundy and I get more done in one day in the White House than they do in six months in the State Department."

1. THE INSTITUTIONALIZATION OF FOREIGN POLICY

Kennedy had come to the Presidency determined to make the Department of State the central point, below the Presidency itself, in the conduct of foreign affairs. McGeorge Bundy emphasized that the President wanted no question to arise concerning "the clear authority and responsibility of the Secretary of State, not only in his own Department, and not only in such larges cale related areas as foreign aid and information policy, but also as the *agent of coordination* in all our major policies toward other nations."*

In embarking on this course, Kennedy was influenced not only by a desire to clarify and concentrate the making of foreign policy but also, I believe, by a basic respect for the skills of the Foreign Service. No doubt his attitude toward professional diplomats was mixed. He probably recalled his father's complaints as ambassador to England, and his visit to Southeast Asia as a young Congressman in 1951 had left him, as he said on his return, with an impression that Foreign Service officers often knew all too little about the nations to which they were accredited, were indifferent to their language and customs, did not represent contemporary America and spent too much time at tennis and cocktails.** Nevertheless there were always the Charles Bohlens, Llewellyn Thompsons and Edmund Gullions; and Kennedy's disappointment about the State Department as President sprang in part, I think, from a special sympathy for the diplomatic enterprise. In other circumstances he would have liked to be an ambassador himself.

The Foreign Service, after all, was the elite unit of the American government. It was in great measure a self-administered body, selecting, assessing and promoting from within. It had deep pride in its *esprit de corps*. Anyone who had seen the Service in action well knew the intelligence, decency and selflessness of this group of exceptionally devoted men and women. The White House could always win any battle it chose over the Service; but the prestige and proficiency of the Service limited the number of battles any White House would find it profitable to fight.

Still, as his pre-election task forces reminded Kennedy, the Service had its professional deformations. Moreover, both its vast increase in size and the trauma of the Dulles-McCarthy period had had a disturbing impact on its thought and operation. Thus Adlai Stevenson in his foreign policy report mentioned the "tremendous institutional inertial force" in the Department of State. The Foreign Service had failed to keep pace with changing demands in the years since the Second World War. The role of American diplomacy in prewar days had been largely spectatorial and ceremonial. But in the postwar world our diplomats could no longer be merely observers. They were operators in more than a hundred countries around the planet, and they needed regional knowledge and technical skill as well as personal initiative to make their interventions effective. But in many cases the older career men deplored the new tendencies toward

* My italics.

** "Meet the Press," December 2, 1951.

specialization, whether functional or (except for the Russia and China services) regional. They continued to see themselves as gentlemen, not players; the political officer remained the Service's beau ideal. Economic, scientific, cultural, commercial and agricultural attachés made up a rather grubby supporting cast. As for regional expertise, younger officers feared that, the better their qualifications for a particular country, the lower rating they would get under "General Usefulness."

Nearly every problem inherent in the Foreign Service process had been compounded by its prodigious growth. The Department itself had moved from its pleasant and leisured home beside the White House, with its high ceilings, great fireplaces and swinging doors, to a vast, unlovely building in Foggy Bottom. As it grew in size, the Department diminished in usefulness. This was in part the consequence of bureaucratization. 'Layering'—the bureaucrat's term for the imposition of one level of administrative responsibility on top of another—created a system of 'concurrences,' which required every proposal to run a hopelessly intricate obstacle course before it could become policy. Obviously clearance was necessary to avoid anarchy, but it often became an excuse for doing as little as possible.

Franklin Roosevelt and Cordell Hull had started the Department's descent from its traditional place at the summit of the foreign policy process—Roosevelt because he wanted certain things done and Hull because he was not temperamentally able to do them. Thwarted in the Secretary's office, Roosevelt fell into the habit of using other channels. No Secretary of State after the war, not even Acheson or Dulles, was quite able to gather back the vanished powers. By 1961 the State Department was but one of many bodies involved in foreign affairs. The London Embassy, for example, housed representatives of forty-four agencies of the United States government.

Bureaucratization was only part of the explanation for State's malaise when Kennedy came to office. The other part was the shock of McCarthy - or rather the shock of the readiness of Dulles, as Secretary of State, to yield up Foreign Service officers to McCarthyism. The Dulles period was a time of distress and humiliation for the professionals. These years saw the expulsion of experienced and independent-minded diplomats. The McCarthy era, by demonstrating the peril of dangerous thoughts, elevated conformism into a conditioned reflex. Career men stopped telling Washington what they really thought and consecrated themselves to the clichés of the cold war.

The Service was not so much an instrument of action as a way of life. And it was a way of life which not seldom divested career officers of strong views of their own. The way to success lay in the faithful support of established policy. The lack of continuity in assignment—Iceland one year, Tanganyika the next—made it difficult to develop an intense interest in new policies. It was no coincidence that the Russia and China services, where the necessity of learning a difficult language compelled continuity, were precisely the services where the professionals were most outspoken on policy matters—and were in consequence most punished in the Dulles-McCarthy years. At times it almost looked as if the Service inducted a collection of spirited young Americans at the age of twenty-five and transmuted them in twenty years into bland and homologous denizens of a conservative men's club.

2. FOGGY BOTTOM IN 1961

This was the situation which confronted Kennedy in his attempt to make the Department the agent of coordination. The new administration almost immediately bogged down in the bureaucratic tangle. Men like Harriman and Kennan, who had known the Department as late as the Truman administration, were startled by the transformation of a decade. The machinery was becoming an end in itself. "The heart of the bureaucratic problem," Rusk once observed, "is the inclination to avoid responsibility." The President used to divert himself with the dream of establishing a secret office of thirty people or so to run foreign policy while maintaining the State Department as a façade in which people might contentedly carry papers from bureau to bureau.

Nor did the Department respond to the President's

own emphasis on the values of specialization. The President had sent the Department a memorandum saying that it was better to let officers build up expertise than to rotate them mechanically every two years, and yet seasoned diplomats with experience in the history, culture and language of a particular nation or region were blindly posted to unfamiliar embassies. Worst of all, bureaucratization and McCarthyism had strengthened the most defensive and conservative impulses within the Foreign Service. I remember when Harriman came back to Washington during a break in the interminable Geneva conference on Laos. The Foreign Service, he said, had declined greatly in purpose, clarity and liberalism since he had last known it.

One almost concluded that the definition of a Foreign Service officer was a man for whom the risks always outweighed the opportunities. Career officers had always tended to believe that the foreign policy of the United States was their institutional, if not their personal, property, to be solicitously protected against interference from the White House and other misguided amateurs; and by 1961 those favored in the Dulles years added to this proprietary instinct an immovable devotion to the attitudes of the past, whether good or bad. The hardest thing of all was to change anything —attitudes, programs, clichés. No one was more annoyed by this fidelity to the past, than Galbraith. "You have no idea," he wrote me from New Delhi in 1961, "how difficult it is to control one's reaction over the smug pursuit of what experience has already shown to be disastrous policies."

This dedication to the past found its ultimate sanction in what seemed the Service's unshakable determination to protect those who, if wrong, were wrong in the right way and to penalize those who, though right, were right out of channels or out of cadence. The Foreign Service operated as a sort of benevolent society, taking care of its worst as well as—sometimes better than—its best. The promotion system was in effect a conspiracy of the conventional against the unconventional. J. Graham Parsons, having drastically misconceived the situation in Laos, was made ambassador to Sweden. His successor as Assistant Secretary for Far Eastern Affairs, a blameless but unimaginative career officer, having displayed no initiative in Washington, was sent as ambassador to a pivotal Asian state.

On the other hand, zeal for good, but new, policies at the expense of bad, but established, ones was likely to gain an officer the reputation for causing trouble and—under the system where the challenged officer wrote the 'efficiency reports'—a place at the bottom of his Foreign Service class. When Kennedy ended the unrelenting American opposition to the center-left coalition in Italy, the Deputy Chief of Mission in Rome, who had been single-handedly responsible for the prolongation of that policy long after it had become obsolete, became ambassador to Czechoslovakia; while an intelligent junior officer who had fought prematurely for the new policy in the Rome Embassy was marked down for insubordination, his offense having been that of carrying the case past the D.C.M. to the ambassador.

Caution even smothered the Department's relations with its own envoys abroad. After the Bay of Pigs I found that Washington had confined itself to sending around bland official 'explanations' couched in language suitable for public release. For what had really happened American diplomats overseas did better to rely on *Newsweek* and *Time*. Even though the Attorney General interested himself in the problem, we were never able to persuade State to level with its own embassies on this matter. This sort of thing was all too common.

3. THE WHITE HOUSE AND FOREIGN POLICY

The center, of course, lay not in Foggy Bottom but in the White House. The act of 1789 establishing the Department of Foreign Affairs provided that the Secretary should manage the business of the Department "in such manner as the President of the United States shall from time to time order or instruct." Kennedy saw the White House and the Department as intimate partners in the enterprise of foreign policy.

The operating link in this partnership was McGeorge Bundy and the now streamlined National Security Council staff. The Council itself met far less regularly than in Eisenhower days and the President convened it only when he was on the brink of decision. He saw no sense in placing unformulated problems before the miscellaneous body of men designated in the statute. Instead he preferred to set up task forces specifically qualified to deal with particular problems. By bringing together working representatives of every agency concerned with the matter and giving one man the job of producing recommendations, the task force could greatly improve the speed and coordination with which policy was made. In time the task force approach led to the formation of the so-called Executive Committee of the National Security Council - a group drawn from the NSC but not including all its statutory members and supplemented by people from outside the NSC as occasion demanded.

But, if the National Security Council played a diminishing role, the National Security Council staff was indispensable.

The Bundy staff was a remarkable body of men—and it was a tribute to Bundy's own clarity of intellect and force of

WALT ROSTOW WHO SERVED AS DEPUTY TO MCGEORGE BUNDY, SPECIAL ASSISTANT FOR NATIONAL SECURTIY AFFAIRS.

character that they so cheerfully deferred to his leadership. Walt Rostow, an economic historian turned social philosopher, served as Mac's deputy. Carl Kaysen applied his brilliant intelligence to security as well as economic issues. Robert Komer, a government career man who had managed to survive the Eisenhower years with undiminished liveliness of wit and hope, covered the uncommitted world. In 1962, Michael Forrestal, the son of Truman's Secretary of Defense, joined the staff and brought intelligent judgment to the baffling issues of southeast Asia. Bromley Smith, a great civil servant, presided calmly as NSC Secretary over the flow of documents and decisions. All of these men had easy access to the President and served him invaluably in alerting him to problems and executing his instructions.

Nor was the work of foreign policy at the White House confined to the Bundy staff. The President wanted Ted Sorensen at his right hand every time there was a major crisis or a major speech. Because of his special concern with Latin America, he directed Richard Goodwin and me and later Ralph Dungan to follow hemisphere developments for him. Dungan, in addition, watched the foreign aid program and advised on the selection of top government officials. Jerome Wiesner and his Science Adviser's staff dealt with armament and disarmament. Myer Feldman kept a hand in on the Middle East and on tariff and trade issues. I acquired the United Nations and occasional European matters, especially Italy, as particular problems.

The Bay of Pigs made us all more aggressive in defending the interests of the President and therefore in invading on his behalf what the foreign affairs bureaucracy too often regarded as its private domain. Bundy insisted from the start that the White House get the flow of raw intelligence from State, Defense and the CIA; this generally gave us enough facts to be able to ask the departments the pregnant questions and not be put off by the sterile answers. We tried to become the President's eyes and ears through the whole area of national security, reporting to him the things he had to know—and this would sometimes include things which the department involved did not wish him to know until it had decided for itself what it wanted him to do. At the same time we tried to uncover in the middle levels of government ideas which we believed deserved a hearing at the top before they had been diluted or choked off by interbureau or interagency rivalry. We were the President's men,

Kennedy's use of his staff provoked much press comment about White House 'meddling'... Kennedy, unmoved, would suggest that people ought to read the Constitution over there and find out who was responsible for foreign affairs and whose government it was anyway.

and the government knew it, in part welcoming it, in part resenting it.

Kennedy's use of his staff provoked much press comment about White House 'meddling'; the very word implied that the White House had no business interfering in the internal affairs of the government. Kennedy, unmoved, would suggest that people ought to read the Constitution over there and find out who was responsible for foreign affairs and whose government it was anyway.

The staff was part of the formal panoply of the White House; but in October 1961 Kennedy acquired a highly informal source of wisdom and support in international matters when his old friend David Ormsby Gore came to Washington as British Ambassador.* Many ties had strengthened their relationship since they first met in London in 1938. After the election, Kennedy told Ormsby Gore that he must come to Washington as ambassador, and in due course he appeared.

The Kennedys (to the irritation of the rest of the diplomatic corps) enjoyed no couple more than they did the Ormsby Gores. The President found the Ambassador a companion for every mood, whether he wanted to sail in Nantucket Sound or brood over the prospects of nuclear annihilation. Like Kennedy and like Macmillan, Ormsby Gore believed in the realistic pursuit of a *détente* with the Soviet Union, and he steadily reinforced Kennedy's skepticism about the clichés of the cold war. Only two men of notable character could have so delicately mingled personal and official relations, for each remained at all times the firm and candid advocate of the policies of his own nation.

Beyond his staff, his task forces, his friends, there was the President himself, increasingly the day-to-day director of American foreign policy. Though he had faithfully served his domestic apprenticeship in Congress, foreign affairs had long since captured his primary imagination, even before he gained his membership on the Senate Foreign Relations Committee. He had had a considerably more varied and extensive international experience than most men elected President. In his twenties he had talked to Franklin Roosevelt, Chamberlain and Baldwin and in his thirties to Churchill, Nehru, Ben Gurion and Fanfani. He knew Europe well and had traveled in Russia, Latin America and the Far East.

It was not accidental that he chose the Under Secretary of State, the Ambassador to the United Nations and the Assistant Secretary for Africa before he named the Secretary of State; he felt this in some particular sense 'his' department. Nor was his early appearance as, in effect, desk officer for Laos uncharacteristic. He wanted to know everything that was going on and, when matters were critical, he often cleared (and redrafted) messages and instructions himself. In the relationship between the President and the ambassadors, there had been, it is true, a slippage since Roosevelt's day. In spite of the Department's effort to insert itself between the President and his ambassadors, Kennedy succeeded in displaying what Edmund Gullion once described as a "direct and sometimes disconcerting personal interest in the problems of particular missions." Ambassadors as different as George Kennan in Yugoslavia and Joseph Farland in Panama later told me that they found the President far more understanding of their problems than the State Department.

Kennedy dealt personally with almost every aspect of policy around the globe. He knew more about certain areas than the senior officials at State and probably called as many issues to their attention as they did to his. He wanted particularly to stay ahead of problems; nothing exasperated him more than to be surprised by crisis. It was at his instance in early 1961, for example, that a task force worked out the first long-range program for Iran; and as early as August 1961 he

* On the death of his father in 1964, Ormsby Gore became Lord Harlech.

sent out a directive saying that the United States should prepare for a more active role in Cyprus if trouble was to be averted in the eastern Mediterranean. More than anyone in the government, he was the source of ideas, initiative and imagination in foreign policy.

This was partly a matter of temperament and curiosity but partly too of necessity. In the modern Presidency, every chief executive, sooner or later, no matter what his background or predilection, is drawn into a particular concern with foreign affairs. It is not just that foreign questions are often more interesting or offer Presidents more scope for personal maneuver and decision; it is above all that the issues are more fateful. And the nuclear age, as Richard Neustadt liked to point out, added a dimension of 'irreversibility' to policy—that is, certain choices, once made, could not be called back. Moreover, the irreversible choices might be, not the final, dramatic decisions, but rather the minor and technical steps taken at a low level a long time back but leading ineluctably to the catastrophic choice. The Bay of Pigs provided Kennedy the warning and confirmed his temperamental instinct to reach deep inside State, Defense and the CIA in order to catch hold of policies before these policies made his choices for him. "Domestic policy," he used to say, "can only defeat us; foreign policy can kill us."

4. THE STRUGGLE FOR COORDINATION

While Kennedy had no doubt that the President's exercise of his seniority in foreign affairs was his constitutional duty, he earnestly hoped that the State Department would really serve as his agent of coordination. He wanted to end the faceless system of indecision and inaction which diffused foreign policy among the three great bureaucracies of State, Defense and the CIA. But, to make coordination effective, it was necessary to strengthen the Department's instrumentalities of control. This was especially important overseas, where the dispersion of power was most acute, visible and mischievous. Kennedy's circular letter to the ambassadors consequently gave them the authority to "oversee and coordinate all the activities of the United States Government" in their countries, except for military forces in the field under a United States area military commander.

This was not an entirely popular move. It was resisted by Defense, the CIA, the Peace Corps and other agencies which liked to act independently—and even by traditional Foreign Service officers who did not want to be responsible for non-traditional operations and preferred not to know, for example, what the CIA was up to. Within State, however, Chester Bowles ardently championed the new approach.

Cuba and Laos had already provided the new administration with horrible examples of the readiness of CIA operatives in the field to go off on policies of their own. This was only the most spectacular expression of the steady growth of the CIA in the 1950s. Its staff had doubled in a decade. It had almost as many people under official cover overseas as State; in a number of embassies CIA officers outnumbered those from State in the political sections. Often the CIA station chief had been in the country longer than the ambassador, had more money at his disposal and exerted more influence. The CIA had its own political desks and military staffs; it had in effect its own foreign service, its own air force, even, on occasion, its own combat forces. Moreover, the CIA declined to clear its clandestine intelligence operations either with the State Department in Washington or with the ambassador in the field; and, while covert political operations were cleared with State, this was sometimes done, not at the start, but after the operation had almost reached the point beyond which it could not easily be recalled.

None of this is to suggest that the CIA constituted, in the title of a popular exposé, an "invisible government" or that its influence was always, or often, reactionary and sinister. In my experience its leadership was politically enlightened and sophisticated. Nonetheless, it had acquired a power which, however beneficial its exercise often might be, blocked State Department control over the conduct of foreign affairs. The President's letter now gave every ambassador for the first time the authority to know everything the CIA people were doing in his country. The directive constituted at least a first step toward bringing secret operations under policy control.

The Bay of Pigs, of course, stimulated a wide variety of proposals for the reorganization of the CIA. Kennedy moved quietly to cut the CIA budget in 1962 and again in 1963, aiming at a 20 percent reduction by 1966. At the same time, anticipating the resignation of Allen Dulles, he began looking for a new director. After a long search, he came up in September 1961 with the name of John McCone, a California Republican who had served Truman as Under Secretary of the Air Force and Eisenhower as chairman of the Atomic Energy Commission. McCone had the reputation of a rigid cold-warrior who viewed the world in moralistic stereotypes, but he turned out to be a cautious, realistic and self-effacing head of the CIA. He repaired morale within the Agency, instituted measures to subject venturesome proposals to critical scrutiny and did his best to keep the CIA and himself out of the newspapers. He restored its relations with the State Department and the Congress, if not altogether with the Department of Defense.

As further evidence of his desire to place responsibility in the diplomatic professionals, Kennedy gave the Foreign Service an unprecedentedly large share of ambassadorial appointments. And during the interregnum he persuaded John Rooney, chairman of the House subcommittee which controlled State Department appropriations, to increase representational allowances so that career officers could afford to take major embassies.

5. THE UNEASY PARTNERSHIP

Yet, in spite of the presidential effort to give the Department the central role in foreign affairs, Richard Neustadt was obliged to testify before the Jackson Subcommittee in 1963: "So far as I can judge, the State Department has not yet found means to take the proffered role and play it vigorously across the board."

Part of the trouble was inherent in the effort, as Neustadt defined it, to make the State Department "at once a department and then something more." The Secretary already had, in the jargon, a 'full plate,' so the process of codification tended toward generalization and ambiguity and rarely provided specific guidance on the hard choices.

Part of the trouble too lay in the attitude of the White House toward the Foreign Service. Talk of the need for specialization was all very well; but Charles Bohlen felt that the President did not make sufficient allowance for the virtues of professionalism. Kennedy wanted quick and personal replies to significant questions, not taking into account the fact that any significant question had a bundle of implications to consider. He wanted ambassadors to know languages, master technical fields and fraternize with the people of the countries to which they were assigned, forgetting that the chief purpose of the diplomat was the transaction of business between governments and that everything else was supporting and subsidiary. Too much emphasis on diplomatic activism per se might lead people to forget the limits of diplomatic action.

The aggressiveness of the White House staff no doubt compounded the trouble. White House 'meddling' struck some of the pros as careless intrusion by impulsive and ignorant amateurs. John Davies would ask, "How can you expect these men to do a good job?" The question was a real one. The Foreign Service obviously had to carry out the policies of the administration; yet 'thought correction,' even in favor of the New Frontier, presented its problems. The President, commenting on the public service in his first State of the Union message, had said, "Let it be clear that this Administration recognizes the value of dissent and daring—that we greet healthy controversy as the hallmark of healthy change."

These structural factors explained part of the State Department's faltering response to its "proffered role." The partnership seemed chronically out of balance. But Kennedy never ceased hoping that it would work. Instead, he repressed his frustrations (at some times more successfully than at others) and kept supposing that by strengthening the direction of the Department he would enable it to sustain its side of the partnership.

6. THE ENIGMA OF RUSK

Kennedy had decided on Dean Rusk as Secretary of State after a single talk. It was an understandable choice. Rusk was a man of broad experience and marked ability. He rarely spoke about himself; but I remember his talking with quiet charm about his boyhood in rural Georgia, a land that had been transformed by public health and electrification. These memories left him a convinced if undemonstrative liberal on domestic issues. To his social and economic convictions he added an earnest concern for the rights of Negroes. War service was followed by government service in the Pentagon and then in the State Department. He was Assistant Secretary for United Nations Affairs and then for the Far East before leaving Washington in 1952 to become president of the Rockefeller Foundation. This background gave him expert knowledge of the Atlantic and the Pacific, Defense and State, the United Nations and the ways that science and medicine could benefit mankind.

A man of exceptional intelligence, lucidity and control, he had a tidy and exact mastery of the technical detail of a bewildering range of foreign problems and a talent for concise and dispassionate exposition. He had great ability to summarize divergent views and put his finger on the heart of a question. His idealism, if subdued and prosaic, was authentic.

As Secretary of State, he worked as long and as hard as anyone in Washington. In negotiations with foreign countries, he was vigilant, impassive, patient and skilled. He displayed the same qualities in his relations with Congress and proved the most effective Secretary of State on the Hill since Cordell Hull. Within the executive branch, he developed excellent relations with McNamara; indeed, Rusk, having spent more than half his government career with the military, disliked cracks about generals and was pleased to have their esteem. As for the general public, he remained deliberately dim until dimness had its effect, repelling controversy and inspiring confidence. Toward the Soviet Union he exhibited a matter-of-fact mistrust which at times seemed automatic inflexibility but still differed from Dulles's conviction of irremediable Soviet evil.

He was, more than anything else, a man bred in the large organizations of mid-century America. But, unlike McNamara, his organizational instinct was for service, not for mastery. Nurtured in the successive bosoms of the university, the Army, the government department, the foundation, he drew reassurance from the solidity of the structure, the regularity of the procedures, the familiarity of the vocabulary. His mind, for all its strength and clarity, was irrevocably conventional. He mistrusted what he called "the flashy or sensational" and rejoiced in the role of "tedium" in diplomacy.

Rusk was a superb technician: this was his power and his problem. He had trained himself all his life to be the ideal chief of staff, the perfect number-two man. The inscrutability which made him a good aide and a gifted negotiator made him also a baffling leader. In consequence, he failed to imbue the Department with positive direction and purpose. He had authority but not command. One telephone conversation with the President was worth a score of meetings with the Secretary. He was equally baffling at the White House. Where McNamara and Dillon would forcefully and articulately assert the interests of their departments in impending foreign policy decisions, Rusk would sit quietly by, with his Buddha-like face and half-smile, often leaving it to Bundy or to the President himself to assert the diplomatic interest. Nearly every time Kennedy faced a major foreign policy decision the views of his Secretary of State remained a mystery. Or so at least was the impression of the White House staff, whose judgment of the Secretary failed, I am sure, to take account of his problems. He was a proud and sensitive man, surrounded in his own Department by figures of greater public note and dominated by a President who wanted to be his own Secretary of State. He lived, no doubt, under threats of humiliation and fears of inadequacy.

His relationship with the President remained formal. Kennedy remarked to a friend in State that Rusk was the only cabinet member he did not call by his first name. When this was repeated to Rusk, he said he liked it better that way. Kennedy was always impressed by Rusk's capacity to define but grew increasingly depressed by his reluctance to decide. Conceivably this was the kind of Secretary of State Rusk thought the President preferred. But, while the President was certainly determined to direct the foreign policy of the nation, he nonetheless wanted someone who could not only mass the State Department but be a constant source of definite recommendations and fresh ideas. Yet, though often perplexed and disappointed by Rusk, Kennedy liked him personally and was protective of him, and felt that dismissal of his Secretary of State would constitute too severe a comment on his own original judgment. All this meant that, if the President were going to get at the "bowl of jelly," reorganization would have to start at a lower level.

DEAN RUSK MEETING WITH GREEK PRESIDENT CONSTANTINE CARAMANLIS IN MAY 1962.

7. THE SACRIFICE OF BOWLES

Chester Bowles, as Under Secretary, had the second place of responsibility in the State Department. Kennedy liked Bowles, appreciated his help in the months before Los Angeles and sympathized with his efforts to redress the balance of our foreign policy toward the underdeveloped world and toward political rather than military solutions. Moreover, Bowles had important assets for the administration. He had unusual gifts for public persuasion. His personal idealism inspired devotion on the part of many who worked for him. He was identified in the United States and through the world with the affirmative impulses of American foreign policy. He was more responsible than anyone else for the distinguished series of ambassadorial appointments. He had been right on Cuba. He retained a strong following in the liberal community.

Bowles, however, had his vulnerabilities too. His ambassadorial choices, though they pleased everybody else, had outraged the oldline professionals. Once the appointments were completed, his role was ill-defined. Though he had shown marked executive ability when he headed the Office of Price Administration in the Second World War, he never received clear-cut authority to run the State Department. To Bowles's supporters—and they were zealous and vocal as his enemies—it seemed that Rusk was unwilling either to manage the Department himself or to let Bowles do it. The relationship between the two men was less close than Bowles had expected.

At the White House the aftermath of the Bay of Pigs had put Bowles in an exposed position. Nor had Bowles made any effort to exploit a personal relationship to the President. More access would not necessarily have improved things, though, for there was a fatal difference in tempo between Bowles and the New Frontier. The New Frontier put a premium on quick, tough, laconic, decided people; it was easily exasperated by more meditative types, like Bowles. Bowles's command of large issues was unfortunately not matched by a command of small issues. "Chet is a fine fellow," the President said to me one day in early May, "but he's just not doing the job.... Because Chet isn't doing his job, Rusk is spreading himself too thin and is not able to do his job either." He added, "Now George Ball is fine. He gets things done. So does Alexis Johnson."

The situation dragged on unhappily for several weeks. One day early in June, the President observed that the present state of affairs really could not be permitted to continue, that Bowles was oriented toward discussion rather than action and therefore only reinforced the vacillating and dilatory habits of the Department. Someone, he said, would have to be put in Bowles's place who could make the Department work; but "of course it will look as if we were throwing out the one man in the State Department who was right on Cuba."

The situation occupied Kennedy and his closest aides for several days, and for a brief time was played out publicly in the press. The staff pondered a number of scenarios that would redistribute responsibility within the department to a number of New Frontiersmen, possibly Arthur Dean, a favorite of Rusk's who had served as a disarmament negotiatior, or George Ball, a lawyer from Chicago who had worked in the Stevenson campaigns. Bowles himself played a role, astutely raising the idea of bringing in Averill Harriman in a more permanent role.

8. THE STATE DEPARTMENT REORGANIZATION

That autumn Bowles was abroad a good deal of the time, and Ball was assuming more and more administrative responsibility within the Department. The final act took place in November. The President was ready to overhead the State Department Staff. George Ball would become Under Secretary; George McGhee would move from the Policy Planning Council to replace Ball as the second Under Secretary (though for Political rather than for Economic Affairs); Harriman would become Assistant Secretary for the Far East; and, from the White House, Walt Rostow would go over to State as counselor and chief of the Policy Planning Council, Fred Dutton as Assistant Secretary for Congressional Relations and Goodwin himself as Deputy Assistant Secretary for Inter-American Affairs. As for Bowles, the President wanted him to take a new assignment in relation to the underdeveloped world. Ted Sorensen, after a long talk, persuaded Bowles to become Special Representative and Adviser to the President for African, Asian and Latin American Affairs.

Bowles, the hapless victim of the conditions which he had diagnosed better than anybody else, behaved with characteristic nobility and was soon hard at work in his new assignment. But he was outside the chain of command, and the job was doomed to frustration. Finally, in December 1962, Bowles decided that his assignment had not worked out and offered his resignation.

The purpose of the reorganization of November 1961, and especially of the blood transfusion from the White House, was to revitalize the Department and redress the imbalance in the foreign affairs partnership; it was one more expression of Kennedy's effort to make the Department the fulcrum of foreign policy.

The upheaval somewhat improved the situation. Though Ball remained a lawyer and not a manager, he had the talents of speed and decision and gave the President at least hope that his questions would be answered and his instructions executed. Rostow, perfectly cast, made the Policy Planning Council a bustle of intellectual activity and helped shape policy on a dozen fronts. Dutton joined policy sophistication with political skill in running congressional relations. Goodwin, until he was eventually cut off and isolated by the bureaucracy, brought new imagination and drive to Latin American affairs. Above all, Harriman not only gave Far Eastern policy a coherence and force it had not had for years but rapidly became the particular champion of the New Frontier within the State Department.

One could not but marvel at the inexhaustible vitality of this man, now in his seventies, the most tested of American diplomats, who, after living at the summit with Roosevelt, Churchill and Stalin twenty years earlier, was now cheerfully settled in a job of lower rank than any he had held for a generation. Inside the government, the New Frontiersmen, within

CHESTER BOWLES, WHO WAS REASSIGNED BY THE PRESIDENT AS SPECIAL REPRESENTATIVE AND ADVISOR FOR AFRICAN, ASIAN AND LATIN AMERICAN AFFAIRS, SPEAKS AT THE WORLD TRADE CONFERENCES OF INTERNATIONAL ASSOCIATION OF MACHINISTS IN WASHINGTON ON NOVEMBER 28, 1961.

and without the State Department, regarded him as their champion. Perhaps no one else, except the President and the Attorney General, had such a stimulating influence on policy. Power continued to gravitate toward him. In 1963, when George McGhee went on to become ambassador to Bonn, Harriman took his place as Under Secretary for Political Affairs.

To the end, the Department remained a puzzle to the President. No one ran it; Rusk, Ball and Harriman constituted a loose triumvirate on the seventh floor and, passing things back and forth among themselves, managed to keep a few steps ahead of crisis. But with all the problems and frustrations, Kennedy had gone far toward infusing a new energy into American diplomacy and a new spirit into the conduct of foreign affairs.

XVII.
PERIL IN THE SKIES

KENNEDY HAD COME TO THE White House without illusion about peace in our time with the communist states. But he did hope that the Soviet leaders, as rational men, might at least agree on the value of moderating the cold war. The Vienna meeting shook this hope, and the Soviet announcement on August 30 of a decision to resume nuclear testing in the atmosphere almost shattered it. The President's response was prompt and bitter. The Soviet course, he said, "presents a hazard to every human being throughout the world by increasing the dangers of nuclear fallout." It "indicates the complete hypocrisy" of Soviet professions about disarmament. It increases "the danger of a thermo-nuclear holocaust." It "will be met with deepest concern and resentment throughout the world."

It certainly was met with the deepest concern in the United States. The next morning, newspapers denounced the Soviet move and Senators demanded that the United States imitate it. The atmosphere was tense in the White House when the President called the National Security Council together at ten o'clock in the Cabinet Room in preparation for a meeting with the congressional leaders at ten forty-five. The faces around the table—Johnson, Rusk, McNamara, General Taylor, General Lemnitzer, Jerome Wiesner, Allen Dulles, Glenn Seaborg of the Atomic Energy Commission, Edward R. Murrow and a few others—were set and anxious. The time was short, and the Secretary of State quickly submitted a draft presidential statement announcing an immediate American decision to resume tests—essential, he thought, both to demonstrate our resolution on Berlin and to satisfy the domestic clamor.

The President dissented. "Why should we put ourselves into this business right away?" he asked. There may be a storm of exasperation in the United States if we don't announce resumption, but we can stand that for a few days." The Russians thus far had only said they would resume testing; they had not yet tested. We speculated as to when their series would begin and what they could expect to learn from it. Kennedy said, "The Russians are not fools. They thought they would lose less than they would gain by this decision. They must believe they will gain most by appearing tough and mean." But he put the statement aside.

Later in the day the President in a brief statement characterized the Soviet announcement as "primarily a form of atomic blackmail, designed to substitute terror for reason in the present international scene," and said nothing about American testing.

1. THE TEST BAN TRAVAIL

The idea of a test ban first arose in the early fifties in response to the development of the hydrogen bomb. In the summer of 1952, Dr. Vannevar Bush, who had mobilized American science during the Second World War, proposed to Dean Acheson, then Secretary of State, that, before trying out the new bomb, the United States seek a no-testing agreement with the Soviet Union. Bush's effort failed, and the United States shortly began a series of nuclear explosions in the atmosphere.

The fission bombs dropped at Hiroshima and Nagasaki in 1945 had produced little radioactive debris. But the hydrogen super-bombs of the fifties were another matter. The detonation of the first fission-fusion-fission bomb in the Bikini Atoll in 1954 sent great sinister clouds floating over the lonely Pacific; and, when the "ashy rain" fell on the Japanese tuna fishermen of the *Lucky Dragon,* leaving them with charred skins and a terrible sickness, the world suddenly learned about the new horror of radioactive fallout. And the physiological argument for a test ban was soon reinforced by a political argument: that the only way to crack Soviet resistance to comprehensive schemes, like the Baruch Plan for the international control of atomic energy, was to demonstrate cooperation and create confidence in smaller and more manageable areas. The test ban seemed the ideal 'first step' toward general disarmament.

LEFT: PROTESTERS PICKET AGAINST RUSSIAN NUCLEAR TESTING OUTSIDE THE SOVIET UNITED NATIONS DELEGATION HEADQUARTERS IN NEW YORK CITY.

THE U.S. DETONATES AN ATOM BOMB AT BIKINI ATOLL IN 1946.

By 1958 Eisenhower agreed to join with the British and Russians in a conference in Geneva on the discontinuance of nuclear tests. The meeting opened in November 1958, as the United States and the Soviet Union were completing elaborate test sequences. Washington then announced that, unless Soviet Russia resumed, it would hold no tests for a year. Since then, neither nation, so far as the other knew, had conducted a test.

The object of the conference was to produce a comprehensive test ban treaty—that is, a control system outlawing all nuclear testing, whether in the earth's atmosphere, in outer space, in the oceans or underground.* Tests in air or water were readily detectable, but with the existing state of seismic research, underground testing below a certain level could not be policed without the possibility of inspection at the suspected site.

During 1959 and early 1960, Soviet representatives in Geneva displayed a modest willingness to grapple with the issues. But, while the British earnestly sought agreement, the American government remained divided within itself on the desirability of a treaty. Anti-test ban scientists, like Dr. Edward Teller, showed that it was theoretically possible to muffle the seismic signals by setting off bombs in great cavities deep under the earth and so to 'cheat' the control system.** Moreover, the responsibility for improving the techniques of seismic detection was entrusted to the Air Force, which, of course, was dominated by opponents of the test ban. The President was not sufficiently informed about the issues, nor the Secretary of State sufficiently concerned, to overcome this resistance. As a result, the American delegation in Geneva played a weak and inglorious role in the negotiations.

At the end of 1959, Eisenhower terminated the formal moratorium and declared the United States free to resume testing—an action which, of course, left the Russians technically free to resume two years later. Nevertheless an informal moratorium continued, and negotiations in Geneva through 1960 began to narrow the areas of disagreement. In time the conference succeeded in adopting a preamble, seventeen articles and two annexes of a draft treaty. As the discussions proceeded, the treaty was assuming a new dimension: it was becoming a first step not only toward wider arms control but toward a working arrangement by which the nuclear superpowers could express their common interest in preventing wars between themselves and the dispersion of nuclear weapons to new powers. Harold Macmillan regarded this as an historic opportunity to make progress toward a *détente*, and he may have been right. But the opportunity was lost. A year later Macmillan told Kennedy that it was all the fault of the American 'big hole' obsession and the consequent insistence on a wantonly large number of on-site inspections.

Then Kennedy came to office determined to narrow the differences. He had been sympathetic to the idea of a test ban for some years. Now as President he sent Arthur Dean to Geneva with a new set of American proposals. These included a reduction in our requirements for annual inspections and for control posts, as well as parity of representation on the control commission between the two sides under a neutral chairman. Unfortunately, as American interest grew, Soviet interest declined. Dag Hammarskjöld's role in the United Nations intervention in the Congo had convinced Khrushchev that there was no such thing as a neutral person and turned him against the previously acceptable idea of a neutral chairman. More important perhaps, Soviet generals and scientists were now demanding the resumption of tests in the hope of achieving more compact and efficient warheads.

* With the exception of underground tests producing signals of less than 4.75 seismic magnitude; it was expected that this threshold would be lowered as seismic research improved detection capabilities.

** In 1960 the Scientists' Committee of the Democratic Advisory Council estimated that the hole required to hide a seventy-kiloton explosion would cost $25 to $50 million and require the excavation of an amount of material greater than the country's annual production of anthracite coal. In the Kennedy administration the Atomic Energy Commission, after several years of effort and at the cost of $20 million, detonated an explosion less than one-tenth that size—and discovered that the signal was enhanced in certain directions. In retrospect, the 'big hole' scare could not seem more dubious.

They also probably now feared that inspection within the Soviet Union would expose the myth of the 'missile gap,' which had become so politically beneficial to them, and reveal Soviet missile sites as low in number and high in vulnerability. In any case, by the end of 1960 Moscow had probably begun preparations for a possible test series in 1961.

The Russians at Geneva therefore responded to the Kennedy initiative by repudiating earlier agreements and demanding the *troika*. The Soviet proposals reduced inspection in effect to self-inspection and thus to absurdity. Some time in 1961, probably after the new American Minuteman and Polaris programs were started and after the Vienna meeting, Khrushchev definitely decided to resume testing.

At the end of July, Khrushchev himself told McCloy that he was under strong pressure to test, especially from his scientists, and that the Berlin crisis had increased the pressure. He had been successful thus far, he said, in holding off the decision; but, the more the United States intensified its threats of war, the more arguments it gave those in the Soviet Union who wanted to resume. His scientists favored a one-hundred-megaton bomb as the most economical, and, though they already had the rockets to lift it, the bomb itself needed to be tested. He had cheered his scientists, he said, by telling them that the United States would resume testing and thus release them to try out their own bomb: "Don't piss in your pants—you'll have your chance soon enough."

2. TO TEST OR NOT TO TEST

There was mounting pressure on Kennedy too; Americans as well as Russians chafed under the moratorium. Some really believed that the Soviet Union was cheating in big holes in Siberia. Others, while doubting that the Russians wanted to go to the enormous expense and difficulty of a clandestine program, nevertheless favored American resumption in the interest of American weapons development. It was argued further that resumption would add verisimilitude to our stance of firmness during the Berlin crisis. The growing demand came not just from the Pentagon but from the Congress, especially from members of the Joint Committee on Atomic Energy, and to some degree also from the public.

On the other hand, resumption would create problems. It would legitimatize renewal by the Soviet Union and therefore accelerate the nuclear arms race; and it would permit the world to blame us for having started the cycle of destruction again. The President hated the idea of reopening the race: "We test and then they test and we have to test again. And you build up until somebody uses them." But as President he could not forget his responsibilities for the national security of the United States. The Soviet about-face at Geneva, he explained to a press conference in late June, "raises a serious question about how long we can safely continue on a voluntary basis a refusal to undertake tests in this country without any assurance that the Russians are not testing." He accordingly asked Jerome Wiesner and the Science Advisory Committee to convene a special panel to take a fresh look at the problem.

If it turned out that our military security required testing, the President was concerned to make it clear to the world that we were resuming only because the Russians would not join us in a treaty. He himself remained unconvinced that the military gains of resumption would outweigh the political losses; the whole idea of testing obviously left him cold.

Wiesner's special panel, chaired by the physicist Wolfgang Panofsky, met with the President and the National Security Council early in August. They reported in effect that it was feasible for the Soviet Union to have conducted secret tests, that there was no evidence it had done so (or had not done so), and that there was no urgent technical need for immediate resumption by the United States. The Joint Chiefs of Staff, however, filed a paper questioning both the premises and the conclusions of the Panofsky report. In summarizing it, General Lemnitzer said, "I would like to emphasize that we are not advocating atmospheric testing. Our memorandum is at fault if it suggests otherwise [as indeed it appeared to do]. And we have no objection to a reasonable delay in the resumption of testing. But we do see urgency in testing for small-yield weapons development."

As the session continued, one saw the old disagreement in the scientific community, going back to the argument over the hydrogen bomb in 1949 and now institutionalized in the divergence between the two great nuclear laboratories, Livermore and Los Alamos. This was the scientific side of the strategic debate of the fifties between massive retaliation and flexible response. Livermore, in the spirit of Ernest Lawrence and Edward Teller, believed that American security rested on the unlimited development of nuclear striking power; in the jargon, this was 'infinite containment.' Los Alamos, in the spirit of Robert Oppenheimer, believed that nuclear power should be only one component in a varied national arsenal; this was 'finite containment.' Though only a minority of the scientific community followed Teller, the Livermore position retained strong allies in the Congress and the press; and the perseverance of its advocates, given emotional edge by their conviction of persecution, had won them access to a formidable sector of public opinion.

With Wiesner as Kennedy's Science Adviser, the doctrines of finite containment and flexible response were clearly in the ascendancy. But, in forming the special panel, Wiesner had taken care to assemble a balanced group, including John Foster, the head of Livermore, as well as Norris Bradbury, the head of Los Alamos. Oddly enough, the Livermore scientists, who a year earlier had discoursed most eloquently on the ease and convenience for the Soviet Union of testing in secret cavities underground, were now most insistent in proclaiming the inadequacy of underground testing for the United States and demanding that we go into the atmosphere as soon as possible. Foster argued vigorously to the President that immediate resumption was necessary in order to develop the neutron bomb—that is, a fissionless bomb killing by neutron rays with very limited blast and radiation effect. The President remarked that he had understood that atmospheric testing was not indicated for the neutron bomb for at least another eighteen months. Wiesner added that the feasibility of the basic idea could be determined in a laboratory. It was the problem of 'staging' which required tests, he said, and going at this problem at once would be like building the body of a car before the motor had been invented.

The President then cross-examined the panel, and listened to the range of scientific and political arguments both for and against the resumption of testing. Eventually, John McCloy, who was in charge of disarmament negotiations, remarked that it would be unwise to resume testing with the UN General Assembly about to meet and that the discussion had satisfied him that the decision could be postponed to the first of the year without impairing national security. This appeared to sum up the sense of the meeting, and we adjourned, the President warning that any indications that we might renew testing would undercut our effort to get a treaty in Geneva.

3. THE SOVIET EXPLOSIONS

I came away with the feeling that, while there was no irresistible short-run case for resumption, everyone regarded a return at least to underground testing as inevitable in the long run if the Russians continued to reject the treaty. Kennedy wrote Macmillan early in August that he was still reviewing the evidence but was not very hopeful that it would be possible to wait much beyond the first of the year. If we did resume, the President continued, it would be underground, unless and until the Soviets resumed atmospheric tests. He also mentioned an idea which Ambassador Thompson had sent from Moscow—that we try once again for a limited ban, outlawing tests in the atmosphere and under water. These were the ones that caused fallout; they did not require inspection; and they were presumably the tests which would help the Russians the most.

This proposal greatly attracted both Bundy and me. But Arthur Dean feared that any retreat from the comprehensive treaty would be taken as a general weakening of our position. When the matter was brought to the President, he readily came up with a compromise—that Dean should fight for the whole treaty in Geneva, but, if nothing happened, we could come out for the limited ban later.

On August 28, the Foreign Broadcast Information Service recorded a Soviet broadcast warning aircraft to stay out of a designated area over Siberia. This bulletin seemed an indication we were soon to have a Russian test in the atmosphere. Two days later came Moscow's official announcement of its decision to resume. We were still waiting for the actual tests. At three o'clock on September 1, Bundy called to say that it looked as if the first Soviet explosion had taken place. You had better come over."

An argument was taking place in Bundy's office when I arrived. Arthur Dean, who had just returned from Geneva, and McCloy favored an immediate announcement of our own determination to resume. Murrow, Wiesner, Bundy and the others favored a declaration calling on the world to condemn the Russians for their action. After discussion it was decided to bring both statements to the President.

As it turned out, Kennedy was in no mood to listen to prolonged debate. Knowing what each side was going to say, he completed our sentences, slashed each statement to bits and said that, while he was not inclined to announce our resumption at this point, he did not know how much longer he could refrain from doing so. Then he briskly ushered us out.

He still hoped to avert a new sequence of atmospheric testing and spare the world a new rain of radioactivity. The time had now come for the Thompson proposal. On September 3 he joined with Macmillan in offering Khrushchev an agreement not to conduct tests which produced fallout, pointing out that such a pact could rely on existing means of detection and would not require additional controls. But later the same day, while cruising off Hyannis Port, he received word of a second Soviet test. If a Soviet series were to constitute the only answer to the offer of an atmospheric ban, Kennedy saw no choice, given the Berlin crisis, but to order United States resumption. When on Monday our detection system picked up a third Soviet test, Kennedy, back in Washington, immediately announced American preparation for tests "in the laboratory and underground, with no fallout.... In view of the acts of the

Soviet Government, we must now take those steps which prudent men find essential." He wrote Macmillan that we had to show both our friends and our own people that we were ready to meet our own needs in the face of these new Soviet acts; at this hour the gravest danger was that we might seem less determined than Khrushchev.

On September 9 Khrushchev made his formal reply to the Kennedy-Macmillan proposal. "Cessation of one kind of test only—in the atmosphere," he wrote, "—would be a disservice to the cause of peace." So, in the name of peace, he reopened the nuclear race.

Between September 1 and November 4 the Soviet Union carried out at least thirty major tests, nearly all in the atmosphere. By this time, though there had been fewer Russian than western tests since testing began, the Soviet Union had discharged more radioactive poison into the air than the United States, Britain and France together. As the new series continued, I noted. "I fear that Khrushchev has decided to make the USSR the embodiment of terror and power in the world in the expectation that all 'lovers' of peace, terrified of war and recognizing the futility of trying to alter Soviet policy, will concentrate their energies on making the west give way over Berlin. This is brinksmanship with a vengeance, and it may get us very close indeed to war."

4. APPEAL TO THE UNITED NATIONS

But the President was not ready to accept the challenge of terror without one more appeal to reason. There still remained the General Assembly of the United Nations, gathering in New York in mid-September for its sixteenth session.

In July Kennedy had asked me to follow United Nations matters for the White House. This put me in the not unfamiliar but still sometimes uncomfortable position of middleman between Kennedy and Stevenson—two men whom I so much admired but whose own rapport was perhaps less than perfect. In this assignment I had the good fortune to work closely with Assistant Secretary of State Harlan Cleveland and the excellent staff of his Bureau of International Organization Affairs.

Kennedy, who had an essential respect and liking for Stevenson, tried, when he thought of it, to make their relationship effective. He understood Stevenson's standing in the world and his influence on liberal opinion in the United States, admired his public presence and wit, valued his skills as diplomat and orator, and considered him, unlike most of the State Department, capable of original thought.

Kennedy fully expected, moreover, that people (including some of his own loyalists who still had not forgiven Stevenson for Los Angeles in 1960) would try to make trouble between Adlai and himself, and generally shrugged off the tales helpfully repeated to him of petulance or discontent in New York. On the other hand, certain of Stevenson's idiosyncrasies did try him; and his own effect on Stevenson in face-to-face encounter was unfortunately to heighten those which tried him most. The relationship was of course harder for Stevenson. He was the older man, and in one way or another Kennedy had denied him his highest hopes. Though Stevenson greatly respected the President's intelligence and judgment, he never seemed wholly at ease on visits to the White House.

Quite apart from the amiable but sometimes formal personal contacts, there were problems inherent in the relationship between Washington and any ambassador to the UN. Stevenson was of course invited to meetings of the cabinet and the National Security Council, but he was very often detained at the UN when large decisions impended at the Department or the White House. Cleveland and I did our best to see that the UN interest was represented in policy discussions, but we were often not in the room ourselves. Washington, moreover, had an ineradicable tendency to think of foreign policy as a matter between the United States and another nation or, at most, as between the United States and an alliance. The Foreign Service particularly appeared to regard multilateral diplomacy as somehow inferior and nonprofessional.

If the atmosphere in Washington made people think too little about the UN, the atmosphere in the headquarters in New York made people think of nothing else. To outsiders the UN often seemed a vast and picturesque form of make-believe, whose excitements bore little connection with serious issues; but to those who lived every day in the all-enveloping UN environment, it became the ultimate reality. It was a world of its own, separate, self-contained and in chronic crisis.

Stevenson, presiding over this hectic outpost of American diplomacy, had a far more arduous and exhausting job than most Washingtonians appreciated; and, because he had the grace of making everything look easy and the habit of disparaging his own success, people in Washington did not realize how superbly he was discharging an impossible assignment. In New York, however, his public stature, his exceptional personal charm and his realistic faith in the UN as an institution enabled him to recover quickly from the embarrassments of the Bay of Pigs and to assume a role of leadership. He had a gifted group of associates at the United States Mission, especially Ambassador Charles W. Yost, a superb Foreign Service officer, quiet, reflective and tough. On political and press matters the White House often dealt with Clayton Fritchey, an old friend of the President's and my own.

FREDERICK BOLAND, PRESIDENT OF THE 15TH GENERAL ASSEMBLY OF THE UNITED NATIONS; KENNEDY; STEVENSON AND DAG HAMMARSKJÖLD IN NEW YORK ON APRIL 28, 1961.

The 15th General Assembly resumed its session after the inauguration; and the President was quick to note that, next to himself, his ambassador to the United Nations was the most conspicuous voice of American foreign policy. Day after day, UN stories would dominate the front page of the *New York Times.* The UN was now as much a fact of international life as NATO or Khrushchev's nuclear tests in Siberia; and this Kennedy fully recognized. Yet his interest in the UN, however, was primarily as an instrument of political and economic action. Here and elsewhere, the idea of 'institution-building,' which meant so much to a political scientist like Harlan Cleveland, did not have great reality for him.

5. STATE OF THE UN

The UN remained a congeries of institutions, and it was now, as it had been since 1945, in a state constitutional evolution. The San Francisco Charter had envisaged a benign, great-power overlordship, with the Security Council as the organization's executive arm. But it had also given each permanent member of the Security Council a veto, and this could render the Council impotent whenever the permanent members were in serious disagreement. The General Assembly had proved too divided and unwieldy for executive action; despite the later theories about the dominance of the Assembly in this period, nearly all UN peace-keeping operations continued to be authorized by the Council.

The single clear point in the confusion was the Secretary-General. Dag Hammarskjöld, especially after his re-election in 1957, disclosed a presidential conception of the Secretary-General's "duty to use his office and, indeed, the machinery of the Organization to its utmost capacity." He considered it his obligation to act on his own, without guidance from the organization or the Charter, if this should seem "necessary in order to help in filling any vacuum that may appear in the systems which the Charter and traditional diplomacy provide for the safeguarding of peace and security." He charged this conception with the quasi-messianic passion of an extraordinary personality. His sense of mission was invincible. With the resourcefulness of a bureaucrat and the fervor of a saint, he sought to make the UN the chosen instrument of mankind in its quest for salvation.

Keeping out of areas of direct Soviet-American confrontation, like Berlin, he concentrated instead on peacekeeping in the third world—in the Middle East, Southeast Asia and Africa. He saw the new nations, which entered the General Assembly in increasing numbers after 1954, as his special constituency and sought to persuade them that the UN was their fortress. His initiative succeeded brilliantly until his entry into the Congo in 1960. Then Khrushchev, perceiving that UN intervention would prevent a communist victory, reached his conclusion that there was no such thing as a neutral person—above all Hammarskjöld—and opened the campaign first to force Hammarskjöld's resignation and then to replace the single Secretary-General with the *troika*.

The United States strongly backed Hammarskjöld, partly no doubt because we agreed with what he was doing in the Congo, but partly also because of a genuine desire to strengthen the capacity of the UN to keep the peace. From our viewpoint the UN, however much it may have fallen short of the dreams of 1945, had amply vindicated itself as a force for stability in a highly unstable world. In its more purposeful moments it had played an indispensable role in averting clashes between the Soviet Union and the West, both by offering a cover for quiet talks, like those which ended the Berlin blockade in 1949, and by containing local crises before the nuclear powers were irretrievably involved, as in the Suez affair in 1956. And the UN represented the best hope of keeping the newly independent nations from sliding into aggression or collapse and of incorporating them into an order of rational development. Despite the rush of the ex-colonial states into the organization, we remained confident that we could mobilize the one-third plus one of the General Assembly necessary to block action against our interests. The meeting of the 16th General Assembly now offered the new President an opportunity to affirm the American concern for peace and to recall the world to its senses.

6. THE DRIVE FOR DISARMAMENT

"I can think of no better position for the United States in the forthcoming General Assembly," Stevenson had written Kennedy in early July, "than the earnest advocacy of disarmament as our top priority national interest.... [We must] seize the initiative in disarmament which the Russians have held too long.... The United States must appear second to none in its desire for disarmament."

This theme Kennedy himself had expounded for a long time. But the quest for disarmament had been long and discouraging. Men of goodwill had preached the perils of the arms race for many years. After the First World War the great powers had engaged in ritualistic disarmament discussions and even completed some treaties; but little had happened. Now nuclear weapons were giving disarmament a new and dreadful urgency. For the first time in history one nation could absolutely obliterate another, and very likely the rest of the world in the process. The arms race, which realists could plausibly dismiss in earlier years as no more than a reflection of international rivalries, had clearly become in the nuclear age a source of tension in itself.

But still little happened. The failed efforts of the fifties produced a spreading frustration about the theory of total disarmament by a single agreement. At the same time, the development of the intercontinental ballistic missile was introducing a new factor which had to be incorporated into disarmament doctrine. In the United States especially, the new strategic analysis carried out in the Rand Corporation and elsewhere was yielding important insights into the character of the arms problem. The men who had invented nuclear weapons now began to give hard thought to the idea, not of abolishing them at one stroke, but of regulating them in the interest of stability. Out of this discussion emerged a new approach to the arms race under the banner of 'arms control.' The thinking was particularly hard along the banks of the Charles River, where Jerome Wiesner, Thomas C. Schelling, Henry Kissinger and others worked out the strategy of equilibrium in the nuclear age. A series of seminars and study groups at the end of the fifties culminated in a highly influential paper by Wiesner in *Daedalus* magazine in the winter of 1960.

The essence of arms control was 'stable nuclear deterrence'—the view, that is, that the best hope for peace and for ultimate disarmament lay in creating a situation where, in Wiesner's words, "a surprise attack by one side cannot prevent retaliation by the other." The temptation of surprise attack in a nuclear age was the hope of knocking out the opposing nuclear capability. If each side knew that both its own and the enemy nuclear forces could survive any conceivable assaults—through making missile bases, for example, 'hard' or mobile—then neither side would rationally initiate an attack which would only result in its own destruction. Stable deterrence had interesting implications—among them that the United States would be better off if the Russian striking force were invulnerable than if it were vulnerable—and most of its proponents were prepared to follow their logic to this conclusion. A stable deterrent system, they further agreed, would make it possible to limit the size of the deterrent and thereby end the nuclear race.

The gospel of stable deterrence enlisted support in the Navy, which saw an expanded role for its Polaris missiles, and in the Army, which resented the funds channeled to the Air Force. But it antagonized those, as in the Air Force, who yearned for unlimited American nuclear supremacy. It also for subtler reasons antagonized some who yearned for total disarmament. An extreme school of 'disarmers' pronounced stable deterrence a dangerous deception. It might be a defense against rational enemy decision, they said, but it was little use against irrationality; so long as missiles rested on launching pads, accident or insanity might still rush the world to nuclear holocaust. This school objected in addition that stable deterrence would make disarmament forever impossible by requiring each side to maintain a sizable nuclear establishment. The argument was that, the smaller the opposing nuclear

MORE THAN 2,000 PEOPLE GATHERED IN FRONT OF THE UN HEADQUARTERS IN NEW YORK ON THE 15TH ANNIVERSARY OF HIROSHIMA TO PROTEST AGAINST NUCLEAR WEAPONS TESTS.

forces became, the more unstable the equilibrium; for the reason that, as the level of force declined, the capacity of cheating to upset the balance increased. If each side, for example, had five hundred legal missiles, hiding two more from the inspectors would make little difference, but, if each side had only five legal missiles, the extra two might be decisive. On these various grounds the once-and-for-all disarmers condemned arms control as an elegant rationalization for a permanent arms race and proclaimed the need for immediate and total abolition of nuclear weapons.

Some arms controllers did indeed think that stabilization of the arms race was the most the world could realistically hope for. But others, like Wiesner himself, rightly doubted that total disarmament was at the moment politically relevant and saw stable deterrence as the best means of creating the atmosphere in which tensions could be reduced, further agreement achieved and, eventually, total disarmament attained. Walt Rostow coined the term 'transitional deterrent' to make this point. As the experience of agreement developed the habits and techniques of inspection and enlarged mutual confidence, the world could begin to cut back military forces and stockpiles and move toward final disarmament. For the interim period, the arms controllers had a variety of proposals designed to reduce the dangers of surprise attack and accidental war.

The Charles River doctrine, in short, appeared to offer a way of reconciling the objective of comprehensive disarmament with the interim requirements of national security. Its evident practicality appealed to Kennedy, and its emergence in 1960 gave him the opportunity for a new start in disarmament policy.

7. ORGANIZING FOR DISARMAMENT

After the election the President-elect had first to decide how to organize his disarmament effort in order to give it the power and priority it had lacked under Eisenhower. Knowing he had to protect disarmament against suspicions of softness, idealism, one-worldism and so on, he followed his customary practice of seeking a conservative to execute a liberal policy. The appointment of John J. McCloy as his special disarmament adviser was thus a deliberate effort to prepare the political ground by placing disarmament in charge of a figure whose background unassailably combined the Republican party, the Pentagon, the Ford Foundation, the Chase Manhattan Bank, and old established banks and law firms.

The disarmament agency came into being as a semi-detached part of State. Because of his commitments as a lawyer, McCloy could not give full time to Washington; so Adrian Fisher, who had once clerked for Justice Frankfurter and had later been Legal Adviser to the State Department under Acheson, and Edward Gullion became his deputies. At this point, McCloy had to return to his private affairs and William Foster was appointed head of what was now the Arms Control and Disarmament Agency.

The basic problem was to weld balanced deterrents and total disarmament into a single negotiating proposal. Stevenson, Wiesner and Gullion all felt that arms control by itself would not be enough, that the United Nations and world opinion demanded that the sword of Damocles be not only balanced but eventually lifted. After all, the United States had nominally accepted "general and complete disarmament" in the 1959 UN resolution, even if our actual proposals before and after had suggested that we were interested only in partial measures and unwilling to go the distance. Any retreat from the goal of general and complete disarmament by the new administration, Stevenson warned, would be disastrous, and we had to put forward a strong and convincing plan if we were to strengthen allied unity and beat the Soviet Union in the UN.

In the early spring Stevenson and Gromyko agreed that there should be an exchange of views between the United States and the Soviet Union to permit a renewal of disarmament negotiations. In July McCloy went to Moscow and engaged in extensive talks with V. A. Zorin, the Deputy Foreign Minister of the Soviet Union. For a long time Zorin had declined to entertain the idea of any negotiation at all until both countries agreed on the basic provisions of a specific plan; but in Moscow McCloy finally got the Soviet Union to change its position and consider a statement of principles. Many specifics were left unresolved, but concurrence became possible on a general statement defining the framework for future multilateral talks. The Americans now accepted the Russian point that disarmament should be "general and complete," leaving nations only the forces necessary to maintain internal order; while the Russians accepted two theses which McCloy had made the center of his argument—that the process should take place in stages "under such strict and effective international control as would provide firm assurance that all parties are honoring their obligations," and that it should go hand in hand with the development of international peace-keeping institutions.

During the spring and early summer, while this was going on, Washington had been involved in a complicated effort to work out the details of a new disarmament plan. Panels were convened, experts summoned from all over the country, studies commissioned, meetings held. Finally Wiesner and Spurgeon Keeney of his staff spent a weekend assembling all the ideas of value, including anything of interest they could find in the Soviet disarmament proposals of the five years preceding, and put together a plan.

The matter was one of fantastic complexity, and the plan was a remarkable intellectual feat. It was based on Wiesner's conviction that arms control and stabilized deterrence offered the way to general and complete disarmament. With immense ingenuity it worked out in three stages the progressive reduction and eventual abolition of all kinds of national armed force. It laid primary stress on the elimination of delivery vehicles for weapons of mass destruction—and also on unilateral and reciprocal measures to lessen the risk of war by accident or miscalculation. It provided for the parallel development and strengthening of peace-keeping institutions. In its essence, so far as one could judge, it was a serious and realistic proposal, at least in the first two stages.

I found myself, however, in the unaccustomed position of sharing the doubts of the Joint Chiefs of Staff about Stage III. By this time, according to the plan, disarmament and international law would develop to a point where "no State would have the military power to challenge the progressively strengthened United Nations Peace Force and all international disputes would be settled according to the agreed principles of international conduct." I suppose some attempt had to be made to visualize a world without national armaments; but Stage III seemed essentially an exercise in millennial rhetoric, and I tried in vain to persuade McCloy to abandon at least a phrase contemplating the day when the United Nations would be able "to assure peace and the just settlement of differences in a disarmed world." It appeared doubtful whether, short of the millennium, any human contrivance would be able to "assure" justice, but the objection glanced off McCloy's faith in the rule of law.

The plan circulated around the government and was vetted, revised, diluted and supplemented, and early in August a final meeting of the Principals approved the plan in substance. In mid-August the President cleared it. Early in September the American program for "General and Complete Disarmament in a Peaceful World" was ready for submission to the United Nations.*

*After further revision, designed mostly to make the political changes between the stages more explicit, the American disarmament plan in its final form was submitted to the eighteen-nation Disarmament Committee in Geneva on April 18, 1962.

XVIII. NO TRUCE TO TERROR

AUGUST 5 WAS A gray and dreary Saturday in Hyannis Port when Adlai Stevenson, Harlan Cleveland and I arrived at the Kennedy compound to discuss United States strategy in the impending session of the United Nations General Assembly. We found the President in a blue sports shirt and chinos, determined, despite the sullen weather, to take us all out for luncheon on his boat in the sound. A chilling wind sprang up over the water, and, while Jacqueline and two of her sisters-in-law huddled forward, the rest of us talked about the UN in the stern.

The first problem was choosing the major theme of the American presentation. Stevenson renewed his proposal of disarmament. Kennedy observed that disarmament did not seem a popular issue in the United States; he could detect no great congressional ardor, for example, for the bill establishing the Disarmament Agency. On the other hand, he knew how much the hope of disarmament meant to the rest of the world. Moreover, it was an issue on which we could make time against the Soviet Union.... Stevenson of course agreed but added earnestly, "We can't do this effectively if we ourselves equivocate. Only total disarmament will save the world from the horror of nuclear war as well as from the mounting expenses of the arms race. Your basic decision must be to identify yourself with a new approach to disarmament. This must be our principal initiative in the United Nations."

1. STRATEGY FOR THE GENERAL ASSEMBLY

For several years the United States had been staving off the entry of Communist China into the UN, and the question was certain to arise with new intensity this year. Kennedy, who considered the state of our relations with Communist China as irrational, did not exclude the possibility of doing something to change them in the course of his administration. But he never supposed that admission to the UN would work any miraculous conversion in Peking, and he had no doubt in 1961 that the international gains (if any) of admission would be far outweighed by the uproar it would cause at home. Eisenhower, for example, had told him in their last meeting before the inauguration that he hoped to support the new administration on all foreign policy issues but would consider it necessary to return to public life if Communist China threatened to enter the UN. With his slim majority, Kennedy felt that he could not take on the China problem this year.

The strategy of keeping Peking out in 1961 involved the question of Outer Mongolia, a pro-Russian communist state on China's western border. Chester Bowles had argued persuasively that it would be to the American interest to recognize Outer Mongolia, both to gain an observation post in central Asia and to nourish the growing mistrust between Russia and China. But Nationalist China bitterly opposed this idea, as did its Republican allies in the American Congress—so much so that the recognition plan was dropped in midsummer. In addition, however, Outer Mongolia was itself a candidate for admission to the UN. If Nationalist China used its power as a permanent member of the Security Council to veto the application, the Soviet Union would presumably retaliate by vetoing Mauritania, and the African members might in turn retaliate by backing the admission of Communist China. We needed African votes, or at least abstentions, to keep Communist China out, and we therefore wanted Outer Mongolia in.

2. THE PRESIDENT AT THE UNITED NATIONS

The Soviet resumption of testing four weeks later gave the September session of the General Assembly even more importance than we had expected. After the Russian tests, the President decided to go to New York and address the General Assembly later in the month. On September 5, the day he ordered the resumption of our own underground tests, he called in Rusk, Stevenson, Cleveland, Bundy, Sorensen and me to consider what he might say.

Over the next week we began work on the President's UN speech. But, as the days passed, opposition began to arise to the idea of his going to New York, or, if he did go, to his making disarmament his major theme. On September 18 the tragic news of Dag Hammarskjöld's death in a plane crash in Africa settled whatever doubts the President may have had about going to New York. Hearing the word while receiving a delegation at the White House, he expressed deep sorrow, adding sadly, "I expect my whole time in office to be filled with dangers and difficulties." The Russians would now undoubtedly use the struggle over the succession to press their campaign to replace a single Secretary-General with the *troika*. Ted Sorensen, taking drafts from Cleveland and myself, began to prepare the final version of the speech.

A week later the President went to New York. "Let us here resolve," he began, "that Dag Hammarskjöld did not live, or die, in vain." He called on the General Assembly to reject the *troika*. To install a triumvirate, he said, would be to "entrench the Cold War in the headquarters of peace." It would paralyze the United Nations; and in the nuclear age the world needed the United Nations more than ever before. For "a nuclear disaster, spread by wind and water and fear, could well engulf the great and the small, the rich and the poor, the committed and the uncommitted alike. Mankind must put an end to war—or war will put an end to mankind. ... Let us call a truce to terror."

The goal of disarmament, he continued, "is no longer a dream—it is a practical matter of life or death. The risks inherent in disarmament pale in comparison to the risks inherent in an unlimited arms race." He set forth the American plan and asked that negotiations continue "without

DAG HAMMARSKJÖLD, SECRETARY GENERAL OF THE UNITED NATIONS, IN 1959.

interruption until an entire program for general and complete disarmament has not only been agreed but has been actually achieved." The logical place to begin, he said, was a test ban treaty. He called further for contributions to a United Nations peace-keeping force, the improvement of UN machinery for the peaceful settlement of disputes, the extension of world law to outer space and the support of the UN Decade of Development.

In his conclusion, he reminded the Assembly of its historic opportunity. "We in this hall shall be remembered either as part of the generation that turned this planet into a flaming funeral pyre or the generation that met its vow 'to save succeeding generations from the scourge of war.' ... The decision is ours. Never have the nations of the world had so much to lose, or so much to gain. Together we shall save our planet, or together we shall perish in its flames. Save it we can—and save it we must—and then we shall earn the eternal thanks of mankind and, as peacemakers, the eternal blessings of God."

The President spoke with particular intensity, and the delegates, many seeing him for the first time in person, were moved by his handsomeness, spirit and commitment. They responded with deep and sustained applause. Kennedy himself, as he looked out at the representatives of the world community, understood more vividly than ever before the power and potentiality of the United Nations. He said later that he was surprised by the majesty of the occasion and the impact of his remarks. His speech, moving beyond the clamors of the day, transcending the crises of Berlin and Southeast Asia, abolishing the memories of the Bay of Pigs, established him as a leader of humanity's party of hope.

The momentum of his words, sustained by Stevenson's effective leadership in New York, continued throughout the session. The *troika* was defeated, and U Thant of Burma became the new Secretary-General with unaltered authority. The application of Communist China for membership was turned back by a decisive vote, and the Assembly resolved that any proposal to make a change in the representation of China was an "important question" requiring a two-thirds majority. Outer Mongolia was admitted, Nationalist China abstaining. The groundwork was laid for new negotiations on disarmament. The Assembly called for a treaty to ban nuclear tests under effective international measures of verification and control and asked the Soviet Union to refrain from exploding its 50-megaton bomb. And, to deal with the financial problems caused by the UN operation in the Congo, the Assembly authorized a $200 million bond issue to be taken up by the member nations.

3. INTERLUDE IN BERMUDA

The urgencies of security, however, remained at war with the dreams of disarmament. Kennedy had felt that the Soviet atmospheric tests left him no choice but to authorize underground testing of our own. Now, as one explosion in the skies above Siberia followed another through the autumn, it became increasingly difficult to hold the line at underground tests. The Joint Chiefs of Staff in particular wanted to resume American tests in the atmosphere as speedily as possible. Early in October they forwarded a paper calling for atmospheric testing in November.

On the morning of October 30 a call from the White House awakened me to report the largest detonation so far—probably that of Khrushchev's threatened 50-megaton bomb. This proved to be the case, though Khrushchev archly said the next day that his scientists had miscalculated: "Instead of fifty megatons it proved to be more, but we will not punish them for that." Our own scientists told us that, if the Soviet super-bomb had had a uranium casing, the explosion would have had the force of one hundred megatons. This final atrocity made it impossible to put off our own preparations for atmospheric testing any longer. Kennedy now directed Ted Sorensen to draft a statement saying that, while we would test in the atmosphere only if required to do so by overriding arguments of national security, contingency preparations should begin at once. Three days after the great Soviet explosion, the paper was laid before the National Security Council for discussion.

At the end of the day the President announced publicly that preparations were under way for atmospheric tests "in case it becomes necessary to conduct them." They would not be undertaken, Kennedy emphasized, "for so-called psychological or political reasons." But if "the orderly and essential scientific development of new weapons has reached a point where effective progress is not possible without such tests," then they would be undertaken "within limits that restrict the fallout from such tests to an absolute minimum."

The machinery of government was thus set for resumption. But preparation was one thing, actual testing another. The President still hoped to avoid further corruption of the atmosphere and further stimulus to the nuclear race. "Personally, I hate the idea of resuming atmospheric tests," he said. "But it's going to be damned hard to stave off the pressure, especially when the news gets out that the big Soviet explosion was relatively clean. This will show that they have something we don't have, and we will be under intense pressure to test in the atmosphere ourselves. But I have made no final decision, and I have told everybody that I have made no decision."

The critical question, as the matter crystallized in the President's mind, became not the Soviet round of 1961 but the rounds which might follow in 1962 or 1963. It was evident that the current series would not by itself enable Khrushchev to reverse the balance of nuclear power. But if the Russians, on the basis of the knowledge so acquired, were to conduct a new series while the United States refrained from atmospheric testing, the next one might well put them in the lead. However much Kennedy loathed the idea of atmospheric tests, any President who stood aside and allowed the enemy to achieve nuclear superiority would plainly have taken an unacceptable risk in the face of his constitutional obligations.

This, I believe, was the President's state of mind when, after several weeks of racking contemplation, he discussed the problem with Harold Macmillan in Bermuda on December 21. We needed British support in the decision to go ahead. The British colony of Christmas Island in the central Pacific offered an ideal site for testing in the atmosphere; and, in any case, it would be politically difficult for the United States to resume without British concurrence. But the nightmare of nuclear holocaust stirred more than ever underneath Macmillan's Edwardian flippancies, and he opened the talks by evoking the awful prospects of an indefinite nuclear race.

If all those talented scientists were to continue going about their business, the Prime Minister said, the only result would be more and deadlier bombs. Was this the goal to which the next generation of man should dedicate itself? If these horrible weapons were not fired off, it would be a hopeless economic waste; if they were, it would be the end of civilization. And, while the United States and the Soviet Union were having this sophisticated competition, many other nations in a few years would begin to acquire their own simpler bombs. Berlin, Macmillan said, seemed to him small beer compared to the destruction of humanity. The world could not continue down this path. You and I, he said to Kennedy with emotion, could not sit in an ordinary little room four days before Christmas and talk about these terrible things without doing something about it. Before we went into the atmosphere ourselves, should we not make one more effort to break the cycle? The arms race was a "rogue elephant" against which we all must act.

Perhaps you and I, he told Kennedy, should meet at the summit with Khrushchev and really push for disarmament. We might fail, but we would have lost only a few months. Macmillan added that, after reading Russian novels and everything else he could find about Russia, he felt that they might come around. Moreover, the nuclear effort was costing the Soviet Union ferociously. And the Soviet position itself was changing. The Russians were halfway between Europe and Asia and watching the rise of China with foreboding. The west thought of them as enormously different, but their economic and social structure was not that alien. After all, mines and railroads were nationalized through most of Western Europe, and one saw already in Russia a spread of unequal privileges through society; the children of the ruling class were going to elite schools, as they did in Britain. Without yielding, could we not provide time to allow the forces of humanity to exert their influence?

Macmillan was eloquent, and Kennedy was moved. But he had to face realities. The problem, he pointed out, was what would happen in 1964 if the Russians continued to test and the west didn't. We could not afford to be taken twice. Even though he was himself a "great anti-tester," he saw no alternative but to prepare for resumption and, if there was no progress with regard either to Berlin or disarmament, to resume.

Later, the Prime Minister asked that the final decision be postponed to permit one last try at disarmament. Kennedy replied that a new effort would only enable the Russians to stall things for many more months. Our case would be no better a year from now, and in the meantime the Russians could get ready for a new series of tests. He concluded later in the day by asking whether Macmillan would agree to atmospheric tests on Christmas Island if the situation did not change. Macmillan responded that this was a decision for the cabinet; but Britain and America were partners, we were in this together; he only wished that the announcement would seem less a threat than a hope.

4. MACMILLAN'S LAST TRY

The decision was now almost, but not quite, firm. Some of us in Washington still thought after Bermuda that one more effort should be made to avert what Wiesner called the "slide into chaos." After consulting with Wiesner and others, I proposed to the President that we announce a decision to resume but offer to cancel our atmospheric tests if the Soviet Union would sign the Geneva treaty. This, it seemed to me, would either get us the treaty or put the Russians in the position of triggering the American test series.

A week after New Year's, Macmillan returned to the battle. In a deeply personal letter to Kennedy, the Prime Minister argued again that resumption would probably lead the Russians to carry out their next series; we would be forced to do the same; the contest would intensify; and, as the burden of the race mounted, one side or the other, when it thought it had attained superiority, might be tempted to put the issue to the test. As the test programs of the great powers continued, he went on, there would be no hope of preventing the spread of nuclear weapons to non-nuclear states. If this capacity for destruction ended up in the hands of dictators, reactionaries, revolutionaries, madmen around the world, then sooner or later, possibly by the end of this century, either by error or folly or insanity, the great crime would be committed. It would seem to any ordinary person, Macmillan continued, that humanity was setting out on a path at once so fantastic and so retrograde, so sophisticated and so barbarous, as to be almost incredible.

It might be, he concluded, that we were condemned, like the heroes of the old Greek tragedies, to an ineluctable fate from which there was no escape; and that like those doomed figures we must endure it, with only the consolation of the admonitory commentaries of the chorus, the forerunners of the columnists of today. But in his view the situation demanded a supreme effort to break the deadlock. Amplifying the thoughts he had advanced in Bermuda, he proposed that the three leaders—Kennedy, Khrushchev and himself—convert the impending eighteen-power disarmament meeting, scheduled for Geneva in March, into a final try for general disarmament, a test ban treaty and an agreement not to transfer nuclear weapons or information to non-nuclear powers. It was, of course, he said, easy to do nothing. But, on the whole, it was not the things one did in one's life that one regretted but rather the opportunities missed.

The Macmillan letter made clear both the extent of his anxiety and the magnitude of the decision which confronted us. Any reply, Rusk said, must contain three elements: an affirmation that our concern equaled Macmillan's; a rejection of any link between the use of Christmas Island and a new disarmament initiative; and an initiative we might offer ourselves as a substitute for what seemed to us the questionable notion of a grandiose disarmament conference. Bundy then prepared an excellent reply along these lines, concluding: "We are ready to examine with you the possibilities for new efforts toward disarmament on the most urgent basis."

5. THE RESUMPTION OF ATMOSPHERIC TESTING

In the course of February Kennedy received an analysis of the Soviet tests by a panel of leading scientists, including so prominent an advocate of the ban as Hans Bethe. Their report disclosed a highly advanced nuclear technology, with new designs and techniques, including some unknown to the west—or at least unexplainable on the basis of the information available—as well as substantial gains in weaponry. The technical basis had evidently been laid for a new series which might enable the Soviet Union to develop bombs whose yield per weight of explosive would be somewhat higher than ours. While this would not give any substantial military advantage to the Soviet Union, the knowledge that the Russians had better weapons would have given them a political and diplomatic advantage the President was disinclined to accept. With a heavy heart, he decided that we would have to resume atmospheric testing. As for the tests themselves, he made it clear he wanted low-yield detonations concentrated in short periods. In the next months, he spent a good deal of time reviewing and revising the proposals for the American atmospheric series.

The next question was when the world should be notified. After lengthy consideration, the President decided to declare his readiness to trade off our atmospheric series, not for a partial, but for a comprehensive test ban treaty.

On February 27 Kennedy informed Macmillan that he planned a television talk on the subject to the nation on March 1. The Prime Minister had still hoped somehow to stave off American resumption, and Kennedy's message came as a shock. The Prime Minister asked the President again for postponement, but Kennedy could not see his way to delay the announcement for more than another twenty-four hours.

The President himself was hardly in a gay mood about his decision. He told me later that he had phoned Truman and Eisenhower. Truman, he said, was sympathetic and seemed to understand how hard the judgment had been. Eisenhower, cold and grumpy, said, "Well, I thought you should have done this a long time ago."

On March 2, Kennedy made his speech. He described the precautions taken to restrict fallout, adding: "I still exceedingly regret the necessity of balancing these hazards against the hazards to hundreds of millions of lives which would be created by a relative decline in our nuclear strength." The United States, he said, would come to Geneva with a series of concrete plans for a major "breakthrough to peace." In particular, it would once again offer a comprehensive test ban treaty. If the Soviet Union were now ready to "accept such a treaty, to sign it before the latter part of April, and apply it immediately—if all testing can thus be actually halted—then ... there would be no need for our tests." That action, he added, would be "a monumental step toward peace—and both Prime Minister Macmillan and I would think it fitting to meet Chairman Khrushchev at Geneva to sign the final treaty."

Khrushchev quickly declined the offer. On April 25, as dawn broke over Christmas Island, the United States began a new round of tests in the atmosphere.

The rogue elephant was loose again, and neither Kennedy nor Macmillan was content to let him rampage unchecked.

6. DISARMAMENT AND THE DEFENSE BUDGET

The rogue elephant was loose again, and neither Kennedy nor Macmillan was content to let him rampage unchecked.

Yet Kennedy persisted in the struggle for disarmament. I do not think he quite saw the arms race in the image of Macmillan's rogue elephant; for the race was not in fact so insensate as that. Staggering as defense expenditures were, they remained a relatively small proportion of the total national output in both the United States and the Soviet Union; and of money spent on defense, only a fraction—in the United States, perhaps one-fifth—went to nuclear striking power. Nor was the 'overkill' idea—the notion that each side was compulsively engaged in piling up more and more nuclear bombs—justified, at least in its more nightmarish form. Actually each side (outside the air forces) was coming to realize that it had more than enough; and a good deal of the new expenditure went, not to increase stockpiles, but for replacement, modernization of weapons systems, research into new weapons and the maintenance of a higher state of alert.

In short, if there was an arms race, neither side was galloping as fast or as frantically as it could. But this provided only comparative consolation. For his part, Kennedy was sure that we had enough for nearly any conceivable contingency; he regarded the balance of terror, however ingeniously safeguarded, as deeply fragile; and he used to say that he would consider it "the ultimate failure" if he ever had to order the use of a single nuclear weapon. Moreover he was increasingly concerned about the diversion to armaments of resources which could be better put to more beneficent uses. All these considerations made him even more determined to lead the world toward arms reduction.

The experience of the spring and summer of 1961, moreover, had convinced him that running faster in the race would only provoke his opponent to run faster too and thereby increase the strain without necessarily altering the gap. He had seen no alternative to higher defense spending in order to liberate American strategy from its predominant reliance on nuclear weapons; but the rise in Washington's defense budget had now produced a comparable rise in Moscow's. Increases and decreases in the two capitals had paralleled each other before, and the administration, as time went on, began to draw a significant conclusion: that the defense budget itself might be used as an instrument of arms limitation. For it was evident that the budget was the most effective means of signaling to the Soviet Union our intentions, whether defensive or first-strike, as well as the kinds of weapons and strategies which might be mutually advantageous and the kinds of limitation that might be mutually possible.* These considerations were much in the minds of Kaysen and Wiesner when the first full Kennedy defense budget came under consideration within the government in the late summer and fall of 1961.

Within the magnitudes of the budget the President, of course, retained a series of choices about weapons systems. He had a profound aversion to weapons which could be used effectively only in a first strike and which for that reason might invite a pre-emptive strike from the other side—like the Jupiters which had been sitting for some years on soft bases in Turkey and Italy. As Bundy remarked later, "he always preferred the system which could survive an attack against the system which might provoke one." The budget communicated this preference to the Soviet Union; and McNamara drove the point home in statements and speeches, especially in an address at Ann Arbor, Michigan, in June 1962. Here he argued forcefully for "a strategy designed to preserve the fabric of our societies if war should occur." By this he meant that the targets of nuclear war should be military forces and installations, not civilian populations. This 'counterforce' strategy required us to have the capacity to hold in reserve, even after a massive surprise attack, sufficient striking power to destroy the enemy society if driven to it; this would give an opponent "the strongest imaginable incentive to refrain from striking our own cities." At the same time McNamara reorganized the control system so that, instead of investing all striking power in a single presidential push button, the command structure could retain after attack the ability to respond in a number of ways besides blowing up the world.

The counterforce doctrine had its ambiguities. But no one who listened to the anguished musings of Kennedy and McNamara on nuclear weapons could doubt their unalterable opposition to preventive or pre-emptive nuclear war. The Berlin situation prevented the President from making a public declaration against the first use of nuclear weapons once war had begun; as he had explained to de Gaulle and Macmillan, he was prepared to go to nuclear weapons if Soviet conventional forces began a war in Europe. But Kennedy and McNamara well knew that no American first strike could wipe out the Soviet capacity to retaliate and that retaliation, even from a doomed opponent, would be dreadful beyond imagination. They were seeking a second-strike capacity and, both for deterrent and for political reasons, one large enough to exceed the weight of any first strike directed against the United States. We probably attained this state of beatitude by 1962, but the administration took no chances. The decisions of the Kennedy years gave the United States by 1964 an arsenal that dwarfed that of the Soviet Union.

7. THE DISARMAMENT FIGHT GOES ON

Kennedy faced no harder problem of public education than that of convincing both Capitol Hill and the Kremlin that his demands for strength and for disarmament, far from being contradictory, were complementary. His view was that, unless we convinced the Russians we could stay in the arms race as long as they could, we would remove the incentive most likely to make them accept general disarmament; for obviously, if we let them win the arms race, they would see no reason to abandon their military superiority and expose their society to external inspection. Both the securing of a second-strike capacity and the diversification of the defense establishment seemed to him, moreover, vital parts of the strategy of deterrence and arms control.

But the notion that these were all actions for peace and not for war required a more sophisticated analysis of the strategic situation than existed in Moscow—or for that matter in Western Europe. And even some in the United States tended to feel there was an inconsistency between building military strength, on the one hand, and working for disarmament, on the other. If this inconsistency bewildered Americans, it doubtless bewildered the Russians even more. But the budget remained a solid indicator of something; and in the end budget-watching—what Khrushchev came to call the "policy of mutual example"—may have been the most effective means of slowing down the arms race in these years, especially as the Soviet analysis of the American budget became more sophisticated. Still, this form of indirect communication and tacit restraint was slow and chancy, and it did nothing to build the international machinery of peace.

The President therefore maintained a steady pressure on the executive branch to keep the negotiating effort alive. Wiesner and Kaysen, flourishing the White House mandate, were tireless in needling the bureaucracy and forcing disarmament issues; and Bundy intervened valuably at critical moments. Wiesner often carried the brunt of the argument against the Pentagon in meetings before the President. Next to the President, McNamara, with the able backing of John McNaughton, probably did more than anyone else to sustain the disarmament drive. With his sense of the horror of nuclear conflict, his understanding of the adequacy of existing stockpiles, his fear of nuclear proliferation, his analytic command of the weapons problem and his managerial instinct to do something about an irrational situation, he forever sought new ways of controlling the arms race. His contribution was especially crucial in dealing with the Joint Chiefs of Staff, possessed as they were by the conviction that they alone understood the requirements of American safety.

William Foster, while sensitive to congressional reactions, proved a calm director of ACDA, and in Adrian Fisher he had a stalwart and effective deputy. Among the civilians concerned, the Secretary of State proved the main source of indifference. He often gave the impression that he regarded disarmament as an essay in futility, if not in folly. One colleague later reported his impression that Rusk "feared living in a world in which predominant military power was not his major tool."

It was easy to understand this skepticism, and a number of thoughtful people shared it. Senator Fulbright, for example, dismissed "general and complete disarmament" as "an exercise in Cold War fantasy, a manifestation of the deception and pretense of the new diplomacy." Yet in retrospect those long, laborious talks at Geneva played, I believe, a vital role in widening understanding between the United States and the Soviet Union.

Certainly the disarmament talks forced the Russians to think through the intricate problems of nuclear survival, to

* A number of points in this discussion have been clarified by Thomas C. Schelling; see especially "The State of the Arms Race" in J. E. Dougherty, ed., *The Prospects for Arms Control* (New York, 1965), 52–55.

examine their own strategic limitations and capabilities, and to ponder the riddle of the nuclear equilibrium. In time they evidently began to master the concept of stable nuclear deterrence and to see that arms control might be a means of approaching rather than avoiding general and complete disarmament. The talks may also have done something to convince them that the Americans honestly wanted to stabilize the weapons situation. Even though so little appeared to be accomplished at the time in the antiseptic conference rooms beside the quiet lake at Geneva, the disarmament negotiations turned out in the end to be a good deal more than exercises in political warfare or theological disputation. They became a form of communication and education, a means of overcoming the cultural lag, an encouragement to parallel voluntary action by the two great nuclear powers and even perhaps a prelude to *détente.*

XIX.
NEW DIRECTIONS IN THE THIRD WORLD

THOUGH KENNEDY WAS deeply concerned with the conflict between the United States and the Soviet Union, he did not consider that conflict the source of all mankind's troubles. In 1961 this was still rather a novel viewpoint for an American President. The tendency in the years after the Second World War had been to see the planet as tidily polarized between America and Russia. In the 1950s John Foster Dulles had transmuted this from an assumption into a dogma. The Dulles world rested on unitary conceptions of the opposing blocs: on the one hand, the 'free world,' capaciously defined to include such places as Spain, Paraguay, Batista's Cuba and Mississippi and destined ultimately for the private enterprise of the Secretary of Commerce and the god of the Secretary of State; and, on the other, the 'communist camp,' a monolithic conspiracy with headquarters in Moscow, enslaving captive peoples and orchestrating global crises according to a comprehensive master plan.

Countries which did not fit into one category or the other were regarded as anomalies. Summing up his creed in 1956, Dulles described neutralism as the principle "which pretends that a nation can best gain safety for itself by being indifferent to the fate of others" and excommunicated its devotees as "immoral." Though the Dulles doctrine was considerably tempered in application, he succeeded in implanting both in American policy and in opinion the idea that those who were not with us around the earth were against us.

Of the various transformations wrought in the Kennedy years none was less noted or more notable than the revolution in American attitudes toward the uncommitted world.

1. KENNEDY AND THE THIRD WORLD

As Senator, Kennedy had come to object to the Dulles doctrine both as morally self-righteous and as politically self-defeating.

Thus, where Dulles saw neutralism as immoral, Kennedy felt that the new states, absorbed in the travail of nationhood, were as naturally indifferent to the 'moral' issues in the cold war as Americans in a comparable stage of development had been to the moral issues in the Napoleonic wars. The spread of neutralism consequently neither surprised nor appalled him. He felt, moreover, that the third world had now become the critical battleground between democracy and communism and that the practical effect of Dulles's bell, book and candle against neutralism could only be to prejudice the American case and drive the developing nations toward Moscow and Peking. The battle for Europe, Kennedy believed, had been, except for Berlin, essentially won by the end of the forties. "Today's struggle does not lie there," he told Paul-Henri Spaak of Belgium in the spring of 1963, "but rather in Asia, Latin America and Africa." Where Dulles divided the world on the question of whether nations would sign up in a crusade against communism, thereby forcing the neutrals to the other side of the line, Kennedy, by making national independence the crucial question, invited the neutrals to find a common interest with us in resisting communist expansion.

As for anti-colonialism, which Dulles approved only so long as it remained within the bounds of gentility, Kennedy saw it as inherently non-genteel and probably inseparable from disorder, excess and a certain bitterness toward the west. The issue, he said in 1959, "is one of timing—and whether once that freedom is achieved, they will regard the United States as friend or foe." Even if the new countries declined to adopt the free enterprise system or enlist in the cold war, the strengthening of their independence was still likely to be a positive good for the United States. In the end, the secure achievement of national identity, he thought, could only set back the Soviet conception of the future world order and strengthen the American. It was partly knowledge of these views and partly also his youth and the sense he gave of freedom from preconception which led the third world to take heart from his election in 1960.

Kennedy became, in effect, Secretary of State for the third world. With his consuming intellectual curiosity, he generally knew more about the Middle East, for example, than most of the officials on the seventh floor of the State Department; and the Assistant Secretaries in charge of the developing areas dealt as much with him as with the Secretary of State. Moreover, he conducted his third world campaign to an unprecedented degree through talks and correspondence with heads of state. He well understood that personalities exert a disproportionate influence in new states without stable political systems, and he resolved to turn this situation to his own purposes. The leaders of the new nations, it must be said, did not always make this task any easier. They were often ungenerous and resentful, driven by historic frustrations and rancors and brimming over with sensitivity and vanity. Moreover, anti-American bravado was always a sure way to excite a crowd and strike a pose of national virility. The President, understanding this as part of the process, resolved not to be diverted by pinpricks.

And so the new President set out to adjust American thinking to a world where the cold war was no longer the single reality and to help the new countries find their own roads to national dignity and international harmony. But in his own government he immediately ran head-on against a set of inherited policies on colonialism, on neutralism and on foreign assistance, deeply imbedded in the minds of government officials and the structure of the executive branch.

2. KENNEDY AND COLONIALISM: THE ANGOLA RESOLUTION

The first problem was colonialism. This was, in one sense, a dying issue. In the fifteen years of the United Nations some forty countries, containing nearly a billion people, had won their independence. In Africa, the colonial continent par excellence, there were twenty-two new states. Yet these successes had only increased the sense of grievance in Asia and Africa about the dependencies which remained. And anti-colonialism was still the most convenient outlet for the revolt of the rest of the world against the historic domination of the West—that revolt so long suppressed, now bursting out on every side.

Since the time of Franklin Roosevelt American policy had had a nominal commitment to anti-colonialism. But the State Department had been dominated by men who, regarding NATO as our top priority, flinched from anything which might bruise the sensibilities of our European allies, some of whom still had colonial possessions. Even in those parts of the Department presumably devoted to the business of the developing world, the aim of helping the new nations meet their problems jostled uneasily with pressure to defend the sanctity of American overseas investment. Such tensions had prevented the formation of a clear American position.

In the December preceding Kennedy's inauguration, forty-three Asian and African states had submitted to the General Assembly a resolution on "the granting of independence to colonial countries and peoples." The resolution declared that "all peoples have the right of self-determination," that "inadequacy of political, economic, social or educational preparedness should never serve as a pretext for delaying independence" and that "immediate steps shall be taken" in all non-self-governing territories "to transfer all powers to the peoples of those Territories, without any conditions or reservations, in accordance with their freely expressed will." The resolution passed by 89-0, with the United States and eight other nations abstaining.

In February the session of the General Assembly resumed with Adlai Stevenson as ambassador. Almost immediately the new administration was confronted by a new colonial issue. For some time the nationalist forces in Angola had been in revolt against the Portuguese authorities. Of all the classical colonial countries, Portugal was far the most impervious to the winds of change. Indeed, the Salazar government, hopelessly anchored in its medieval certitudes, had been the real if unstated target of the December resolution. Now, as the fighting in Angola grew more fierce and sustained, Liberia placed before the Security Council a resolution calling on Portugal to comply with UN policy against colonialism and proposing a UN inquiry into the situation. This resolution incorporated by reference the anti-colonialism resolution of December.

Stevenson and Kennedy both saw the opportunity to intimate a change in American policy. There was token opposition from the Europeanists at State; but Kennedy took care that everything should be done with due concern for the feelings of Portugal and the solidarity of NATO. Salazar was informed of the American intention a week before the vote. The resolution failed in the Security Council, but the new administration was now free of automatic identification with colonialism.

As troubles mounted in Angola, the same resolution came before the General Assembly a month later and this time passed with American support. Our UN votes produced anti-American riots in Lisbon and a mild surge of criticism in the United States. The New York foreign policy crowd feared that Kennedy was opening a gap in the Atlantic Alliance. Unimpressed by such reactions, Kennedy had authorized a White House statement two days after the first vote pointing out that the decision had not been taken in haste and that our NATO allies had been notified in advance. In the third world the new administration was acclaimed as the friend of oppressed peoples.

3. KENNEDY AND NEUTRALISM: LAOS

While these early moves were showing the third world a new American attitude toward colonialism, Kennedy was demonstrating in Laos a new American support of neutralism.

The Laos talks had started in Geneva following the cease-fire of early May 1961. The conference opened in a contentious atmosphere. The Russians insisted that the Pathet Lao be seated on a basis of equality with the representatives of Prince Souvanna Phouma, the neutralist, and General Phoumi, the protégé of the Eisenhower administration, and the British were ready to go along. But the Americans objected at first, and everything seemed blocked. When Rusk, with Kennedy's approval, finally consented to seating the Pathet Lao, the right-wing delegates walked out. Eventually the three Laotian factions met in Laos and agreed on triple representation.

After a few days Rusk returned to Washington, leaving Averell Harriman in charge. The Geneva meeting recessed while Kennedy and Khrushchev met in Vienna. Laos was, of course, the sole beneficiary of their conversations, and the talks resumed in June, spurred on by the Kennedy-Khrushchev commitment to "a neutral and independent Laos under a government chosen by the Laotians themselves." Harriman now plunged into the serious stretch of negotiation. As he saw it, the neutralization policy confronted several obstacles: the Chinese, who wanted the Pathet Lao to win; the Pathet Lao, who hoped to evade the cease-fire and complete the conquest of the country; General Phoumi, who could not believe that Washington was serious about neutralization; and a few people in the State Department, who still considered neutralization a mistake.

Harriman was determined to keep the talks in low key: he saw no advantage in turning the conference into a shouting match. But the negotiations proved long and tortuous. Though the United States had few tangible bargaining assets, Harriman had skill, persistence and cool logic, and he conceived his task in terms not of victory but of settlement. In time, his perseverance began to have effect. G. M. Pushkin, the Soviet representative, finally agreed that Moscow would assume responsibility for the observance of the agreement by the communist signatories; and then both Russia and China agreed that, while recommendations by the International Control Commission had to be unanimous, the minority could not veto majority reports on questions of the violation of the agreement. They agreed further to prohibit the entrance of foreign troops and the use of Laos as a corridor into South Vietnam. By early December the conference completed a draft Declaration on the Neutrality of Laos.

The problem remained of establishing a government of national union. Harriman's belief that Souvanna was the only possible head of a coalition displeased the diehards in Washington. In December negotiations broke down. Though the Geneva conference persuaded the Laotians to resume talks in January 1962, and Harriman finally got the State Department to say publicly that defense and interior should go to Souvanna, Phoumi continued his resistance.

But Harriman persevered. Speaking with brutal frankness, Harriman informed Phoumi that he could not expect American troops to come to Laos and die for him and that the only alternative to a neutral Laos was a communist victory. Phoumi was still unyielding until April, when the Thai government, which had hitherto backed him, accepted the Harriman logic and urged him to join a government under Souvanna.

No sooner had Phoumi declared a readiness to negotiate than the Pathet Lao broke the cease-fire in a major way, which brought a prompt reaction in Washington. Harriman now proposed that a contingent of Marines be sent to

Thailand. Kennedy was at first reluctant, fearing that once the Marines were installed in Thailand it would be difficult to find an occasion to withdraw them, but decided to go ahead. The commitment of limited force on May 15 had an immediate effect. The Pathet Lao came to a halt, and negotiations started up again. On June 12 a coalition government was formed with Souvanna as prime minister and Phoumi and Prince Souphanouvong of the Pathet Lao as vice premiers.

On July 23 the Declaration on the Neutrality of Laos was finally ratified in Geneva. Kennedy described it as "a heartening indication that difficult and at times seemingly insoluble international problems can in fact be solved by patient diplomacy." If the settlement could be made to work, "it would encourage us to believe that there has been a change in the atmosphere, and that other problems also could be subjected to reason and solution."

The settlement did not 'work' in the sense that the signatories observed the Geneva declaration. In 1962 coalition labored under terrific disadvantages which had not existed five years earlier. As a result, the Geneva settlement on Laos never went into effect. The Pathet Lao representatives soon withdrew from Vientiane and resumed their effort to take over the country by force; the International Control Commission failed to close the corridor to South Vietnam or otherwise assure neutralization; and Laos fell into a state of *de facto* partition. The Soviet Union did not—perhaps could not—fulfill its pledge to secure compliance by the communist states.

Yet, depite the systematic violation of the Geneva Agreement, the new policy brought clear gains. The Kennedy strategy ended the alliance between the neutralists and the Pathet Lao. Souvanna, Kong Le and other neutralist leaders became the defenders of Laotian independence no longer against the United States but now against communism. The result was to localize the crisis, stop an imminent communist take-over, place the Pathet Lao in the role of breakers of the peace, block the southward expansion of China and win the American position international support. By 1965, General Phoumi, after the failure of his last intrigue, had fled the country; William Sullivan was now American Ambassador in Vientiane; and Souvanna Phouma was receiving active American assistance in Laos and stoutly supporting American policy in South Vietnam.

The result expressed Kennedy's ability to see the world in terms more complex and realistic than total victory or total defeat. Laos was neither won nor lost, but it was removed from the area of great-power confrontation. The Laos experiment illustrated both the advantages and problems of neutrality.

4. KENNEDY AND NEUTRALISM: BELGRADE

Washington's tolerance of neutralism was not based on any sort of *New Statesman* belief in the moral superiority of neutrals. The President was entirely unsentimental in this respect. But in the case of Laos he saw no other way out, and, with his understanding of the historical inevitability of neutralist attitudes, he was quite prepared, when feasible, to build neutralism as an alternative to communist expansion. Moreover, he had no doubt about the value to the United States of neutralist support in the various disputes with the Soviet Union. This led to considerable White House interest in a meeting of unaligned nations, called by Nehru, Tito, Nasser and Sukarno for Belgrade in early September 1961.

By this time, Kennedy was deep in the year's troubles with the Soviet Union. As the American fight for a test ban met Soviet resistance in the spring and Khrushchev gratuitously reopened the Berlin crisis in the summer, the President was beginning to wonder why American policy had so little backing, or apparently even understanding, among the neutrals. Therefore, a fortnight before Belgrade, he addressed a series of pointed questions to Stevenson and Bowles, as the chief local champions of the third world policy, and also to Galbraith, as his specialist on Nehru. He asked, in effect, why we were failing to put across our position on Berlin to the third world; why the neutrals seemed to equate our firmness with belligerence, as over Berlin, and our moderation with weakness, as over Laos; and why they appeared to judge American actions with such severity and Soviet actions with such apparent charity.

The replies showed considerable convergence of diagnosis. The trouble with Berlin, everyone agreed, was that it was so far away. "These European quarrels," Galbraith said, "are not for Asia. The outcome short of war has little implication for the Indian national interest." If we seemed more belligerent, it was because our papers reported so much about the agony of decision. Moreover, as Stevenson emphasized, when questions involved the danger of war but not their own interests, "neutrals will almost inevitably favor compromise between Western and Communist positions with little regard for the rights and wrongs of the case." The experts suggested that we could strengthen our case in Berlin if we would say something about negotiation, base our argument on self-determination rather than on legalistic talk about rights of conquest and prove the genuineness of our devotion to self-determination by extending the principle from white men in Berlin to black men in Angola and to Indians in Goa. As for the double standard, we should not be unhappy if the neutrals implicitly expected better behavior from us than from the Russians; and we had no choice but to accept the less agreeable fact that they knew us to be responsive to public criticism as the Russians were not. All this would naturally lead them to concentrate their pressure on us. In general, the consultants concluded, our wealth and power, the color of our skins and our association with the colonial nations of Europe, condemned us to an almost irreducible barrage of heckling, and we should have to grin and bear it.

These remarks coincided, I believe, with Kennedy's own fundamental view. But it was hard to be philosophical in the midst of the Berlin crisis, and even harder when, after the Soviet Union resumed nuclear testing, the neutral leaders gathering at Belgrade reacted with stupefying forbearance. We all knew how they would have blackened the skies with resolutions if we had been the first to resume.

As it turned out, the Belgrade conference disappointed Moscow about as much as it did Washington. The Soviet Union conspicuously failed to win neutral support for its positions on Berlin, on disarmament and on the *troika* approach to the UN; there was considerable resentment in the corridors about the Soviet resumption of nuclear testing; and anti-American speeches and statements were notable for their absence. Indeed, the Belgrade meeting disappointed everybody, even its sponsors, for it revealed such internal differences among the twenty-eight participating nations that it destroyed the dream of a neutral bloc as a unified force in world affairs. In their devotion to the principle of non-alignment, the new states were evidently prepared to apply it to each other.

Their final declaration dealt very largely with colonial questions, the one great bond which held the very motley group together. Then Nehru, with Nkrumah of Ghana, was dispatched to Moscow and Sukarno, with Keita of Mali, to Washington to carry the Belgrade gospel to the great powers. Kennedy observed, "Khrushchev certainly drew the pick of the litter," but he received the emissaries politely and ended up having a spirited and enjoyable talk with the African.

American interest lay primarily in building the independence the unaligned countries, in steering their energies toward internal development and in leading them into long-term association with the West. This, he added, was one vital role of foreign aid. Keita and Sukarno had told Kennedy that the unaligned countries, in their positions on international issues, did take into account where the aid came from; and, in analyzing the Belgrade conference, Rostow was able to show that, of the eighteen moderates, the great majority had either received most of their aid from the United States or were hoping for increased American aid, while, of the six extremists, all except Yugoslavia (and including Indonesia) had received substantially more aid from the Soviet Union.

This, I believe, made great sense to Kennedy, and the Belgrade meeting did not deflect him long from his chosen course.

5. NEHRU

Of all the neutral countries, Kennedy was most interested in India, which he had long regarded as "the key area" in Asia. The spectacle of this great nation, weighed down by legacies of centuries, making a brave attempt to achieve economic modernization within a democratic polity captured his imagination. The struggle between India and China "for the economic and political leadership of the East, for the respect of all Asia," he said in 1959, would determine the Asian future.

Yet this desire to aid India coexisted with a certain skepticism about Indian leadership. When Kennedy had visited New Delhi in 1951, Nehru for some reason—perhaps because all he could see was an unknown young Congressman—treated him with marked indifference. The visitor had been warned that, when Nehru became bored, he would tap his fingers together and look at the ceiling. Kennedy was in the office, he later liked to recall, for about ten minutes when Nehru started to tap his fingers and gaze abstractedly at a spot over his visitor's head. Moreover, Nehru's talent for international self-righteousness led Kennedy in some moods to view him as almost the John Foster Dulles of neutralism. Still, Nehru was unquestionably one of the great men of the century; and, even if he were not, India remained the key area of Asia.

In sending Galbraith as his ambassador to New Delhi, Kennedy deliberately chose a man who could be depended upon to bring to Indian problems his own mixture of sympathy and irony. Kennedy was delighted by Galbraith's wit, effrontery and unabashed pursuit of the unconventional wisdom, and they were now exceptionally good friends. Nor did the President appear to mind Ken's guerrilla warfare against the ikons and taboos of the Department of State. From time to time, the President took pleasure in announcing that Galbraith was the best ambassador he had.

Galbraith went to New Delhi with several advantages: an acquaintance with Nehru, his own prestige as an economic and social philosopher, and the President's strong belief in increased economic assistance to India—this last quickly result-

PRESIDENT HARRY TRUMAN SHAKES HANDS WITH PRIME MINISTER JAWAHARLAL NEHRU ON HIS VISIT TO THE UNITED STATES IN 1949.

ing in a $500 million appropriation for Indian development. But he also had the disadvantage of the Dulles legacy and especially of the policy of American military aid to Pakistan.

Very early Galbraith decided that the best way to erase memories of Dulles was to expose Nehru to Kennedy. The two leaders shared that address, patrician instinct and long historical view which made them, next to Churchill, the two greatest statesmen on the British model of their day. But by 1961 Nehru, alas, was no longer the man he had once been. His strength was failing, and he retained control more by momentum of the past than by mastery of the present.

Galbraith insisted that Nehru really would wish to be received in a home. Hyannis Port seemed a little too depressing to the Kennedys, and they decided to invite him to Newport. Nehru arrived in New York on November 5, 1961, was promptly subjected to a sharp and unceremonious inquisition by Lawrence Spivak on "Meet the Press," and the next morning departed for Rhode Island.

The President met him at the naval base and brought him back to the Auchincloss residence on the *Honey Fitz*. Along the way, he gestured at the great mansions shining in the sun, their green lawns stretching down to the seawall, and said, "I wanted you to see how the average American family lives." Nehru responded that the American Ambassador had been giving him special instruction in the affluent society. When they arrived at Hammersmith Farm, Jacqueline and Caroline were waiting at the front door. The little girl had picked a flower and now she made a curtsy and presented

NEHRU AND HIS DAUGHTER, INDIRA GANDHI, ON THEIR VISIT TO THE U.S. IN NOVEMBER 1961.

it to him. He smiled and was briefly gay with Mrs. Kennedy. But when the talk turned to Vietnam during luncheon, he fell into remote silence. It was heavy going, then and later.

They all went back to Washington in the afternoon for a state dinner. The President, unperturbed, gave one of his graceful and witty toasts. "We all want to take this opportunity to welcome you to America, Mr. Prime Minister," he began, "though I doubt whether any words of mine can embellish the welcome already extended to you by Larry Spivak." Nehru listened without expression. His own toast was discursive and overlong, though rather touching. In conversation he displayed interest and vivacity only with Jacqueline. I had the impression of an old man, his energies depleted, who heard things as at a great distance and answered most questions with indifference. The private meetings between the President and the Prime Minister were no better. Nehru was terribly passive, and at times Kennedy was hard put to keep the conversation going. It was, the President said later, like trying to grab something in your hand, only to have it turn out to be just fog. It was all so sad: this man had done so much for Indian independence, but he had stayed around too long, and now it was all going bit by bit.

The following spring, reminiscing about the meeting, Kennedy described it to me as "a disaster ... the worst head-of-state visit I have had." It was certainly a disappointment, and Kennedy's vision of India had been much larger before the visit than it would ever be again. Though Kennedy retained his belief in the necessity of helping India achieve its economic goals, he rather gave up hope, after seeing Nehru, that India would be in the next years a great affirmative force in the world or even in South Asia.

6. GOA AND AFTER

Five weeks after Nehru left the United States he ordered his army to occupy the ancient Portuguese colony of Goa on the west coast of India. Galbraith, in a valiant last-minute effort to

JACQUELINE KENNEDY TOURS THE PALACE OF THE MAHARAJAH DURING HER VISIT TO INDIA IN MARCH, 1962.

stop the military action, got it put off for three or four days. But Washington only authorized him to offer vague diplomatic pressure on Portugal in exchange for a six-month standstill by India. To be effective he needed more specific assurance that sooner or later we would get the Portuguese out.

In Paris, where NATO was meeting, Dean Rusk conversed with Dr. Franco Nogueiria, the Portuguese foreign minister, on the eve of the invasion. It was not a high point of American diplomacy. At no time did the Secretary express any reservations about permanent Portuguese control of Goa or even acknowledge that the Indians might have a legitimate point in resenting the Portuguese presence.

Franco Nogueiria had concluded his talk with Rusk in Paris by warning him that the Goanese would fight to the end; they all might die in the resulting slaughter but not until each had killed ten Indians. At midnight on December 17 the invasion began. It was over in twenty-four hours. Forty-five Portuguese and twenty-two Indians were killed. The historical and political reasons for the invasion were understandable enough; but the contrast between Nehru's incessant sanctimony on the subject of non-aggression and his brisk exercise in *Machtpolitik* was too comic not to cause comment.

Obviously we had to condemn the Indian resort to force in unequivocal language. The only issue was whether we should stop there or go on to say, as Galbraith had recommended and Stevenson now urged, that we regarded the Portuguese enclave as anachronistic and looked forward to a peaceful termination of Portuguese colonialism in India. The State Department, over Stevenson's protest, insisted that he not make allusions in his speech to Portuguese colonialism, and this made the speech when delivered at the Security Council seem all the more unfeeling to the Indians.

Nehru himself sent the President a long and plaintive letter at the end of the month. "Why is it," he asked, "that

MRS. KENNEDY AND HER SISTER PRINCESS LEE RADZIWILL ATTEND MASS IN INDIA.

something that thrills our people should be condemned in the strongest language in the United States?" He had been "deeply hurt," he remarked, by the "extraordinary and bitter attitude of Mr. Adlai Stevenson."

The President took his time about replying. In three weeks he wrote: "All countries, including of course the United States, have a great capacity for convincing themselves of the full righteousness of their particular cause. No country ever uses force for reasons it considers unjust.... I fear that the episode in Goa will make it harder to hold the line for peace in other places." He concluded by suggesting that one difficulty was that the invasion followed so soon after Nehru's visit to the United States. "I confess to a feeling that we should have discussed this problem."

Nehru hastily answered that he had said nothing then because he had no intention of taking action; the Portuguese provocations at the end of November had brought the matter to a head. This seemed a little disingenuous. On October 23, a fortnight before he departed for America, he had said in Bombay that "the time has come for us to consider afresh what method should be adopted to free Goa from Portuguese rule." The whole episode further diminished Kennedy's hope that India had a serious role to play in the struggle for peace. Yet, with his usual realism, he avoided recriminations; and, indeed, Indian sensitivity lasted longer than American.

Kennedy, in any case, had no desire to protract resentments. In November Nehru had invited Jacqueline to visit India, and she made the trip with Lee Radziwill in March.

It was a happy journey. Nehru was in a gentle and winning mood, much more himself than he had been in Newport or Washington. He was delighted by his guests, evidently welcomed the relief from pressure and liked to take them for strolls through his gardens. He scrupulously avoided politics and did not lobby about Goa, Kashmir or Pakistan. Jacqueline and Lee then went on to Pakistan as part of Washington's policy of non-discrimination within the subcontinent.

Jacqueline's trip disposed of the lingering pique about Goa and re-established the process which was making the President so popular a figure throughout India. In this era of Nehru's decline, with India receding from the world stage, young Indians in particular were fixing their hopes more and more on the American President. Even the communist press treated Kennedy with respect.

Then in the autumn the Chinese themselves provided valuable cooperation by invading India from the north. Nehru, forgetting the virtues of non-alignment, sent a desperate appeal for American help. With Kennedy's strong backing, Galbraith took the opportunity to consolidate the American friendship with India. Acting with great sense and skill, and after the usual arguments with the dilatory Department, he succeeded in working out air defense arrangements and otherwise making clear that, in case the war intensified, India could expect American assistance.

Nehru, now frail and sick, was less and less in active command of his government. But, with Galbraith's expert management, the Chinese invasion and then the soothing ministrations of Chester Bowles, his relations with Kennedy were stabilized by 1963. If India were not to be the positive international force for which Kennedy had hoped, nevertheless it had acquired a sober confidence in the American government and a tremendous admiration for the American President.

XX.
TANGLE IN SOUTHEAST ASIA

INDIA REMAINED the most reasonable of the developing nations of Asia: British imperialism had not been in vain. The Dutch and French, however, had not created political traditions or institutions calculated to smooth the transition to self-government; nor were they prepared to retreat from empire with the relative skill and tact of the British after the Second World War. The nationalist reaction in Indonesia and Indochina was in consequence fierce and angry.

Indonesia won its independence in 1949, Indochina, after an especially nasty war, in 1954. At Djakarta President Sukarno proceeded to gather the emotions of nationalism unto himself and used them without scruple to establish his power. In Indochina, Cambodia and Laos went their separate paths; and Vietnam, divided by the Geneva Agreements of 1954, now consisted of two hostile states, with North Vietnam stimulating and supporting a civil war south of the border.

In different ways, Indonesia and Vietnam presented Kennedy with problems to which there were no clear or easy answers and which harassed him throughout his administration.

1. SUKARNO

The 'guided democracy' which Sukarno had proclaimed in the fifties grew more and more every year into a capricious personal despotism. Sukarno was a great nationalist demagogue, adored by his people and basking in their adoration. His deep mistrust of the white West was understandably compounded in the case of the United States by his knowledge that in 1958 the CIA had participated in an effort to overthrow him. His internal problems were complex and multitudinous. He looked on them with insouciance and, in the manner familiar to despots, sought to forget them by seeking international victories. By 1961 he was threatening attack on the Dutch colony of West New Guinea, withheld when the rest of the Netherlands East Indies achieved independence. Sukarno suspected that the Dutch had retained West New Guinea as a point of reentry in case his government might collapse, and, seeing the Dutch presence as an intolerable threat to Indonesian security, he was determined to force them out.

He came to Washington in the spring of 1961 and again in September after Belgrade. The meetings with Kennedy were no great success. The Indonesian leader's vanity was unconcealed, and his interest in reasoned exchange seemed limited. He gave the impression of a clever politician who had squandered the opportunity to promote the development of his country in favor of posturing on the world scene and personal self-indulgence. For all this, though, the President regarded Indonesia, this country of a hundred million people, so rich in oil, tin and rubber, as one of the potentially significant nations of Asia. He was anxious to slow up its drift toward the communist bloc, and was therefore immediately responsive when Robert Komer proposed that the United States take the initiative in trying to settle the West New Guinea argument before it blew up into a crisis. Like Laos, West New Guinea did not seem to him a part of the world in which great powers should be rationally engaged. In December Kennedy wrote Sukarno offering to help find a solution by direct negotiation.

In February Robert Kennedy went to Indonesia, bearing a presidential letter urging the Indonesians to come to the conference table without preconditions. Sukarno and the Attorney General got on surprisingly well. Robert Kennedy's directness and candor made a distinct impression in Djakarta; and, in later years when relations between the United States and Indonesia took a bad turn, he was the American who could talk most effectively to the Indonesian leader.

American pressure on Sukarno and on the Dutch finally brought the principals reluctantly to the conference table in the spring of 1962. There followed five months of negotiation, accusation, interruption and provocation. "Everybody is displeased, really, with our role," Kennedy said in April. "...The role of the mediator is not a happy one, and we're

LEFT: A PHOTOGRAPH OF PRESIDENT KENNEDY MEETING WITH PRESIDENT SUKARNO HANGING IN JAKARTA.

PRESIDENT SUKARNO ADDRESSES THE INTERNATIONAL YOUTH SOLIDARITY MEETING IN JAKARTA TO OPPOSE THE FEDERATION OF MALAYSIA.

prepared to have everybody mad, if it makes some progress." But progress was made slowly. The agreement of August 1962, based on an idea of Bunker's, called in the United Nations to provide an interim administration while sovereignty passed, over an eight-month period, from the Dutch to the Indonesians. The agreement provided further that in 1969 the Papuans should be permitted a free choice as to whether they wished to continue as part of Indonesia. Critics could plausibly attack the settlement as a shameful legalization of Indonesian expansion, and indeed it was; but the alternative of a war over West New Guinea had perhaps even less appeal.

Kennedy now moved to take advantage of the improved atmosphere. For a time relations between Djakarta and Washington improved. In an effort to persuade the Indonesians to turn inward and grapple with their development problems, the United States offered aid to the Indonesian stabilization program. Sukarno remained slippery and temperamental; but he was flattered by Kennedy's attention and stayed precariously within the orbit of communication.

Only later, after Sukarno determined to make the Federation of Malaysia his next target and after the United States had permitted itself to become identified with Malaysia against Indonesia, did the downward slide of relations resume, leading Sukarno eventually out of the United Nations and into the communist camp. The problem was intractable, but the Kennedy policy succeeded in delaying the slide and preserving for a time a basis of contact within Indonesia.

2. DIEM

Most intractable of all was the problem of Vietnam. In the end this was to consume more of the President's attention and concern than anything else in Asia. The American commitment to the Saigon government was now of nearly seven years' standing. After the Geneva Agreements of 1954 had split Vietnam along the 17th parallel, President Eisenhower had written Prime Minister Ngo Dinh Diem of South Vietnam pledging American support "to assist the Government of Viet-Nam in developing and maintaining a strong, viable state, capable of resisting attempted subversion or aggression through military means." The United States, Eisenhower continued, though without particular emphasis, expected that this aid would be met "by performance on the part of the Government of Viet-Nam in undertaking needed reforms." The object of this American effort, Eisenhower concluded, was to "discourage any who might wish to impose a foreign ideology on your free people."

It was never clear that the people were so free or the ideology so foreign as Eisenhower supposed, but his language defined the mood in which Washington began the Vietnam adventure. That mood was essentially moralistic, and war reinforced by the 'domino' theory. "You have a row of dominoes set up," Eisenhower explained to a press conference, "you knock over the first one, and what will happen to the last one is that it will go over very quickly. So you have a beginning of a disintegration that would have the most profound influences."

This was a moment of the supremacy of abstract principles, without much consideration of the concrete situation in Vietnam. A more discriminating view might have regarded Ho Chi Minh, the boss of North Vietnam, less as the obedient servant of a homogeneous Sino-Soviet bloc than as a leader of nationalist communism, historically mistrustful of the Chinese and eager to preserve his own freedom of action. It might have taken a more relaxed attitude toward the evolution of Vietnam; and it might have decided to draw the American line on the Siamese side of the Mekong River, where both the political and military foundations for an American position were a good deal stronger. But abstractions prevailed, and the commitment was made, and, after Washington accepted Diem's refusal to take part in the all-Vietnam elections promised by the Geneva Agreements for 1956, it became increasingly a commitment to one man.

It cannot be said that Diem had altogether kept his side of the bargain, especially in the performance of "needed reforms," nor can it be said that the Eisenhower administration brought this omission very urgently to his attention. Diem, a profound traditionalist, ran a family despotism in the oriental manner. He held power in his own hands, regarded opposition as treason, showed disdain for the shallow institutions of western democracy and aimed to restore the ancient Annamese morality. "If we open the window," his sister-in-law, the lovely and serpentine Madame Nhu once said, "not only sunlight but many bad things will fly in." On the other hand, he had kept the country together in difficult circumstances, and, with American aid, brought about a measure of economic growth and social improvement. Living standards, indeed, had risen faster in South than in North Vietnam, where Ho Chi Minh concentrated on investment rather than consumption. And Diem himself seemed a man of rectitude and purpose, devoted and incorruptible.

PRESIDENT DWIGHT EISENHOWER MEETING WITH PRESIDENT NGO DINH DIEM OF SOUTH VIETNAM IN MAY 1957.

The civil war had begun the year after the cancellation of the elections. Diem's authoritarianism, which increasingly involved manhunts, political re-education camps and the 'regroupment' of population, produced a spreading resistance. At first the communists hung back, but, as the success of Diem's economic policies convinced Ho Chi Minh that he could not wait passively for the Diem regime to collapse, he sent word to his comrades in the south to join the guerrillas. In March 1960 the Viet Cong, as the rebels were known, established a National Liberation Front, and in September the Communist Party of North Vietnam bestowed its formal blessing and called for the liberation of South Vietnam from American imperialism. By this time Ho Chi Minh was supplying the Viet Cong with training, equipment, strategic advice and even men. Most of the Viet Cong in any case continued to be recruited in South Vietnam; and most Viet Cong arms and equipment were captured from Diem's army.

The Viet Cong unquestionably expressed a strain of fanatic idealism. "We are peasants in soldiers' clothing," they sang, "waging the struggle for a class oppressed for thousands of years. Our suffering is the suffering of the people." Nationalists fought side by side with communists. But the Viet Cong did not precisely represent a movement of rural uplift. They extended their power as much by the fear they incited as by the hope they inspired. It was warfare in the

PRESIDENT HO CHI MINH OF NORTH VIETMAN IN BULGARIA IN 1957.

shadows, ambush and murder and torture, leaving behind a trail of burned villages, shattered families and weeping women.

American assistance to Diem in the fifties averaged about $300 million a year. This was mostly economic aid, which South Vietnam, unlike Laos, put to fairly good use, though only a fraction got to the countryside where most of the South Vietnamese lived. On the military side, our advisers, many of them veterans of the Korean War, conceived their mission as that of training a conventional army designed, not to fight guerrillas, but to repel a Korean-style invasion from the north. They accompanied this by a systematic barrage of self-serving reports. Cheered by such bulletins, a Senate committee concluded in 1960, "that the U.S. Military Assistance Advisory Group (MAAG) can be phased out of Vietnam in the foreseeable future."

Some officers, like Brigadier General Edward Lansdale, dissented with vigor from both MAAG's strategy and its complacency. Lansdale thought that it was essentially a guerrilla war and that it was going very badly. The guerrilla attacks were increasing in audacity and scope; the success of the Pathet Lao had opened up the corridor of assistance from North Vietnam to South Vietnam through Laos; there were now perhaps 15,000 Viet Cong in South Vietnam, and they were overrunning half the country, and more by night.

In Saigon there was increasing dissatisfaction with Diem, his government and the conduct of the war. In November 1960 a military coup almost succeeded in overthrowing the regime. Diem rode this out. Once back in control, he cracked down on all varieties or potentialities of opposition. Trusting no one, he based himself more and

VICE PRESIDENT JOHNSON ARRIVES IN SAIGON ON MAY 11, 1961. HERE HE INSPECTS DIEM'S HAND-PICKED GUARD.

more narrowly on his family, especially on his able and aggressive younger brother, Ngo Dinh Nhu.

3. JOHNSON IN SAIGON

Vietnam confronted the new American President, not with an immediate crisis, like Laos, but rather with a situation of deepening military and political shakiness. Kennedy had long believed, and Khrushchev's January speech had confirmed that belief, that the main communist reliance in the coming period would be on neither nuclear nor conventional but on guerrilla war. The battle in Vietnam was obviously not along the frontier but in the villages; and it could be won only by a flexibility and mobility which matched that of the guerrillas themselves. Moreover, it could not be won by military means alone. Guerrilla warfare was essentially political war. Effective counterinsurgency action, for example, depended on swift and sure intelligence from the countryside. The Viet Cong could never be defeated unless the Saigon regime could enlist the support of the peasants.

A counterinsurgency plan for Vietnam, prepared in the winter of 1960 and approved by Kennedy in early 1961, proposed an extensive program of military and social reforms; if these recommendations were carried out, the report said, the war could be won in eighteen months. A Vietnam Task Force, set up in April, reduced the report to forty points; Frederick Nolting was sent to Saigon as ambassador, his predecessor being accounted too anti-Diem; and in May the Vice-President visited in Saigon as part of a general tour of Southeast Asia. There, Johnson discussed the military and economic situation with Diem; and in an address to the National Assembly he urged the importance of meeting the needs of the people in education and rural development.

Johnson went on to Thailand and India, where he had useful talks with Nehru, and then back to Washington. "Our mission arrested the decline of confidence," he reported to Kennedy on his return. "It did not—in my judgment—restore any confidence already lost." Time was running out, and "the basic decision in Southeast Asia," he told Kennedy, "is here. I recommend that we move forward promptly with a major effort to help these countries defend themselves."

He did not consider Southeast Asia lost, "and it is by no means inevitable that it must be lost." In each country, he said, it was possible to "build a sound structure capable of withstanding and turning the Communist surge." But this could only be done if the nations of Southeast Asia had "knowledge and faith in United States power, will and understanding." The long-term danger, he added, came not from communism but "from hunger, ignorance, poverty and disease. We must—whatever strategies we evolve—keep those enemies the point of our attack, and make imaginative use of our scientific and technological capacity."

As for Vietnam, he found Diem a complex figure beset by many problems. "He has admirable qualities, but he is remote from the people, is surrounded by persons less admirable than he. The country can be saved—if we move quickly and wisely." The Vice-President did not envisage the

TROOPS TRAINING IN SOUTH VIETNAM IN 1961.

commitment of American troops beyond training missions. He favored the reorientation of the military effort along with programs of political and economic reform. "It would be useful," he said, "to enunciate more clearly than we have—for the guidance of these young and unsophisticated nations—what we expect or require of them."

Under the pressure of Johnson and Nolting, Diem agreed in May to a number of points in the task force report in exchange for American support on an increase in the Vietnamese Army. However, Diem's assurances led to little or nothing in the way of performance. This was increasingly the pattern of Washington's relations with the Diem regime. Indeed, American attempts to advise Diem became a classical exercise in what anthropologists might call cross-cultural frustration. The Americans did tend to regard Vietnam, in the Vice-President's words, as a "young and unsophisticated" nation, populated by affable little men, unaccustomed to the modern world, who, if sufficiently bucked up by instruction and encouragement, might amount to something. The Vietnamese, regarding their nation as infinitely older and more sophisticated than the United States, looked on the Americans as impatient, naïve and childlike, lacking all sense of form or history. Diem in particular viewed the Americans with a mandarin's disdain and increasingly responded to their advice by the simple but powerful device of doing all the talking himself. What perhaps began as a tactic soon became a disease.

Diem seemed unwilling or unable to undertake, for example, the programs of rural reform designed to close the gap between the president's palace in Saigon and the people in the villages. Most likely the whole conception of seeking 'popular support' seemed to him one of those western delusions with no relevance to life in Asia. In his view it was the moral obligation of the people to respect their government. As for the Vietnamese Army, though it continued to regard Diem's one-man rule with periodic restlessness, his divisive strategy kept it from acting against him. Moreover, the officers had been so well persuaded by American advisers of the virtues of conventional war that most had little heart for the chancy life of night patrols, small-unit action and hit-and-run tactics.

The Johnson trip was followed by an economic mission, headed by Eugene Staley, and still more recommendations. But it seemed impossible to stop the disintegration. "The situation gets worse almost week by week," Theodore H. White wrote us in August. "If a defeat in South Vietnam is to be considered our defeat, if we *are* responsible for holding that area, then we must have authority to act. And that means intervention in Vietnam politics.... If we do decide so to intervene, have we the proper personnel, the proper instruments, the proper clarity of objectives to intervene successfully?"

4. THE TAYLOR-ROSTOW MISSION

In September the Viet Cong seized a provincial capital and beheaded the governor. Morale in Saigon sank even lower. Diem was plainly losing the war, and Theodore White's questions were now more relevant than ever. Kennedy, absorbed as he was in Berlin and nuclear testing, faced a series of inescapable decisions in Vietnam.

There seemed a strong case for trying Johnson's approach and making an increased effort to stabilize the situation in South Vietnam. Early in October Kennedy sent General Maxwell Taylor and Walt Rostow on a mission to Saigon to see if this could be done. He charged them to find out whether Vietnamese nationalism had turned irrevocably against us or still might serve as a basis for the fight against communism.

The very composition of the mission—headed by a general, with a White House aide as deputy and no figure of comparable rank from the State Department—was significant. The effect was to color future thinking about Vietnam in both Saigon and Washington with the unavowed assumption that Vietnam was primarily a military rather than a political problem. The mission went about its work in an orderly way. Their collective answer to Kennedy's question was that South Vietnam had enough vitality to justify a major United States effort. The trouble, as Taylor and Rostow diagnosed it, was a double crisis of confidence: doubt that the United States was really determined to save Southeast Asia; doubt that Diem's methods could really defeat the Viet Cong.

GENERAL MAXWELL TAYLOR SIGHTS A CANNON DURING A TOUR OF THE SOUTH VIETMAN BORDER AREA IN OCTOBER 1961.

To halt the decline, they recommended increased American intervention—in effect, a shift from arm's-length advice to limited partnership. While only the Vietnamese could finally beat the Viet Cong, Americans at all levels, Taylor and Rostow argued, could show them how the job was to be done.

The report concentrated on military matters. As for Diem, the report gave a candid account of his political and administrative idiosyncrasies but rejected any idea that he be replaced. While it outlined a number of desirable political reforms—especially broadened participation in government and more work in the villages—it relied mainly on the expectation that the new system of limited partnership could work *de facto* changes in Diem's methods of government and gradually narrow the gap between the regime and the people.

Taylor and Rostow hoped that this program would suffice to win the civil war—and were sure it would if only the infiltration from the north could be stopped. But if it continued, then they could see no end to the war. Rostow argued forcibly for a contingency policy of retaliation against the north, graduated to match the intensity of Hanoi's support of the Viet Cong.

The President was impressed by the idea of stiffening the Diem regime through an infusion of American advisers. He did not, however, like the proposal of a direct American military commitment. The war in Vietnam, he said could be won only so long as it was *their* war. If it were ever converted into a white man's war, we would lose as the French had lost a decade earlier.

Though the Taylor report offered political as well as military remedies, the thrust of its argument and recommendation was that the crisis of confidence was military in its origins and could be ended by the commitment of American troops or at least by American partnership in the conduct of Vietnamese field operations. J. K. Galbraith and Averell Harriman were sure on the contrary that the crisis of confidence was political in its origins and had resulted from Diem's repressive and reactionary policies in face of a communist-managed peasant insurrection.

Kennedy, still undecided about next steps, asked Galbraith to stop by in Saigon on his way back to India. Galbraith reported to Washington that the fundamental problem was the total ineffectuality of the Diem regime. If there were effective government in Saigon, the situation would be far from hopeless; for, with support from the countryside and something to fight for, the well-equipped Vietnamese Army of a quarter of a million could deal with the fifteen thousand or so lightly armed irregulars opposing them. Galbraith could see no long-term solution which did

TOP: SOUTH VIETNAMESE TROOPS BOARDING HELICOPTERS DURING A TRAINING SESSION.

BOTTOM: U.S. SOLIDERS TRAIN SOUTH VIETNAMESE SOLIDERS IN AMBUSH TECHNIQUE ALONG THE LAOS BORDER IN 1962.

not involve a change of leadership. Diem, a significant man in his day, had passed the point of rehabilitation.

Reflecting on the situation and reposing particular confidence in McNamara and Taylor, Kennedy prepared to go ahead. Moreover, given the truculence of Moscow, the Berlin crisis and the resumption of nuclear testing, the President unquestionably felt that an American retreat in Asia might upset the whole world balance. In December he ordered the American build-up to begin. General Paul Harkins, as the new American commander in Saigon, and Ambassador Nolting worked closely together. Both saw Diem as the key to success, and both were convinced that attempts to bring pressure on him would be self-defeating. The proper policy in their view was to win Diem's confidence by assuring him unswerving support and then try to steer him gently and gradually toward reform; if Diem felt this backing to be anything less than whole-hearted, the policy would not work. This became known, in the phrase of Homer Bigart of the *New York Times*, as the period of "sink or swim with Ngo Dinh Diem."

The result in 1962 was to place the main emphasis on the military effort. When the social and economic program developed in Washington in 1961 encountered the usual resistance in Saigon, it was soon dropped. In place of a serious attack on the central problems of land and taxation, the regime announced a number of marginal and largely meaningless reforms to placate the Americans and did very little to put even these into effect.

The military advisers flocked in with the weapons of modern war, from typewriters to helicopters. They worked

GENERAL MAXWELL TAYLOR AND ROBERT MCNAMARA DEBRIEF WITH THE PRESIDENT AFTER THEIR TOUR OF VIETNAM.

with local 'counterparts' in all sections of the government in Saigon. In the field, they lived with the Vietnamese Army, helped plan military actions and sometimes participated themselves. The military assignment was frustrating, because the power to advise was not the power to command. It was also thankless, because as a matter of policy the American role was systematically played down. But the advisers themselves were brave and devoted as well as anonymous; their courage and selflessness were deeply impressive; and they made a difference.

Morale rose in Saigon. Viet Cong activity declined in the countryside. No more provincial capitals were attacked. "Every quantitative measurement we have," Robert McNamara said on his first visit to Vietnam in 1962, "shows we're winning this war." Maxwell Taylor, when he returned for a fresh look a year after his first visit, thought he detected "a great national movement" rising to destroy the Viet Cong. No one could doubt a widespread and substantial improvement in the military situation. In Washington, the President, who had other matters on his mind, accepted the cheerful reports from men in whom he had great confidence. His 1963 State of the Union message summed up the mood at the turn of the year: "The spearpoint of aggression has been blunted in South Vietnam."

XXI.
AFRICA: THE NEW ADVENTURE

IN NO PART of the third world did Kennedy pioneer more effectively than in Africa. Of all the continents this one had stayed longest on the outer fringes of the American consciousness. As late as 1960, our direct interests in Africa, political or economic, military or intellectual, were meager. No traditional doctrines guided our African policies. No alliances committed our troops. Our foreign aid programs made only token contributions to African development. Our very sense of the continent below the Mediterranean rim was vague and dim. No historic ties bound us to black Africa except the slave trade. Even Americans of African descent were not much interested.

The explosion of African nationalism after the Second World War had at first only a limited impact. As we considered Latin America primarily our own responsibility, so we considered Africa primarily a Western European responsibility. Our nominal sympathy with the anti-colonial movement did lead us to occasional exhortations about the virtues of orderly transition to self-government; but, when the chips were down, as with the United Nations anti-colonial resolution of December 1960, we gave priority to NATO. Our African policy remained general and perfunctory.

Still African nationalism was now a burning fact in the world—never more than in the months of September and October 1960, when sixteen new African states flocked into the UN. During this year the Congolese leader Patrice Lumumba became the bright symbol of nationalist militance; and Lumumba's murder a few weeks after Kennedy's inauguration set off a reaction of outrage through the continent. The martyrdom of Lumumba at the presumed hands of an imperialist agent raised the mistrust of the west to a sudden frenzy of hatred. In Moscow Khrushchev lost no time in embracing the protest and demanding the punishment of the imperialists, hoping thereby to capture the energies of African nationalism. By March 1961 the Congo was in turmoil; a number of the new states, especially Guinea, Mali and Ghana, seemed well launched on the Marxist road; and most of the rest of Africa was consumed with bitterness toward the West. The Atlantic countries had never stood lower nor the Soviet Union higher in the minds of politically conscious Africans.

1. KENNEDY IN AFRICA

Kennedy arrived in office, however, with a record on Africa unique among American politicians. His broad interest in colonial problems had gone back a long way—to childhood tales of Ireland's long struggle for independence and, in the contemporary world, at least to the trip he had taken as an inquisitive young Congressman to Indochina in 1951. In the mid-fifties he had begun to see in Algeria the same pattern of colonial decay he had already inspected in Southeast Asia; and he feared that French intransigence would have the same outcome of uniting the nationalists with the communists. In addition, he had just come on the Senate Foreign Relations Committee and no doubt wanted to move into foreign affairs in a way that would at once be arresting and useful and demonstrate a basic liberalism.

He therefore thought a good deal in the spring of 1957 about a speech on the Algerian struggle for self-determination. Rising in the Senate in July, he pointed out that the French government was repeating its errors of the past—above all, in its refusal to accept the reality of nationalism; and he bluntly criticized the American policy of full support to France in the struggle against the Algerian rebels. The Atlantic nations, he said, must understand that "this is no longer a French problem alone," and the United States must use its influence to work for a solution based on a recognition of "the independent personality of Algeria."

It is hard now to recall the furor his remarks caused. The Algerian speech brought Kennedy more mail, both from the United States and abroad, than any other address he made in the Senate. It produced great irritation not just in official circles in Paris and Washington but throughout the foreign policy establishment in the United States—the Council on Foreign Relations, the *New York Times,* the Department of State. Kennedy had criticized an ally; he had imperiled the unity of NATO. Even Democrats drew back. Dean Acheson attacked him scornfully. Adlai Stevenson thought he had gone too far. For the next year or two, respectable people cited Kennedy's Algerian speech as evidence of his irresponsibility in foreign affairs.

But there were other reactions. French critics of the official policy were pleased to have their hands strengthened by this evidence of international concern. In Europe the speech identified him for the first time as a fresh and independent voice of American foreign policy. And Africans, of course, were deeply excited.

Soon Kennedy became chairman of the African Subcommittee of the Senate Foreign Relations Committee. In this capacity he warned his colleagues about the new energies bursting forth in the dark continent. He advocated sympathy with the independence movement, programs of economic and educational assistance and, as the goal of American policy, "a strong Africa."

In 1960, for the first time in American history, Africa figured prominently in a presidential election. Kennedy charged repeatedly that "we have lost ground in Africa because we have neglected and ignored the needs and aspirations of the African people." Once elected, Kennedy moved forward swiftly to lay the groundwork for a new African policy. His first State Department appointment was G. Mennen Williams as Assistant Secretary for African Affairs. He described this as "a position of responsibility second to none in the new administration," which expressed a new sense of urgency about Africa—and was so received by African leaders. Williams, of course, was well known as a progressive governor of Michigan and battler for civil rights; and his designation expressed Kennedy's desire to take African policy out of conventional channels and give it fresh energy and purpose. In March the President seized the opportunity afforded by the Angola resolution in the UN to dramatize the new American attitude toward African colonial questions. And on African Freedom Day in April he told a reception of African ambassadors of his "profound attachment to the great effort which the people of Africa are making in working toward political freedom." Kennedy's concern with Africa necessarily remained marginal, except when, as in the Congo, problems erupted into crisis. But his curiosity was unremitting. He cared very much, for example, about the performance of his African ambassadors and rarely failed to see them when they came home on consultation. "He was really interested in what they thought," as Ralph Dungan once remarked, "and he always wanted to check their judgment against his."

PATRICE LUMUMBA, PRIME MINISTER OF THE REPUBLIC OF CONGO IN JULY 1960.

The President's interest was not widely shared in the United States, except by African specialists and, to an increasing degree, by Negro leaders. No one in Congress, for example, showed the concern for Africa that Kennedy himself had shown as Senator. Kennedy was not able to increase American assistance to Africa as he would have liked. But, as the magazine *West Africa* later put it, the Africans "considered that Mr. Kennedy's political attitudes were even more important than his efforts to aid their economies." And in communicating these political attitudes Kennedy used a weapon more powerful than the most generous aid programs. That weapon was his own personal contacts with African leaders.

2. PRESIDENTIAL DIPLOMACY

Under Eisenhower presidential meetings with foreign leaders had not ordinarily been for the transaction of business; this was left to the Secretary of State and the pros. They were rather for the purpose of generating goodwill—what came to be called "high-level massage." The purely ceremonial aspects of official visits bored Kennedy. With the help of Angier Biddle Duke, his skillful Chief of Protocol, he cut down on the number of full-dress state visits and devised a new category of less formal meetings. The essence for him was, not the warm handclasp and the smiling photograph, but private communication and candor. He wanted to find out how foreign leaders saw their problems, to get them to understand something of his own problems and to establish personal relations which could be continued by correspondence. We had the impression that he was sometimes impatient with his European guests, who could be long-winded and self-important. But he went to endless lengths to be friendly to visitors from Latin America, Asia and Africa. Nowhere did his efforts have more striking success than with the Africans. Beginning with Nkrumah of Ghana in March 1961, African leaders flowed through the White House in what appeared an unending stream.

They would arrive at the White House, proud, tense and unsure, not knowing what to expect from the head of the most powerful state in the world. Kennedy, with instinctive charm and consideration, put them instantly at ease. For one thing he conveyed an intimate understanding of the force of African nationalism. He talked to Africans as an American and not as a partner of the European colonial powers; and, at the same time, his insight into the African mood enabled him to see African problems, not as outsiders saw them, but as Africans saw them themselves.

He spoke simply and directly, as one world leader talking in confidence to another. He set forth American policy without apology, even when he knew it might disturb or displease his visitor. He made clear his understanding of their determination to stay out of the cold war and made it just as clear that the United States was going to meet its own commitments in the world. At the same time, he treated his visitors as members of the fraternity of working politicians and did not hesitate to discuss the limitations placed on his own action by the Congress or the balance of payments or public opinion.

He inquired into his visitors' problems with disarming frankness: "Well, now that you've got your independence, aren't you finding that your troubles are just beginning?" He realized that their internal pressures sometimes forced them to do things—of an anti-American sort, for example—which they might rather not do. Indeed, he was the first American President for whom the whole world was, in a sense, domestic politics.

His knowledge startled his visitors by its sweep and detail. He would mention personalities and issues, cite facts and statistics and comment on past or present in a way which led some of his guests to say afterward that the American President knew more about their countries than they did themselves. There were never reprimands or homilies: his respect for the dignity of his visitors was complete. He did not ask them to do things they could not do nor promise them things he could not deliver. He gave the impression that he was looking for areas where he and they could work together; where disagreement was unavoidable, then let each side understand the reasons and respect the differences.

He invited their opinions and, whatever the crises on his desk, heard them out with undivided attention. The African leaders responded with astonishingly free and open accounts of their uncertainties and hopes. One after another, they left his presence with admiration for his "sensibility," pride in what they now felt to be a special relationship, a conviction that Kennedy's America, even if it could not do everything at once, was basically with them, and, most of all, a fascination with Kennedy himself. Kennedy's personal friends soon encircled the continent.

3. AFRICA VS. EUROPE

The problem of balancing the relative claims of our NATO allies and the new African states was always tricky. It especially affected our policy in the United Nations, confronting Adlai Stevenson, the State Department and the President with a series of delicate decisions. The vote on the Angola resolution in March 1961 had liberated the United States from its position of systematic deference to the old colonial powers. Nonetheless, each new issue had to be met on its merits.

Kennedy was thus considerably concerned in the early months of 1961 with his old problem of Algeria. He watched with sympathy de Gaulle's careful and circuitous effort to bring his nation to the acceptance of Algerian independence. When the French generals in Algeria mutinied at the end of April and there seemed for a panicky moment the prospect of a paratroop attack on Paris, Kennedy promptly offered de Gaulle his assistance. The collapse of the revolt permitted de Gaulle to move forward; but in the next months, as France finally began talks with the Algerian nationalists, Tunisia took the opportunity to try to drive the French out of their military base at Bizerte. When the French responded by a large and bloody attack, the matter came before the United Nations. In August a special session of the General Assembly met to consider an Afro-Asian resolution calling for the withdrawal of French armed forces from Tunisian territory.

De Gaulle, of course, pronounced the debate no business of the UN and declined to let France take part. In New York Stevenson felt that we should vote for the Afro-Asian resolution. In Washington the Bureau of European Affairs recommended abstention. The President said "With all his faults, the General is the only hope for a solution in Algeria. Tell Adlai that our sympathy is with the anti-colonial nations; but their cause won't be helped by the overthrow of de Gaulle, nor will our position in Berlin. Let's sit this one out."

We abstained without undue damage to our position in Africa. Kennedy then asked the State Department to prepare a letter to Habib Bourguiba, the wise president of Tunisia, in order to "reestablish with you a communication which seems to have been partially interrupted by the incidents of Bizerte." Our relations with Tunisia were soon repaired; in another year France was out of Bizerte, Franco-Tunisian relations were restored and Algeria was independent.

The Portuguese colonies were not so easy. Angola, Mozambique and Portuguese Guinea were all in conditions of incipient revolt, and the new African states were determined to help them gain their freedom. Our own capacity to act in this situation, however, was limited by our dependence, or alleged dependence, on the military and naval installations which Portugal made available to us in the Azores. The Azores lease was due to expire at the end of 1962, and this gave these discussions a certain frenetic quality that autumn until Dr. Salazar finally decided to extend American access to the facilities without formal renewal of the agreement.

This dilemma left us no choice but a moderating policy on Portuguese questions in the UN—never enough for the nationalists in Africa and always too much for the Pentagon and Dr. Salazar. The situation dragged on inconclusively through the Kennedy years, trailing an aura of general dissatisfaction on both sides. Nevertheless Kennedy's effectiveness in making his African visitors understand the American dilemma over the Azores base limited the harm that restraint on the Portuguese colonies did to our general position in Africa.

Kennedy always mistrusted UN resolutions which promised big things but could not be carried out. He used to quote a Chinese proverb: "There is a great deal of noise on the stairs, but nobody comes into the room." He wanted, not hortatory rhetoric against colonialism, but realistic resolutions which could help lay the economic, educational and institutional foundations for self-government.

4. NORTH AFRICA

Once countries had gained their independence, Kennedy believed that the sensible thing was to try to live with the new nations and their new leaders. Not domination or preachment but adjustment and rapprochement seemed to him the fruitful relationship. He saw this as a long-term investment and was ready in the meantime to put up with a certain amount of nonsense.

On July 3, 1962, five years and a day after Kennedy had given his speech in the United States Senate, Algeria became free, but the long war against France had radicalized the political leadership and ravaged the economic and administrative system. Ahmed Ben Bella, who quickly acquired ascendancy in the new Algeria, was a passionate nationalist and socialist presiding over a turbulent and divided land.

Still, even this wilder Algeria had not forgotten the American who had once championed its cause. In 1962, when Ben Bella made his first major trip outside Algeria, he went straight to Washington. After a cordial meeting with Kennedy, the Algerian leader left more ardent than ever in his enthusiasm. Unfortunately Ben Bella's almost fanatical admiration for the American President did not extend to American foreign policy. When the Algerian leader left Washington, he went on—to Kennedy's surprise and annoyance—to visit Fidel Castro. Kennedy, who had found Ben Bella sincere and congenial, was perplexed by what seemed either hopeless naïveté or calculated insult. In the next months, the Algerian government, in between Ben Bella's fraternal greetings to the American President, applauded the Cubans and the Viet Cong and fulminated against American imperialism.

With his personal stake in the outcome of the Algerian revolution, Kennedy followed Algerian developments with special care. His disappointment over Ben Bella's erratic behavior did not divert him from his course. He felt that the anti-imperialist extravagance of Algeria was more the result of mood than of doctrine or discipline; that the present state of affairs was not necessarily permanent; that the United States should maintain a presence and help direct Ben Bella's energies toward the welfare of his own people. He pursued this policy throughout North Africa, meeting with leaders from Tunisia and Libya. And it was the President's intention, when political conditions permitted, to invite President Nasser of Egypt to the United States.

The Nasser story is more a part of Middle Eastern than of African policy. High in a list of problems for the New Frontier was the question of whether better relations were possible with the most powerful leader of the Arab world. In August, when Nasser sent an unexpected and lengthy reply to a circular message Kennedy had sent to the Arab chiefs of state the previous spring, a correspondence sprang up between the two Presidents which went on intermittently through the Kennedy years and served as a substitute for a face-to-face encounter.

Middle Eastern policy was complicated not only by Nasser's dreams of empire and by the decay of medieval oligarchies in states like Yemen and Saudi Arabia but also, of course, by the inordinate Arab hatred of Israel. Kennedy believed strongly in America's moral commitment to Israeli security and took steps to strengthen Israel's ability to resist aggression. But he wished to preserve an entrée to Nasser in order both to restrain Egyptian policy toward Israel and to try to work more closely with the modernizing forces in the Arab world.

Kennedy's deeper hope, as with Sukarno and Ben Bella, was to persuade Nasser to concentrate on making progress at home rather than trouble abroad. As in Algeria, our main tool of economic assistance was Food for Peace. For a time the policy of selective cooperation had an encouraging effect. In June 1962, when Nasser wrote Kennedy expressing his tacit acceptance of the American interest in a free Israel, marking a considerable advance in mutual understanding.

Then the Imam of Yemen died in September 1962, and Nasser's involvement in the ensuing power struggle dominated American relations with Egypt in 1963 and interrupted Kennedy's effort to turn Egyptian energies inward.

5. BLACK AFRICA: SÉKOU TOURÉ AND NKRUMAH

The policy of staying in close, keeping at work and waiting for the breaks had its most notable success in Guinea. Under the influence of Sékou Touré, a left-wing trade union leader, Guinea alone among the former French colonies had voted in 1958 against de Gaulle's idea of transforming the old French empire into a French community. In a fit of irritation, de Gaulle responded by ordering a total French evacuation. He even placed Guinea on an international blacklist. Sékou Touré, even if he were not a Marxist, had no choice but to turn east—and, of course, then considering himself a Marxist, he found this alternative highly agreeable. The Russians, delighted at the chance to establish themselves on the Atlantic coast of Africa, obliged with an extensive program of technical assistance. By 1960 Washington had consigned Guinea to the communist bloc.

Kennedy took another view. He felt that Sékou Touré remained a nationalist at heart; and, before William Attwood departed as his ambassador to Conakry, the President asked him to verify this as best he could. Attwood found the American position less hopeless than it seemed from Washington. He reported a slow disillusionment and recommended a small American aid program to show Sekou Touré that the United States was willing to go along with genuine non-alignment. In December, 1961, after a clumsy Russian intervention into Guinean politics, Sékou Touré expelled the Soviet Ambassador. By the spring of 1962, American aid was beginning to arrive: food, teachers, money. And, when Touré came to New York in October for the UN General Assembly, the President asked him down to Washington. Kennedy met him at the airport and took him back to the White House, where they talked over the problems of Guinea for an hour in the Cabinet Room. Then Kennedy brought him over to the Mansion, introduced him to Jacqueline and Caroline and gave him a formal luncheon.

From this time on Touré felt that he had a friend at the White House and sent personal messages at the slightest pretext. The Attwood-Kennedy policy was able to succeed, of course, because it came at the right time. But, if Washington had persisted in its conviction that Guinea was irreclaimable, we would not have been in the position to take advantage of the Soviet errors.

In the case of Nkrumah of Ghana, the new American policy found harder going. Relations between Ghana and the United States were already poor, and by the time Kennedy's ambassador arrived in Accra at the end of January, the Ghanian cabinet met to consider whether he should be allowed to present his credentials at all. The murder of Lumumba brought a well-organized outburst of anti-American rioting, following which Nkrumah served as the gracious host for Leonid Brezhnev, the president of the Soviet Union.

At the same time, there remained one great foothold for the west in Ghana, and this was the project, originally conceived by the British colonial administration, for a dam on the Volta River. A Volta dam would not only create a great lake to help meet internal needs for irrigation, fish and transport, but could generate hydroelectric power and make possible the installation of a smelter to convert Ghana's bauxite resources into aluminum; it would be the key to Ghana's economic future.

The British and Canadian aluminum industry had considered aiding the Volta Dam until the increase in the British bank rate in 1958 made participation too costly. Then Nkrumah appealed to Washington, and appeared at the White House early in March, 1961. The visit was a success. The Kennedys liked him, and Nkrumah was so moved that on the plane to New York he scrawled Kennedy a warm personal note on a yellow lined pad expressing his pleasure at the meeting and his hope for future friendship. In July Kennedy wrote him that the United States planned to go ahead with the Volta project.

In the meantime, Nkrumah had set forth on a swing around the communist circuit. With each statement in each new communist capital he seemed to move further from a position of non-alignment. When he reached Peking in September, his communiqué after a talk with Mao actually included some of the same phrases he had scribbled to Kennedy on the plane in March: the sands of the cold war were indeed constantly shifting. The Iron Curtain tour resulted in so apparently fervent an embrace of the communists as to raise new questions about the Volta Dam at just the moment when the agreement had come to the point of signature. Nor did Nkrumah strengthen his case by undertaking new measures of internal repression on his return to Ghana.

Kennedy now began to wonder whether it was appropriate to invest a large share of the limited funds set aside for Africa in a single project in a single country—above all, in a country which was not providing stirring examples either of liberalism at home or non-alignment in the world. Congress was increasingly unhappy; public opinion was critical; Robert Kennedy was opposed; even Adlai Stevenson suggested that aid to the project be suspended. Only Chayes, Bowles, Williams and Fredericks at State were solidly in favor. On the other hand, construction industry representatives, whom Kennedy sent to Accra in October for tough talk with Nkrumah, returned with his cordial assurances that Ghana would stay on a course of true neutrality; and a circular inquiry to our other African embassies showed that most African governments, including some of Nkrumah's political enemies, hoped we would go ahead. Kennedy now sent a special mission to Ghana.

At the same time, the British weighed in heavily. Macmillan wrote Kennedy in November that he did not believe Nkrumah had yet gone over to the Russians. If the United States were now to pull out, Macmillan said, the Africans would regard it as an attempt to use financial power to dictate the national policy of independent African states; the Russians would move in; and cancellation might have the same consequences in West Africa that John Foster Dulle's repudiation of the Aswan Dam had in Egypt in 1956. But, if the west backed the Volta Dam, it would be convincing proof to the Africans, who were tending to regard the Soviet system as peculiarly well designed to bring about industrialization, that industrial development could be combined with freedom.

The President, as usual, was interested in the long run. He probably had made up his mind early in the year to support the project. He well understood that cancellation of the Volta Dam now would set back his whole African policy, while support would dramatize the new American attitude toward non-alignment throughout Africa. He hoped that this policy would preserve a positive American presence within Ghana and that Nkrumah's nationalism would in the end prevail over his leanings toward the east. He made the final decision to go ahead in November. The agreement was signed in Accra in January. The total American government investment—all in the form of loans—amounted to somewhat over $40 million.

The policy did not allow for the vagaries of Nkrumah. The Ghanian leader proceeded in the next years to transform his country in the direction less of African socialism than of African totalitarianism. The *Osagyefo* or Redeemer, as he called himself, established a dictatorship, crushed all opposition, turned violently against the west and set himself up as a virtual deity. Kennedy watched these developments with deepening concern, and in 1963 Kennedy evidently wished that he had been tougher in the first place. By this time he instructed AID to extend no more long-term credits to Ghana. Yet even then his view was that the final beneficiaries of the Volta Dam would be not the government of Kwame Nkrumah but the people of Ghana.

6. THE CONGO

Of all the African problems, the one that most commanded the President's attention was the Congo. Independence had descended like a hurricane on the unprepared country in July 1960. In a few days the new state was in chaos: the Force Publique had mutinied; Katanga and other provinces were proclaiming their independence; Belgian paratroopers were coming back to restore order. In desperation Prime Minister Lumumba appealed to the United Nations. On July 14 the Security Council voted to provide the central government with enough military assistance to pacify the country.

Lumumba also cabled N. S. Khrushchev "to watch hourly over the situation"; and Khrushchev responded in his own way. By September several hundred Soviet 'technicians' were in Leopoldville, Russian military equipment was going to Lumumba's army, and communist sympathizers were moving into the central government. Lumumba obviously preferred this to assistance from the United Nations; and in consequence President Joseph Kasavubu dismissed him early in September. In another week Kasavubu, closing the Soviet and Czech embassies, placed his main reliance on the UN peace-keeping force. The Russians, having just missed establishing a powerful military and political presence in this rich, large and strategic land, now turned savagely against the UN. Khrushchev, still watching hourly over the situation, vetoed subsequent Security Council action, launched violent attacks against Hammarskjöld and soon advanced the *troika* proposal. He accompanied this barrage by vigorous support for Lumumba and, after Lumumba's arrest and murder, for his heir, Antoine Gizenga.

In January 1961 Kennedy inherited a Congo still in chaos, divided among the Kasavubu government in Leopoldville, the Gizenga group in Stanleyville and the pro-Belgian secessionist regime of Moise Tshombe in Elisabethville. Overshadowing everything was the prospect that Soviet meddling in the chaos might lead to a Russian base in the heart of Africa. From the start the new President had a simple and constant view: that, unless the United Nations filled the vacuum in the Congo, there would be no alternative but a direct Soviet-American confrontation. The UN could not bring the great powers together in the Congo, but at least it could keep them apart. A unified Congo, with a strong central government, therefore seemed the condition for the success of the UN policy.

In the summer of 1961 the Congolese parliament elected a coalition government under a sober trade unionist named Cyrille Adoula. At the request of the new government, the UN forces now began action to end the secession. UN troops took over key installations in Elisabethville and, as they extended their operations in September, they encountered resistance from Tshombe's forces.

The outbreak of hostilities brought down a storm of criticism on the UN. Hammarskjöld, concerned by the fighting, flew to the Congo to arrange a cease-fire and promote negotiations between Leopoldville and Elisabethville. This was his last mission. In the meantime, Edmund Gullion arrived in the Congo in August as Kennedy's new ambassador. Kennedy, with confidence in Gullion, subdued occasional doubts to give consistent support to the UN policy. He was backing the UN, as he once explained to Macmillan, as the best insurance against the conflict of great powers in the Congo. Our own national experience, he added, demonstrated that, if a compact of government was to endure, it must provide the central authority with at least the power to tax and the exclusive power to raise armies; we could not argue with the Congolese to the contrary.

Hostilities continued in the Congo despite a nominal UN ceasefire until in mid-December 1961 Tshombe sent Washington a message requesting the President's help in arranging a meeting with Adoula. The result was the signing in January of the Kitona agreement in which Tshombe accepted the authority of the central government.

Gullion, however, remained skeptical. He felt that Tshombe was playing for time and would not abide by the agreement. This forecast turned out to be right, as Tshombe began systematically to evade the accord. During the summer of 1962 British, Belgian and American officials worked together on a new unification plan which U Thant put into final form and sponsored in September. Once again Tshombe accepted the plan and once again stalled on its execution. But the President was still determined to use American influence to bring about unification. Fearing, however, that neither his European allies nor American public opinion would countenance a renewal of the UN war against Katanga, he bent every effort to achieve a political solution. Matters dragged unhappily on, with the Adoula government growing feebler every day, till the time limit which U Thant had attached to his plan expired in December. Tshombe now denounced the plan and declaimed, with flourishes, about a "scorched earth" policy. On Christmas Eve his troops resumed the harassment of the UN forces. After four days of accepting Katangan fire without retaliation, the UN army received U Thant's reluctant permission to respond.

Things were tense in the White House in the few days after Christmas. There was strong pressure throughout Washington to stop the UN forces from taking the offensive. If we did so, it would mean the end of American influence in the Congo and drive the central government (even if without Adoula) to accept Soviet assistance. But the fighting around Elisabethville suddenly acquired a momentum of its own. Before we really knew what was happening, Tshombe's resistance collapsed. It all occurred so quickly that it outstripped both instructions from the UN headquarters in New York and any revolt in western public opinion as well as any intervention by Moscow. I do not know what Kennedy would have done if the fighting had stretched out. But he had already decided to lend American fighter planes to the

U.N. SECRETARY GENERAL DAG HAMMARSKJÖLD VISITING THE CONGO IN 1961.

UN force if they were requested; and this suggests that he was ready, if necessary, to go very far down the military road to secure a unified Congo.

The Katanga secession thus came to an end. In time, the Adoula government fell, and in another year Tshombe, who had fled the country in June 1963, renounced his secessionism and returned as Prime Minister of the unified Congo. With impressive agility, Tshombe, having lost his principle, at least recovered what he evidently valued a good deal more—his power.

The Congo policy did more, however, than simply settle a constitutional argument and preserve the Congo as a nation. It gave the United Nations its greatest success in peace-keeping and its greatest effort in technical assistance. More than that, it averted a possible Soviet-American clash in the heart of Africa. Above all, it consolidated the growing confidence of the new African states in the American President.

7. THE STRUGGLE AGAINST APARTHEID

Of all the preoccupations of African nationalism, the most obsessive was with South Africa, where *apartheid*—the policy of systematic exclusion of Africans and Asians from the life of the community—was becoming each year more cruel and abhorrent. Blocked from doing anything about apartheid on the spot, the other African states had long since appealed to the United Nations, which for some years had responded by passing resolutions of exhortation and condemnation. This ritualistic exercise had no effect on South Africa, and by 1961 the other African states were concluding that something more was required. The African resolutions of that year therefore demanded political and economic sanctions against apartheid. But even Asian nations considered this an extreme use of UN power, and the resolution as finally voted left it to individual states to consider such action as was open to them.

The American President's speeches about freedom and justice and his use of American troops to protect Negro rights made a deep impression in Africa. It made Africans perceive the United States for a moment as "the defender of liberty, equality and fraternity."

As South Africa, far from showing any inclination to abandon its practices, proceeded to tighten its system more each year, the question of sanctions was bound to recur. In the autumn of 1962, after more repression, the African states put in a new resolution calling on UN members to break their political and economic relations with South Africa and even asking the Security Council to consider expelling South Africa from the UN if it did not change its policies.

The United States had joined regularly in the ceremonial condemnation of apartheid. We also sought through diplomatic channels to persuade the South African government of the hopelessness of its course. An *aide mémoire* to Pretoria in September 1961 thus recorded our inability to cooperate with South Africa in ways which would lend support to apartheid. But a program of UN sanctions presented other questions; and the 1962 resolution embodying this program was one of those unrealistic declarations, at once grandiose and ineffectual, which made Kennedy so impatient. So long as South Africa's major trading partners declined to participate, for example, the call for an economic boycott would be meaningless. Our refusal to support sanctions in 1962 was readily accepted by the Africans, though the General Assembly passed the resolution by a heavy majority.

We knew, however, that the matter would come up with fresh intensity in 1963. The first all-African association, the Organization of African Unity, met at Addis Ababa in May and called, in effect, for the United States to choose between Africa and the colonial powers. After the meeting, friendly African leaders like Houphouët-Boigny and Nyerere warned us that in the case of South Africa we could no longer rest on purely verbal condemnation of apartheid. Reflecting on these developments, Mennen Williams wrote a memorandum in mid-June arguing that we must now prepare to back up disapproval with action. The indicated area, in his view, was the sale of arms.

The proposal of a total arms embargo encountered instant opposition in the upper levels of the State Department. One high official argued that it would gain us only a transitory political truce with the African leaders, who would be satisfied with nothing less than a full economic embargo, and that it would lose us the tangible advantages of our present cooperation with South Africa on a wide range of defense matters. An even higher official suggested that, if we embarked on the policy of sanctions against nations whose internal arrangements we disapproved, we must logically end by severing relations with perhaps half the existing community or states.

These were not easy questions; and they involved, of course, the Portuguese colonies as well as South Africa. The choice seemed almost to be between the military risk of losing the Azores and the South African tracking stations and the political risk of losing Africa. The Portuguese and South African cases were, however, separable; and, of the two, the Portuguese problem was the more difficult.

But South Africa was a different matter; and, indeed, pressure here could do something in African eyes to make up for restraint in the case of Portugal. After debating many options with his cabinet and staff, Kennedy, in a brilliant stroke, went further and proposed a unilateral declaration that as a matter of national policy the United States would sell no additional arms to South Africa after the first of the year, so long as South Africa practiced apartheid. On August 2 Stevenson announced this decision in the Security Council. Five days later he cast the American vote for a resolution calling on all states "to cease forthwith the sale and shipment of arms, ammunition of all types and military vehicles to South Africa." Britain and France abstained. This action could not long satisfy the insatiable African demand for stronger measures against apartheid; but it preserved the new African faith in American policy.

At the same time, developments within the United States were further increasing African confidence in Kennedy. The distance between the American and African Negro had narrowed greatly since 1956. The acceleration of the American civil rights struggle cast Kennedy himself more and more as the champion of the American Negro against his traditional oppressors. The American President's speeches about freedom and justice and his use of American troops to protect Negro rights made a deep impression in Africa. The struggle against segregation at home gave substance to our condemnations of apartheid in the United Nations and helped the Africans accept our reasoned objection to sanctions. But, more than this, it made Africans perceive the United States for a moment as "the defender of liberty, equality and fraternity." The American President's gallant leadership in the civil rights fight sealed the vast regard and affection for him in African hearts.

XXII.
THE WORLD OF DIVERSITY

KENNEDY'S THIRD WORLD POLICY—the policy of helping the new nations to strength and independence—involved more than a change in American attitudes toward colonialism and non-alignment. For the travail of nationhood required above all economic and social progress. To throw serious weight behind the independence movement, the President had to redesign our existing programs of economic assistance, devise new instruments of social betterment and infuse the whole effort with a fresh idealism.

American assistance to foreign nations had gone through a number of phases since the Second World War. Immediately after the war, during the UNRRA period, foreign aid went mostly for humanitarian purposes. At the end of the forties, in the era of the Marshall Plan, it went for the reconstruction of developed economies shattered by the war. In the fifties attention shifted to the underdeveloped countries of Asia, and aid went mainly for military assistance. This was for several reasons. The Korean War gave priority to the military aspect of the communist offensive in the third world. John Foster Dulles's diplomacy, moreover, conceived aid in large measure as a means of enlisting allies and establishing strong military positions (as in Laos). And the annual agony of getting the aid bill through Congress was somewhat eased when it could be presented as a hard, anti-communist, military program.*

1. NEW DIRECTIONS IN FOREIGN AID

In the meantime, a new analysis of the aid problem was emerging from the universities and the foundations. At the start, development had been seen as a relatively self-contained economic process, calling only for the injection of capital and technical skill** into a dormant economy. In time economists began to see that development had to be studied in a broader institutional and cultural context. The substantial increase of output and living standards, it was becoming evident, required the modernization of entire social structures and ways of thought and life—and for this capital was not enough.

As in the case of military strategy, the new approach was most fully explored along the banks of the Charles River. Here a group of economists at Harvard and the Massachusetts Institute of Technology were evolving a comprehensive view, shaped in great part by their own experience, of the development process.

Out of this there came the argument that the true role of foreign aid was neither military nor technical assistance but the organized promotion of national development. The Charles River analysis made several contributions of great significance. First of all, it offered the aid program what it had long lacked—specific criteria for assistance. The goal, the Charles River economists said, was to enable underdeveloped nations, to "take off" into self-sustaining economic growth. This, they believed, was feasible for most countries; and, when it was reached, the need for special external assistance would end. Next they pointed out that non-economic as well as economic factors determine growth. Thus, in addition to the familiar range of economic issues—industrialization, agricultural methods, sources of energy, the internal market, inflation, balance of payments and so on—they brought in structural change, land reform, the roles of the public sector and of private entrepreneurship, political development and other social and cultural adjustments required to ease the modernization process. Both economic and non-economic factors were to be subsumed under national development plans. The emphasis on national development was not intended to divorce foreign aid from the political interests of the United States. But it looked to long-term rather than short-term political effects. In this view, foreign aid, instead of being a State Department slush fund to influence tactical situations, should aim at the strategic goals of a stronger national independence, an increased concentration

*This process of letting political necessity shape the aid program had actually begun in the last Truman years. In 1951, Harriman, with whom I had worked in Paris in 1948 on the Marshall Plan, called me to Washington to help on the President's aid message. There I first met David E. Bell, Richard Neustadt and Harlan Cleveland and participated with them in the invention of the concept of 'defense support'—a means of bringing in economic aid which could be justified as militarily essential.

**Odiously termed 'know-how' in the bureaucracy.

on domestic affairs, greater democracy and a long-run association with the West.

Pointing out that capital assistance alone could not do the job, Galbraith laid heavy emphasis on four other things as equally crucial: a substantial degree of education within the country; a substantial measure of social justice; a reliable apparatus of public administration; and a purposeful theory of national planning. The stress on education assumed particular importance in the next years. The stress on country planning and social reform similarly became central, especially in Latin America.

The Charles River approach represented a very American effort to persuade the developing countries to base their revolutions on Locke rather than Marx. Perhaps this was a dream, but it was not impossible of fulfillment in all countries. Certainly it represented an immense improvement over the philosophy of the country store. It gave our economic policy toward the third world a rational design and a coherent purpose. It sought to remove our assistance from the framework of the cold war and relate it to the needs of nations struggling for their own political and economic fulfillment. It laid out fields for research and priorities for action. Its spirit was generous and humane. It may have fallen short of the ferocities of the situation. But, given the nature of our institutions and values, it was probably the best we could do.

2. KENNEDY AND FOREIGN AID

In the late fifties a few people in the Eisenhower administration were growing dissatisfied with the American foreign aid programs. As the decade progressed, Kennedy's interest in aid problems had steadily increased. His concern with India soon led him to larger reflections about the challenge of modernization. He readily accepted the Cambridge thesis that the American interest would be best served by the development of strong and independent states. He knew that money was essential but insisted repeatedly that it was not enough. Along with capital, he wanted education and social change. The political payoff, in his view, would come in the long run and as a result of other things than aid appropriations. He doubtless agreed with Machiavelli: "The friendship which is gained by purchase and not through grandeur and nobility of spirit is bought and not secured."

He also had a deepening sense of the urgency of the aid effort. In 1959, after mentioning the national preoccupation with the missile gap, he called attention to another gap which, he said, "constitutes an equally clear and present danger to our security"—the economic gap. By this he meant "the gap in living standards and income and hope for the future ... between the stable, industrialized nations of the north, whether they are friends or foes, and the overpopulated, under-invested nations of the south, whether they are friends or neutrals."

Kennedy as President faced the task of reorganizing the aid effort. He had inherited an organization, or rather a congeries of organizations; he had inherited a congressional conviction that foreign aid was primarily part of the cold war; and he had to work within that inheritance.

"The fundamental task of our foreign aid program in the 1960s," Kennedy said, "is not negatively to fight communism: its fundamental task is to help make a historical demonstration that in the twentieth century, as in the nineteenth—in the southern half of the globe as in the north—economic growth and political democracy can develop hand in hand." To meet this challenge, he continued, the effort must base itself on new principles—especially national development planning and long-term authorization and financing. It must also have unified administration and operation; and this meant, Kennedy explained, a single aid administration absorbing not only the International Cooperation Administration and the Development Loan Fund but Food for Peace, the Peace Corps and even certain functions of the Export-Import Bank. He assembled a task force on foreign economic assistance, which worked through the spring and summer to lay the groundwork for the new Agency for International Development (AID).

The establishment of AID inaugurated a long period of turmoil and frustration. The unification of the aid agencies was the inevitable consequence of the decision to encourage

One AID economist calculated that in certain countries every dollar invested in birth control would be 200 times as productive as the same dollar invested in foreign aid.

national development planning in the countries aided; but a further consequence had to be the organization of the new agency along regional rather than technical lines in Washington. This posed a mortal threat to the vested ideas, interests and routines of the aid bureaucracy.

The search began for a director, someone conservative enough to reassure Congress but liberal enough to carry forward the program—a business image, as it was put, without a business mentality. The choice fell upon Fowler Hamilton, a New York lawyer and a Democrat with government experience in the Second World War who had been under consideration for the directorship of CIA.

3. EVOLUTION OF AID

Hamilton focused first on recruitment, then spent most of his time dealing with Congress. This was a heartbreaking job. Fanatical foes of foreign aid, chief among them Congressman Otto Passman of Louisiana, did their best to block the new aid bill, but the administration staged a vigorous drive, and Congress finally agreed that the Kennedy recommendations deserved a try.

There followed a year of disappointment. Changing the direction of an agency while it continues its day-to-day operations is one of the hardest tricks in government; it has been likened to performing surgery on a man while he hauls a trunk upstairs. AID, despite the new legislation and leadership, remained sluggish and appeared ineffectual. The President often grew exceedingly impatient over its seeming inability to act, especially in Latin America. Returning ambassadors would tell of the enthusiasm with which the local governments had proposed one program or another, the excitement of planning, the filing of applications—and then the endless silence, interrupted only by the arrival of new technical missions or the request for further feasibility studies, until the government lost interest in the project and faith in Washington.

AID's apparent failure to show significant results during its year of grace gave Passman a chance to return to the battle in 1962. He did this with undiminished zest, producing a congressional mood that cut the President's 1962 request from $4.9 to $3.9 billion and reduced development loans by more than 20 percent.

The President was coming to the conclusion that the basic weakness lay in the program itself and its execution. It was mostly in this respect that he found Hamilton wanting. Hamilton had taken on the assignment as a lawyer takes a case; he even occasionally spoke of the President as "my client." But he had no special knowledge of the technical intricacies of the development effort; and his activities as reorganizer, recruiter and salesman left him little time to worry about the substance of AID's work. Then the congressional debacle of 1962 weakened his standing as the program's attorney.

In any case, Hamilton had presided over the organizational transition with considerable success. Yet at the end the program was substantively no more convincing than before and politically weaker than ever. This situation convinced Kennedy that extreme measures were necessary to get the aid bill through Congress in 1963. He was having difficulties with business community for other reasons, and he resorted to the familiar device of a blue-ribbon panel of bonded conservatives set up to cast a presumably cold eye on the aid effort and then to recommend its continuance as essential to the national interest. He selected General Lucius Clay to head the group.

At the same time, the President had to choose a successor to Hamilton. The other obvious candidate within the government was David Bell. Bell had exceptional qualifications. He had the practical experience of having run the Ford Foundation mission in Pakistan; and his superb record as director of the Bureau of the Budget had won him the total confidence of the President.

As some in the administration had feared, Clay's group did not achieve the desired effect. After holding hearings, which at least afforded Bell the chance to get a quick and useful briefing in his new responsibilities, the group submitted a report which ultimately weakened support for the President's bill. By the end of the Kennedy years funding for foreign aid was at its lowest point since 1958. Yet, philosophically and operationally, the program was in better shape than it had been for some time. Testifying before the House Foreign Affairs Committee in 1963, David Bell pointed out that, of the forty countries which had received the major share of American development aid since 1945, fourteen no longer depended on external assistance and ten others were steadily reducing such dependence. In these twenty-four countries, Bell said, "democratic institutions have been strengthened or less democratic regimes liberalized." He concluded with characteristic precision that, while economic progress could not guarantee democracy, "it seems clear that without economic progress the chances for strengthening democratic processes in the less developed countries would be greatly diminished."

The success of the aid program—both in getting support at home and results abroad—remained as elusive as its continuation seemed imperative. But David Bell more than vindicated Kennedy's confidence. In the end, he stayed longer as aid administrator than anyone else in the history of the effort.

4. DEVELOPMENT VS. POPULATION

The struggle for economic growth encountered more than the well-advertised obstacles of ignorance, disease, corruption and inertia. Even when countries had the will to reshape attitudes and institutions, there was still the constant threat that population would increase faster than output, producing a decline in per capita income and therefore in the savings available for capital formation. Indeed, this threat actually became more acute as nations began to modernize. Improvements in sanitation and public health—from the boiling of water and the swatting of flies to penicillin and DDT—often neutralized the old Malthusian checks before economic growth could take up the slack. One AID economist calculated that in certain countries every dollar invested in birth control would be 200 times as productive as the same dollar invested in foreign aid.

This problem had nagged the consciousness of foreign aid people for some time. In the very long run, industrialization and affluence might bring down the birth rate; but in the short run the situation seemed to require a more specific and purposeful attack. But the Eisenhower staunchly refused to allow the incorporation of birth control into any of its aid programs.

The election in 1960 of a Roman Catholic President might have been supposed to place population control even further outside the realm of public policy. Actually Kennedy had long been concerned about the implications of population growth for economic development. Early in 1960 what he stated that the solution was "for the United States and other powers to help them get ahead of their population increase. If they make a judgment that they want to limit their population under those conditions, that is a judgment they should make, and economic assistance which we give permits them to make that judgment, if that is their choice."

In the autumn of 1962 Sweden laid before the UN General Assembly a resolution calling on the Secretary-General to conduct an inquiry on population problems. This meant that, for the first time, the General Assembly would debate population policy. The United States voted for the Swedish resolution in the General Assembly, balking only at a section calling for UN "technical assistance" on population problems; we abstained here because the UN already had all the authority it needed to give its members technical assistance and the inclusion of this superfluous language might raise fears that the UN was about to go into the business of distributing contraceptive devices. AID soon adopted a policy that did not allow the United States to impose any obstacles to another country's efforts to address their population concerns, nor to dictate the means of dealing with those concerns, superseding the Eisenhower ban against action on population questions. This activity slowly awakened public interest. In April 1963 someone asked Kennedy at a press conference whether he thought the United States should supply funds for international birth control studies. The President replied: "If your question is: Can we do more, should we know more about the whole reproduction cycle, and should this information be made more available to the world so that everyone can make their own judgment, I would think that it would be a matter which we could certainly support."

Kennedy's statement represented a significant revolution in the attitude of the American government. He affirmed two principles: freedom of research on population matters and freedom of every nation to use the resulting knowledge in determining its own policy. In handling the question this way, he dispelled all doubt, if any remained, about the capacity of a Catholic President to decide public issues on their merits. Actually, with the growing reappraisal within the Church itself, the policy provoked little criticism among his co-religionists. Catholic concern seemed now to narrow to the relatively small point—and one on which they received reassurance—that the government should not ship out contraceptives. The Kennedy years thus further strengthened the American attack on world poverty by preparing the means to keep population growth from nullifying the development effort.

5. FOOD AND PEOPLE

The original plan for aid reorganization had contemplated absorbing both Food for Peace and the Peace Corps into the Agency for International Development. After all, they too provided forms of assistance; and the logic of those who wanted to run government by the book was to put them all in the centralized operation. This logic was not perhaps irresistible. Nothing could take the heart out of new ideas more speedily than an old bureaucracy. The heads of both agencies vigorously shared this view, and each had strong support in his fight for autonomy—George McGovern from the agricultural committees on the Hill, and Sargent Shriver from the Vice-President, as chairman of the Peace Corps's National Advisory Committee.

Food for Peace was the great unseen weapon of Kennedy's third world policy. McGovern's imaginative direction of the program received Kennedy's direct and personal support; and, after McGovern was elected Senator from South Dakota in 1962, the work was carried forward by Richard Reuter of CARE. Shipments under Public Law 480 averaged nearly $1.5 billion annually in the Kennedy years. This assistance not only played a notable humanitarian role in averting mass starvation in India, Egypt, Algeria and other nations; but the use of food as wages carried it beyond a relief program to serve, in effect, as a means of financing development. In addition to its profound impact abroad, the program greatly eased the problems created by American agricultural productivity, reduced surplus storage charges, increased farm income and purchasing power and even, under the stipulation that the food be transported in American ships, helped subsidize the maritime industry. Food for Peace, as Hubert Humphrey once put it, was "a twentieth century form of alchemy."

But the part of the aid effort which best expressed the distinctive spirit of the New Frontier was the Peace Corps. In the late fifties Humphrey and Richard Neuberger in the Senate and Henry Reuss in the House had advanced variations on the general idea of sending volunteers overseas for technical assistance work. Kennedy advanced the idea during the campaign and the response was unexpectedly warm. "I want to demonstrate to Mr. Khrushchev and others," he said toward the end of the campaign in Chicago, "that a new generation of Americans has taken over this country ... young Americans [who will] serve the cause of freedom as servants of peace around the world, working for freedom as the communists work for their system." He often envied the communist capacity to mobilize popular idealism, especially of the young. He was sure there was a comparable fund of idealism among the youth of America; and the Peace Corps seemed a means of demonstrating the reality of this idealism to the world.

On March 1, 1961, Sargent Shriver submitted a report to Kennedy recommending immediate establishment. The objectives of the Peace Corps, according to the report, were threefold:

It can contribute to the development of critical countries and regions.

It can promote international cooperation and good will toward this country.

It can also contribute to the education of America and to more intelligent participation in the world.

On the same day Kennedy set up the Peace Corps by executive order and sent a message to Congress requesting legislation. By the spring of 1961 recruitment and training were well under way. Soon the volunteers began to leave on their assignments. The original authorization of 500 grew to 5000 by March 1963 and to 10,000 in another year, and volunteers were soon working in forty-six countries.

The Peace Corps in action was an immensely moving sight. Here were young American men and women who had given two years of their lives to serve in unknown places in remote lands, with little recognition or reward beyond their own sense of achievement and growth. I saw them in India in 1962 and again in Venezuela in 1963. In the Punjab they were agricultural specialists, working with the farmers in the villages. In Caracas I was taken deep into a *barrio,* along alleys turned into mud by several days of rain. We finally reached a playground, at one end of which a young Negro from Denver was presiding over twenty-five dead-end kids sawing and hammering away on pieces of lumber. A soap-box derby was impending, and Jerry Green, and Peace Corps man, had dug up some boards and set the boys to work. We talked about the boys and their prospects. He described an alliance he had struck with the local Catholic priest both to encourage the boys to stay in school and also to make the local school better. Later he drove us in a battered jeep to his quarters. The walls along the way were chalked with amiable slogans—*Muera Betancourt* and *Muera Kennedy**—but Jerry received friendly waves and greetings every few steps. I later asked Allan Stewart, our ambassador in Caracas, about the

*"Death to Betancourt," "Death to Kennedy."

THE FIRST MEMBERS OF THE PEACE CORPS VOLUNTEERS LEAVE FOR OVERSEAS DUTY ON AUGUST 29, 1961.

Peace Corps. He said, "It has been wonderful here. It has worked miracles in changing the Venezuelan image of North Americans. Before the Peace Corps, the only Americans the poor Venezuelans ever saw were riding around in Cadillacs. They supposed them all to be rich, selfish, callous, reactionary. The Peace Corps has shown them an entirely different kind of Americans. It is transforming the whole theory they have of the United States."

This was the point—this, and the extent to which the experience gave the volunteers a new understanding of the world and themselves. Watching the volunteers as they carried to dark slums and sullen villages examples of modesty, comradeship, hard work and optimism, one wondered whether they were not bringing some inkling of the meaning of a democratic community to places hitherto inaccessible to the democratic idea, and whether future Nyereres and

Sékou Tourés, even perhaps future Nkrumahs and Castros, might not catch fire from their liveliness and devotion. One simply could not dismiss what the foreign minister of Thailand called "this important idea, the most powerful idea in recent times, of a Peace Corps, of youth mingling, living, working with youth," nor discount his surprise that this idea should come from the mightiest nation on earth, the United States. Many of us who did not know about the United States thought of this great nation as a wealthy nation, a powerful nation, endowed with great material strength and many powerful weapons. But how many of us know that in the United States ideas and ideals are also powerful?

6. DOGMATISM VS. PRAGMATISM

Kennedy's third world policy represented a considerable break from the Washington world view of the fifties, and it foreshadowed a fundamental reconstruction of our total foreign policy. In the Eisenhower years the conduct of foreign affairs had rested on a set of abstract and unitary doctrines—about the uncommitted world, which we regarded as immoral; about the 'free world,' or, as it was known in public documents, the Free World, which we hoped would conform to the principles upon which we fancied American society was based; and about the communist world, which we saw as a centralized conspiracy. Now each of these dogmas was undergoing revision.

As we stopped regarding neutralism as a sin, so we receded from the insistence that nations which received our aid should adopt our economic creed. In the fifties Washington had been deeply convinced of the superiority, not to say sanctity, of the system of free private enterprise. No one seemed to care that this system, as described in the official literature, did not correspond to the reality of our own society, which had long since evolved into a mixed economy and a welfare state, or even to the actuality of our own past, marked in pre-takeoff days by considerable initiative on the part of the so-called public sector.

Kennedy's own views were strictly empirical. Declining to regard the choice between private and public means as a matter of moral principle, he rejected equally the theologians of the private sector and the theologians of the public sector—those on the right who regarded public enterprise as inherently sinful and those on the left who regarded private enterprise as inherently sinful. In his judgment, the only issue was which means could best achieve the desired end, and this to be answered not by doctrine but by experiment. We were not, in short, to worry too much about the ideological character of economic development.

It was not easy to bring even the executive branch of the government, steeped in ancient habits, to tolerate other economic systems or, at first, to describe our own with much accuracy. The United States Information Agency until well into 1961 dispatched a weekly economic commentary portraying the American economy, as if George Humphrey still reigned in Washington, as a system of rugged individualism unhampered by government control. Edward R. Murrow did not need prompting, to begin his revamping of USIA. He proved a brilliant chief, and in Donald M. Wilson he had an exceptionally able deputy. One felt that Murrow finally came into his own in Washington. In the fifties he had been a solitary voice of courage and reason in commercial television; but there had seemed to be gathering within him a searing disgust with the medium and a sad frustration about his own life. All this now changed quickly in Washington. He revitalized USIA, imbued it with his own bravery and honesty and directed its efforts especially to the developing nations, where, instead of expounding free-enterprise ideology, it tried to explain the American role in a diverse and evolving world. USIA became one of the most effective instruments of Kennedy's third world policy; and Murrow himself was a new man, cheerful, amused, committed, contented. Under Ed Murrow the Voice of America became the voice, not of American self-righteousness, but of American democracy.

7. UNIFORMITY VS. DIVERSITY

No great power could run the world: variety was the stubborn and irreducible reality. The policy of the two blocs was played out. And, if the monolithic vision was against the grain of history, the pluralist universe was of its essence. Kennedy felt more than ever that the time was coming to crystallize a new view of the world.

Where the unitary American dogma of the fifties had dismayed our allies and, in effect, excommunicated the unaligned nations, Kennedy's doctrine of diversity now offered a common cause which even carried its appeal far beyond the Iron Curtain itself. As no one since Roosevelt, he was identifying the United States with the movement toward national independence and popular democracy and, perhaps even more than Roosevelt, with the hopes and aspirations of distant peoples. He made their longing for bread and schools and dignity his own. Most of all, he was giving the younger generation around the earth, as the foreign minister of Austria, Dr. Bruno Kreisky, later put it, "the courage to test their mettle in a field which had been barred to too many of them too long." Around the earth the young looked to him increasingly as their leader. Always he spoke for reason, recognizing the intractable diversity within the human family, eschewing the moralistic crusade, striving, in an age when war could mean the end of civilization, to move beyond war and offer humanity a chance to control its own destiny.

In seeking to build the world community on the idea, not of uniformity, but of diversity, the President expressed his own sense of the grand dynamic of modern history; and, in summoning history as his witness, he struck hard at the heart of the Marxist case.

In his vision of a world of diversity united by allegiance to peace, Kennedy established the basis for a wise and strong American policy—a basis from which he could move with equal ease toward conciliation or confrontation with the Soviet Union. Whichever way circumstances compelled him to move, he could act with the deep conviction he set forth: "No one can doubt that the wave of the future is not the conquest of the world by a single dogmatic creed but the liberation of the diverse energies of free nations and free men."

XXIII. THE COUNTRY MOVING AGAIN

The fifties had hardly been a notable season of innovation in our national life. The politics of boredom had produced widespread public apathy. National policy had been complacent and lethargic. Young people had become so circumspect that they were known as the 'silent generation.' Economic growth had puttered along at an average rate of 2.5 to 3 per cent a year. There had been recessions in 1954 and 1958. In the early spring of 1960, the economy had begun to sink into another recession. Gross national product stagnated. Unemployment increased by 1.2 million between February and October. If Kennedy were to start the country moving again, he would have to begin with the economy.

1. KENNEDY AND ECONOMICS

In the presidential years, it was easy to forget that Kennedy's pervading congressional concern was with domestic affairs. His House issues were those of urban and industrial liberalism: the minimum wage, social security, unemployment compensation, housing, labor reform. As Senator he added a growing concern with the structural problems of his state and region—the decay of older industries, like shoes and textiles; the stagnation of historic mill towns; the losing competition with the low-wage South.

The special character of his New England problems led him in the fifties to think less about fiscal and monetary and more about structural remedies—in other words, direct attempts to strengthen New England's position in the national economy. In general, he looked for programs which he thought would at once benefit New England and the nation, like redeveloping depressed areas or raising the minimum wage or repealing the Taft-Hartley Act. On occasion, he would vote against what Massachusetts considered its local interest, and sometimes, he was ready to help New England at possible expense to the general welfare.

Another influence on his economic thought must be added, though his advisers were always uncertain when it would come into play and how much weight the President gave it himself. This was the practical business wisdom he had heard so long—and from time to time continued to hear—from his father.

As President, he meant to assure himself a wide range of intelligent advice. Having chosen Douglas Dillon as Secretary of the Treasury, he chose Walter Heller as chairman of the Council of Economic Advisers. "I need you both," he told Heller, "for a proper balance in economic matters." Diverging institutional interests created in any case a balance, or at least a tug of war, between the Council, charged by statute with working "to promote maximum employment, production and purchasing power," and the Treasury, primarily involved in taxation, the management of the debt and the protection of the dollar. But Kennedy was further pleased by the personal contrasts: the economics professor vs. the investment banker; the liberal vs. the moderate; the man who worried about deflation vs. the man who worried about inflation; the Democrat vs. the Republican.

2. THE DEBATE OVER EXPANSION

The first problem was the recession. It had deepened throughout 1960, and Kennedy had made it a central issue in the campaign. Kennedy had argued that the resumption of economic progress was "the number one domestic problem which the next President of the United States will have to meet."

He threw out a variety of suggestions during the campaign to bring the growth rate up to 5 percent: using the budget "as an instrument of economic stabilization"; reversing the tight money policy of the Eisenhower years; providing special assistance to areas hit by economic decline and technological change; making "the public investments which provide a solid foundation for the private investment which is the key to our free enterprise economy"; developing the country's resources; encouraging plant modernization; training manpower for an increasingly automated economy; improving the educational system; assuring equal opportunity for employment.

Now as President he had to make good. The recession had continued to deepen in the weeks after the election. By February 1961 unemployment reached the astonishing figure of 8.1 percent of the labor force. In deciding how to set in motion the processes of recovery and re-employment, Kennedy met again in the world of economists the two currents of thought he had already brushed in his own experience—the structural and the fiscal schools.*

The first school attributed unemployment below a certain level—say, 4 percent—to structural transformations in the economy. It argued that, given the pace and progress of automation, the scarcity of educated and skilled labor would constitute a bottleneck in an expanding economy, forcing an expansion stimulated by fiscal and monetary policies alone to stop short of full employment. Thus there might be a shortage of highly skilled labor in Detroit while there was unemployment in Appalachia; nor would aggregative policies solve the problem of the San Diego aircraft worker

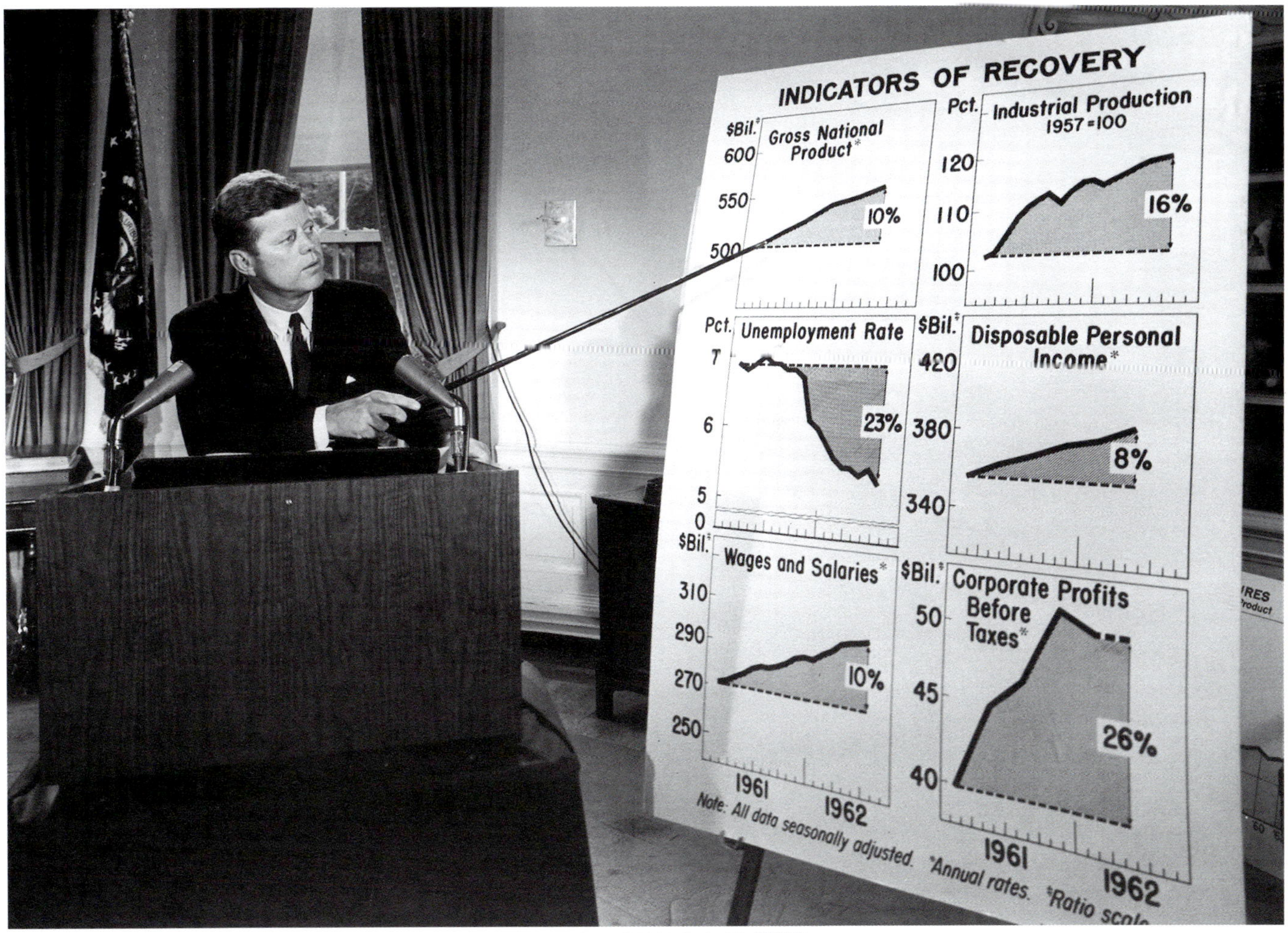

KENNEDY ADDRESSES THE NATION ABOUT THE ECONOMY IN WASHINGTON, D.C. IN 1962.

* Historians will note that the debate between the structuralists and the fiscalists was a new and more analytical phase of the old New Deal debate between the institutionalists of the First New Deal (Tugwell, Berle, Hugh Johnson), who wanted to restore the economy through reorganization of social structure, and the Keynesians of the Second New Deal (Eccles, Currie, Ben Cohen, Henderson), who proposed to end the depression through deficit spending.

displaced in the missile age, or of untrained teenagers or Negroes in a time of increasing technical demand.

The fiscal school, on the other hand, attributed stagnation and unemployment to deficiencies in aggregate demand; and it came to place particular emphasis on the theory, popularized by Heller, of the 'fiscal drag'—the theory, that is, that with rising levels of output high tax rates drained away needed purchasing power and thereby forced expansion to stop short of full employment.

Most government economists in the end sought a combination of fiscal and structural positions—enough of a deficit to produce new jobs, enough redevelopment or retraining to equip men for the jobs. But a critical issue arose as to the best way to create the deficit. Here fiscalists especially sensitive to political urgencies favored tax reduction on the ground that it would slide down congressional throats more easily. Those especially sensitive to structural deficiencies argued, on the other hand, that the deficit should be brought about by an increase in public spending designed to improve education, labor mobility and so on.

3. POLICY: 1961

In the President's mind what was theoretically desirable had to be tempered by what was politically feasible. His campaign had emphasized discipline and sacrifice; his victory had been slim; his Congress was conservative; and, at least in the mind of the business community, his party had a reputation for fiscal irresponsibility.

Kennedy's special message to Congress on February 2 therefore concentrated on the extension of unemployment insurance, area redevelopment, the increase of the minimum wage, housing and community development, acceleration of procurement and construction and the like. More novel though hardly more radical was a proposal for special tax incentives to investment. The message even catered somewhat to congressional fears about the budget, promising balance "over the years of the economic cycle." Later messages through the spring called for other institutional measures. And Congress proved responsive to the structural approach. Within six months it passed an area redevelopment bill, an omnibus housing bill, a farm bill, a rise in the minimum wage, the liberalization of social security, temporary unemployment benefits, benefits for dependent children of unemployed parents and a program to combat water pollution—a record of action on the domestic front unmatched in any single sitting since 1935. Still, this was a program of welfare, perhaps a program to end the recession, but not a program of economic expansion.

To the administration's surprise, however, businessmen recoiled from the proposal; having counted on a liberalization of depreciation allowances, they considered the investment credit a poor substitute. Actually the administration had depreciation revision in mind too and was postponing it only because it involved too great a revenue loss if enacted apart from general tax revision. Yet, despite Washington's placatory policy, business opposition blocked the investment credit in the 1961 Congress, and the bill was finally postponed to 1962.

4. KENNEDY AND BUSINESS

This miscarriage set the tone for Kennedy's relations with business. The resistance to the investment credit had sprung fundamentally from the inability of businessmen to believe that Democrats would ever do anything for business. His first steps were not reassuring to business. His series of distinguished appointments to the regulatory agencies expressed the theory that these agencies should respond to the public interest rather than to the industries regulated. This naturally outraged businessmen who, in earlier years, had grown used to regarding regulatory agencies as adjuncts of their own trade associations.

Kennedy had, I believe, considerable respect for the experience of businessmen. He felt that this experience gave them clues to the operations of the American economy which his intellectuals, for all their facile theories, did not possess. On the other hand, he had no great respect for the ideas of businessmen, and the respect declined the further their ideas moved away from their experience. And he regarded the pressure to play up to businessmen with recurrent exasperation.

5. STEEL

The President had been much concerned to keep costs and prices down both to prevent inflation at home and to relieve the balance of payments by promoting exports abroad. Inflation created by excess demand was not very likely in an economy only beginning to emerge from a recession; but 'cost-push' inflation, touched off on occasion in the fifties when wages rose faster than productivity, remained a threat. And steel obviously played a key role in the strategy of price stability because increases in steel prices reverberated so far, wide and fast through the economy. Accordingly Kennedy wrote the presidents of the leading steel companies in September 1961, describing steel as "a bellwether, as well as a major element in industrial costs," and suggesting that the industry "forgo a price increase." He followed this by a letter to David J. McDonald of the United Steelworkers proposing that wage demands be kept "within the limit of advances in productivity."

Early in 1962, Secretary of Labor Goldberg, who himself had been the Steelworkers' general counsel, helped negotiate a non-inflationary settlement which both the union and the industry accepted in April. Everyone concerned assumed that, in return for what one student has called "the least costly agreement in many years,"* the industry would never dream of raising prices. Then, on April 10, Roger Blough, chairman of the board at United States Steel, made his famous call at the White House and, without advance warning, handed the President of the United States a four-page mimeographed statement announcing the decision to raise steel prices $6 a ton. Blough's whole demeanor suggested a genuine belief that an increase in steel prices was no more the business of government than an increase in the price of the lemonade a child might sell in front of his house. Kennedy's reaction was a mixture of incredulity over what he saw as the selfishness and stupidity of the steel industry and anger over what he regarded as its premeditated deceit. Honorable people, he felt, did not behave in this fashion.

He called in his advisers on domestic policy and swung into action. If he accepted the steel decision, it would mean a grave threat to the wage-price guideposts, price stability, the program of economic expansion, the balance of payments, the trust the labor movement had in him and the prestige of the Presidency. He was coldly determined to mobilize all the resources of public pressure and private suasion to force steel to rescind the increase.

The next morning Bethlehem Steel, the second largest company, announced an increase, and four others quickly followed. At his press conference that afternoon Kennedy described these actions as "a wholly unjustifiable and irresponsible defiance of the public interest" by "a tiny handful of steel executives whose pursuit of private power and profit exceeds their sense of public responsibility." In the meantime, he had mounted a campaign of pressure against the steel magnates. Dillon, McNamara, Hodges, Clark Clifford and others were making phone calls all over the country. The Defense Department started shifting its steel purchases from the United States Steel to companies which had not yet raised prices. The Department of Justice began inquiries into whether the steel companies had acted in violation of the anti-trust laws.** The Federal Trade Commission announced an informal investigation to see whether the steel companies had broken regulations against collusive price-fixing. Congressional anti-trust committees promised hearings. Ted Sorensen started work on emergency wage-price legislation. Public opinion rallied behind the President.

On Friday, April 13, Inland, Kaiser and the Armco Steel Corporation all let it be known that they were prepared to hold the line. Shortly, word came that Bethlehem had rescinded its price increase. Before the afternoon was over, United States Steel surrendered. It was seventy-two hours after Blough's call on Kennedy.

The steel fight confirmed the worst suspicions on each side about the other. The business community knew that the President was not 'one of ours'; they felt that business was not understood in Washington; and they construed Kennedy's pro-business efforts as based on the need for economic and political placation and not on the belief that the true business of America was business.*** They felt, in short, that they were outsiders again.

As for the President, the steel fight showed once again his cool understanding of the uses of power. He had, in fact, *no* direct authority available against the steel companies. Instead, he mobilized every fragment of quasi-authority he could find and, by a bravura public performance, converted weakness into strength. And his victory was a durable one. In winning this victory, Kennedy answered the question with which the business community had confronted every activist Chief Executive since Jackson: "Who is President anyway?" He delivered his answer at a cost, but the cost of not answering would have been greater. And, if the domestic cost was significant, in foreign policy his triumph over steel was an unmixed gain. Kennedy had left the world no doubt that he was equally independent of the American business community—and in a world indoctrinated with fears of aggressive American capitalism this won new trust for his leadership in foreign affairs.

* Grant McConnell, *Steel and the Presidency—1962* (New York, 1963), 75.

** In 1965 eight major companies, headed by U. S. Steel, pleaded *nolo contendere* to charges of price-fixing between 1955 and 1961. Each company received the maximum fine under the anti-trust laws.

*** The Research Institute of America on June 30, 1962, reported the results of a survey of 6000 business executives. Fifty-two percent described the administration as "strongly anti-business," 36 percent as "moderately anti-business," and only 9 percent as "neutral" or "pro-business."

XXIV. THE NATIONAL AGENDA

UNDERNEATH THE CLAMOR the President had been thinking intensively about the problems of communication on economic problems. One Sunday in May 1962 he took André Malraux out to Glen Ora for luncheon, and, as Kennedy later described it, they fell into a discussion of the persistence of mythology in the contemporary world. The real issue today, Kennedy commented, was the management of industrial society—a problem, he said, not of ideology but of administration. This conversation remained in his mind. A few days later, when he spoke to the White House conference on national economic issues, the "difference between myth and reality" provided the theme for his remarks.

> *The fact of the matter is that most of the problems, or at least many of them, that we now face are technical problems, are administrative problems. They are very sophisticated judgments which do not lend themselves to the great sort of 'passionate movements' which have stirred this country so often in the past.... How can we look at things as they are, not through party labels, or through position labels, but as they are—and figure out how we can maintain this economy so that it moves ahead?*

1. REASON AT YALE

In another few days he decided to make this the theme of a major address at the Yale Commencement. The central issues of our time, Kennedy said in New Haven, "relate not to basic clashes of philosophy or ideology but to ways and means of reaching common goals." As every past generation had to disenthrall itself from an inheritance of truism and stereotype, 'so in our own time we must move on from the reassuring repetition of stale phrases to a new, difficult, but essential confrontation with reality."

> *For the great enemy of the truth is very often not the lie—deliberate, contrived and dishonest—but the myth, persistent, persuasive and unrealistic. Too often we hold fast to the clichés of our forebears. We subject all facts to a prefabricated set of interpretations. We enjoy the comfort of opinion without the discomfort of thought.*

In particular, the dialogue between government and business was "clogged by illusion and platitude." It failed "to reflect the true realities of contemporary American society."

He then dealt with several prevalent myths. As against the myth that government was growing relatively bigger, he pointed out that, excepting defense and space expenditures, the federal government had expanded less than any other major sector of the economy since the Second World War. As against the myth that federal deficits created and surpluses prevented inflation, he cited the historical record of the postwar years. As against the myth that the national debt was growing at a dangerously rapid rate, he pointed out that it had declined sharply since the war, both per person and as a proportion of gross national product. As against the myth that 'confidence' in the national administration was the condition for economic prosperity, he pointed out that such confidence had not prevented recessions in 1929, 1954, 1958 and 1960, and that corporate plans were "not based on a political confidence in party leaders but on an economic confidence in the nation's ability to invest and produce and consume."

> *What is at stake [he concluded] is not some grand warfare of rival ideologies which will sweep the country with passion but the practical management of a modern economy. What we need is not labels and clichés but more basic discussion of the sophisticated and technical issues involved in keeping a great economic machinery moving ahead....*
>
> *The debate of the thirties had its great significance and produced great results, but it took place in a different world with different needs and different tasks. It is our responsibility today to live in our own world and to identify the needs and discharge the tasks of the 1960s.*

In the course of the speech, Kennedy remarked that the governments of Western Europe were prepared "to face technical problems without ideological preconceptions" and therefore could "coordinate the elements of a national economy and bring about growth and prosperity." Our own nation, he said, should begin "a serious dialogue of the kind which has led in Europe to such fruitful collaboration among all the elements of economic society and to a decade of unrivaled economic progress."

2. THE NEW SOCIETY

The nation at mid-century, urban, industrial, mobile, technologically kinetic, spiritually hyperbolic, contained a swarm of hard and insistent problems. Kennedy used to speak almost with envy of the relatively predictable statecraft of the nineteenth century. Now the United States faced "new problems, entirely different from those that have faced the Eisenhower administration, or that of Harry Truman, or Franklin Roosevelt or Woodrow Wilson ... new problems, requiring new people, new solutions, new ideas,"

The problems, of course, were not all that different, nor were the answers he offered in 1960 all that new—the improvement of the educational system, the strengthening of public provisions for social security and medical care, attention to the decaying cities, a more rational farm program, the conservation and development of natural resources, recognition of the Negro revolution. This was, in effect, the unfinished business of Franklin Roosevelt's New Deal. Yet Kennedy's spirited presentation imbued it with his own intense contemporaneity. The program, taken as a whole, offered a systematic identification of the fundamental problems of modern America in terms of a deeply critical assessment of the moral, intellectual and institutional failures of American society. And, despite his support of economic growth and his concern over persisting privation, the thrust of his preoccupation was less with the economic machine and its quantitative results than with the quality of life in a society which, in the main, had achieved abundance.

This, as he fully realized, was a subtle preoccupation, not easily convertible into the coin of politics. With 94 percent of the labor force employed and national income steadily rising, it would be difficult to persuade a largely conservative Congress and a largely contented people of the need for federal action to improve the quality of society. It would require, as he saw it, a long and patient program of public education. This he promptly began in an extraordinary series of messages to the Congress on domestic affairs in the spring of 1961. In addition to his strictly economic documents, he sent the Hill messages on health and hospital care, education, natural resources, highways, housing and community development, agriculture, regulatory agencies and an omnibus message on urgent national needs. In subsequent years he sent further messages on many of these subjects and added a variety of other issues: civil rights, transportation, public welfare, the protection of the consumer, mental illness and retardation, youth, the elderly.

His intimate acquaintance, of course, was with urban and industrial issues. He approached the farm problem with suspicion, but he liked and trusted Orville Freeman and, in time, developed an authentic intellectual interest in farm matters. In 1960 national agricultural policy was in an evident cul-de-sac. The farmer was the victim of his own fantastic technological efficiency. Production per man-hour in American agriculture was increasing at a rate twice as fast as in industry; public storage of surplus agricultural commodities, especially wheat and feed grains, was overflowing every available bin and elevator. Yet at the same time people in the United States and abroad were going hungry; only one American farmer in nine was earning wages comparable to those of skilled factory workers; total farm income was declining; and unemployment and poverty were twice as bad on the countryside as in the cities. Moreover, the farmer himself, in spite of his immense contribution, was increasingly regarded as a cadger and parasite on the rest of the economy.

Freeman tackled the problem with energy and intelligence, and a new agricultural policy began to emerge. The surpluses were put to use through Food for Peace abroad and enlarged distribution of surplus foods to the needy at home, soon accompanied by a revival of the Food Stamp plan of the thirties. New policies both reduced surpluses to the level of a prudent national reserve and increased net farm income by the average of almost $1 billion a year during the Kennedy Presidency. In the meantime, Freeman's rural areas development program began the work of improving and modernizing life on the countryside. The result was a series of changes which re-established the farmer in the national polity and offered for the first time in years the hope of a rational policy for agriculture.

The President approached conservation with a good deal more initial warmth, though with similar abstractness. He had enjoyed pointing out during the presidential campaign that "the two Americans in this century who have done more to develop the resources of the west" were both easterners, Theodore Roosevelt and Franklin Roosevelt, and he was determined to carry on this tradition. Early in March 1961; dedicating the National Wildlife Federation Building, he affirmed the responsibility "to hand down undiminished to those who come after us, as was handed down by those who went before, the natural wealth and beauty which is ours."

These were heartfelt words. Kennedy cared deeply about the loveliness of lakes and woods and mountains and detested the clutter and blight which increasingly defaced the landscape. But, in the pressures of presidential life in the sixties, conservation had a rather low priority. "Intellectually he is fine," Udall said to me one day. "He knows the issues and recognizes their importance. When the problems are brought to him, his response is excellent. But he doesn't raise them himself." He did, however, call the first White House Conference on Conservation in fifty-four years, and he gave Udall's vigorous direction of the Department of the Interior strong support; the annual outlays for natural resources were 16 per cent higher than in Eisenhower years. As one who loved ocean beaches, gulls wheeling in the sky, dunes baking in the sun, gleaming surf and salt spray, he was particularly pleased to establish three national seashores, above all the one covering white beaches and serene inland ponds of his own Cape Cod.

3. YOUTH AND THE FUTURE

Yet, except on holiday, he remained unregenerately a city man, deeply anxious about the mess and tangle of urban America. This could be only in part a matter for the national government; and the Attorney General wrought a decisive change in the capacity of cities to provide for themselves by bringing apportionment cases to the Supreme Court and challenging the system of rural over-representation in state legislatures. The Housing Act of 1961, the most extensive piece of housing legislation for a dozen years, gave the federal government new weapons and resources in its attack on urban squalor. The President's attempts to persuade Congress to authorize a Department of Urban Affairs failed in 1961 and 1962, in part because of the expectation that he would give the new cabinet post to his Housing Administrator, Dr. Robert C. Weaver, eminently qualified in every way save, in the view of some, by the color of his skin.

But the President's particular concern was how to turn the urban and suburban communities, so often chaotic and demoralized, into places where young people could grow up with a sense of purpose in their lives and a belief in the rationality of their society. When he would say that the key to the American future was its youth, this was not a passing piety. It was a central fact as vividly perceived as Orville Freeman's wheatfields or Stewart Udall's dams. He knew (and would rattle off the statistics) that each year 4 million boys and girls were born in the United States; that one out of three who completed the fifth grade would drop out before graduation from high school; that nearly 3 million in their teens would come every year into the labor market; that workers under the age of twenty-five, though less than one-fifth of the labor force, were one-third of the unemployed; that the social cost in aimless defection from society, like that of the beats, or insensate anger against it, like that of the delinquents, was growing; that arrests of the young had increased 86 per cent in a decade; that juvenile delinquency, as his Secretary of Health, Education and Welfare, Abraham Ribicoff, told Congress in 1961, was not so much criminality as "a system of belief and values with a strong and stable tradition of its own"; and that, as the President summed it up, "youth unemployment poses one of the most expensive and explosive social and economic problems now facing this country." The terror of being young and poor or young and cynical or young and hopeless was much on his mind. He understood the power of a glittering society to tantalize and thwart the deprived young, to give them the world on a television screen and slam the door in their faces, to take people already confused by broken homes, overcrowded schools, hostile communities and fill them with such desperate resentment that, to affirm their own impalpable identities, they could not stop short of violence and murder.

In Robert Kennedy, eight and a half years his junior, who cared, if possible, even more intensely about youth trapped in a careless society, the President had both a passionate ambassador to the young and a determined instrument of action. It was the Attorney General who ran the President's Committee on Juvenile Delinquency and Youth Crime (with his old schoolmate from Milton, David Hackett, as director) and did so not as a cop but as a comrade; it was the Attorney General who headed the cabinet study group in 1962 which devised the National Service Corps, later known as Volunteers in Service to America (VISTA); it was the Attorney General who led the national campaign against school dropouts, roamed the streets of Harlem, fought for schools and playgrounds in Washington and talked to the young at every opportunity. Because of the personal concern of the Kennedys, much of the youth program took place outside the Department of Health, Education and Welfare, but that sprawling and disheveled department played a growing role.

If youth constituted the key to the future, "the most direct, rewarding and important investment in our children and youth," as the President once put it, "is education." Education was essential to employment in a high-technology society where among the unemployed 40 per cent had eight years of schooling or less (and where only 1.4 percent had college training). More than that, education was essential to the fulfillment of talented individuals. As the war generation of babies now pressed upon the colleges, with their younger brothers and sisters beginning to crowd the schools, little seemed more important than the expansion and improvement of the nation's educational facilities. By 1970 there would be a 25 percent increase in school children and a 75 percent increase in college students. Nor would building more schoolrooms help much by itself if teachers and curricula remained mechanical and boring. Little disappointed the Kennedys more in domestic policy than their failure to make significant legislative progress in federal aid to education.

Underneath all this lay the President's acute sense of the rising issue of generations in American life. By 1966 half the population would be under the age of twenty five. Having seized power themselves from a resentful older generation, the Kennedys understood the emotions of the young crowding into a capricious and incomprehensible society. Many of the legislative measures of the New Frontier may have been left over from the New Deal. But the generational perception was new and original. It reinforced the President in his determination to transform a wealthy society into a civilized community and gave his program its distinctive design and theme. American politics would never be the same again.

XXV.
IN THE WHITE HOUSE

THE PRESIDENT RETURNING TO WORK AFTER A WALK AROUND THE WHITE HOUSE GROUNDS.

BY THE SUMMER OF 1962 Kennedy was well settled in the Presidency. He had changed somewhat physically in this year and a half. The face was more lined and furrowed; the features were heavier, less handsome but more powerful. The first eighteen months is always the period of presidential definition, and for Kennedy the succession of crises had tied an already disciplined personality ever more irrevocably to the responsibilities for which he held himself accountable to the future. The experience deepened him and gave emphasis to a certain somber side of his nature. At the same time, it liberated him. He could at last be himself; the private face, somewhat subdued and withheld during the congressional years, became fully the public face. The force of his intelligence, gaiety and wit, now displayed without inhibition, made people wonder how two years earlier they could possibly have confused him with Richard Nixon.

1. IN THE MANSION

The day began at quarter to eight. George Thomas, his devoted and humorous Negro valet, would knock at the door of the Kennedy bedroom. As he sat down before his breakfast tray, surrounded by the morning papers and urgent cables and reports which may have come in during the night, Caroline and John would rush in, greet their father and turn on the television to watch animated cartoons. Then more presidential reading, with the television going full blast. At nine o'clock a calisthenics program came on, and Kennedy liked to watch the children tumble on the bedroom floor in rhythm with the man on the screen. Then, taking one of the children by the hand, he would walk over to the presidential office in the West Wing.

After a morning of work and a swim, often with David Powers, in the White House pool, he returned to the Mansion for luncheon. He preferred to lunch alone or with Jacqueline; very occasionally he brought guests. After luncheon came the nap. Impressed by Churchill's eloquence in praise of afternoon rest, he had begun this practice in the Senate. It was a genuine sleep, in pajamas and under covers. He went off at once; and in forty-five minutes would awaken and chat as he dressed. This was Jacqueline's hour of the day, as the morning was the children's.

This historian, it must be said, had not realized how constricted the living quarters of an American President were.

JOHN JR. VISITS HIS FATHER AND EVELYN LINCOLN IN THE OVAL OFFICE.

THE WHITE HOUSE POOL WHERE THE PRESIDENT TOOK HIS MORNING SWIM.

The first floor of the Mansion was given over to public rooms and reserved for state occasions. The third floor was rarely mentioned. The private life of the Kennedys took place on the second floor under conditions which an average Park Avenue tycoon would regard as claustrophobic. A long dark corridor, brightened by a set of Catlin's Indian paintings, transected the floor. Bedrooms debouched from each side. A yellow oval room, marvelously light and lovely, was used for tea or drinks before dinner; it had served earlier Presidents as an office. Another room at the west end of the corridor was Jacqueline's room by day and the sitting room in the evening. Dinner guests resorted to the President's own bathroom. It was not a house for spacious living. Yet, until Theodore Roosevelt persuaded the Congress to build the West Wing, Presidents not only raised their families in these crowded quarters but ran the country from them.

It never seemed unduly crowded in these days. The atmosphere was always one of informality. When his family was away, the President used to have his afternoon appointments on the second floor. But generally he returned to the West Wing after his nap, where he worked until seven-thirty or eight at night. Jacqueline liked to guard the evenings for relaxation, and the President welcomed the relief from the incessant business of the day.

After the first year, they left the White House very seldom for private dinners elsewhere, though Kennedy always enjoyed the food and conversation at Joseph Alsop's. Instead, Jacqueline would arrange small dinners of six, eight or ten in the Mansion. They were informal and gay, the most agreeable occasions in the world. One memorable evening celebrated Stravinsky's seventy-fifth birthday. On less formal evenings Jacqueline would sometimes put on phonograph records and there might be a moment of dancing. The President often vanished silently into his bedroom to work or make phone calls, reappearing in time to bid his guests goodnight. Occasionally there were films in the projection room in the East Wing. Kennedy was not a great movie fan and tended, unless the film was unusually gripping, to walk out after the first twenty or thirty minutes.*

* He was interested, however, that one of his staff should contribute film reviews to *Show* magazine, and with his curiosity about everything he would often have suggestions about critiques he thought should be written. Before beginning the assignment, I sent him a memorandum asking whether it would be any embarrassment to him if I became a film critic on my own time. The message came back through Evelyn Lincoln: "The President says it is fine for you to write for *Show* as long as you treat Peter Lawford with respect."

The state dinners were inevitable, but Jacqueline made them bearable by ending the old regimented formality of solemn receiving lines and stilted conversation and changing them into elegant and cheerful parties, beautifully mingling informality and dignity. When asked about White House dinners, people would now say with surprise that they really had a very good time. But the gala occasions were the small dinner dances. Jacqueline conceived them as a means of restoring a larger social gaiety to her husband's life. When several months of unrelenting pressure had gone by, she would feel that the time had come for another dancing party and begin to look for a pretext to give one, whether to say hello or farewell to the Radziwills, welcome Kenneth Galbraith or honor Eugene Black. There were not many such parties—only five in the whole time in the White House—and they were all blithe and enchanting evenings. The President seemed renewed by them and walked with a springier step the next day.

The Kennedys liked to preserve the weekends as much as possible for themselves and the children. In 1961 they took a house at Glen Ora in Virginia; but the President found it confining and in later years preferred to go to Roosevelt's old refuge of Shangri-La at Catoctin Mountain in Maryland, renamed by Eisenhower Camp David after his grandson. In the winter there was Palm Beach, where they went for longer periods at Christmas and Easter, and in the summer Hyannis Port and Newport. Sailing relaxed him most of all—the sun, the breeze, the water; above all, no telephone. He could get along quite happily even without the sun and used to insist on taking his friends out on dark and chilly days. The guests would huddle together against the cold while the President sat in the stern in a black sweater, the wind blowing his hair, blissfully happy with a steaming bowl of fish chowder.

The weekends and holidays, despite his battered black alligator briefcase stuffed with papers, gave him time for the children, but he saw them as much as possible during the week, and his delight in them was unconcealed. He loved children and told Jacqueline before their marriage that he wanted at least five; she had four in seven years. He liked young children in particular and always wanted a baby coming along when its predecessor was growing up. Caroline and John were, as the world came to know, wonderfully spirited and original, and they cast their spell throughout the White House. One often encountered them in the corridors going out to their morning nursery school. One morning I said to Caroline, "Who is your friend?" She replied with dignity, "He's not my friend; he's my brother." They invaded the West Wing, took candies from a box kept for them on Evelyn Lincoln's desk and liked to hide from their father under the cabinet table.

Often at the end of the day the President would leave his desk, throw open the French windows leading into the Rose Garden, walk out on the colonnade and clap his hands. At this signal every child and dog in the vicinity would rush across the green lawn into his arms. He would encourage John to dance, clapping his hands again as the accompaniment. In the evening he made up stories for them about Caroline hunting with the Orange County hounds and winning the Grand National and John in his PT boat sinking a Japanese destroyer. He would tell them about Bobo the Lobo, a giant, and about Maybelle, a little girl who hid in the woods, and about the White Shark and the Black Shark. The White Shark lived off people's socks, and one day, when the President and Caroline were sailing with Franklin Roosevelt, Jr., off Newport, Kennedy pretended to see the White Shark and said, "Franklin, give him your socks; he's hungry." Franklin promptly threw his socks into the water, which made a great impression on Caroline.

For her part Jacqueline was determined that the children lead as normal lives as possible. This was not an easy

A VIEW OF THE ROSE GARDEN FROM THE OVAL OFFICE.

JACQUELINE GIVING ONE OF HER TELEVISED TOURS OF THE WHITE HOUSE.

goal for the young children of a President, but she did her best, arranging the White House nursery school where they could fraternize with their contemporaries and taking them off in her blue Pontiac station wagon on quiet expeditions to shops or parks. On Halloween evening in 1962, the doorbell rang at my house in Georgetown. When my fourteen-year-old daughter opened the door to the trick-or-treaters, she found a collection of small hobgoblins leaping up and down. One seemed particularly eager to have her basket filled with goodies. After a moment a masked mother in the background called out that it was time to go to their next house. Christina suddenly recognized the voice. It was, of course, Jackie, and the excited little girl was Caroline out with her cousins. They had just rung Joe Alsop's bell; Dean Acheson was the next stop.

Such adventures varied their lives. John and Caroline were not, if their mother could help it, the little prince and princess, any more than she and the President were royalty. She disapproved of the term "First Lady," which had come into semi-official usage in the previous administration. When she heard the servants referring to her by the title, she told them her name was "Mrs. Kennedy." She constantly reminded the children that the White House was their temporary residence, not their permanent home.

The White House was temporary for the Kennedys but permanent for the nation. Mrs. Eisenhower had taken her successor on a trip around the Mansion in December 1960. It was too soon after John's birth, and Jacqueline was desperately weak after the Caesarean operation. She trudged through the historic rooms, long since emptied of the authentic past, now filled with mediocre reproductions; it seemed almost as if this were a house in which nothing had ever taken place. She resolved on the spot to establish the President's residence thereafter as unequivocally the nation's house and transform it into a house of which the nation could be thoroughly proud. She asked the Library of Congress to send books about the historic White House to her at Palm Beach. Between Christmas and the inauguration she immersed herself in the literature. The restoration of the White House became her special project. Her hope was to recover as many as possible of the old and beautiful objects which past Presidents had cherished and make the President's house both a distillation of American history and an expression of American excellence.

The President gave her his full support, applauded as the inherited furniture was carted away and watched the transformation with mounting pride. He was rather complacent about the knowledge of décor he had acquired under her tutelage and liked to point out to visitors the objects which she had brought back to their original home. The success of the guidebook pleased him, and he kidded those on the staff who had said gloomily that it would never do to sell a guidebook in the White House. He congratulated her as the number of people going through the White House steadily rose: in 1962 the total was nearly two-thirds greater than in 1960. In February 1962, when Mrs. Kennedy took the whole nation on a television tour of the new White House, the President viewed the program with great satisfaction. (As for Jacqueline, when Norman Mailer complained about her voice in *Esquire* and wrote that she walked through the program "like a starlet who is utterly without talent," she took no offense and thought he was probably right.)

KENNEDY AND DAUGHTER CAROLINE.

Her husband's delight in her was visible. His eyes brightened when he talked of her or when she unexpectedly dropped by the office. He was even entertained by her occasional bursts of undiplomatic candor. "Whenever a wife says anything in this town," he remarked in high amusement one night at dinner at the White House, "everyone assumes that she is saying what her husband really thinks. Imagine how I felt last night when I thought I heard Jackie telling Malraux that Adenauer was *'un peu gaga'!"*

He adored her because she remained utterly faithful to herself—and the nation, for all its earlier reservations, came to adore her for the same reason. The things people had once held against her—the unconventional beauty, the un-American elegance, the taste for French clothes and French food—were suddenly no longer liabilities but assets. She represented all at once not a negation of her country but a possible fulfillment of it, a suggestion that America was not to be trapped forever in the bourgeois ideal, a dream of civilization and beauty. She had dreaded coming to the White House, fearing the end of family and privacy. But life for herself and her husband and children was never more intense and more complete. It turned out to be the time of the greatest happiness.

2. IN THE OFFICE

It has been traditional for Presidents to curse the Presidency. Washington said he felt like "a culprit, who is going to the place of his execution." Jefferson called the Presidency a "splendid misery," Buchanan "a crown of thorns"; for Truman the White House was "the finest prison in the country." Such melodramatic lamentations never escaped the lips of John F. Kennedy. He had wanted to become President, he loved being President and at times he could hardly remember that he had ever been anything else. He never complained about the 'terrible loneliness' of the office or its 'awesome burdens.' I do not think he felt terribly lonely; as he once remarked to William Manchester, "In many ways I see and hear more than anyone else." (He regarded his life, I think, as threatened more by confinement than by solitude; occasionally at the end of the day he would say, almost wistfully, "What are you doing tonight?" and then enjoy a moment of gossip about old friends in Georgetown.) As for those 'awesome burdens,' he had asked for them, knowing more or less what he was getting into, and would not repine now.

His presidential life was instinct with action. "He did everything around here today," James Reston wrote of a not uncharacteristic day, "but shinny up the Washington Monument." Once, driving with Ben Bradlee during the interregnum, while a small Bradlee child scrambled between the front and back seats, Kennedy said, "I suppose if you had to choose just one quality to have that would be it: vitality." But his own vitality was under sure control. He had written years before about his brother Joe: "Even when still, there was always a sense of motion forcibly restrained." This was preëminently true of the President himself.

Seated at his desk or in the rocking chair in front of the fireplace, immaculately dressed in one of his two-buttoned, single-breasted suits, he radiated a contained energy, electric in its intensity. Occasionally it would break out, especially during long and wandering meetings. His fingers gave the clue to his impatience. They would suddenly be in constant action, drumming the table, tapping his teeth, slashing impatient pencil lines on a pad, jabbing the air to underscore a point. Sometimes the constraint of the four walls seemed too much, and he would stride across the room, pausing wryly to look at the mass of indentations left on the floor by his predecessor's golf cleats, throw open the doors to the lawn and walk up and down the colonnade. One day, while talking, he rose from his desk, picked up his cane, inverted it and started making golf swings; then, looking up with a smile, he said, "I'm getting to be more like Ike every day!"

He had to an exceptional degree the talent for concentration. When he put on his always surprising horn-rimmed glasses and read a document, it was with total intentness; in a moment he would have seized its essence and returned to the world he had left. He was for the same reason a superb listener. "Whoever he's with," someone said, "he's with them completely." He would lean forward, his eyes protruding slightly, concerned with using the occasion not to expound his own thoughts but to drag out of the talker whatever could be of use to him. Isaiah Berlin was reminded of a remark made about Lenin: that he could exhaust people by listening to them. In this way he ventilated problems in great detail without revealing his own position and without making his visitors conscious that he was holding back.

His manners were distinguished, and the more timid or lowly the people, the greater his consideration. "Mr. Kennedy's almost awesome egalitarianism," Secret Service Chief Baughman later wrote, was "in some ways even greater than Mr. Truman's." His moments of irritation were occasional but short. They came generally because he felt that he had been tricked, or because a crisis caught him without warning, or because someone in the government had leaked something to the press. The air would rock for a moment; his years in the Navy and in Massachusetts politics had not been in vain and, when pressed, his vocabulary was vivid. But, though he got mad quickly, he stayed mad briefly. He was a man devoid of hatred. He detested qualities but not people. Calm would soon descend, and in time the irritation would become a matter for jokes.

RIGHT: KENNEDY AT EASE IN HIS ROCKING CHAIR.

"Humour," said Hazlitt, "is the describing the ludicrous as it is in itself; wit is the exposing it, by comparing or contrasting it with something else. Humour is, as it were, the growth of nature and accident; wit is the product of art and fancy." Franklin Roosevelt was a man of humor, Kennedy a man of wit. His irony could be gentle or sharp, according to mood, and it was directed at himself as often as at others. It helped him to lighten crises and to hold people and problems in balance; it was an unending source of refreshment and perspective, and an essential part of his own apparatus of self-criticism. Detachment was one of his deepest reflexes.

He came to the Presidency almost without break of stride. Yet the Presidency, as he once put it, is a "mysterious institution." "There is no experience you can get," he said at the end of 1962, "that can possibly prepare you adequately for the Presidency." He himself came to feel the mystique of the Presidency strongly enough to doubt whether the quality of the presidential experience could be understood by those who had not shared it.

Now he sat in the presidential office himself and knew he was facing the appraisal of future historians. He had come in without illusions about the job; and experience soon reinforced what history had indicated. "Every President," he wrote in his foreword to Ted Sorensen's perceptive essay *Decision-Making in the White House,* "must endure the gap between what he would like and what is possible." He quoted Franklin Roosevelt's remark on Lincoln—"a sad man because he couldn't get it all at once. And nobody can." Yet this insight never threw him. He was a natural President, as other men were natural writers or outfielders or steeplechase riders.

Our last natural President had been Franklin Roosevelt. Roosevelt and Kennedy had so much in common: both were patrician, urbane, playful, cultivated, inquisitive, gallant; both were detached from the business ethos, both skeptical of the received wisdom, both devoted to politics but never enslaved by it, both serene in the exercise of power, both committed to the use of power for the ends of human welfare and freedom; both too had more than their share of physical suffering. Yet, as an historian who had written about Roosevelt, I could not but notice the differences as well as the resemblances.

Roosevelt was born thirty-five years earlier in a different century and a different world. He had grown up in those days of glowing hope which were shattered but not wholly extinguished by the First World War. He remained buoyant, expansive, spontaneous, audacious, theatrical, overflowing with a careless confidence about the future; if life was filled with trouble, action and passion could overcome it. Like Churchill, Roosevelt rallied the certitudes of the nineteenth century to fight the duplicities of the twentieth.

Kennedy, the child of a darker age, was more disciplined, more precise, more candid, more cautious, more sardonic, more pessimistic. His purpose was hardened and qualified by the world of ambiguities and perils. Underneath the casualness, wit and idealism, he was taut, concentrated, vibrating with inner tension under iron control, possessed by a fatalism which drove him on against the odds to meet his destiny. One could only speculate about the roots of this fatalism—the days of danger, the months of sickness, the feeling that life was short, the cool but tormented sense of the importunities and frustrations of the age in which he lived. The shadow was never far from him: that rendezvous at midnight in some flaming town. One never knows to what extent retrospect confers significance on chance remarks; but he said so many things attesting to a laconic sense of the transience of the Presidency, if not to a haunted conviction of human mortality. Nor could anyone interest him much in details of personal protection. "If someone is going to kill me," he would say, "they are going to kill me." President Kennedy never appeared ruffled or hurried. But time was his enemy, and he fought it to the end.

3. IN THE EXECUTIVE BRANCH

As a natural President, he ran his presidential office with notable ease and informality. He did this by instinct, not by theory. He always shrank from portentous discussions of himself and the Presidency (or anything else). Pressed, he turned questioners aside: "I have a nice home, the office is close by and the pay is good." In the autumn of 1961 Kennedy was sitting on the lawn of his mother-in-law's house in Newport, smoking a fragrant pre-Castro cigar, while in the background the sun was setting and a great aircraft carrier was entering the bay. It was the time of Berlin and the Soviet resumption of testing; in California Nixon was having his troubles with former Governor Goodwin Knight in internal Republican politics. As the warship steamed along, the American flag flying high, a friend felt a patriotic glow and was moved to ask Kennedy: "What do you *feel* at a moment like this? What is it *like* to be President?" The President smiled, flicked the ash from his cigar and said, "Well, it's a lot better than mucking around with Goody Knight in California."

In order to get the country moving again, he had to get the government moving. He came to the White House at a time when the ability of the President to do this had suffered steady constriction. By 1961 the tension between the permanent government and the presidential government was deep in our system.

The permanent government included men and women of marked devotion, quality and imagination. Kennedy knew this, seized many occasions to say so publicly and gave John Macy, the chairman of the Civil Service Commission, every support in improving the morale of the career services. Yet, though a valuable reservoir of intelligence and experience as well as a valuable guarantee against presidential government's going off the tracks, the permanent government remained in bulk a force against innovation with an inexhaustible capacity to dilute, delay and obstruct presidential purpose. Only so many fights were possible with the permanent government. The fighters were gradually weakened, cut off, surrounded and shot down, as if from ambush, by the bureaucracy and its anti-New Frontier allies in Congress and the press. At the start we had all felt free to 'meddle' when we thought that we had a good idea or someone else a poor one. But, as the ice began to form again over the government, free-wheeling became increasingly difficult and dangerous. At the time, I noted, "Every important mistake has been the consequence of excessive deference to the permanent government. In too many areas we have behaved as the Eisenhower administration would have behaved." The problem of moving forward seemed in great part the problem of making the permanent government responsive to the policies of the presidential government.

In the long run, the problem of the permanent government could no doubt be solved by permeation and attrition. "Getting the bureaucracy to accept new ideas," as Chester Bowles once said, "is like carrying a double mattress up a very narrow and winding stairway. It is a terrible job, and you exhaust yourself when you try it. But once you get the mattress up it is awfully hard for anyone else to get it down." But it also required day-to-day direction and control. This was Kennedy's preferred method: hence his unceasing flow of suggestions, inquiries, phone calls directly to the operating desks and so on. This approach enabled him to imbue government with a sense of his own desires and purposes. A Foreign Service officer once remarked on the feeling that "we were all reading the cables together"—the man at the desk, the Secretary of State and the White House. Nothing was more invigorating and inspiring, especially for the imaginative official, than personal contact with the President.

Kennedy tried in a number of ways to encourage innovation in the permanent government. His call for "dissent and daring" in the first State of the Union message concluded: "Let the public service be a proud and lively career." He took particular pleasure in the rehabilitation of government servants who had been punished for independence of thought in the past. But Kennedy's habit of reaching into the permanent government was disruptive as well as exciting for the bureaucracy. For the permanent government had its own set of requirements and expectations—continuity of policy, stability of procedure, everything within channels and according to the book. These were essential; without them government would collapse. Yet an active President, with his own requirements and expectations, was likely to chafe under the bureaucratic minuet.

Kennedy considered results more important than routine. His purpose in his time of almost constant crisis was to control and stimulate a vast and unwieldy government in order to produce wise decision and efficient execution. He designed his methods to suit his purpose.

4. THE WHITE HOUSE STAFF

His first instrument was the White House staff. This was a diverse group, and Kennedy wanted it that way. Bundy liked to compare the staff to prisms through which the President could look at public problems; and he knew precisely the angle of each refraction. One of his talents was the capacity to attract natural oppositionists—Galbraith, Kaysen, Murrow and others—and put them to work for government. He had some of these on his staff, along with some who were natural public servants; together they provided the mix which met his needs.

He was infinitely accessible to the Special Assistants. One could nearly always get him by phone; and, while Ken O'Donnell guarded one entrance to the presidential office with a wise concern for the President's time and energy, Evelyn Lincoln presided over the other with welcoming patience and warmth. For the half hour or so before luncheon and then again in the last hour of the afternoon, the door between Mrs. Lincoln's office and the President's room was generally ajar—a signal to the staff that he was open for business. In the early evening, however, after the Huntley-Brinkley news program, the pressure would be off. Then he would frequently be in a mood to lean back in his chair and expand on the events of the day.

He liked to regard his staff as generalists rather than specialists and had a distressing tendency to take up whatever happened to be on his desk and hand it to whoever happened to be in the room. He expected his staff to cover every significant sector of federal activity—to know everything that was going on, to provide speedy and exact answers to his questions and, most of all, to alert him to potential troubles. When a crisis was sprung without notice, there would be ejaculations of incredulity or despair; "For God's sake, do I have to do everything around here myself?" These passed swiftly; he wasted little time in recrimination and always buckled

For those who failed him, remorse was a far sharper spur than reprimands would have been.

down promptly to the problem of what to do next. For those who failed him, remorse was a far sharper spur than reprimands would have been. Above all, the responsibility of the staff, Kennedy said, was to make certain that "important matters are brought here in a way which permits a clear decision after alternatives have been presented." He added, "Occasionally, in the past, I think the staff has been used to get a pre-arranged agreement which is only confirmed at the President's desk, and that I don't agree with."

When a decision was in the offing, the next step was to call a meeting. Kennedy disliked meetings, especially large ones, and insisted that they be honed to the edge of action. He convened the cabinet far less even than Roosevelt. "Cabinet meetings," he once told John Sharon, "are simply useless. Why should the Postmaster General sit there and listen to a discussion of the problems of Laos? ... I don't know how Presidents functioned with them or relied on them in the past." (Very few good ones had.) If he had to have a meeting, he preferred a small one with candid discussion among the technicians and professionals who could give him the facts on which decision was to be based. Policy people were less essential because he could supply policy himself. Kennedy would listen quietly to the presentation, then ask pertinent questions and expect precise replies. He had a disconcerting capacity, derived in part from his larger perspective and in part from his more original intelligence, to raise points which the experts, however diligently they had prepared themselves, were hard put to answer. Rambling made him impatient, but his courtesy was unshakable; there were only those drumming fingers. At the end, he would succinctly sum up the conclusions.

5. KENNEDY AND SPEECHES

Dean Acheson once said of presidential addresses, "This is often where policy is made, regardless of where it is supposed to be made." The presidential speech was automatically a declaration of national intent, addressed not only to Congress, the country and the world but also (sometimes equally important) to the executive branch of the government.

Kennedy's speeches covered a whole range of occasions from greeting delegations of foreign students to warning the world of the perils of nuclear war. Though he was a perfectly competent writer, he rarely had time to compose his own speeches any longer (except when he spoke extemporaneously, as he very often did). Ted Sorensen was, of course, his main reliance. They had worked closely together for a decade, and on these matters their minds rolled in unison. I do not know which of them originated the device of staccato phrases ("We shall pay any price, bear any burden, meet any hardship, support any friend, oppose any foe to assure the survival and success of liberty") or the use of balanced sentences ("Never have the nations of the world had so much to lose or so much to gain. Together we shall save our planet or together we shall perish in its flames"); but by the time of the Presidency their styles had fused into one.

Next to Sorensen, Richard Goodwin was Kennedy's best writer. After Goodwin's departure to the State Department, I found myself increasingly involved in speech drafting. The President somewhat mistrusted my efforts, however, as "too Stevensonian," by which he meant too complicated in syntax and fancy in language. He felt that his voice had too narrow a range to permit rhetorical flight and used to envy Stevenson his greater inflection of tone. Actually his own range steadily expanded during the Presidency, and he rapidly became an orator of unusual force and eloquence.

He would begin work on a speech by calling in the writer and sketching out his ideas. When the occasion was serious, he would read the draft with intense care, scribble illegibly on the margin and then go over the result with the writer.

If the occasion was political or festive, he would approach the speech with greater casualness, quite often using the prepared text only as a point of departure or, as he had done so often in the 1960 campaign, abandoning it entirely.

The speech process often brought his miscellany of curious knowledge into play. In September 1962 he asked me to prepare something for a talk he had to make at Newport at the dinner before the America's Cup races. He suddenly said, "I understand that there is about the same amount of salt in the human blood as there is in sea water, and that is a proof of our origin in the sea." This sounded like an old wives' tale to me, but I said I would check into it. I called one of Jerome Wiesner's specialists, who was skeptical too but agreed to look further. In an hour he called back, rather excited, and said, "It seems as if you have got on to something there." When I later asked Kennedy where in the world he had heard this, he said he couldn't remember. In Newport he converted it into poetry: "All of us have in our veins the exact same percentage of salt in our blood that exists in the ocean, and, therefore, we have salt in our blood, in our sweat, in our tears. We are tied to the ocean. And when we go back to the sea—whether it is to sail or to watch it—we are going back from whence we came."

XXVI.
DOWN PENNSYLVANIA AVENUE

ALL THESE DEVICES—White House staff, meetings, speeches—were familiar presidential tools. But by themselves they were only the beginning of the system of presidential control. Every activist President devises further methods, often peculiar and personal, to reach out beyond the White House into the executive branch and beyond that to the Congress. Kennedy's most efficacious means of management and stimulus had no precedent since the age of Jackson and Taney and did not fully exist then—that is, the use of the Attorney General as a prime presidential agent on policy across the board.

In spite of the eight and a half years' difference in their ages, John and Robert Kennedy had achieved by 1961 an extraordinary partnership. Their communication was virtually telepathic and their communion complete. One is not sure when this all started. Robert, the seventh of the nine Kennedy children, was also, among the brothers, the smallest, lightest and, perhaps in consequence, tensest. One had the impression that the family competition had been hardest on him, forcing him to scramble for everything and giving his character at an early point the style of bantam-cock determination. Possibly because of this, and even though the gap in ages could not have permitted mush comradeship in the early years, his older brother was obviously fond of him. A letter from the South Pacific after PT-109 when Robert, then seventeen, joined the Navy from Milton Academy suggests the relationship. "The folks sent me a clipping of you taking the oath," Jack Kennedy wrote. "The sight of you there, just as a boy, was really moving particularly as a close examination showed that you had my checked London coat on. I'd like to know what the hell I'm doing out here while you go stroking around in my drape coat, but I suppose that [is] what we are out here for." He added lightly: "In that picture you looked as if you were going to step outside the room, grab your gun, and knock off several of the houseboys before lunch. After reading Dad's letter, I gathered that the cold vicious look in your eye was due to the thought of that big blocking back from Groton."

1. BOBBY

That "cold vicious look" stayed in Robert Kennedy's photographs for some time; his public role in the fifties was that of a prosecutor and investigator. After the Navy, he went on to Harvard and then to the University of Virginia Law School. After law school he briefly joined Truman's Department of Justice. When the Republicans took over in 1953, he moved on to the staff of the Subcommittee on Investigations of the Senate Committee on Government Operations, chairman, Senator Joseph McCarthy. Here he worked primarily on an investigation of trade by allied nations with Communist China. Though this investigation was considerably disputed, it was less disputed than McCarthy's other investigations into the alleged disloyalty of government employees. Partly because he genuinely liked McCarthy, Robert Kennedy watched the committee steer this second course with mounting disapproval. After six months, he told McCarthy that he disagreed with the way the committee was being run, predicted that it was headed for disaster and resigned. Subsequently he returned as counsel for the Democrats on the committee and wrote the minority report condemning McCarthy's investigation of supposed Communist shenanigans at Fort Monmouth. In 1957 he became counsel for the Senate Rackets Committee in its long and angry investigations into "improper activities" on the part of labor and management. Here his bitter duel with Jimmy Hoffa of the Teamsters attracted national attention.

Robert's close working association with his older brother began in 1952, when he managed the Senate campaign, and flourished in the Rackets Committee, where John Kennedy was a leader among the senatorial members. In November 1959, Jack naturally turned to Robert to organize his drive for the presidential nomination. Bringing along such colleagues from the Rackets Committee staff as Kenneth O'Donnell

LEFT: ROBERT KENNEDY CONSULTING WITH HIS BROTHER OUTSIDE THE OVAL OFFICE.

ROBERT KENNEDY, SERVING AS CHIEF COUNSEL FOR THE SPECIAL SENATE COMMITTEE AT THE RACKETEERING HEARINGS.

and Pierre Salinger, Bobby took over. In the next year he mobilized the Kennedy forces, brought pressure on undecided party leaders, gave people orders, blew them up if the execution was slow or slipshod, became the candidate's no-man and took on himself the onus for the hard judgment and the unpleasant decision. By the end of 1960 he had thus embellished the public impression of the remorseless prosecutor by stirring in that of the relentless politician.

When, to the general indignation of the bar and the press, he was appointed Attorney General, he was widely regarded as a ruthless and power-hungry young man, devoid of principle or scruple, indifferent to personal freedom or public right, who saw life in rigidly personal and moralistic terms, divided people between the 'white hats' and the 'black hats' and found his greatest pleasure in harassing his fellow citizens. A cluster of legends arose to reinforce this theory: thus his father was supposed to have said with paternal pride, "Bobby hates the same way I do." And Bobby's public bearing—the ominous manner, the knock-the-chip-off-my-shoulder look, the stony blue eyes, clenched teeth, tart, monosyllabic tongue—did not especially dispel the picture of a rough young man suddenly given national authority.

I do not know of any case in contemporary American politics where there has seemed to me a greater discrepancy between the myth and the man. The public theory of Robert Kennedy could only appear to those who knew him, as James Wechsler later described it, a case of mistaken identity. No doubt Robert's first political heroes were Herbert Hoover and Douglas MacArthur; no doubt he once considered Yalta a national betrayal; no doubt he regarded (and continued to regard) professional liberals with suspicion. But in my experience he did not hold grudges, cherish a black-and-white view of life, scorn issues of personal freedom or believe that anyone who was not with him was against him. This was true neither of his personal relations nor (as was plainly shown by his leadership in changing the American line on neutral countries) of his policy judgments. He was emotionally more intense than his older brother, but he had all of John Kennedy's laconic candor and increasing shares of his objectivity and his deadpan, throwaway wit.

Indeed, as one came to know him better, what seemed most characteristic were his gentleness, consideration, sobriety, idealism and, if the word had not been hopelessly degraded by political oratory, compassion. At home in Hickory Hill, with his happy and spirited wife, surrounded by multiplying sons, daughters and pets (David Ormsby Gore once said that he had known Bobby and Ethel so long that he could remember when the dogs outnumbered the children), or in shirtsleeves in his office, children's drawings thumbtacked on the wall, a litter of souvenirs from foreign travel strewn around the room, a large dog somnolent on the floor, he hardly seemed the demon of the liberal imagination. Most striking of all was what one of his first liberal friends, William O. Douglas, called his "unique capacity for growth." Thus at some point Robert Kennedy grew aware of the world of mind and sensibility in which his brother had been so long at ease; and he determined to explore this world for himself. He began reading extensively, especially history and biography; he started listening to music and attending ballet; and he was responsible for organizing one of the pleasantest of the New Frontier exercises, the so-called Hickory Hill seminar.

The purpose here was to remind public officials that a world existed beyond their in-boxes. The regulars, consisting of about twenty cabinet members, agency chiefs and lesser government people, plus the Ormsby Gores, met once a month or so to hear an authority speak on a subject of his own choosing so long as it did not involve the day-to-day business of government. Two of the sessions—with Isaiah Berlin of Oxford and David Donald of Johns Hopkins—were held at the White House, and Jacqueline occasionally came to others. The evenings were lively and generally disputatious. The seminars summed up a good deal of the humane and questing spirit of the New Frontier.

2. THE ATTORNEY GENERAL

As Attorney General, Robert Kennedy was determined to make the Department of Justice professionally the best department in the government. The quality of appointments had not been so high since the New Deal—Byron White and then Nicholas Katzenbach as Deputy Attorney General, Archibald Cox as Solicitor General and, among the Assistant Attorney Generals, Burke Marshall for the Civil Rights Division, John Douglas for the Civil Division, Louis Oberdorfer for the Tax Division, Herbert Miller for the Criminal Division, William Orrick for Anti-Trust, Ramsey Clark for Lands and Norbert Schlei for the Office of Legal Counsel. In addition, two Pulitzer Prize newspapermen, John Seigenthaler and Edwin O. Guthman, were in charge of public information.

It was an exceptionally able staff, and Robert Kennedy told it to make the Department an example of impartial law enforcement. The Attorney General's readiness, for example, to bring cases against Democratic politicians confounded his critics of 1960. Along with civil rights and juvenile delinquency, he took a particular personal interest in the fight against organized crime, and nonetheless, the anti-crime effort had more élan and effect than it had had for years.

The relationship with J. Edgar Hoover was always a problem for Attorney Generals. For a quarter of a century the FBI had operated as if it were an independent agency, choosing its own cases, nourishing its own relations with the Congress and the press and bypassing its Attorney Generals to report directly to the President. The exceptional proficiency of Hoover's investigations and certainly of his public relations had made him an almost sacrosanct national figure. John F. Kennedy regarded the FBI as an element in the panoply of national power requiring both propitiation and control. While he preserved friendly relations with Hoover and invited him from time to time to the White House, he also wholeheartedly supported his brother's view that the Bureau be restored to the Department of Justice. For the first time in a generation, communications from the Bureau to the White House went through the office of the Attorney General. Moreover, Robert Kennedy directed the FBI to join the Department by moving not only into the drive against organized crime but also, considerably more alien to the Bureau's folkways, into the enforcement of the civil rights laws.

The question of the indigent defendant was another of Robert Kennedy's personal concerns. Through legislation and the establishment of an Office of Criminal Justice, he now sought to make sure that poor men charged with crime would have free counsel, reasonable bail and a fair opportunity to prepare a defense; he wanted, as he liked to say, a Department of Justice, not a Department of Prosecution.

On civil liberties questions, contrary to liberal fears, Robert Kennedy proved concerned and responsive. Like all Attorney Generals since 1940, he wanted wiretapping legislation; but, after imprudent endorsement of a broad bill in 1961, the Department restudied the problem and came up the next year with a far more careful and confined approach. For the rest, he presided over a quiet and thorough liquidation of the McCarthyite heritage. "I think that the Communist party as a political organization is of no danger to the United States," he said. "It has no following and has been disregarded by the American people for many, many years." Insofar as its relationship to the Soviet Union made it a danger, that was a matter for the FBI. Anti-communist vigilantes, he continued, "perform a disservice to the United States," and he attacked "those who, in the name of fighting Communism, sow seeds of suspicion and distrust by making false or irresponsible charges, not only against their neighbors, but against courageous teachers and public officials." Within the government he argued for the dismissal of unsupported security charges and recommended a pardon for the last Smith Act defendant in federal prison, the ex-Communist Junius Scales; he did this over the opposition not only of Hoover, who insisted that Scales should not be released until he cooperated by naming names, but of his successive Deputy Attorney Generals. "For the first time since the rise of McCarthyism," said Joseph Rauh, Washington's leading civil liberties lawyer, "an Attorney General has refused to treat a man's unwillingness to inform on others as a ground for withholding favorable governmental action in his case."

In the Washington judgment, he turned out to be the best Attorney General since Francis Biddle twenty years earlier. But this was a lesser part of his services to the President. When he first decided to appoint his brother to the cabinet, I do not know how much John Kennedy expected Robert to do besides run the Department of Justice and be available for private advice and commiseration. The Bay of Pigs, however, changed all that. Thereafter the President wanted Bobby at every crucial meeting. He did not necessarily agree with his younger brother; the Attorney General was one more prism which he read like the others. But the President trusted him more than anyone else to get to the bottom of an idea or project, to distinguish what was operational from what was literary, to anticipate consequences, to ride herd on execution, to protect the presidential interest and, above all, to be candid.

Within the cabinet, Robert Kennedy became a constant and steady liberal force, no matter how much it irritated him to have this pointed out. Whatever the issue, one could expect a reaction on the merits, without regard to vested intellectual or administrative interests. One could expect a reaction on political feasibility also; but the two were kept carefully separate. Gradually the New Frontiersmen came to see him as their particular champion, knowing that he was

ROBERT KENNEDY DURING A MORNING MEETING WITH HIS ADVISERS AT THE JUSTICE DEPARTMENT. FROM LEFT ARE BURKE MARSHALL, NICOLAS KATZENBACH AND NORBERT SCHLEI.

often free to say and do things which the President, in the nature of things, could not say or do. Soon he had his allies scattered throughout the administration. An unfriendly observer wrote, "Kennedy, a student of guerrilla warfare, was applying its techniques to intergovernmental relations." But he did not plant these men; he won them.

He was also increasingly the voice of New Frontier idealism to young people at home and abroad. His programs for poor children through the President's Committee on Juvenile Delinquency, with their concern for education and emphasis on what intellectuals would later call 'participatory democracy,' represented a genuine innovation in American social policy.

Especially in foreign affairs, if a good idea was going down for the third time in the bureaucratic sea, one turned more and more to Bobby to rescue it. His distinctive contribution was to fight unremittingly for his brother's understanding that foreign policy was not a technical exercise off in a vacuum but the expression of a nation's internal policy and purpose. He freely attacked the policy of association "with tyrannical and unpopular regimes that had no following and no future." To students coming to his office he would say, "Two thirds of the world today goes to bed hungry. The benefits of the world can't be concentrated on the few. Such a solution would be intolerable. We in the United States have a responsibility to help others." He left his mark in a dozen areas of foreign policy from cultural exchange to counterguerrilla warfare.

The myth of ruthlessness persisted. But the man grew; his horizons enlarged; his identity evolved. "He is an active principle," Norman Mailer wrote. "... Something compassionate, something witty, has come into the face. Something of sinew." He was in these years his brother's total partner and, more than anyone else, enabled the President to infuse the government with the energy and purpose of the New Frontier.

3. THE VICE-PRESIDENT

However surprised John Kennedy had been in Los Angeles when Lyndon Johnson accepted his invitation to go on the ticket as candidate for Vice-President, he soon had reason to rejoice in the selection. In the autumn of 1960 Johnson proved a powerful and tireless campaigner, especially in the South. Indignantly rejecting suspicions of the presidential candidate as a Yankee and Catholic, he would say in the regional idiom, "Kennedy's a man to go to the well with."* Employing his whole oratorical range—first hunched over the rostrum, talking in a low, confiding, pleading voice, telling a repertory of stories unmatched since Alben Barkley, then suddenly standing erect, roaring, gesticulating, waving his arms—he carried the message of confidence with panache across the southern states. Without Johnson, Kennedy would have lost Texas and perhaps South Carolina and Louisiana:** without these three states, the electoral vote would have been evenly split and the result at the mercy of unpledged electors from Mississippi and Alabama. Kennedy fully appreciated all this and was grateful.

After the inauguration, both Kennedy and Johnson confronted the problem of the vice-presidential role in the new administration. Thirty-four previous Presidents had faced this problem with only indifferent success; the real difficulty lay in the Constitution itself. If the Vice-Presidency was an office without power (the duty of presiding over the Senate, whatever that was worth, derived technically from the constitutional provision assigning the Vice-President another and distinct post as President of the Senate), it remained one of absolute potentiality. "I am Vice-President," John Adams continued. "In this I am nothing. But I may be everything." As Harry Truman once put it, "the President, by necessity, builds his own staff, and the Vice-President remains an outsider, no matter how friendly the two may be.... Neither can take the other completely into his confidence." It was in a way a doomed relationship. Probably no

* A reference to the hazards of replenishing the water supply when an encampment was under Indian assault in frontier days.

** In Louisiana, however, the Catholic and Negro vote seems to have been chiefly responsible for Kennedy's gains over Stevenson in 1956.

President and Vice-President since Jackson and Van Buren had wholeheartedly liked and trusted each other.

Nevertheless one did not have the impression that Kennedy worried unduly about his relations with Johnson. He recognized of course that the former majority leader might have difficulty in reconciling himself to the upward rush of the young back-bencher. And he was well aware too that the Vice-President was temperamental, edgy and deeply sensitive. On the other hand, ever since their confrontation on the Tuesday of convention week, Kennedy had no doubt, I think, that Johnson would accept his primacy. Moreover, he liked Johnson personally, valued his counsel on questions of legislation and public opinion and was determined that, as Vice-President, Johnson should experience the full respect and dignity of the office. He took every care to keep Johnson fully informed. He made sure he was at major meetings and ceremonies. Nor would he tolerate from his staff the slightest disparagement of the Vice-President.

His sympathetic friend William S. White has written that Johnson set out "to be first of all a loyal Vice-President."*

This was clearly so, and Johnson clearly succeeded. White suggests that Johnson would have handled certain matters differently—Vietnam, Latin America, the steel crisis—but Johnson rigorously kept disagreement to himself. He cleared all important speeches with the White House, held few press conferences and rarely gave stories to newspapermen. At meetings of the cabinet or the National Security Council, he kept his peace until the President asked his view. Then he would faithfully back the President's policies and reserve his own comment for questions of political or congressional management.

The problem still remained of finding things for the Vice-President to do. As Senator, Johnson had helped shape the space program, and as Vice-President he was now able to carry it forward. Johnson also served as chairman of the President's Committee on Equal Employment Opportunities, as Nixon had before him. Above all, as Kennedy sent the Vice-President on trips abroad. In the Kennedy years Johnson visited thirty-three countries and delivered more than 150 speeches. The equal employment and overseas assignments, as Johnson must have noticed, gave him an opportunity to build himself up in areas where he had been conspicuously weak when he had tried for the Presidency in 1960.

Johnson's vice-presidential performance was a triumph of self-discipline, and it exacted its psychic price. Underneath the self-imposed constraint, Johnson remained a proud and imperious man of towering energies and passions. Self-effacement was for him the most unnatural of roles; and the foreign visits became one great escape. He sought his missions abroad, adored them and whirled through his thirty-three countries, scattering ballpoint pens, cigarette lighters and general pandemonium in his wake and returning with trunks of gifts for his friends. He was effective in his meetings with foreign leaders and had a bracing impact on the correct young men of the Foreign Service.

But life in Washington was harder. In later years he would describe the Vice-Presidency as the most valuable time in his career—the time which enabled him to take over the Presidency with such skill and purpose—and doubtless this was so; but at the time one felt an increasing moroseness and unhappiness.

Probably Johnson's greatest frustration lay in his role, or lack of it, in relationship to Congress. Beyond his deep emotional identification with the New Deal, somewhat tempered in the fifties by the conservatism of the country and the politics of Texas, Johnson had displayed no consuming interest in the substance of policies. But, once the substance was given, he was the great legislative prestidigitator of his time, skilled in modifying a measure to enlist the widest possible support, so adept at the arts of wheedling, trading and arm-twisting, so persistent and so persuasive. Yet these extraordinary talents went largely unemployed in the Kennedy years. Once the necromancer had left his senatorial seat, the old black magic evidently lost some of its power.

There were, however, deeper reasons for steering the energies of the Vice-President in other directions. If Kennedy had allowed Johnson to conduct his congressional relations, he would in effect have made the Vice-President the judge of what was legislatively feasible and thereby have lost control over his own program. This was something no sensible President would do. Kennedy therefore relied on his own congressional liaison staff under Lawrence O'Brien, calling on the Vice-President only on particular occasions. Could Johnson have been used more? He thought so and used to say privately with sad incredulity about one or another administration measure or tactic in Congress, "You know, they never once asked me about that!" But in public he remained co-operative and steadfast.

4. KENNEDY AND THE CONGRESS

As Kennedy's comment on Theodore Roosevelt and Wilson as against Polk and Truman had suggested, he felt that in some sense the real test of a President was his ability to get his program through Congress. In the mood of the early sixties this would be the hardest test of all.

In the years since the Second World War, Congress, through its enlarged use of its powers of appropriation and investigation, had become increasingly involved in the details

* W. S. White, *The Professional: Lyndon B. Johnson* (Boston, 1964), 228.

of executive administration, thereby systematically enhancing its own power and diminishing that of the President. Moreover, the more foreign policy required money, the more Congress acquired a means of veto. No one wished to change the system; but it was hard to deny that contemporary Presidents, hedged round by an aggressive Congress and an unresponsive bureaucracy, had in significant respects notably less freedom of action than their predecessors.

On top of this, Kennedy's margin in Congress was exceedingly nominal. The figures looked fine—64 Democrats to 36 Republicans in the Senate, 263 to 174 in the House—but were deceptive. For one thing, in a number of states Kennedy had run behind the Democratic candidates for Congress. "The people in Congress do not feel that they owe the President anything," a Democratic Congressman told *U.S. News and World Report*. "A good many of them were elected in 1960 in spite of his presence on the ticket rather than because his name was there. They feel that they have more of a mandate for their point of view than he does for his program." Moreover, the apparent Democratic majorities in both House and Senate included many members of the old anti-New Deal coalition of conservative Democrats and Republicans. "Some Democrats," as the President observed in 1962, "have voted with the Republicans for twenty-five years, really since 1938 ... so that we have a very difficult time, on a controversial piece of legislation, securing a working majority."

He could never escape the political arithmetic. The Democrats had lost twenty seats in the 1960 congressional election, all from the North, nearly all liberal Democrats, nearly all defeated because of the religious issue. Many times in the next two years Kennedy desperately needed these twenty votes. Without them he was more than ever dependent on the South. The old Confederacy was represented by ninety-nine Democratic Congressmen and twenty-one Democratic Senators. This meant in the House that, if the administration carried every northern, western and border Democratic vote, which it rarely did, it would still require a minimum of fifty-five southern votes to preserve a Democratic majority. It meant that he had hardly more Democratic Congressmen from the northern and western states (132) than from the border states and the South (131). Moreover, the old Confederacy, by virtue of seniority, controlled most of the critical committee chairmanships and thereby had further leverage over legislation. The legislative progress of the New Frontier was thus largely in the hands of aging men, mostly born in another century, mostly representing rural areas in an urban nation (and, indeed, mostly coming from states where less than 40 per cent of persons of voting age had cast ballots in the 1960 election). For an edifying four months in 1962 a feud between Representative Clarence Cannon (eighty-three years old) and Senator Carl Hayden (eighty-four years old), each of whom angrily declined to go to the office of the other, held up House-Senate agreement on appropriation bills and left a number of government agencies without money to meet their payrolls.

Nothing brought the precariousness of the administration's position home more grimly than the first congressional battle—the fight in January 1961 to enlarge the House Rules Committee in order to make sure the administration would have the power to bring its program to the floor. In spite of Kennedy's victory in the national election to the floor. In spite of Kennedy's victory in the national election two months earlier, it took twenty-two Republican votes and a personal plea by Speaker Rayburn from the well of the House for the administration to squeak through by five votes. Sixty-four southern Democrats were on the other side. It was a close and bitter business, and the memory of this fight laid a restraining hand on the administration's legislative priorities for some time to come. Every President, moreover, has to husband his bargaining power for its most effective use. Thus in 1962 Kennedy decided—perhaps mistakenly—to use his for the trade expansion bill first of all; he thereby had less left over for other parts of his program.

Kennedy used to quote Jefferson: "Great innovations should not be forced on slender majorities." Nor was he one to see great virtue in losing. "There is no sense," he once said, "in raising hell, and then not being successful. There is no sense in putting the office of the Presidency on the line on an issue, and then being defeated." Yet, despite such aphorisms, he did, in fact, submit to Congress an astonishing number of innovations, doing so less perhaps in the expectation of immediate enactment than in the knowledge they would never be enacted without a long campaign of congressional and national education. I doubt, for example, whether he really counted on getting Medicare in 1961 to 1962. But he knew that if he sent up a message and a bill, there would be debate and hearings; Congress would begin to accustom itself to unfamiliar ideas; the legislation would be revised to meet legitimate objections; the opposition would in time expend itself and seem increasingly frantic and irrelevant; public support would consolidate; and by 1964 or 1965 the bill would be passed. This is not to say that he would not have preferred immediate results, did not fight for them (while always balancing them against desired results in other areas) and did not, in many cases, achieve them. But, even if he did not get action on all his requests, the educational processes thus set in motion would make the passage of most of them inevitable in the years to come.

Yet one result of his flow of proposals was very likely to increase congressional anxieties. There were too many new ideas, coming too fast, couched in too cool and analytical a tone and implying too critical a view of American society. Instead of being reassured, many Congressmen felt threatened. And the President himself, despite those fourteen years in Congress, had always been something of an alien on the Hill. This had been especially true in the House, where he had had least contact with the leadership, where his experience was most out of date and which now confronted him with his toughest problems. Even in the Senate, where he was liked and respected, he had never been one of the cloakroom boys. He did not act, talk or look like a Senator, or regard the Senate as the climax of human evolution. Now he had shot up over the heads of his seniors, and the congressional elders, who had been great men when he arrived as a gangling first-termer, were sometimes discomfited by dealing with him as President. A few resented his intellectualism, his wealth and the style of his world.

On his side, Kennedy cultivated his congressional relations with diligence and cheer, though with a certain fatalism. He enjoyed the Tuesday morning breakfasts with congressional leaders, often had congressional groups at the White House and threw himself with necessary vigor into the congressional battles. He particularly liked and valued Mike Mansfield, approved of Mansfield's announced principles of "courtesy, self-restraint and accommodation" and considered him underrated because he did his job with so little self-advertisement and fanfare. He liked Carl Albert, the House leader, for the same reasons. He also liked and was entertained by Everett Dirksen, the Republican leader in the Senate. He respected the standards and the craftsmanship of the Hill. He spent more of his time than people realized working with Congress. But it cannot be said that this was the part of the Presidency which gave him the greatest pleasure or satisfaction.

This made his congressional liaison staff all the more important, and it served him well. Lawrence O'Brien, a man of great decency and character, assembled a first-class group of people—Henry Hall Wilson, Richard Donahue, Mike Manatos, Charles Daly, Claude Desautels—and gave the White House a more organized legislative role than it had ever had before. Kennedy sometimes said himself that in his fourteen years in Congress he had had little useful contact with members of the White House staff, and he wished to change that now. He sought to centralize the organization of legislative pressure. While the departments and agencies retained primary responsibility for their bills, each gave O'Brien every Monday morning a report on activities and plans. Digested and analyzed, these reports went to the President before the Tuesday breakfasts.

O'Brien did not have the most enviable job in the government. From the congressional perspective the White House agents on the Hill were always doing too much or too little. Complaints about absence of presidential leadership alternated with complaints about excess of presidential pressure. Larry suffered the constantly shifting winds with equanimity and worked for the program with tact and devotion. It remained a constant battle.

The fact that Kennedy accepted his congressional compromises and defeats fatalistically instead of raging back in the manner of the Roosevelts led some observers to suppose that, if he had only fought harder, he would have had greater success. But Kennedy, knowing the arithmetic of Congress and the entrenched power at that time of the conservative coalition, knew that he just did not have the votes for his more controversial proposals—and that he could not afford to alienate Congressmen gratuitously if he wanted to save his less controversial bills. Nor did he rest great hope in the measures for congressional reform urged by Senator Joseph Clark and others. He was basically resigned to the existing structure and hoped to make it work by getting better people in Congress. In September 1962, when James MacGregor Burns submitted a resolution to the American Political Science Association proposing a presidential commission to investigate executive-congressional relations, Kennedy remarked that this seemed to him the wrong approach; Congress had to be persuaded to reform itself, and there was very little the executive could do about it. It would help greatly, he added, if we could gain a few seats in the election; but nothing really fundamental could be done until after 1964. "We can make loyalty to the ticket the test in 1964, and then we can deal with those who failed to support the ticket."

Congress remained his great frustration. But the extent of that frustration has been exaggerated. The myth grew up in later years that, for all the loftiness of its design, the New Frontier was unusually ineffective in enacting its proposals. While Kennedy did not get everything he wanted, he knew that in many cases the ground had to be sowed in 1961 and 1962 if the crop were to be harvested in 1964 and 1965. And the things he did get even before the 1962 election constituted a legislative record unmatched in some respects since the days of Roosevelt.*

* 1961: Peace Corps; Alliance for Progress; Arms Control and Disarmament Administration; area redevelopment; general housing act; extension of unemployment compensation; aid to dependent children of unemployed; increase in minimum wage; water pollution control; juvenile delinquency program; community health facilities. 1962: Trade Expansion Act; UN bond issue; tax bill; investment tax credit; communications satellite; manpower development and training; accelerated public works; drug labeling; restraints on conflict of interest; federal pay reform; federal assistance for the immunization of children; constitutional amendment abolishing the poll tax in federal elections; farm bill with wheat controls.

The statistics for these two years show 53 total major recommendations in 1961, of which 33 were enacted into law; 54 in 1962, of which 40 were enacted into law. "Summary of the Three-Year Kennedy Record and Digest of Major Accomplishments of the 87th Congress and the 88th Congress First Session," 88 Cong., 1 Sess., Sen. Doc. No. 53, 55–60.

XXVII.
THE BULLY PULPIT

PRESS SECRETARY PIERRE SALINGER ANSWERS QUESTIONS FROM THE PRESS.

THE MOST COMMON CRITICISM of Kennedy during his Presidency was that he had failed as a public educator. It was said that he concentrated on 'selling' himself and his family rather than his ideas; that he was excessively preoccupied with his 'image'; and that he was unwilling to convert personal popularity into political pressure for his program. He was compared invidiously with the Roosevelts, Wilson and other Presidents celebrated for their skill in rallying the electorate behind controversial policies.

Yet in later years the age of Kennedy was seen as a time of quite extraordinary transformation of national values and purposes—a transformation so far-reaching as to make the America of the sixties a considerably different society from the America of the fifties. And, instead of hearing that Kennedy did too little as a public educator, one heard more often in retrospect that he had tried to do too much too quickly, to put over too many new ideas in too short a time, that he had unnecessarily affronted the national mood and pushed ahead so fast that he lost contact with public opinion. Clearly the paradox of Kennedy and public education deserves examination.

1. PUBLIC EDUCATION: THE CONVENTIONAL THEORY

Memory had left an impression of F.D.R. as incessantly on the air and of Theodore Roosevelt and Wilson constantly using the White House, in T.R.'s phrase, as a "bully pulpit." Compared to these glowing recollections, Kennedy's efforts seemed meager and perfunctory. In fact, in three years, Kennedy made nine television reports to the nation from the White House, therefore averaging 50 percent higher than F.D.R.'s peacetime rate; and he gave far more public speeches each year than the Roosevelts or Wilson had given. He also held frequent private meetings at the White House with editors, businessmen, labor leaders, organization representatives and other panjandrums of the opinion mafia. And he used television and the press with skill and resource.

Like all modern Presidents, Kennedy found the newspapers a major educational instrument. Only 16 percent had backed him in 1960; but the working press had been strongly for him. Kennedy liked newspapermen; they liked him; and he recognized that they provided him a potent means of appealing to readers over the heads of publishers. In Pierre Salinger he had an engaging and imaginative press secretary. While Salinger sometimes lacked the total knowledge of high policy which his very able predecessor under Eisenhower, James Hagerty, had enjoyed, and while newspapermen claimed he lacked Hagerty's proficiency in making their technical arrangements, he admirably conveyed Kennedy's own insouciant spirit to the White House press room, bore patiently with Kennedy's occasional outbursts against the press and prescribed an open-door policy for newspapermen in the White House and throughout the government.

The press conferences were the central forum of presidential contact. Kennedy averaged twenty-one a year, far fewer than Roosevelt and somewhat fewer than Eisenhower. Though at times oddly resistant when the time came for another press conference, he was the most skilled presidential practitioner in this medium since Roosevelt. Moreover, while Roosevelt's press conferences were intimate off-the-record sessions around the presidential desk in the oval office, Kennedy's were mass public affairs, often on live television; he achieved his success under far more exacting conditions.

Success was the product of study as well as of art. Salinger organized a meticulous briefing process, drawing in predicted questions and recommended responses from information officers across the government. The President would then convene a press conference breakfast, ordinarily attended by Salinger, Sorensen, Bundy, Heller and Robert Manning, the State Department's Assistant Secretary for Public Affairs. Here the President would try out his answers, often tossing off replies which convulsed the breakfast table but which, alas, could not be diplomatically made on the occasion.

Later in the day he would go over to the auditorium of the State Department, and the fun would begin: the forest of hands waving from the floor; the questioner recognized by a brisk jab of the presidential forefinger; then the answer—statistics rolling off the presidential tongue, or a sudden glint in the eye signaling the imminence of a throwaway joke, or, very occasionally, an abrupt frostiness of countenance; then the next questioner recognized almost before the answer to the first was completed—it was a superb show, always gay, often exciting, relished by the reporters and by the television audience.

One felt at times that the President missed chances to make points to the nation for fear of boring the men and women in the room by telling them things he supposed they already knew. F.D.R. had never hesitated to cast elementary statement or homely metaphor—lend-lease and the neighbor's firehose—before the sophisticates of the Washington press corps, knowing that the key phrases would filter through to the people who needed them. In Kennedy's case, the uninitiated, instead of learning something about a public issue, often only witnessed abstract and cryptic exchanges between reporter and President. Nonetheless, the conferences offered a showcase for a number of his most characteristic qualities—the intellectual speed and vivacity, the remarkable mastery of the data of government, the terse, self-mocking wit, the exhilarating personal command. Afterward he liked to relax, watch himself in action on the evening news and chat about the curious habits of the press.

His relations with the press, like those of all Presidents, had its ups and downs. Kennedy read more newspapers than anyone except perhaps Roosevelt,* and very often with appreciation; but like Presidents Hoover, Roosevelt, Truman and Eisenhower—indeed, like most politicians—he retained an evidently inexhaustible capacity to become vastly, if briefly, annoyed by hostile articles or by stories based on leaks. When this happened there would be complaints to the staff, calls to reporters, searches for the sources of stories and even the cancellation for a time of the *New York Herald Tribune*. Nor were relations improved when the information officer of the Defense Department talked imprudently about news as "part of the arsenal of weaponry" and affirmed "the inherent right of the government to lie ... to save itself when faced with nuclear disaster."

Washington reporters, with their acute sense of contemporaneity, always believe that each new administration is plotting an assault on the freedom of the press with a determination and malignity never before seen in the republic; the iniquities of past Presidents fade quickly in retrospect. So for a time in 1962 they proclaimed a deep sense of grievance over the 'hypersensitivity' of the President and the administration. For its part the administration used to wonder about the hypersensitivity of reporters, who seemed to feel that, if a government official dared disagree with a story, it was an attempt to 'manage' the news. This guerrilla warfare between press and government was, of course, inherent in the situation; it was also a great bulwark of national freedom.

2. PROBLEMS OF THE CONVENTIONAL THEORY

Kennedy thus used the conventional instruments of public education with freedom and skill. But he felt that press conferences and public addresses could not work for him as they had worked for the Roosevelts and Wilson—that hortatory and explicit public education was simply not suited to the mood of the 1960s. For, as a student of history, he understood that public education did not take place in a vacuum. To move a nation, a President had first to have the nation's ear; and there was no quicker way to dissipate presidential influence than to natter away when no one was listening.

Thus a decade of reformers and muckrakers, working in the cities and states, had given the nation's ear to Theodore Roosevelt and Wilson, and a depression touching nearly every family in the country had given the nation's ear to Franklin Roosevelt. The early thirties in particular had been a time when visible and tangible crisis had generated a hunger for national action. With people hanging on every presidential word, public education offered no great problem to a President who had something to say. But no President, not even one of the Roosevelts or Wilson, could create by fiat the kind of public opinion he wanted. Effectiveness in public education required leverage in the nation to begin with.

Kennedy had very little leverage. No muckraking agitation had prepared the way for his Presidency; no national economic collapse was making his constituents clamor for action. His was an invisible and intangible crisis. The economy was moving forward, 95 percent of the labor force had jobs, American troops were not fighting in foreign lands, the country was bathed in physical contentment; and, except for racial minorities, spiritual disquietude floated about without commitment to issues. This acquiescent nation had elected him President by the slimmest of margins; no one could possibly claim his victory as a mandate for radical change.

Timing remained the key. In the absence of visible crisis Presidents had to wait for some event to pierce the apathy and command the nation's ear; experience was a more potent teacher than exhortation. At moments one felt that it was nearly impossible to change people or policies in advance of disaster, because only disaster could sufficiently

* And expected everyone else to do likewise. No experience was more frequent for members of his staff than to be called by the President early in the morning for discussion of an item in the papers; in my case the calls regularly came before I had had a chance to read the papers. Averell Harriman once told a congressional committee, "A man cannot serve President Kennedy unless he reads the newspaper carefully. He won't last very long if he doesn't, in this administration."

intimidate and overcome those with vested interests in existing people and policies. So we read every day in the newspapers about the decay of the Diem regime in Vietnam. But, so long as the Secretaries of State and Defense endorsed the policy of unconditional support of Diem, it was hard for the President to act until some dreadful blow-up made the failure of the policy manifest—and by that time it might be too late. So too in Negro rights: if the President committed his prestige to congressional action before the nation was ready to listen to his arguments, he might squander the hope of later influence. In a sense, things had to get worse before there was a possibility of putting them better. Thus Estes Kefauver's bill for the control of the marketing of drugs lingered in committee to immense public indifference until the thalidomide scandal provoked national anger and congressional action. Francis Keppel, the Commissioner of Education, used to express the hope that Congress would pass federal aid to education before some catastrophe—150 schoolchildren, for example, burned to death in a firetrap—came along to stir overdue national concern.

Public education in the explicit manner of the Roosevelts and Wilson was thus not, in Kennedy's judgment, particularly well adapted either to the times or to his special congressional dilemma—or to himself. This last is a subtler matter; for a period of visible domestic crisis like 1933 would doubtless have called forth different aspects of his own personality. But a politician lives in continuous interaction with his age; and the chemistry of the sixties confirmed Kennedy in temperamental traits already well marked—an aversion to what he called "highly charged" political positions, a scorn for histrionics, a recoil from corniness, a determination not to become a national scold or bore. These traits were rooted partly, as Richard Neustadt has suggested, in a rationalist's "mistrust of mass emotion as a tool in politics." Kennedy feared overexciting people about public issues, as he came to believe that his call for an air-raid shelter program had done during the Berlin crisis of 1961; and he was embarrassed on the rare occasions when he succumbed to public emotion himself, as he did when the Cuban Brigade, freed from Castro's prisons, presented its flag to him at Miami in December 1962. They were rooted too in that qualified historical fatalism which led him to doubt whether words, however winged, would by themselves change the world.

One other factor entered in, and this I find hardest of all to assess. Contrary to a widespread impression, Kennedy did not perceive himself as a partisan President, nor did he wish the country so to perceive him. He perceived himself rather as a man who, unlike the Trumans and Robert Tafts of American politics, generally saw reason on both sides of complex issues. By taking a non-partisan stance, he aimed at erasing the picture of the power-hungry young careerist and winning the national confidence he felt he lacked. As President, he replenished that strategy whenever he feared that any actions might revive the picture or weaken the confidence: thus his propitiatory course in the aftermath of the steel controversy.

At the time it seemed that Kennedy suffered from the illusion so common to new Presidents that he, unlike any of his predecessors, could really be President of all the people and achieve his purposes without pain or trauma. Some of us, however, thought national argument the best way to break national apathy and communicate the reality of problems, and argued the inevitability and superiority of the politics of combat as against the politics of consensus. But, while he did not dispute the points, he plainly saw no reason for rushing prematurely into battle.

I think now he had deeper reasons for this than I understood at the time—that his cast of mind had a profounder source than a pragmatist's preference for a law over an issue, than a rationalist's distaste for give-'em-hell partisanship, or even than a statesman's need to hoard national confidence against the possibility that foreign crisis might require swift and unpopular presidential decisions. I believe today that its basic source may have been an acute and anguished sense of the fragility of the membranes of civilization. His hope was that it might be possible to keep the country and the world moving fast enough to prevent unreason from rending the skin of civility. But he had peered into the abyss and knew the potentiality of chaos.

3. THE KENNEDY APPROACH

The fact that neither his time nor his temperament encouraged Kennedy to be a public educator in the explicit manner of the Roosevelts and Wilson did not mean that he renounced the presidential responsibility of public education. On the contrary: he pursued it in his own fashion—a fashion which so subtly permeated national attitudes and so quietly penetrated individual lives that no one realized how much he had changed things until his time was over. The essence of his attack was not admonition and remonstrance, in the earlier style, but example.

It was this which led to the familiar charge that Kennedy and his administration were preoccupied, to use the odious word, with 'image.' Noting the discrepancy between Kennedy's personal popularity and the support for his policies, observers concluded that he was reluctant to spend his popularity for result. Critics compared him to a matinee idol. One Republican Congressman dismissed the enthusiasm in which he was held: "It's like that of a movie actor—it's not related to legislation." Yet the Kennedy image was not, of course, anything like that of a movie actor. It was packed with a whole set of intellectual implications which were preparing the nation for legislative change as surely as Theodore Roosevelt's muckrakers or Franklin Roosevelt's depression. In an age of pervasive contentment, his personality was the most potent instrument he had to awaken a national desire for something new and better. The extraordinary effect with which he used it became apparent only in later years: thus Howard K. Smith in retrospect pronounced Kennedy not a failure in public education but a "brilliant communicator."

Kennedy communicated, first of all, a deeply critical attitude toward the ideas and institutions which American society had come in the fifties to regard with such enormous self-satisfaction. Social criticism had fallen into disrepute during the Eisenhower decade. In some influential quarters it was almost deemed treasonous to raise doubts about the perfection of the American way of life. But the message of Kennedy's 1960 campaign had been that the American way of life was in terrible shape, that our economy was slowing down, that we were neglectful of our young and our old, callous toward our poor and our minorities, that our cities and schools and landscapes were a mess, that our motives were materialistic and ignoble and that we were fast becoming a country without purpose and without ideals. As President, he proceeded to document the indictment. In so doing, he released the nation's critical energy. Self-criticism became not only legitimate but patriotic.

The literature of protest in the Kennedy years poked freely into sacrosanct or shadowed corners of American society—the persistence of poverty (Michael Harrington, Herman P. Miller, Ben Bagdikian, Edgar May, Harry Caudill and many others), racial inequities (a whole bookshelf), taxation (Philip Stern, Stewart Alsop), the spoiling of land, air, water and environment (Stewart Udall, Peter Blake, Howard Lewis, Lewis Herber, Donald Carr), the drug industry (Richard Harris, Morton Mintz); it even challenged such national ikons as television (Newton Minow, Merle Miller and others), the pesticide (Rachel Carson), the cigarette (Maurine Neuberger) and the funeral parlor (Jessica Mitford). There had not been such an outpouring of self-examination since the New Deal. While Presidents cannot claim entire credit for the social criticism of their day, and while in certain fields, notably Negro rights, schools and cities, the process had begun before Kennedy, nonetheless the presidential stance has a pervasive effect on the national mood.

Facts thus collected were one weapon in the dissolution of the established pretensions. Wit was another. The fifties had constituted probably the most humorless period in American history. A President and Vice-President who might have been invented by H. L. Mencken were viewed with invincible solemnity. Adlai Stevenson, a truly serious man who expressed part of his seriousness in humor, was regarded with suspicion. The zone of the acceptably comic had never been so contracted. This gloom permeated the decade.

For Kennedy wit was the natural response to platitude and pomposity. He once told me that the political writers he enjoyed most were Murray Kempton and Bernard Levin, who were by way of being the Menckens of their day. His whole personal bearing communicated a delight in satire; and in his wake came an exuberant revival of American irreverence. This had had its underground beginnings at the end of the fifties in small San Francisco and Greenwich Village nightclubs—Mort Sahl and the hungry i, Mike Nichols and Elaine May—but now it flourished, bringing Art Buchwald back to the United States and ending in the murky and ambiguous depths of black comedy. Like muckraking, satire forced the nation to take a fresh look at itself and helped prepare the ground for change.

A third component of the Kennedy image was respect for ideas. The fifties had been a decade of anti-intellectualism. For his belief in the trained intelligence Stevenson was ridiculed as an egghead. Neither ideas nor the men who had them were welcome in the places where respectable men fingered the levers of authority. But Kennedy had long hoped, as he said in January 1960, to "reopen the channels of communication between the world of thought and the seat of power." He felt this, I think, both technically essential in a world imposing novel and complex demands on policy and morally essential to assure civilized government. As President, he carried Roosevelt's brain-trust conception further than it had ever been carried before. The intellectual was no longer merely consultant or adviser but responsible official, even in areas so remote from traditional academic preoccupations as the Department of Defense. Some imports from the campuses worked out better than others; but the reversal of national form in a decade could hardly have been more spectacular. No President had ever made such systematic use of the nation's intellectual resources: and under his tutelage both academics and 'practical' men discovered that they had something to learn from the other.

The combination of self-criticism, wit and ideas made up, I think, a large part of the spirit of the New Frontier. It informed the processes of government, sparkled through evenings at the White House and around town, refreshed and enlivened the world of journalism, stimulated the universities, kindled the hopes of the young and presented the

WALTER CRONKITE INTERVIEWING THE PRESDIENT AT HYANNIS PORT IN AUGUST 1963.

nation with a new conception of itself and its potentialities. From the viewpoint of the fifties, it was almost a subversive conception, irreverent and skeptical, lacking in due respect for established propositions and potentates. Perhaps only a President who was at the same time seen as a war hero, a Roman Catholic, a tough politician and a film star could have infected the nation with so gay and disturbing a spirit. But Kennedy did exactly this with ease and grace; and, in doing so, he taught the country the possibilities of a new national style. If he did not get the results he would have liked at once, he was changing the climate in directions which would, in time, make those results inevitable.

4. THE KENNEDYS AND THE ARTS

He did this only partly by doubting the perfection of existing institutions. His more powerful weapon was his vision of the truly civilized community America might become. This vision animated his efforts to improve the quality of American life. It reached its climax in the unprecedented concern which the President and his wife gave to the place of the intellect and the arts in the national society.

"The artist," William Faulkner had said at the American Academy of Arts and Letters in 1957, "has no more actual place in the American culture of today than he has in the American economy of today, no place at all in the warp and woof, the thews and sinews, the mosaic of the American dream." The Kenneds came to the White House with a lively desire to help meet this problem. They were wholly unaffected in their attitude toward the arts. The President's curiosity and natural taste had been stimulated by Jacqueline's informed and exquisite responses: art had become a normal dimension of existence. The art to which Kennedy responded most deeply and spontaneously, I think, was literature; but he had a growing interest in architecture, and he had acquired some knowledge of painting—he liked the impressionists, though he was baffled by non-objective art—and sculpture. Serious music, it must be said, left him cold. But even here he believed it important for the President of the United States to lend his prestige to distinction of creation and performance.

Indeed, the character of his personal interest was less important than his conviction that the health of the arts was vitally related to the health of society. He saw the arts not as a distraction in the life of a nation but as something close to the heart of a nation's purpose. Excellence was a public necessity, ugliness a national disgrace. The arts therefore were, in his view, part of the presidential responsibility, and he looked for opportunities to demonstrate his concern. Thus when Stewart Udall early in December 1960 suggested that Robert Frost be invited to read a poem at the inauguration, Kennedy instantly responded. The combination of Frost on the rostrum and W. H. Auden, Alexis Léger, Paul Tillich, Jacques Maritain, Robert Lowell, John Hersey, John Steinbeck, Allen Tate and fifty other writers, composers and painters in the audience did seem to prefigure a new Augustan age of poetry and power.

The inauguration was the first step in the unfolding policy of presidential recognition of the arts. Then came a series of White House dinners. In November 1961, Pablo Casals, who had long declined to play his cello in public as a badge of mourning for Spanish democracy, agreed to perform at the White House on an evening honoring Muñoz Marín. Other dinners followed—for Stravinsky; for the western hemisphere Nobel prize-winners (whom Kennedy called "the most extraordinary collection of talent, of human knowledge, that has ever been gathered together at the White House, with the possible exception of when Thomas Jefferson dined alone"); for André Malraux—all memorable affairs. He encouraged the cabinet to arrange a series of cultural evenings—readings, recitals, dramatic performances. Never before had any President sought to identify the White House with the whole range of the nation's intellectual life. Thornton Wilder, who inaugurated the cabinet series, remarked that the administration had created "a whole new world of surprised self-respect" in the arts.

To complete the process of national recognition, Kennedy rehabilitated the Presidential Medal of Freedom in an effort to honor those "whose talent enlarges the public vision of the dignity with which life can be graced and the fullness with which it can be lived."

5. THE ARTS AND GOVERNMENT

Kennedy well understood that honoring the masters would not solve the problems of the young artist or the elevation of artistic standards or the economic sustenance of the arts. Nor did he suppose that these were problems to which government had the solution. But within its own domain the national government did all sorts of things, from designing stamps to erecting public buildings, which bore upon the arts; and these things, the President felt, ought to serve as an example to the rest of the country. In the busy summer of 1961 he asked Pierre Salinger and me to consider how the White House might take hold of this problem. We recommended that he commission a special consultant to survey the areas where public policy had impact on cultural life and to define the elements of a national cultural program.

I had in mind for the assignment August Heckscher of the Twentieth Century Fund. Heckscher combined artistic sensibility with an astute practical sense of the way government operated. The President invited Heckscher to conduct an inquiry "without fanfare" into the resources, possibilities and limitations of national policy in relation to the arts. "Obviously government can at best play only a marginal role in our cultural affairs," Kennedy told Heckscher. "But I would like to think that it is making its full contribution in this role." Kennedy's caution expressed, as Heckscher later noted, his fear of the vague generalization and the empty gesture.

Heckscher began work as part-time Special Consultant on the Arts in 1962. "The statement of a philosophy of government and the arts," Kennedy told him, "won't be enough. We have to go beyond that now." In the spring of 1963, he assembled numerous practical recommendations—including, as "the logical crowning step in a national cultural arts policy," the establishment of a National Arts Foundation—in a report on "The Arts and the National Government." A few days later Kennedy set up the Advisory Council on the Arts by executive order and prepared to make the Special Consultancy on the Arts a fulltime and permanent office. Since Heckscher wished to return to the Twentieth Century Fund, it was the President's intention to appoint Richard Goodwin to the post.

Kennedy and Heckscher had strong support throughout the government in this effort, especially from two members of the cabinet, Arthur Goldberg and Stewart Udall. Najeeb Halaby, the administrator of the Federal Aviation Agency, set up an expert committee to supervise the design and decoration of airports. In the House of Representatives Frank Thompson and John Lindsay and in the Senate Hubert Humphrey, Claiborne Pell, Joseph Clark and Jacob Javits all fought hard for the cultural effort.

The President and the Attorney General had a particular interest in television. As Senator, Kennedy had told a group of broadcasters that politics and television presented the practitioner with similar problems. "Will the politician's desire for reelection—and the broadcaster's desire for ratings—cause both to flatter every public whim and prejudice—to seek the lowest common denominator of appeal—to put public opinion at all times ahead of the public interest? For myself, I reject that view of politics, and I urge you to reject that view of broadcasting." In order to encourage the industry in this course, Kennedy appointed Newton N. Minow, the old associate of Adlai Stevenson's, as chairman of the Federal Communications Commission; and Minow promptly told the National Association of Broadcasters that, if they would ever watch television from morning to night, "I can assure you that you will observe a vast wasteland." The powers of the FCC chairman were limited; but in the next years Minow not only hit them again and again but obtained laws providing federal aid for educational television and requiring that new television sets receive channels in the ultra-high frequency range. "You keep this up," Kennedy told him on one occasion. "This is one of the really important things." The Attorney General had a special concern for the quality of children's programs. When, to the President's great regret, Minow resigned in 1963, E. William Henry, a protégé of Robert Kennedy's, carried forward his work with comparable humor and force.

The President's commitment to the arts reached its climax in the city of Washington itself. Most Presidents since Jefferson had remained astonishingly indifferent to their immediate surroundings. But Kennedy, with his strong architectural instincts, had a consuming interest in the physical appearance of the capital, and involved himself in plans for the preservation of Lafayette Square and the restoration of Pennsylvania Avenue. "You, sir," said J. Roy Carroll, Jr., the president of the American Institute of Architects, to Kennedy in the spring of 1963, "are the first President of the United States—except, possibly, the first and third ones—who has had a vision of what architecture and its allied arts can mean to the people of the nation, and of what the careful nurturing of the architecture of the city of Washington can mean to the millions who come here to pay homage to the heart of their country." And, in 1964, speaking where Faulkner had spoken exactly six years before, Lewis Mumford described Kennedy as "the first American President to give art, literature and music a place of dignity and honor in our national life."

XXVIII. THE POLITICS OF MODERNITY

THE KENNEDY MESSAGE—self-criticism, wit, ideas, the vision of a civilized society—opened up a new era in the American political consciousness. The President stood, in John P. Roche's valuable phrase, for the politics of modernity. "Liberalism and conservatism," Kennedy remarked one night, "are categories of the thirties, and they don't apply any more.... The trouble with conservatives today is that most of their thinking is so naïve. As for the liberals, their thinking is more sophisticated; but their function ought to be to provide new ideas, and they don't come up with any." His effort was to dissolve the myths which had masked the emerging realities in both domestic and foreign affairs. His hope was to lead the nation beyond the obsessive issues of the past and to call forth the new perceptions required for the contemporary world.

1. THE PRESIDENCY OF THE YOUNG

It was no accident therefore that he made his most penetrating appeal precisely to those who were coming of age in this contemporary world and who were most free of the legacies of historic controversy. Indeed, nothing in the Kennedy years was more spectacular than the transformation of American youth.

In the fifties the young men and women of the nation had seemed to fall into two groups. The vast majority were the 'silent generation,' the 'uncommitted generation,' the 'careful young men,' the 'men in the gray flannel suits'—a generation fearful of politics, incurious about society, mistrustful of ideas, desperate about personal security. A small minority, rejecting this respectable world as absurd, defected from it and became beats and hipsters, 'rebels without a cause.' Pervading both groups was a profound sense of impotence—a feeling that the social order had to be taken as a whole or repudiated as a whole and was beyond the power of the individual to change.

Probably attitudes were all beginning to change; but the coming of Kennedy certainly made them change very much faster. He was the first President since Franklin Roosevelt who had anything to say to men and women under the age of twenty-five, perhaps the only President with whom youth could thoroughly identify itself—and this at a time when there were more young people both in the population and the colleges than ever before. His very role and personality, moreover—his individuality in a homogenized society, his wholeness in a specialized society, his freedom in a mechanized society—undermined the conviction of impotence. If the President of the United States seemed almost a contemporary, then political action—even picketing—no longer appeared so ludicrous or futile.

The New Frontier gospel of criticism and hope stirred the finest instincts of the young; it restored a sense of innovation and adventure to the republic. The silent campuses suddenly exploded with political and intellectual activity. Young people running for office explained that Kennedy had made politics respectable; what perhaps they more often meant was that he had made it rational. The Civil Service Commission reported a great increase in college graduates wanting to work for the government. The Peace Corps was only the most dramatic form of the new idealism.

The very qualities which made Kennedy exciting to the youth made him disturbing to many of his contemporaries and elders. For his message was a threat to established patterns of emotion and ideology. The politics of modernity was intolerable for the true believers. This accounts, I believe, for the ambiguity with which the radical left regarded Kennedy and the hatred which the radical right came to concentrate on him.

2. KENNEDY AND THE LEFT: IDEAS

From the start of the republic American progressivism had had two strains, related but distinct. The pragmatic strain accepted, without wholly approving, the given structure of society and aimed to change it by action from within. The utopian strain rejected the given structure of society, root and branch, and aimed to change it by exhortation and example from without. Both were impatient with established complacencies and pieties. Both recognized that the great constant in history was change. But the problem of power split them. The pragmatists accepted the responsibility of power—and thereby risked corruption. The utopians refused complicity with power—and thereby risked irrelevance.

Both strains were much alive in the Kennedy years. The administration itself expressed the spirit of liberal pragmatism; and other liberal pragmatists in Congress and elsewhere urged only that it do so with greater audacity and force. Hence mild tensions sometimes existed between the administration and its logical allies. Kennedy and much of the White House staff retained a suspicion of the ritualistic liberal as someone more intent on virtuous display than on practical result; moreover, criticism was harder to take from friends than from enemies. As for the liberals on the Hill, they were sometimes hurt and resentful, as their predecessors had been toward Roosevelt a quarter-century earlier, when the President seemed to be compromising too much and sticking too close to the southern Democrats in the leadership. Hubert Humphrey was our most effective liberal in Congress; after one bitter debate he said wearily to me, "It's hard for us down here to keep on defending the things we think the White House believes in when the White House seems to spend its time saying nice things about the other side."

But the pragmatic liberals, if they often wished the administration to move faster, had no doubt that it was *their* administration and held faith in the President's basic purpose and therefore an unwillingness to draw drastic conclusions from temporary tactics. As for Kennedy, despite occasional annoyance over the refusal of some liberals to understand the constraints on presidential action, he knew at bottom that over the long run pressure from the left increased his freedom of maneuver.

The liberals who did not like power constituted a different problem. The nuclear age had given the recoil from power new intensity. Since Hiroshima many liberals and

THE COVER OF *LOOK* MAGAZINE, JANUARY 2, 1962, DEPICTING KENNEDY AS THE PRESIDENT OF THE VERY YOUNG.

intellectuals had been reluctant to identify themselves with anything done by government.

Such people now viewed the Kennedy administration with deep suspicion. The President in their mind was the Tempter, using the allurements of power, charm, wealth and flattery to seduce their brethren into betraying their vocation and becoming the tools of what C. Wright Mills had called "the power elite." Kennedy's air of interest in ideas and the arts seemed only the latest and most diabolical Establishment ruse to defeat dissent by absorbing it. Those who succumbed to the temptation, the critics argued, would pay a heavy price both in weakening that principled opposition to power which was the duty of an intellectual community and in debasing themselves. Alfred Kazin concluded in a piece not without some highly perceptive passages, "Kennedy's shrewd awareness of what intellectuals can do, even his undoubted inner respect for certain writers, scholars and thinkers, is irrelevant to the tragic issues and contributes nothing to their solution. To be an 'intellectual' is the latest style in American success, the mark of our manipulable society."

Kazin expressed a wholly legitimate belief that one role for intellectuals was that of unremitting hostility to power. But was that the only role? It seemed to me that there was also a strong case for intellectuals so inclined to take part in government if only to provide a link between the political and the intellectual communities. The process of mediation might well give the intellectual community more impact on the political process than if it remained in solid and permanent opposition. It seemed hard to argue, moreover, that serious intellectuals were inexorably corrupted by public responsibility; this had hardly happened to Keynes or to MacLeish or to Berle in the thirties, to Murrow or Galbraith or Heller now. That was not to say that intellectuals made a great deal of difference to government, or that intellectuals in government always kept faith with their own ideals. Nonetheless, if intellectuals decided to abandon government to non-intellectuals, they would have only themselves to blame for the result.

3. KENNEDY AND THE LEFT: POLICIES

Where the utopian left felt more than a generalized mistrust of power, it objected to both the foreign and domestic policies of the administration. In foreign affairs, some regarded the cold war as the invention of the military-industrial complex and supposed that, if only Washington changed its course, Moscow and Peking would gladly collaborate in building a peaceful world. This had been somewhat the Indian view—or at least until the Chinese crossed the Himalayas and reality broke out. Others, while seeing communism as a problem and the cold war as a reality, felt that resistance involved too great a risk and were gloomily prepared to endure a communist world if that would avert a nuclear holocaust: better red than dead. Both groups condemned the policy of nuclear deterrence. Both identified themselves a bit self-righteously with 'peace' as if everyone who disagreed with them wanted to blow up the world. Both yearned for total solutions. And for both the proper United States policy was unilateral disarmament and neutralism.

Thus Professor Stuart Hughes, the Harvard historian, advised the United States in his book *An Approach to Peace* to seek "a new model for foreign policy in the experience of Sweden or of Switzerland, or even of India." The mission of the American intellectual, as Hughes saw it, was to do what the Asians and Africans had thus far failed to do and define neutralism "as a faith and a way of life."

In domestic affairs, the contribution of the utopian left was unimpressive, except in the civil rights effort, in which its members played a brave and valuable part. On other relevant issues the left made few original contributions. They acted as if they were crying out great ideas in the wilderness which the political leaders studiously ignored. In fact, the political leaders themselves were begging for usable ideas—and not finding any. Even Michael Harrington's book on poverty came along half a dozen years after Averell Harriman had begun a poverty program as governor of New York.

The utopian critique still had value perhaps in its sheer intransigence, though nothing more infuriated the utopians than to be patted on the shoulder and told that society needed their nonconformity. The crime of 'incorporating the critic into the consensus' was quite naturally regarded as the dirtiest trick of all. If dissent was punished, terrible; if embraced, worse.

The Bay of Pigs had quite understandably thrust the utopian left into bitter opposition; and a curious episode later in 1961 turned its members even more bitterly against the administration. This was the furor which followed the President's request, made originally in May and repeated with emphasis in his July speech on the Berlin crisis, for a fallout shelter program. The proposal was sensible enough. Any President, living in a world of possible nuclear war and knowing that things could be done to save the lives of twenty or thirty million people if war came, would have been plainly delinquent if he had declined to ask for them. Earlier both Truman and Eisenhower had urged civil defense measures, only to have the nation regard the problem with supreme boredom. Now in the Berlin context it acquired, or seemed to acquire, a frightening reality. Before anyone was aware what was happening, a condition of national panic seemed to be boiling up. Get-rich-quick shelter manufacturers arose on every side. Many on the utopian left feared that the program, if it were not actual preparation for a surprise nuclear attack on the Soviet Union, would at the very least give the American people a false sense of security and therefore encourage them in reckless foreign adventures. Within the United States itself they perceived it as an incitement to vigilantism if not a means by which the radical right could seize control of local communities. The program, in short, became in their minds a portent of preventive war and fascism.

Civil defense policy, in the meantime, was in a state of unjustifiable confusion. As the Defense Department had first conceived the problem, each family was to dig for itself. To advance the cause the Pentagon hired Madison Avenue specialists to prepare a shelter instruction booklet intended for distribution to every householder. This was a singular document. In the draft submitted to the White House, it did not make clear that American policy was to avoid a holocaust; and it offered a relatively sanguine picture both of life in the shelter and of the world into which people would emerge after the attack. Moreover, it seemed to be addressed exclusively to the upper middle class—to people owning houses with gardens or basements; there was nothing in it for those who lived in tenements.

Kennedy, while unshaken in his belief that defense against fallout was a necessary form of national insurance, was dismayed both by the booklet and the public reaction. He remarked ruefully that he wished he had never said the things which had stirred the matter up and wanted to diminish the excitement as expeditiously as possible. Carl Kaysen and I, who were following the problem for the White House, concluded that the do-it-yourself family shelter theory was a disaster and that the only fair and rational policy would be one of public community shelters. The Defense Department itself was reaching the same conclusion. The President speedily decided in favor of the public program. The Defense Department rewrote its pamphlet and, instead of putting it in every mailbox, left copies at post offices for concerned citizens. Thereafter the shelter panic subsided.

This episode, following too soon after the Bay of Pigs, seemed to many on the left a further horrible revelation of the inner essence of the administration. Kennedy was well aware of this disaffection among the radical intellectuals. He used to say that Adlai Stevenson could still beat him in Madison, Wisconsin, or in Berkeley, California—even perhaps in Cambridge, Massachusetts. Yet, most of the radicals, even at their most critical, felt a sense of reluctant kinship with the President. Kennedy was too bright, too attractive, too *contemporary* to be wholly disowned. He had fortified their own feelings of self-respect. He had made them feel in some way more at home in their own country.

4. KENNEDY AND THE RADICAL RIGHT

There was no question of a family quarrel with the radical right—and the fury of the right-wing response to Kennedy was a measure of his impact on the nation. If the intellectuals did not always recognize a friend, the reactionaries lost no time in recognizing an enemy.

The burst of right-wing activity in the early sixties was a predictable historical phenomenon. In conservative periods, like the fifties, the radical right was characteristically disorganized and dormant. Its members were soothed by the eternal hope that a conservative administration might do something they would like. The existence of friends—or at least of nodding acquaintances—in Washington restrained them from major organizational efforts on their own.

But the election of a progressive administration generally has a galvanizing effect on the radical right. It grows desperate, convinced that the nation is in mortal danger, that it is five minutes before midnight, that it must rally and resist before it is too late. This happened in the early thirties under Roosevelt. It happened again under Kennedy in the sixties.

I first heard of the John Birch Society in an early-warning letter in December 1960 from that fine old progressive Republican Alfred M. Landon. One heard a great deal more of it and similar groups in the months following. The radical right appealed especially to the incoherent resentment of the frightened rich and the anxious middle class. It flourished particularly in states like California and Texas, overflowing with raw new money; in states like Arizona and Florida, where older people had retired on their pensions; and in small towns in the mountain states, where shopkeepers felt themselves harassed by big business, big labor and big government. The mood was one of longing for a dreamworld of no communism, no overseas entanglements, no United Nations, no federal government, no labor unions, no Negroes or foreigners—a world in which Chief Justice Warren would be impeached, Cuba invaded, the graduated income tax repealed, the fluoridation of drinking water stopped and the import of Polish hams forbidden.

In domestic policy the philosophy of the radical right was well stated by Senator Strom Thurmond, who stated that "many of the domestic programs advocated in the United States, and many of those adopted, fall clearly within the category of socialism." In foreign policy the radical right, like the radical left, derived much of its early impetus from the Bay of Pigs, though it drew the opposite conclusion. It now rallied behind Senator Barry Goldwater, echoing his opposition to a "no-win" policy and his call for "total victory."

President Kennedy felt deep concern at the spread of extremism, right and left. This concern was related, I feel sure, to his sense of the latent streak of violence under the surface of American life: the sun o'ercast with blood, the nation torn asunder and dismembered. "We are a frontier country," James V. Bennett, the federal director of prisons, told the Senate Subcommittee on Juvenile Delinquency, "and we have certain elements in our background and culture that incline us to the use of weapons more than some other countries in the world." The tension and anonymity of urban life had further sharpened the impulse to violence. Every day the television industry instructed the children of the nation how easily problems could be solved by revolver shots. Fortifying the Gunsmoke ethic was a mood of national self-righteousness—the happy conviction of American uniqueness, which smoothed out and washed away the cruelties and sins of the past and which now licensed for Americans acts which, if performed by Russians or Chinese, would have seemed instinct with evil.

Early in November 1961 the President observed that an age of insoluble problems, he observed, breeds extremism, hysteria, a weakness for simple and passionate solutions. "There are two groups of these frustrated citizens," he soon said at the University of Washington in Seattle, one group urging the pathway of surrender, the other the pathway of war.

> *It is a curious fact that each of these two extreme opposites resembles the other. Each believes that we have only two choices: appeasement or war, suicide or surrender, humiliation or holocaust, to be either Red or dead.*

Against the left he urged the indispensability of strength; against the right, the indispensability of negotiation. But the challenge to the right was the main burden of the speech. "At a time when a single clash could escalate over night into a holocaust of mushroom clouds, a great power does not prove its firmness by leaving the task of exploring the other's intentions to sentries."

4. THE POLITICS OF RESENTMENT

A few days later 1800 delegates attended a meeting of the National Indignation Convention at the Memorial Auditorium in Dallas, Texas. One speaker, to the delight of the crowd, complained that the chairman of the meeting had turned moderate: "All he wants to do is impeach Warren—I'm for hanging him."* General Walker himself had now retired to Dallas to advocate the cause of the John Birch Society. Other right-wing organizations were trundling their wares across the country, like the Christian Anti-Communism Crusade of Dr. Fred Schwarz and the Christian Crusade of the Reverend Billy James Hargis. Even further to the right the Minutemen were drilling their members in guerrilla tactics to deal with Soviet invasion or other unspecified contingencies. In the outskirts of Washington itself, George Lincoln Rockwell was recruiting pimply youths for an American Nazi party.

The spectrum of the right ran all the way from the amiability of Barry Goldwater to the lunacy of the outer fringe. The press reported much of this with surprising solemnity. In the summer of 1962 New York right-wingers, convinced that Nelson Rockefeller and Jacob Javits were beyond redemption, organized the Conservative Party. When *Life* ran a skeptical story about Fred Schwarz, the outcry from Schwarz's backers, some of whom were national advertisers, induced *Life*'s publisher, C. D. Jackson, to fly to a Schwarz rally in the Hollywood Bowl and offer a public apology. Aided by such reverent treatment, the right wing grew, if not more popular, at least richer, and the contributors included a number of leading industrial families and their family foundations.

The more frenetic right-wing agitation focused more and more directly on the President and his family. Every President, of course, provokes his quota of more or less good-natured jokes, and so did Kennedy. In Texas businessmen passed out cards saying "I MISS IKE" and then, in lower case, "Hell, I even miss Harry." The Kennedy cocktail? Stocks on the rocks. "Caroline Kennedy is certainly a nice kid. But that's the last time we should let her plan a Cuban invasion." The Kennedy rocking chair as the symbol of the New Frontier: you get the feeling of moving but you don't go anywhere. If Jack, Bobby and Teddy were on a sinking boat, who would be saved? The country. "Truman showed that anyone can be President, Ike that no one could be President, Kennedy that it can be dangerous to have a President."

But in the domain of the radical right it all became much sicker and nastier. Not since the high point of the hate-Roosevelt enthusiasm of the mid-thirties had any President been the target of such systematic and foul vilification. Everything about Kennedy fed resentment: his appearance, his religion, his wealth, his intelligence, his university, his section of the country, his wife, his brothers, his advisers, his support of the Negroes, his determination to de-emotionalize the cold war, his refusal to drop the bomb.

All this encouraged the unthinking and the vicious to cherish their threats and hatreds. In the two years after November 1961 the Secret Service investigated thirty-four threats against the President's life from the state of Texas alone.

Kennedy, who disliked the very thought of an 'age of hate,' mobilized the weapons of reason to fight the spreading hatreds of his own land, beginning his education of the public before his first year was over. But he knew that reason by itself could not be enough. Once again, he fell back on his most powerful weapon—himself; on his own willingness to attest by example his faith in American rationality and

* The speaker was J. Evetts Haley, whose book, *A Texan Looks at Lyndon*, was one of the more scurrilous contributions to the 1964 campaign.

decency, on his own determination, as Norman Mailer said in a flash of insight, to define "the nature of our reality for us by his actions." Kennedy was in this sense the existential hero, though the term would have amused or depressed him. So in November of 1961 he chose to carry his attack on extremism into the city of Los Angeles where four weeks before the publisher of *Life* had publicly apologized to Fred Schwarz. So in the future he never hesitated to define America by his presence and courage in the heart of the enemy's country.

5. THE TRIAL OF 1962

In this swirling mood of emotion Kennedy prepared to confront his first national electoral test—the congressional elections of 1962. The radical right, despite the Conservative Party of New York, constituted, of course, a tiny minority of the electorate and the radical left, despite Stuart Hughes, a tinier still. The great majority of the voters remained in the orbit of conventional politics. But the probabilities were always against the party in power in a mid-term election.

"History is so much against us," Kennedy mused at a press conference. "[Yet] if we can hold our own, if we can win five seats or ten seats, it would change the whole opinion in the House and in the Senate." No one thought this likely. In August the Gallup poll reported that twenty-four of the thirty-five marginal Democratic seats were in danger. Meanwhile Kennedy pondered his own role in the campaign. In 1962, the President asked me to check the record on presidential intervention in mid-term elections. I reported back that, while presidential intervention had steadily increased in the course of the century, there was no evidence that it had ever played a significant role. Roosevelt, for example, had made only 'non-political' speeches during the great Democratic triumph of 1934; while Eisenhower's campaigns of 1954 and 1958—the most extensive ever undertaken by a President in mid-term elections—had not succeeded in staving off Democratic victories. My memorandum suggested that "the most fruitful form of presidential participation" was the non-political tour, quoting Theodore Roosevelt: "'The most effective political speeches are often those that are nominally not political speeches at all.' History," the memorandum concluded, "suggests that it would be a mistake … to turn the 1962 mid-term election into a test of personal confidence by actively intervening in the form of personal endorsement or advocacy of (or opposition to) individual candidates."

Kennedy wisely ignored both the memorandum and history. He already planned a non-political tour to dedicate dams in mid-August, and he undertook another in early September. But he plainly felt under wraps. Given his sense of the politics of modernity, he may subconsciously have perceived that he himself was the best argument for his issues and that the best hope was to turn the mid-term election precisely into a test of personal confidence. Campaigning, moreover, was a refreshing experience; he always returned cheerful and rejuvenated. I can remember his coming back enormously invigorated from New Jersey after his last-minute entry into the gubernatorial campaign in 1961, saying that the crowds lining the streets reminded him where his support really lay—and that most of them couldn't care less whether the budget was balanced or not. He acknowledged that in the past "fate usually didn't seem to be affected" by what Presidents had done; but "I've never believed that precedents really mean anything in politics. From my own personal experience as well as for other reasons, just because it happened this way in the past doesn't mean anything. The question really is, can we interest enough people to understand how important the congressional election of 1962 is? And that is my function."

In the end he traveled more miles in the campaign of 1962 than Eisenhower had in 1954 and 1958 put together. His central theme was to establish the difference in domestic policy between the two parties. "We have won and lost vote after vote by one or two or three votes in the Senate, and three, four or five votes in the House of Representatives," he would say, "and I don't think we can find jobs for our people, I don't think we can educate our younger people, I don't think we can provide security for our older citizens, when we have a party which votes 'no.'" He would conclude with sharpening voice and stabbing hand: "And that's why this election is important."

XXIX. BATTLE FOR THE HEMISPHERE

1962 HAD NOT BEEN A BAD YEAR: the Berlin crisis over, a settlement in Laos, aggression checked in Vietnam, the Congo straightening out, favorable developments in the rest of Africa, United States Steel chastened, expansion resuming in the American economy. But the problems of the western hemisphere remained acute. "I regard Latin America," the President said early in 1963, "as the most critical area in the world today." The Alliance for Progress, announced with such hope in the brisk March of 1961, had offered Latin America the possibility of a democratic revolution. But in many countries the practical foundations of the Alliance were shaky. Moreover, since the Alliance by its very existence warned Fidel Castro that he could no longer count on the Latin American states falling to Marxist revolution of their own weight, the *Fidelistas* and their communist allies were redoubling their efforts to disrupt the democratic effort and seize the energies of change for themselves. The struggle for the future of Latin America was well joined—and the outcome thus far indeterminate.

The President sought to place our hemisphere policy in the ablest possible hands. Adolf Berle as chairman of the Task Force on Latin America continued to recommend the creation of the post of Under Secretary of State for Latin American Affairs, controlling both political and economic lines of policy; but this was predictably opposed by the State Department on bureaucratic grounds. When Thomas Mann left Washington shortly before the Bay of Pigs to become ambassador to Mexico, Kennedy wanted to persuade some figure of public consequence to take his place as Assistant Secretary of State for Inter-American Affairs. The search was frustrating and lost many valuable weeks. During this time the daily conduct of Latin American affairs remained in the hands of the permanent government—blasé officials in the State Department and the aid agency who believed that they alone understood the *Latinos* and dismissed the Alliance for Progress as a slogan left over from the presidential campaign.

They were decent and hard-working people. But their uncritical commitment to the conceptions of the fifties—to conservative regimes in politics and to private initiative and technical assistance in economics—hardly equipped them to compete with Fidel Castro for the allegiance of a continent in revolutionary ferment. And, as they began to realize that the new President meant business, they seemed to feel threatened by the new policy, as if they feared it would swallow up their own responsibilities and sense of significance.

1. THE CHARTER OF PUNTA DEL ESTE

The conviction among the bureaucrats that, if only they sat tight, the Alliance for Progress would go away left the initiative to the White House, to Berle's Task Force, increasingly isolated within State, and to the Treasury Department, where Douglas Dillon's long and enlightened interest in Latin America now had the able support of Assistant Secretary John Leddy. It was this situation which led in the spring to the stream of complaints from the State Department, about 'meddling' in hemisphere policy. It can be flatly said that without such meddling there would have been no Alliance for Progress.

The Alliance rested on the premise that modernization in Latin America required not just injections of capital or technical assistance but the breaking of the bottlenecks of economic development through reform of the political and social structure. It was formally organized in August 1961 at an Inter-American Economic and Social Council conference held in Punta del Este, Uruguay. In his message to the conference Kennedy defined his conception of the occasion with great clarity. "We live in a hemisphere," he said, "whose own revolution has given birth to the most powerful forces of the modern age—the search for the freedom and self-fulfillment of man. We meet to carry on that revolution to shape the future." This meant "full recognition of the right of all the people to share fully in our progress. For there is no place in democratic life for institutions which benefit the few while denying the needs of the many, even though the elimination of such institutions may require far-reaching and difficult changes such as land reform and tax reform and a vastly increased emphasis on education and health and housing. Without these changes our common effort cannot succeed." No President of the United States had ever spoken such words to Latin America before. He concluded with an appeal for the participation "of workers and farmers, businessmen and intellectuals and, above all, of the young people of the Americas."

Douglas Dillon, the head of the United States delegation, struck the same note. "This is a revolutionary task," he told the Latin Americans, "but we are no strangers to revolution.... The fruits of the American revolution have not yet been extended to all our people. Throughout the hemisphere millions still live with hunger, poverty and despair. They have been denied access to the benefits of modern knowledge and technology. And they now demand those benefits for themselves and for their children. We cannot rest content until these just demands are met."

Che Guevara was there too, smoothly arguing the case for the competing revolution. Some Latin Americans, indeed, wanted to include Cuba in the Alliance. But others, led by Pedro Beltrán of Peru, the conference's chairman, countered the Cubans with a Declaration to the Peoples of America placing the principles of the Alliance in a firm context of representative democracy and political freedom. The confrontation between Guevara and Dillon in the last session gave the meeting its moment of drama. Guevara told the Latin Americans that they had Castro to thank for this sudden offer of massive United States aid. Observing that

DOUGLAS DILLON, THE HEAD OF THE U.S. DELEGATION TO PUNTA DEL ESTE.

Cuba was in sympathy with many of the Alliance's objectives, he said that, as the instrument of imperialism, the Alliance was bound to fail; Cuba would therefore abstain. Guevara's moderation was itself striking evidence of the Alliance's initial appeal. Dillon was cool and effective in rebuttal. Then twenty American republics pledged themselves to a series of quite startling goals:

To improve and strengthen democratic institutions through application of the principle of self-determination by the people.
To accelerate economic and social development....
To carry out urban and rural housing programs to provide decent homes for all our people.
To encourage ... programs of comprehensive agrarian reform, leading to the effective transformation, where required, of unjust structures and systems of land tenure and use; with a view to replacing latifundia and dwarf holdings by an equitable system of property....
To assure fair wages and satisfactory working conditions to all our workers....
To wipe out illiteracy....
To press forward with programs of health and sanitation....
To reform tax laws, demanding more from those who have most, to punish tax evasion severely, and to redistribute the national income in order to benefit those who are most in need, while, at the same time, promoting savings and investment and reinvestment of capital....
To maintain monetary and fiscal policies which ... will protect the purchasing power of the many, guarantee the greatest possible price stability, and form an adequate basis for economic development.
To stimulate private enterprise....
To find a quick and lasting solution to the grave problem created by excessive price fluctuations in the basic exports....
To accelerate the integration of Latin America....
To this end the United States will provide a major part of the minimum of 20 billion dollars, principally in public funds, which Latin America will require over the next ten years from all external sources in order to supplement its own efforts....
For their part, as a contribution to the Alliance for Progress, each of the countries of Latin America will formulate a comprehensive and well-conceived national program for the development of its own economy.

The Charter of Punta del Este was a summons to a democratic revolution—nor was revolution a word feared by the architects of the Alliance, even though it continued to dismay the Department of State. Of course most of the governments endorsing this summons were far from revolutionary. Some no doubt joined because they considered American aid worth a signature; others because, as President Alberto Lleras Camargo of Colombia once put it, "In Latin America, perhaps more than anywhere else in the world, political leaders have the habit of carrying revolutionary statements beyond the point to which they are really prepared to go." The American negotiators had no illusions about the mixture of motives, nor did they suppose that setting fine words down on parchment would have magical effects. But they knew that the commitment of twenty governments to this unprecedented set of goals strengthened those in each country who sought democratic progress.

This included the government in Washington. The trip to Vienna, the Berlin crisis, the debate over nuclear test resumption, the reform of the aid program—all the problems of the summer of 1961 had further slowed the reorganization of our own Latin American management. Failing to find an outsider of sufficient stature as Assistant Secretary for Inter-American Affairs, the President in July appointed Robert F. Woodward, an intelligent and liberal-minded career officer, wholeheartedly devoted to the Alliance, then serving as ambassador to Chile. Berle, his assignment valuably completed, resigned. In the fall Kennedy sent Richard Goodwin over to serve as Woodward's deputy. In the White House the President himself, with some help, after Goodwin's departure, from Ralph Dungan and me, continued to keep an exceedingly vigilant eye on hemisphere developments.

In November, Kennedy appointed as AID Deputy for Latin America Teodoro Moscoso, who had been Economic Development Administrator under Governor Luis Muñoz Marín in Puerto Rico and was now ambassador to Venezuela.

He could have found no one more deeply dedicated to the spirit of Punta del Este. The Puerto Rican experience, indeed, was an important source of the ideas behind the Alliance. Puerto Rico was being transformed from miserable circumstances into a thriving community. During the fifties it provided both a refuge and something of an inspiration for democratic Latin Americans exiled by their own countries. Muñoz, convinced that these progressive leaders offered the best hope for the continent, now argued forthrightly that in the long run only the democratic left could make the Alliance work. They constituted the one group "which *wants* it to succeed in its entirety ... the group which seeks social advances and higher living standards for *all* the people in a framework of freedom and consent...the only nontotalitarian element which understands the depths of the revolutionary ferment in Latin America and which can provide responsible leadership to shape this revolution into constructive channels."

2. THE DEMOCRATIC REVOLUTION

Muñoz's formulation was a succinct statement of the philosophy implicit in the Punta del Este Charter. Though the Alliance included dictatorial regimes like those of Stroessner in Paraguay and Duvalier in Haiti, its principles were progressive democratic principles and its affinities were with progressive democratic governments. Adolf Berle made the point in his final report as chairman of the Task Force:

THE PRESIDENT MAKES HIS REMARKS UPON THE DEPARTURE OF THE DELEGATION TO PUNTA DEL ESTE, AUGUST 2, 1961.

The present struggle will not be won, and can be lost, by opportunist support of transitory power-holders or forces whose objectives are basically hostile to the peoples they dominate. Success of the American effort in Latin America requires that at all times its policy be based on clear, consistent, moral democratic principles. I do not see that any other policy can be accepted or indeed stands any real chance of ultimate success. The forces sweeping Latin America today demand progress, and a better life for the masses of their people, through evolution if possible, or through revolution if that price must be paid. A preponderance of these forces want the resulting forms to provide liberty, rejecting tyranny whether from the right or from the left.

In Latin America the democratic left comprised two major strains: the *partido populares*, which had battled for social democracy in various countries of Central and South America since the Second World War under far-sighted men like Rómulo Betancourt of Venezuela and José Figueres of Costa Rica but which now was becoming a little the movement of an older generation; and the Christian Democrats, emerging as a significant force in Chile and Venezuela and appealing to younger people in other countries. In Venezuela the two strains combined in support of the Betancourt government. For this and other reasons, some of us in Washington saw Venezuela as a model for Latin American progressive democracy (remembering always that its oil revenues gave it a margin of wealth the other republics lacked). Betancourt, who had spent a good share of his exile in Puerto Rico, had brought back to Venezuela plans and institutions derived from the Puerto Rican experience. A rugged fighter for democracy, he was hated by both right and left: Trujillo's assassins had tried to kill him, and Castro's terrorists were seeking now to destroy his government. Resisting radical action urged by both sides, he vowed not to deviate from the course laid down for me by the fundamental law of Venezuela and by my own conscience."

No one in Washington understood this course better than the President. He wholly accepted the thesis of the democratic revolution and therefore on his first presidential trip to Latin America in December 1961 chose to visit two presidents notable for their commitment to progressive reform—Betancourt in Caracas and Alberto Lleras Camargo in Bogotá.

No one need have worried. Wildly enthusiastic crowds lined the streets in Caracas and the next day in Bogotá. "Do you know why those workers and *campensinos* are cheering you like that?" Lleras Camargo asked Kennedy. "It's because they believe you are on their side." That night at the San Carlos Palace the American President set forth the promise of the Alliance. "We in the United States," he said, "have made many mistakes in our relations with Latin America. We have not always understood the magnitude of your problems, or accepted our share of responsibility for the welfare of the hemisphere. But we are committed in the United States—our will and our energy—to an untiring pursuit of that welfare and I have come to this country to reaffirm that dedication." Then he said, "The leaders of Latin America, the industrialists and the landowners, are, I am sure, also ready to admit past mistakes and accept new responsibilities."

Each year he made a Latin American trip, with the democratic revolution his constant theme. He seized every opportunity to signify his respect for men like Betancourt and Lleras.

3. THE SHOWCASE THAT FAILED

The President's emphasis was absolutely correct. Democratic leadership in the Latin countries was fundamental to the success of the Alliance. Without it United States aid and exhortation could do little. If anyone had doubted this proposition, it received full verification in the tribulations of the Dominican Republic. Since 1930 Rafael Trujillo had operated a cruel and efficient dictatorship on the eastern half of the lovely but tragic old Spanish island of Hispaniola. His oppression of his own people was considered beyond the reach of the Organization of American States; but, when he sent his agents to Caracas to kill Betancourt, the OAS rallied and in August 1960 recommended that its members break ambassadorial relations with Trujillo and embargo the import of arms and petroleum. In early 1961 Washington began to hear increasing reports of unrest on the island. On May 30 a group of disgruntled army officers stopped Trujillo's car late one night and shot him down.

The assassination took Washington by surprise. The President, who was then in Paris on his visit to de Gaulle, was confronted on his return by a Dominican regime under Joaquín Balaguer, who had been the nominal president under Trujillo, with Trujillo's son Ramfis still in charge of the armed forces. Kennedy examined the situation realistically. "There are three possibilities," he said, "in descending order of preference: a decent democratic regime, a continuation of the Trujillo regime or a Castro regime. We ought to aim at the first, but we really can't renounce the second until we are sure that we can avoid the third."

The problem was whether a country where potential political leadership had been suppressed, murdered or exiled for more than a generation could easily acquire the instincts and skills of self-government. For the next three months the President endeavored to assess the democratic prospects. The accumulating information suggested that Balaguer was making an honest attempt to bring about a transition to democracy. The presence of young Trujillo remained troubling, however; and his control of the army presumably limited our capacity to do anything about him. Toward the end of August the State Department proposed that we try to induce the army, Balaguer, Ramfis Trujillo and the moderate opposition to stick together in order to lay the foundations for movement toward self-government. Kennedy agreed. "Balaguer is our only tool," he said. "The anti-communist liberals aren't strong enough. We must use our influence to take Balaguer along the road to democracy." The intricate factional differences within the opposition represented enormous obstacles, but Kennedy counseled patience and vigilance, emphasizing that the whole key in all those countries is the emergence of a leader—a liberal figure who can command popular support as against the military and who will carry out social and economic reform—a Nehru or a Muñoz. No such figure has emerged. We don't know who he will be. The great danger in the next six months is a take-over by the army, which could lead straight to Castro.

In the Dominican Republic the democratic opposition insisted on the expulsion of Ramfis Trujillo as the condition for any rapprochement with Balaguer. Washington instructed its representatives there to support this view. Finally in mid-November Ramfis agreed to leave the country. But the next day two of his uncles made an unexpected return to the island, Ramfis canceled his departure and the developments seemed to portend a military coup to restore the Trujillo family to power. Washington read the cables with rising concern. The President directed the Secretary of State to put out a statement saying that the United States would not remain indifferent if the Trujillos attempted to "reassert dictatorial domination." Then Kennedy decided on a bold stroke: the dispatch of eight American ships, with 1800 Marines on board, to steam visibly off Santo Domingo just outside the three-mile limit, ready to go in if the Balaguer government asked for them. Given the ingrained Latin American hatred of gunboat diplomacy, this course involved obvious risks. On the other hand, it would be, for once, Yankee intervention to sustain a democratic movement rather than to destroy it, and the President was prepared to take his chance.

We waited with some apprehension until surprising and heartening word came in from Santo Domingo. It must have been a unique moment in Latin American history: the people dancing in the streets, cheering the United States fleet and shouting enthusiastic *vivas* for the *gringos*. The presence of the fleet encouraged General Pedro Rodríguez Echavarría of the air force to rise against Ramfis. The Trujillos quickly fled, this time for good; and Kennedy's action won commendation throughout Latin America. Only Fidel Castro objected. The incident provided striking evidence of the change in Latin American attitudes Kennedy had wrought in the seven months since the Bay of Pigs.

But the ordeal of Dominican democracy was just beginning.* As Washington saw the problem, transition to democracy required the broadening of the Balaguer government by the incorporation of representatives of the disparate democratic groups opposed to *Trujillismo*.

Strenuous efforts were made after the Trujillos' downfall to bring these elements together, but the animosities and suspicions engendered by the *Trujillista* period made mediation a thankless task. Eventually President Kennedy made a personal appeal to Balaguer and Rodríguez Echavarria. His intervention was the catalyst that made possible the establishment of a Council of State, committed to a program of political democracy and the preparation of elections. When Rodríguez Echavarría, who hated the Unión, Cívica, then attempted a coup, the popular reaction defeated him.

The Council was never a strong government; but it brought peace and personal freedom to the Dominican Republic and in December 1962, with the technical assistance of the OAS, it held the only democratic election that the people had known in generations. The election resulted in the victory of Juan Bosch, who had returned the year before from twenty years of exile. An old friend of Muñoz, Figueres and Betancourt, Bosch was strongly in the progressive democratic tradition. "The Alliance for Progress," he said after the election, "is a political and economic ideal for which we, the democratic, revolutionary leaders of Latin America, have been fighting for a long time." Kennedy instructed our government to give Bosch full support, hoping that the Dominican Republic might become a democratic showcase in the Caribbean.

But Bosch was essentially a literary figure, better as short story writer than as statesman. In spite of the invasion of the islands by swarms of Washington economists and engineers, of foundation experts and private consultants, in spite of grants and loans and blueprints, the Bosch government was not able in 1963 to reduce unemployment or prepare a national development program. Even had he been a Nehru or a Muñoz he would have confronted problems of overwhelming difficulty: a nation without democratic tradition or experience, a government without trained administrators, an army dominated by *Trujillistas* and an economy burdened by a staggering inheritance of foreign debt.

Kennedy watched the Dominican troubles with disappointment but not with much surprise. It confirmed his sense both of the limited capacity of the United States to work unilateral miracles and of the dependence of the Alliance on Latin American leadership.

4. COMMUNISM IN THE WINGS

The Alliance for Progress represented the affirmative side of Kennedy's policy. The other side was his absolute determination to prevent any new state from going down the Castro road and so giving the Soviet Union a second bridgehead in the hemisphere.

It was idle to suppose that communism in Latin America was no more than the expression of an indigenous desire for social reform. Latin America had long occupied an honored place in Leninist meditations about the future of world politics. Not only were Marxist ideas far more relevant to Latin American feudalism than they were, for example, to African tribalism, but communist success in Latin America would deal a much harder blow to the power and influence of the United States. Communist parties had existed for forty years in the major countries. Latin Americans, regularly summoned to training schools in Moscow or Prague, learning everything from political doctrine to paramilitary warfare, carried their lessons back to their homelands. Khrushchev himself made no secret of his hopes for the western hemisphere.

Communism had both targets of priority and targets of convenience in Latin America. Venezuela and Brazil, for example, seemed to be the chief targets of priority. The main target of convenience in 1961—that is, one which became attractive less for intrinsic desirability than because it was there—was a small country, still an English colony, British Guiana. Here, Kennedy's convictions to aid nations as needed regardless of their economic systems, were put to the test. The country, on schedule to become independent of Britain shortly, was sorely in need of American aid. But the administration had little confidence in the likely leader there, Dr. Cheddi Jagan, a man publicly committed to neutralism, but imbued with a fervent, if somewhat naïve, socialist attitude. The British had convinced the United States that Jagan was the safest man to back in British Guiana, but Kennedy doubted Jagan's ability to maintain his position as a parliamentary democrat in a country experiencing economic and social upheavals, and he insisted on a careful reevaluation of the situation before any aid commitments were made.

* John Bartlow Martin, whom Kennedy soon sent to Santo Domingo as United States Ambassador, will tell the story in detail in his book *Overtaken by Events*.

The decision came perilously close to forcing Jagan and his supporters to turn towards Moscow, but it turned out to be sagacious. By the end of 1964, elections produced a coalition government under Forbes Burnham, perceived as a less impressionable and more responsible leader. British Guiana, after a tense and unhappy period of turbulence, seemed to have passed safely out of the communist orbit.

5. THE SECOND PUNTA DEL ESTE

British Guiana, however, was a marginal problem. The central threat remained Fidel Castro, whose broadcasters were now inveighing daily and agents conspiring nightly against the democratic regimes of Latin America. "The duty of every revolutionary," as Castro's Second Declaration of Havana put it in February 1962, "is to make revolution." Fidel himself, who had talked wistfully in 1960 about converting the Andes into "the Sierra Maestra of the American continent," now predicted in 1962 on the first anniversary of the Bay of Pigs that Betancourt and his regime would be overthrown in a year. Nor were such statements merely exercises in abstract prophecy—as the Venezuelan government learned when it found a great cache of weapons, unquestionably Cuban in origin and provenance, secreted for terrorists at a point along the Caribbean coast.

The Organization of American States had handled all this in 1960 and 1961 in somewhat gingerly fashion. The United States favored some form of collective action, or at least exhortation, against Castro; but when this was proposed at a meeting of foreign ministers at San José, Costa Rica, in August 1960, most of the American republics demurred. Some, like Mexico and Argentina, cherished the principle of non-intervention in the internal affairs of their fellow republics; others, like Bolivia, feared the domestic political repercussions of an anti-Castro stand; still others did not want to antagonize Castro or make him further dependent on the Soviet Union. In some cases, no doubt, there was a furtive sympathy for David against Goliath, especially when Goliath seemed primarily agitated about economic properties he had previously appropriated himself. The tendency was to regard the Cuban matter as a private quarrel between Washington and Havana rather than as an inter-American responsibility. The resolution finally adopted at San José condemned interference by extra-continental powers in the hemisphere but said nothing about Cuba.

Castro's growing fierceness during 1961, however, began to disturb his Caribbean neighbors. Venezuela and Colombia broke off diplomatic relations, and Lleras Camargo, increasingly concerned, called for a new meeting of foreign ministers to consider the Cuban problem. By a vote of 14 to 2, with five nations abstaining, the OAS Council resolved in December to hold such a session in January 1962. Again the resolution did not mention Cuba by name, and the split vote—the fact that such significant nations as Argentina, Brazil, Chile and Mexico all either abstained or were opposed—showed the division in the hemisphere.

Kennedy called his advisers together to debate strategy for the meeting. The goal would be to balance a hard line on Cuba with the need to achieve and consensus and maintain harmony within the OAS. With his appreciation of internal political problems in other countries, he said that he did not want a hard line at Punta del Este to set off a chain reaction of government crises across the continent. Also he expressed concern that the voting of sanctions by a narrow margin made up of small states representing a minority of the population of Latin America would be regarded as a victory for Castro.

And so we flew south through the equatorial night, arriving in Montevideo on January 21. A motorcade took us on to Punta del Este, a placid town dotted with palm trees meandering amiably along a wind-swept beach. In a few hours the tactical problem began to fall into shape. The Central American foreign ministers were committed to a hard line; some were under instruction to walk out if sanctions were not voted. Argentina, Brazil and Mexico were passionately opposed to sanctions. Within the United States delegation, Morrison, Senator Bourke B. Hickenlooper and Congressman Armistead Selden favored an all-out effort for sanctions. Speaking with a certain sour force at the first delegation meeting, Hickenlooper said he saw no point in his trying to talk to delegates from other countries because he did not know what our policy was. "I don't even know that we have a policy. It seems to be like the father who told his son, 'Sell the cow for $25 if you can; but, if you can't sell it for 25 accept 15.' That is no policy. I still don't understand why we can't go all out for sanctions." He later said, "The Washington bureaucracy doesn't understand the depth of public feeling on this matter. But Congress knows how deeply people care. If we do not come back with very strong action against Castro, the whole Alliance for Progress will be in trouble." Rusk suggested that fourteen votes—the bare two-thirds necessary—for sanctions might not be enough but, if we could get sixteen, it would be different. Goodwin observed that the meeting had two objectives—to get an immediate condemnation of Castro and to strengthen the future capacity of the OAS to deal with Castro; if we pushed the first objective too far, we might lose the second.

The conference displayed Rusk at his best. Here all his qualities—his intelligence, command of detail, inexhaustible patience and effortless inscrutability—precisely fitted the requirements of the occasion. With members of Congress and the Caribbean foreign ministers harassing him on one side and representatives of the most important South American states harassing him on the other, he strove coolly to work out the best possible combination of condemnation and consensus. There were twelve sure votes for a hard policy; but among the dissenters were the largest countries of the hemisphere—Brazil, Argentina, Mexico, Chile—as well as Bolivia and Ecuador. Uruguay and Haiti hung uncertainly in the middle.

In the meantime a new idea was emerging out of the incessant buzz of talk in the lobbies and corridors of the San Rafael Hotel—that the government of Cuba be excluded from the inter-American system. This idea had been informally advanced by Argentines seeking an alternative to mandatory sanctions. This proposition, along with partial economic sanctions and the establishment of a special security committee, now became the heart of the United States resolution. The congressional delegation, after 48 hours' exposure to the atmosphere of the conference, agreed that this was the best we could get and said they would defend it in Washington.

My own particular assignment was to prepare, with Walt Rostow and Goodwin, Rusk's address to the conference. The Secretary's speech, with its social and economic emphasis, provided a relief, welcome even to the Latin Americans, from the juridical disquisitions standard for such gatherings; and it went over very well. Rusk concluded by asking the foreign ministers to recognize that Cuba's alignment with "the Sino-Soviet bloc" was "incompatible" with the inter-American system, to exclude the Castro regime from the organs and bodies of that system, to end trade, especially in arms, between Cuba and the rest of the hemisphere and to seek means to defend the Americas against Castro's indirect aggression.

The result was a substantial success. Though only fourteen nations voted explicitly to exclude Cuba from the inter-American system, all twenty republics—the whole hemisphere except for Cuba itself—supported the declaration of incompatibility and the exclusion of the Castro government from the Inter-American Defense Board; nineteen voted to create a Special Consultative Committee of Experts on Security Matters to combat Cuban subversive activities; seventeen voted to suspend arms traffic with Cuba; and sixteen voted to follow this up with study looking toward further extensions of the trade embargo. The resolution on security, calling on the OAS to take all appropriate steps for "individual or collective self-defense" against "the continued intervention in this hemisphere of Sino-Soviet powers," turned out to be of particular importance. Much more progress was made toward the isolation of Cuba within the hemisphere than could have been anticipated a few months before.

6. THE RETURN OF THE MILITARY COUP

Punta del Este I had set in motion the grand project for the democratic modernization of Latin America; Punta del Este II now launched the indispensable supporting policy for the containment of Castro. But the meeting did not avert a political chain reaction.

The trouble began in Argentina, which should have been the most stable democracy in Latin America. But the landed oligarchy had stunted the country's democratic development for generations; and then after the war Peron, while breaking the grip of the oligarchy, also wrecked Argentina's economy, debauched its politics and corrupted its administration. The military, having first installed and then ejected Peron, had acquired the habit of intervention in civil politics. The military now arrested Frondizi and installed the president of the senate, the next in the line of constitutional succession, as the new President of Argentina, and their action now confronted Washington with a difficult decision. Frondizi's overthrow had been greeted with vast apathy by the Argentine people, and the United States reluctantly accepted the constitutional validity of the new government.

Soon, a problem at once clearer and harder arose in Peru. Unlike Argentina, Peru, with its high degree of illiteracy, its low per capita income, its unassimilated Indian population and its feudal system of land tenure, seemed destined for upheaval. In July 1962, officers trained in the United States, commanding tanks built in the United States, knocked down the iron gates of the Presidential Palace, arrested President Manuel Prado and set up a military junta.

Washington, in accordance with previous planning, now suspended diplomatic relations. The President issued a strong statement explaining that the military coup had contravened the purposes of the inter-American system. In a second statement the State Department announced the suspension of various assistance programs. Washington brought pressure on the junta to return to constitutionalism. Responding to this pressure, the junta guaranteed freedom of the press and of political opposition, even for the *Apristas,* promised free elections for June 9, 1963, and soon released most of those arrested at the time of the coup, including President Prado.

Representatives of the junta appeared before the Council of the OAS, formally set forth the steps taken to restore civil liberties and promised solemnly to hold free elections within a year and abide by the results. On the basis of these assurances, we soon resumed relations with the Peruvian government. Though Kennedy was criticized at the time for seeming to begin one policy—non-recognition—and then to go back on it, the fact was that the suspension of relations produced exactly the desired result. There were no reprisals, civil freedom was restored, free elections were guaranteed. While most American businessmen in Peru wanted unconditional recognition of the regime, the United States government showed its independence of business pressure and its opposition to military dictatorship. The action further consolidated the confidence of democratic Latin Americans in the progressive purpose of the American President. And the Peruvian election was held, as pledged, in June 1963. This time Fernando Belaunde Terry of the democratic left won a clear victory and began to give his country the programs of social reform it had so long needed.

7. TROUBLES OF THE ALLIANCE

On March 12, 1962, the anniversary of his first proposal of the Alliance for Progress, the President spoke again to the Latin American diplomats assembled at the White House.

Our "most impressive accomplishment" in the seven months since Punta del Este, he said, had been the "dramatic shift in thinking and attitude" through the hemisphere. The Charter of Punta del Este had posed the challenge of development in a way that could no longer be ignored, and had laid down the principle of "collective responsibility for the welfare of the people of the Americas." A second accomplishment was the creation of the institutional framework within which development would take place. The United States, moreover, had committed its pledged billion dollars to the first year of the Alliance. But the "ultimate responsibility for success," Kennedy declared with emphasis, "lies with the developing nation itself...." The men of wealth and power in poor nations, the President continued, "must lead the fight for those basic reforms which alone can preserve the fabric of their own societies. Those who make peaceful revolution impossible will make violent revolution inevitable. These social reforms are at the heart of the Alliance for Progress."

While he spoke, criticism of the Alliance was already rising on the ground that results thus far had been disappointing both in reform and in development.

In the case of reform, it was unrealistic to expect Latin American governments to enact overnight land and tax reforms revising the basic structure of power in their societies when in our own country, for example, it had taken a strong government several years of savage political fighting to pass the relatively innocuous reforms of the New Deal. As for development, a long period was inevitable before plans and projects, separately initiated in a score of nations, proceeding in different sectors and at different paces, could generate cumulative momentum. Given the most favorable circumstances, the seeds planted by the Alliance in 1961 and 1962 could not hope to bear visible fruit before 1964 or 1965.

Nor was the Alliance given the most favorable circumstances. In addition to the problems created by the communist threat, by rapid population growth and by internal political instability, the effort was beginning at a time of decline in world commodity prices—and in a continent where most nations depended excessively on one or two commodities as a means of earning foreign exchange.

In these early years, moreover, only Venezuela and Colombia (at least through Lleras's presidential term) and some Central American states, notably Costa Rica and El Salvador, had governments fully responsive to the aims of the Alliance. Brazil, the nation in Latin America with the greatest potentiality, was the one on which we expended most money and concern; but, after the odd departure of Quadros in 1961, the government had fallen into the hands of his vice-president, João Goulart, a weak and erratic demagogue; and it required all the persuasion of two brillant ambassadors, Lincoln Gordon in Rio and Roberto Campos in Washington, to preserve any rationality in Brazilian-American relations. Argentina, the second largest nation, remained in melancholy stagnation and disarray.

There were problems too in Washington. The aid bureaucracy was not accustomed to running revolutions and crusades; and Moscoso, always a little at sea in Washington, was hard put to reconcile the conflicting pressures swirling around him. Though he committed the billion dollars each year in program and project loans, the stipulations and rigidities in the aid legislation held up actual disbursement. And the Latins themselves, who were often slow to produce good projects and effective development programs, excused their own delinquencies by blaming everything on the Washington bureaucracy.

Moreover, the North American business community had not been, with notable exceptions, enthusiastic about the Alliance. As foreign private investment in Latin America diminished in 1961 and as Latin America's own private capital continued to flow out of the hemisphere into Swiss banks, the Alliance in Washington was under growing pressure from United States companies doing Latin American business to talk less about social reform and more about private investment. But the effect was further to belittle the crusade, to attenuate the mystique and zeal of Punta del Este and to lead Latin Americans to see the Alliance, despite its Latin origins, not as a great adventure of their own, but as a bilateral money lending operation, 'made in the U.S.A.,' to serve the interests of North American business.

As a consequence, the Alliance sometimes seemed bureaucratic and incomprehensible south of the border. "The present lingo of economic technocracy," wrote Morales-

Carrión, "simply does not reach the average Latin American. His slogans come from the world of nationalism, not the world of technocracy." The biggest obstacle the Alliance faced was "that it had not been wedded to Latin American nationalism, the single most powerful psychological force now operating in Latin America....Unless the Alliance is able to ally itself with nationalism, to influence it in a constructive direction, to translate its abstract terminology into familiar concepts related to nation-building, the Alliance will be pouring money into a psychological void."

One sometimes felt that the communists, operating on a shoestring in city universities or back-country villages, were reaching the people who mattered for the future—the students, the intellectuals, the labor leaders, the nationalist militants—while our billions were bringing us into contact only with governments of doubtful good faith and questionable life expectancy. Latin American democratic leaders themselves began to express increasing concern about the "degeneration" of the Alliance into a bilateral and technical program without political drive or continental vision. In October 1962 the Inter-American Economic and Social Council proposed that leading Latin American statesmen review the Alliance in the hope of promoting its multilateralization and Latin-Americanization and giving it a vital political base in the hemisphere.

Yet in our gloom we underestimate the extent to which things were already stirring underneath the surface. For imperceptibly the Charter of Punta del Este was transforming the politics of Latin America, imprinting the issues of modernization on the consciousness of the political and intellectual community and channeling the energies of both public and private agencies as never before. All the time, things were happening: development plans submitted, reform laws passed, teachers trained, schoolbooks circulated, roads and houses built, water supplies purified, land redistributed, savings and loan associations organized, economic integration among blocs of countries advanced, embers of hope kindled—never enough but a beginning. The shadows of communism, military adventurism and ancient privilege still obscured a gathering consensus which might in time bring the goals of the Alliance into reach.

Moreover, the President himself was winning in Latin America a faith and affection enjoyed by no other North American leader except Franklin Roosevelt in the long history of the Americas. His policies at home were validating his efforts in the hemisphere. Professor Albert O. Hirschman of Harvard, the expert on Latin American economic development, reported, for example, that his clash with United States Steel made a strong impression south of the border; "if Kennedy took on a real fight with a major segment of the U.S. business community, perhaps he meant what he said when he proposed social reforms for Latin America?" Moreover, the President, with his understanding of the crucial role of the Latin American intellectuals, seized opportunities to meet with academic and artistic groups at the White House.

In 1900 the Uruguayan writer José Enrique Rodó in his essay *Ariel* had articulated a favorite South American view of the United States: "Titanic in its concentration of will, with unprecedented triumphs in all spheres of material aggrandizement, its civilization yet produces as a whole a singular impression of insufficiency, of emptiness." Now for a moment the United States appeared no longer in the guise of Caliban but as a culture worthy in its own right of the leadership of the Americas.

XXX. AGAIN CUBA

IN 1962 THE ALLIANCE FOR PROGRESS was still an uncertainty. As for Castro, increasingly isolated within the hemisphere, he was more bent than ever on the course he had pursued since 1959. "I am a Marxist-Leninist," he said on December 2, 1961, "and I shall be a Marxist-Leninist until the last day of my life"; nor was there any reason to doubt his word. Within Cuba life had settled into drab routine. Economic planners fumbled ineffectually with agricultural and industrial programs. Popular enthusiasm diminished, even if organized opposition did not materially increase. Toward Latin America the regime maintained tenuous relations with half a dozen states and denounced the rest. Toward the United States invective was undefiled.

1. THE GAMBLE

On July 2, 1962, Raúl Castro, the Minister of the Armed Forces, arrived in Moscow. Either before his arrival or very soon thereafter the Soviet and Cuban governments arrived at a startling decision: that Soviet nuclear missiles were to be secretly installed in Cuba in the fall.

The Soviet Union had never before placed nuclear missiles in any other country—neither in the communist nations of Eastern Europe, nor, even in the season of their friendship, in Red China. Why should it now send nuclear missiles to a country thousands of miles away, lying within the zone of vital interest of their main adversary, a land, moreover, headed by a willful leader of, from the Russian viewpoint, somewhat less than total reliability? Castro, with characteristic loquacity, later produced a confusion of explanations, claiming at different times that it was a Cuban idea, a Russian idea or a mutual decision.

As for the Russians, Khrushchev told the Supreme Soviet in December 1962, "We carried weapons there at the request of the Cuban government ... including the stationing of a couple of score of Soviet IRBMs [intermediate-range ballistic missiles] in Cuba. These weapons were to be in the hands of Soviet military men.... Our aim was only to defend Cuba." The presence of the missiles, Khruschev continued, was designed to make the imperialists understand that, if they tried to invade Cuba, "the war which they threatened to start stood at their own borders, so that they would realize more realistically the dangers of thermonuclear war." This was all very noble, and the defense of Cuba was certainly a side effect of the Soviet action. But the defense of Cuba did not really require the introduction of long-range nuclear missiles.

In a general sense, the decision obviously represented the supreme Soviet probe of American intentions. No doubt a 'total victory' faction in Moscow had long been denouncing the government's 'nowin' policy and arguing that the Soviet Union could safely use the utmost nuclear pressure against the United States because the Americans were too rich or soft or liberal to fight. Now Khrushchev was prepared to give this argument its crucial test. Since a successful nuclearization this would still leave the United States with at least a 2 to 1 superiority in nuclear power targeted against the Soviet Union, the shift in the military balance of power would be less crucial than that in the political balance. Every country in the world, watching so audacious an action ninety miles from the United States, would wonder whether it could ever thereafter trust Washington's resolution and protection. More particularly, the change in the nuclear equilibrium would permit Khrushchev, who had been dragging out the Berlin negotiation all year, to reopen that question with half the United States lying within range of nuclear missiles poised for delivery across the small stretch of water from Florida. It was a staggering project—staggering in its recklessness, staggering in its misconception of the American response, staggering in its rejection of the ground rules for coexistence among the superpowers which Kennedy had offered in Vienna.

The decision having been made, the next problem was the development of a plan. Moscow evidently saw the operation in two stages—first, the augmentation of Cuban defensive capabilities by bringing in surface-to-air anti-aircraft (SAM) missiles and MIG-21 fighters; then, as soon as the SAMs were in place to protect the bases and deter photographic reconnaissance (a SAM had brought down the U-2 over Russia in 1960), sending in offensive weapons, both ballistic missiles and Ilyushin-28 jet aircraft able to deliver nuclear bombs. The first stage, involving only defensive weapons, required no special concealment. The second stage called for the most careful and complex program of deception. One can only imagine the provisions made in Moscow and Havana through the summer to ship the weapons, to receive them, unload them, assemble them, erect bases for them, install them on launching pads—all with a stealth and speed designed to confront the United States one day in November or December with a fully operational Soviet nuclear arsenal across the water in Cuba.

2. THE SURVEILLANCE

By late July the Soviet shipments began to arrive. Three weeks later CIA sent an urgent report to the President that "something new and different" was taking place in Soviet aid operations to Cuba. There were perhaps 5000 Soviet 'specialists' now in Cuba; military construction of some sort was going on; more ships were on their way with more specialists and more electronic and construction equipment. The data suggested that the Soviet Union was refurbishing the Cuban air defense system, presumably by putting up a network of SAM sites.

The intelligence community concluded that Moscow, having resolved after a time of indecision that it had a large stake in Castro's survival, had decided to insure the regime against external attack. It could thereby hope to secure the Soviet bridgehead in the western hemisphere, strengthen Castro's prestige in Latin America and show the world Washington's inability to prevent such things at its very doorstep. No one in the intelligence community (with one exception; for the thought flickered through the mind of John McCone) supposed that the Soviet Union would conceivably go beyond defensive weapons. The introduction of nuclear missiles, for example, would obviously legitimatize an American response, even possibly an invasion of Cuba. Our best Soviet experts in State and CIA considered Khrushchev too wary and Soviet foreign policy too rational to court a risk of this magnitude.

Nonetheless, when a U-2 flight on August 29 showed clear evidence of SAM sites under construction, the President decided to put Moscow on notice. The statement read that, while we had no evidence of "significant offensive capability either in Cuban hands or under Soviet direction," should it be otherwise, "the gravest issues would arise."

CIA DIRECTOR, JOHN MCCONE, ARRIVES AT THE WHITE HOUSE FOR A MEETING WITH THE PRESIDENT ON OCTOBER 24, 1962.

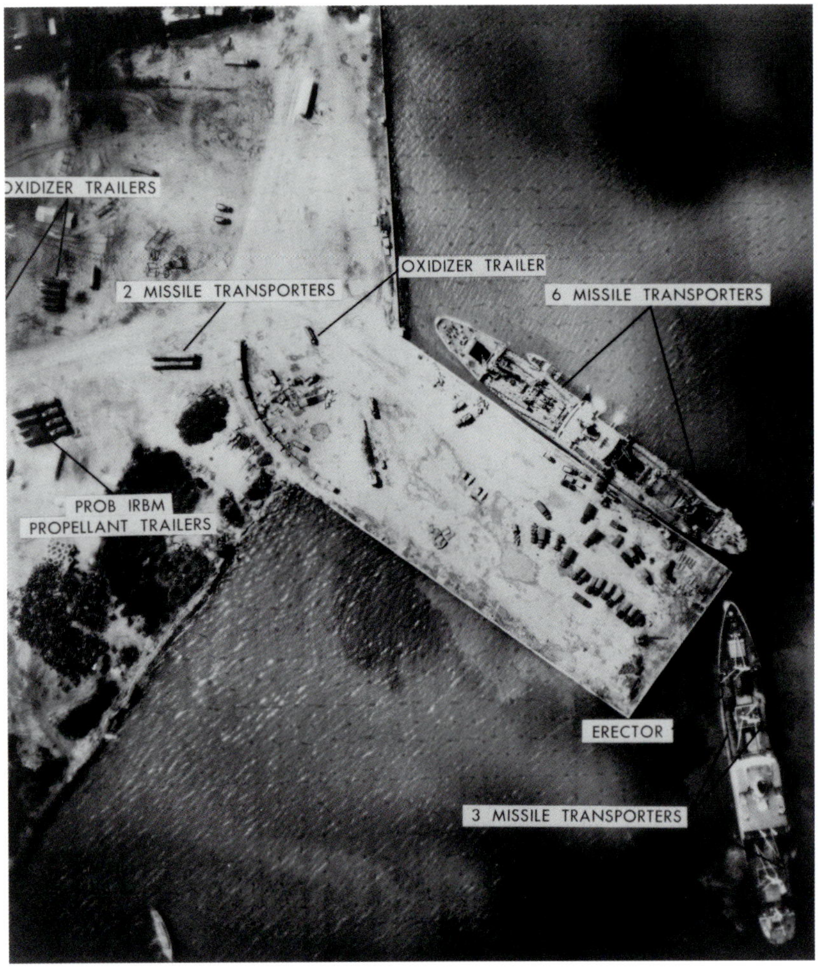

U-2 SURVEILLENCE PHOTOS REVEAL MISSILES BEING INSTALLED IN CUBA.

He had also taken the precaution of doubling the frequency of the U-2 overflights of Cuba. The evidence from flights on September 5, 17, 26 and 29 and October 5 and 7, as well as from other sources, indicated a continuing military build-up large in its proportions but still defensive in its character. The government saw no reason as yet to believe that Khrushchev intended anything beyond this; he had not, so far as we knew, lost his mind.

And, across the world, ships were sliding out of Black Sea harbors with nuclear technicians in their cabins and nuclear missiles in their holds. Khrushchev, having done his best to lull Kennedy by public statements and private messages, now in early September put the second stage of his plan into operation. He could hope that the hurricane season might interfere with the U-2 overflights and that the fall political campaign might inhibit the administration from taking drastic action. Moreover, he had an advantage unknown to us: Soviet engineering had enormously reduced the time required for the erection of nuclear missile sites.

In the meantime, Washington had been receiving a flow of tales about nuclear installations through refugee channels. Such reports had been routine for eighteen months. No one could be sure whether the sources in Cuba could tell a surface-to-air from a surface-to-surface missile; moreover, this government recalled that it had been misled by Cuban refugees before. Lacking photographic verification, the intelligence community treated the information with reserve. After consideration, it recommended on October 4 a U-2 flight over western Cuba. The recommendation was approved on October 10, and from the eleventh to the thirteenth the pilot and plane waited for the weather to break. Sunday the fourteenth dawned beautiful and cloudless.

On the same day the Soviet Ambassador in Washington gave the Attorney General an unusual personal message from Khrushchev for the President. The Soviet leader pledged in effect that he would stir up no incidents before the congressional elections in November. Then a week later, in the midst of a long and wearying disquisition on world affairs, Moscow said flatly that the "armaments and military equipment sent to Cuba are designed exclusively for defensive purposes." The statement continued truculently by accusing the United States of "preparing for aggression against Cuba and other peace-loving states," concluding that "if the aggressors unleash war our armed forces must be ready to strike a crushing retaliatory blow at the aggressor." The President responded calmly on September 13 at his press conference that the new shipments did not constitute a serious threat but that if at any time Cuba were to "become an offensive military base of significant capacity for the Soviet Union, then this country will do whatever must be done to protect its own security and that of its allies." In the meantime, he asked Congress for stand-by authority to call up the reserves.

When the U-2 plane returned from its mission, the negatives went swiftly to the processing laboratories, then to the interpretation center, where specialists pored over the blown-up photographs frame by frame. Late Monday afternoon, reading the obscure and intricate markings, they identified a launching pad, a series of buildings for ballistic missiles and even one missile on the ground in San Cristóbal.

3. THE EXECUTIVE COMMITTEE

The President was having breakfast in his dressing gown at eight forty-five on Tuesday morning when Bundy brought the news. Kennedy asked at once about the nature of the evidence. As soon as he was convinced that it was conclusive, he said that the United States must bring the threat to an end: one way or another the missiles would have to be removed. He then directed Bundy to institute low-level photographic flights and to set up a meeting of top officials. Privately he was furious: if Khrushchev could pull this after all his protestations and denials, how could he ever be trusted on anything?

The meeting, beginning at eleven forty-five that morning, went on with intermissions for the rest of the week. The group soon became known as the Executive Committee, presumably of the National Security Council; the press later dubbed it familiarly ExCom, though one never heard that phrase at the time. It carried on its work with the most exacting secrecy: nothing could be worse than to alert the Russians before the United States had decided on its own course. For this reason its members—the President, the Vice-President, Rusk, McNamara, Robert Kennedy, General Taylor, McCone, Dillon, Adlai Stevenson, Bundy, Sorensen, Ball, Gilpatric, Llewellyn Thompson, Alexis Johnson, Edwin Martin, with others brought in on occasion, among then Dean Acheson and Robert Lovett—had to attend their regular meetings, keep as many appointments as possible and preserve the normalities of life. Fortunately the press corps, absorbed in the congressional campaign, was hardly disposed or situated to notice odd comings and goings.

In the Executive Committee consideration was free, intent and continuous. Every alternative was laid on the table for examination, from living with the missiles to taking them out by surprise attack, from making the issue with Castro to making it with Khrushchev. In effect, the members walked around the problem, inspecting it first from this angle, then from that, viewing it in a variety of perspectives. They had, it was estimated, about ten days before the missiles would be on pads ready for firing. The deadline defined the strategy. It meant that the response could not, for example, be confided to the United Nations, where the Soviet delegate would have ample opportunity to stall action until the nuclear weapons were in place and on target. It meant that we could not even risk the delay involved in consulting our allies. It meant that the total responsibility had to fall on the United States and its President.

A MEETING OF THE EXECUTIVE COMMITTEE ON OCTOBER 29, 1962.

On the first Tuesday morning the choice for a moment seemed to lie between an air strike or acquiescence—and the President had made clear that acquiescence was impossible. Listening to the discussion, the Attorney General said aloud that the group needed more alternatives: surely there was some course in between bombing and doing nothing; suppose, for example, we were to bring countervailing pressure by placing nuclear missiles in Berlin? The talk continued, and finally the group dispersed for further reflection.

The next step was military preparation for Caribbean contingencies. A Navy-Marine amphibious exercise in the area, long scheduled for this week, provided a convenient cover for the buildup of an amphibious task force, soon including 40,000 Marines; there were 5000 more in Guantanamo. The Army's 82nd and 101st Airborne Divisions were made ready for immediate deployment; altogether the Army soon gathered more than 100,000 troops in Florida. SAC bombers left Florida airfields to make room for tactical fighter aircraft flown in from bases all over the country. Air defense facilities were stripped from places outside the range of the Cuban missiles and re-installed in the Southeast. As the days went by, 14,000 reservists were recalled to fly transport planes in the eventuality of airborne operations.

In the meantime, the Pentagon undertook a technical analysis of the requirements for a successful strike. The conclusion, as it evolved during the week, was that a limited "surgical" strike therefore might expose the United States to nuclear retaliation. Military prudence called for a much larger strike to eliminate all sources of danger. Anything less, the military urged, would destroy our credibility before the world and leave our own nation in intolerable peril. Moreover, this was a heaven-sent opportunity to get rid of the Castro regime forever and re-establish the security of the hemisphere.

It was a strong argument, urged by strong men. But there were arguments on the other side. The Soviet experts pointed out that even a limited strike would kill the Russians manning the missile sites and might well provoke the Soviet Union into drastic and unpredictable response, perhaps nuclear war. The Latin American experts added that a massive strike would kill thousands of innocent Cubans and damage the United States permanently in the hemisphere. The Europeanists said the world would regard a surprise strike as an excessive response. Even if it did not produce Soviet retaliation against the United States, it would invite the Russians to move against Berlin in circumstances where the blame would fall, not on them, but on us. It would thereby give Moscow a chance to shift the venue to a place where the stake was greater than Cuba and our position weaker. In the Caribbean, we had overwhelming superiority in conventional military force; the only recourse for the Soviet Union there would be to threaten the world with nuclear war. But in Berlin, where the Russians had overwhelming conventional superiority, it was the United States which would have to flourish nuclear bombs.

All these considerations encouraged the search for alternatives. When the Executive Committee met on Wednesday, Secretary McNamara advanced an idea which had been briefly mentioned the day before and from which he did not thereafter deviate—the conception of a naval blockade designed to stop the further entry of offensive weapons into Cuba and hopefully to force the removal of the missiles already there. Here was a middle course between inaction and battle, a course which exploited our superiority in local conventional power and would permit subsequent movement either toward war or toward peace.

As the discussion proceeded through Thursday, the supporters of the air strike marshaled their arguments against the blockade. They said that it would not neutralize the weapons already within Cuba, that it could not possibly bring enough pressure on Khrushchev to remove those weapons, that it would permit work to go ahead on the bases and that it would mean another Munich. The act of stopping and searching ships would engage us with Russians instead of Cubans. The obvious retort to our blockade of Cuba would be a Soviet blockade of Berlin. Despite such arguments, however, the majority of the Executive Committee by the end of the day was tending toward a blockade.

That afternoon, in the interests of normality, the President received the Soviet Foreign Minister Andrei Gromyko. It was one of the more extraordinary moments of an extraordinary week. Kennedy knew that there were Soviet nuclear missiles in Cuba. Gromyko unquestionably knew this too, but did not know that Kennedy knew it. His emphasis was rather grimly on Berlin, almost as if to prepare the ground for demands later in the autumn. When the talk turned to Cuba, Gromyko heavily stressed the Cuban fears of an American invasion and said with due solemnity that the Soviet aid had "solely the purpose of contributing to the defense capabilities of Cuba"; "if it were otherwise," the Russian continued, "the Soviet Government would never become involved in rendering such assistance." To dispel any illusion about possible American reactions, the President read the Foreign Minister the key sentences from his statement of September 13. He went no further because he did not wish to indicate his knowledge until he had decided on his course.

In the evening the President met with the Executive Committee. Listening again to the alternatives over which he had been brooding all week, he said crisply, "Whatever you fellows are recommending today you will be sorry about a week from now." He was evidently attracted by the idea of the blockade. It avoided war, preserved flexibility and offered Khrushchev time to reconsider his actions. It could be carried out within the framework of the Organization of American States and the Rio Treaty. Since it could be extended to nonmilitary items as occasion required, it could become an instrument of steadily intensifying pressure. It would avoid the shock effect of a surprise attack, which would hurt us politically through the world and might provoke Moscow to an insensate response against Berlin or the United States itself. If it worked, the Russians could retreat with dignity. If it did not work, the Americans retained the option of military action. In short, the blockade, by enabling us to proceed one step at a time, gave us control over the future. Kennedy accordingly directed that preparations be made to put the weapons blockade into effect on Monday morning.

The next day the President, keeping to his schedule, left Washington for a weekend of political barnstorming.

4. THE DECISION

Kennedy left behind a curiously restless group of advisers. This became evident when they met at the State Department at eleven on Friday morning. Over Ted Sorensen's protest that a decision had been reached the night before and should not be reopened now, several began to re-argue the inadequacy of the blockade.

Secretary McNamara, however, firmly reaffirmed his opposition to a strike and his support for the blockade. Then Robert Kennedy, speaking with quiet intensity, said that he did not believe that, with all the memory of Pearl Harbor and all the responsibility we would have to bear in the world afterward, the President of the United States could possibly order such an operation. For 175 years we had not been that kind of country. Sunday-morning surprise blows on small nations were not in our tradition. Thousands of Cubans would be killed without warning, and hundreds of Russians too. We were fighting for something more than survival, and a sneak attack would constitute a betrayal of our heritage and our ideals. The blockade, the Attorney General concluded, would demonstrate the seriousness of our determination to get the missiles out of Cuba and at the same time allow Moscow time and room to pull back from its position of peril. It was now proposed that the committee break up into working groups to write up the alternative courses for the President—one to analyze the quarantine policy, the other to analyze the strike. Then everyone dispersed to meet again at four o'clock for a discussion of the competing scenarios.

At the second meeting the balance of opinion clearly swung back to the blockade (though, since a blockade was technically an act of war, it was thought better to refer to it as a quarantine). In retrospect most participants regarded Robert Kennedy's speech as the turning point. The case was strengthened too when the military representatives conceded that a quarantine now would not exclude a strike later. There was brief discussion of a *démarche* to Castro, but it was decided to concentrate on Khrushchev. Then they turned to the problem of the missiles already in Cuba. Someone observed that the United States would have to pay a price to get them out; perhaps we should throw in our now obsolescent and vulnerable Jupiter missile bases in Italy and Turkey, whose removal the Joint Congressional Committee on Atomic Energy as well as the Secretary of Defense had recommended in 1961. After a couple of hours, Adlai Stevenson, who had had to miss the day's meetings because of UN commitments, arrived from New York. He expressed his preference for the quarantine over the strike but wondered whether it might not be better to try the diplomatic route also. We must, he said, start thinking about our negotiating position; for example, a settlement might include the neutralization of Cuba under international guarantees and UN inspection; demilitarization would, of course, include our own base at Guantanamo as well as the Soviet installations. The integrity of Cuba should be guaranteed. He also echoed the suggestion that we might want to consider giving up the Italian and Turkish bases now, since we were planning to do so eventually.

The President, still campaigning, received reports from his brother in Washington. The schedule now called for a speech to the nation on Sunday night. By Saturday morning, however, it was evident that preparations would not be complete in time, so it was decided to hold things for another twenty-four hours. Meanwhile, the President, pleading a cold, canceled the rest of his political trip and returned to Washington.

That afternoon he presided over the Executive Committee and its final debate. McNamara impressively presented the case for the blockade. The military, with some civilian support, argued for the strike. Stevenson spoke with force about the importance of a political program, the President agreeing in principle but disagreeing with his specific proposals. A straw vote indicated eleven for the quarantine, six for the strike. Then he issued orders to get everything ready for the quarantine. On Sunday morning a final conference with the military leaders satisfied him that the strike would be a mistake. His course was now firmly set.

5. THE CRISIS

I knew nothing about any of this until late Friday, October 19, when Adlai Stevenson phoned me, saying casually that he was in Washington and wondered when we could get together. On Saturday morning, he asked, "Do you know what the secret discussions this week have been about?" I said I knew of no discussions; the President was out campaigning; I had presumed that everything was fine. Adlai, observing gravely that there was trouble and he had the President's permission to tell me about it, described the seesaw during the week between the diplomatic and military solutions. The quarantine, he now felt, was sure to win. He would have to make a speech early in the week at the Security Council, and he wanted me to help on it. He outlined the argument and, with due discretion, I set to work.

The secret had been superbly kept. But later in the day, when the President returned from the campaign and Rusk canceled a speech that night, a sense of premonitory excitement began to engulf Washington. Already those whose business it was to sniff things out were on the track. The President himself intervened with the publisher of the *New York Times* to keep the lid on a speculative story they were preparing to publish. By Saturday night the town was alive with speculation and anticipation.

On Sunday Stevenson, contemplating the problems of gathering UN backing for the quarantine, wrote down his thoughts about our UN strategy. He saw no hope of mustering enough votes in the UN to authorize action against Cuba in advance; but the OAS offered an opportunity for multilateral support, and OAS approval could provide some protection in law and a great deal in public opinion. As for the UN, he said, we must seize the initiative, bringing our case to the Security Council at the same time we imposed the quarantine. In order to avert resolutions against the quarantine, he continued, we should be ready to propose a political path out of the military crisis. His negotiating program, following his remarks to the Executive Committee, centered on the removal of Soviet military equipment and personnel under UN observation and the introduction of UN influence into Cuba in the hope of ending communist domination of the Cuban government. He would throw a non-invasion guarantee and Guantanamo into the bargain to evidence our restraint and good faith. Exercising the prerogative freely employed that week by nearly all his colleagues, he now wrote that Turkey and Italy should not be included; this would only divert attention from the Cuban threat to the general issue of foreign bases.

The President, however, rightly regarded any political program as premature. He wanted to concentrate on a single issue—the enormity of the introduction of the missiles and the absolute necessity for their removal. Stevenson's negotiating program was accordingly rejected.

I spent all day Sunday till well after midnight working at the State Department with Harlan Cleveland, Joseph Sisco and Thomas Wilson on the UN speech. At ten o'clock on Monday morning the President called me in to instruct me to go to New York and assist Stevenson on the UN presentation. He was in a calm and reflective mood. It was strange, he said, how no one in the intelligence community had anticipated the Soviet attempt to transform Cuba into a nuclear base; everyone had assumed that the Russians would not be so stupid as to offer us this pretext for intervention. I asked why he thought Khrushchev had done such an amazing thing. He said that, first, it might draw Russia and China closer together, or at least strengthen the Soviet position in the communist world, by showing that Moscow was capable of bold action in support of a communist revolution; second, that it would radically redefine the setting in which the Berlin problem could be reopened after the election; third, that it would deal the United States a tremendous political blow. When I remarked that the Russians must have supposed we would not respond, Kennedy said, "They thought they had us either way. If we did nothing, we would be dead. If we reacted, they hoped to put us in an exposed position, whether with regard to Berlin or Turkey or the UN."

I met with him again at eleven to go over the draft of the UN speech with Rusk, Robert Kennedy and others. The President suggested a few omissions, including a passage threatening an American strike if the Soviet build-up in Cuba continued; he preferred to leave that to Moscow's imagination. The Attorney General drew me aside to say, "We're counting on you to watch things in New York.... We will have to make a deal at the end, but we must stand absolutely firm now. Concessions must come at the end of negotiation, not at the beginning." Then, clutching the speech, I caught the first plane to New York.

In Washington everything awaited the President's television broadcast that night to the nation.

At five o'clock Kennedy saw the congressional leaders, many of whom had flown in from their home states in Air Force planes. He showed them the U-2 photographs and told them what he proposed to do. The President listened courteously to some who called for an invasion, but was in no way shaken in his decision.

Then at seven o'clock the speech: his expression grave, his voice firm and calm, the evidence set forth without emotion, the conclusion unequivocal—"The purpose of these bases can be none other than to provide a nuclear strike capability against the Western Hemisphere." He recited the Soviet assurances, now revealed as "deliberate deception," and called the Soviet action "a deliberately provocative and

PRESIDENT KENNEDY SIGNS A PROCLAMATION FORMALLY PUTTING INTO EFFECT THE U.S. ARMS QUARANTINE AGAINST CUBA.

unjustified change in the status quo which cannot be accepted by this country, if our courage and our commitments are ever to be trusted again by either friend or foe." Our "unswerving objective," he continued, was to end this nuclear threat to the Americans. He then laid out what he called with emphasis his *initial* steps: a quarantine on all offensive military equipment under shipment to Cuba; an intensified surveillance of Cuba itself; a declaration that any missile launched from Cuba would be regarded as an attack by the Soviet Union on the United States, requiring full retaliatory response upon the Soviet Union; an immediate convening of the Organization of American States to consider the threat to hemisphere security; an emergency meeting of the UN Security Council to consider the threat to world peace; and an appeal to Chairman Khrushchev "to abandon this course of world domination, and to join in an historic effort to end the perilous arms race and to transform the history of man."

He concluded with quiet solemnity. "My fellow citizens: let no one doubt that this is a difficult and dangerous effort.... No one can foresee precisely what course it will take or what costs or casualties will be incurred. ...But the greatest danger of all would be to do nothing.... Our goal is not the victory of might, but the vindication of right—not peace at the expense of freedom, but both peace *and* freedom, here in this hemisphere, and, we hope, around the world. God willing, that goal will be achieved."

After the broadcast the President returned to the Mansion, sought out Caroline and told her stories until it was time for dinner. He dined alone with Jacqueline.

6. THE REACTION

We listened to the speech clustered around a television set in Stevenson's office in New York. I had found Adlai unperturbed in the midst of pandemonium. The Mission was a frenzy of activity in preparation for the Security Council. From the moment of the President's statement, Stevenson had to talk so much to UN delegates from other nations that he had little time left for his own speeches and strategy. Through Monday evening and Tuesday morning he snatched moments to revise and edit his remarks for the Security Council. It was reminiscent of his presidential campaigns: the last part of his address was still in the typewriter at the Mission on Tuesday afternoon when he had already begun to speak across the street at the UN.

The speech began at four o'clock. The OAS had been meeting since nine that morning, and no one could doubt the OAS sentiment, but a number of ambassadors had not yet received instructions from their governments. As a result, the resolution establishing the legal basis for United States action was not passed until Stevenson was well into his speech.*

The text of the resolution was placed on the desk in front of him.

Stevenson, who had been speaking with extraordinary eloquence to a hushed chamber, now read the OAS resolution. In another moment he concluded: "Since the end of the Second World War, there has been no threat to the vision of peace so profound, no challenge to the world of the Charter so fateful. The hopes of mankind are concentrated in this room.... Let [this day] be remembered, not as the day when the world came to the edge of nuclear war, but as the day when men resolved to let nothing thereafter stop them in their quest for peace."

And now the tension was rising. In Cuba workmen were laboring day and night to complete the bases. Forty-two medium-range nuclear missiles were being unpacked and prepared for launching pads with desperate speed. IL-28 aircraft were being assembled. On the Atlantic at least twenty-five Soviet merchant ships, some no doubt loaded with intermediate-range missiles, were steaming toward Cuba, their courses thus far unaltered after the President's speech. Ninety ships of the American fleet, backed up by sixty-eight aircraft squadrons and eight aircraft carriers, were moving into position to intercept and search the onrushing ships. In Florida and neighboring states the largest United States invasion force since the Second World War was gathering. In Moscow, the Soviet government in a long and angry statement insisted that the weapons in Cuba were defensive, ignored the charges of nuclear missiles and savagely denounced the American quarantine.

The United Nations was only the first step in gaining world understanding of the American position. Africa now assumed vital strategic importance because Soviet flights to Cuba would have to refuel at African airports. Both Sékou Touré in Guinea and Ben Bella in Algeria sent Kennedy their assurances that they would deny Russian aircraft transit rights. (Touré later added that the problem must be kept in a Soviet-American context; if it became a Cuban-American problem, we would lose support in the uncommitted world.) Most African states, moved no doubt by their faith in the American President, indicated private sympathy. In Western Europe support was general, though there were waverings in Britain and Italy.

The British had received their first notification on Saturday, October 20. At Sunday noon Kennedy called David Ormsby Gore to the White House and outlined the alternatives. Ormsby Gore expressed strong support for the quarantine and, with his knowledge of Macmillan, assured the President of a sympathetic British reaction. Later the same day Kennedy explained directly to Macmillan that he had found it essential in the interests of security and speed to make his first decision on his own responsibility, but that from now on he expected to keep in the closest touch. He added that, if Khrushchev tried anything in Berlin, the United States would be ready to take a full role there as well as in the Caribbean.

Macmillan responded on Monday that Britain would give all the support it could in the Security Council, though he did not then or later offer to take part in specific action on the Atlantic. He added that two aspects of the problem particularly troubled him. European opinion, he said, would need attention, because Europeans had grown so accustomed to living under the nuclear gun that they might wonder what all the fuss was about. The other and more worrying point was that, if it came to a negotiation, Khrushchev might try to trade Cuba for Berlin. The President, no doubt detecting an element of reserve in Macmillan's tone, tried to reassure him that the Cuban decision was not simply a response to aroused public opinion or to private passion against Cuba; he had no interest in a squabble with Castro. This was something very different: a major showdown with Khrushchev, whose action had so contradicted all the Kremlinologists had prophesied that it was necessary to revise our whole estimate of his desperation or ambition or both.

*It was passed unanimously. Uruguay, still awaiting instructions, abstained on Tuesday but changed its vote to affirmative on Wednesday.

THE PRESIDENT SOLEMNLY INFORMS AMERICANS THAT THIS IS A "DIFFICULT AND DANGEROUS EFFORT."

IN NEW YORK, A GROUP OF CUBAN REFUGEES WATCH THE PRESIDENT'S ADDRESS.

LEFT: ADLAI STEVENSON ADDRESSES THE U.N. SECURITY COUNCIL ON OCTOBER 23.
RIGHT: BRITISH DAILYS ANNOUNCE THE U.S. BLOCKADE OF CUBA.

Thereafter Macmillan did not falter, and his counsel and support proved constant through the week.

On Tuesday night Kennedy dined quietly at the White House with English friends, including David Ormsby Gore. In a while Robert Kennedy walked in, bleak, tired and disheveled. He had just been to see Ambassador Dobrynin in an effort to find out whether the Soviet ships had instructions to turn back if challenged on the high seas. The Soviet Ambassador, the Attorney General said, seemed very shaken, out of the picture and unaware of any instructions. This meant that the imposition of the quarantine the next day might well bring a clash.

The three old friends talked on. Ormsby Gore recalled a conversation with Defense Department officials who had declared it important to stop the Soviet ships as far out of the reach of the jets in Cuba as possible. The British Ambassador now suggested that Khrushchev had hard decisions to make and that every additional hour might make it easier for him to climb down gracefully; why not, therefore, make the interceptions much closer to Cuba and thereby give the Russians a little more time? If Cuban aircraft tried to interfere, they could be shot down. Kennedy, agreeing immediately, called McNamara and, over emotional Navy protests, issued the appropriate instruction. This decision was of vital importance in postponing the moment of irreversible action. They soon parted, looking forward with concern to the crisis of the morrow.

And so around the world emotions rose—fear, doubt, incertitude, apprehension. In the White House the President went coolly about his affairs, watching the charts with the Soviet ships steadily advancing toward Cuba, scrutinizing every item of intelligence for indications of Soviet purpose, reviewing the deployment of American forces. In this manner he preserved a taut personal control over every aspect of the situation; the Bay of Pigs had not been in vain. He said to someone, "I guess this is the week I earn my salary."

He never had a more sober sense of his responsibility. It was a strange week; the flow of decision was continuous; there was no day and no night. In the intervals between meetings he sought out his wife and children as if the imminence of catastrophe had turned his mind more than ever to his family and, through them, to children everywhere in the world. This was the cruel question—the young people who, if things went wrong, would never have the chance to learn, to love, to fulfill themselves and serve their countries. One noon, swimming in the pool, he said to David Powers, "If it weren't for these people that haven't lived yet, it would be easy to make decisions of this sort."

XXXI.
THE GREAT TURNING

STEVENSON DESCRIBES THE LOCATION OF MISSILE SITES IN CUBA TO THE U.N. SECURITY COUNCIL USING AERIAL PHOTOGRAPHS.

WITHIN THE KREMLIN, so far as one could tell, there was confusion. The Russians had obviously anticipated neither the quick discovery of the bases nor the quick imposition of the quarantine. Their diplomats across the world were displaying all the symptoms of improvisation, as if they had been told nothing of the placement of the missiles and had received no instructions what to say about them. Ambassador Anatoly Dobrynin himself gave every indication of ignorance and confusion. As late as Wednesday a message to Robert Kennedy from Mikoyan repeated that Cuba was receiving no weapons capable of reaching the United States. Georgi Bolshakov, who transmitted the message and who had seemed to us all an honest fellow, assured the Attorney General that he believed this himself.

In New York on Wednesday Stevenson was continuing the battle for the American resolution in the United Nations. Then U Thant made an unexpected intervention, proposing that the Soviet Union suspend its arms shipments and the United States its quarantine to allow an interlude for negotiations. Khrushchev accepted this thought at once and with evident pleasure; but, from our viewpoint, it equated aggression and response, said nothing about the missiles already in Cuba, permitted work to go forward on the sites and contained no provisions for verification. Still, while New York and Washington agreed in rejecting U Thant's proposal, the manner of the rejection caused debate. Some in Washington appeared to fear any response which would 'entrap' us in a negotiating process; it seemed to us in New York that they must be bent to clear the road for an air strike and an invasion. Stevenson and McCloy strongly recommended a response to U Thant which would keep the diplomatic option alive.

1. WAITING

On Wednesday night, as we were pondering these matters at the U.S. Mission in New York, I received a telephone call from Averell Harriman. Speaking with unusual urgency, he said that Khrushchev was desperately signaling a desire to cooperate in moving toward a peaceful solution. Harriman set forth the evidence: Khrushchev's suggestion of a summit meeting in his reply to Bertrand Russell; his well-publicized call on the American singer Jerome Hines the night before after a Moscow concert; his amiable if menacing talk with an American businessman, William Knox of Westinghouse International; the indications that afternoon that the nearest Soviet ships were slowing down and changing course. This was not the behavior of a man who wanted war, Harriman said; it was the behavior of a man who was begging our help to get off the hook. Khrushchev had sent up similar signals after the U-2 affair in 1960, Harriman continued, and Eisenhower had made the mistake of ignoring him; we must not repeat that error now. "If we do nothing but get tougher and tougher, we will force him into countermeasures. The first incident on the high seas will engage Soviet prestige and infinitely reduce the chance of a peaceful solution." "We must give him an out," Harriman said again. "If we do this shrewdly, we can downgrade the tough group in the Soviet Union which persuaded him to do this. But if we deny him an out, then we will escalate this business into a nuclear war."

Kennedy called him the next morning, and I imagine that Harriman's counsel may have strengthened his own inclination to go further along the diplomatic road. At any rate, his reply to U Thant on Thursday, while stressing that the "threat was created by the secret introduction of offensive weapons into Cuba, and the answer lies in the removal of such weapons," authorized Stevenson to continue discussions on whether satisfactory arrangements could be assured to this end. This was a second vital decision.

In Washington they had meanwhile been seeking to provide for every contingency the quarantine might create. By involving us directly with the Russians, it contained a great variety of potential risks; and the Executive Committee

THE AIRCRAFT CARRIER *ENTERPRISE* WAS REPORTED TO BE AMONG THE WARSHIPS HEADING TO THE CARIBBEAN TO SERVE IN THE U.S. BLOCKADE OF CUBA.

undertook the most intensive consideration of all possible gradations and configurations: where, when and how to stop ships, how much force to use, when to board, whether to disable the propeller and tow the ship to port. Soon they ascertained that Soviet submarines were following the ships; as quickly as possible, we put a destroyer on the tail of every submarine. It was all an amazing naval deployment, conducted with skill and efficiency. Among the destroyers to take part, apparently in the natural line of duty, was the *Joseph P. Kennedy, Jr.*

As they plotted the courses and studied the charts, Thursday seemed to confirm the encouraging signs of Wednesday and to justify Ormsby Gore's suggestion of Tuesday night that the line of interception be drawn closer to Cuba. Half the Soviet ships, the Executive Committee noted with a flood of relief, had put about and were heading home. Others were evidently waiting for further orders. Only one had entered the quarantine zone—a tanker, obviously not carrying nuclear weapons. In Washington some felt that we must react to this challenge with full military vigor; but the President decided to give Khrushchev more time and said that the tanker, once it had identified itself and thereby established the quarantine, should be permitted to proceed without boarding and search—a third vital decision.

There were other portents, and to them our intelligence community turned like Roman haruspices to the entrails of a sacrificial victim. For the first time all that long week Soviet diplomatic behavior across the world was beginning to conform to a pattern; this indicated that Moscow had at last sent out instructions.

The essence of the emerging pattern seemed to be concern for a peaceful settlement, but the situation was still loaded with danger. Work continued on the sites; unless this was stopped, the missiles would soon be on their launching pads. Nor had the Soviet Union yet admitted the presence of nuclear missiles in Cuba at all. On Thursday evening at the UN Stevenson returned to the debate in the Security Council. He crisply dismissed the communist argument that the United States had created the threat to the peace: "This is the first time that I have ever heard it said that the crime is not the burglary, but the discovery of the burglar." As for those who thought the quarantine too extreme a remedy: "Were we to do nothing until the knife was sharpened? Were we to stand idly by until it was at our throats? ... The course we have chosen seems to me perfectly graduated to meet the character of the threat."

Zorin made a cocky but evasive reply. Now Stevenson took the floor again. Ironically regretting that he lacked his opponent's "talent for obfuscation, for distortion, for confusing language and for double-talk," saying sternly "those weapons must be taken out of Cuba," he turned on the Russian with magnificent scorn:

> *Do you, Ambassador Zorin, deny that the USSR has placed and is placing medium and intermediate-range missiles and sites in Cuba? Yes or no? Don't wait for the translation. Yes or no?*

Zorin muttered something about not being in an American courtroom. Stevenson, cold and controlled:

> *You are in the courtroom of world opinion. You have denied they exist, and I want to know if I understood you correctly. I am prepared to wait for my answer until hell freezes over. And I am also prepared to present the evidence in this room—now!*

It was a moment of tremendous excitement. At Stevenson's order, aerial photographs were wheeled on easels into the council chamber, showing the transformation of San Cristóbal from a peaceful country spot into a grim nuclear installation. Other pictures added further evidence. Zorin wanly denied the authenticity of the display. Stevenson wondered savagely why the Soviet Union did not test its denial by permitting a United Nations team to visit the sites.

Then, in a moment, Stevenson concluded: "We know the facts and so do you, sir, and we are ready to talk about them. Our job here is not to score debating points. Our job, Mr. Zorin, is to save the peace. And if you are ready to try, we are."

The Stevenson speech dealt a final blow to the Soviet case before world opinion.

2. THE LETTERS

But on Friday work still continued on the sites. In Florida the American army prepared for invasion. In Washington the pressure to attack mounted as each passing moment brought the installations closer to operation. And in Moscow there must have been deep anxiety and bitter debate.

Khrushchev had now evidently abandoned the effort to bring in more nuclear weapons. But some of the men around him—perhaps the Soviet military—were apparently determined to make the missiles already there operational as speedily as possible. Indeed, this group may have gone along with the pacific gestures of Wednesday and Thursday precisely to gain time to complete the sites. In any case, once the missiles were on launching pads, Moscow might be able to drive a better bargain.

Khrushchev himself, however, seems to have reached a different position. He knew by now that his essential gamble had failed. Whatever he had once supposed, the Americans were ready to fight. His own options were narrowing before his eyes. If he were to strike at Berlin, he would only expose the Soviet Union to nuclear attack. If he did not compose matters quickly in the Caribbean, then the great army, massing so visibly in Florida, would descend on Cuba. It was now beyond the realm of tactical maneuver: all roads led to the abyss. The Soviet Chairman and the American President were the two men in the world with ultimate responsibility for nuclear war. Like Kennedy, Khrushchev had peered into the abyss before. "Immediate action," as he later told the Supreme Soviet, "was needed to prevent an invasion of Cuba and to preserve peace."

At one-thirty on Friday John Scali, the State Department correspondent for the American Broadcasting Company, received a call from Aleksander Fomin, a counselor at the Soviet Embassy, insisting on an immediate meeting. Scali, who had lunched occasionally with Fomin in the past, joined him at once at the Occidental Restaurant. The usually phlegmatic Russian, now haggard and alarmed, said, "War seems about to break out. Something must be done to save the situation." Scali replied that they should have thought of that before they put the missiles in Cuba. The Russian sat in silence for a moment. Then he said, "There might be a way out. What would you think of a proposition whereby we would promise to remove our missiles under United Nations inspection, where Mr. Khrushchev would promise never to introduce such offensive weapons into Cuba again? Would the President of the United States be willing to promise publicly not to invade Cuba?" When Scali said he did not know, Fomin begged him to find out immediately from his State Department friends. Then, reaching for a pencil, he wrote down his home telephone number: "If I'm not at the Embassy, call me here. This is of vital importance."

Scali carried the proposal to Roger Hilsman at State, and Hilsman carried it to Rusk. After discussion with the Executive Committee, Rusk asked Scali to tell the Russian that we saw "real possibilities" for a negotiation but they must understand that time was short—no more than forty-eight hours. At seven-thirty Friday evening Scali passed this word along. They met this time in the coffee shop of the Statler Hilton. Fomin, once he had satisfied himself about the authenticity of Scali's message and after a brief attempt to introduce the idea of UN inspection of Florida as well as Cuba, rose and, in his haste to get the word back, tossed down a five-dollar bill for a thirty-cent check and speeded off without waiting for the change.

Two hours later a long letter from Khrushchev to the President began to come in by cable. The Soviet leader started by insisting that the weapons shipments were complete and that their purpose was defensive. Then he declared his profound longing for peace; let us, he said with evident emotion, not permit this situation to get out of hand. The enforcement of the quarantine would only drive the Soviet Union to take necessary measures of its own. But if the United States would give assurances that it would not invade Cuba nor permit others to do so and if it would recall its fleet from the quarantine, this would immediately change everything. Then the necessity for a Soviet presence in Cuba would disappear. The crisis, Khrushchev said, was like a rope with a knot in the middle: the more each side pulled, the more the knot would tighten, until finally it could be severed only by a sword. But if each side slackened the rope, the knot could be untied.

The letter was not, as subsequently described, hysterical. Though it pulsated with a passion to avoid nuclear war and gave the impression of having been written in deep emotion, why not? In general, it displayed an entirely rational understanding of the implications of the crisis. Together with the Scali proposal, it promised light at the end of the cave. And in New York on Friday we heard that Zorin had advanced the same proposal to U Thant, and that the Cubans at the UN were beginning to hint to unaligned delegates that the bases might be dismantled and removed if the United States would guarantee the territorial integrity of Cuba. The President probably had his first good night's sleep for ten days; certainly the rest of us did.

But when the Executive Committee assembled on Saturday morning, prospects suddenly darkened. The Moscow radio began to broadcast a new Khrushchev letter containing, to everyone's consternation, an entirely different proposition from the one transmitted through Scali and embodied in Khrushchev's letter of the night before. The Soviet Union now said it would remove its missiles from Cuba and offer a non-aggression pledge to Turkey if the United States would remove its missiles from Turkey and offer a non-aggression pledge to Cuba. The notion of trading the Cuban and Turkish bases had been much discussed, but Kennedy regarded the idea as unacceptable, and the swap was promptly rejected. This proposal was perplexing enough; but, far more alarming, word soon came that a U-2 was missing over Cuba, presumably shot down by the Russians. American planes had thus far flown over the missile sites without interference. The Soviet action now, some felt, could only mean one thing: that the confrontation was entering its military phase. The bases were becoming operational, and the Russians were evidently determined to use force to maintain them. We had no choice, it was argued, but a military response; and our tactical analysis had already shown that strikes at the bases would be little use without strikes at the airfields, and strikes at the airfields of little use without further supporting action, so, once the process began, it could hardly stop short of invasion.

The President declined to be stampeded. Obviously, if they shot down U-2s, we would have to react—but not necessarily at once. Again he insisted that the Russians be given time to consider what they were doing before action and counteraction became irrevocable. There remained the Khrushchev letters, and the Executive Committee turned to them again with bafflement and something close to despair. It was noted that Defense Minister Rodion Malinovsky had mentioned Cuba and Turkey together as early as Tuesday, and that *Red Star,* the army paper, had coupled them again on Friday. Could the military have taken over in Moscow? Rusk called in Scali and asked him to find out anything he could from his Soviet contact. Scali, fearful that he had been used to deceive his own country, upbraided Fomin, accusing him of a double cross. The Russian said miserably that there must have been a cable delay, that the Embassy was waiting word from Khrushchev at any moment. Scali brought this report immediately to the President and the Executive Committee at the White House.

In the meantime a new crisis: another U-2 on a routine air-sampling mission from Alaska to the North Pole had gone off course and was over the Soviet Union; it had already attracted the attention of Soviet fighters and was radioing Alaska for help. Would the Russians view this as a final reconnaissance in preparation for nuclear attack? What if they decided to strike first? Roger Hilsman brought the frightening news to the President. There was a moment of absolute grimness. Then Kennedy, with a brief laugh, said, "There is always some so-and-so who doesn't get the word." (The plane returned safely; but perhaps Khrushchev did interpret the flight exactly as Hilsman feared; perhaps this too, along with the invasion force massing in Florida and an unauthorized statement on Friday by the State

LOCAL PROFESSIONAL WOMEN DEMONSTRATING OUTSIDE THE U.N. IN NEW YORK CITY.

MORE PROTESTERS OF THE CUBAN BLOCKADE IN WASHINGTON, D.C. PICKETING OUTSIDE THE WHITE HOUSE.

Department press officer threatening "further action" if work continued on the bases, reinforced his determination to bring the crisis to an end.)

Later that afternoon the Executive Committee met again. Robert Kennedy now came up with a thought of breathtaking simplicity and ingenuity: why not ignore the second Khrushchev message and reply to the first? forget Saturday and concentrate on Friday? This suggestion may, indeed, have been more relevant than anyone could have known. For, as Henry Pachter has argued,* the so-called second letter, from internal evidence, appears to have been initiated as the immediate follow-on of Khrushchev's reply to U Thant; it began with a reference to Kennedy's reply to U Thant on Thursday and took no note of events on Friday. Moreover, its institutional tone suggested that it was written in the Foreign Office. Might it not have been drafted in Moscow on Thursday and Friday with an eye to Saturday morning release in New York? Then the so-called first letter, which reflected the movement of events well beyond the U Thant proposal and which was clearly written by Khrushchev himself, may well have been composed late Friday night (Moscow time) and transmitted immediately to Kennedy while the 'second' letter was deep in the bureaucratic pipelines. Knowing heads of state and foreign office bureaucracies, one could take anything as possible.

At any rate, on October 27 Kennedy now wrote Khrushchev, "I have read your letter of October 26th with great care and welcomed the statement of your desire to seek a prompt solution." As soon as work stopped on the missile bases and the offensive weapons were rendered inoperable under UN supervision, Kennedy continued, he would be ready to negotiate a settlement along the lines Khrushchev had proposed. Then, in a sentence profoundly expressive of his desire to retrieve something out of crisis, he added: "If your letter signifies that you are prepared to discuss a detente affecting NATO and the Warsaw Pact, we are quite prepared to consider with our allies any useful proposals."

And so the message shot inscrutably into the night. Robert Kennedy carried a copy that evening to the Soviet Ambassador, saying grimly that, unless we received assurances in twenty-four hours, the United States would take military action by Tuesday. No one knew which Khrushchev letter superseded the other; no one knew whether Khrushchev was even still in power. "We all agreed in the end," Robert Kennedy said afterward, "that if the Russians were ready to go to nuclear war over Cuba, they were ready to go to nuclear

* In his brilliant essay on the missile crisis *Collision Course* (New York, 1963), 67–68.

war, and that was that. So we might as well have the showdown then as six months later." Saturday night was almost the blackest of all. Unless Khrushchev came through in a few hours, the meeting of the Executive Committee on Sunday might well face the most terrible decisions.

Sunday, October 28, was a shining autumn day. At nine in the morning Khrushchev's answer began to come in. By the fifth sentence it was clear that he had thrown in his hand. Work would stop on the sites; the arms "which you described as offensive" would be crated and returned to the Soviet Union; negotiations would start at the UN. Then, no doubt to placate Castro, Khrushchev asked the United States to discontinue flights over Cuba. (As for the errant U-2 which had strayed over Russia the day before, he warned that "an intruding American plane could be easily taken for a nuclear bomber, which might push us to a fateful step.") Looking ahead, he said, "We should like to continue the exchange of views on the prohibition of atomic and thermonuclear weapons, general disarmament, and other problems relating to the relaxation of international tension."

It was all over, and barely in time. If word had not come that Sunday, if work had continued on the bases, the United States would have had no real choice but to take action against Cuba the next week. No one could discern what lay darkly beyond an air strike or invasion, what measures and countermeasures, actions and reactions, might have driven the hapless world to the ghastly consummation. The President saw more penetratingly into the mists and terrors of the future than anyone else. A few weeks later he said, "If we had invaded Cuba ... I am sure the Soviets would have acted. They would have to, just as we would have to. I think there are certain compulsions on any major power." The compulsions opened up the appalling world of inexorability. The trick was to cut the chain in time. When Kennedy received Khrushchev's reply that golden October morning, he showed profound relief. Later he said, "This is the night to go to the theater, like Abraham Lincoln."

3. THE ELECTION

The President issued immediate instructions that there should be no claiming of victory, no cheering over the Soviet retreat. That night he limited himself on nationwide television to a few unadorned words about "Chairman Khrushchev's statesmanlike decision" and the "compelling necessity for ending the arms race and reducing world tensions."

The next morning he told me he was afraid that people would conclude from this experience that all we had to do in dealing with the Russians was to be tough and they would collapse. The Cuban missile crisis, he pointed out, had three distinctive features: it took place in an area where we enjoyed local conventional superiority, where Soviet national security was not directly engaged and where the Russians lacked a case which they could plausibly sustain before the world. Things would be different, he said, if the situation were one where they had the local superiority, where their national security was directly engaged and where they could convince themselves and others they were in the right. "They had no business in putting those missiles in and lying to me about it. They were in the wrong and knew it. So, when we stood firm, they had to back down. But this doesn't mean at all that they would back down when they felt they were in the right and had vital interests involved."

What worried Kennedy particularly was the inconceivable way each superpower had lost hold of the reality of the other: the United States absolutely persuaded that the Soviet Union would never put nuclear missiles into Cuba; the Soviet Union absolutely persuaded that it could do so and the United States would not respond. But he believed that rationality had triumphed; he hoped that Khrushchev's deceit and recklessness signified some awful aberration, and that the consequence would be to end Soviet illusions about American behavior under pressure. And, indeed, the alacrity with which Khrushchev had managed his retreat suggested that Harriman may have been right in surmising that the Cuban adventure was less his own idea than a project pressed on him by his hard-liners. Perhaps, like Kennedy after the Bay of Pigs, he was now sitting in the Kremlin wondering how in the world he could ever have embarked on so crazy an undertaking.

BY DECEMBER, RUSSIA HAD BEGUN SHIPPING ITS WEAPONS OUT OF CUBA.

"There are few higher gratifications," Dr. Johnson once said, "than that of reflection on surmounted evils." Kennedy was well satisfied by the performance of his government. The Executive Committee had proved a brilliant instrument of consideration and coordination. He was particularly proud of his brother, always balanced, never rattled, his eye fixed on the ultimate as well as on the immediate. McNamara, as usual, had been superb. Llewellyn Thompson had provided wise counsel; Edwin Martin had managed the Latin American side with tact and efficiency. If the President was disappointed in others, he was not, I think, especially surprised. As a whole, the government could hardly have performed better. For the rest, life went on.

The crisis had for a moment suspended the political campaign. It is hard to estimate the impact of the Cuba week on the election, though foreign crisis usually strengthens the administration in office. Certainly it was a rebuke to extremism on both the left and the right. The outcome left the internal composition of the Congress little changed, but, in light of the losses usually suffered by incumbent administrations in mid-term elections, the President's personal mandate was triumphantly refreshed. And Richard Nixon's declaration of hatred of the press and 'withdrawal' from politics after losing the governorship of California gave the White House a special fillip of entertainment.

4. LOOSE ENDS

But the problems of the missile crisis were far from over. In New York Stevenson and McCloy were deep in intricate negotiation. In Havana Castro, unconsulted by Khrushchev, furious over the Soviet idea that the UN should verify the dismantlement and removal of the missiles and determined to hold on to the IL-28 bombers, which he now claimed as Cuban property, was doing all he could to upset the Soviet-American settlement. The Russians themselves seemed less than forthcoming on verification and on the removal of the IL-28s. But on November 20 Khrushchev finally agreed that the IL-28s would go within thirty days, and the United States terminated the quarantine.

Castro's resistance, however, made it impossible to establish the UN inspection Khrushchev had proposed, and the United States therefore never completed the reciprocal pledge not to invade Cuba. Discussions dragged desultorily on till in January 1963 the United States and the Soviet Union, accepting the impossibility of resolving "all the problems which have arisen in connection with this affair," formally removed the Cuban missile question from the Security Council. In the months to come, however, the original Khrushchev-Kennedy plan was in a sense put into effect at one remove. Instead of UN inspection, American aerial reconnaissance served as the means of verification; "the camera," the President said in December, "... is actually going to be our best inspector." The Soviet Union tacitly accepted this by instructing the Russians at the SAM sites to leave the U-2s alone. For its part, the United States, without formal commitment, refrained from invasion and, indeed, took measures in the spring of 1963 to prevent hit-and-run attacks by Cuban refugees from United States territory.

5. AFTERMATH

The President had one other item of unfinished Cuban business—this one left over from the Bay of Pigs. He had never forgotten the men his government had put on the Cuban beaches, and he had been determined in one way or another to free them from Castro's prisons. In May 1961, when Castro had proposed an exchange of the surviving members of Brigade 2506 for five hundred bulldozers, or, as he soon said, $28 million, Kennedy had instigated the organization of a private Tractors for Freedom Committee led by Mrs. Roosevelt, Walter Reuther and Milton Eisenhower. But the project soon bogged down in domestic political controversy.

At the end of March 1962, the captives went on trial in Havana. Members of the Brigade who had escaped to Florida now made a new attempt to seek government support. They found an immediate sympathizer in Robert Kennedy, who, with Richard Goodwin's assistance, set to work to mobilize hemisphere opinion to persuade Castro to spare the lives of the prisoners. Then the possibility of ransoming the Brigade revived in Havana, though Castro now lifted the price to $62 million. This sum seemed beyond hope of raising, and in June the Attorney General recommended that the Cuban exiles ask James B. Donovan of New York, a lawyer who had been general counsel of OSS in the Second World War, to intercede with Castro. Donovan, flying to Havana in late August, persuaded Castro to accept food and drugs instead of money. Negotiations dragged on into October and into the missile crisis; but Donovan persisted and arranged a deal. After the crisis, the Attorney General, taking personal command, mobilized the Department of Justice, much of the rest of the government and much of the drug industry to get the men out by Christmas. Time was pressing; for the prisoners themselves, underfed and sick, were beginning to look, as one who had visited them told Robert Kennedy, like animals who were about to die. It was an undertaking of extraordinary drive and enterprise, and it succeeded. On December 21 Donovan and Castro signed a memorandum of agreement. Two days later the first prisoners arrived in Florida. After Christmas the Brigade leaders, gaunt and wasted, were received by the President at Palm Beach.

But the ultimate impact of the missile crisis was wider than Cuba, wider even than the western hemisphere. To the whole world it displayed the ripening of an American leadership unsurpassed in the responsible management of power. From the moment of challenge the American President never had a doubt about the need for a hard response. But throughout the crisis he coolly and exactly measured the level of force necessary to deal with the level of threat. Defining a clear and limited objective, he moved with mathematical precision to accomplish it. At every stage he gave his adversary time for reflection and reappraisal, taking care not to force him into 'spasm' reactions or to cut off his retreat.

Moreover, despite strong pressure to take action repugnant to our national traditions, he always linked his use of power to the ideals of the country and to the necessities of the world which would have to go on after the conflict. By his own composure, clarity and control, he held the country behind him. It was almost as if he had begun to reshape the nation in his own image, for the American people, so many of whom had been in a frenzy about air-raid shelters a year before, so many of whom still longed for total solutions, went through the Cuba week without panic or hysteria, with few cries of "better red than dead" and fewer demands (until the crisis was safely over) for "total victory."

In a toast to Chancellor Adenauer two weeks afterward, Kennedy spoke of "an important turning point, possibly, in the history of the relations between East and West." He meant, as he later explained, that this was the first time that the United States and the Soviet Union had ever directly challenged each other with nuclear weapons as the issue; and in his sense of "a climactic period" he associated the missile crisis with the growing conflict between China and Russia and the Chinese attack on India. All this, he said, was "bound to have its effects, even though they can't be fully perceived now."

He did not exaggerate the significance of the Cuban victory in itself. He recognized that he had enjoyed advantages in this specific contest—because Cuba did not lie within the reach of Soviet conventional power or within the scope of Soviet vital interests, and because the Russians knew they could not sustain this particular course of deceit and irresponsibility before the world. These conditions might not be present the next time. But he hoped that he had made to Khrushchev in the Atlantic in October 1962 the point he had failed to make sixteen months before in Vienna—that neither side dare tamper carelessly with the delicate and complex equilibrium of world power. "If we suffer a major defeat, if they suffer a major defeat," he mused with newspapermen at Palm Beach on the last day of the year, "it may change the balance of power.... It also increases possibly the chance of war."

This was why, when Khrushchev backed down, Kennedy refrained from calling the American victory a victory or the Russian rout a rout. "Every setback," Kennedy said later, "has the seeds of its own reprisal, if the country is powerful enough." So the German invasion of Czechoslovakia in the winter of 1939 had led to the British guarantee of Poland. "We tried to make their setback in Cuba not the kind that would bring about an increase in hostility but perhaps provide for an easing of relations."

It was this combination of toughness and restraint, of will, nerve and wisdom, so brilliantly controlled, so matchlessly calibrated, that dazzled the world. Before the missile crisis people might have feared that we would use our power extravagantly or not use it at all. But the thirteen days gave the world—even the Soviet Union—a sense of American determination and responsibility in the use of power which, if sustained, might indeed become a turning point in the history of the relations between east and west.

XXXII. THE NOT SO GRAND DESIGN

YET, EVEN AS THE PRESIDENT had won the most decisive victory of west over east since the start of the cold war and in a style which promised the relief rather than the rise of international tension, he faced a setback within the west itself. The concept of a unified democratic Europe as part of a freely trading Atlantic community had been a basic element of Kennedy's world strategy. In a sympathetic and illuminating book of 1962 called *The Grand Design,* Joseph Kraft had set forth the administration's vision of North America and Western Europe happily joined by policies and institutions in common pursuit of economic expansion and military defense. Now in the moment of triumph the Grand Design was shaken by brusque challenge bursting out of the heart of the western alliance itself.

On January 14, 1963, eleven weeks after his prompt support of the United States during the missile crisis, General Charles de Gaulle held one of his periodic press conferences. In two sharp and elegant strokes, he knocked out the economic and military pillars of Atlantic unity. If Great Britain were admitted to the Common Market, the General said, it would transform the character of the European Economic Community and "finally it would appear as a colossal Atlantic community under American domination and direction." As for a coordinated western nuclear policy, "France intends to have her own national defense.... For us, in present circumstances, integration is something which is not imaginable." He concluded suavely about the French nuclear force: "It is entirely understandable that this French enterprise should not seem very satisfactory to certain American quarters. In politics and strategy, as in economics, monopoly naturally appears to him who enjoys it as the best possible system."

1. THE METAMORPHOSIS OF WESTERN EUROPE

The de Gaulle press conference was the ironic result of a series of changes the United States itself had set in motion fifteen years earlier. The Second World War had left Western Europe in a state of spiritual and physical shock: France, Italy and Germany had suffered deep national humiliation; Britain was weary and spent; the smaller countries realized more than ever their helplessness in the modern world. The loss of overseas empires intensified the sense of impotence; so too did Western Europe's knowledge of its absolute dependence on the United States for economic reconstruction and military protection.

The Marshall Plan and the North Atlantic Treaty Organization constituted the two sides of the American response. Behind the NATO shield, the nations of Western Europe with Marshall aid set to work rebuilding and modernizing their economies. In France Jean Monnet laid down the bases for national planning. The unification of Europe, sooner or later, seemed to him a necessity of history. With quiet American collaboration, Monnet began a step-by-step realization of his vision. The Coal and Steel Community was set up in 1951; Monnet became its first president. The failure of the project of a European Defense Community in 1954 only confirmed his belief that economic integration had to precede political integration. The next year he resigned his official post in order to work for economic unity through the Action Committee for a United States of Europe, whose membership included political and labor leaders from the six nations. In 1957, France, West Germany, Italy, Belgium, the Netherlands, and Luxembourg signed the Treaty of Rome, organizing the European Economic Community. The EEC further stimulated the renaissance of Western Europe. Soon the EEC's Common Market became the world's largest importer and greatest trading community.

By 1960 the economic dependence on the United States had largely disappeared. And, at the same time, the military dependence had taken new and perplexing forms. If the prospect of a Soviet invasion of Western Europe had ever been real, few Europeans believed in it any longer. Moreover, the Soviet nuclear achievement, putting the United States for the first time in its history under threat of devastating attack, had devalued the American deterrent in European eyes. These developments meant that the conditions which had given rise to the Marshall Plan and NATO were substantially gone. The new Europe would not be content to remain an economic or military satellite of America. The problem now was to work out the next phase in the Atlantic relationship.

This problem received much hard thought on both sides of the Atlantic in the late fifties; and the search for a solution began to move in two somewhat different directions. Those concerned with the economic and political aspects of the relationship were thinking more and more in terms of a dual Atlantic partnership resting on two distinct entities, the United States and the European Economic Community.* Those concerned with the military aspects were thinking more and more in terms of a single Atlantic community based on NATO and the indivisibility of the nuclear deterrent. The divergence was, in the language of the American civil rights movement, between 'separate but equal' and 'integration.'

2. PARTNERSHIP

The existence of the Common Market and its external tariffs, creating the need for reciprocal tariff adjustments with other nations and areas, made the idea of Atlantic partnership almost irresistible to economists both in Europe and the United States. George Ball had begun to formulate the revision of trade policy required to prepare the American economy to live with a unified Western Europe. In 1961, he became Under Secretary of State for Economic Affairs and his first move was to secure the ratification of the convention establishing the Organization for Economic Cooperation and Development. The OECD, Kennedy said, would become "one of the principal institutions through which we pursue the great aim of consolidating the Atlantic community."

The next step was taken in London. When Harold Macmillan came to Washington in April 1961, he informed the President that Britain had resolved to apply for membership in the Common Market. This was an extraordinary decision; it represented the reversal of a thousand years of English history. The decision had two main grounds: the economic hope that the competitive stimulus of continental industry in a larger market would speed the modernization of British industry; and the political hope that, in the twilight of empire, Britain could find a new role of leadership in Europe.

From Washington's viewpoint, the second reason was more attractive than the first; for the Common Market presented the United States with economic problems which British membership would only enhance. But these were, in his mind, overborne by the political benefits. With British membership, the Market could become the basis for a true political federation of Europe.

3. INTERDEPENDENCE

At the same time that economics was prescribing a transatlantic partnership between two separate and equal entities, defense strategy was arguing for a unified Atlantic military community based on the American nuclear deterrent. The discrepancy between these two conceptions was not always clearly recognized. But it led to continuous though murky debate within the American government and the west, and it represented a lurking vulnerability within the Grand Design.

Secretary McNamara laid down the strategic position in his forthright way at the Athens NATO ministerial meeting in the spring of 1962 and repeated it publicly in his Ann Arbor speech in June. The nature of nuclear war, in McNamara's view, made a unified deterrent imperative. He regarded "relatively weak national nuclear forces with enemy cities as their targets" as perilous in peace, because they might invite preemptive first strikes, and disastrous in war. The rational policy, in his belief, was in peace to avoid "the proliferation of nuclear power with all of its attendant dangers" and in war to enforce a no-cities strategy on the enemy. His conclusion was clear: "Limited nuclear capabilities, operating independently, are dangerous, expensive, prone to obsolescence, and lacking in credibility as a deterrent."

* Hopefully to be enlarged by the addition of Great Britain and other members of the European Free Trade Association. Proponents of this conception mysteriously insisted for a time on calling it the 'dumbbell' theory.

Actually the McNamara doctrine saw little role even for dependent national deterrents; and the President had privately urged on Macmillan in February 1962 that a British effort to maintain its deterrent through the sixties might both confirm de Gaulle in his own course and hasten the day when the Germans would demand nuclear weapons for themselves. The French independent deterrent, weaker and cruder than the British, was left as the target of American public disapproval, an impression which did not stir pro-American feelings at the Elysée.

The indispensability of nuclear centralization, called for a NATO solution in order to head off independent national aspirations; or, as McNamara put it at Ann Arbor, it emphasized the "interdependence" of national security interests on both sides of the Atlantic. With this mellifluous but misleading term McNamara indicated the line of debate between the strategists and the economists: Atlantic interdependence vs. transatlantic partnership. "Interdependence" was misleading because what McNamara mean at bottom was precisely the *dependence* of western security on a nuclear deterrent under American control. Yet his resort to the word also suggested his recognition of a problem, even if, in stating the problem: "We want and need a greater degree of Alliance participation in formulating nuclear weapons policy to the greatest extent possible." But what Alliance participation would be possible, except in marginal and symbolic forms, so long as the United States retained its veto over the use of nuclear weapons?

In 1957, Britain, Turkey and Italy accepted nuclear missiles under an agreement by which the United States retained custody of the warheads and both the United States and the recipient could veto their use: these were the Jupiters which caused such argument during the Cuba crisis. No one liked the Jupiters very much, but the emergence of the submarine-based Polaris missile at the end of the decade introduced new possibilities. But a discontent with the American monopoly was rising in top European military and government circles. Given the uncertainties of American politics, the new vulnerability of America to Soviet nuclear attack and the new self-confidence of Western Europe, why should not Western Europe have nuclear resources of its own?

By 1960 the sharing of nuclear control was thus a live issue.

4. FLEXIBLE RESPONSE VS. NUCLEAR CENTRALIZATION

After reflection, the new administration decided to continue along these lines. In Ottawa in May 1961 Kennedy said that the United States was ready to commit to NATO five or more Polaris atomic missile submarines, "subject to any agreed NATO guidelines on their control and use, and responsive to the needs of all members but [sic] still credible in an emergency"; beyond this, he looked forward to the possibility of a NATO seaborne force, "truly multilateral in ownership and control, if this should be desired and found feasible by our Allies, *once NATO's non-nuclear goals have been achieved.*"

The control problem in this formulation remained, however, as obscure as ever. In any case the last clause (my italics) contained a major catch from the European viewpoint, and therefore the Ottawa proposal elicited no immediate European enthusiasm. The Eisenhower multilateral force had been within the context of massive retaliation, empty as that doctrine had become by 1960. But the Kennedy proposal was within the context of the novel and unfamiliar doctrine of flexible response. This new doctrine made the strengthening of the conventional forces of the Alliance, as Kennedy said at Ottawa, the "matter of the highest priority" if, in McNamara's phrase, western strategy was going to multiply its options.

The Berlin crisis of the summer of 1961 revealed some of the difficulties of the European reaction. McNamara, despite heroic efforts, could not bring the Pentagon and the NATO command to consensus on the western military response. And, while everyone agreed that we might eventually have to go on to nuclear war, there was disagreement between those who favored a single definitive salvo against the Soviet Union and those who favored careful and discriminate attack.

Washington had been persuading Western Europe for a decade of the infallibility of nuclear protection. The new American passion for conventional force now led many Europeans to believe, or profess to believe, that, in view of our own vulnerability to nuclear attack, we were no longer prepared to go to nuclear war at all. They contended that the Soviet Union would be far more effectively deterred if it knew the United States had no alternative to instant nuclear retaliation. Moreover, conventional forces, it was argued, were expensive; they were politically unpopular; they could never be large enough to defeat the Red Army; their use would convert Europe into a battleground while America and Russia remained privileged sanctuaries; and in any case no one believed in the likelihood of a Soviet invasion of Western Europe unless the Russians thought themselves exempt from nuclear reprisal.

Kennedy tried to counter this current of thought by assuring de Gaulle and others that the United States would use nuclear weapons in case of a massive conventional attack on Western Europe. But de Gaulle, thinking always in terms of the narrow interests of the nation-state, did not see why the United States should do so unless its own territory was under assault. He believed all the more fervently in the necessity of the French independent deterrent. Even the British in early

1962 officially suggested to the Defense Department that a substantial increase in conventional forces in Europe might discredit the deterrent.

The Kennedy-McNamara strategy, brilliantly designed to reduce the threat of nuclear war and to cope with the world-wide nuances of communist aggression, thus caused confusion and concern. In European eyes the question of nuclear control became more crucial than ever. A multilateral force conditioned on the achievement of NATO's non-nuclear goals had no great appeal; but the multilateral force in itself implied an entry into the nuclear club, and this did have appeal, especially for Bonn, so long excluded from membership.

If the Ottawa formula had no widespread impact in Europe outside Bonn, it had dramatic impact in Washington. For the idea of a multilateral force—MLF, as it was soon familiarly known—met a number of internal problems in our own policy. Though it served no strictly military function it appealed to the advocates of strategic interdependence as a means of preserving the unity of the deterrent and at the same time of giving NATO allies a nuclear role. Thus very early the MLF acquired a powerful convert in Thomas K. Finletter, our ambassador to NATO. At the same time, the MLF attracted advocates of economic partnership because it brought new and urgent pressure on the European governments to move toward federation. The reason for this was that the only body to which we would possibly yield our nuclear veto was the government of a united Western Europe. Thus the Europeanists, whether tending toward interdependence, like Finletter, or toward partnership, like Ball, began to see in the MLF a useful vehicle—in time, *the* vehicle—for resolving the contradictions of our Atlantic policy.

In September 1962, however, McGeorge Bundy, striking out in another direction in a speech at Copenhagen, declared that the United States was willing to accept a European nuclear force "genuinely unified and multilateral," provided that it was integrated with the American deterrent; this, unlike MLF, meant a force without American participation.

Kennedy saw all this debate, both at home and abroad, as entirely exploratory. Despite his strong ties to Europe, had no absolute doctrines about it. He combined a strong sense of ultimate Atlantic solidarity with a wide tolerance of means.

His basic attitude toward Europe was to do what he could to strengthen the hand of modern-minded Europeans in their quest for unity—not to tell Europe what it ought to do but to adjust American policy to the needs and tempo of rational European self-determination. This was the spirit of his moving address at Independence Hall in Philadelphia on July 4, 1962. Here he mingled the Europeanist themes, speaking both of the "Atlantic partnership" which would be made possible when Europe formed "a more perfect union" and of a "Declaration of Interdependence" based on "the indivisible liberty of all." In Europe, where the speech made a deep impression, it was correctly read as an affirmation of the American desire for close relationship with whatever sort of united Europe the genius of its people might evolve.

5. SKYBOLT

The President's Philadelphia speech came at a time of rising optimism about European unity. Then in the weeks after the missile crisis the concepts of partnership and interdependence entered into unexpected conflict. The issue was, in its first appearance, technical: the decision of the United States government to cancel an agreement made by President Eisenhower provide Great Britain with Skybolt missiles. But the problem very quickly became profoundly political. It involved other things than partnership and interdependence—most notably the relationship between Washington and London. Its solution, however, compelled the President to choose between those in his own government whose main interest lay in transforming Western Europe, including Britain, into a unified political and economic entity and those whose main interest lay in guarding the Anglo-American special relationship and integrity of the deterrent.

Skybolt, a two-stage ballistic missile launched from a bomber, originated as the Air Force's answer to Polaris in our permanent inter-service competition over the strategic deterrent. Though Britain could probably have had Polaris in 1960, it preferred Skybolt, which would prolong the life of the Royal Air Force's V-bombers, while Polaris would force the Royal Navy to divert its resources from aircraft carriers to submarines. Moreover, Skybolt seemed more likely to maintain the 'independence' of the British deterrent; Polaris was already being mentioned in a NATO context. The agreement bound the United States to pay all the costs of Skybolt's research and development. Britain had only to pay for the operational missiles she would eventually acquire. At the same time, Britain opened the Holy Loch naval base to American Polaris submarines. Though provisions were made for terminating the Skybolt agreement and though Skybolt and Holy Loch were nominally separate undertakings, the British left Camp David with the conviction that their loan of Holy Loch obligated the Americans to assist the British deterrent by providing one form of missile or another.

Skybolt was an extraordinarily intricate device, and in the early months of 1962 the project involved more money and less progress than anyone had supposed, and by August McNamara's cost-effectiveness studies convinced him that further investment would be a mistake. By the time of the missile crisis McNamara had substantially concluded to end American support for Skybolt. Rumors began to circulate, some reaching the British, who communicated deep concern about possible difficulties between our two countries and emphasized the importance of our taking the initiative in devising a substitute. On November 7 McNamara formally recommended cancellation to the President. Secretary Rusk, who was present, agreed with the decision. There was brief talk about other weapons systems which might be offered in place of Skybolt—possibly Polaris. Initially, London's response to the decision was muted. For a time, the special relationship was at an impasse as each partner lingered by the telephone, expecting the other to come forth with alternative proposals. At the end of the month London and Washington jointly announced a meeting between the Prime Minister and the President for Nassau on December 18, three days after Macmillan was to meet with de Gaulle in France; but this was for other matters. Skybolt was not even on the original agenda.

McNamara, supposing wrongly that the British were hard at work on contingency planning, had directed his own people to appraise possible substitutes for Skybolt. They fixed quickly on Polaris; for, in the view of those who cared about a unified deterrent, the addition of Polaris to a British nuclear force which, as McNamara had pointed out after Ann Arbor, was for all practical purposes integrated with our own, raised no serious problem. The Europeanists in State, however, were now organizing to defend the conception of transatlantic partnership. They had regretted the cancellation of Skybolt, fearing that it would overthrow the government in London committed to bring Britain into Europe. But, if Skybolt had to go, at least let it carry the special relationship down with it; this would place the British and the Germans on a level of equality in the missile age, make Bonn more manageable and facilitate British entry into Europe. What worried the Europeanists was the thought that the United States by offering a replacement for Skybolt—Polaris, for example—would prolong the British deterrent, intensify Bonn's demand for a nuclear role and prove to de Gaulle that Britain preferred the United States to Europe. Some Europeanists were chiefly concerned with the Common Market, others with the MLF. But both British entry into the Market and the MLF were now, in their view, at stake, and Skybolt offered the grand opportunity to terminate the special relationship and force Britain into Europe.

But these were still mostly flurries behind the scenes. With no evidence of special concern from London, Washington concluded that the British were not too unhappy, and the Skybolt problem receded from official minds. McNamara went to London on December 11. When his careful explanation of Skybolt's technical shortcomings failed to conclude in any substitute offer which the British with dignity could accept, the Minister of Defense, Peter Thorneycroft, took the offensive. He concentrated on the political consequences of cancellation: for the Tory government, for Anglo-American understanding. Those who had always been saying that it was impossible to rely on the United States would be confirmed; those who had argued for that reliance would be betrayed. Thorneycroft asked if the United States were cancelling Skybolt for technical reasons, would it be prepared to state publicly that it would do everything possible to help Britain preserve its independent nuclear role? He claimed that the United States lay under a moral obligation, if it announced the demise of Skybolt, to announce at the same time some other means of sustaining Britain's deterrent.

And in the December drizzle at Rambouillet the Prime Minister met the General. De Gaulle no longer saw how Britain could possibly join the Common Market: better let it apply for association rather than membership. Macmillan valiantly argued the case for Britain in Europe. The Prime Minister also brought up Skybolt and told the General that he planned to maintain the British deterrent, hopefully on the basis of Polaris. This was a point with which de Gaulle, cherishing his own deterrent, would presumably sympathize. But the talks were not a success, and the parting was as chilly as the weather: now on to the sunlight of the Caribbean.

6. NASSAU AND AFTER

When Kennedy arrived in Nassau, the atmosphere was tense. Henry Brandon of the London *Sunday Times* reported in the British delegation a "resentment and suspicion of American intentions such as I have never experienced in all the Anglo-American conferences I have covered over the past twenty years." When the formal talks began the next morning, Macmillan with weary eloquence invoked past glories of the Anglo-American relationship and suggested that a straight switch of Polaris for Skybolt would keep that relationship alive. More eloquent than ever, Macmillan insisted that Britain was determined to stay in the nuclear club. His nation had a great history and would not give up now. If the United States would not help, Britain would continue on its own at whatever cost, including the inevitable rift with the United States.

By now the President had very likely made up his own mind that the British had to have Polaris. The only question was how to reconcile this with the claims of multilateralization and European partnership. Macmillan had suggested at one point a willingness to put his Polaris force in NATO if he retained the right to draw it back in case of an emergency. This formula offered a possibility of harmonizing independence

STATE OF THE UNION ADDRESS ON JANUARY 14, 1963 IN WHICH KENNEDY HAILED THE EUROPEAN ALLIANCE. ON THIS SAME DAY, CHARLES DE GUALLE DECLARED WAR AGAINST THE GRAND DESIGN.

and NATO. The drafters now set to work and outdid themselves in masterly ambiguity. Article 6 of the Statement on Nuclear Defense Systems contemplated a NATO multinational force—that is, allocations from national forces to the NATO command. Article 7 pledged both nations to use their "best endeavors" toward a multilateral force—that is, a mixed-manned force from which national withdrawals would be impossible. Article 8 agreed that the United States would make Polaris missiles (minus warheads) available to the British and that the resulting British force might be included in either the multinational or the multilateral system. The communiqué concluded by expressing the joint Anglo-American conviction that "the nuclear defense" of the western alliance was "indivisible."

For Macmillan it was a great victory. For Kennedy it was a reasonable adjustment to a thorny problem, leaving policy free to move in a number of directions. For our own Europeanists, it was a missed opportunity and bitter defeat: instead of forcing the British to an MLF commitment, we had saved their deterrent, thrust an issue into the hands of de Gaulle and set back the cause of European integration.

For France it might, despite Macmillan's mention of Polaris at Rambouillet, have devastating effect; so it was decided at Nassau to offer de Gaulle Polaris on the same terms as to Macmillan—i.e., assignment to NATO but with the escape clause of emergency withdrawal. The President and others hoped that it might throw the French a bridge back to NATO. During December and the first two weeks of the new year those in Washington who based themselves on Nassau's Article 6 remained quite optimistic about the chance of the French joining a NATO multinational force. The MLF, they hoped, was dead. But the Europeanists were meanwhile rallying from their post-Nassau gloom to mount a new campaign, based on Nassau's Article 7, to retrieve the MLF and defend the Grand Design against both de Gaulle and Macmillan. Kennedy, impressed by their contention that Nassau had given Bonn a dangerous sense of exclusion, agreed that a modest refloating of the MLF might pull West Germany back toward the alliance and offset Adenauer's growing fascination with de Gaulle.

In January 1963, Kennedy in his State of the Union address hailed the alliance: "Free Europe is entering into a new phase of its long and brilliant history … moving toward a unity of purpose and power and policy in every sphere of activity." In Paris the same day de Gaulle held his press conference and declared war against the Grand Design.

XXXIII.
TWO EUROPES: DE GAULLE AND KENNEDY

THE BRUTALITY OF DE GAULLE'S ATTACK left an impression that he was overcome by sudden anger and caused much speculation over possible irritants. It seemed unlikely that the policy of January 14 was the product of passing annoyance. Its roots, as I endeavored to persuade the President, lay deep in the view of Europe and the world de Gaulle had stated and restated throughout his career. Kennedy asked for a memorandum on this point. My report to him concluded: "There is very little we could have done to divert him from what has plainly been the cherished objective of his life."

1. DE GAULLE'S EUROPE

He had set forth as recently as 1959 in *Le Salut,* the third volume of his magnificent memoirs, what he called "the great plan I have conceived for my country." The elements were clearly stated.

a) Britain and the United States wanted "to relegate us to a secondary place among nations responsible for constructing the peace. But I had no intention of letting this happen."

b) "I intended to assure France primacy in Western Europe."

c) I intended "to prevent the rise of a new Reich that might again threaten the safety" of France;

d) I intended "to co-operate with East and West and, if need be, contract the necessary alliances on one side or the other without ever accepting any kind of dependency";

e) I intended "to persuade the states along the Rhine, the Alps, and the Pyrenees to form a political, economic, and strategic bloc; to establish this bloc as one of the three world powers and, should it become necessary, as the arbiter between the Soviet and Anglo-American camps."

De Gaulle could hardly have made his purpose more solemn or emphatic. "Since 1940," he wrote, "my every word and act have been dedicated to establishing these possibilities; now that France was on her feet again, I would try to realize them."

No one had predicted his own course more lucidly than de Gaulle himself. Why then had January 14 astonished so many people? One reason, I discovered to my dismay, was that few people in the State Department appeared to have read de Gaulle. Another surely was that de Gaulle liked to put about an impression of himself as a lonely, unyielding, messianic figure, set in his views, oblivious of tactics, prepared to wait in Colombey-les-deux-Eglises until the great world came round to him. No impression could be more misleading. Actually he was one of the consummate political tacticians of the twentieth century.

De Gaulle, who had perceived for a long time the fatal contradiction within the Grand Design between interdependence and partnership, now was moving to exploit it. But why had he chosen this moment to come into the open? Probably the Cuban missile crisis was a precipitating factor. On the one hand, it showed that the United States in emergencies would act on its own, without NATO consultation or 'integration,' on matters affecting not only American security but world peace. This undoubtedly reinforced the General's old belief that America did not regard Europe as a primary interest; no nation could ever be expected to look out for anything but itself. At the same time the outcome of Cuba paradoxically renewed his faith in the broad efficacy of the American deterrent. And the outcome also reconfirmed his view that there was no danger of war over Berlin. All this left him free to pursue his own ends in Europe.

In addition, if Cuba were to be followed by a *détente,* de Gaulle wanted to be in on the peacemaking. Moreover, if Western Europe were irrevocably tied to the Atlantic, the division of Europe would become permanent, and de Gaulle's dream of rebuilding "Europe from the Atlantic to the Urals" would be forever frustrated. And within the Common Market Britain was steadily acquiring the votes for admission—a result which, if achieved, would end French primacy in the Economic Community and consolidate Atlantic influence on the continent. Europe must be for the Europeans; action was necessary: Nassau provided the pretext.

I believe the President could never rid his mind of the thought that, if this or that had been done differently, it might have been possible to avoid the impasse of 1963. His interest in de Gaulle never flagged. The General was one of the heroes. Nevertheless, if Kennedy had his troubles with him as he said at the Malraux dinner in 1962 he came in the end to feel that de Gaulle was operating out of a consistent, if not convincing, conception of France's interests and that the General evidently believed he needed some sort of friction with the United States. Kennedy, however, never regarded him as beyond rational discourse, a visit was scheduled for February 1964.

2. MLF

January 14 unavoidably produced the usual reaction—"what can you do with a man like that?"—but in a short while Kennedy accepted the new reality. The Europeanists, however, did not want to let the dust settle. Ball's January visit to Adenauer had given a new spurt of life to the MLF. If de Gaulle meant to make West Germany choose between France and the United States, the MLF in Washington's view was the way to make it clear that Bonn would find greater security in the Atlantic relationship. To strengthen this point, Kennedy decided in mid-January to visit Germany on a spring trip to Europe. Soon afterward Ambassador Livingston Merchant, an experienced career officer, was directed to work with Finletter in preparing and negotiating American proposals on the MLF.

Kennedy accepted the need to reassure the Germans and show NATO that there were alternatives to Gaullism. But he retained a certain skepticism about the MLF. He felt first of all that the MLF campaign diverted interest from more serious problems of the planet. "The whole debate about an atomic force in Europe," he told Spaak of Belgium in May, "is really useless, because Berlin is secure, and Europe as a whole is well protected. What really matters at this point is the rest of the world." As for the MLF per se, he really considered that, so long as the United States retained its veto, the MLF was something of a fake. Though he was willing to try it, he could not see why Europeans would be interested in making enormous financial contributions toward a force over which they had no real control.

The MLF advocates replied primarily by talking about West Germany. Bonn wanted the MLF because it was a status symbol, marking a form of accession to the nuclear club; because it gave West Germany an indissoluble nuclear association with the United States and a sense of nuclear equality with Britain; because it would avert pressures for an independent German deterrent; because they hoped that in a few years the control issue would be re-examined on its merits; in short, because MLF provided a self-respecting role in nuclear deterrence.

All this rested on the premise that the Germans were hell-bent on having nuclear weapons and, if they could not get them multilaterally, would seek them bilaterally, even at the expense of the American relationship. Though this proposition had been hackneyed around the American government, it did not seem to some, especially the British, all that self-evident. Some British political leaders feared that the American effort to promote the MLF having the effect of generating such a demand where none existed before. They added ominously that, if such a demand ever came into being, it was not likely to be satisfied by the secondary symbolism of mixed-manning.

Ever the pragmatist, Kennedy understood that the MLF was the best available tool to reconcile interdependence—the indivisibility of the deterrent—with partnership—the building of a united Western Europe; moreover, it would fill a vacuum into which, otherwise, Gaullism might seep. In press conferences Kennedy said, "We think the multilateral force represents the best solution to hold the alliance together," though always emphasizing that if "Europe decides that this isn't what they want, we would be glad to hear other proposals." MLF in his view was not a demarche but a response. When he sent emissaries to discuss it with European leaders, he instructed them not to talk as if they were reflecting a personal preoccupation of the American President's.

But our Europeanists, seeing the MLF as the last chance of strengthening allied cooperation and of securing Adenauer against the temptation of de Gaulle, pushed the idea with greater zeal than the President intended. The Merchant mission of March and April charged around Europe in a Convair, giving the impression of a major American campaign and stirring opposition wherever it went. Apart from Germany, the response was meager; and, as the MLF appeared likely to dwindle into a Washington-Bonn operation, which the President would never have accepted, its supporters had to redouble their efforts elsewhere.

In October 1963 when Lord Home, soon to be translated into Sir Alec Douglas-Home and Prime Minister, visited Washington, he said that the British saw the point of MLF but were bothered by the insistence with which the American government was pushing it. Kennedy, a little taken aback, said he had no desire to bring pressure. The President reaffirmed his feeling that MLF's basic principle was interesting and important; it would give non-nuclear powers a sense of participation in nuclear decisions without making them nuclear powers. But in his view we should go at it slowly.

3. ITALY

If anything was clear about the new Europe, it was that the economic revival was transforming the mood and expectations of the working classes. By showing that a free economic system could raise mass living standards, it was attenuating their commitment to classical socialism. At the same time, it was inciting them to demand larger shares of the affluence they saw flowing around them. And meanwhile the very abundance of consumer goods was creating a spiritual disquietude among the intellectuals, fearful of materialism and seeking some higher public purpose. All this was producing a ferment in the broad political zone lying between traditional conservatism on one side and communism on the other.

The two great groups historically inhabiting the center-left were the Christian democrats and the social democrats. Though they had long been at odds over such issues as government aid to church schools, the fellowship of the Resistance during the war had encouraged tentative experiments in collaboration. If they could only work steadily together now, might they not give Western Europe the social leadership it needed to meet its new problems? At the moment such a rapprochement seemed most likely in Italy. If the center-left coalition succeeded there, the alliance between progressive Catholics and democratic Socialists might offer a model for other nations—for Germany after Adenauer, for France after de Gaulle, even for Spain after Franco. The consolidation of a Western European center-left would also be the best guarantee against the communist effort to revive the prewar united front with the Socialists.

The Soviet intervention in Hungary in 1956 proved too much for Pietro Nenni, the main Socialist leader, and many of his comrades. In 1957 Nenni began to move away from the Communist Party. By 1960 his break was complete.

The movement of the Nenni Socialists led some in the democratic parties to see at last the chance to end the immobilism which had long cursed Italian politics. The thesis thus arose among the Christian Democrats of an *apertura a sinistra*—an opening to the left—calling for a center-left government, composed of the Christian Democratic, Social Democratic and Republican parties with, initially, 'outside' support (i.e., benevolent parliamentary abstention) by the Nenni Socialists, to be followed in due course by active voting support and eventually by participation in a governing coalition.

The policy of the United States before Kennedy had been one of purposeful opposition to the opening to the left.

That policy was appropriate for the Eisenhower administration and possibly even for the conditions of the fifties. But by 1961 no one could doubt Nenni's break with the Communists. Moreover, by ingenious reinterpretation, Nenni had defined his party's traditional neutralism as meaning the preservation of the existing European equilibrium; since Italian withdrawal from NATO would threaten that equilibrium, Nenni explicitly opposed such withdrawal as an unneutral act. Moreover, a progressive administration in Washington should certainly not be in the position of discouraging progressive policies in Rome, especially when social reform was required to isolate the Communists, eliminate the conditions which bred them and begin the reclamation of the working class for democracy.

For all these reasons it seemed that the time had come to end the American opposition to the *apertura* and make it clear that the United States welcomed a government in Italy which addressed itself to the social and economic needs of the people. Prime Minister Amintore Fanfani's visit to Washington in June 1961 provided an obvious opportunity to signalize the new departure. Though the *apertura* was not on the formal agenda, Kennedy told Fanfani privately that, if the Italian Prime Minister thought it a good idea (as he did), we would watch developments with sympathy.

The presidential decision was, of course, at once communicated to the State Department, and this should have ended the matter. In fact, it only marked the beginning of a long and exasperating fight. In the end it took nearly two years to induce the Department of State to follow the President's policy. The stratagems of obstruction and delay were manifold, and the motives mixed. It was partly, I imagine, the chronic difficulty of changing established policies; partly the patriotic conviction on the part of certain Foreign Service officers that

PRESIDENT KENNEDY WAVES TO A CROWD OF MORE THAN 300,000 CHEERING PEOPLE GATHERED TO HEAR HIM SPEAK IN BERLIN.

they owned American foreign policy and, in any case, knew better than the White House; partly an innate Foreign Service preference for conservatives over progressives along with a traditional weakness for the Roman aristocracy.

It was an endless struggle. Meetings would be called, decisions reached, cables sent; then the next meeting would begin with the same old arguments. One felt entrapped as in a Kafka novel. It finally came to an end when Averell Harriman became Under Secretary for Political Affairs in the spring of 1963. With his expert knowledge of the Italian situation and his administrative vigor, he turned the bureaucracy around. By the time that Nenni and his party eventually entered the Italian government in December 1963, the Department of State was at last in accord.

The leaders of the center-left parties had no doubt from mid-1961 on that a change of administration had occurred in Washington; and, if they sometimes found little evidence of it in the Department of State, they knew well enough from their own experience that foreign offices suffered from cultural lags. Kennedy, moreover, appealed greatly to them as both a Catholic and a progressive; the coincidence that he and Pope John came on the world stage about the same time strengthened them both. And the idea of a New Frontier in America was exciting to those who sought new frontiers for their own nation.

4. THE EUROPEAN TRIP

The rising confidence in Kennedy among the democratic left was not confined to Italy. Anti-Americanism, so long epidemic in these circles throughout Western Europe, was suddenly suspended. The American President was becoming a hope, if not a hero, for progressives in England, West Germany and France. Many on the left were not only Kennedyites but McNamaraites: they preferred an American nuclear monopoly and, like the Labour Party, opposed the MLF, not because it promised Europe too little control over nuclear weapons, but because it promised too much; the last thing they wished was for Washington to surrender the veto. Most of these people, outside England, were also sympathetic to the movement for a united Europe. But they were not excited by the technocratic Europe of civil servants, high commissions and supranational bureaucracies. They sought

PRESIDENT KENNEDY DURING HIS TRIP TO IRELAND VISITING WITH HIS IRISH COUSINS AT DUNGANSTOWN. FROM LEFT ARE MARGARET KIRWAN; EUNICE SHRIVER (THE PRESIDENT'S SISTER); JOSEPHINE RYAN; MARY RYAN; JFK; MARY ANNE RYAN; MARGARET WHITTY; AND JOAN KIRWAN.

neither the European chauvinism of de Gaulle nor the benign Eurocracy of Monnet but an open and democratic European union, charged with political purpose.

The startling reversal of the democratic left seemed to indicate our real opportunity in European policy—to support the Europe of democracy and freedom against the Europe of paternalistic authoritarianism.

The President, his European trip approaching, saw it as an opportunity, with all delicacy, to talk beyond governments to people, especially to the young and idealistic. Obviously the President had to talk about Germany, European unity, our undying commitment to the defense of Europe, the indivisibility of Europe and the United States, Atlantic partnership, low tariffs, and the other respectable issues. But I suggested anything he said about them ought to be stated with "due recognition of the fact that Europe considers itself a big boy now—that Europeans are fed to the teeth with what they regard as the American habit of deciding unilaterally what European policy should be and setting out to impose it regardless of what Europe thinks." The most important thing was to take advantage of his own issues—to remember that the reason for the rise of pro-American feeling in Europe was not the MLF or our support for British entry into the Common Market but the fact that a young, vigorous, progressive administration had taken over in Washington and was doing things, not for the few, but for the many.

On June 23 the President left for Germany, and the triumphal journey began. On June 25 he addressed himself to European issues in Frankfurt. He multiplied his options, speaking about a "democratic European Community," a "unified free Europe," "a united Europe in an Atlantic partnership—an entity of interdependent parts, sharing equally both burdens and decisions."

Then on to Berlin and the wildest reception of all, three-fifths of the population of West Berlin streaming into the streets, clapping, waving, crying, cheering, as if it were the second coming. Before paying the ordained visit to the city hall and signing the Golden Book, Kennedy made his first inspection of the Wall. No one is ever prepared for the Wall: it shocked and appalled the President, and he was still angry when he came out of the city hall and faced the seething crowd in the Rudolf Wilde Platz, compressed into a single excited, impassioned mass. His words were true but unwontedly harsh:

There are many people in the world who really don't understand, or say they don't, what is the great issue between the free world and the communist world.

Let them come to Berlin!

There are some who say that communism is the wave of the future.

Let them come to Berlin!

And there are some who say in Europe and elsewhere we can work with the communists.

Let them come to Berlin!

And there are even a few who say that it is true that communism is an evil system, but it permits us to make economic progress.

Lass sie nach Berlin kommen! Let them come to Berlin! The crowd shook itself and rose and roared like an animal. Absorbed in his short remarks, Kennedy hurried on. In a moment he concluded: "All free men, wherever they may live, are citizens of Berlin, and, therefore, as a free man, I take pride in the words *'Ich bin ein Berliner.'*" The hysteria spread almost visibly through the square.

On to Dublin the same night, where he began a blissful interlude of homecoming, at once sentimental and ironic. I imagine that he was never easier, happier, more involved and detached, more complexly himself, than in the next few days. So at Wexford, in the county which his great-grandfather had left on an inexplicable adventure across the Atlantic in the 1840s, when the town presented him with an engraved silver and gold box, John Fitzgerald Kennedy said: "I am proud to have connected on that beautiful golden box the coat of arms of Wexford, the coat of arms of the kingly and beautiful Kennedys, and the coat of arms of the United States." He paused, then, "That is a very good combination." Speaking before the Irish Parliament, he reminded his audience that Joyce had called the Atlantic a bowl of bitter tears. "This is not the land of my birth," Kennedy said, "but it is the land for which I hold the greatest affection, and I certainly will come back in the springtime."

Then to Birch Grove in England, where Macmillan said no on the multilateral force and yes on British Guiana; and to Italy for the last lap.

The trip represented President Kennedy's effort to move the European discussion beyond the technicalities of structure to the realities of life. As he knew better than anyone, the impact of an outsider on a continent at once so ancient and so alive as Europe could only be meager. His objectives were limited, but he attained most of them. He defined a democratic alternative to de Gaulle. He made it clear that Europeans must build European unity. He also made it clear that America was not obsessed with the nuclear issue to the exclusion of the urgent social questions of the new Europe. He surmounted the barriers of diplomacy to carry his message to the people. He left behind an indelible memory of a young, vibrant, tough-minded and idealistic America.

Before the Irish Parliament, he had recalled the lines from *Back to Methuselah:* "You see things; and you say 'Why?' But I dream things that never were; and I say 'Why not?'" Shaking off the splintered fragments of the doctrinaire Grand Design of 1961, he now rescued its essence—the hope of a creative west united in common allegiance to progressive democracy—and gave it new identity and purpose. In the summer of 1963, John F. Kennedy could have carried every country in Europe.

ABOVE: A VISIT TO CHECKPOINT CHARLIE TO SURVEY THE BERLIN WALL.
BELOW: THE PRESIDENT VISITS WITH PRIME MINISTER MACMILLAN AT THE PRIME MINISTER'S SUMMER RESIDENCE AT BIRCH GROVE.

XXXIV. THE PURSUIT OF PEACE

THE PROBLEMS WITHIN THE WESTERN ALLIANCE, as Kennedy well understood, were part of the price the west was paying for a certain ebbing in the cold war. His first instinct after the missile crisis had been to restore communication with his adversary and resume the search for areas of common interest.

Though Kennedy did not suppose that the humiliation of the missile crisis would transform the Kremlin overnight, he did hope that his restraint in the aftermath might convince the Russians that the American menace to their security was hardly enough to justify the desperate act which had brought on the crisis. Still, with his capacity to understand the problems of others, the President could see how threatening the world might have looked to the Kremlin.

1. INTIMATIONS OF DÉTENTE

Khrushchev's retreat on Cuba meant a clear victory of the American over the Soviet definition of the status quo. And, by accepting the status quo in the form of the existing equilibrium of power rather than of the communist revolution, Khrushchev swallowed not only the dialectic of Vienna but the rhetoric of his flamboyant speech six months earlier proclaiming the historic inevitability of a communist world.

By the summer of 1962 the communist empire's offensive was in ruins. The third world remained obstinately a third world. Nationalism had proved stronger than Marxism; and communism had encountered one frustration after another in Laos, in the Congo, in Latin America. Kennedy's firmness over Berlin had re-established the credibility of the deterrent (for the Russians, if not for General de Gaulle) and handed Moscow still another frustration. The Cuban adventure represented a bold effort to turn the western flank at Berlin by altering the nuclear balance. At the same time, it was a tacit confession of Soviet nuclear inferiority. Its failure struck from Soviet hands, one hoped permanently, the weapon of nuclear blackmail Khrushchev had brandished so long and so jovially and forced the Russians to re-examine their whole strategic position. In the meantime, while the United States was recovering economic momentum and political purpose, the Soviet Union was sinking into ever more worrying agricultural, industrial and intellectual difficulties. The communist empire itself, after the truce of 1960, was clearly splitting into hostile blocs. The high hopes of January 1961 were giving way to bleak realities.

So on November 19, 1962, a month after his defeat in the Caribbean, Khrushchev, in a 30,000 word report to the central committee of the Soviet Communist Party, implicitly called off the world offensive and demanded concentration on the tasks of the Soviet economy. In January 1963 in East Berlin he said that the erection of the Wall had diminished the need for a separate German peace treaty.

Clearly the Soviet leaders had decided on a breathing spell. Half a century had transformed the Soviet Union from a revolution dedicated to overturning the existing order to an establishment with heavy vested interests in the status quo. Moreover, in the last decade the revulsion against Stalinism, against forced labor camps, against arbitrary arrests, against the drabness and meanness of daily life, had coincided with the emergence of technical and managerial groups who insisted on a predictable and comfortable existence and whose active loyalty was indispensable to the power of the state. And, the decay of Marxist legitimacy around the world reduced the Soviet Union itself to just another state scrapping for leadership within the communist empire.

These changes both inside the Soviet Union and inside the communist world placed Khrushchev's desire for a breathing spell in a new frame. And the onset of the nuclear age completed the transformation of the context. Sitting on a nuclear stockpile was not the most comfortable position in the world. Only two men on the planet had been exposed to the absolute pressure of nuclear decision; and even for them it was not till the missile crisis that what was perceived intellectually was experienced emotionally. Cuba thus made vivid the sense that all humanity had a common interest in the prevention of nuclear war—an interest far above those national and ideological interests which had once seemed ultimate.

2. BACK TO THE TEST BAN

Though the United States had resumed atmospheric testing in the Pacific in April 1962, both Kennedy and Macmillan continued to keep the idea of a test ban alive between themselves, exchanging through the year thoughts about the form and timing of a new approach to Moscow. The President was particularly interested in the possibility of lowering the required quota of annual on-site inspections from the existing figure of twenty. Spurred on by presidential concern, scientists worked to refine techniques of detection and identification.

The question of on-site inspections was political as well as technical. A test ban treaty required Senate ratification. To win the necessary two-thirds vote, in view especially of the strong military opposition, the treaty would have to give every appearance of safeguarding national security against Soviet cheating. But the inspection issue pertained, of course, to a comprehensive test ban. In the meantime, the idea of a limited ban, covering self-policing environments, remained under consideration. At the end of July Kennedy consequently proposed to Macmillan the possibility of offering simultaneous treaties at Geneva: a comprehensive ban with much reduced on-site inspection—this Kennedy preferred because of its greater effect on nuclear proliferation—with an atmospheric test ban as a reasonable second best. The Russians, however, lost no time in turning both down at the end of August.

No doubt Soviet minds were in the Caribbean at this point; but, when the disarmament conference resumed a month after Cuba, one hoped that the mood might be changing. By this time the Soviet Union was winding up its 1962 series of atmospheric tests. We were also completing our own series; and the President's sense of the meagerness of their results after the clamor about their necessity—all the tests seemed to have proved was the need for more tests—made him more determined than ever to bring the whole thing to an end.* Conceivably Khrushchev might have similar feelings. Moreover, the Soviet Union had accepted the principle of international verification in the case of the Cuban missiles, and had come to believe that the United States would accept a minimal number of inspections.

"It seems to me, Mr. President," Khrushchev wrote Kennedy on December 19, 1962, "that time has come now to put an end once and for all to nuclear tests, to draw a line through such tests." We believe, Khrushchev continued, that national means of detection are sufficient to police underground as well as atmospheric tests; but we understand your need for "at least a minimum number" of inspections for the ratification of the treaty. "Well, if this is the only difficulty on the way to agreement, then for the noble and humane goal of ceasing nuclear weapons tests we are ready to meet you halfway." Citing the Kuznetsov-Dean conversations, Khrushchev proposed agreement on two to three annual inspections limited to earthquake areas. If this were accepted, "the world can be relieved of the roar of nuclear explosions."

Kennedy, who received the letter at Nassau, was exhilarated: it looked as if the Russians were really interested in a *modus vivendi*. However, the inspection quota still presented difficulties. Wiesner and a number of scientists had arrived at the "firm opinion ... that the possibility of five inspections per year would have provided adequate security against clandestine nuclear testing"; and McNamara was ready in February to settle for six. But with the intense military and partisan opposition to a test ban and the senatorial battle looming ahead, it seemed impossible politically to go below eight or, at the least, seven. As for the Russians, they not only declined to go above three. The conclusion in the State Department and the Foreign Office was that the Kremlin, immobilized by its problems with China, could not conceivably join hands with the nation China hated most in permanently excluding China from the nuclear club. The announcement of a Russo-Chinese ideological conference for Moscow in July convinced the experts that for the time being the ban was out of the question.

But, despite the failure of the New York negotiations and the pessimism of the professional diplomats, Kennedy

* He was also dissatisfied with the programs of underground testing, which had advanced nuclear technology little and had been by no means so fallout-proof as advertised. In the year after September 1961 there were seventeen cases of venting—that is, the discharge of radioactive debris, primarily iodine 131, into the atmosphere—at the Yucca Flats Proving Ground in Nevada.

He meant peace which enabled men and nations to grow and to hope and to build a better life for their children, "not merely peace in our time but peace for all time."

and Macmillan persisted in their pursuit of a treaty. In March and April the President and the Prime Minister passed back and forth across the Atlantic drafts of a new approach to Khrushchev. In mid-April, the new Kennedy-Macmillan letter arrived in Moscow. The Anglo-American proposal noted that the west had already reduced its inspection quota from twenty to seven and mentioned an idea, backed by the neutral nations at the disarmament conference, of spreading the quota over several years. We all, Kennedy and Macmillan said, owe a duty to our own security, but we also have a duty to humanity, and this requires one more serious attempt to stop testing and prevent the further proliferation of nuclear weapons. The letter concluded by saying that the writers would be ready in due course to send to Moscow very senior representatives empowered to speak for them directly with Khrushchev.

Khrushchev's reply in early May could hardly have been more declamatory and rude. To judge your position by your proposals, Khrushchev told the western leaders, the only conclusion could be that you were not serious: one wondered whether you were not going through the motions for domestic political reasons. If there were no real hope for agreement, the Soviet Union had no choice but to take measures to strengthen its own security. In a perfunctory final paragraph, Khrushchev, referring to the notion of sending senior representatives to Moscow, said, in effect, so be it; the Russians were even prepared to try this method of discussion.

Kennedy began to feel that the test ban was slipping away. Washington and London meanwhile brooded over the reply to Khrushchev's latest unpromising message. David Ormsby Gore, picking up Khrushchev's grudging final paragraph, suggested bypassing the debate and concentrating instead on the special emissaries. Macmillan strongly supported this view, and Kennedy readily agreed. Finally on May 30 a brief letter went to Khrushchev, centering on the proposal that American and British emissaries go to Moscow at the end of June or early in July.

3. APPEAL AT AMERICAN UNIVERSITY

In the meantime, the debate in the United States had been producing a certain clarification of issues. A resolution in the Senate voiced support for a limited test ban, and while the President had some concern that this approach might undercut the effort to achieve a comprehensive test ban, he was gratified for the overall strengthening of the anti-testing case, which he continued to press. In press conferences and in conversations with leaders of opinion, Kennedy hammered away at the dangers of nuclear proliferation.

One day late in May McGeorge Bundy told several of us that the President had decided the time had come for a major address on peace. He had evidently concluded that a fresh context was required to save the dying negotiation. We were asked to send our best thoughts to Ted Sorensen and to say nothing about this to anybody. The President meanwhile outlined his own views to Ted, who set to work. The speech was scheduled for the American University commencement on the morning of Monday, June 10.

Then on Saturday morning Khrushchev unexpectedly replied to the proposal about the special emissaries. His letter, ungracious and sulky, still doubted the sincerity of the Anglo-American effort and still complained about inspection. But he said at least that he would receive the emissaries. For all the querulousness, he had agreed to let the negotiations begin.

On Monday the President addressed himself in the open air on the American University campus to what he called "the most important topic on earth: world peace." By peace, he said, he did not mean "a Pax Americana enforced on the world by American weapons of war," nor did he mean the peace of the grave or the security of the slave. He meant peace which enabled men and nations to grow and to hope and to build a better life for their children, "not merely peace in our time but peace for all time." In the nuclear age, peace had become "the necessary rational end of rational men." It was said, he continued, that it was idle to dream of peace until the Soviet leaders adopted a more enlightened attitude. "I hope they do. I believe we can help them do it." He added, in a sentence capable of revolutionizing the whole American view of the cold war, "But I also believe that we must reexamine our own attitude—as individuals and as a Nation—for our attitude is as essential as theirs."

Too many Americans, he went on, regarded peace as impossible and therefore war as inevitable. "We need not accept that view. Our problems are manmade—therefore, they can be solved by man." Nor was it correct to suppose that peace would end all quarrels and conflict. It "does not require that each man love his neighbor—it requires only that they live together in mutual tolerance."

The communists were of course trapped in conspiratorial hallucinations about the United States; but that should warn us "not to fall into the same trap as the Soviets, not to see only a distorted and desperate view of the other side, not to see conflict as inevitable, accommodation as impossible and communication as nothing more than an exchange of threats. No government or social system is so evil that its people must be considered as lacking in virtue." Among many traits Americans and Russians had in common was an abhorrence of war. "No nation in the history of battle," he reminded his listeners, "ever suffered more than the Soviet Union suffered in the course of the Second World War." If world war should come again, all both sides had built, "all we have worked for, would be destroyed in the first twenty-four hours." Yet "we are both caught up in a vicious and dangerous cycle in which suspicion on one side breeds suspicion on the other, and new weapons beget counterweapons."

In short, both countries had "a mutually deep interest in a just and genuine peace and in halting the arms race. ... If we cannot end now all our differences, at least we can help make the world safe for diversity. For, in the final analysis, our most basic common link is that we all inhabit this small planet. We all breathe the same air. We all cherish our children's future. And we are all mortal."

To move toward peace would "require increased understanding between the Soviets and ourselves ... increased contact and communication." In particular, it would require new progress toward general and complete disarmament. And in the area of disarmament one problem "where the end is in sight, yet where a fresh start is badly needed, is ... a treaty to outlaw nuclear tests." The President then announced that discussions would soon begin in Moscow "looking toward early agreement on a comprehensive test ban treaty" and that the United States would conduct no atmospheric tests so long as other states did not do so; "we will not be the first to resume." No treaty could provide "absolute security" against deception and evasion; but if it were sufficiently effective in its enforcement and sufficiently in the interests of its signers, it could "offer far more security and far fewer risks than an unabated, uncontrolled, unpredictable arms race."

4. MISSION TO MOSCOW

Secretary Rusk somewhat tentatively mentioned Averell Harriman to be the American negotiator in Moscow. For reasons which the White House could never understand, or perhaps understood all too well, Harriman, in spite of his almost unsurpassed Russian experience, was rather systematically excluded in the State Department from Soviet affairs. Yet from the viewpoint not only of ability and qualification but of persuading the Russians we meant business, he was the ideal choice. "As soon as I heard that Harriman was going," someone from the Soviet Embassy remarked to me, Harriman set about his preparations in his usual astute, detailed and all-encompassing manner. The question whether we should try for a comprehensive or limited ban was still unresolved. The British were in favor of reducing the inspection quota still further, but Harriman, was sure the Russians would not agree to an inspection quota acceptable to us unless he had, as he liked to put it, "some goodies in his luggage."

The problem of China was increasingly on the President's mind. By 1963 Kennedy and Macmillan were reaching the conclusion that China presented the long-term danger to the peace. Kennedy told Harriman that he could go as far as he wished in exploring the possibility of a Soviet-American understanding with regard to China. Averell responded that he would more than ever need something to sweeten the package.

In the meantime, the Russians had had a chance to study the American University speech. One cannot know; but it seems probable that that address reassurance and a weapon he could use against the Chinese. Khrushchev himself later told Harriman with evident feeling that it was "the greatest speech by any American President since Roosevelt." At any rate, on July 2 in Berlin, he offered his answer—a limited ban, outlawing tests in the atmosphere, in outer space and under water. "If the western powers now accept this proposal," he said, "the question of inspection no longer arises." He did not this time insist on a concurrent and unpoliced moratorium on underground tests; but he said that "on the conclusion of a test ban agreement" it would also be necessary "to take another big step toward easing international tension"—a non-aggression treaty between the NATO and the Warsaw Pact states. A test ban agreement, "combined with the simultaneous signing of a non-aggression pact," would create a "fresh international climate."

Two days later Khrushchev, turning his face from west to east, said that "only madmen" could hope to destroy capitalism by nuclear war; "a million workers would be destroyed for each capitalist.... There are people who see things differently. Let them. History will teach them." The next day the delegation of those who saw things differently arrived in Moscow, and the Russo-Chinese ideological talks began. They dragged on in the greatest secrecy from July 5 to adjournment, without communiqué, on July 20. But a long and emotional statement by the central committee of the Soviet Communist Party on July 14 suggested how things were going. Citing Mao Tse-tung as prepared to sacrifice millions of lives in nuclear war, the Russians replied that they could not "share the views of the Chinese leadership about creating 'a thousand times higher civilization' on the corpses of hundreds of millions of people." Such views were "in crying contradiction to the ideas of Marxism-Leninism." The nuclear bomb "does not distinguish between imperialists and working people: it devastates entire areas."

This was the mood in Moscow when on the following day the American and British delegations began discussion of the test ban.

The opening talk cleared away a certain number of issues. Then the hard negotiation began. Several issues gave special trouble. One arose from foggy language in the preamble seeming to ban the use of nuclear weapons even in self-defense. Harriman, knowing that this was inconsistent with our own stated policy and would cause trouble on the Hill, demanded that the wording be cleared up. A second problem was that of the withdrawal clause, which Harriman knew we needed because of the probability that China would refuse to sign and then might become a nuclear power on its own, would insist on such a clause. In the end he flatly told Gromyko that, without a withdrawal clause, there could be no treaty. A third problem was that of accession to the treaty. The issue here was how to arrange for states not recognized by other states to join them in signing the treaty without thereby receiving implicit recognition. Our concern, of course, was to avoid conferring an inadvertent blessing on East Germany and China.

The discussions proved long and difficult. Harriman, who dominated the negotiations on the western side, was evidently at his best—correct, forceful, his restraint masking a capacity for toughness and even anger. A member of the British delegation later called him "the great man of the meeting." He would not give ground. Harriman, however, had negotiated with the Russians before and knew precisely what he was doing. "I am always right when I *know* I am right," he said on his return. "Sometimes I only *guess* I am right, and then I may be wrong. This time I *knew* I was right." At the White House, a call came in from Moscow just as the President initiated a call to Macmillan in London. The report was optimistic. The Russians had accepted a revision of the preamble eliminating the language which we had disliked. As for accession, the lawyers had worked out an ingenious system of multiple depositaries, leaving every signatory free to sign only in association with nations of which it approved. The President nodded his approval to Bundy, who was conducting the conversation. Just at this point, the London call was completed. Macmillan came on the phone with a certain elaborateness: he was terribly sorry, he told the President, but he had had to ask David to express his concern about the progress of the Moscow negotiations. Kennedy, a broad smile on his face, broke in: "Don't worry. David is right here. It's been worked out, and I've told them to go ahead." Macmillan, having accomplished one of the dreams of his life was deeply moved. On his return Harriman went straight to Hyannis Port. The President, without ceremony, said, "Well, this is a good job."

It *was* a good job, and it would not have come about without the intense personal commitment of Kennedy and Macmillan. America and Britain had offered the Soviet Union a limited test ban four times in four years; now it was accepted the fifth time around. Left to itself, the Soviet Union, to judge from Khrushchev's attitude in the spring of 1963, would not have perceived that a test ban was to its own interest and would not have understood its potentialities as a key to the future. Left to itself, the Department of State would not have persevered with the issue, nor would it have ever proposed an American University speech—that speech which, in its modesty, clarity and perception, repudiated the self-righteous cold war rhetoric of a succession of Secretaries of State. Mao Tse-tung was also entitled to credit for his indispensable assistance in making the treaty possible.

One more man deserved mention. When Harriman arrived in Washington on July 28, his Georgetown neighbors staged an impromptu welcome for him. One girl with a very small baby in her arms said to him, "I brought my baby because what you did in Moscow will make it possible for him to look ahead to a full and happy life."

NIKITA KHRUSHCHEV TOASTS THE SIGNING OF THE LIMITED TEST BAN TREATY ON AUGUST 5, 1963.

5. THE TEST BAN ON THE HILL

Negotiation, however, was only half the problem; ratification remained. The President regarded the test ban treaty as the most serious congressional issue he had thus far faced. He was, he told us, determined to win if it cost him the 1964 election. But the opposition was organized and strong; and, while he felt sure the great majority of the people were for it, he was not sure they could make themselves heard in time.

Addressing the nation the day after the treaty was initialed in Moscow, Kennedy recalled mankind's struggle "to escape from the darkening prospects of mass destruction." "Yesterday," he said, "a shaft of light cut into the darkness." He did not exaggerate the significance of the agreement. It was not the millennium: it would not resolve all conflicts, reduce nuclear stockpiles, check the production of nuclear weapons or restrict their use in case of war. But it was "an important first step—a step toward peace—a step toward reason—a step away from war." He concluded with the Chinese proverb he had put to Khrushchev two years before in Vienna: "A journey of a thousand miles must begin with a single step."

The prospective end of radioactive fallout was, of course, an immense boon for humanity. But I think that Kennedy saw the main point of the treaty as a means of moving toward his Vienna goal of stabilizing the international equilibrium of power. After all, both America and Russia knew that each had enough nuclear strength to survive a surprise attack and still wreak fearful destruction on the other: the test ban now indicated a mutual willingness to halt the weapons race more or less where it was. And, in addition to slowing down the bilateral arms race, the treaty held out the hope of preventing the spread of nuclear weapons to new nations. Moreover, the effect, both practical

SIGNING THE LIMITED TEST BAN TREATY. LOOKING ON FROM LEFT ARE SENATOR JOHN PASTORE, RI; AVERELL HARRIMAN; SENATOR WILLIAM FULBRIGHT, AR; SENATOR GEORGE SMATHERS, FL.

and symbolic, of Soviet-American collaboration in stopping nuclear tests and dispersion might well lead to future agreement on more general disarmament issues.

So the supporters of the treaty saw it. But sections of the military and scientific community continued in strong opposition. Some argued that true security lay in unlimited nuclear supremacy, and this required unlimited testing.

Given such opposition, ratification would be impossible without the support of the Joint Chiefs of Staff, for which they were determined to exact a price. The Chiefs accordingly attached "safeguards" to their support: vigorous continuation of underground testing; readiness to resume atmospheric testing on short notice; strengthening of detection capabilities; and the maintenance of nuclear laboratories. The President, determined that the treaty should be ratified, gave his "unqualified and unequivocal assurances" that the conditions would be met. Senators, reluctant to be associated with what critics might regard as disarmament, seized with delight on the chance of interpreting the renunciation of atmospheric tests as a green light for underground tests. The effect for a moment, as Richard Rovere put it, was to turn "an agreement intended to limit nuclear testing into a limited warrant for increasing nuclear testing."

The President was prepared to pay this price to commit the nation to a treaty outlawing atmospheric tests. He had called the treaty a "step toward reason." For all the concessions in the presentation to the Senate, his reliance on reason was now being broadly vindicated. For two and a half years he had quietly striven to free his countrymen from the clichés of the cold war. In speech after speech he had questioned the prejudices and platitudes of the fifties, cautioned against extreme solutions and defined the shape of terror in the nuclear age. The American University speech was the climax of a long campaign.

6. FURTHER STEPS ON THE JOURNEY

If the treaty were to have its full effect, it would have to include all present and potential nuclear powers. This gave Khrushchev the problem of signing up China, as it gave Kennedy the problem of signing up France. These were not easy assignments. Neither Peking nor Paris shared the Washington-London-Moscow view that the treaty was a noble and selfless act on behalf of humanity. After all, America, Britain and Russia had all the nuclear weapons they needed: now, in effect, they proposed to close down the store. To Mao Tse-tung and de Gaulle, the treaty sounded more like a hypocritical conspiracy by the nuclear monopolists to make their supremacy permanent lest new nations enter the club and challenge their control of world affairs.

One does not know what effort, if any, Khrushchev made to get China to sign, or North Korea, North Vietnam and Albania, or even Cuba, where Castro, still smarting from the missile crisis, took the occasion to make clear that Moscow could not deliver him on the world scene. The rest of Khrushchev's flock ambled in without delay. As for France, Kennedy made a determined attempt to persuade de Gaulle by offering him the technical data atmospheric testing would otherwise give him. He declared France a nuclear power in the terms of the Atomic Energy Act, thereby making it eligible for nuclear assistance without new legislation and, as soon as the treaty was initialed, sent Paris a formal proposal.

The General rejected Kennedy's offer, arguing that the treaty and even nuclear cooperation with the United States would violate the apparently infinitely violable sovereignty of France. As Kennedy told Macmillan, de Gaulle's answer made it clear that he wished neither Anglo-American nuclear assistance nor even a serious discussion. But though the President was not surprised, he was nonetheless bitterly disappointed. The French declination, on top of the Chinese, meant that the treaty would fail as a means of stopping major proliferation. "Charles de Gaulle," Kennedy told David Brinkley, "will be remembered for one thing only, his refusal to take that treaty."

Yet, if the test ban was not to stop national nuclear weapons development completely, it still denied at least its signatories—soon more than a hundred—the most convenient means of pursuing the nuclear dream. And it still offered the prospect of a *détente* between the two superpowers.

In the long run, the promise of détente was never quite fulfilled. The non-aggression pact discussed as part of the planning for the Moscow talks fell by the wayside, and in time, despite the reduction in tensions, the two nations gradually fell into old patterns. Everyone felt more secure in the old rubrics, and foreign policy slipped back from men to institutions.

XXXV. THE TRAVAIL OF EQUAL RIGHTS

HISTORIANS OF THE TWENTY-FIRST CENTURY will no doubt struggle to explain how nine-tenths of the American people, priding themselves every day on their kindliness, their generosity, their historic consecration to the rights of man, could so long have connived in the systematic dehumanization of the remaining tenth—and could have done so without not just a second but hardly a first thought.

The answer to this mystery lay in the belief, welling up from the depths of the white unconscious, in the inherent and necessary inferiority of those of a darker color. This belief was fortified by the failure of institutions—the church, the university, the government, the business firm—to live up to their own ideals and by the narrow views of the federal system which could lead a President like William Howard Taft to say with function in his inaugural address, "It is not the disposition or within the province of the Federal Government to interfere with the regulation by Southern States of their domestic affairs." By such means white America virtuously succeeded in cutting the Negro out of conscience and even, except for servants, entertainers and athletes, out of sight.

"I am an invisible man," cried the hero of Ralph Ellison's novel in 1953. "… I am invisible, understand, simply because people refuse to see me."

1. INTO THE LIGHT

In the first decade of the twentieth century outbursts of race rioting in Illinois reminded some white Americans of the existence of outcasts in their midst. In the next years the national ethos began slowly to change. In the thirties Franklin Roosevelt gave the Negroes a sense of national recognition. He did so more in terms of their interests in economic and social justice than of their title to equal rights. Yet he threw open the gate of hope; and the Negroes themselves, who had been stirring restlessly for a generation, now began to shake off the psychological manacles with which white society had so long made them accomplices in their own subjection. The future at last was spreading out before them, and they moved to take history into their own hands.

Then the Second World War offered Negro militants the great opportunity to force the moral issue on the white conscience. For that war called on the American Negro to fight the idea of a master race in defense of rights denied them by their own master race; and the paradox proved too manifest even for the white man to ignore. After the war, President Truman, abandoning the prejudices of his upbringing, set forth the first comprehensive legislative program for civil rights. In these years segregation disappeared in the armed forces. In 1954 a unanimous Supreme Court, including three southerners, outlawed segregation in public schools.

It should have surprised no one that, as the Negroes began to gain some of their rights, their determination to claim *all* their rights hardened. Revolutions accelerate not from despair but from hope. When barriers began to fall, the Negro leadership, ever more able and aggressive, pressed more and more urgently for full membership in American society. The national creed gave them their moral leverage, and politics increasingly responded to their pressure. By the 1950s the northern Democratic leaders recognized that historic injustices had to end, but they thought that steady and rational progress step by step over a period of years would suffice to satisfy the victims of injustice and contain their incipient revolution.

The school desegregation decision, now to be carried out, in the delphic words of the Court, with "all deliberate speed," was one such step. The next was the Civil Rights Act of 1957, the first congressional enactment on civil rights for eighty-seven years. The Supreme Court decision and the Civil Rights Acts were essentially the result of the strategy of the NAACP and its executive director, Roy Wilkins, a man of exceptional sagacity and purpose. Regarding law as the most effective and lasting way of securing Negroes their rights, Wilkins concentrated on persuading the courts to take a fresh look at old law (as through Thurgood Marshall and the NAACP legal bureau) and on persuading Congress to enact new law (as through Clarence Mitchell and the NAACP Washington office). Yet progress in the courts and Congress, though of a sort unimaginable a generation earlier, was beginning to be slow and abstract for the awakening Negro militancy. The "deliberate speed" of the desegregation decision seemed to mean no movement at all. In the first years neither the Civil Rights Act of 1957 nor the Civil Rights Commission produced notable federal action.

In the meantime, the experience of a Negro bus boycott in Montgomery, Alabama, in the winter of 1955–56 had suggested another strategy. Martin Luther King, Jr., a young Baptist minister precipitated into the leadership of the boycott, preserved Negro purpose and discipline during the long weeks by preaching the gospel of non-violent resistance, derived from his reading of Thoreau and Gandhi. A superb orator, deeply sensitive to the woe and weariness of his race, King drew from the religious traditions of southern Negroes a strength which now enabled them to defy white society without giving it the pretext to respond in customary manner with whip and rope. The spirituals which had once sustained Negroes in servitude now nerved them for battle. Though in fact King's approach supplemented and supported that of the NAACP (indeed, it took an NAACP suit to secure the goal of the bus boycott), his appeal released new energies in the struggle. Where the NAACP used legal means to attack the power points in southern society, King and his Southern Christian Leadership Conference went into the communities, called for mass action and brought the Negroes into the streets.

Then in February 1960 four Negro students at the Agricultural and Technical College in Greensboro, North Carolina, were denied service at a lunch counter. Their decision to stay in their seats until the place closed launched the new technique of 'sit-ins' across the South and brought another organization, the Congress of Racial Equality (CORE), into prominence. A year later James Farmer, who had been program director for the NAACP, became CORE's national director. The sit-ins led to kneel-ins, pray-ins and other forms of non-violent protest and soon to the formation of still another group, intense in its emotions and radical, if often obscure, in its doctrines, the Student Nonviolent Coordinating Committee (SNCC).

ROY WILKINS, EXECUTIVE DIRECTOR OF THE NAACP, SPEAKING BEFORE THE DEMOCRATIC PLATFORM COMMITTEE IN CHICAGO, 1956.

By 1960 the Negro was no longer the invisible man. The Negro leadership—Wilkins, King, Farmer, Whitney Young of the Urban League and the veteran head of the Brotherhood of Sleeping Car Porters, A. Philip Randolph, were as gifted and impressive a group as one could find in the country. The movement for equal rights rushing along. But no one—certainly not the white politicians, not even the established Negro leadership—could foretell at what pace or with what intensity.

2. KENNEDY AND CIVIL RIGTHS

Kennedy had collaborated with the movement for civil rights in the fifties. In the later part of that decade, civil rights advocates regarded him as sympathetic, but detached.

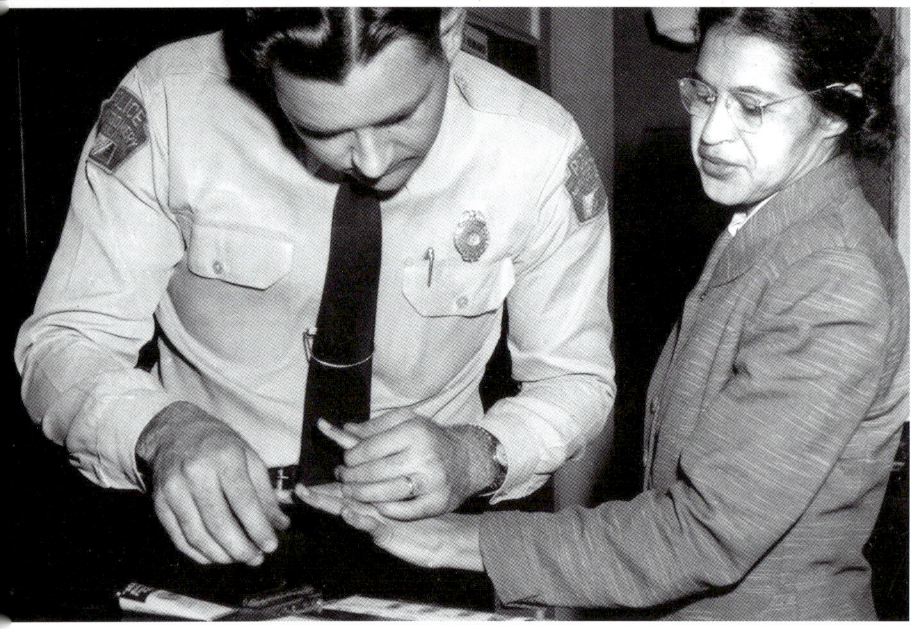

TOP: DR. MARTIN LUTHER KING, JR. (BACK, LEFT) AND REVEREND RALPH D. ABERNATHY (FRONT, LEFT) ARE AMONG THE FIRST TO RIDE ON A BUS AFTER THE SUPREME COURT'S INTEGRATION ORDER WENT INTO EFFECT IN MONTGOMERY, ALABAMA. WITH THEM ARE REVEREND GLENN SMILEY OF NEW YORK AND AN UNIDENTIFIED WOMAN.

MIDDLE: ROSA PARKS IS FINGERPRINTED ON FEBRUARY 22, 1956, TWO MONTHS AFTER REFUSING TO GIVE UP HER SEAT ON A BUS FOR A WHITE PASSENGER.

BOTTOM: FRANKLIN MCCAIN (LEFT) AND DAVID RICHMOND, TWO OF THE FOUR COLLEGE STUDENTS WHO STARTED DEMONSTRATIONS AGAINST SEGREGATED LUNCH COUNTERS IN GREENSBORO, NORTH CAROLINA IN 1960.

Kennedy's sense of his weakness with the Negroes led him in the spring of 1960 to ask Harris Wofford of the Notre Dame Law School, who had joined his campaign staff as an expert on Asian matters, to shift over to civil rights.

Wofford now arranged a series of meetings between Kennedy and Negro leaders. Each session advanced the candidate a little in his own commitment. At the convention he insisted on a strong civil rights plank; and after the August special session he joined twenty-three other Democratic Senators in a statement condemning the Republican civil rights record. The statement concluded: *"we pledge action to obtain consideration of a civil rights bill by the Senate early next session that will implement the pledges of the Democratic platform."*

In the campaign Kennedy incorporated the plight of the Negro into his general critique of American society. "Only a President willing to use all the resources of his office," he said in California, "can provide the leadership, the determination and the direction ... to eliminate racial and religious discrimination from American society." He emphasized that "the greater opportunity" lay "in the executive branch without congressional action." Here he mentioned the housing order and, repeatedly, mentioning the stroke of the presidential pen. He also advocated more vigorous measures to win the Negro the right to vote, the right to employment in companies doing business with the federal government and the right to federal appointments.

These proposals probably counted less in the election than his phone call to Mrs. Martin Luther King, Jr. "I am deeply indebted to Senator Kennedy," King soon said, "who served as a great force in making my release possible." On election day Kennedy received an overwhelming share of the Negro vote.* And, if King thought himself indebted to Kennedy before the election, Kennedy, reflecting on his margin, must have known after the election how indebted he was to King and the Negroes. Had only whites gone to the polls in 1960, Nixon would have taken 52 percent of the vote. In the electoral college Kennedy could not have carried Illinois and Michigan, not to mention Texas, South Carolina and possibly Louisiana. He needed to lose only the first two of those states to have lost the election.

Setting forth Negro expectations in an article in the *Nation* soon after Kennedy's inauguration, King ascribed the "intolerably" slow progress in civil rights as much "to the limits which the federal government has imposed on its own action" as to the segregationist opposition. In the legislative area, he demanded that the President fight for a "really far-reaching" civil rights program with particular emphasis on the right to vote. In the area of executive action, he called on the President to "give segregation its death blow through

* Gallup and Harris, the two main polling organizations, give figures ranging from 68 to 78 percent.

PRESIDENT KENNEDY MEETS WITH THE PRESIDENTS OF NEGRO COLLEGES.

a stroke of a pen"—especially by stopping the use of federal funds to support housing, hospital and airport construction in which discrimination was open and notorious. "We must face the tragic fact," King said, "that the federal government is the nation's highest investor in segregation." Describing housing as "the most tragic expression of discrimination," King laid special stress on the necessity for a housing order.

Confronted by such proposals, the new President faced a most difficult problem. While he did not doubt the depth of the injustice or the need for remedy, he had read the arithmetic of the new Congress and concluded that there was no possible chance of passing a civil rights bill. Moreover, he had a wide range of presidential responsibilities; and a fight for civil rights would alienate southern support he needed for other purposes (including bills, like those for education and the increased minimum wage, of direct benefit to the Negro). And he feared that the inevitable defeat of a civil rights bill would heighten Negro resentment, and place a perhaps intolerable strain on the already fragile social fabric. He therefore settled on the strategy of executive action.

He explained his position frankly to Wilkins, King and other Negro leaders. "Nobody needs to convince me any longer," he told King, "that we have to solve the problem, not let it drift on gradualism. But how do you go about it? If we go into a long fight in Congress, it will bottleneck everything else and still get no bill."

Undoubtedly he wanted to keep control over the demand for civil rights and this, unlike the demand for federal spending, might well, if stimulated, get out of hand. Some also thought that the President, precisely because he perceived civil rights as a moral issue, may have felt that criticism of the administration, which in the field of economic policy would seem a mere disagreement over tactics, might carry here a suggestion of deficient moral energy.

3. THE STRATEGY OF 1961

Kennedy thus began by hoping that a strong and declared presidential commitment to civil rights, accompanied by the appointment of Negroes to government posts and by vigorous action on behalf of Negro rights by the White House and the Department of Justice, would move things along fast enough to hold the confidence of the Negro community.

MEMBERS OF THE PRESIDENT'S COMMITTEE FOR EQUAL EMPLOYMENT OPPORTUNITY.
IN FRONT, FROM LEFT: LUTHER HODGES, SEC. OF COMMERCE; ARTHUR GOLDBERG, SEC. OF LABOR; KENNEDY, AND VICE PRESIDENT JOHNSON.

He seized a variety of small opportunities to communicate his personal contempt for racial prejudice. He issued a strong executive order against discrimination in federal employment and made a special effort to seek Negroes for high federal jobs including Assistant Secretaries in the Cabinet, and Ambassadors. In October Thurgood Marshall was nominated to the Second Circuit Court, the first of five Negroes made lifetime judges in the Kennedy years. Requesting reports from all departments and agencies on Negro employment, especially in the higher grades, he was appalled by the result and instructed the cabinet in the spring of 1961 to take immediate steps to improve the situation.

The President also established a single President's Committee on Equal Employment Opportunity under the Vice-President. Johnson, conceivably noting that the assignment would give him a chance to build a record where he had previously been regarded with mistrust, saw an opportunity. Actually, though Johnson had regularly voted against civil rights bills till 1957 and had even described Truman's civil rights program in 1948 as "a farce and a sham—an effort to set up a police state in the guise of liberty," this attitude reflected Texas politics rather than personal bias. The Vice President was wholly devoid of racial prejudice, took pride in the support he received from Negroes and Mexicans and wanted now to do his best for his fellow man. He summoned the heads of firms doing business with the government and urged them to join in Plans for Progress providing for the training and employment of Negroes. The deliberations of the Committee were on occasion contentious. But the record far surpassed that of a committee headed by Nixon in the previous administration.

The Department of Justice, however, was the center of federal action and in the year of the Bay of Pigs, Laos, Berlin and test resumption Kennedy left civil rights policy pretty much to his brother. Robert Kennedy, like the President, had a clear sense of historic injustice and a strong feeling of political obligation; but he was relatively new to the problem. Yet, if some of his southern judicial appointments in 1961 were unfortunate, he rapidly showed his deep belief in the idea of equal opportunity. Discovering fewer than ten Negro attorneys in the Department, he laid on a special recruiting campaign and quintupled the number by the end of the year. He also had appointed at once—and for the first time in history—Negroes as United States Attorneys and enlarged the staff of the Civil Rights Division.

Kennedy and Burke Marshall, the Assistant Attorney General in charge of the Civil Rights Division decided from the start that, before taking situations to the courts, they would first try to negotiate with local officials, thereby giving full respect to the federal system and full opportunity for local self-correction. Indeed, in the field of school integration, where they lacked authority to initiate suits, they had ordinarily no other choice. In September schools were desegregated without violence in Atlanta, New Orleans, Memphis and Dallas. In Prince Edward County, Virginia, where white resistance to integration had closed all the schools, the Department of Justice sought court action to bring about their reopening.

The Department gave first priority, however, to voting rights. Many observers had concluded by 1960 that the franchise was the keystone in the struggle against segregation. Negro voting did not incite social and sexual anxieties; and white southerners could not argue against suffrage for their Negro fellow citizens with quite the same moral fervor they applied to the mingling of races in schools. Concentration on the right to vote, in short, seemed the best available means of carrying the mind of the white South. Then, once Negroes began to go to the polls, politicians would have to temper their views or lose their elections. The Department was not alone in regarding voting as, if not the key to civil rights, at least the indispensable conditions for the assertion of other federal rights. Though the NAACP still worried more about school integration, Martin Luther King, Jr., in November 1961, declared: "*The central front, however, we feel is that of suffrage.* If we in the south can win the right to vote it will place in our hands more than an abstract right. It will give us the concrete tool with which we ourselves can correct injustice."

The denial of Negro suffrage had long been an accepted southern scandal. In at least 193 counties fewer than 15 percent of eligible Negroes were permitted to register; in Mississippi this was true in seventy-four out of eighty-two counties. In thirteen southern counties not one Negro was on the rolls. The civil rights legislation of 1957 and 1960 had equipped the Attorney General with a measure of authority to intervene in such cases; but the Eisenhower administration had brought only ten suits and none at all in Mississippi. By mid-1963, however, Kennedy and Marshall had filed forty-two suits, eight of them in Mississippi. The Attorney General fully realized that winning suits would not make much difference if apathy, ignorance or fear still prevented the mass of Negroes from registering. Accordingly, the administration, with helpful assistance from the Taconic Foundation and collaboration from the Southern Regional Council, persuaded the leading Negro organizations to undertake a drive which in 1963 registered a considerable number of Negro voters across the South.

It was not easy, however, to keep the turbulence of civil rights in the ordered channels of due process, and there

LEFT: JAMES FARMER, ONE OF THE FOUNDERS OF CONGRESS OF RACIAL EQUALITY (CORE).
RIGHT: FREEDOM RIDERS ARRIVE IN NEW YORK FROM JACKSON, MISSISSIPPI.

were other issues than voting and schools. In the spring of 1961 James Farmer and CORE sent out groups of 'freedom riders' to challenge segregation in interstate bus terminals—in their restaurants, waiting rooms, restrooms. The first band, led by Farmer himself, proceeded through the Carolinas and Georgia, with occasional fights and arrests, but without serious trouble until it reached Alabama. At Anniston a white mob burned up one of the buses. At Birmingham the riders were attacked and beaten. By now SNCC, King's Southern Christian Leadership Conference and other groups had their own riders on the road to Alabama, and there was every prospect of serious violence. On May 20, when a delegation of agitators arrived in Montgomery, a mob greeted them with clubs and pipes. A number of freedom riders and local Negroes were beaten; John Seigenthaler, whom Robert Kennedy had sent to the scene, was knocked unconscious. Since the state of Alabama, despite gubernatorial assurances, obviously could not maintain order, Robert Kennedy sent more than 600 deputy federal marshals to Montgomery.

The height of the crisis was over, though the rides continued; in the end over a thousand people were involved. Robert Kennedy had meanwhile petitioned the Interstate Commerce Commission to issue regulations requiring desegregation of all facilities in terminals used in interstate bus travel. On September 22 the ICC put out such orders. When a few cities pleaded local laws as excuse for non-compliance, the Department of Justice brought suits; and at the same time it proceeded against segregation in airports and railroad stations. In time, in a quiet revolution, travel terminals of all sorts through the South were open on equal terms to white and Negro.

4. MINORITY REPORT

The strategy of executive action was thus proving adaptable to new problems. But it was also producing an undercurrent of criticism both within the government and without.

The Civil Rights Commission had been established in 1957 as a propitiatory gesture to hold off pressure for more far-reaching legislation. Its authority was limited to investigation (including the holding of hearings) and recommendation. But facts had a power which no one had foreseen. Increasingly the Commission construed its obligations as not only technical but moral; it saw itself as, in director Berl Bernhard's phrase, "the duly appointed conscience of the government in regard to civil rights." Father Theodore Hesburgh, president of Notre Dame and a member of the commission, well summed up its mood in his closing statement in the 1961 report: "Americans might well wonder how we can legitimately combat communism when we practice so widely its central folly: utter disregard for the God-given spiritual rights, freedom and dignity of every human person."

A FREEDOM RIDER BUS IS FIRE BOMBED IN ALABAMA.

The Commission shared the Department of Justice's concern for voting rights, but also gave great weight to its inquiries into housing, education, employment and law enforcement. As Bernhard put its view in November 1961, "There can be no single approach which will bring an end to discrimination"; inequalities in political participation, education, employment, housing and the administration of justice all reinforced one another. This meant that, while the Commission applauded Justice's work in the field of voting rights (apart from the Department's evident determination to keep the Commission out of that field), its members began to worry whether the government was concentrating on voting to the neglect of other problems equally vital.

The Commission's 1961 report's chief recommendation was that the President issue the executive order forbidding discrimination in housing; and that it cover not just federally financed housing—that is, mortgages insured by the Federal Housing Administration and the Veterans Administration—but the conventional mortgage activities of federally assisted financial institutions, such as banks whose deposits were guaranteed by the Federal Deposit Insurance Corporation. In the view of the Commission, housing was as much a key to Negro inequality in the North as voting was in the South.

The Commission was an agency of recommendation while the Department of Justice was an agency of action. The Commission moved out ahead to define new areas and offer new proposals; the Department acted to solve immediate problems. Despite occasional arguments between them, it seemed to the outsider a good combination. If annoying at times, the pressure of the Commission probably enabled the Department to do a better job.

The civil rights groups were meanwhile pressing even harder for the executive order on housing. Recalling Kennedy's campaign assurances about "a stroke of the pen," people began sending pens to the White House in a sarcastic effort to ease the President's task. Kennedy had, I think, intended to put out the order when Congress adjourned in the fall of 1961, but delayed for various reasons, aggrieving the civil rights leadership. By declining to issue the order, Martin Luther King, Jr., said, "The President did more to undermine confidence in his intentions than could be offset by a series of smaller accomplishments." In similar vein Wilkins, while praising the President for "his personal role in civil rights and very plain indications of his concern that conditions be improved," declared his "disappointment with Mr. Kennedy's first year" as a result of the failure to issue the housing order and even more of the "basic error" of the strategy of "no legislative action on civil rights."

Yet, despite the discontent of the leadership, the Negro community on the whole seemed well satisfied, and Kennedy's personal popularity was obviously increasing. The President

GOVERNOR ROSS BARNETT OF MISSISSIPPI.

himself, sensitive to the need of maintaining momentum, observed in his 1962 State of the Union message that there was much more to be done "by the Executive, by the courts and by the Congress." In particular he expressed administration interest in bills to end the use of literacy tests and poll taxes as means of denying Negroes the right to vote.

5. THE BATTLE OF OXFORD

On January 20, 1961, a veteran of nine years in the Air Force named James Meredith, his spirit quickened by Kennedy's inaugural address, wrote to the University of Mississippi requesting an application for admission. "I am an American-Mississippi-Negro citizen," he explained when he returned his form. "With all of the occurring events regarding changes in our educational system taking place in our country in this new age, I feel certain that this application does not come as a surprise to you. I certainly hope that this matter will be handled in a manner that will be complimentary to the University and to the State of Mississippi. Of course, I am the one that will, no doubt, suffer the greatest consequences of this event."

Ole Miss, as the university at Oxford was known through the state, had never (to its knowledge*) admitted a Negro, and now offered complicated academic reasons for rejecting Meredith. But Meredith, encouraged by Medgar Evers, director of the NAACP in Mississippi and represented in court by the NAACP Legal Defense Fund, filed suit on the ground that he had been turned down because of his race. When the federal district judge dismissed Meredith's plea, he appealed, and the Fifth Circuit Court, finding in June 1962 that he had been rejected "solely because he was a Negro," reversed the lower court's decision. After a summer of legal maneuver Justice Hugo Black, an Alabaman, upheld the court of appeals. Governor Ross Barnett of Mississippi promptly declared, "We will not surrender to the evil and illegal forces of tyranny."**

Robert Kennedy thereupon phoned the Governor, pointing out that he was proposing to defy a federal court order, and suggested they try to work out a solution together. But Barnett's neo-Confederate rhetoric, echoed by most of the legislature and most of the newspapers of the state, had already incited a wave of panic and hate among his fellow-Mississippians; and this encouraged the Governor in his course. On September 20, when James Meredith, accompanied by federal marshals, presented himself at Oxford for registration, students were marching around the campus singing "Glory, Glory, Segregation." Barnett grandiloquently read aloud a long proclamation rejecting Meredith's application. Concluding, he handed the document to Meredith: "Take it and abide by it."

This action in Oxford gave Washington a new states rights crisis—and also me a new assignment. Up to this point, though my personal concern was of very long standing, my participation in civil rights matters at the White House had been slight. Now both the Mississippi impasse and the impending centennial of the Emancipation Proclamation, set for September 22 at the Lincoln Memorial, drew me into civil rights.

In the meantime, two days after Ross Barnett turned back James Meredith in Oxford, the country marked the first century of the Emancipation Proclamation. The President, in a message to the gathering at the Lincoln Memorial, placed special emphasis on the Negro role in the long fight for equal rights since the abolition of slavery. "The essential effort, the sustained struggle," he said, "was borne by the Negro alone with steadfast dignity and faith. ...It can be said, I believe, that Abraham Lincoln emancipated the slaves, but that in this century since, our Negro citizens have emancipated themselves." But the task was not finished: "like the proclamation we celebrate, this observance must be regarded not as an end, but a beginning."

Robert Kennedy had already responded to Barnett's defiance by citing the three top officers of the University of Mississippi for contempt of court. Once in the courtroom the academic administrators readily agreed to register Meredith. But the Governor, furious at this pusillanimity and

* Walter Lord's *The Past That Would Not Die* (New York, 1965) provides a careful, accurate and lively account of the Meredith affair. See also, for further detail, Michael Dorman, *We Shall Overcome* (New York, 1965), 11–143.

** Harry S. Murphy, Jr., a light-skinned Negro, later revealed that he had studied at Ole Miss in 1945–46 as a Navy V-12 student. Doubtless there had been others in the years since the university was founded in 1848.

unimpressed by federal law, told the Attorney General, "I consider the Mississippi courts as high as any other court and a lot more capable.... I am going to obey the laws of Mississippi." Robert Kennedy replied, "My job is to enforce the laws of the United States—I intend to fulfill it." The next day he obtained a restraining order from the Fifth Circuit Court enjoining Barnett and other state officials not to interfere with the registration of Meredith. But when Meredith again tried to register, Barnett physically barred his way. As Meredith and the Department of Justice officials departed, the mob surrounding the building shouted, "Communists.... Go home, nigger." That night Barnett told Robert Kennedy, "It's best for him not to go to Ole Miss." The Attorney General replied softly, "But he likes Ole Miss."

In the next days the Department of Justice made one more attempt to find a solution. After complicated negotiation through intermediaries, Barnett assured the Attorney General that a sufficient show of federal force—the appearance, for example, of marshals who, when the governor confronted them, would promise to draw their guns—would give him the excuse he needed for retreat. But the state was now aflame, and the excitement was bringing to Oxford country folk from miles around, many armed, all determined to keep the nigger out of Ole Miss. Recruits were on their way even from more distant points.

As Meredith, flanked by a group of armed marshals, prepared to make his third try, Barnett decided that the situation was too dangerous, the crowd might break out of control. The Attorney General, who had never much liked the play-acting, instructed Meredith and the marshals to pull back. The next day Barnett was found guilty of civil contempt and ordered to purge himself by the following Tuesday or face arrest and a fine of $10,000 a day. On Friday, September 28, Robert Kennedy met with General Maxwell Taylor to provide for the necessary troop movements.

Later that afternoon he asked me to come over to the Department of Justice to work on a statement explaining the necessity for federal intervention. Preparations were being made with great secrecy. Edwin Guthman spirited me into the Department through a side entrance and installed me in a room behind the Attorney General's office. In a moment Bobby came in and said he understood better now how Hitler had taken over in Germany. "Everyone in Mississippi is accepting what that fellow is doing," he said. "There are no protests anywhere—from the bar or from professional men or from the professors. I wouldn't have believed it." He described with incredulity the latest proposition from Barnett: that Mississippians would raise money for Meredith to go to any university he desired outside the state if the Attorney General would persuade him to give up on Ole Miss.

The next afternoon, Saturday, September 29, I was called over to the President's office. The Attorney General, Burke Marshall and Kenneth O'Donnell were there. Matters were now rushing to climax. In a final effort to get a peaceful settlement and avert the sending of troops, the President himself had put in a call to Governor Barnett, and now spoke plainly to him. "Here's my problem, Governor. I don't know Mr. Meredith, and I didn't put him in there. But under the Constitution I have to carry out the law. I want your help in doing it." Barnett said that Tom Watkins, the Mississippi lawyer who had served as intermediary in the show-of-force scheme, was ready to come to Washington with a new plan.

As the two brothers discussed the Barnett proposal, they concluded that there was no point in Watkins's coming to Washington unless he was prepared to negotiate a change in Barnett's position. The Attorney General then called Watkins. He had, he said crisply, two questions: "Will the Governor defy or follow the order of the Court? If he means to defy that order will we have a pitched battle down there when we arrest the Governor?" After a moment, "Is there any possibility of finding out what we need down there? Must we send an army, a division or what? This depends on what the Governor will do. We are at least entitled to know that. If the Governor is going to stand up and bar the way, that's one situation. If he is going to tell everyone to go home, that's an entirely different situation." Watkins said his understanding was that Barnett would physically bar Meredith; he would also try to quiet the mob. Robert Kennedy: "He can't do that. You can't tell others to behave if you yourself are obstructing the order of the court." Before concluding the conversation, he asked Watkins whether Barnett would take responsibility for maintaining law and order.

They waited for a while to give Watkins a chance to talk to Barnett. Then the President called Barnett again. For some reason Watkins had not called the Governor; so the Attorney General, going to the phone, recapitulated his conversation with Watkins. "I said that, unless he had concrete proposals which might form a basis for agreement, he was wasting his time in coming to Washington. These proposals would have to include strong and vocal action on your part ... at minimum an order that people could not congregate in Oxford in groups larger than three or five; that students who commit disorders are liable for expulsion; that all people carrying guns or clubs in Oxford be arrested." Barnett then suggested that, while he himself would go with a flourish to Oxford, Meredith should be registered at Jackson, the state capital. Robert Kennedy said,

"Sneaking Meredith off to Jackson for registration doesn't meet the problem. It doesn't really make much sense, does it?"

In a minute the President went on the phone. "I know your feeling about the law of Mississippi and the court order," he said. "What we are concerned about is whether you will maintain law and order—prevent the gathering of a mob and action taken by a mob. Can you stop that? What about the Attorney General's proposals to stop a mob?" His voice was dispassionate and stern. Barnett evidently said that he would do his best. The President: "As I understand it, you will do everything you can to maintain order. Next, Governor, *can* you maintain order?" Barnett then suggested a cooling-off period. The President: "Would you undertake to register him in two weeks? Unless we have your support and assurance ..." The conversation trailed off.

At seven that night there was a third phone call. Barnett brought up again the idea of registering Meredith secretly in Jackson, assuring the President that the state police could keep everything under control. With reluctance, the President decided to accept the subterfuge. Then three hours later Barnett phoned Robert Kennedy canceling the deal. There was now no alternative to a collision between the state of Mississippi and the national government. After midnight the President issued orders federalizing the Mississippi National Guard and sending troops of the United States Army to Memphis. He also requested national television time for Sunday evening.

Mississippi, throbbing with righteous emotion, prepared as if for war. But Barnett, whose rhetoric constantly outran his resolution, drew back once again, calling the Attorney General on Sunday morning with a more elaborate version of the show-of-force proposal, this time a staged capitulation of Mississippi forces to the Army. Robert Kennedy coldly dismissed it as "a foolish and dangerous show." He added that the President planned to report Barnett's repudiation of their earlier agreement in his television speech. Alarmed at this, Barnett quickly came up with a substitute proposal: that Meredith be quietly flown into Oxford that afternoon. He told the Attorney General that the state police would keep outsiders off the campus; and that, while he would have to say that he had yielded to overwhelming force, he would condemn any talk of violence and urge that the fight be carried forward in the courts.

In a few hours Meredith and the federal marshals, led by their brave and humorous chief, James McShane, arrived on the campus in Oxford. While Meredith went off to a dormitory, Deputy Attorney General Nicholas Katzenbach and the federal officials waited in the Lyceum, an imposing ante-bellum building which housed the university's administrative offices. As the sun set, a crowd, without challenge from the state police, began to collect menacingly around the Lyceum: first, "2-4-1-3, we hate Ken-ne-dy"; then a rising growl of taunts and curses—"Kill the nigger-loving bastards"; then, as it grew dark, bottles and bricks. For an hour and a half the marshals, though a number were hurt and bleeding, stood impassively under the attack. But after a time, as the mob, now numbering 2500, began to surge toward the Lyceum, the order was given to respond by tear gas.

In Washington the President, unaware of the troubles in Oxford, had gone on the air to say that Meredith was safely on the campus and explain why the federal government had massed its power to put him there. "If this country," he said, "should ever reach the point where any man or group of men by force or threat of force could long defy the commands of our court and our Constitution, then no law would stand free from doubt, no judge would be sure of his writ, and no citizen would be safe from his neighbors." He concluded with a direct appeal to the students of the university: "The honor of your University and State are in the balance. I am certain that the great majority of the students will uphold that honor."

In Oxford students jeered. Other outsiders joined the mob, some with shotguns and rifles. At the Lyceum the marshals were running out of tear gas. As Katzenbach heard the sounds of shots through the confederate howls, he concluded that the time had come to call in the troops. In Washington the President issued the order. The battle raged on until the troops arrived. Hundreds were wounded, including more than a third of the marshals; two men, one a French reporter, were killed. The President stayed in his office at the other end of the telephone until dawn.

The next morning James Meredith appeared before the registrar in the Lyceum and was duly inducted into the University of Mississippi. A fellow student shouted, "Was it worth two lives, nigger?" For weeks troops stayed on campus, for months marshals accompanied Meredith to classes, reprisals were attempted against his family; but with heroic tenacity he pursued his chosen course. Some of the faculty, led by the undaunted historian James W. Silver,* gave Meredith support. But it was a long lonely time until he graduated in August 1963.

Yet he had established the principle; and President Kennedy's action had a profound effect around the world, most of all in Africa. Three weeks after Oxford, Sékou Touré and Ben Bella were prepared to deny refueling facilities to Soviet planes bound for Cuba during the missile crisis.

Though some American Negroes felt Kennedy might have acted sooner and did not much like his television appeal to Mississippians to honor their traditions, this was

* Whose book *Mississippi: The Closed Society* (New York, 1964) contains an invaluable account of these days as well as of the atmosphere in Mississippi.

JAMES MEREDITH IS ESCORTED TO THE UNIVERSITY OF MISSISSIPPI CAMPUS BY CHIEF U.S. MARSHAL JAMES MCSHANE, LEFT.

quickly forgotten in the memory of the dispatch of the Army and the admission of Meredith. In the fall elections the Democrats won more Negro votes than ever. Then on November 20 Kennedy finally issued the executive order on housing. While limited to housing owned or directly insured by the federal government and thus covering only 15 per cent of savings and loans residential mortgage holdings, it still marked a new step toward equal opportunity.

In the middle of 1963, when the Louis Harris polling organization asked Negroes who had done most for Negro rights, the first three in the judgment of the rank and file were the NAACP, Martin Luther King, Jr., and President Kennedy.

XXXVI. THE NEGRO REVOLUTION

IN THE WINTER OF 1962–63 the civil rights leaders, more bent than ever on legislation, watched the success of the President's strategy with understandable frustration. Martin Luther King, Jr., sorrowfully described 1962 as "the year that civil rights was displaced as the dominant issue in domestic politics.... The issue no longer commanded the conscience of the nation." He attributed this to the readiness to accept token victories as evidence of genuine progress. "In fairness," he added, "it must be said that this Administration has outstripped all previous ones in the breadth of its civil-rights activities. Yet the movement, instead of breaking out into the open plains of progress, remains constricted and confined. A sweeping revolutionary force is pressed into a narrow tunnel."

1. NEW DIRECTIONS IN LEGISLATION

However, the President, recognizing the discontent and perceiving a need for new action if he were to preserve his control, had decided to seek legislation himself. On February 28, 1963, he sent a message to Congress setting forth in moving detail the national shame of inequality not only in voting and education but in employment and public accommodations. Racial discrimination, he said, hampered our economic growth and our world leadership; it increased the costs of public welfare, crime, delinquency and disorder; it marred the atmosphere of a united and classless society. "Above all, it is wrong." But, after this eloquent start, the actual legislative recommendations disappointed the civil rights leaders—piecemeal improvements in existing voting legislation, technical assistance to school districts voluntarily seeking to desegregate, an extension of the life of the Civil Rights Commission. The Commission itself, though warmly praised in the President's message, shared this disappointment. It felt that the time was approaching to attack the broad problem of which the housing order had been a symbol: that is, the extent to which federal programs and activities themselves supported the structure of segregation.

At the same time the Commission was in a wrangle with the Department of Justice on the question whether it should be permitted to hold hearings in Mississippi. The Commission felt that drawing national attention to terror might to some degree deter it. But the Department feared that the hearings would stir local trouble and prejudice its own complicated litigations, especially those arising from the Oxford affair. Accordingly the Attorney General on three occasions asked the Commission to delay its Mississippi hearings.

But the Commission's statutory existence was running out, and by March it seemed too late to prepare for hearings. When the Commissioners met in Indianapolis at the end of the month, they were in a state of considerable irritation. The members therefore took the unusual step of preparing an interim report. It began by describing the defiance of the Constitution in Mississippi:

> *Citizens of the United States have been shot, set upon by vicious dogs, beaten, and otherwise terrorized because they sought to vote. Since October, students have been fired upon, ministers have been assaulted ... children, at the brink of starvation, have been deprived of assistance by the callous and discriminatory acts of Mississippi officials administering Federal funds.*

Given this situation, the Commission (including its southern members) concluded unanimously that "only further steps by the Federal Government can arrest the subversion of the Constitution in Mississippi." In particular, it proposed that the President strengthen the administration's efforts to provide federal protection for the citizens in the exercise of their constitutional rights; that he "consider seriously" the desirability of legislation to "assure that Federal funds contributed by citizens of all States not be made available to any State which continues to refuse to abide by the Constitution," and further that he "explore" his legal authority as chief executive "to withhold Federal funds from the State of Mississippi until the State of Mississippi demonstrates its compliance with the Constitution."

In a few days, Dr. Hannah, as chairman of the Commission, and Berl Bernhard, as director, presented the document to the President. Kennedy asked whether the report was unanimous and whether the Commission was adamant about putting it out. Assured on both points, he said he thought the part about cutting off funds was "subject to misunderstanding. I am not sure it is constructive.... I know some of the agencies have been dragging [their feet]. I am doing everything I can to see that they get in line. Your Commission doesn't understand I can't do it alone. The Commission report would be better directed at the Congress." Bernhard said that he gathered the President would prefer that the Commission not publish the report. "That is correct," Kennedy said. "If the Commissioners have made up their mind, I presume they will issue the report anyway. I think they are off track on this one, but I wouldn't try to suppress it. That would be wrong—couldn't do it anyway. It is independent, has a right to be heard, but I do wish you could get them to reconsider."

2. FEDERALISM AND FREEDOM

The report of the Civil Rights Commission called attention to one tragic gap in the administration design: the difficulty of protecting individuals in the South in the assertion of their federal rights. For most of the time since Reconstruction this had hardly been a problem; the rights had not been fully defined by the courts, and in any case the southern Negro had not protested their denial. Neither condition prevailed now. Recent events had proved several things: the readiness of the courts to define the rights, the unalterable purpose of the Negro to claim them, the brutality with which some southern whites were determined to withhold them, and, most troubling of all, the evident intention of local police authority, especially in Alabama and Mississippi, to support those who would frustrate the law against those who would fulfill it.

The last phenomenon confronted the Department of Justice with intricate problems of the relationship between national and local jurisdictions under the federal system. Robert Kennedy could send federal marshals to protect the freedom riders in Alabama in the spring of 1961 because the Interstate Commerce Act gave the national government clear responsibility to safeguard interstate travel. He could send federal marshals and the Army itself to Mississippi in the autumn of 1962 because state officials were defying federal court orders. But what could the Department do when defiance of the national government was less flagrant or the breakdown of local law enforcement less manifest? What could it do in particular with what Burke Marshall called the "double standard in the daily administration of law," so deeply imbedded in southern folkways, so routine and so automatic, so pervasively affecting not only the citizens involved but the very concept of government held by the law enforcement officials?

Shortly after Kennedy came into office, for example, a Negro Air Force captain in a southern city visited the house of a white major with whom he had served; the police, on the complaint of a neighbor, arrested them both for disturbing the peace. In Clinton, Louisiana, twelve Negroes who sent a wholly respectful letter to the mayor asking for the establishment of a biracial committee on community relations were arrested on the charge of intimidating public officials. In addition to cases of this sort there was the normal incidence of police brutality, falling more heavily on Negroes than on any other group in American society. When cases went to trial, it was always before white judges and all-white juries. Often Negroes could not obtain adequate counsel. Often bail was excessive. Yet the double standard, while in many cases "clearly beyond the very large limits of permissibility set by federal constitutional standards," was presently, Marshall said, "almost outside the reach of federal action" except when individuals themselves fought state criminal convictions up to the Supreme Court.

Though William Howard Taft's coarse formula about "the regulation by Southern States of their domestic affairs" was extinct, the Department of Justice felt a responsibility to preserve an appropriate balance between national and state powers in the federal system. This feeling inclined it to question proposals that the national government be given authority to enjoin interference with constitutional protests against racial injustice. The feeling also, in the eyes of some critics, discouraged the Department from using to the hilt laws already on the books. As for prosecutions of police abuses, the Department feared that, every time a southern grand jury refused to return an indictment requested by a federal attorney, it only invited further police brutality.

Yet the bitter problem remained. In too many civil rights cases the police themselves were perpetrators of crimes or protectors of criminals. Even when local authorities in the South met their minimum responsibilities for public order, they sometimes refused to give effect to the federal rights at issue, assuming that litigation would be so complex, burdensome and protracted that in the meantime, as Marshall put it, "the federal rights would atrophy." Marshall did not think that the federal system interposed insuperable obstacles to the right to vote; this could be secured "with enough money, enough energy, enough lawyers, and enough months or years." But the abuse of local police power and criminal processes for the purpose of frustrating federal court orders or the purpose of punishing those who agitated against the segregation system (and even those who, without agitation, quietly declined to abide by it) provided, he concluded, "a new test of the ability of the federal system" to meet its responsibilities.

Nothing gave Robert Kennedy and Marshall greater distress than their sense of the constitutional impotence of the national government in face of what the Attorney General called "the heartless, organized mistreatment of our fellow Americans who are Negroes." They well understood the fury of Negroes and civil rights workers who, after watching local authorities humiliate, beat and even murder their comrades, unavailingly demanded instant and massive retaliation by Washington.

Loss of faith in government by the Negroes themselves was the overhanging threat. Whites who looked only at the things in American life which had changed in a generation drew one conclusion; Negroes who looked only at the things which were the same drew another. However impressive—however truly unprecedented—the achievements of the Kennedy administration between 1961 and 1963, terrible facts remained. Seven and a half years after the school desegregation decision, spread of *de facto* segregation (defined by James Baldwin as meaning "that Negroes are segregated but nobody did it") was actually reducing integration in northern schools. The right to vote?—still smothered in litigation and constitutional hair-splitting. Employment?—Negroes, still the last to be hired and the first to be fired, had an unemployment rate two and a half times that of whites. Housing?—still hopeless. The federal government?—still subsidizing discrimination through a wide range of federal programs, and still incapable, short of major outrages like Meredith at Oxford, of protecting Negroes in the exercise of their constitutional rights in the South. The Emancipation Proclamation?—a hundred years gone, and the Negro still in bondage.

3. THE RAGE WITHIN

And more and more Negroes perceived these facts at a time when the sit-in demonstrators and the freedom riders and James Meredith, Roy Wilkins and A. Philip Randolph and Martin Luther King, Jr., had given them a new pride in themselves and a new sense of the power of direct action. The hoarded anger of generations, so long starved by despair, was now fed by hope.

The whites wondered why, when the Negroes had come so far, they pushed so hard. They could wait no longer: each year rotted away more of the Negro future. Boys and girls whose lives had been crippled by ten could not be easily redeemed at twenty.

Martin Luther King, Jr., had called 1961 "a year of the victory of the non-violent method: though blood flowed, not one drop was drawn by a Negro from his adversary." How long could this last? Negro militants were impatient not only of Kennedy and his strategy of executive action but of Roy Wilkins and his strategy of law, soon perhaps of King himself and his strategy of non-violence. The rise in these years of the Muslims in the steaming black ghettos of the North, where Elijah Muhammad and Malcolm X preached the ineradicable evil of the white man, contained chilling portents for the future. And, new generation of extremists, leapfrogging over the sedate Moscow faith of the American Communist Party, were approaching a quasi-Maoist belief in the virtues of violence.

And now in April 1963 in Birmingham, Alabama, a new crisis was developing. Under the leadership of Martin Luther King, Jr., the Negroes of Birmingham were launching a great campaign to end discrimination in shops, restaurants and employment. But sit-ins and marches were producing sharp retaliation. When King called for a protest march on Good Friday, April 12, Police Commissioner Eugene "Bull" Connor obtained an injunction, harassed the marchers with police dogs and arrested King and other leaders. A new and more moderate city administration was about to take office, and the Attorney General three times counseled the Birmingham

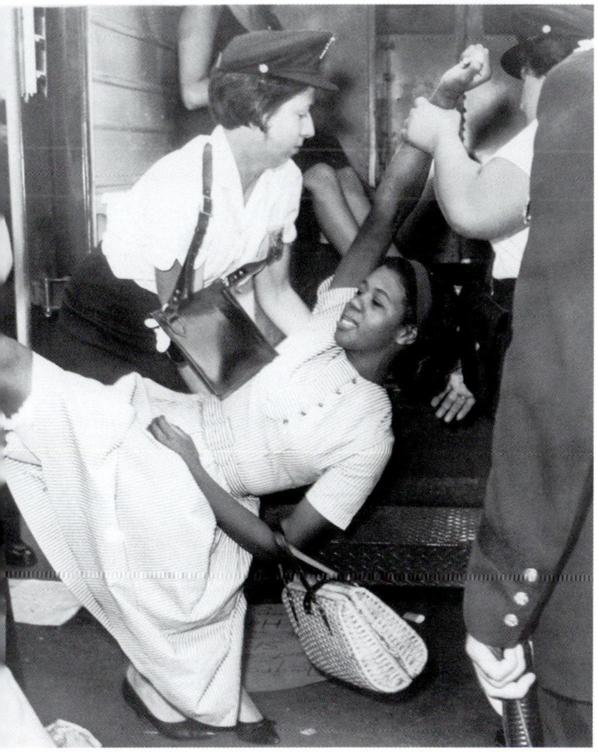

TOP: ONE OF THE MANY IMAGES OF POLICE DOGS ATTACKING BLACK DEMONSTRATORS IN BIRMINGHAM IN THE SPRING OF 1963.

MIDDLE LEFT: A FEMALE DEMONSTRATOR IS DRAGGED INTO A POLICE VAN.

MIDDLE RIGHT: BLACK LEADERS POSE OUTSIDE THE WHITE HOUSE AFTER MEETING WITH THE PRESIDENT IN SEPTEMBER 1963 TO DISCUSS THE CRISIS IN BIRMINGHAM. FROM LEFT ARE REVEREND J.L. WARE, REVEREND FRED SHUTTLESWORTH, DR. A.C. GASTON, REVEREND MARTIN LUTHER KING, JR., REVEREND RALPH D. ABERNATHY, DR. LUCIUS PITTS, AND BISHOP H. I. MURCHISON.

BOTTOM: A POLICE OFFICER FRISKS A DEMONSTRATOR FOR AN ATTEMPTED SIT-IN AT A DOWNTOWN LUNCH COUNTER IN BIRMINGHAM IN APRIL 1963.

JAMES BALDWIN (RIGHT) DURING A PRESS CONFERENCE IN SEPTEMBER 1963. WITH HIM IS BAYARD RUSTIN, DEPUTY DIRECTOR OF THE MARCH ON WASHINGTON.

leaders not to force issues while Bull Connor was still in charge. But the movement by now had a momentum of its own. King told Robert Kennedy that the Negroes had waited one-hundred years and could wait no longer. The demonstrations increased. So did the arrests. On May 2 about 500 Negroes, many of them high school students and younger, were hauled off to jail, some in school buses. The next day more students paraded. This time white bystanders threw bricks and bottles. The police turned fire hoses on the marchers, and Bull Connor released his growling police dogs. On Saturday, May 4, newspapers across the United States and around the world ran a shocking photograph of a police dog lunging at a Negro woman.

That morning the President received an Americans for Democratic Action group. They pressed him hard on civil rights. He said that the picture had made him "sick," but that at this point there was nothing he could constitutionally do. Then he added, "I am not asking for patience. I can well understand why the Negroes of Birmingham are tired of being asked to be patient."

Burke Marshall flew to Birmingham the same day in an effort to compose the situation. Finding total separation between the white and Negro communities, he worked in quiet talks to open up channels of communication. Meanwhile, the President, McNamara and Dillon tried to persuade business leaders with branches in Birmingham to use their influence toward mediation. Washington meanwhile refrained from public comment lest it undercut Marshall's effort. On May 10 an agreement was reached. But Governor George C. Wallace quickly announced that he would not be a party to any "compromise on the issues of segregation." The next night white patriots bombed houses and hotels in the Negro district. Rioting continued until dawn. In Washington President Kennedy sent federal troops into Alabama and prepared to federalize the state's National Guard.

The events in Birmingham abruptly transformed the mood of the nation. Churchmen, whose piety had studiously overlooked what John Quincy Adams had called the foul stain on the American conscience, idealistic students, recently preoccupied with disarming the United States and leaving the Soviet Union the great nuclear power in the world, ordinary citizens, complacent in their assumptions of virtue, were for a season jerked into guilt and responsibility. Bull Connor's police dogs accused the conscience of white America in terms which could not longer be ignored. But the awakening was so belated that it could hardly claim moral credit.

No one assailed the moral confusion and shame of white America more effectively than the Negro writer James Baldwin. In a long piece for the *New Yorker* in November 1962 called "Letter from a Region of My Mind," later published in the book *The Fire Next Time,* Baldwin evoked with penetrating power the fate of the Negro in white society—the past of rope, fire, torture, castration, infanticide, rape; death and humiliation; fear by day and night, fear as deep as the marrow of the bone; doubt that he was worthy of life, since everyone around him denied it; sorrow for his women, for his kinfolk, for his children, who needed his protection, and whom he could not protect; rage, hatred and murder, hatred for white men so deep that it often turned against him and his own, and made all love, all trust, all joy impossible; and the present of wine-stained and urine-splashed hallways, knife and pistol fights, clanging ambulance bells, helplessness and terror. "For the horrors of the American Negro's life," Baldwin said, "there has been almost no language." Neither civilized reason nor Christian love had persuaded the whites to treat Negroes with decency. The power of the white world was a criminal power; "the Negro's experience of the white world cannot possibly create in him any respect for the standards by which the white world claims to live." Only the fear of retaliation could deter the white man, protect the Negro's dignity and assert his individuality.

Baldwin described meetings with Elijah Muhammad and Malcolm X; while rejecting their racism, he unwillingly acknowledged their appeal. "Things are as bad as the Muslims say they are—in fact, they are worse, and the Muslims do not help matters—but there is no reason that black men should be expected to be more patient, more forbearing, more farseeing than whites; indeed, quite the contrary." The real reason that non-violence was considered a virtue in Negroes was that white men did not want their lives, their self-image or their property threatened. "The price of the liberation of the white people is the liberation of the blacks—the total liberation, in the cities, in the towns, before the law, and in the mind." He concluded in the words of an old spiritual: *God gave Noah the rainbow sign. No more water, the fire next time!*

Then in May 1963 the Attorney General, whose concern for civil rights had steadily deepened as his duties had confronted him with the horror of Negro inequality, sought to extend his contacts with Negro intellectuals. Accordingly he invited Baldwin to meet with him in New York, and to bring along knowledgeable people with concrete suggestions. The next day Baldwin and a number of Negro writers and show people—Professor Kenneth Clark, Lorraine Hansberry, Lena Horne, Harry Belafonte and others—met Robert Kennedy in his New York apartment.

In the Negro group was also Jerome Smith, a young freedom rider who had recently been savagely beaten in the South. Smith opened the meeting by saying, as the Attorney General understood it, that being in the same room with Robert Kennedy made him feel like vomiting. What Smith was apparently trying to say was that he felt like vomiting to have to plead before the Attorney General for the rights to which he was entitled as an American, but it came through to Kennedy, who had been fighting hard himself for these rights, as a gratuitous expression of personal contempt. The Attorney General showed his resentment; the group rallied around the freedom rider; and from this already low point the conversation went rapidly down hill.

Jerome Smith added that, so long as Negroes were treated this way, he felt no moral obligation to fight for the United States in war. The group applauded this sentiment. Some spoke of sending arms into the South. Baldwin said that the only reason the government had put federal troops in Alabama was because a white man had been stabbed. Burke Marshall, who was present, said that he had consulted with Dr. King about the use of federal troops; the group laughed at him. When Robert Kennedy, recalling his talk with Baldwin the day before, tried to seek their ideas about civil rights policy, they showed no interest. Baldwin was evidently not even aware that the President had given a civil rights message in February. "They didn't know anything," Bobby said to me later. "They don't know what the laws are—they don't know what the facts are—they don't know what we've been doing or what we're trying to do. You couldn't talk to them as you can to Roy Wilkins or Martin Luther King. They didn't want to talk that way. It was all emotion, hysteria. They stood up and orated. They cursed. Some of them wept and walked out of the room."

As for Baldwin, he felt that Kennedy was just unable to understand the sense of urgency of the Negro people—and this once again confirmed his thesis about the white man. Kenneth Clark, more thoughtfully, said later, "The fact that Bobby Kennedy sat through such an ordeal for three hours proves he is among the best the white power structure has to offer. There were no villains in that room—only the past of our society."

4. THE PRESIDENT IN COMMAND

On May 18, speaking at Vanderbilt University in Tennessee, the President glanced at the recent events in Birmingham. "No one can deny the complexity of the problems involved in assuring to all of our citizens their full rights as Americans," he said. "But no one can gainsay the fact that the determination to secure these rights is in the highest traditions of American freedom." His remark appeared to acknowledge that the revolution was overflowing its banks and to give nonviolent resistance presidential sanction. In any case, the momentum after Birmingham now seemed irresistible. In Nashville, Tennessee, in Raleigh and Greensboro, North Carolina, in Cambridge, Maryland, Albany, Georgia, Selma, Alabama, Negroes marched, prayed, sat in for their rights. During the summer 14,000 demonstrators were arrested in the states of the old Confederacy.

Then on May 21 a federal district judge ruled that the University of Alabama must admit two Negroes to its summer session in June. "I am the embodiment of the sovereignty of this state," Governor George Wallace replied, "and I will be present to bar the entrance of any Negro who attempts to enroll." It looked as if Alabama were going to follow Mississippi down the road of nullification. In the end, Wallace judiciously retreated in the face of National Guardsmen, and the students were registered. That evening—it was the day after the American University speech—Kennedy went on television to discuss civil rights.

After describing the events of the day at Tuscaloosa, the President expressed the hope that every American would examine his conscience. The nation, he said, was founded "on the principle that all men are created equal, and that the rights of every man are diminished when the rights of one man are threatened." It ought to be possible, he said,

> for American students of any color to attend any public institution without having to be backed up by troops. It ought to be possible for American consumers of any color to receive equal service in places of public accommodation, such as hotels and restaurants and theaters and retail stores, without being forced to resort to demonstrations in the street, and it ought to be possible for American citizens of any color to register and to vote in a free election without interference or fear of reprisal.... In short, every American ought to have the right to be treated as he would wish to be treated, as one would wish his children to be treated.
>
> But this is not the case.

In burning language he set forth the plight of the American Negro. If the Negro could not enjoy the full and free life which all of us want, "then who among us would be content to have the color of his skin changed and stand in his place? Who among us would then be content with the counsels of patience and delay?" We said to the world and to each other that we were the land of the free; did all we mean was that it was a land of the free except for the Negroes? "that we have no second-class citizens except Negroes; that we have no class or caste system, no ghettos, no master race except with respect to Negroes?"

This was, he said, "a moral issue"—"as old as the scriptures and ... as clear as the American Constitution." The time had come for the nation to fulfill its promise. The fires of frustration and discord were burning in every city where legal remedies were not at hand. The moral crisis could not be quieted by token talk or moves; it could not be left to demonstrations in the streets. "A great change is at hand, and our task, our obligation, is to make that revolution, that change, peaceful and constructive for all." Next week, he said, he would ask Congress to make the commitment it has not yet fully made in this century—the commitment to the proposition "that race has no place in American life or law."

It was a magnificent speech in a week of magnificent speeches. Some criticized Kennedy for not having given it earlier. But the timing was a vindication of his approach to mass education. He had prepared the ground for that speech ever since he became President. His actions, his remarks, the concern for Negro rights and scorn for racism implicit in his personality and bearing—all had subtly entered and transformed national expectations and attitudes. He had quietly created an atmosphere where change, when it came, would seem no longer an upheaval but the inexorable unfolding of the promise of American life. Yet he did not call for change in advance of the moment. If he had made his June speech in February, it would have attracted as little attention as his civil rights message that month. But Birmingham and the Negroes themselves had given him the nation's ear.

The night of Kennedy's speech, Medgar Evers of Mississippi, James Meredith's friend and counselor, a brave, gentle and responsible man, was murdered by a white killer in front of his house in Jackson. A week later the President invited his wife, children and brother-in-law, Charles Evers, who was taking Medgar's place as director of the Mississippi NAACP, to the White House. Robert Kennedy attended Medgar Evers's funeral in Arlington Cemetery and, giving Charles Evers his telephone numbers at the office and at home, said to call any time, day or night, if Negroes were being harassed or intimidated. (Charles Evers said later, "Whenever I had the need to call him, I've never found it too late or too early.")

The President had already begun to mobilize leaders of opinion in a succession of meetings, first with governors and then with hotel, restaurant and theater owners, labor leaders, religious leaders, educators, lawyers, women and with the Business Council. They sat on the gilt chairs in the East Room of the White House while the President, the Vice-President and the Attorney General sought in their various styles to explain the urgency of the situation and seek their support in meeting the problem—the President controlled and terse, the Vice-President evangelical and often very moving, the Attorney General blunt and passionate.

On June 19 the President sent his civil rights bill to the Hill. In addition to his February proposals, he now called for equal accommodations in public facilities, the grant of authority to the Attorney General to initiate school desegregation suits, new programs to assure fair employment, the establishment of a Community Relations Service, and a provision authorizing the federal government to withhold funds for programs or activities in which discrimination occurred. These recommendations did not produce universal satisfaction. The Vice-President had doubts about sending up any civil rights bill at this time, at least until the appropriations were passed. The civil rights leaders, on the other hand, while acknowledging that this was the most comprehensive civil rights bill ever to receive serious consideration from the Congress, wanted even stronger measures.

But even the administration bill had no assurance of an easy passage. We were first beginning to hear this summer about the phenomenon of the 'white backlash.' Rumors spread of middle-class whites concerned about the pace of integration. Politicians described widespread panic in traditional Democratic districts over the prospective inundation of their neighborhoods and schools by Negroes; some thought that civil rights might very well lose the election for Kennedy in 1964. The Louis Harris poll reported in the autumn that the civil rights issue had already turned some 4.5 million white voters against the administration. In the South, of course, bitterness toward the Kennedys reached new heights of virulence.

The President never had any illusions about the political advantages of equal rights. But he saw no alternative to leading the fight in order to prevent the final isolation of the Negro leadership and the embitterment of the Negro people. Every day that summer new and ominous tendencies seemed to appear in the colored masses. The President observed gloomily that the progress since Birmingham had been made possible by the awakening of the middle-class white conscience and the belated rallying to the civil rights cause; now the mindless radicalism of the Negro militants might well drive this new middle-class support away and postpone the hope of progress.

5 WE SHALL OVERCOME

Civil rights filled his mind, even in the summer of the test ban treaty. On June 22, the day before he left on his European trip, he invited the civil rights leaders to a meeting in the Cabinet Room to discuss the tactics of the bill now before the Congress. It was the best meeting I attended in my years in the White House. The President began with a crisp account of the parliamentary situation. If the bill was to pass, he said, it had to reach out beyond the traditional civil rights groups. He concluded by saying that, for reasons he well understood, Negro patience was at an end and that substantial progress had to come in 1963.

The civil rights group had been talking about a peaceful march on Washington, like the one A. Phillip Randolph had proposed to Franklin Roosevelt twenty years earlier. Whitney Young of the Urban League now said that the President's comments about demonstrations in the streets were being interpreted to mean he was against the march on Washington. "We want success in Congress," Kennedy replied, "not just a big show at the Capitol. Some of these people are looking for an excuse to be against us. I don't want to give any of them a chance to say, 'Yes, I'm for the bill, but I'm damned if I will vote for it at the point of a gun.' It seemed to me a great mistake to announce a march on Washington before the bill was even in committee. The only effect is to create an atmosphere of intimidation—and this may give some members of Congress an out."

A. PHILIP RANDOLPH SPEAKS DURING A NEWS CONFERENCE IN WASHINGTON, D.C.

A. Philip Randolph, speaking with the quiet dignity which touched Kennedy as it had touched Roosevelt before him, discussed the attempt to shift the civil rights drive from the streets to the courts. "The Negroes are already in the streets," Randolph said. "It is very likely impossible to get them off. If they are bound to be in the streets in any case, is it not better that they be led by organizations dedicated to civil rights and disciplined by struggle rather than to leave them to other leaders who care neither about civil rights nor about non-violence? If the civil rights leadership were to call the Negroes off the streets, it is problematic whether they would come."

The President agreed that the demonstrations in the streets had brought results; they had made the executive branch act faster and were now forcing Congress to entertain legislation which a few weeks before would have had no chance. "This is true. But now we are in a new phase, the legislative phase, and results are essential. The wrong kind of demonstration at the wrong time will give those fellows a chance to say that they have to prove their courage by voting against us. To get the votes we need we have, first, to oppose demonstrations which will lead to violence, and, second, give Congress a fair chance to work its will."

The Vice-President then remarked that many people had wrong ideas about the way Congress made up its mind. "Not many votes are converted in the corridors. Most fellows vote for what they think is right and for what they think their states want. We have about 50 votes for us in the Senate and about 22 against us. What counts is the 26 or so votes which remain. To get those votes we have to be careful not to do anything which would give those who are privately opposed a public excuse to appear as martyrs. We have to sell the program in twelve crucial states—and we have less than twelve weeks."

James Farmer of CORE said, "We understand your political problem in getting the legislation through, and we want to help in that as best we can. But the civil rights forces have their problems too. We would be in a difficult if not untenable position if we called the street demonstrations off and then were defeated in the legislative battle. The result would be that frustration would grow into violence and would demand new leadership."

"It is not a matter of either/or," Martin Luther King, Jr., now said, "but of both/and. Take the question of the march on Washington. This could serve as a means through which people with legitimate discontents could channel their grievances under disciplined, non-violent leadership. It could also serve as a means of dramatizing the issue and mobilizing support in parts of the country which don't know the problems at first hand. I think it will serve a purpose. It may seem ill-timed. Frankly, I have never engaged in any direct action movement which did not seem ill-timed. Some people thought Birmingham ill-timed." The President interjected wryly, "Including the Attorney General."

Someone brought up the question of police brutality. The President said sardonically, "I don't think you should all be totally harsh on Bull Connor." For a moment, there was an audible intake of breath around the cabinet table. "After all," Kennedy went on, "he has done more for civil rights than almost anybody else." He continued: "This is a very serious fight. The Vice-President and I know what it will mean if we fail. I have just seen a new poll—national approval of the administration has fallen from 60 to 47 percent. We're in this up to the neck. The worst trouble of all would be to lose the fight in the Congress. We'll have enough troubles if we win; but, if we win, we can deal with those. A good many programs I care about may go down the drain as a result of this—we may all go down the drain as a result of this—so we are putting a lot on the line. What is important is that we preserve confidence in the good faith of each other. I have my problems with the Congress; you have yours with your own groups. We will undoubtedly disagree from time to time on tactics. But the important thing is to keep in touch."

In a few moments he excused himself to go to a meeting on his European trip. "What seems terribly important," he said as he left, "is to get, and keep, as many Negro children as possible in schools this fall. It is too late to get equality for their parents, but we can still get it for the children—*if* they go to school, and take advantage of what educational opportunity is open to them. I urge you to get every Negro family to do this at whatever sacrifice."

The conference with the President did persuade the civil rights leaders that they should not lay siege to Capitol Hill. Instead, Bayard Rustin, the organizer of the March, made plans for a mass demonstration in front of the Lincoln Memorial. When asked about the march at a press conference in mid-July, Kennedy, noting that the participants intended "a peaceful assembly calling for a redress of grievances" and that it was "not a march on the Capitol," said, "I think that's in the great tradition." A. Philip Randolph outlined the tradition in a moving speech in Washington two days before the March. The event was "an outcry for justice, for freedom." It would serve "as a witness of commitment on the part of Negroes all over America, as well as our white brothers and sisters, in a great moral protest against racial bias." There was no way, he concluded, to stem such demonstrations until Negroes had acquired "the same things that white citizens possess—all their rights. They want no reservations."

A few days before the March the President expressed some concern that it might not be large enough. The leaders had committed themselves to producing 100,000 people. If it fell materially short of this, Kennedy remarked, it might persuade some members of Congress that the demand for action on civil rights was greatly exaggerated. He need not have worried. On August 28, nearly a quarter of a million people, black and white, came to Washington. They arrived by plane and bus and automobile and foot from almost every state in the union. The concern and mutual consideration of the marchers invested everything they did with an immense and lovely dignity. Nothing marred the beauty of the day.

In the afternoon they gathered in front of the Lincoln Memorial. "Even though we still face the difficulties of today and tomorrow," said Martin Luther King, Jr., the last of the speakers, "I still have a dream.... I have a dream that on the red hills of Georgia the sons of former slaves and the sons of former slave-owners will be able to sit together at the table of brotherhood.... I have a dream that even the state of Mississippi, a state sweltering with the heat of injustice, will be transformed into an oasis of freedom.... I have a dream that one day every valley shall be exalted, every hill and mountain shall be made low, the rough places will be made plain, and the crooked places will be made straight, and the glory of the Lord shall be revealed and all flesh shall see it together." The crowd, joining hands, rocking back and forth, cried, almost ecstatically, "Dream some more." Then in the dusk the vast assemblage quietly dispersed. Snatches of the poignant old Baptist hymn which the movement had made its own hung in the air:

We shall overcome, we shall overcome,
We shall overcome, some day.
Oh deep in my heart I do believe,
We shall overcome some day.

6. THE REVOLUTION

The President congratulated the leaders at the White House in the evening. Publicly he said, "This nation can properly be proud." But the March, though so splendid an affirmation, worked no miracles on the Hill. After long weeks of discussion and infighting, the President called in the House leaders in late October and, with the help of Charles Halleck, the Republican leader, personally worked out a compromise. The best civil rights bill in American history thus passed the first obstacles on its road to enactment. The House vote in January 1964 was the fulfillment of the agreement the Democratic and Republican leaders had made with Kennedy in the October White House meetings.

Yet, even when enacted, the new program would meet only part of the causes of the growing unrest. Its provisions were designed for the Negroes of the South. To the Negroes of the North the rights it offered were those they nominally possessed already. And to the heart of the now boiling northern unrest—to the frustrations in the black ghettos of the cities—it offered nothing.

Negroes had been moving north in increasing numbers since the First World War. By 1963 probably more than half lived outside the old Confederacy. They had drifted mostly into the great northern cities in search of jobs, hopes, excitement, oblivion. The 1960 census showed Washington more than half Negro, Baltimore and St. Louis a third, Philadelphia and Chicago a quarter, with the proportion steadily growing as the last wave of white immigrants, moving out to the suburbs, left the newcomers the decaying tenements, the filth and rats of the central city.

For the Negro the North was different from the South—more freedom but less purpose. The northern ghettos lacked the institutions which had to some degree stabilized life in the South. "The northern Negro," James Baldwin wrote, "is much more demoralized than the southern Negro is, because, there being no signs ["white" and "colored"], you have to play it by ear entirely.... Negroes do, in the north, go mad for just that reason." Moreover, there was still, Baldwin continued, "the Negro family in the south, and there is no Negro family, effectively speaking, in the north."

The South, moreover, still had the Negro church with its quietist traditions and devout following; it still had preachers like Martin Luther King, Jr. But in the ghettos the old-time religion was losing its potency, at least among the young, or else becoming an instrument for racists or racketeers. And in the South the mass action of 1963 had nourished Negro self-discipline and given shape to the sense of a Negro community negotiating with a white community to secure Negro rights. But in the North the sense of a united Negro community had perished in the long distances between the Negro upper class, with its prosperous insurance men and bankers and doctors, and the apathetic, despairing mass. The well-to-do Negro could now take advantage of the guilt of white society and enter universities and professions, hotels and golf courses; he could begin to identify himself with prevailing values. But the poor Negro, hedged in by *de facto* segregation in the schools, watching the gap between his own and the white worker's income and employment steadily widen, felt he was falling further and further behind and was losing his remnants of loyalty to the existing order. The angry Negro intellectuals could not hold the northern ghettos together; and the civil rights leaders had few ties to the rootless Negro urban proletariat.

The ghettos thus lacked internal structures of self-discipline and self-help; here they differed from the communities of European immigrants with their strong family ties and their networks of internal organization. They were swamps of incoherent resentment and despair, responding to prophets and demagogues, seeking identity in crime or surcease in a

THE MARCH ON WASHINGTON ARRIVES AT THE LINCOLN MEMORIAL.

slug or a fix. Civil rights bills had little to say to the unemployed, undereducated, untrained Negroes wandering aimlessly down the gray streets of Harlem or Watts, to boys and girls in their teens abandoned by their fathers and adrift in a desolation of mistrust and corruption, to the hoods and junkies and winos and derelicts.

The fulfillment of the Negro revolution plainly demanded much more than the achievement of the Negroes' legal rights. In April 1963 the unemployment rate for non-whites was 12.1 percent, for whites, 4.8 percent. Poverty afflicted half the non-white population, less than one-fifth of the white population. Three out of five non-white families lived in deteriorating or dilapidated buildings or without plumbing. The racial and social problems were inextricably intermingled. Bayard Rustin observed that the civil rights movement could not succeed "in the absence of radical programs for full employment, abolition of slums, the reconstruction of our educational system, new definitions of work and leisure." The deeper problems of inequality were "the result of the total society's failure to meet not only the Negro's needs, but human needs generally."

The President was keenly aware of the larger contexts. When civil rights leaders had reproached him in 1961 for not seeking legislation, he told them that an increased minimum wage, federal aid to education and other social and economic measures were also civil rights bills. He knew that a slow rate of economic growth made every problem of equal rights more intractable, as a faster rate would make every such problem easier of solution. In 1963 he counted on his tax cut to reduce Negro unemployment; he reviewed and enlarged his educational program—vocational education, adult basic education, manpower development, youth employment—to help equip Negroes for jobs; and his concern for the plight of the Negro strengthened his campaigns against juvenile delinquency, urban decay and poverty.

The Negro leaders had never doubted that Kennedy was on their side. But they had feared he regarded the civil rights problem as only one among many problems. By the summer of 1963 he had clearly made it the major problem next to the pursuit of peace itself.

Every great period of social change in American history has been set off by the demand of some excluded but aggressive group for larger participation in the national democracy: in the age of Jackson by the frontier farmer, the city worker, the small entrepreneur; in the progressive era by the bankrupt farmers of the middle border and the by-passed old upper classes of the cities; in the New Deal by labor in mass-production industries, the unemployed and the intellectuals. The uprising of the Negroes now contained the potentiality of ushering in a new era which would not only win Negroes

DR. KING DELIVERING HIS NOW FAMOUS "I HAVE A DREAM" SPEECH ON THE STEPS OF THE LINCOLN MEMORIAL.

their rights but renew the democratic commitment of the national community. It also contained the potentiality, if the anger of the Negroes exceeded the will of the government to redress their grievances and the capacity of their own leadership to retain their confidence, of rending and destroying the fabric of American society.

By 1963 the revolution was enlisting the idealism not only of the Negroes but of the universities and churches, of labor and the law. It was also attracting some who, as one put it, if they could not get their places around the table, threatened to knock its legs off. A generation ago Roosevelt had absorbed the energy and hope of the labor revolution into the New Deal. So in 1963 Kennedy moved to incorporate the Negro revolution into the democratic coalition and thereby help it serve the future of American freedom.

XXXVII.
AUTUMN 1963

THE SUMMER OF 1963 ended in sadness. In early August Jacqueline gave birth prematurely to a five-pound boy. Young Patrick Bouvier Kennedy came into the world with respiratory troubles. After thirty-nine hours of struggle, the labor of breathing proved too much for his heart, and he died in a Boston hospital. The President's anguish for his wife and their dead son gave August a melancholy cast. Early in September he and Jacqueline quietly observed their tenth wedding anniversary in Newport.

But in public policy the Presidency of John F. Kennedy was coming into its own. He was doing at last in the summer of 1963 what he had been reluctant to do before: putting the office of the Presidency on the line at the risk of defeat. He was staking his authority and his re-election on behalf of equal rights, the test ban, planned deficits in economic policy, doing so not without political apprehension but with absolute moral and intellectual resolve. As he had anticipated, the civil rights fight in particular was biting into his popularity. In November Gallup would report that national approval of his administration was down to 59 percent. Most of this decline was in the South; there, if the Republicans, as he came to believe they would, nominated Barry Goldwater, Kennedy expected to carry only two or three states. Moreover, this had been the hardest of his congressional sessions. At the end of July, according to the *Congressional Quarterly*, 38 percent of the administration's proposals had not yet been acted on by either house. Civil rights and tax reduction were making very slow progress. Knives were sharpening for foreign aid. Even routine appropriation bills were held up.

Then Senate ratification of the test ban treaty in September gave his leadership a new access of strength. "There is a rhythm to personal and national and international life," he had said in the winter, "and it flows and ebbs." It had ebbed for many weeks. Now perhaps it was beginning to flow again.

1. JOURNEY TO THE WEST

On the day the Senate ratified the treaty, Kennedy left Washington for a trip to the West. It was ostensibly a nonpolitical tour, its pretext conservation. This was a genuine, if somewhat abstract, concern, and he welcomed the chance to see the condition of the national estate at first hand. But the trip had other motives too. Of the eleven states on his itinerary, he had lost eight in 1960; with the South turning against him, he needed new sources of support. Furthermore, ten had senatorial contests in 1964, and in several the John Birch Society was active. Above all, the trip offered him a chance to reestablish contact and purpose with the people.

He conscientiously pursued the conservation theme for several speeches. Then late on the second day, at Billings, Montana, he struck, almost by accident, a new note. Mike Mansfield was present and in his third sentence Kennedy praised the Senate leader for his part in bringing about test ban ratification. To his surprise this allusion produced strong and sustained applause. Heartened, he set forth his hope of lessening the "chance of a military collision between those two great nuclear powers which together have the power to kill 300 million people in the short space of a day." The Billings response encouraged him to make the pursuit of peace increasingly the theme of his trip.

In Great Falls, Montana, he discussed the illusions of isolationism.

Then to Hanford, Washington, and on September 26 to Salt Lake City, where he defined America's role in the modern world. I had worked on this speech. The President wanted to concentrate on extremism in foreign policy—a masked comment, in effect, on Goldwater.

The President received an unusually cordial reception on the streets of a city that Washington regarded as a stronghold of the radical right. Then, before an immense crowd at the Tabernacle of the Latter Day Saints, he began his speech.

"We find ourselves," he said, "entangled with apparently unanswerable problems in unpronounceable places. We discover that our enemy in one decade is our ally in the next. We find ourselves committed to governments whose actions we cannot often approve, assisting societies with principles very different from our own." It was little wonder that in a time of contradiction and confusion we looked back to the old days with nostalgia. But those days were gone forever; science and technology were irreversible. Nor could we remake the new world simply by our own command. "When we cannot even bring all of our own people into full citizenship without acts of violence, we can understand how much harder it is to control events beyond our borders." Our national interest was "best served by preserving and protecting a world of diversity in which no one power or no one combination of powers can threaten the security of the United States."

The forces of diversity, he added, were "in the ascendancy today, even within the Communist empire itself.... The most striking thing about our world in 1963 is the extent to which the tide of history has begun to flow in the direction of freedom. To renounce the world of freedom now, to abandon those who share our commitment, and retire into lonely and not so splendid isolation, would be to give communism the one hope which, in this twilight of disappointment for them, might repair their divisions and rekindle their hope." At the end the audience stood at their seats and cheered for many minutes.

He had hit his stride, reached the deeper concerns of his audience, and the rest of the journey was a triumphal procession. He always found journeys "out there" refreshing, but this time he returned in a state of particular exhilaration. Whatever the stalemate in Congress, he knew now that he had immense resources of affection and strength in the people. He knew too that peace, economic growth and education would be powerful themes for 1964.

2. THE VIETNAM QUANDARY

Nothing was tougher at the moment than the situation in South Vietnam, where the abrupt collapse of the hopes of 1962 had provided the unpleasant surprise of 1963.

Our policy in 1962 had been dominated by those who saw Vietnam as primarily a military problem and who believed that its solution required unconditional support of Diem. The reports rendered by Ambassador Frederick Nolting and General Paul Harkins to Washington conveyed the picture of a regime led by an unquestionably difficult but statesmanlike and, in any case, irreplaceable figure making steady progress in winning over the peasants, pacifying the countryside and restoring the stability of government. The local opposition, in this view, consisted of intellectuals, neutralists and agents of the Viet Cong, concerned more with their own petty grievances and ambitions than with winning the war. The only way to improve things, they believed in all sincerity, was to reassure Diem about the constancy of American support.

Through most of 1962 this policy appeared to be producing results. The Saigon government, so near collapse at the end of 1961, had recovered much of its authority. The strategic hamlet program, in the considered judgment of the Departments of State and Defense, was bringing the countryside into firm alliance with the regime. The Viet Cong were presumably making little progress. Indeed, in the spring of 1963 Alexis Johnson claimed that 30,000 casualties had been inflicted on the guerrillas in 1962—a figure twice as large as the estimated size of the Viet Cong forces at the beginning of the year. In the same month Secretary McNamara authorized the Defense Department to announce "we have turned the corner in Vietnam," and General Harkins predicted that the war would be won "within a year." The communists themselves acknowledged 1962 as "Diem's year." The American advisers and the helicopter war had increased the cost of guerrilla action, and the Viet Cong almost reached the point of giving up in the Mekong delta and withdrawing to the mountains.* Kennedy, beset by the missile crisis, congressional elections, Skybolt, de Gaulle, Latin America, the test ban negotiations and the civil rights fight, had little time to focus on Southeast Asia. His confidence in McNamara, so wholly justified in so

* See the testimony of the Australian Communist writer, W. T. Burchett, in *Vietnam: Inside Story of the Guerrilla War* (New York, 1965).

many areas, led the President to go along with the optimists on Vietnam.

Not everyone shared this optimism, and dissent arose first among the American newspapermen in Vietnam.* The reporters were bright, inquisitive, passionate young men in their late twenties or early thirties with careers to make—Malcolm Browne of the Associated Press, Cornelius Sheehan of the United Press International, David Halberstam of the *New York Times,* Charles Mohr of *Time,* François Sully of *Newsweek.* They saw Diem not as a selfless national leader but as an oriental despot, hypnotized by his own monologues and contemptuous of democracy and the west. They detested the Nhus. They considered the strategic hamlet program a fake and a failure; and their visit to dismal stockades where peasants had been herded, sometimes at bayonet point, to engage in forced labor confirmed their worst misgivings. They did not believe Diem's communiqués; and, when Harkins and Nolting insisted they were true, they stopped believing Harkins and Nolting.

In time the disagreement between the officials and the newspapermen hardened into deep antagonism. Nolting, a conscientious Foreign Service officer, honestly saw no alternative to working with Diem. Diem, who supposed that the American press was as controlled as his own, believed, or pretended to believe, that the newspaper stories were expressing the secret views of the United States government and used his fury over lost face as one more excuse for resisting American advice. The reporters, as Nolting and Harkins saw it, were therefore damaging the war effort; instead of making carping criticisms, they ought, as patriotic Americans, to help the Embassy build up Diem and strengthen his national control and international reputation. In their reports to Washington the officials even gave the astonishing impression that there would be no trouble in Vietnam if only the newspaper fellows would follow the line.

As for the newspapermen, they resented the view that their duty was to write stories in support of official policy. They could never get over Admiral Felt's reproach to Malcolm Browne: "Why don't you get on the team?" They angrily refused to become, as they thought, myth-makers and invoked with solemn indignation the traditions of a free press. "The U. S. Embassy," David Halberstam wrote in a characteristic outburst, "turned into the adjunct of a dictatorship. In trying to protect Diem from criticism, the Ambassador became Diem's agent. But we reporters didn't have to become the adjuncts of a tyranny. We are representatives of a free society, and we weren't going to surrender our principles to the narrow notions of a closed society." One encounter after another made the newspapermen more certain that the Embassy was deliberately lying to them. They did not recognize the deeper pathos, which was that the officials really believed their own reports. They were deceiving not only the American government and people but themselves.

Not everyone in Washington, however, was deceived. Averell Harriman as Assistant Secretary for the Far East had long felt, as by the pricking in his thumbs, that we were on the wrong course. Roger Hilsman, as head of the State Department Office of Intelligence and Research, also doubted whether things were really as splendid as they appeared in Embassy dispatches. In the White House Michael Forrestal shared this skepticism. And, as 1962 gave way to 1963, it seemed increasingly evident that, despite the communiqués and the statistics and the dispatches, the Viet Cong were as omnipresent and the Saigon government as ineffectual as ever. The point was made with some vividness on January 2, 1963, at Ap Bac, fifty miles from Saigon, when a considerable force of Diem's regulars encircled a Viet Cong battalion one-tenth its size, declined to close with them and finally permitted the Viet Cong to escape in the night after they had knocked down five American helicopters and killed three American advisers. A senior American adviser present later surmised that the Vietnamese commander was "reluctant to attack for fear he would take casualties, incur the displeasure of political leaders in Saigon and ruin his military career." Though General Harkins tried to claim Ap Bac as a Vietnamese victory, the newspapermen at the scene reported otherwise, and their reports were not implausible.

Those in Saigon and Washington who saw Vietnam as primarily a military problem thought that the answer to Ap Bac was an intensified military effort. After all, the American presence was still negligible—11,000 troops in all and, in the last two years, a total of thirty-two killed in battle and eighty wounded. But the Harriman group now questioned the exclusively military strategy more insistently than ever. "Fighting a guerrilla war in an underdeveloped nation," Hilsman, the veteran of jungle warfare in Burma, had argued the previous September, "requires as much political and civic action as it does military action." The more elaborate the American military establishment, the doubters feared, the more it would be overwhelmed by brass, channels and paperwork, the more it would rely on conventional tactics and the more it would compromise the Vietnamese nationalism of Diem's cause. Worse, the growth of the military commitment would confirm the policy of trying to win a political war by military means.

What was lacking, the Harriman group felt, was any consuming motive to lead the South Vietnamese to fight for

* For details, see Malcolm W. Browne, *The New Face of War* (Indianapolis, 1965), David Halberstam, *The Making of a Quagmire* (New York, 1965), John Mecklin, *Mission in Torment* (New York, 1965) and Robert Shaplen, *The Lost Revolution* (New York, 1965).

Saigon. Why, for example, should peasants die for a government which, when it recovered territory from the Viet Cong, helped the local landowners collect their back rent? General Edward Lansdale wrote, "that there must be a heartfelt *cause* to which the legitimate government is pledged, a cause which makes a stronger appeal to the people than the Communist cause.... When the right cause is identified and used correctly, the *anti*-Communist fight becomes a *pro*-people fight."

3. THE BUDDHISTS

This was a minority view. The Secretary of State was well satisfied with military predominance in the formation of United States policy toward Vietnam. As late as April 22, 1963, in a speech in New York, Rusk discerned a "steady movement [in South Vietnam] toward a constitutional system resting upon popular consent," declared that "the 'strategic hamlet' program is producing excellent results," added that "morale in the countryside has begun to rise," assured his listeners that "to the Vietnamese peasant" the Viet Cong "look less and less like winners" and concluded, "The Vietnamese are on their way to success" (meaning presumably the South Vietnamese). So too Alexis Johnson, speaking for right-thinking officials, cited the strategic hamlet program as "the most important reason for guarded optimism." "Perhaps the most important result," Johnson declared, "is the intangible knitting together of Government and people."

Intangible the knitting together certainly was. Exactly a month after this piece of official wisdom and a fortnight after Rusk's assurances a group of Buddhists gathered in Hue to protest a Diem order forbidding them to display their flags on Buddha's 2587th birthday. Diem's troops fired indiscriminately into the crowd, leaving a moaning mass of dead and wounded. Indignation spread through the towns of South Vietnam; and, when Diem proved unyielding and unrepentant, the anger took appalling forms, culminating in the spectacle of Buddhist *bonzes* dousing themselves in gasoline and burning themselves to death.

Though the Buddhists had suffered legal discrimination in South Vietnam, they had not been actively persecuted. The upheaval, while religious in pretext, was social in its origins and quickly became political in its objectives. It went beyond *bonzes* and students to militant young army officers exasperated by the caprice and confusion of Diem's direction of the war. As the protests spread, the Buddhist revolt threatened to become the vehicle by which all those opposed to the regime, including, no doubt, fellow travelers of the Viet Cong, might hope to bring it down. It was at bottom an uprising, wholly unanticipated by American diplomats, against the hierarchical structure of traditional Vietnamese society—against the older generation of Vietnamese nationalists who, like Diem and Nhu, were upper-class, Catholic, French-speaking, in favor of a new nationalist generation, drawn largely from the middle and lower classes, anti-western, radical, impassioned: it was, in effect, the angry young men massing to throw out the mandarins.

The Buddhists, with their fiery adventures in self-immolation, engaged the sympathy of the American newspapermen and through them of many people in the United States. Diem helped this process by refusing gestures of contrition or conciliation lest, as usual, he lose face. Washington now instructed the Embassy to bring pressure on him to compose the Buddhist quarrel, warning that, if the situation grew worse, the United States might have to disavow his Buddhist policy publicly. In Saigon, Nolting, to Kennedy's irritation, had departed on a long-planned holiday cruise in the Aegean. His absence, however, permitted his able Deputy Chief of Mission, William Trueheart, to state the American position more bluntly than Diem had ever heard it before.

In response, Diem began to make a few nominal concessions, if with visible resentment. The Nhus, who wanted him to crush the uprising altogether, were even more resentful. In the steaming Saigon summer the incipient hysteria in the presidential palace boiled over. Diem and the Nhus saw plots everywhere: the Buddhists were Viet Cong agents; the American reporters were communists or agents of the CIA; the CIA was even collaborating with the Viet Cong. Madame Nhu said gaily that she clapped her hands whenever more *bonzes* "barbecued" themselves and only wished that David Halberstam would follow their example. Nhu told Morris West, the Australian novelist, that the Americans should get out and that he was in touch with some fine nationalist communists in Hanoi. About this time John Mecklin, the USIA chief, had a nightmare about an American diplomatic mission which gradually discovered it was dealing with a government of madmen, whose words meant nothing, where nothing that was supposed to have happened had actually happened; yet there seemed no escape from dealing with the madmen forever.

The paranoia in Saigon strengthened the Harriman position in Washington. Kennedy himself, who had been doubting the official optimism for some time, used to say dourly that the political thing there was more important than the military, and no one seemed to be thinking of that. When Mecklin visited Washington in the spring, the President asked him why there was so much trouble with the reporters and, after hearing the explanation, personally instructed the Saigon Embassy to change its attitude and start taking American newspapermen into its confidence. Now he began to conclude that the new situation required a new ambassador. Six months before, Nolting had asked, for personal reasons, to be relieved; and, after the Buddhist outburst, the President reluctantly decided that the time had come.

I have the impression that he wanted to send next to Saigon Edmund Gullion, from whom he had first learned about Indochina a dozen years before and who had performed with such distinction in the Congo; Gullion was certainly the candidate of at least some at the White House. But Dean Rusk, in a rare moment of self-assertion, determined to make this appointment himself. He did not want Gullion, and his candidate, to the astonishment or dismay of the White House staff, turned out to be Henry Cabot Lodge.

Lodge, who had been a liaison officer with the French Army during the Second World War, spoke fluent French. In his capacity as reserve officer, he had written a paper on Vietnam in the spring of 1962 and had wanted to take his tour of duty in Vietnam. Yet as Ambassador to the United Nations in the Eisenhower years he had displayed no great understanding of the third world and no great talent in dealing with the representatives of new nations. The White House staff feared that once in Saigon he would instinctively side with General Harkins and Diem. But the President was attracted by the idea for political reasons, and so the appointment was made late in June.

Since Lodge could not leave until late August, it was decided to send back Nolting, who had finally arrived in Washington from his holiday, for one last try of the pro-Diem policy. Nolting, angered by Trueheart's forthright representations to Diem in his absence, felt when he got back to Saigon on July 11, that his labor of two years lay in ruins. Nor had the recent troubles altered in the slightest his estimate of the situation. He considered the Buddhists unappeasable, believing their goal to be the overthrow of the regime. He felt American pressure on their behalf, especially any public disavowal of Diem's anti-Buddhist actions, would only incite Diem to more stringent repression or his opponents to a coup. Any effort to divorce Diem from the Nhus would be useless.

In Washington, meanwhile, Kennedy sought to put Saigon's problems in perspective by reminding a press conference that Vietnam after all had been at war for twenty years. "Before we render too harsh a judgment on the people, we should realize that they are going through a harder time than we have had to go through." Our goal, he continued, was "a stable government there, carrying on a struggle to maintain its national independence. We believe strongly in that.... In my opinion, for us to withdraw from that effort would mean a collapse not only of South Vietnam but Southeast Asia. So we are going to stay there."

Neither Nolting's return nor Kennedy's temperate words had much effect, though, before Nolting left in mid-August, Diem did assure him there would be no more attacks on the Buddhists. Then six days later, Diem's troops assaulted the pagodas, arresting hundreds of *bonzes* and seizing the temples of worship in a night of violence and terror. It was, Mecklin wrote later, "ruthless, comprehensive suppression of the Buddhist movement." Madame Nhu described it to a reporter as "the happiest day in my life since we crushed the Binh Xuyen [a private army of brigands] in 1955."

The Americans were caught completely by surprise. General Harkins had noted the Vietnamese troop movements but thought they were being deployed for an attack on the Viet Cong. "We just didn't know," the CIA chief told Halberstam. It was an act of calculated contempt for the Americans. The next evening in the midst of a hot, soggy drizzle of rain Cabot Lodge arrived in Saigon.

4. THE SOUND OF MUTINY

The White House doubters had been mistaken about Lodge. We had forgotten his patrician's preference for fair play and his patriot's pride in the dignity of his country. Both had been considerably affronted as he read through the Saigon cable file in preparation for his mission. Now Diem and Nhu had obviously carried out their attack against the pagodas the day before his arrival in order to present him with a *fait accompli*, expecting that the Americans would give in, as they had always done before. But Lodge in Saigon agreed with Harriman and Hilsman in Washington that, if we were to retain any credibility in Vietnam, we had to stand up this time.

In Vietnam the brutality of the assault sent a shudder even through the Diem regime itself. The foreign minister resigned and, in a gesture of defiance, shaved his head like a *bonze*. Madame Nhu's father resigned as ambassador to Washington with a denunciation of his daughter. Above all, the action crystallized the dis-affection of the generals who, in the confusion, had been themselves blamed (by, among others, the Department of State) for the atrocity. Now they began sending clandestine messages to the new ambassador. They first wanted it made clear that they had nothing to do with the raids. Then they inquired with oriental suavity what our attitude would be if they were to take action against the regime, should Nhu, for example, make a deal with Hanoi. Lodge cabled Washington for instructions.

The reply was drafted on August 24. The American government, it suggested, could no longer tolerate the systematic repression of the Buddhists nor the domination of the regime by Nhu. The generals could be told that we would find it impossible to support Diem unless these problems were solved. Diem should be given every chance to solve them. If he refused, then the possibility had to be realistically faced that Diem himself could not be saved. We would take no part in any action; but, if anything happened, an interim anti-communist military regime could expect American support.

August 24 was a Saturday. The President was on Cape Cod; McNamara and Rusk were out of town; McCone was on vacation. The draft was cleared through all the relevant departments but not at the top level. Defense accepted it because it understood that the cable had already gone; McNamara, if he had been consulted, would have opposed it. So also would McCone. No one is sure what Rusk's position would have been. The President saw the draft at Hyannis Port without realizing that the departmental clearances did not signify the concurrence of his senior advisers.

On his return to Washington Kennedy felt rather angrily that he had been pressed too hard and fast. He discussed the situation with Robert Kennedy, who talked in turn with McNamara and Maxwell Taylor. The Attorney General reported back with great concern that nobody knew what was going to happen in Vietnam and that our policy had not been fully discussed, as every other major decision since the Bay of Pigs had been discussed. The President thereupon called a meeting on Vietnam for the following day and asked that Nolting be invited.

The former ambassador gave a dignified and uncritical statement of the case for Diem and expressed doubt whether the generals involved could carry off a coup. He suggested that we should not jump unless we knew where we were jumping. The President agreed and began a process of pulling away from the cable of August 24. Vietnam meetings continued for several days, and messages flashed back and forth between Washington and Saigon. While the talks went on, the coup itself gradually evaporated. Nolting had been right: these generals could not carry it through.

Diem and Nhu proceeded quickly to exploit their victory. There were more arrests, especially among students, thousands of whom, including boys and girls of high school age, were carted off to indoctrination centers. In Washington policy weakly reverted to collaboration with Diem, encouraged by CIA's suggestion that Diem might have been sufficiently alarmed by the coup rumors to do some of the things we wanted. The President, however, did not wish to leave Diem in any doubt about how he felt, especially about Nhu. In a television interview on September 3, he tossed

TOP: HENRY CABOT LODGE, SECOND FROM LEFT, ARRIVES IN VIETNAM.
BOTTOM: LODGE SHAKES HANDS WITH PRESIDENT NGO DINH DIEM IN THE PRESIDENTIAL PALACE IN SAIGON.

GENERAL TAYLOR (LEFT) AND MCNAMARA (SECOND FROM LEFT) ARE SENT ONE MORE TIME TO WITNESS THE WAR AGAINST THE VIET CONG. GENERAL PAUL HARKINS, COMMANDER OF THE U.S. FORCES IN VIETNAM, IS AT MCNAMARA'S LEFT.

aside a moderate statement his staff had prepared in light of his reaction to the August 24 telegram. Instead, he said:

I don't think that the war can be won unless the people support the effort and, in my opinion, in the last two months, the government has gotten out of touch with the people.

The repressions against the Buddhists, we felt, were very unwise.... It is my hope that this will become increasingly obvious to the government, that they will take steps to try to bring back popular support.... With changes in policy and perhaps with personnel I think it can. If it doesn't make those changes, I would think that the chances of winning it would not be very good.

No one could misinterpret the reference to changes in personnel. Kennedy also emphasized that "in the final analysis, it is their war. They are the ones who have to win it or lose it. We can help them, we can give them equipment, we can send our men out there as advisers, but they have to win it, the people of Vietnam."

The contrast between this statement and his reaction to the August 24 cable suggested Kennedy's own perplexity; and, in a new effort to find out what the situation was, he sent another mission early in September. It consisted this time, not of the usual senior officials, but of two old Vietnam hands, General Victor Krulack of the Marines and Joseph Mendenhall of State, a Foreign Service officer. After a frenzied weekend of inspection and interrogation, the two men flew back to Washington. Mecklin, who came back with them, observed that "the general and the FSO not only appeared to dislike each other, but also disagreed on what should be done about Vietnam. On the whole flight they spoke to each other only when it was unavoidable." They reported immediately to the National Security Council. Krulack told the assembled dignitaries the war was going beautifully, that the regime was beloved by the people and that we need have no undue concern even about Nhu. Mendenhall told them that South Vietnam was in a desperate state, that the regime was on the edge of collapse and that Nhu had to go. The President listened politely and finally said, "Were you two gentlemen in the same country?" And so the meetings on Vietnam continued.

5. THE FALL OF DIEM

Lodge had begun his Saigon tour with the usual calls on Diem and Nhu. When he got nowhere with them, he stopped calling on them. "They have not done anything I asked," he would explain. "They know what I want. Why should I keep asking? Let them come to ask me." The anti-Diem section of the Embassy and American press in Saigon, enormously cheered, said to each other: "Our mandarin is going to beat their mandarin." Lodge kept cabling Washington that the situation was getting worse and that the time had arrived for the United States to increase its pressure. He recommended in particular the suspension of American aid.

McNamara and Rusk were at first opposed. The suspension of aid, they said, would hurt the war effort. And Lodge did not help his case by a Bostonian high-handedness which not only turned his embassy into a one-man show but also made him uncommunicative and at times almost derisive in response to inquiries from Washington. But Kennedy, I believe, came to the conclusion in mid-September that Lodge, Harriman, Hilsman and Forrestal were right on the question of pressure, though he remained wary of anything which might involve the United States in attempts against the regime. Accordingly he decided to send McNamara and Taylor on one more trip on the Saigon shuttle in the hope that exposure to Lodge and the facts would convince them too that pressure was essential.

MCNAMARA VISITS WITH DIEM IN SAIGON ON SEPTEMBER 29, 1963.

In the past, McNamara's susceptibility to quantification had led him to take excessive comfort in General Harkins's statistical optimism, embodied, for example, in tables purporting to correlate government and Viet Cong casualties; and Nolting had done little to assert the importance of things which could not be quantified. In Saigon, as in Washington, the State Department had acquiesced in the theory that Vietnam was basically a military problem. But Lodge considered intangibles like political purpose and popular support as of the highest importance. For a few days after McNamara's arrival, Lodge and Harkins engaged in a quiet duel for the Secretary's ear. In the end Lodge made the political case so effectively that McNamara agreed there was no alternative to pressure; indeed, McNamara returned to Washington doubting whether Diem could last even if he took corrective action. But he also thought that the political mess had not yet infected the military situation and, back in Washington, announced (in spite of a strong dissent from William Sullivan of Harriman's staff who accompanied the mission) that a thousand American troops could be withdrawn by the end of the year and that the major part of the American military task would be completed by the end of 1965.

This announcement, however, was far less significant than McNamara's acceptance of the Lodge pressure program. Some thought had already been given to the problem of picking out of the aid effort the cuts which would do the least harm to the war, and early in October a selective suspension went quietly into effect. Madame Nhu now appeared in the United States to lobby against the new policy; for a moment she won support from right-wing politicians, though in the end her extravagances injured her own cause. In Saigon her husband apparently renewed his efforts to make contact with Hanoi. Speculation bubbled up again about possible successors to Diem.

As for Diem, there is some suggestion that the program of pressure, so belatedly adopted, was having effect. "With or without American aid," he said in mid-October, "I will keep up the fight, and I will always maintain my friendship toward the American people." On the last day of the month Diem and Lodge made a trip together to dedicate an experimental

A MEMBER OF SOUTH VIETMAN'S REBEL MILITARY IS SHOWN IN THE PRESIDENTIAL PALACE, WHICH WAS DESTROYED IN THE COUP AGAINST DIEM ON NOVEMBER 1, 1963.

reactor at Dalat. Diem for the first time indicated an interest in compromise and asked Lodge what he had to do. Lodge told him to send Nhu out of the country and institute some reforms. Diem, instead of turning this down out of hand, said that he needed a little time to think about it. It was too late. The next day the generals struck. Diem and Nhu were murdered, and the history of Vietnam entered a new phase.

It is important to state clearly that the coup of November 1, 1963, was entirely planned and carried out by the Vietnamese. Neither the American Embassy nor the CIA were involved in instigation or execution. What lay behind the coup was not the meddling of Americans, quiet or ugly, but the long history of Vietnamese military resentment against Diem, compounded now by the fear that Nhu, with his admiration for totalitarian methods of organization, might try to transform South Vietnam into a police state. It was almost inevitable that, at one point or another, the generals would turn against so arbitrary and irrational a regime.

I saw the President soon after he heard that Diem and Nhu were dead. He was somber and shaken. I had not seen him so depressed since the Bay of Pigs. No doubt he realized that Vietnam was his great failure in foreign policy, and that he had never really given it his full attention. But the fact that the Vietnamese seemed ready to fight had made him feel that there was a reasonable chance of making a go of it; and then the optimism of 1962 had carried him along. Yet, with his memory of the French in Indochina in 1951, he had always believed there was a point at which our intervention might turn Vietnamese nationalism against us and transform an Asian civil conflict into a white man's war. When he came into office, 2000 American troops were in Vietnam. Now there were 16,000. How many more could there be before we passed the point? By 1961 choices had already fatally narrowed; but still, if Vietnam had been handled as a political rather than a military problem, if Washington had not listened to General Harkins for so long, if Diem had been subjected to tactful pressure rather than treated with

VIOLENT PROTESTS IN SAIGON DURING THE NOVEMBER 1 COUP.

uncritical respect, if a Lodge had gone to Saigon in 1961 instead of a Nolting, if, if, if—and now it was all past, and Diem miserably dead. The Saigon generals were claiming that he had killed himself; but the President, shaking his head, doubted that, as a Catholic, he would have taken this way out. He said that Diem had fought for his country for twenty years and that it should not have ended like this.

6. TROUBLES IN THE HEMISPHERE

Cuba was another unsolved problem. Fidel Castro did not cease to call for revolution in Latin America. But Fidel's appeal to the hemisphere had steadily waned. His opposition to the Alliance for Progress had cast doubt on the selflessness of his interest in social betterment. Then the missile crisis displayed him as a rather impotent and ignominious Soviet tool, warned other Latin revolutionists that they could not count on Soviet support once the chips were down and demonstrated to non-communists the danger communist bridgeheads brought to all Latin America. At the same time, Washington pursued its measures of economic, diplomatic and military containment. Kennedy's policy of isolating and ignoring Castro worked well. By 1963 he was hardly even a thorn in the flesh. Once his influence in Latin America was destroyed, the survival of a mendicant communist regime in the Caribbean was not important.

As for the future, Kennedy, as usual, refused doctrinaire conclusions in a world where history produced such astonishing and unforeseen reversals. He continued to keep the door open to those within the Castro regime itself who might want to return to the hemisphere. For his part, Castro continued to denounce Washington and the CIA. Still, of Kennedy, Castro said he could "be an even greater President than Lincoln.... I will say this: he has come to understand many things over the past few months; and then too, in the last analysis, I'm convinced that anyone else would be worse." He concluded: "As a man and as a statesman, it is my duty to indicate what the bases for understanding could be." And so the matter rested, with lines of communication still open.

Kennedy followed the Alliance for Progress with ever watchful eye. The recommendation of the Inter-American Economic and Social Council in 1962 had led to a review of the Alliance by Lleras Camargo of Colombia and Kubitschek of Brazil. While the two Latin American leaders disagreed on certain issues, they united in recommending the establishment of an inter-American development committee to preside over the Alliance. When the IA-ECOSOC met in November 1963 at São Paulo in Brazil, it established the Inter-American Committee for the Alliance for Progress (CIAP). This body, on which Walt Rostow became the United States representative, marked the 'Latinization' of the Alliance and gave it new coherence and purpose.

But the road to democracy remained hard. On September 25, 1963, the Dominican military overthrew Juan Bosch in the Dominican Republic. A week later another military coup overthrew the regime of Ramón Villeda Morales in Honduras. Kennedy promptly recalled our ambassadors and economic and military aid chiefs from Santo Domingo and Tegucigalpa.

Still, despite political setbacks, the Alliance for Progress continued to gain. In 1963 eight countries attained increases in per capita income of nearly 5 percent—almost twice the target of Punta del Este. In 1964 Latin America as a whole fulfilled the Punta del Este goal. And the rise of new leaders like Eduardo Frei Montalva in Chile and Belaunde in Peru expressed the vitality of the democratic revolution.

The President was more troubled than ever by the organization of Latin American affairs within our own government. Late in October he discussed with Richard Goodwin and me the old problem which Berle had raised in 1961 of an Under Secretaryship of State for Inter-American Affairs, embracing both the Alliance and the political responsibilities of the Assistant Secretary. Kennedy, remarking sharply that he could not get anyone on the seventh floor of the State Department to pay sustained attention to Latin America, dictated a plain-spoken memorandum to Rusk saying that he wanted to create the new Under Secretaryship.

He had in mind for the job Sargent Shriver or perhaps Averell Harriman, whom he had just designated to lead the United States delegation to the São Paulo meeting. We later learned that Rusk sent the presidential memorandum to the Assistant Secretary for Administration, who passed it along to some subordinate, and it took Ralph Dungan's intervention to convince the Secretary that this was a serious matter requiring senior attention. Receiving no response, the President after a fortnight renewed the request.

7. REVOLUTION IN FISCAL POLICY

The year 1963 was one of initiatives not only in the pursuit of peace and in the struggle for equal rights but in national economic policy.

In the autumn of 1962 the administration had quietly committed itself to a radical principle: the deliberate creation of budgetary deficits at a time when there was no economic emergency—when, indeed, the budget was already in deficit and the economy was actually moving upward. This idea was the wildest heresy to those who used to predict a depression to curl a man's hair if the government did not balance its books. It would have seemed extreme to the contracyclical spenders of the New Deal, who were prepared for deficits in depression in order to offset declines but supposed that the proper policy in prosperity was to keep taxes up and retire the national debt. Kennedy was even moving beyond his own theory in 1961 of a budget balanced "over the years of the economic cycle" when he adopted the theory of deficits at the peak of the cycle so long as unemployment remained high.

Because the principle was so revolutionary, it exacted a price, or rather a series of prices. The first had been the decision to create the deficit through tax reduction rather than through social spending. Kennedy, in spite of his sympathy with the Galbraithian concern for the public sector, simply considered the expenditures route politically impossible and accepted Walter Heller's argument that the increased revenues produced by the tax route would eventually increase public benefits. The second price, not so serious, was the decision to stretch out the projected cut of about $10 billion over three years. The third price was more serious: an assurance to Wilbur Mills that tax reduction would be accompanied by an "ever-tighter rein on Federal expenditures."

A fourth price was the gradual erosion in Congress of most of the tax reforms to which Dillon and Mills had devoted so much attention in the years preceding. The tax reform program, in essence, was an effort to close loopholes in the tax laws in exchange for a reduction in the surtax rates. Kennedy was prepared to pay this price for the tax cut. But the President reserved the problem in his own mind for treatment in the longer run.

Even with all these concessions, the principle of the planned deficit remained too startling for easy acceptance. Mythology died hard. In May 1963 President Eisenhower in an agitated magazine article expressed his "amazement" about this "vast, reckless" plan for "a deliberate plunge into a massive deficit." "What can those people in Washington be thinking about? Why would they deliberately do this to our country? I ask myself." The deficit road, the former President grimly warned, "through history has lured nations to financial misery and economic disaster." And in the business community, a number of leaders, while applauding the idea of tax reduction, especially for higher brackets and for corporations, insisted that it be accompanied by a parallel reduction in government expenditures. It required patient explanation before they began to understand that this approach, by taking out of the spending stream with one hand what was being put in by the other, would nullify the stimulative value of the cut.

The bill made slow progress through Congress. Public reaction at first was muted. Still, when the House of Representatives passed the tax bill by 271 to 155 on September 25, 1963, the worst was over. Though Senator Byrd showed every intention of dragging out the hearings before the Senate Finance Committee, enactment sometime in early 1964 was reasonably assured. The Yale speech had not been in vain; and the American government, a generation after *General Theory*, had accepted the Keynesian revolution. But a problem remained. The steady increase in national output since the bottom of the 1960–61 recession had not been accompanied by any equivalent lessening of unemployment. Would the tax cut do any better in cutting into chronic unemployment?

This question had worried Kennedy ever since the primaries in the spring of 1960 had carried him into the blasted valleys of West Virginia. Repeatedly through the campaign he called for "an economic drive on poverty."

Now as President he confronted an economic system which seemed to be able to do everything but give all its people jobs and decent lives. Population growth compounded the challenge. The progress of automation further complicated the problem by bringing the period nearer when technology would begin to destroy more jobs than it created. How could an increasingly computerized economy, using fewer people to produce more goods, provide useful employment to those displaced by technological change, to those traditionally discriminated against in the labor market and to those entering that market for the first time? This question did not worry him politically, because he was sure the unemployed would never turn to the Republicans to create jobs for them. But it worried him socially. Unemployment was especially acute among Negroes, already so alienated from American society, and among young people, and it thereby placed a growing strain on the social fabric.

Tax reduction, in short, was the first part of the assault on unemployment. After the artillery barrage, the structural troops were then expected to move in and mop up remaining pockets of resistance. A basis for structural action had already been laid by legislative enactment: the Area Redevelopment Act, passed in 1961 after having been twice vetoed in the Eisenhower administration, and the Accelerated Public Works Act of 1962. In addition, the Manpower Training and Development Act was passed in 1962, and bills for vocational education and youth employment were moving through Congress in 1963.

Kennedy, who never forgot West Virginia, followed developments in the spreading economic decay in the hills and valleys of the Appalachian mountains with particular interest. This region, as he once put it, would be "very hard to reach even if the economy is going ahead at a strong rate." From the start, he steered a great variety of government programs—ARA, highway construction, Army Corps of Engineers, TVA, food stamp—into Appalachia. In the spring of 1963 he established a joint federal-state Committee on the Appalachian Region and, with nice historical eye, appointed Franklin D. Roosevelt, Jr., the Under Secretary of Commerce, as chairman. Roosevelt took hold of the project with ability and energy. It seemed in 1963 that the Appalachia program might become a model for comparable programs in other parts of underdeveloped America, such as the upper Great Lakes region and the Ozarks.

Within the executive branch the President's Committee on Juvenile Delinquency had been developing under Robert Kennedy's goading perhaps the most imaginative attack on the structure of poverty. The Committee decided to use its funds—$10 million a year—to stimulate cities to come up with coordinated plans, uniting federal, municipal and private instrumentalities in an effort to help boys and girls in the slums. In order to make sure that they would not just be schemes benevolently imposed by social workers and welfare agencies, Robert Kennedy insisted on bringing the poor into planning and execution—an innovation of great significance, stoutly resisted in many cases by city administrations. The Committee concentrated on sixteen cities in the course of 1963 and approved plans in ten of them. Mobilization for Youth and the Haryou program in Harlem were among the best known. Out of this experience there emerged the concept of 'community action' as a fundamental part of the war against deprivation.

Yet, apart from the Committee on Juvenile Delinquency, none of the structural efforts quite worked. The Area Redevelopment Administration received inadequate appropriations and, because of political pressure as well as human need, had to spread them too thin over too wide an area. After a year and a half, only slightly more than 150,000 were in training under the Manpower Development and Training Act. The youth employment bill, proposing a Youth Conservation Corps, passed the Senate in April 1963 but bogged down in the House. And the Appalachia program threatened to be dominated by the state governors, who flinched from offending the absentee corporate owners of the area and wanted to put the bulk of government funds into highway construction.

8. THE WAR AGAINST POVERTY

As Kennedy reflected on these matters in the spring of 1963, he began to feel that the problem was one not only of greater investment in private industry but of greater investment in public services and human beings, not only of distressed areas but of distressed individuals, not only of vocational training but of elementary education, medical care, civil rights, community action and personal morale. He was reaching the conclusion that tax reduction required a comprehensive structural counterpart, taking the form, not of piecemeal programs, but of a broad war against poverty itself. Here perhaps was the unifying theme which would pull a host of social programs together and rally the nation behind a generous cause.

Kennedy knew that unemployment and poverty were in part separate problems (indeed statistics showed that a majority of the unemployed were not below the poverty line and a majority of the poor were not unemployed); but the problems overlapped in the area of structural remedy. This concern for poverty as a problem distinct from unemployment—for chronic or, in bureaucratese, 'hardcore' poverty—was relatively new.

It was not till toward the end of the 1950s—and especially with the publication in 1958 of Galbraith's *The Affluent Society* and its chapter xxiii on "The New Position of Poverty"—that chronic poverty began to impinge on the national consciousness as a distinct issue. Galbraith warned that the poor, unlike the ambitious immigrants of the nineties or the politically aggressive unemployed of the thirties, were now a demoralized and inarticulate minority who in many cases had inherited their poverty and accepted it as a permanent condition. Because of their apathy and invisibility they had ceased to be objects of interest to the politician. Nor would the increase of the gross national product of itself solve their problems. But he insisted that an affluent society, through investment in the public sector, could begin to take measures which might at least keep poverty from being self-perpetuating. Then in 1962 *The Other America,* a brilliant and indignant book by Michael Harrington, translated the statistics into bitter human terms. If Galbraith brought poverty into the national consciousness, Harrington placed it on the national conscience.

Kennedy read both Galbraith and Harrington; and I believe that *The Other America* helped crystallize his determination in 1963 to accompany the tax cut by a poverty program. Galbraith's unremitting guerrilla warfare in support of the public sector against "reactionary" Keynesianism certainly played its part too.

New data, as Heller explained in a memorandum to Kennedy on May 1, underlined the drastic slowdown in the rate at which the economy was taking people out of poverty. In spite of the remarkable increase in the gross national product, the absolute number of the poor appeared to be slightly larger than in 1957 and the proportion only 1 per cent lower. By reasonable definitions—an annual income of

$3000 for a family or $1500 for an individual—one-fifth of the nation lived in an underworld of poverty beyond the reach of most government programs, whether housing, farm price supports, social security or tax reduction.

It puzzled Kennedy that the poor were not angrier and more politically demanding. But, as he said to Heller, the time had come for action. There were doubts in other parts of the government, even in Heller's own staff. Ted Sorensen, however, told Heller, "This is the President's kind of program. Go ahead on it." Early in June Heller circulated a memorandum within the Council of Economic Advisers asking "what lines of action might make up a practical Kennedy anti-poverty program in 1964?" Through the summer and fall the Council carried on its work. During the cabinet meeting on October 29, 1963, the President scribbled, as usual, on a yellow lined pad; the doodles show the word "poverty" half a dozen times, encircled and underlined. On Armistice Day, 1963, Kennedy told Heller, "First we'll have your tax cut; then we'll have my expenditures program." One day in November, musing about the 1964 State of the Union message, he remarked to me, "The time has come to organize a national assault on the causes of poverty, a comprehensive program, across the board"; this, he suggested, would be the centerpiece in his 1964 legislative recommendations. Between tax reduction and the war against poverty, Kennedy believed that he had finally put together the elements of a total program for economic growth and opportunity.

Already the policies of the Kennedy years had resulted in the longest American peacetime expansion of the economy in the century of recorded business cycle history. The average increase of the gross national product in real terms was 5.6 per cent a year*—measurably more than the 5 per cent Kennedy had talked about in the 1960 campaign. Profits, wages and salaries were higher than ever before; yet costs and prices remained stable, and wage rates on the average rose no faster than productivity.

The sources of this triumph can be briefly enumerated. The steady rise in expenditures, averaging over $5 billion a year, contributed basic economic stimulus.** The investment tax credit and the liberalized depreciation allowances encouraged investment. The Federal Reserve Board followed the elections returns and, where the balance of payments permitted, pursued a policy of monetary ease. The guideposts and the steel fight restrained the wage-price spiral. Roosa's legerdemain defended the dollar. Neither of the right-wing bogies of the fifties—the passion for a balanced budget or the fear of inflation—was allowed to abort the boom. Then the tax cut promised to infuse the body economic with new energies for consumption and investment and the poverty program to open the gates of escape from deprivation and squalor.

It was, indeed, an unprecedented performance in economic management; and its success was due to Heller and Dillon, whose creative debates first illuminated the choices and then led to consensus, and above all to Kennedy, whose political instinct determined the timing of policies and whose intellectual leadership made them acceptable to the country. The job of public education which Kennedy had begun so brilliantly at Yale was yet to be completed. Still, these years equipped the republic with policies which promised to advance economic growth, move toward full employment and relieve the age-old burdens of poverty.

9. ONE ACQUAINTED WITH THE NIGHT

On a beautiful autumn Saturday at the end of October the President flew to Amherst College in Massachusetts to take part in a ceremony in honor of Robert Frost. He had decided to speak about Frost's inaugural theme of poetry and power. When we were talking over what he might say, we had chatted about Frost's poems. He recalled *"I have been one acquainted with the night"* and said, "What a terrific line!" Soon we landed and motored over to the college. It was Indian summer, golden and vivid but with forebodings of winter. "The men who create power," Kennedy told his Amherst audience, "make an indispensable contribution to the nation's greatness, but the men who question power make a contribution just as indispensable ... for they determine whether we use power or power uses us." And then he offered his vision of the American promise.

I look forward to a great future for America, a future in which our country will match its military strength with our moral restraint, its wealth with our wisdom, its power with our purpose.

I look forward to an America which will not be afraid of grace and beauty, which will protect the beauty of our natural environment, which will preserve the great old American houses and squares and parks of our national past, and which will build handsome and balanced cities for our future.

I look forward to an America which will reward achievement in the arts as we reward achievement in business or state-craft....

I look forward to an America which commands respect throughout the world not only for its strength but for its civilization as well. And I look forward to a world which will be safe not only for democracy and diversity but also for personal distinction.

* This figure is from the first quarter of 1961 to the third quarter of 1963.

** The administrative deficits were $3.9 billion in 1961, $6.4 billion in 1962 and $6.3 billion in 1963.

Many thoughts drifted through his mind about the future—publishing a newspaper (he sometimes joked with Ben Bradlee about buying the *Washington Post*), returning to Congress like John Quincy Adams, traveling around the world, writing a book.

This was his sense of the future, and he embraced it as if on a rising tide of confidence. For all the congressional problems of 1963, he knew he had had a good year, and he anticipated 1964 with relish. So much beckoned: the enactment of the civil rights and tax reduction bills; the war against poverty; education and Medicare; the pursuit of peace beyond the test ban; the advance of the Alliance for Progress; a visit from de Gaulle in February; a trip with Jacqueline to the Far East in the spring; the presidential election in the fall.

He had little real doubt, I think, that he would win the election with ease, especially against Goldwater. This would give his second term the congressional margin and the popular mandate the first had lacked. He saw his second administration, like Theodore Roosevelt's, as the time of great legislative action, when the seeds planted in the first term would come to fruition. He expected, of course, to make some changes in his administration, some notable, though none, so far as I know, in the cabinet (unless he could not persuade his brother to stay on as Attorney General). Then after the election, he could not only complete his present program but move forward to new problems—tax evasion was one, an attack on the structure of government subsidies was another, the rationalization of the city, the promotion of the arts and the protection of the natural environment, others. In foreign affairs he looked forward particularly to the possibility, if the *détente* held, of a journey to the Soviet Union.

Sometimes he would muse about life beyond 1968. He had remarked early in his administration that, "whether I serve one or two terms in the Presidency, I will find myself at the end of that period at what might be called the awkward age—too old to begin a new career and too young to write my memoirs." Many thoughts drifted through his mind about the future—publishing a newspaper (he sometimes joked with Ben Bradlee about buying the *Washington Post*), returning to Congress like John Quincy Adams, traveling around the world, writing a book. As the plans for his presidential library at Harvard took shape, he began to visualize the future with more particularity. They would, he thought, live part of each year in Cambridge. Here he could use his offices in the Library, work on the history of his administration, hold seminars and talk to students. He hoped that the Library might become a center where academicians, politicians and public servants could challenge and instruct one another, thereby realizing his old dream of bringing together the world of thought and the world of power.*

But 1969 was a long time away, and there remained the hurdle of 1964. The President looked forward with high anticipation to running against Goldwater. As the election year approached, Kennedy looked to Johnson for particular help in the Vice-President's own state. There John Connally, who had resigned as Secretary of the Navy to run successfully for governor, and Senator Ralph Yarborough were engaged in the latest phase of the quarrel which had plagued the Texas Democratic party ever since Garner had opposed a third term for Roosevelt in 1940. The conservative Democrats of Texas were increasingly based on the oil industry, the young suburban businessmen and the rural conservatives, while the liberal Democrats had joined the old populist tradition with the new force of organized labor. The conservatives had won out in the late forties and fifties; this had been reflected in Johnson's own movement from the aggressive young New Dealer to the cautious middle-of-the-roader of the Eisenhower years. Yet, though in the course of this journey he had estranged many Texas liberals, his heart had remained with the New Deal. Kennedy looked to him to use his personal influence with Connally and his ideological affinity with Yarborough to end

* This intention will now be carried out in the John F. Kennedy Institute of Politics under the direction of his friend Richard Neustadt.

the wracking fight within the Texas Democratic party. By going to Texas himself, the President hoped to use the presidential authority to help the Vice-President bring the warring Texans together.

On November 19 he had the usual breakfast with the congressional leaders. Chatting about his trip, he said that the Texas feuds would at least create interest and bring people out. He added, "Things always look so much better away from Washington." The next night was Robert Kennedy's thirty-eighth birthday. At the party at Hickory Hill, Ethel Kennedy, instead of making her usual chaffing toast about her husband, asked us all, with simplicity and solemnity, to drink to the President of the United States. The next morning the President and Mrs. Kennedy flew to Texas, with stops scheduled for San Antonio, Houston, Dallas, Austin.

10. DALLAS

Exactly four weeks before, Adlai Stevenson had gone to Dallas for a meeting on United Nations Day. The National Indignation Convention, still active on the radical right, decided to counter this visit by holding a "United States Day" meeting the previous day with General Edwin A. Walker as the main speaker. That night General Walker denounced the United Nations. The next day handbills with photographs of the President of the United States—full-face and profile—were scattered around Dallas: "WANTED FOR TREASON. THIS MAN is wanted for treasonous activities against the United States," followed by a scurrilous bill of particulars.

That evening many of Walker's patriots returned to the same auditorium to harass Stevenson. While Adlai spoke, there was hooting and heckling; placards and flags were waved, and noisemakers set off. When the police removed one of the agitators from the hall, Stevenson, with customary poise, said, "For my part, I believe in the forgiveness of sin and the redemption of ignorance." At the close he walked through a jostling crowd of pickets to his car. A woman screamed at him, and he stopped for a moment to calm her down. The mob closed in on him. Another woman crashed a sign down on his head. A man spat at him. As the police broke through to him, Stevenson, wiping his face with a handkerchief, said coldly, "Are these human beings or are these animals?"

The next day, I talked with some of the leading people out there. They wondered whether the President should go to Dallas, and so do I." After all, the assault on Stevenson was by no means an isolated event. During the 1960 campaign Lyndon Johnson himself, accompanied by his wife, had been hissed and spat upon by a screaming mob in the lobby of the Adolphus Hotel.

Still, as Kenneth O'Donnell said later, the President "could not possibly go to Texas and avoid Dallas. Dallas plainly was a peculiar place. It was the newest rich city in the country, and was dominated by raw new wealth flowing from the oil fields into banking, insurance, utilities and real estate. The manners of the Dallas plutocracy had been somewhat refined by Neiman-Marcus, but its politics had been kept in a primitive and angry state by the *Dallas Morning News*, whose publisher two years before had told Kennedy at the White House that the nation needed a man on horseback while he was riding Caroline's tricycle. A white collar city, it had neither a traditional aristocracy nor a strong labor movement to diversify its opinions or temper its certitudes. The fundamentalist religious background of many of its inhabitants had instilled a self-righteous absolutism of thought; and the whole community, with bank clerks and real estate hustlers sporting Stetsons and sombreros, carefully cultivated the myth of the old Texas and its virile, hard-riding, hard-shooting men taking the law into their own hands.* Texas had one of the highest homicide rates in the country—far higher, for example, than New York—and Dallas, which murdered more people some years than England, doubled the national average. It was a city of violence and hysteria, and its atmosphere was bound to affect people who were already weak, suggestible and themselves filled with chaos and hate.

But not all Texas was in the image of Dallas. San Antonio, where the President stopped early Thursday afternoon, had recently sent Henry Gonzalez, a liberal Democrat, to Congress, and it greeted Kennedy with great enthusiasm. Even conservative Houston was almost as friendly later that same day. Kennedy, delighted by the warmth of his reception, remained, however, in a mood of puzzlement and annoyance over the backbiting of Texas Democratic politics. Kennedy, counted on Johnson to compose matters. But Johnson had lost much of his standing in Texas: in the limbo of the Vice-Presidency, he was now only a name and a memory. Probably the President overestimated the Vice-President's capacity to deal with the situation. In any case, in a brief but cogent private talk in Houston on Thursday afternoon Kennedy expressed his discontent with the situation.

Later the President spoke to the League of United Latin-American Citizens, recalling the Good Neighbor policy and the Alliance for Progress. Then, "in order that my words may be even clearer," he introduced Jacqueline who said a few words in Spanish. As they left for a dinner in honor of Congressman Albert Thomas, a group of Cuban refugees held signs and shouted slogans. In their midst,

* About this time the December issue of *Redbook* came on the newsstands. An article by Jhan Robbins recorded the impressions of European children about Americans. The first answer to the question "What are Americans like?" was: "The average American is, of course, a Texan. He eats lots of breakfast and gets fat so he has to go on a diet because he likes to look skinny. He calls everyone 'sweetheart' and is bad to colored people. If he doesn't like who is his President, he usually shoots him."

Ronnie Dugger of the *Texas Observer* saw one old man waving over his head a small sign: "Welcome Kennedy."*

Later that night the presidential party went on to Fort Worth. Before breakfast the next morning, Friday, November 22, Kennedy read the *Dallas Morning News*. The day before a sports columnist in the *News* had suggested that the President talk about sailing in Dallas in order to avoid trouble. "If the speech is about boating you will be among the warmest of admirers. If it is about Cuber, civil rights, taxes or Vietnam, there will sure as shootin' be some who heave to and let go with a broadside of grape shot in the presidential rigging." This morning the News ran a full-page advertisement headed: WELCOME MR. [sic] KENNEDY TO DALLAS. It claimed to speak for the "America-thinking citizens of Dallas" who still had, "through a Constitution largely ignored by you," the right to disagree and criticize. It then set forth a series of questions: why had Kennedy "scrapped the Monroe Doctrine in favor of the 'Spirit of Moscow'"? why had the foreign policy of the United States "degenerated to the point that the C.I.A. is arranging coups and having staunch Anti-Communist Allies of the U.S. bloodily exterminated"? why had Kennedy "ordered or permitted your brother Bobby ... to go soft on Communists, fellow-travelers, and ultra-leftists in America, while permitting him to persecute loyal Americans who criticize you"? why had Gus Hall, head of the American Communist Party, "praised almost every one of your policies and announced that the party will endorse and support your re-election"? why, why, why—a list designed to suggest that the President was systematically pro-communist if not a traitor. Kennedy pushed the paper aside with disgust. He asked, "How can people write such things?"

But he was light and bantering when he addressed the citizens of Fort Worth a little later in the soft rain in front of the Texas Hotel. "Mrs. Kennedy is organizing herself," he said. "It takes longer, but, of course, she looks better than we do when she does it." Then he went on to speak at a breakfast of the Fort Worth Chamber of Commerce. At the conclusion the chairman of the meeting presented him with a cowboy hat. The President, who never put on funny hats, looked at it with suspicion and finally said, "I'll put it on at the White House and you can photograph it there." Back at the Texas Hotel, he chatted with Jacqueline and Kenneth O'Donnell about the role of the Secret Service. All they could do, he said, was to protect a President from unruly or overexcited crowds. But if someone really wanted to kill a President, it was not too difficult; put a man on a high building with a telescopic rifle, and there was nothing anybody could do to defend a President's life. O'Donnell said afterward that Kennedy regarded assassination as a risk inherent in a democracy; "it didn't disturb him at all."

During the short trip to Dallas, the men in the plane discussed the city's aberrant atmosphere. Fanaticism was what he detested most—as the reason and poise he incarnated were what distraught and rootless people, drawn to Dallas by the climate of alienation and anger, might find most intolerable.

When they arrived at Love Field, Congressman Henry Gonzalez said jokingly, "Well, I'm taking my risks. I haven't got my steel vest yet." The President, disembarking, walked immediately across the sunlit field to the crowd and shook hands. Then they entered the cars to drive from the airport to the center of the city. The people in the outskirts, Kenneth O'Donnell later said, were "not unfriendly nor terribly enthusiastic. They waved. But were reserved, I thought." The crowds increased as they entered the city—"still very orderly, but cheerful." In downtown Dallas enthusiasm grew. Soon even O'Donnell was satisfied. The car turned off Main Street, the President happy and waving, Jacqueline erect and proud by his side, and Mrs. Connally saying, "You certainly can't say that the people of Dallas haven't given you a nice welcome," and the automobile turning on to Elm Street and down the slope past the Texas School Book Depository, and the shots, faint and frightening, suddenly distinct over the roar of the motorcade, and the quizzical look on the President's face before he pitched over, and Jacqueline crying, "Oh, no, no ... Oh, my God, they have shot my husband," and the horror, the vacancy.

11. THE DRUMS OF WASHINGTON

On Friday morning I had flown to New York with Katharine Graham, whose husband Philip had died three months before, for a luncheon with the editors of her magazine *Newsweek*. Kenneth Galbraith had come down from Cambridge for the occasion. We were still sipping drinks before luncheon in an amiable mood of Friday-before-the-Harvard-Yale game relaxation when a young man in shirtsleeves entered the room and said, a little tentatively, "I am sorry to break in, but I think you should know that the President has been shot in the head in Texas." For a flash one thought this was some sort of ghastly office joke. Then we knew it could not be and huddled desperately around the nearest television. Everything was confused and appalling. The minutes dragged along. Incomprehensible bulletins came from the hospital. Suddenly an insane surge of conviction flowed through me: I felt that the man who had survived the Solomon Islands and so much illness and agony, who so loved life, embodied it, enhanced it, could not possibly die

* For Dugger's vivid record of the Kennedy trip, see the *Texas Observer*, November 29, 1963; also "Dallas, After All," *Observer*, March 6, 1964.

PRESIDENT AND MRS. KENNEDY DRIVING FROM LOVE FIELD TO DOWNTOWN DALLAS WITH GOVERNOR JOHN CONNALLY ON NOVEMBER 22, 1963.

now. He would escape the shadow as he had before. Almost immediately we received the irrevocable word.

In a few moments Galbraith and I were on Katharine Graham's plane bound for Washington. It was the saddest journey of one's life. Bitterness, shame, anguish, disbelief, emptiness mingled inextricably in one's mind. When I stumbled, almost blindly, into the East Wing, the first person I encountered was Franklin D. Roosevelt, Jr. In a short time I went with my White House colleagues to Andrews Field to await the return of Air Force One from Texas. A small crowd was waiting in the dusk, McNamara, stunned and silent, Harriman, haggard and suddenly looking very old, desolation everywhere. We watched incredulously as the casket was carefully lifted out of the plane and taken to the Naval Hospital at Bethesda. Later I went to my house in Georgetown. My weeping daughter Christina said, "Daddy, what has happened to our country? If this is the kind of country we have, I don't want to live here any more." The older children were already on their way back from college to Washington.

Still later I went back to the White House to await the last return. Around four in the morning the casket, wrapped in a flag, was brought from the Naval Hospital and placed on a stand in the East Room. Tapers were lit around the bier, and a priest said a few words. Then Jacqueline approached the bier, knelt for a moment and buried her head in the flag. Soon she walked away. The rest of us waited for a little while in the great hall. We were beyond consolation, but we clung to the comradeship he had given us. Finally, just before daybreak, we bleakly dispersed into the mild night.

We did not grieve alone. Though in Dallas school children applauded the news* and in Peking the *Daily Worker* ran a savage cartoon entitled "Kennedy Biting the Dust" showing the dead President lying in a pool of blood, his necktie marked with dollar signs, sorrow engulfed America and the world. At Harvard Yard the bells tolled in Memorial Church, a girl wept hysterically in Widener Library, a student slammed a tree, again and again, with his fist. Negroes mourned, and A. Philip Randolph said that his "place in history will be next to Abraham Lincoln." Pablo Casals mused

THE PLANE CARRYING PRESDIENT KENNEDY'S COFFIN LANDS IN WASHINGTON, D.C.

that he had seen many great and terrible events in his lifetime—the Dreyfus case, the assassination of Gandhi—"but in recent history—and I am thinking of my own lifetime—there has never been a tragedy that has brought so much sadness and grief to as many people as this." "For a time we felt the country was ours," said Norman Mailer. "Now it's theirs again." Many were surprised by the intensity of the loss. Alistair Cooke spoke of "this sudden discovery that he was more familiar than we knew." "Is there some principle of nature," asked Richard Hofstadter, "which requires that we never know the quality of what we have had until it is gone?" Around the land people sat desperately in front of television sets watching the bitter drama of the next four days. In Washington Daniel Patrick Moynihan, the Assistant Secretary of Labor, said, "I don't think there's any point in being Irish if you don't know that the world is going to break your heart eventually. I guess that we thought we had a little more time.... Mary McGrory said to me that we'll never laugh again. And I said, 'Heavens, Mary. We'll laugh again. It's just that we'll never be young again.'"

In Ireland, "Ah, they cried the rain down that night," said a Fitzgerald of Limerick; he would not come back in the springtime. David Bruce reported from London, "Great Britain has never before mourned a foreigner as it has President Kennedy." As the news spread around London, over a thousand people assembled before the embassy in Grosvenor Square; they came in endless thousands in the next days to sign the condolence book. That Was The Week That Was on television, unwontedly serious: "the first western politician to make politics a respectable profession for thirty years—to make it once again the highest of the professions, and not just a fabric of fraud and sham.... We took him completely for granted." "Why was this feeling—this sorrow—at once so universal and so individual?" Harold Macmillan later asked. "Was it not because he seemed, in his own person, to embody all the hopes and aspirations of this new world that is struggling to emerge—to rise, Phoenix-like, from the ashes of the old?" In West Berlin people lighted candles in darkened windows. In Poland there was a spontaneous mass mourning by university students; church bells tolled for

* The children were not responsible; they expressed the atmosphere of the city.

JACQUELINE AND CAROLINE KNEEL BY THE CASKET.

fifteen minutes on the night of the funeral. In Yugoslavia Tito, so overcome that he could hardly speak, phoned the American chief of mission; later he read a statement over the state radio and went in person to the embassy to sign the book. The national flag was flown at half-mast, and schools were instructed to devote one full hour to a discussion of the President's policies and significance. In Moscow Khrushchev was the first to sign the book, and the Soviet television carried the funeral, including the service in the church.

Latin America was devastated. Streets, schools, housing projects were named after him, shrines set up in his memory; his picture, torn from the newspaper, hung on the walls of workers' shacks and in the hovels of the *campesinos.* "For Latin America," said Lleras Camargo, "Kennedy's passing is a blackening, a tunnel, a gust of cloud and smoke." Castro was with Jean Daniel when the report came; he said, *"Es una mala noticia"* ("This is bad news"). In a few moments, with the final word, he stood and said, "Everything is changed.... I'll tell you one thing: at least Kennedy was an enemy to whom we had become accustomed." In Cambodia Prince Sihanouk ordered court mourning; "a light was put out," he later said, "which may not be re-lit for many years to come." In Indonesia flags flew at half-mast. In New Delhi people cried in the streets. In Algiers Ben Bella phoned Ambassador

Porter in tears and said, "I can't believe it. Believe me, I'd rather it happen to me than to him." In Guinea Sékou Touré said, "I have lost my only true friend in the outside world." The embassy reported, "People expressed their grief without restraint, and just about everybody in Guinea seemed to have fallen under the spell of the courageous young hero of far away, the slayer of the dragons of discrimination, poverty, ignorance and war." In N'zérékoré in the back country, where one would hardly think they had heard of the United States let alone the American President, a group of natives presented a sum of money to their American pastor to buy, according to the custom of the Guerze people, a rush mat in which to bury President Kennedy. In Kampala Ugandans crowded the residence of the American Ambassador; others sat silently for hours on the lawns and hillsides waiting. In Mali, the most left-wing of African states, President Keita came to the embassy with an honor guard and delivered a eulogy. In the Sudan a grizzled old Bisharine tribesman told an American lawyer that it was terrible Kennedy's son was so young; "it will be a long time before he can be the true leader." *Transition,* the magazine of African intellectuals, said, "In this way was murdered the first real chance in this century for an intelligent and new leadership to the world.... More than any other person, he achieved the intellectual's ideal of a man in action. His death leaves us unprepared and in darkness."

In Washington grief was an agony. Somehow the long hours passed, as the new President took over with firmness and strength, but the roll of the drums, when we walked to St. Matthew's Cathedral on the frosty Monday, will sound forever in my ears, and the wildly twittering birds during the

THE FUNERAL PROCESSION.

PRESIDENT JOHN F. KENNEDY IS BURIED AT ARLINGTON NATIONAL CEMETERY.

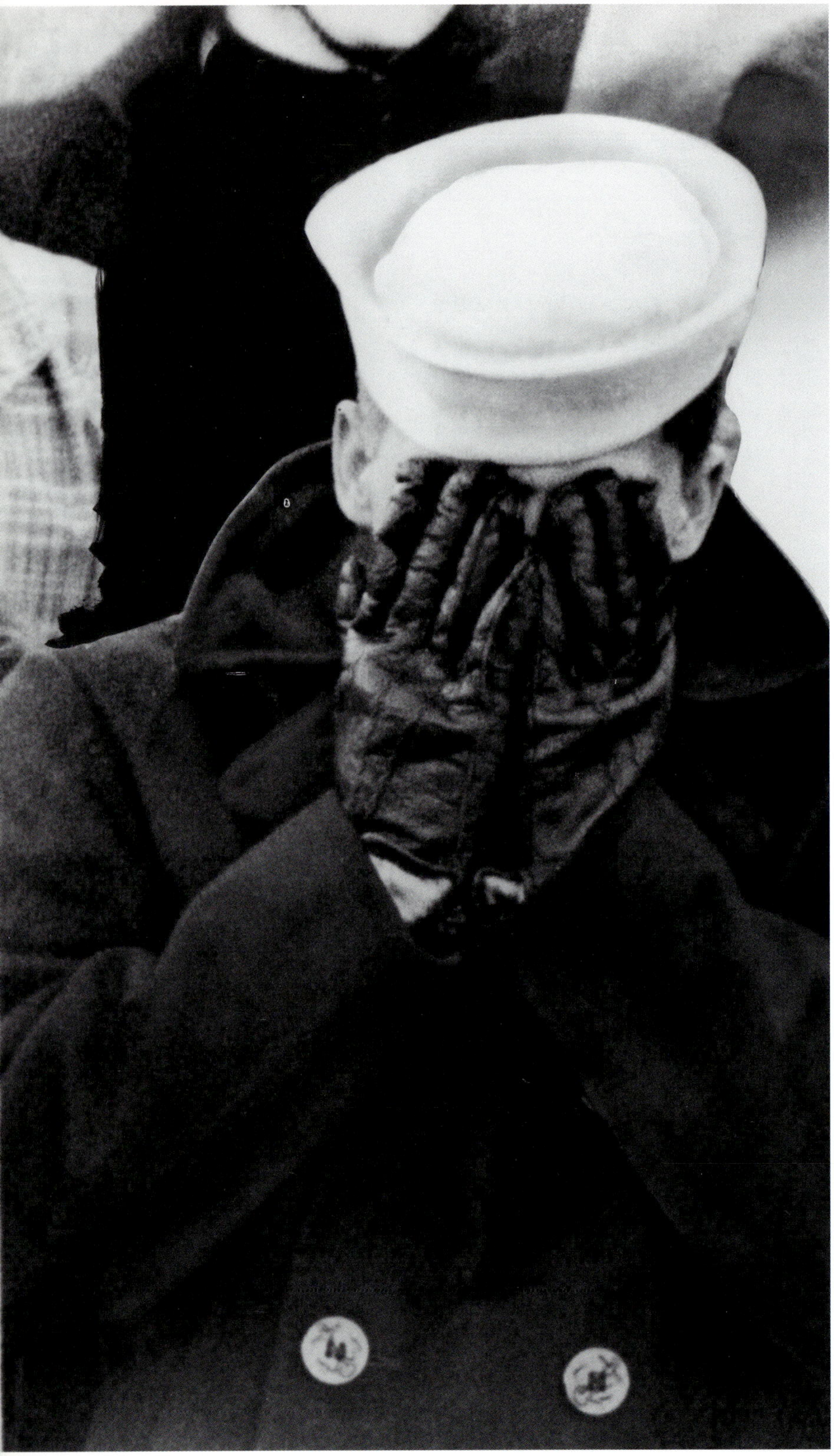
AN UNIDENTIFIED SOLIDER WEEPS AT THE BURIAL.

interment at Arlington while the statesmen of the world looked on. It was all so grotesque and so incredible. One remembered Stephen Spender's poem:

I think continually of those who were truly great....
The names of those who in their lives fought for life,
Who wore at their hearts the fire's center.
Born of the sun they traveled a short while towards the sun,
And left the vivid air signed with their honour.

It was all gone now—the life-affirming, life-enhancing zest, the brilliance, the wit, the cool commitment, the steady purpose. Richard Neustadt has suggested that two years are the period of presidential initiation. He had had so little time, yet he had accomplished so much: the new hope for peace on earth, the elimination of nuclear testing in the atmosphere and the abolition of nuclear diplomacy, the new policies toward Latin America and the third world, the reordering of American defense, the emancipation of the American Negro, the revolution in national economic policy, the concern for poverty, the stimulus to the arts, the fight for reason against extremism and mythology. Lifting us beyond our capacities, he gave his country back to its best self, wiping away the world's impression of an old nation of old men, weary, played out, fearful of ideas, change and the future; he taught mankind that the process of rediscovering America was not over. He re-established the republic as the first generation of our leaders saw it—young, brave, civilized, rational, gay, tough, questing, exultant in the excitement and potentiality of history. He transformed the American spirit—and the response of his people to his murder, the absence of intolerance and hatred, was a monument to his memory. The energies he released, the standards he set, the purposes he inspired, the goals he established would guide the land he loved for years to come. Above all he gave the world for an imperishable moment the vision of a leader who greatly understood the terror and the hope, the diversity and the possibility, of life on this planet and who made people look beyond nation and race to the future of humanity. So the people of the world grieved as if they had terribly lost their own leader, friend, brother.

On December 22, a month after his death, fire from the flame burning at his grave in Arlington was carried at dusk to the Lincoln Memorial. It was fiercely cold. Thousands stood, candles in their hands; then, as the flame spread among us, one candle lighting the next, the crowd gently moved away, the torches flaring and flickering, into the darkness. The next day it snowed—almost as deep a snow as the inaugural blizzard. I went to the White House. It was lovely, ghostly and strange.

It all ended, as it began, in the cold.

THE ETERNAL FLAME BURNING AT THE LINCOLN MEMORIAL.

INDEX

PHOTO CREDITS

AP/WIDEWORLD:
pp. 2 (both), 3, 5 (bottom, left), 6, 8, 9, 12, 13 (both), 15, 16, 18, 21, 22, 23 (top), 24 (left), 27 (both), 28, 29, 30, 33, 35 (top right and bottom), 37, 38, 39 (both), 49, 54, 56, 59, 60, 61, 63, 64, 81, 82, 84, 87, 92, 100, 104 (bottom, left and right), 105, 106, 107, 111, 119, 125, 133, 134, 135, 136, 138, 140, 141, 145, 150, 154 (both), 156, 163, 165, 166, 168, 172, 174, 177, 189, 190, 191, 192, 194, 196, 197, 198, 199, 201, 202, 205, 211, 219, 223, 235, 244, 246, 265, 275, 284 (bottom left), 305, 306, 307 (both), 313, 314, 317, 318 (both), 322, 323, 324, 327, 330 (top, middle right, bottom), 332, 335, 338, 339, 345 (both), 346, 347, 348, 357

CORBIS:
p. 104 (top)

JOHN F. KENNEDY LIBRARY:
pp. 4, 5 (top and middle), 23, 32, 34(both), 35 (top left), 36 (both), 38, 44, 45, 50, 52, 55, 58, 64, 67, 68, 77, 78, 79, 90, 101, 112, 117, 124, 126, 126 (all), 130, 142, 159, 230, 232, 233, 250, 255, 267, 277, 283, 292, 301, 319, 320, 349, 358, 359, 360, 361, 353

LIBRARY OF CONGRESS:
pp. 24, 40, 42, 50, 73, 98, 116, 122, 146, 152 (both), 200, 202, 203, 234, 237, 242, 276, 281, 284 (top and bottom right), 286, 288, 291, 293, 330, 362

LOOK MAGAZINE:
pp. 231, 259